Cambridge Archaeological and Ethnological Series

THE HEROIC AGE

MAP OF CENTRAL EUROPE
illustrating the Heroic Age of the Teutonic Peoples

Where the same name occurs both in capitals and italics the former denote a
position occupied in the early part of the Heroic Age, while the latter
mark a change or extension of territories.

THE HEROIC AGE

BY

H. MUNRO CHADWICK

ELRINGTON AND BOSWORTH PROFESSOR OF ANGLO-SAXON,
AND FELLOW OF CLARE COLLEGE, CAMBRIDGE

Cambridge :
at the University Press
1926

CAMBRIDGE
UNIVERSITY PRESS
LONDON : Fetter Lane

NEW YORK
The Macmillan Co.
BOMBAY, CALCUTTA and
MADRAS
Macmillan and Co., Ltd.
TORONTO
The Macmillan Co. of
Canada, Ltd.
TOKYO
Maruzen-Kabushiki-Kaisha

First Edition 1912
Reprinted 1926

PRINTED IN GREAT BRITAIN

TO

JAMES RENDEL HARRIS

IN GRATITUDE AND FRIENDSHIP

PREFACE

THE type of poetry commonly known as heroic is one which makes its appearance in various nations and in various periods of history. No one can fail to observe that certain similar features are to be found in poems of this type which are widely separated from one another both in date and place of origin. In view of this fact it has seemed worth while to attempt a comparative study of two groups of such poems with the object of determining the nature of the resemblances between them and the causes to which they are due. Occasional illustrations have been taken from other groups of poems belonging to the same type.

The first part of the book deals with the early heroic poetry and traditions of the Teutonic peoples, more especially with those stories which were the common property of various Teutonic peoples. It is pointed out that these stories all relate to a period with definite limits—a period for which a considerable amount of information is available from external sources. The subjects discussed include the distribution of the stories and the relationship between the various versions of them, the antiquity of the earliest poems and the conditions under which they were produced. Lastly, an attempt has been made to estimate the significance of the various elements, historical, mythical and fictitious, of which the stories are composed.

The second part deals with Greek heroic poetry and traditions. These relate to a period for which little or no external evidence is available; and consequently they present many problems, the bearings of which can hardly be estimated without reference to the existence of similar phenomena elsewhere. In general I have followed the same plan as in the first part, and made use throughout of the results obtained there. If some excuse is necessary for dealing with so well worn a theme I may plead that, so far as my knowledge goes, it has not hitherto been approached from this point of view.

In the third part attention has been called to the existence of a number of somewhat striking characteristics common to the two groups of poems and an attempt made to account for them. The conclusion to which I have been brought is that the resemblances in the poems are due primarily to resemblances in the ages to which they relate and to which they ultimately owe their origin. The comparative study of heroic poetry therefore involves the comparative study of 'Heroic Ages'; and the problems which it presents are essentially problems of anthropology.

In this conclusion I am glad to find myself in agreement with Dr Haddon, who suggested to me that a comparative study of this kind would be a suitable subject for the Cambridge Archaeological and Ethnological Series. I take this opportunity of thanking him for bringing the matter before the Syndics of the University Press and for the interest which he has kindly taken in the progress of the work.

Owing to the pressure of teaching and other duties a considerable time has unfortunately elapsed since the earlier portions of the book were printed. I would therefore respectfully call the reader's attention to the list of Addenda at the end, where references will be found to several important works which have appeared in the meantime.

In a work, such as this, which deals with records preserved in a number of different languages, difficulties necessarily arise with regard to the spelling of proper names. In the representation of Teutonic names the system adopted in my previous books has in general been retained. Any such system is of course open to objections, of the cogency of which I am quite aware; and consequently I have not felt inclined to carry out my scheme with rigid consistency. The same remarks apply to the representation of Greek names—which will doubtless displease many critics. South Slavonic names and words are given according to the usual Croatian orthography.

I cannot attempt here to enumerate the various scholars to whose writings I am indebted. It will be seen that they are many and that much of what I have had to do is in the nature of criticism. One name however, that of Professor Ridgeway, I cannot leave unmentioned, since it is largely to his inspiring influence—by no means through his writings alone—that my interest in these subjects is due.

It remains for me to record my obligations to a number of friends who have generously responded to my requests for information or criticism on various points. In particular I must mention Miss A. C. Paues, Mr A. B. Cook, Dr W. H. R. Rivers, Mr S. A. Cook, Professor J. W. H. Atkins, Professor A. Mawer, Mr E. H. Minns and Mr F. W. Green. Above all I am indebted to Mr E. C. Quiggin and Mr F. G. M. Beck, who have most kindly read through a considerable part of the book in proof and several chapters even in manuscript. It is scarcely necessary to add that in the sections dealing with Celtic history and poetry Mr Quiggin's criticism has been of the greatest value to me. My thanks are due, further, to my pupils, Mr C. A. Scutt, of Clare College, and Mr Bruce Dickins, of Magdalene College, for similar kind services in the proofs of the later chapters. From the staff of the University Library—in particular I must mention Mr A. Rogers and Mr O. Johnson —I have received the same unfailing and courteous attention as in the past. Lastly, I have to thank the Syndics of the University Press for undertaking the publication of the book and the staff for the efficient and obliging way in which the printing and corrections have been carried out.

H. M. C.

December, 1911.

CONTENTS

NOTES.

———

MAPS.

CHAPTER I.

THE EARLY NARRATIVE POETRY OF THE TEUTONIC PEOPLES.

THE remains of English poetry which have come down to us from times anterior to the Norman conquest are mainly of a religious character and deal with the lives of saints or with subjects derived from the Bible or ecclesiastical tradition. The secular poems are comparatively few in number and, with one exception, of inconsiderable length. Most of them are narrative poems and admit of a very obvious classification according to the choice of subjects with which they are concerned. One group deals with the exploits of English kings and noblemen of the tenth century, the other with the exploits and adventures of persons who did not belong to this country. We will take the second group of poems first, as it is admitted by all authorities to be the earlier of the two.

The longest poem of this class is Beowulf, an epic of 3183 verses, the subject of which briefly is as follows: Hrothgar, king of the Danes, has built a splendid hall, but is unable to enjoy the use of it on account of the ravages of a monster named Grendel, who attacks the hall by night and devours all whom he finds there. Beowulf, a nephew of Hygelac, king of the Geatas, hearing of Hrothgar's distress comes to his help and destroys first the monster himself and then his mother who had come to exact vengeance. He is thanked and rewarded for his exploits by Hrothgar, and returns to his own home. After this a long period is supposed to elapse. Hygelac has perished in an expedition against the Frisians, and his son Heardred has been slain by the Swedes. Beowulf has succeeded to the throne and reigned many years. In his old age he resolves to attack a dragon which is ravaging the land, and in spite of the cowardice of his followers, of whom all except one forsake him, he eventually succeeds in destroying it, though not before he has himself received a mortal wound. The poem ends with an account of his funeral.

The action is interrupted a good many times by references to incidents in the history of the royal families of the Danes and the Geatas, particularly to Hygelac's fatal expedition and to the dealings of his family with the Swedish kings Ongentheow, Onela and Eadgils. We find also a number of allusions to heroes of the past such as Sigemund, Eormenric, Finn and Offa, who are known to us from other sources.

To the same class of poetry belong some fragments dealing with the stories of Finn and Waldhere. The fragment relating to Finn is very obscure and indeed would be quite unintelligible were it not for a passage in Beowulf (vv. 1068—1159) where the same story is introduced as the subject of a recitation by Hrothgar's minstrel. A certain Hnaef, represented as a vassal of Healfdene, Hrothgar's father, was slain in a fortress belonging to Finn, king of the Frisians. His followers made so brave a defence that Finn was compelled to come to terms with them. Subsequently, when an opportunity presented itself they took vengeance upon Finn and slew him. The fragment gives an account of the fighting which took place, probably in the encounter immediately after Hnaef's death.

The story of Waldhere is well known from German sources which we shall have to mention presently. One of the fragments is taken up by an altercation between Waldhere and the Burgundian king Guthhere, before they begin to fight, while the other contains an exhortation to Waldhere by the lady to acquit himself bravely.

Widsith, though not an epic poem itself, refers to a large number of the characters which figure in Beowulf, Finn and Waldhere. It is stated that the poet was in the service of a certain Eadgils, prince of the Myrgingas, and that in company with Ealhhild, apparently a princess of the same family, he visited the court of the Gothic king Eormenric. The greater

This card was in:

I would like to ha
this field, and also:

Would you please write yo

Name

Address

Date

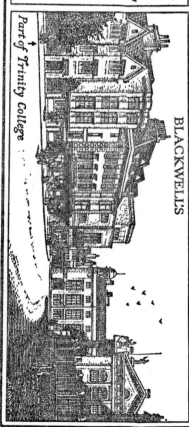

B·H·
BLACKWELL
Ltd
48 to 51
Broad Street
OXFORD

BLACKWELL'S

Part of Trinity College :

THERE, in the Broad, within whose booky house

BUSINESS REPLY CARD
Licence No. 6947

BLACKWELL'S

Broad Street

OXFORD

England

I would like to receive the
following Catalogues as issued :

☐ Antiquarian and Modern Press Books
☐ Bibliography ☐ Topography & Travel
☐ English Literature ☐ Fine Arts
☐ Greek & Latin Classics ☐ Political
Science ☐ Near East ☐ Africana ☐ Far East
☐ Semitica ☐ History ☐ Theology
☐ Philosophy ☐ Science ☐ Law
☐ Education ☐ Philology ☐ Economics
☐ French Literature ☐ German Literature
☐ Medicine and Surgery ☐ Technical
☐ Natural History and Gardening

*If you are interested in foreign books
on these subjects, please mark F here* ☐

CHAPTER I.

THE EARLY NARRATIVE POETRY OF THE TEUTONIC PEOPLES.

THE remains of English poetry which have come down to us from times anterior to the Norman conquest are mainly of a religious character and deal with the lives of saints or with subjects derived from the Bible or ecclesiastical tradition. The secular poems are comparatively few in number and, with one exception, of inconsiderable length. Most of them are narrative poems and admit of a very obvious classification according to the choice of subjects with which they are concerned. One group deals with the exploits of English kings and noblemen of the tenth century, the other with the exploits and adventures of persons who did not belong to this country. We will take the second group of poems first, as it is admitted by all authorities to be the earlier of the two.

The longest poem of this class is Beowulf, an epic of 3183 verses, the subject of which briefly is as follows: Hrothgar, king of the Danes, has built a splendid hall, but is unable to enjoy the use of it on account of the ravages of a monster named Grendel, who attacks the hall by night and devours all whom he finds there. Beowulf, a nephew of Hygelac, king of the Geatas, hearing of Hrothgar's distress comes to his help and destroys first the monster himself and then his mother who had come to exact vengeance. He is thanked and rewarded for his exploits by Hrothgar, and returns to his own home. After this a long period is supposed to elapse. Hygelac has perished in an expedition against the Frisians, and his son Heardred has been slain by the Swedes. Beowulf has succeeded to the throne and

reigned many years.   In his old age he resolves to attack a
dragon which is ravaging the land, and in spite of the cowardice
of his followers, of whom all except one forsake him, he
eventually succeeds in destroying it, though not before he has
himself received a mortal wound.   The poem ends with an
account of his funeral.

The action is interrupted a good many times by references
to incidents in the history of the royal families of the Danes and
the Geatas, particularly to Hygelac's fatal expedition and to the
dealings of his family with the Swedish kings Ongentheow,
Onela and Eadgils.   We find also a number of allusions to
heroes of the past such as Sigemund, Eormenric, Finn and Offa,
who are known to us from other sources.

To the same class of poetry belong some fragments dealing
with the stories of Finn and Waldhere.   The fragment relating
to Finn is very obscure and indeed would be quite unintelligible
were it not for a passage in Beowulf (vv. 1068—1159) where the
same story is introduced as the subject of a recitation by
Hrothgar's minstrel.   A certain Hnaef, represented as a vassal
of Healfdene, Hrothgar's father, was slain in a fortress belonging
to Finn, king of the Frisians.   His followers made so brave a
defence that Finn was compelled to come to terms with them.
Subsequently, when an opportunity presented itself they took
vengeance upon Finn and slew him.   The fragment gives an
account of the fighting which took place, probably in the
encounter immediately after Hnaef's death.

The story of Waldhere is well known from German sources
which we shall have to mention presently.   One of the fragments
is taken up by an altercation between Waldhere and the
Burgundian king Guthhere, before they begin to fight, while the
other contains an exhortation to Waldhere by the lady to acquit
himself bravely.

Widsith, though not an epic poem itself, refers to a large
number of the characters which figure in Beowulf, Finn and
Waldhere.   It is stated that the poet was in the service of a
certain Eadgils, prince of the Myrgingas, and that in company
with Ealhhild, apparently a princess of the same family, he
visited the court of the Gothic king Eormenric.   The greater

part of the poem is taken up with lists of peoples which he
had visited and of famous princes whom he knew personally or
by report.

The elegy of Deor consists of a number of brief notices of
misfortunes which had befallen various persons, Weland and
Beaduhild, Geat, Theodric and the subjects of Eormenric. Each
notice ends with a refrain expressing the belief or hope that the
poet will be able to survive his misfortunes as they did. At the
end he says that he had been the bard of the Heodeningas, but
that his office had been taken away from him and given to a
skilful minstrel named Heorrenda.

In a later chapter we shall have to discuss the question when
these poems were composed. At present it will be enough to
remark that though the MSS. in which they are preserved date
only from the tenth or eleventh centuries almost all scholars
agree that the poems themselves cannot be later than the eighth
century, while probably the majority would refer their composition, in part at least to the seventh. In their present form they
cannot be earlier than this, for with the exception of the Finn-
fragment all of them contain Christian allusions.

The later group of secular narrative poems may best be
described as historical. The earliest of them celebrates the
battle of Brunanburh won by Aethelstan in 937 over the
Scottish king Constantine II and his Scandinavian allies.
Others describe Edmund's conquest of the Five Boroughs, the
coronation of Edgar, the glories of his reign, the troubles which
followed, and lastly the death of Edward the Confessor. The
longest of all is a detailed account of the disastrous battle
of Maldon, in which Byrhtnoth, earl of Essex, lost his life.
All these pieces except the last are found inserted in texts
of the Saxon Chronicle and all without exception appear to
have been composed soon after the events which they commemorate.

In addition to the above there are a number of other short
poems which are not essentially of a religious character. The
most important of these are the Wanderer, the Wife's Complaint,
the Husband's Message and the Ruin—to which we may perhaps add the first half of the Seafarer. They are probably all of

fairly early date, but they differ from the poems we have been
discussing in the fact that they contain no proper names. Those
of them which can be called narrative deal apparently with
typical characters or situations. A certain amount of magical
and gnomic poetry has also survived, while metrical riddles are
numerous, but these need not concern us here.

It is scarcely open to doubt that a large amount of Anglo-
Saxon narrative poetry has perished. Several historical poems
and ballads of the tenth and eleventh centuries, now lost, can be
traced in texts of the Saxon Chronicle and in Latin works[1].
Attempts have been made also to show that narrative poems
were used by the compilers of the early part of the Chronicle
and by several Latin histories referring to the same period, but
the evidence adduced is very doubtful. Perhaps the most likely
case is the story of Hengest and Horsa, especially in the form in
which it appears in the Historia Brittonum. On the other hand
it is probable that parts of the Vitae Duorum Offarum, a
St Albans work dating from the beginning of the thirteenth
century, are derived ultimately from poems which described
Offa's single combat and marriage—incidents to which we find
brief references in Widsith and Beowulf respectively. A similar
origin may perhaps be claimed for Walter Map's story (*De Nugis
Curialium*, II 17) of Gado (Wada). A few corrupt verses of a
poem on this subject, obviously of late date, have been preserved
in a Latin homily[2].

The earlier and later groups of narrative poems have in
general[3] the same metrical form and on the whole a very similar
terminology. The love of battle-scenes is also common to both.
In other respects however they differ greatly. Here we need
only notice the entire difference in subject-matter ; the poems of
the second group contain no allusion to the subjects of the first.
Much greater changes however, both in form and matter, are
noticeable when English poetry reappears in the thirteenth and
fourteenth centuries. The majority of these poems are of French

[1] Cf. Brandl in Paul's *Grundriss d. germ. Philol.*[2], II pp. 1083 ff., 1087 f.

[2] Academy, 1896, I 137 ; cf. Brandl, *op. cit.*, p. 1085.

[3] This remark applies more especially to the poems on Brunanburh and Maldon
in the later group.

origin. But even when the scene is laid in England, the subjects are usually drawn from written sources—which is certainly not the case with the historical poems of the tenth century. To the subjects of the earlier group of Anglo-Saxon poems there is scarcely a reference.

The period of German literature which corresponds chronologically to the Anglo-Saxon period in England is far inferior to the latter in remains of secular narrative poetry. We possess only one fragment of a poem somewhat similar to the Finn-fragment, preserved in a MS. dating from about 800, and one poem of somewhat later date, celebrating a victory of Ludwig III, king of the West Franks. To these we may add three or four very short metrical charms, similar to the Anglo-Saxon magical pieces mentioned above.

The subject of the first of these poems is as follows: Hildebrand (*Hiltibrant*) is an old warrior who has left his country with Dietrich (*Theotrih*) and served with the Huns. On his return from exile, thirty years later, he is challenged by a young warrior named Hadubrand. In the altercation with which the piece opens Hildebrand discovers that his opponent is his own son, acquaints him with the fact and tries to dissuade him from the combat with offers of rich presents. But the young man refuses to believe him, and taunts him with cowardice and guile in trying to put him off his guard. Hildebrand is therefore obliged to fight, and the fragment comes to an end in the midst of the encounter.

The Ludwigslied is a poem of fifty-nine verses celebrating the praises of Ludwig III, with special reference to his victory over the Northmen at Saucourt in 881, and seems to have been composed before the king's death in the following year. It is not in the old Teutonic alliterative metre which we find in Anglo-Saxon poetry and in the Hildebrandslied, but in the later rhyming verse. The religious element is prominent throughout.

There is no doubt that a considerable amount of secular narrative poetry once existed in German. Einhard in his Life of Charlemagne (cap. 29) states that the emperor collected native and very ancient poems in which were related the deeds

and battles of kings of former times¹.   But during the following
centuries poetry of this kind seems to have gone entirely out of
favour among the higher classes.   We do indeed find occasional
references to such poems in later Latin works.   In particular the
Annals of Quedlinburg have incorporated from them a number
of notices relating to Eormenric, Theodric (*Thideric de Berne*)
and other heroes of antiquity.   But here it is expressly stated
that it was among the peasants (*rustici*) that these poems were
known.   Other Latin chronicles cite lost poems relating to
persons and events of the tenth century, which may have been
somewhat similar to the contemporary Anglo-Saxon poems,
though generally they appear to have been of a less serious
character.

Some compensation for the loss of early German poetry is
afforded by the preservation of a few Latin poems, of which the
most important is *Waltharius manu fortis*, composed probably
about 930 by Ekkehard of St Gall.   The subject is the same as
that of the Anglo-Saxon Waldhere fragments.   Waltharius and
Hiltgund, the son and daughter respectively of two princes in
Gaul, were betrothed in their childhood, but had to be given up
as hostages to Attila, king of the Huns.   After many years they
escaped and carried off with them much treasure.   Hearing of
this, King Guntharius, who dwelt at Worms, determined to
waylay them and set out with twelve warriors, among them
the brave Hagano who had formerly shared Waltharius' exile.
Waltharius is overtaken in a defile of the Vosges and slays
eleven of the warriors in single combat.   In his final encounter
with Hagano and Guntharius all three are crippled, but
Waltharius is able to make his way home with Hiltgund.   There
are other poems, one of which combines German with Latin in
each verse, celebrating the deeds of the contemporary Saxon
emperors and their relatives.

The second period of German literature, beginning in the
twelfth century, is incomparably superior to the first in the

---

¹ Saxo Poeta, who wrote about 890, speaks of *uulgaria carmina* which celebrated
Pippinos Carolos Hludowicos et Theodricos et Carlomannos Hlothariosque (Mon. Germ.,
Script. 1 268).   But it is usually held that these words are due to a mistaken inference
from Einhard, whose work he was using.

amount of secular narrative poetry which it has left behind.
Here we need only concern ourselves with those poems which
draw their subjects from ancient native traditions.   These are
mostly anonymous and come from the southern districts,
especially Austria and Bavaria.   Their metrical form is modern
and similar to that of other poetry of the same period.   The
best known of these poems is the Nibelungenlied, which dates
from the beginning of the thirteenth century.   Only a very brief
résumé of its contents can be given here.

Siegfried (*Sîvrit*), the son of Siegmund, comes from Xanten
to Worms and asks for the hand of Kriemhild, the sister of the
Burgundian king Gunther.   He joins Gunther in his campaigns
and by magical arts enables him to win the amazon Brünhild
(*Prünhilt*) for his bride.   The two wives quarrel, and Brünhild
learns from Kriemhild of the part played by Siegfried towards
her.   On hearing this she begins to long for his death, and
eventually he is murdered at a hunting party by Hagen
(*Hagene*), the chief of Gunther's knights.   Hagen also deprives
Kriemhild of Siegfried's treasure (*der Nibelunge hort*) and sinks it
in the Rhine.   Kriemhild is afterwards married to Etzel, king of
the Huns and, burning for vengeance, persuades him to invite
Gunther on a visit, together with his brothers Gernot and
Giselher and also Hagen.   Soon after their arrival she brings
about a quarrel, and after a huge slaughter on both sides,
Gunther and Hagen, who have lost all their men, are captured
by Dietrich von Bern, Etzel's vassal.   Kriemhild puts them to
death, violating the oath which she had given to spare them, and
in anger at this treachery Hildebrand, Dietrich's old retainer,
slays her.

Closely connected in subject with the Nibelungenlied is the
Klage, which describes the funeral of those slain in the fighting
with Gunther and the lamentation over them.   Here too we may
notice the Seyfridslied, though in the form in which it has come
down to us it belongs to a much later period.   In reality it is
clearly a combination of two different ballads, both of which
deal with Siegfried's early years.   The first relates how he was
brought up by a smith and slew a dragon.   The second gives
an account of another similar adventure—this time with a fiery

dragon which had carried off Kriemhild from her father's home. Siegfried kills the dragon and at the same time takes possession of the treasure of certain dwarfs, the sons of Nybling.

A number of other medieval poems deal with the adventures of Dietrich von Bern and his knights. Alpharts Tod tells the story of the young knight Alphart, Hildebrand's nephew, and his encounter with two of Ermenrich's warriors named Witege and Heime, by the former of whom he was treacherously slain. Dietrichs Flucht relates how Ermenrich (*Ermrich*) was instigated by an evil counseller named Sibeche to plot destruction for his nephew Dietrich. Though the plot fails, Hildebrand and several of Dietrich's other knights are captured and imprisoned, and in order to obtain their release Dietrich is forced to go into exile. In the Rabenschlacht we are told how Dietrich with the help of Etzel set out to recover his inheritance. While he is engaged in battle with Ermenrich, his brother Diether and two young sons of Etzel are slain by Witege. Dietrich rides after Witege to exact vengeance, but Witege disappears in the sea. Virginal describes how Dietrich was imprisoned by a giant in a castle called Muter and rescued by Hildebrand, Witege, Heime and others. Further adventures with giants and dwarfs are related in the Eckenlied, Sigenot and Laurin. In the Rosengarten Dietrich is made to fight with Siegfried.

The story of Wolfdietrich and Ortnit has come down to us in several different forms, but the outline may be given briefly as follows. Wolfdietrich, the son of king Hugdietrich, is kept out of his inheritance by his brothers or their guardian Saben on the ground of illegitimacy. He betakes himself to a faithful old knight, Berchtung of Meran, who raises an army to help him. But in the battle that ensues Berchtung and his sons are all slain or captured, and Wolfdietrich has to go into exile. He then marries the widow of a king named Ortnit and destroys the dragon which had killed him. Eventually he succeeds in winning his father's kingdom and releasing his faithful followers. Some elements of this story appear to have been incorporated in the romance of King Rother.

The story of the poem Kûdrûn falls naturally into two parts. In the first Hetel (*Hetele*), king of Denmark, hears of Hilde, a princess of Ireland and desires to marry her. As her father, the fierce Hagen, will not consent, Hetel's warriors Wate, Fruote and Hôrand carry her off. Hagen pursues them to Denmark, but in the fight which follows he is nearly killed by Wate. Finally a reconciliation takes place and Hilde is allowed to marry Hetel. In the second part Hartmuot and Herwig are suitors for Kûdrûn, the daughter of Hetel and Hilde. The latter is at length accepted, but Kûdrûn is carried off by Hartmuot and his father Ludwig (*Ludewîc*). A pursuit follows and Hetel is killed by Ludwig. Kûdrûn is kept at Hartmuot's home for seven years, harshly treated by his mother Gerlind, because she will not consent to become his wife. At last Herwig and her brother Ortwîn with the warriors Wate, Fruote and Hôrand come and rescue her. Ludwig is killed but Hartmuot is spared at Kûdrûn's intercession.

In conclusion mention must be made of some fragments o. a poem dealing with Walther and Hildegund. The subject seems to have been identical with that of Ekkehard's Waltharius. Reminiscences of other ancient stories are occasionally to be found in poems of a romantic character. Among these we may note especially the poem Herzog Friedrich von Schwaben, a portion of which seems to be derived from the story of Weland.

The North German dialects have no poetry of this type, except a few ballads dating from much later times, of which the most important is one on Eormenric's death. But a great mass of legend, derived chiefly from North German sources, is preserved in the Norse work Thiðreks Saga af Bern, which dates from about the middle of the thirteenth century. The characters are for the most part identical with those which figure in the High German epics, Dietrich von Bern, Ermenrich, Witege, Walther, Siegfried etc. Traces of poems of much earlier date have been sought in several Latin chronicles. Besides the references in the Annals of Quedlinburg, to which we have already alluded, mention may be made of the Saxon stories given by Widukind and the Translatio S. Alexandri, especially that of the victory over the Thuringian king Irminfrith.

The vernacular poetry of the Langobardi has entirely perished, but a number of stories given by the Latin historians are thought to be based on early poems. The first and most striking of these is the account of the battle with the Vandals, in which the two armies appeal for victory to Wodan and Fria respectively[1]. A similar origin has been claimed for several other narratives, such as that of Alboin's visit to Turisind, king of the Gepidae, and more especially the story of Authari and Theudelinda[2].

The Gothic historian Jordanes states (cap. 5) that his compatriots were wont to celebrate the deeds of their famous men in poetry, and it is probable that many of the legends which he gives were ultimately derived from such poems. Among them we may include not only the story of Filimer and the migration to the Black Sea (cap. 4)—in which case ancient poems are expressly mentioned—but also perhaps that of the first migration under Berig (*ib.*) and some part of the account of Ostrogotha (cap. 16 f.), as well as the incidental reference to Vidigoia's death (cap. 34). In the story of Hermanaricus also several incidents, notably the death of Sunilda and the vengeance subsequently exacted by her brothers Sarus and Ammius (cap. 24), suggest a tradition preserved in poetic form.

No Scandinavian country except Iceland[3] has preserved any early poems in its native language. The ancient literature of Iceland however is peculiarly rich in secular narrative poetry. Moreover though the earliest of these poems are probably quite two centuries later than Beowulf, they are entirely free from Christian influence. Indeed it can hardly be doubted that a considerable proportion of them date from heathen times.

It will be convenient to begin with the collection of poems usually known as the Older Edda. These are all anonymous; but most of them are generally believed to belong to the tenth century, while a few may really have been composed in Norway at a still earlier date. Eleven of these poems deal exclusively, or almost exclusively, with gods, giants and other supernatural

---

[1] Origo Gentis Langobardorum (Mon. Germ., Script. Rerum Langobard., p. 2 f.); Paulus Diaconus, *Hist. Lang.* I 8.

[2] Cf. Kögel, *Geschichte d. deutschen Litteratur*, I p. 115 ff.

[3] The poems were not all composed in Iceland. Many of the earliest doubtless came from Norway, others perhaps from the British Isles, while others again are referred to Greenland.

beings, and hence stand quite apart from the class of poetry with which we are concerned. But since we shall have to refer to them occasionally in the following pages it will be convenient here to give a brief synopsis of their contents.

Völuspá is a mythological poem in the form of a speech delivered to the god Othin by a sibyl whom he is consulting. It deals with the origin of the world, the history of the gods and their coming fate. Hávamál is a collection of proverbial wisdom and moral precepts of the heathen age, with occasional references to myth and ritual. Vafþrúðnismál describes how Othin visited the giant Vafþrúðnir and entered into a contest with him in mythological lore. The subject of Grímnismál is a visit paid by Othin in disguise to a king named Geirröðr, who tortures him. Othin gives a long discourse on mythological matters and finally reveals himself, whereupon the king stumbles over his sword and dies. Skírnismál relates how Skírnir, the servant of the god Frey, was sent to obtain for his master the hand of the giantess Gerðr, of whom he had become passionately enamoured. Hárbarðslióð is taken up with an altercation between the god Thor and a ferryman called Hárbarðr (generally supposed to be Othin), who refuses to take him over a strait. Hýmiskviða gives an account of Thor's adventures when he went to visit the giant Hýmir. Lokasenna is occupied with a number of scandalous charges brought by Loki against various gods and goddesses who have been invited to a feast by Aegir. Thrymskviða relates how the giant Thrymr, having obtained possession of Thor's hammer, demanded the goddess Freyia as his bride, and how Thor came disguised as Freyia and slew the giant. Alvíssmál is a dialogue between Thor and the dwarf Alvíss, who is a suitor for his daughter. Thor detains the dwarf with questions on the various names of natural objects and phenomena until the fatal moment of daybreak. Vegtamskviða describes how Othin went to consult a sibyl on the impending fate of Balder.

In addition to these pieces, all of which probably come from one collection, there are two semi-mythical poems contained in other works. Rígsmál or Rígsþula relates how a certain Rígr (identified in the introduction with the god Heimdallr) became the progenitor of the three classes of men—the characteristics of which are described at length.   Hyndlulióð is mainly a genealogical poem, narrating how Freyia went to consult the giantess Hyndla as to the ancestry of her devotee, Óttarr the son of Innsteinn.   It contains also some purely mythological matter which is generally supposed to have come from a separate poem. Here also we may mention two pieces known as Grógaldr and Fiölsvinnsmál, which clearly belong together.   In the former Svipdagr calls up the spirit of Gróa, his mother; in the latter he comes to the enchanted abode of Menglöð and, after many questions with the gatekeeper, is at length recognised as her destined lover.   In much later times we find Swedish and Danish versions of the same story, and there can be little doubt that it is really a folk-tale.

The purely mythological poems of the Edda are followed by Völundarkviða, which gives a fairly full account of the story of Völundr (Weland).   It describes how Völundr and his brothers obtained as their wives three swan-maidens, who after eight years deserted them.   Then Völundr is captured by a king named Níðuðr, hamstrung and compelled to work as his smith. Völundr executes vengeance on the king's sons and daughter (Böðvildr) and then flies away.

The next poem, Helgakviða Hiörvarðssonar, gives in dialogue form a somewhat complicated story of the adventures of a king named Hiörvarðr and his son Helgi.   A different Helgi, the son of Sigmundr, is the subject of the two following poems, Helgakviður Hundingsbana.   Both poems relate how the hero overthrew a king named Hundingr and how he was afterwards summoned by Sigrún, the daughter of Högni, to save her from marriage to a prince named Höðbroddr, whom she detested. The first poem ends with Helgi's victory over Högni and Höðbroddr; but the second goes on to describe how Dagr, the son of Högni, subsequently slew Helgi in revenge for his father. Sinfiötli, the son of Sigmundr, figures in both poems, but Sigurðr is not mentioned.

The next poem, Grípisspá, probably a late work, gives a summary of the adventures of Sigurðr, the son of Sigmundr, in the form of a dialogue between the hero and his uncle Grípir, who is endowed with prophecy. This is followed by three pieces which may really be parts of one original poem. The first (commonly called Reginsmál) relates how three of the gods, Othin, Hoenir and Loki, killed a certain Otr, the son of Hreiðmarr. Having to pay compensation to the father, Loki robbed a dwarf, named Andvari, of his gold. Andvari laid a curse on the gold, and Hreiðmarr was soon killed by his own son Fáfnir, who subsequently turned into a serpent[1]. Reginn, Fáfnir's brother, betook himself to Sigurðr and became his attendant. The poem then goes on to describe how a certain Hnikarr (Othin) guided Sigurðr on an expedition he undertook against the sons of Hundingr. In the next piece (Fáfnismál) Sigurðr at Reginn's instigation attacks and kills Fáfnir. Then, finding that Reginn is plotting treachery, he slays him also and carries off Fáfnir's gold. In the third (Sigrdrífumál) Sigurðr finds and wakens a maid named Sigrdrífa, a valkyrie who has been punished by Othin with an enchanted sleep. She imparts to him much magical lore; but the close of the poem is lost owing to a lacuna in the MS.

Of the following nine poems six—Sigurðarkviða I (a fragment), Guðrúnarkviða I, Sigurðarkviða II (*hin skamma*), Guðrúnarkviða II (*hin forna*), Atlakviða and Atlamál—deal with practically the same events as the Nibelungenlied. But unfortunately, owing to the lacuna in the MS. several poems at the beginning of the series have been lost. Hence in order to obtain a full account of the story it is necessary to refer to the Völsunga Saga (see below), which used the lost poems as well as the others.

The chief variations from the German version of the story are as follows: (i) Sigmundr has been killed before the birth of Sigurðr (Siegfried) by the sons of Hundingr. (ii) The wife of Sigurðr is called Guðrún, Grímhildr being the name of her mother and Giúki that of her father. (iii) Brynhildr is the sister of Atli (Etzel). In several authorities[2] she is identified with the valkyrie

---

[1] Called a dragon (*dreki*) in Völsunga Saga.

[2] Helreið Brynh. (str. 7 ff.) and the prose versions (Skaldsk. 41, Völs. S. 20). It is a much debated question whether the two are identified also in Fáfnismál, str. 40 ff. In Grípisspá they seem clearly to be separated.

of Sigrdrífumál, and it is stated that she and Sigurðr had exchanged vows of love; but Sigurðr's love was subsequently
turned to Guðrún through a magic potion given him by Grímhildr. (iv) Högni (Hagen) is the brother of Gunnarr (Gunther);
and in place of Gernôt and Gîselher there is another brother
named Guthormr. It is the last-named who actually kills
Sigurðr, and he is himself killed by the dying man. Brynhildr
then puts herself to death and is burned with Sigurðr. (v) The
death of Gunnarr and Högni is attributed to Atli. Guðrún on the
other hand warns her brothers of the treachery awaiting them,
and subsequently avenges their deaths by killing Atli and the
children he had had by her.

Interspersed among these poems are three others connected
with the same story, but dealing with incidents unknown to the
German version. The Helreið Brynhildar describes how Brynhildr on her way to Hell encounters a giantess, to whom she
tells the story of her life. Guðrúnarkviða III relates how
Guðrún was accused to Atli of adultery with Thióðrekr, but
established her innocence by the ordeal. In Oddrúnargrátr a
sister of Atli named Oddrún comes to Borgný, the daughter of
a certain Heiðrekr, to relieve her in her travail, and gives an
account of the relations between herself, Brynhildr and Gunnarr.

The last two poems—Guðrúnarhvöt and Hamðismál—are
concerned with the story of the attack upon Iörmunrekr (Hermanaricus), to Jordanes' account of which we have already
alluded (p. 10). Here the story is connected with the preceding
poems[1] by the fact that Svanhildr (Sunilda) is represented as
the daughter of Guðrún and Sigurðr, while Hamðir and Sörli
(Ammius and Sarus) are said to be the sons of Guðrún and a
certain Iónakr, whom she had married after Atli's death. In
the first poem Guðrún incites her sons to avenge their sister
and then bewails her many misfortunes. The second describes
the actual fighting, preceded however by the account of a quarrel
in which Erpr, a stepson of Guðrún, is killed by his half-
brothers. To his death is attributed the fact that Iörmunrekr,

---

[1] The death of Svanhildr is mentioned also in Sigurðarkviða II, where it is
attributed (as in the prose authorities) to the evil counsel of a certain Bikki, an
adviser of Iörmunrekr.

was able to survive the onslaught, though he lost both hands
and both feet.

The prose Edda (Skaldskaparmál, cap. 43) contains a poem,
Grottasöngr, which gives the story of two giant maidens who
had to grind gold and peace for the Danish king Fróði. At the
end there is an allusion to Halfdan and Hrólfr Kraki (see below).
Besides this we have, both in the prose Edda and elsewhere, a
number of fragments of poems, some of which refer to Sigurðr
and his family and some to other stories. Among the latter
mention may be made especially of a poem Biarkamál, which
celebrated the achievements of the Danish king Hrólfr Kraki
and the heroism of his retinue in the battle wherein he lost his
life. In Hervarar Saga large portions of an early poem relating
to the Goths and Huns have been preserved.

In addition to the poems enumerated above, all of which are
anonymous, we have also a number of works by known poets.
Most of these deal either wholly or in part with contemporary
persons and events. The earliest date from the ninth century
and are of Norwegian origin. Probably the oldest of all are the
fragments of Bragi Boddason, the chief of which is a description
of his shield (Ragnarsdrápa). From the reign of Harold the
Fair-haired several poems are known, though nearly all of them
are in a very fragmentary condition. Among them may be mentioned especially the Ynglingatal of Thióðolfr of Hvín, a genealogical poem which traces the descent of Rögnvaldr, a cousin of
Harold, from the ancient kings of the Swedes and the god Frey.
Another famous work by the same poet was the Haustlöng,
which dealt with mythological subjects. Next perhaps in
importance to Thióðolfr was Thórbiörn Hornklofi, from whom
we have fragments of two poems (Hrafnsmál and Glymdrápa),
celebrating the exploits of Harold. Somewhat later we hear of
a poet named Goðþormr Sindri, who is known chiefly from the
remains of a work (Hákonardrápa) in honour of Haakon I. A
famous fragment (Eireksmál) by an unknown poet, dating from
shortly after the middle of the tenth century, celebrates the
death of King Eiríkr Blóðöx and his reception by Othin in
Valhalla. From this is copied the Hákonarmál of Eyvindr
Skaldaspillir, celebrating the death of Haakon I at the battle of

Fitje (A.D. 961). The same poet also composed a genealogical poem (Háleygiatal) in imitation of Ynglingatal. In it he traced the ancestry of Haakon, earl of Lade, who ruled Norway from about 975 to 995, back through the kings of Hálogaland to Othin and Skaði.

From this time onwards the cultivation of poetry seems to have been almost entirely limited to Icelanders, many of whom resided largely at the courts of various Scandinavian kings. Among them the most noteworthy and almost the earliest was Egill Skallagrímsson, who lived from about 900 to 982. He is known chiefly from the Höfuðlausn, composed for Eiríkr Blóðöx in England, the Arinbiarnardrápa, in honour of his friend Arinbiörn, and the Sonatorrek, an elegy over one of his sons. Of his younger contemporaries perhaps the best known are Kormakr Ögmundarson and Einarr Helgason. The latter is famous chiefly for his poem Vellekla, in which he celebrated the exploits of Earl Haakon. Many other distinguished poets flourished during the following half century—down to the time of Harold III (Harðráði)—but it is not necessary here to discuss their works.

By the time of Harold III the composition of prose narratives or sagas (sögur) had already begun to be cultivated by Icelanders, though it was not until towards the end of the following century that they were first committed to writing. Many sagas are based on old narrative poems; as for instance Ynglinga Saga, which is largely a paraphrase and expansion of Ynglingatal. Völsunga Saga, which gives the stories of Helgi, Sigurðr, Guðrún and Svanhildr, is derived mainly from the poems of the Edda, though it has used other materials. The earlier part, dealing with Sigmundr and his ancestors seems to have drawn upon some lost poems. In Sörla Tháttr[1] we meet with a story—found also in the prose Edda (Skaldsk. 50) and alluded to in Bragi's Ragnarsdrápa—which is clearly connected with that of the first part of the German poem Kûdrûn. Hildr, the daughter of Högni, is carried off in her father's absence by his friend Heðinn. They are overtaken and a battle follows, in which all the combatants are killed. Hildr by magic spells

---

[1] Fornaldar Sögur Norðrlanda, I p. 391 ff.

rouses the slain each night to renew the battle. In Hrólfs Saga Kraka we have an account of the Danish kings Helgi and Hróarr, the sons of Halfdan, and of Helgi's son, Hrólfr Kraki, which seems to be derived ultimately from old poems like Biarkamál. Certain incidents in the story, such as Hrólfr's dealings with the Swedish king Aðils, are related also in other sagas. The same characters figured prominently in Skiöldunga Saga, of which we have little except an abridged Latin trans-lation. This saga also related at length the stories of Haraldr Hilditönn, Sigurðr Hringr and Ragnarr Loðbrók, parts of which are known also from other sources, especially Ragnars Saga Loðbrókar and the Tháttr af Loðbrókar sonum.

Among Latin authorities the most important is the great Danish History (*Gesta Danorum*) of Saxo Grammaticus, which dates from the end of the twelfth century and contains metrical translations or paraphrases of many old poems. Of these perhaps the most noteworthy are the Biarkamál and some of the poems attributed to Starkaðr (Starcatherus), particularly those ad-dressed to Ingialdr (Ingellus). Here also we find a detailed account of the tragic story of Hagbarðr and Signý, which is very frequently alluded to in Old Norse poetry. Hagbarðr belonged to a family which was involved in vendetta with the Danish king Sigarr. But having fallen in love with Signý, the king's daughter, he visited her disguised as a woman—an adven-ture which ended in his being discovered and condemned to death. Signý and all her maidens destroyed themselves when he was led to the gallows. Many other stories are given entirely in prose, among them those of Heðinn and Högni, Iörmunrekr and Helgi Hundingsbani, though no mention is made of Sig-mundr or Sigurðr. The adventures also of Haraldr Hilditönn and Ragnarr Loðbrók are related at considerable length. Lastly, we may mention a story which is not recorded by any Icelandic authority, namely that of the single combat fought by Uffo the son of Wermundus. It deserves notice here on account of its obvious identity with the English story of Offa.

In the course of this chapter we have reviewed briefly the secular narrative poetry produced by the various Teutonic peoples down to the end of the tenth century. In the case of works by historical Norwegian and Icelandic poets, owing to the abundance of material, we have restricted ourselves to mentioning only the leading names.   Elsewhere we have endeavoured to give a more or less complete summary.   On the other hand, among works dating from later than the tenth century, we have taken into consideration only those which are concerned with stories of ancient times.   The stories themselves will be discussed in the following chapters.

CHAPTER II.

THE HEROIC AGE OF THE TEUTONIC PEOPLES.

IT will not have escaped notice that a large proportion of the stories described or alluded to in the preceding chapter are found in the literature of more than one nation. The most casual reader could not fail to observe the identity of the story of Sigurðr and Guðrún, as given in the Edda and Völsunga Saga, with that of Siegfried and Kriemhild related in the Nibelungenlied. Equally obvious is the connection between the story of Iörmunrekr and Svanhildr in the same Scandinavian authorities and that of Hermanaricus and Sunilda given by Jordanes. A still closer resemblance is furnished by the Anglo-Saxon poem Waldhere and the German-Latin Waltharius. The connection between the German poem Kûdrûn and the Scandinavian story of Heðinn and Högni is perhaps less striking, but not open to question. The brief references to the story of Weland and Beaduhild in the Anglo-Saxon poem Deor are quite sufficient to prove its substantial identity with that told in Völundarkviða.

In other cases the same characters appear, though the incidents related are different. Eormenric (Ermenrich) is a prominent figure in Anglo-Saxon and German poetry, as well as in Scandinavian and Gothic records. The Wudga and Hama of Widsith (Waldhere and Beowulf) and the Theodric of Waldhere are clearly identical with the Witege, Heime and Dietrich von Bern oi the German epics, while Theodric figures also, though not prominently, in the Edda. Of all the Edda poems[1] those which show the least connection with non-Scandinavian poetry are the three Helgakviður. Yet Sinfiötli, as well as Sigmundr,

---

[1] Except of course those which deal only with supernatural beings (p. 11 f.).

is mentioned in Beowulf (under the form Fitela) and there are traces that his name was once known in Germany.

We may observe that in Beowulf it is only the persons mentioned in casual references and in episodes lying outside the main action of the story, such as Sigemund, Eormenric, Hama and Weland, to whom we find allusions in German poetry. On the other hand most of the chief characters of the poem are well known from Scandinavian records, though not in connection with precisely the same incidents. There is no doubt as to the identity of the Danish kings Healfdene, his sons Hrothgar and Halga, and Hrothwulf the nephew and colleague of Hrothgar, with Halfdan, his sons Hróarr and Helgi and Helgi's son, the famous Hrólfr Kraki—all likewise kings of the Danes. Equally obvious is the identity of the Swedish prince Eadgils the son of Ohthere with Aðils the son of Óttarr in Ynglingatal, while his uncle and opponent Onela is clearly the same person as Aðils' opponent Áli, although the latter is represented as a Norwegian in Old Norse literature. Further, the episode in which Ingeld is incited by an old warrior to avenge his father Froda is evidently to be connected with certain poems given by Saxo, in which the old warrior Starcatherus rouses Ingellus to avenge his father Frotho. Among other persons mentioned in the poem Scyld is doubtless to be identified with the Skiöldr of Scandinavian tradition; probably also Heremod with the Hermóðr of Hynd-lulióð and Weoxtan with the Vésteinn of the Kalfsvísa[1]. To the identification of Beowulf himself with the Biarki of Scandinavian tradition, which is doubted by some scholars, we shall have to return later.

The characters of the Finn fragment are much less easy to trace elsewhere. Two of Hnaef's warriors named Ordlaf and Guthlaf are probably to be identified with two Danish princes, Oddlevus and Gunnlevus, mentioned in Skiöldunga Saga; but there is nothing to show that Sigeferth is identical with Sigurðr the son of Sigmundr. In Widsith however we find a large number of persons who are well known from Continental and Scandinavian authorities. Besides Eormenric, Wudga, Hama, Offa, Hrothgar, Hrothwulf and Ingeld, of whom we have already spoken,

---

[1] Quoted in the prose Edda (Skaldskaparmál, cap. 66).

we hear of Aetla, king of the Huns (Atli, Etzel), Guthhere and
Gifeca, kings of the Burgundians (i.e. the Gunnarr and Giúki of
the Edda), and Sigehere, king of the Danes (i.e. probably Sigarr,
the father of Signý), as well as the Goths Eastgota the father of
Unwine (i.e. Jordanes' Ostrogotha the father of Hunwil), Becca
(probably Bikki, the evil counsellor of Iörmunrekr) and the
Herelingas, Emerca and Fridla, who are doubtless to be identified
with the Embrica and Fritla, nephews of Eormenric, mentioned
in the Annals of Quedlinburg and elsewhere. It is more than
probable also that in v. 21 : " Hagena ruled the Holmryge and
Heoden (MS. *Henden*) the Glommas," we have an allusion to the
story of Heðinn and Högni (the Hetel and Hagen of Kûdrûn).
We may compare a passage of Deor (v. 35 ff.) which tells of
a skilful minstrel of the Heodeningas named Heorrenda, presumably the Hôrand of the German poem.

These instances, though far from exhaustive, will be sufficient
to show that the same characters recur again and again in the
early narrative poetry of the various Teutonic peoples. In the
last nineteen poems of the Older Edda (viz. those which deal
with human beings) there is but one (Helgakviða Hiörvarðssonar)
which introduces no characters known elsewhere. Among the
early Anglo-Saxon poems treated on p. 1 ff. we find no such
case, and the same is probably true of the German poems
discussed on pp. 5, 7 ff. With the later Anglo-Saxon poems
(p. 3) and the German historical poems of the ninth and
following centuries the case is quite otherwise. The exploits of
Aethelstan and Byrhtnoth are celebrated only in English poems,
those of Ludwig III and other German princes only in the
poetry of their own country. So also with the skaldic poems
of the North. If these introduce any personal names known
in the poetry of England or Germany they are names, like
Sigmundr and Hermóðr, derived from earlier poems and not
belonging to contemporary persons. Similarly neither English
nor German poetry celebrates the deeds of Eiríkr Blóðöx or
Haakon the Good.

The phenomena noted above seem to indicate that the poetic
cycles with which we have been dealing have a common origin
or at least that there was a considerable amount of borrowing

between poets of different nations. In order however to be able to form an opinion on this point it is necessary first to consider the following questions : (i) how far the characters and incidents of these poems are to be regarded as historical, (ii) to what period or periods of history they belong. We may note in passing that no doubt need be entertained as to the historical basis of the later group of Anglo-Saxon poems, of German poems such as the Ludwigslied or of the Northern skaldic poems—however much the true facts may be obscured by poetic embellishments.

It is clear enough that some of the characters of the common cycles are historical persons. Thus there can be no doubt that Aetla (Atli, Etzel), king of the Huns, is the famous Hunnish king Attila who died in 453. Again the Burgundian king Guthhere (Gunnarr, Gunther), who plays so prominent a part in the stories of Waldhere and Sigurðr-Siegfried, is clearly identical with the historical Burgundian king Gundicarius (Gundaharius), whose defeat in 435 by the Roman general Aetius is recorded by contemporary writers. Of his end Prosper says only that the Huns destroyed him together with his family and nation[1], and some scholars have denied that Attila had any part in this event[2]. But our knowledge of the course of events on or beyond the Roman frontier at this period is too slight to justify any confident statement on such a point. Of the other members of the Burgundian royal family Gifeca (Giúki) and Gislhere (Giselher) are mentioned in the laws of King Gundobad who died in the year 516[3].

---

[1] Theodosio XV et Valentiniano IV coss. (A.D. 435): *pax facta cum Vandalis… eodem tempore Gundicarium Burgundionum regem intra Gallias habitantem Aetius bello obtriuit, pacemque ei supplicanti dedit, qua non diu potitus est. siquidem illum Hunni cum populo atque stirpe sua deleuerunt.*

[2] The overthrow of Guthhere is ascribed to Attila by Paulus Diaconus in his *Gesta episc. Mettensium* (Mon. Germ., Scr. II p. 262), *Hist. Misc.* XIV (Muratori, Scr. I p. 97); but he is a late authority. On the other hand an anonymous Gaulish chronicle, which ends in the year 452, attributes the whole of the Burgundian disasters to Aetius : *bellum contra Burgundionum gentem memorabile exarsit quo uniuersa pene gens cum rege per Aetium deleta* (Mon. Germ., Chron. Min. I 660). But this seems to be due to the confusion of two events which Prosper clearly distinguishes (cf. Idatius, *Chron.*, Theodosii ann. XII, XIII).

[3] Liber Legum Gundebati, cap. 3 (Mon. Germ., Leg., Vol. III p. 533): *si quos apud regiae memoriae auctores nostros, id est Gebicam, Godomarem, Gislaharium, Gundaharium, patrem quoque nostrum et patruum, liberos liberasue fuisse constiterit, in eadem libertate permaneant.*

The Gothic king Eormenric (Hermanaricus, Iörmunrekr) is another doubtless historical character. The account of him given by Jordanes seems indeed to be derived from tradition, handed down probably in poetic form ; but the statement that he took his own life through fear of the Huns is confirmed by the strictly contemporary writer Ammianus Marcellinus (xxxi. 3. 1), from whom we gather that the event took place shortly after 370. He also states that Eormenric was a most warlike king and feared by the surrounding nations on account of his many brave deeds.

In Dietrich von Bern (the Theodric of Waldhere and the Thióðrekr of the Edda) we certainly have reminiscences of the Ostrogothic king Theodoric who ruled Italy from 489 to 526. The statement in the Hildebrandslied that he fled from the hostility of Ottachar and the story of the Rabenschlacht recall his campaigns with Odoacer, which culminated in the surrender of Ravenna in 493. But it cannot possibly be true that he was present at Attila's court, where we find him in the Edda and in German poetry, much less that he had any dealings with Eormenric. The former mistake is generally attributed to confusion between Dietrich and his father Dietmar (Thiudemer), who is known to have been with Attila. The other error however is more difficult to account for and will require to be discussed later.

It is commonly held that in the poems dealing with Wolfdietrich[1] the hero and his father Hugdietrich represent a confusion of the Frankish kings Theodberht (r. 534—548) and his father Theodric I (r. 511—534). In this case however it must be confessed that the resemblances are extremely slight. The application of the name Hugo Theodoricus to Theodric I in the Annals of Quedlinburg cannot at best prove more than that the chronicler identified the two.

The identification of characters which figure in stories relating to the northern kingdoms is naturally more difficult, since references to such persons by contemporary Roman

---

[1] This cycle is supposed to have been known in England at one time, owing to the juxtaposition of the names Seaıola (Saben) and Theodric in Widsith, v. 115. Theodric, king of the Franks, is mentioned in the same poem (v. 24).

historians are extremely rare. One safe instance however is
furnished by the incident, referred to several times in Beowulf, of
Hygelac's disastrous expedition against the Franks and Frisians.
Gregory of Tours (III 3) and the Gesta Francorum (cap. 19)
mention a very serious raid on the lower Rhine by a king of the
Danes named Chocilaicus, which ended in his defeat and death
through the arrival of an army under Theodberht. The Liber
Monstrorum (I, cap. 3[1]), a work of perhaps the seventh century,
states that the bones of a certain *Getarum rex Huiglaucus*, who
had been slain by the Franks, were preserved on an island at the
mouth of the Rhine. There can be no question that the person
referred to in these passages is the Hygelac of Beowulf. The
date of the expedition, though not precisely fixed by any
authority, may safely be placed within a few years of 520.

Most of the Danish and Swedish princes common to Beowulf
and the Northern authorities are now generally regarded as
historical characters, though we have no reference to them in
contemporary documents. It is to be noted in the first place
that though the persons themselves are common to the two
traditions, English and Northern, they are not as a rule
mentioned in connection with the same incidents. Further,
there is no evidence for communication between England and
the Baltic during the seventh and eighth centuries. This renders
it probable that the two records go back independently to a
time at which persons who remembered Hygelac's younger
contemporaries might still be alive.

Lastly a few words must be said with regard to the stories of
Haraldr Hilditönn, Sigurðr Hringr and Ragnarr Loðbrók. The
sons of Loðbrók are well known from contemporary historical
documents through their piratical expeditions, more especially
the great invasion of England in 866. Moreover, though
the references to Loðbrók himself are rare and doubtful,
it is clear enough that the king Ella who is said to have put
him to death was the Northumbrian usurper Aella, who reigned
from 863 to 867. Loðbrók's father Sigurðr Hringr has been
identified with a certain Sigifridus whose conflict with another
Danish king named Anulo is recorded in a number of Latin

---

[1] Cf. Berger de Xivrey, *Traditions Tératologiques*, p. 12.

chronicles under the year 812, and Anulo himself with that Óli who is represented as Sigurðr's ally at the battle of Brávík. Lastly, it has been suggested that a reference to Haraldr Hilditönn may quite possibly be preserved in the description of Anulo as *nepos Herioldi quondam regis*[1]; for according to Saxo (p. 250) Óli was the son of Haraldr's sister and eventually succeeded him on the Danish throne.

The above identifications[2] are sufficient to show that historical characters are introduced into most of the stories with which we have been dealing. Further—and this is a very remarkable fact—apart from the last cycles embracing Haraldr Hilditönn and Ragnarr Loðbrók, which are entirely confined to Northern literature, all the historical personages whom we have been able to identify belong to a period extending over barely two centuries. Eormenric flourished in the latter half of the fourth century, Attila and the Burgundian kings in the first half of the fifth; Theodric towards the end of the same century and in the first quarter of the sixth. Hygelac again was a contemporary of Theodric; while Wolfdietrich, if he is rightly identified with Theodberht, died in 548. In the stories which form the common themes of English, German and Scandinavian poets we find no mention of historical persons who lived after the middle of the sixth century.

Now it will be clear that the cycles of stories dealing with Ragnarr Loðbrók and his ancestors are really, like the skaldic poems, to be compared with German and English works such as the Ludwigslied and the poem on the battle of Brunanburh. The difference in tone is sufficiently accounted for by the social conditions of the Viking Age, which were wholly different from those which prevailed in the Christian kingdoms.

The statement that the common cycles of tradition mention no historical characters later than about 550 ought perhaps to be qualified in one case. Paulus Diaconus (*Hist. Lang.* I 27) says

---

[1] Einhardi Ann., 812 (Mon. Germ., Scr. I p. 199). Prof. Olrik (*Nordisches Geistesleben*, p. 44) apparently rejects this identification, as he places Haraldr Hilditönn not long after the time of Hrólfr Kraki.

[2] The list makes no claim to completeness. Thus several of the characters in Hervarar Saga (probably mentioned also in Widsith, v. 116 ff.) have been identified with historical persons of the fifth century. But the evidence is far from satisfactory.

that the praises of Alboin, king of the Langobardi, who died in 572 (or 573), were sung by the Saxons, Bavarians and other peoples; and it has been suggested that his account of certain incidents in Alboin's career is derived from poetic sources. Further, we find the generosity of the same king celebrated in the Anglo-Saxon poem Widsith, where he is apparently the latest person mentioned. Hence there is some ground for including him among the characters of common Teutonic poetry—which will involve our extending the lower of the chronological limits fixed above by about twenty years. Yet it is not clear that Alboin figured in any poems which can properly be called narrative, except perhaps among his own people.

On the other hand some of the Gothic heroes recorded by Jordanes, if we are to trust his chronology at all, must be referred to times long anterior to the middle of the fourth century. Apart from Gothic tradition the only mention of any of these persons occurs in a brief passage in Widsith (v. 113 f.): "(I have visited) Eastgota, the wise and good father of Unwine." Now Ostrogotha is brought by Jordanes into connection with the Emperor Philip (v. 244—249). He is mentioned also by Cassiodorus (*Var.* XI. 1) as one of the ancestors of Amalasuintha and as a prince renowned for forbearance (*patientia*). In spite of his suspicious name what is said of him by Jordanes seems to point to a genuine tradition. But if so, even setting aside both the reference to Philip and the genealogy given by Jordanes in cap. 5, he is probably to be referred to a time anterior to the upper limit fixed above. Into the story of Filimer and the migration we need not enter, as there is no reason for supposing it to be anything but a purely Gothic tradition. The story of the Langobardic victory over the Vandals (cf. p. 10) is probably of a similar character.

There remain of course a number of stories which contain no names of persons mentioned in contemporary records. The story of Finn is in Beowulf connected, rather loosely, with Healfdene, Hrothgar's father. Hence if the incidents which it relates are to be regarded as historical, they must be dated somewhat earlier, though certainly not more than a century earlier, than Hygelac's expedition. The story of Offa and his father Wermund must be referred to a still earlier period if we are to trust the evidence of the Mercian genealogy in which these persons figure. I have tried elsewhere[1] to show that the Athislus, who in Saxo's version of the story appears as Wermund's enemy, is probably to be identified with the Eadgils prince of the Myrgingas mentioned in Widsith. The latter is represented as the contemporary of Eormenric, and the date thus obtained agrees with that given by the genealogy. The story of Weland, if it contains any historical element, should be placed perhaps slightly further back; for in Waldhere, as well as in many German authorities, including Thiðreks Saga, Weland is said to be the father of Widia (Wudga, Witege). The latter is often associated with Eormenric[2], and there can be little doubt that he is to be identified with the Gothic Vidigoia who is mentioned as a hero of the past by Jordanes (cap. 34) in a quotation from Priscus[3]. For the story of Hagbarðr and Signý a date is afforded by a poem attributed by Saxo (p. 214) to Starkaðr. The poet, who in his old age served Ingellus, i.e. Ingeld, the son-in-law of Hrothgar, says that he had followed Haki, the brother of Hagbarðr, in his early youth. In Ynglinga Saga (cap. 23) Haki is made to fight with the Swedish king Iörundr, four generations above Aðils, but this genealogy cannot be entirely correct.

The only important stories which remain are those of Fróði the Peaceful and Heðinn and Högni. In Saxo's history (p. 158 ff.) the two are brought into connection with one another, and it is certainly to be noted that a Fruote von Tenemarke plays rather a prominent part in Kûdrûn, especially the first portion. But Fróði is associated with different sets of persons in different works, and his resemblance to the god Frey rather suggests that he was regarded as the typical representative of a Golden Age in the past. The story of Heðinn and Högni is very difficult to locate, both in regard to time and scene. Widsith however, which is our earliest authority for it, represents

---

[1] *The Origin of the English Nation*, p. 134 f.

[2] But also with Theodric. This is a question to which we shall have to refer later.

[3] *Venimus in illum locum ubi dudum Vidigoia, Gothorum fortissimus, Sarmatum dolo occubuit* (cf. also cap. 5).

Hagena (Högni) as king of the Holmryge, who appear to have dwelt in eastern Pomerania. Since the whole of the south coast of the Baltic had probably become Slavonic by the end of the fifth century, it is at all events unlikely that the story refers to any period after this.

We shall have to discuss later how far these stories are to be regarded as historical and to what extent the characters and incidents with which they deal are to be attributed to myth or fiction. Here it is sufficient to point out that with the exception of the story of Heðinn and Högni, the connections of which are obscure, all the stories which we have just been discussing are referred by our authorities to generations anterior to the characters of Beowulf. Hence we may safely conclude that the period embraced by the common poetry and traditions of the various Teutonic peoples—what we may call the Heroic Age of these peoples—had come to an end by the middle of the sixth century or at least by the death of Alboin. Its upper limit must in view of the evidence given above be set from two to three centuries back—probably three centuries if we include the story of Ostrogotha.

These limitations are clearly such as to call for some attempt at explanation. Why do the cycles of story which are common to the various Teutonic peoples mention no historical character later than Alboin? Before we can hope to give a satisfactory answer to this question, a number of other phenomena will have to be taken into account. One or two observations however will not be out of place here.

The period extending backwards from two to three centuries before the reign of Alboin coincides with what is generally known as the Age of National Migrations (Völkerwanderungszeit). It was during this period that many of the Teutonic nations broke through the frontiers of the Roman empire and carved out for themselves extensive kingdoms within its territories. Among these were the realms of Guthhere and Theodric, and in part also that of Attila. There is no doubt that in all these cases the conquest of the Roman provinces brought with it a great accession of wealth and profoundly affected the life of the invaders.

The same period witnessed the conversion of most of the continental Teutonic peoples to Christianity, another change which produced far-reaching effects upon them. Yet it is not clear at first sight how this change is connected with the chronological limitation of the stories, for while some of the chief characters, Attila for instance and doubtless Eormenric, were heathens, others such as Theodric were certainly Christians. The change of faith is not a motive which plays any part in the stories themselves.

Whatever weight we may be disposed to attach to these observations, it should be noted that they do not seem to apply to every case. Thus we shall see in the course of the next chapter that Danish characters figure more prominently than those of any other nation, not only in Scandinavian but also in English records, throughout the period ending with Hrólfr Kraki. Yet the Danes took no part, collectively at least, in the movements against the Roman Empire, nor did Christianity penetrate to them before the ninth century. It is worth remarking therefore that stories relating to Denmark stop where they do, and that for centuries after the time of Hrólfr we can scarcely give the name of a single Danish prince.

In the following chapters it will be convenient to speak of the period which we have been discussing simply as the Heroic Age. The term 'heroic poetry,' as a translation of Heldendichtung or Heltedigtning, may of course be applied in a sense to such works as Hákonarmál or the poem on the battle of Maldon, just as well as to Beowulf or the Hildebrandslied. But no ambiguity will arise if we limit the term 'heroic' here to what may be called the 'Teutonic' Heroic Age (das germanische Heldenalter), i.e. to the period embraced by the common poetry and traditions of the various Teutonic peoples.

CHAPTER III.

SCENE AND NATIONALITY IN THE HEROIC STORIES.

In the last chapter it was pointed out that the age covered by the heroic poetry and traditions of the Teutonic peoples coincides with a clearly marked period of history, extending over about two or possibly three hundred years, and coming to an end in the latter half of the sixth century. Something must now be said regarding the geographical and ethnographical limitations of the stories—the localities in which the scenes are laid and the nationalities to which the various characters belonged. The scenes are distributed over a considerable part of Europe, extending from Italy to Sweden and from western Russia to the Vosges and the Netherlands. The British Isles however seem to have lain outside the area, though in the late form in which some of the stories have come down to us, we do occasionally find references to them—generally to Scotland or Ireland—which are probably due to confusion with stories of the Viking Age. Indeed it is remarkable that the early Anglo-Saxon poems contain no reference to persons or events connected with this country. Further, except possibly in the case of the story of Hengest and Horsa, we have no evidence worth consideration that poems dealing with such subjects ever existed. Norway also is not made the scene of any of the main stories, though it is mentioned incidentally in English and German as well as Scandinavian poems. The Balkan peninsula figures only in the later German poems, while references to places in Italy are limited practically to the Dietrich (Theodric) and Wolfdietrich cycles.

Turning to the question of nationality we find the following peoples represented : (i) to the Goths belong Eormenric, Theodric, Wudga (Witege) and probably most of the heroes associated with them; (ii) to the Huns Attila; (iii) to the Burgundians Guthhere and his family; (iv) to the Rugii apparently Hagena (Högni), the father of Hild ; (v) to the Franks Hugdietrich and Wolfdietrich, if the identifications are correct ; (vi) to the Frisians Finn ; (vii) to the Angli Wermund and Offa; (viii) to the Danes (a) Fróði the Peaceful, (b) Sigarr and his family, together probably with Hagbarðr and Haki, (c) Hrólfr Kraki and his family, perhaps also Froda (Frotho IV) and Ingeld; (ix) to the Götar Hygelac, Beowulf and their relatives, (x) to the Swedes (Svear) Aðils and his family.

It is somewhat remarkable that we have no stories dealing with Alamannic or Bavarian heroes, since the German poems which have come down to us are almost entirely derived from the territories of these peoples[1]. The Vandals too are unrepresented, and probably also the Visigoths, while the evidence for Frankish heroes is slight and rather unsatisfactory. Frankish nationality is claimed by most scholars for Siegfried, chiefly on the ground that Xanten is represented as his home in the Nibelungenlied[2]. Yet he is never called a Frank, and it is not clear that Xanten was in the possession of the Franks at the time to which the story refers. The same nationality may perhaps be claimed for Waldhere. In several German poems Langres is said to be his home, though he is also called a Spaniard, while Ekkehard makes his father king of Aquitaine[3]. To this question we shall have to return later. In any case both stories refer to a period considerably anterior to the real conquest of Gaul by the Franks, and it is certainly a curious fact that Clovis and his great achievements seem to be entirely unnoticed in poetry.

It appears then that though most of the principal Teutonic nations are represented in our stories the relative prominence

---

[1] These poems do introduce Bavarian characters, such as the Markgraf Rüdiger ; but they are not found elsewhere in heroic poetry.

[2] In the prose piece *Frá dauði Sinfiötla* (in the Older Edda) Sigmundr is said to have held territories in the land oi the Franks.

[3] Hence many scholars regard him as a Visigoth.

assigned to them does not at all correspond to what we should expect. Most remarkable is the fact that in stories relating to the Continent nearly all the chief characters (Eormenric, Theodric, Guthhere, Attila, etc.) belong to nations which had passed out of existence before the end of the sixth century. From Jordanes (cap. 5) we gather that the preservation of the early Gothic traditions was very largely due to the pride taken by that people in its own heroes of the past. Yet it is not easy to see how the survival of the stories which have come down to us can be ascribed to any such feeling.

Let us first examine the Anglo-Saxon poems. In Beowulf the scene is laid first in the land of the Danes and later in that of the Götar. The hero himself belongs to the latter nation, but in the earlier part of the poem the former are decidedly the more prominent. Taking it as a whole the interest is divided between the royal families of these two nations; the only other dynasty which comes in for any considerable share of attention is that of the Swedes. In the story of Finn the interest is centred in a prince and his followers who according to Beowulf were of Danish nationality and involved in hostilities with the Frisians. In Waldhere the hero and heroine, whatever their nationality, belong to Gaul, while their opponents are Burgundians. In Deor the interests are mainly, perhaps exclusively, Gothic. In Widsith the foremost characters are Eadgils, prince of the Myrgingas (a dynasty hostile to the Angli), and the Gothic king Eormenric; after them the English king Ofia, the Danish kings Hrothgar and Hrothwulf, Guthhere, king of the Burgundians, Aelfwine (Alboin, king of the Langobardi) and several Gothic heroes. In all these poems there is no reference, as far as we know, to any person of English nationality except Offa and his relatives (Beow. 1944 ff.), nor except in Widsith is the name of the Angli even mentioned.

If we turn now to the Scandinavian records, which are entirely Norse (Norwegian-Icelandic), so far as the vernacular literature is concerned, the phenomena which confront us are on the whole very similar. As we might expect from the comparative lateness of our authorities the nationality of the various characters is not very clearly indicated. It is remembered that

Atli (Attila) belonged to the Huns and Iörmunrekr (Eormenric) to the Goths, but Gunnarr (Guthhere) is only once called lord of the Burgundians. As for Sigurðr, his later adventures are uniformly located in the Rhineland, but the history of his family is generally connected with Denmark, which is also the scene of Helgi's exploits. Most noteworthy however is the fact that Norway is only mentioned once in the Older Edda, namely in the prose of Helgakviða Hiörvarðssonar. In the sagas it is somewhat more prominent, e.g. in the account of Biarki's origin in Hrólfs Saga Kraka; but these passages are usually regarded as accretions to the original stories. Of course there are numerous other sagas which deal exclusively with Norwegian history and legend. These stories however are peculiar to Norwegian-Icelandic literature, and the earliest persons who figure in them, if we may regard them as historical, cannot have lived before the seventh century. In stories relating to earlier times the scene is practically always laid in Denmark or southern Sweden or in the lands south of the Baltic.

Even in the German poems national feeling has influenced the choice of subjects comparatively little. The poems in their present form are mainly Austrian or Bavarian. Yet except in the second half of the Nibelungenlied this region does not figure prominently[1], and even there the Bavarian characters that occur are generally believed to be rather late additions to the story. The chief characters of the story in its original form were clearly Burgundians and Huns, to whom the Goths may have been added at a fairly early date. The stories which deal with the Rhineland—those of Siegfried and Walther—may be derived ultimately from early Frankish poems; but this cannot be proved. Most of the others are concerned with Gothic heroes, the true scene of whose adventures is to be sought in Poland, Hungary, Italy and other countries which had ceased to be Teutonic before the time of our authorities. Theodric, it is true seems to have become a national hero in the south-east, but this feature is prominent only in the latest poems, and even here it is clearly remembered that he belonged to Italy. But the most

---

[1] Tyrol is the scene of several of Dietrich's and Wolfdietrich's adventures; but generally it is the southern (Italian) part of that country.

remarkable case is that of Kûdrûn. The poem itself is probably Austrian, but the names which it contains show that the story is derived from Frisian sources. The scene is laid first in Ireland, then in Denmark and lastly in Normandy. Yet if we take into account the various Scandinavian versions and the references to the story in Anglo-Saxon poetry, there is every probability that it came originally from the Baltic.

This short discussion will suffice to show how singularly free the poems we have been discussing are from anything in the nature of national interest or sentiment. They are certainly national in the sense that the characters are drawn entirely, or almost entirely, from within the Teutonic world—for even Attila can hardly be regarded as an exception. But nationalism in the narrower sense, i.e. in the interests of the poet's own nation or tribe, seems to be altogether wanting. The interest is centred in one or more individual characters and in the various adventures that befall them. Sometimes, as in Beowulf, it does also embrace the history of the family to which these persons belonged, but the nation, apart from the royal family, is practically disregarded.

The contrast afforded by the historical poems of the ninth and tenth centuries[1] is sufficiently obvious. We have seen that these poems, whether English or German, uniformly deal with the poet's own nation. The poem on the battle of Brunanburh is an expression of national triumph. It is not concerned with the personal adventures of the king or his brother, but with the prowess of the English army as a whole. The bravery of the princes is certainly noticed, but they appear to be regarded as the champions and representatives of the nation. The Ludwigslied breathes on the whole a similar spirit, in spite of its strongly religious tone. Even in the skaldic poetry of the North traces of national pride are clearly discernible, as in Hákonarmál (v. 3), where Haakon, at the head of his Norwegian troops, is described as the terror of the Danes.

It may perhaps be urged that, though the poems which have come down to us have no national interest, they may be derived

---

[1] The poem on the battle of Maldon approximates much more closely than any other of this age to the spirit of the old poetry.

from older poems which originated in the hero's own land.
Thus many scholars believe Beowulf to be of Scandinavian
origin in one sense or another, though the linguistic arguments
which have been brought forward in favour of this view are not
generally admitted. But there is a curious lack of uniformity
in the national interests of the poem, as we have already seen.
If it had been the chief intention of the original poet to glorify
the Danish nation, he would not have ignored it as he has done
in the latter part of the poem. On the other hand if his intention was to glorify the Götar he would hardly have begun with
an account of the early kings of the Danes. The difficulty has
been got over by supposing that the poem as we have it is of
composite formation, and it may very well be that the second
part of the poem is a later addition. But it is to be observed
that somewhat similar phenomena occur in other cases. Thus
the stories of Siegfried and Attila are connected both in the
Nibelungenlied and the Edda, and there can be no doubt that
the connection is of considerable antiquity. Yet the only
common element in the two stories is supplied by the Burgundians, and the portraiture of their princes, especially that of the
king, is hardly of such a character as to suggest its derivation
from a poem composed for the glorification of the Burgundian
nation.

The evidence then of Beowulf alone is scarcely sufficient to
justify us in assuming more than that its author or authors were
interested in the royal families of the North, and that they
possessed a considerable amount of information regarding them.
The account of the early kings of the Danes seems to be in the
nature of a tribal or family tradition—to be compared with the
early stories given by Jordanes, Paulus Diaconus and Widukind.
Traditions of this kind are no doubt generally of a mythical
character, and consequently their origin is to be sought in the
particular locality or family with which they are concerned.
We have no evidence that such traditions formed the main
theme of stories which were common to the poetry of the various
Teutonic peoples. But it is natural enough that a poet who was
well acquainted with some royal family, whether that of his own

nation or not, would also know its traditions, and that he would utilise them incidentally or by way of introduction in a poem largely concerned with the fortunes of that family.

The main story of the poem stands on a different footing. Of course if it could be shown that the Danish princes who figure both in Beowulf and the various Scandinavian records were fictitious persons, who never really existed, we should be bound to hold that they were derived from a common story, probably of Scandinavian origin. But few scholars would now be willing to admit such a proposition. Certain incidents, such as the exhortation of Ingeld (Ingellus) by the old warrior (Starcatherus), may be held to point to a common origin in poem or saga; but most of the events narrated appear to have been either preserved by memory or invented independently.

With the stories of Sigurðr (Siegfried) and Waldhere the case is somewhat different. It is the opinion of the great majority of scholars that both these heroes are mythical or fictitious, in spite of the fact that they are associated with undoubtedly historical characters. If this view is correct—a question which we shall have to discuss later—we may conclude at once that the different versions of the two stories, Scandinavian and German in the one case, English and German in the other, have sprung from a common source, whether in poem or saga. But even if we take the opposite view, viz. that Sigurðr and Waldhere were real persons and that their adventures are founded on fact, it does not by any means follow that the different versions of their stories must have originated independently. Neither hero seems to have belonged to a family of outstanding position, nor were their exploits such as to influence the destiny of nations[1]. In the age of Hunnish supremacy scores of petty princes must have undergone somewhat similar adventures and distinguished themselves by similar deeds of heroism. Hence it can hardly be due to accident that the handful whose names we know were celebrated far and wide in the Teutonic world.

[1] The victories over the Saxons and Danes described in the Nibelungenlied and the Tháttr af Nornagesti have little in common and are scarcely to be regarded as an essential feature in the story of Sigurðr.

The story of Eormenric is again rather a different case. There can be no question that this king was a historical person, but the earliest detailed account which we possess of his doings, viz. that given by Jordanes, dates from nearly two centuries after his death. Now we find what is perhaps the most striking episode in Eormenric's story, namely the account of Swanhild and the vengeance attempted by her brothers, both in Jordanes and the Older Edda (Guðrúnarhvöt and Hamðismál) with comparatively slight variations. The chief feature wanting in Jordanes' account is supplied by the Annals of Quedlinburg[1]. How much truth the story contains we are not in a position to decide. But even if we grant that the main features are historical, the event can hardly have been of the first importance, since the attack seems really to have failed in its object. Ammianus Marcellinus says that Eormenric committed suicide owing to despair at the impending Hunnish invasion, and Jordanes recognises that his death was partly due to this cause. But in the later (Scandinavian and German) accounts it is entirely forgotten. Hence if we bear in mind the close agreement between the Gothic and Scandinavian versions of the story, not only in the names of the characters but also in the description of Swanhild's death, we can hardly help inferring that they are derived from a common narrative source.

In conclusion mention may be made of a story which appears to be definitely at variance with historical truth, namely the account of Attila's death given in the Edda poems Atlakviða and Atlamál. It is there stated that Attila was murdered with his two children by his wife Guðrún in revenge for her brothers (Gunnarr and Högni), whom he had treacherously put to death. Now Jordanes (cap. 49) says that Attila died from the bursting of a blood-vessel on the night of his marriage with a girl named Ildico. As his account is derived from Priscus, a contemporary and trustworthy writer, there can be little doubt that it is correct. Yet it should be observed that the Roman chronicler Marcellinus Comes, who wrote apparently a few years before Jordanes, says

---

[1] *Anastasius annos* XXVII......*Ermanrici regis Gothorum a fratribus Hemido et Serilo et Adaccaro, quorum patrem interfecerat, amputatis manibus et pedibus turpiter, ut dignus erat, occisio* (Mon. Germ., Scr. III p. 31).

that Attila died by the hand of a woman[1]. The account given
in the Edda therefore is no invention of an Icelandic or
Norwegian poet, but founded on a story which was current
among the Romans within a century after Attila's death. Indeed
considering the circumstances it is by no means unlikely that
the story originated immediately after the event.

These examples will be sufficient to show that the subjects of
many of our poems are derived from stories which passed from
one Teutonic people to another and some of which were of great
antiquity. Further, it is a proof of the popularity of these stories
that they were preserved until comparatively late in the Middle
Ages, in spite of the fact that they did not appeal to national
interests. The question how they were preserved and transmitted
is one which we shall have to discuss in the following chapters.
We may note at once however that the most obvious means of
preservation, namely by means of writing, was almost certainly
not used to any great extent. Had that been the case the
divergencies between the different versions of the stories would
be far less noticeable than they are. Even in the case of
Waldhere, which shows probably the least amount of variation,
the Anglo-Saxon fragments show a treatment of the subject
totally different from that which appears in Ekkehard's poem.
Again, there is no evidence that the Roman alphabet was used
in the North, except possibly by a few foreigners here and there,
before the end of the tenth century, while the Runic alphabet,
though it had been known for many centuries, seems not to have
been employed for literary purposes until very late times. But,
as we have already mentioned, some of the Edda poems date
probably from the ninth century, and the story of Heðinn and
Högni is used by the poet Bragi who lived apparently in the
early part of that century. On the Continent of course the case
is somewhat different. We have seen that Charlemagne did
have a number of ancient poems written down ; but there is
nothing to show that his collection had any permanent influence.
When the Quedlinburg annalist or his authority quotes the

---

[1] Ind. VII. Aetio et Studio coss. (A.D. 454): *Attila rex Hunnorum Europae
orbator prouinciae noctu mulieris manu cultroque confoditur. quidam uero sanguinis
reiectione necatum perhibent.*

heroic stories, perhaps some two centuries later, he refers not to any written works but to songs formerly current among the country people. It is doubtless by oral tradition therefore, whether in verse or prose, that the stories of the Heroic Age have mainly been preserved.

There can be no question that a large number of similar stories have perished. A glance through the catalogues of Widsith will show many names which otherwise are entirely unknown to us, and also an appreciable number which are not mentioned elsewhere in Anglo-Saxon literature, though they figure in German and Scandinavian records. It would scarcely be wise however to assume that all the stories of the Heroic Age were common Teutonic property. Thus we have no evidence for the story of Waldhere in the North[1], while stories dealing with Danish heroes seem to have been little known in Germany. The latter observation deserves notice all the more in view of the obvious popularity of such stories in England—a fact proved not merely by Beowulf and Finn, but still more by the prominence assigned to Danish characters in Widsith.

It will be convenient now to summarise briefly the results of our discussion. We have seen that the scenes of the heroic stories are distributed over most of the lands formerly occupied by the Teutonic peoples. Norway and England however, as well as the distant kingdoms of the Visigoths and Vandals, seem to lie outside the area. The heroes also are drawn from many nations, though not in the proportion which we should expect. Thus the Frankish nation, which ultimately became dominant, is but poorly represented, while the most prominent places are taken by peoples such as the Ostrogoths and Burgundians, which lost their nationality in the course of the sixth century.

We have further seen that a very large proportion of the characters of the heroic stories figure in the literature of two or more nations, and that frequently the same stories are told of them. In the latter case it is probable, indeed often practically certain, that the different versions of the story are ultimately derived from a common narrative. On the other hand, where the same characters are known but only in connection with

---

[1] Excluding of course Thiðreks S. af Bern.

different events, such derivation can be proved only if it can be shown that the characters themselves are fictitious. This remark applies especially to a number of characters common to Beowulf and Scandinavian stories relating to Hrólfr Kraki and his times.

It is fully in accord with these facts that the heroic poems are not concerned at all—or at least only to a very slight degree —with local or tribal interests. Their tone indeed may be described as in a sense international, though with the restriction that characters and scenes alike are drawn exclusively from within the Teutonic world.

CHAPTER IV.

THE ORIGIN AND HISTORY OF THE HEROIC POEMS.

IN an earlier chapter (p. 3) it was mentioned that the English heroic poems are usually ascribed to the seventh or eighth centuries. We must now try to see whether any means are to be found of dating their composition more precisely.

Unfortunately very few references to the poems or their subjects occur in works which can be dated with anything like certainty. The most important is contained in a letter from Alcuin to Hygebald, bishop of Lindisfarne, written in the year 797 : "When priests dine together let the words of God be read. It is fitting on such occasions to listen to a reader, not to a harpist, to the discourses of the fathers, not to the poems of the heathen. What has Ingeld to do with Christ? Strait is the house; it will not be able to hold them both. The king of heaven will have no part with so-called kings who are heathen and damned; for the one king reigns eternally in heaven, the other, the heathen, is damned and groans in hell. In your houses the voices of those who read should be heard, not a rabble of those who make merry in the streets[1]." From this passage it is clear that at the end of the eighth century there were current in Northumbria certain poems, probably well known poems, dealing with a heathen king named Ingeld, whom we need not

---

[1] *Verba Dei legantur in sacerdotali conuiuio. ibi decet lectorem audiri, non citharistam; sermones patrum, non carmina gentilium. quid Hinieldus cum Christo? angusta est domus; utrosque tenere non poterit. non uult rex coelestis cum paganis et perditis nominetenus regibus communionem habere, quia rex ille aeternus regnat in coelo, ille paganus perditus plangit in inferno. uoces legentium audiri in domibus tuis, non ridentium turuam in plateis.* Mon. Germ., Epist. Carol. II 124; cf. O. Jänicke, ZfdA. XV 314.

hesitate to identify with Ingeld the son of Froda, who figures in Beowulf. Of course it is not at all likely that the reference is to Beowulf itself, for the part played by Ingeld in that poem is insignificant.

Acquaintance with the subjects of the heroic poems is shown also by a mistake in the Historia Brittonum, 31, which dates probably from about the same period. This passage contains a genealogy, tracing the descent of Hengest and Horsa from Woden and of Woden from Geat. The latter part is known also from many other texts, in which it regularly runs as follows: *Woden Frealafing, Frealaf Frithuwulfing, Frithuwulf Finning, Finn Godwulfing, Godwulf Geating.* In the Historia Brittonum however in place of *Finn Godwulfing* we find *Finn qui fuit Folcwald*—which is clearly due to confusion with Finn the son of Folcwalda (*Finn Folcwalding*), a Frisian king mentioned in Beowulf and Widsith, as well as in the fragment which bears his name.

Further evidence is afforded by names of persons and places. There can be no doubt that even in the seventh century it was customary to take the names of famous men of the past or present. Danihel, bishop of Winchester (d. 745), and Iohannes, bishop of Hexham (d. 721), are instances which no one will dispute. In the Durham Liber Vitae we meet with the names Aethan and Cundigeorn. It must not be assumed that persons bearing such names were necessarily of Celtic blood. Indeed the spelling suggests rather that they were Englishmen called after Aidan and Kentigern. Deusdedit, archbishop of Canterbury (655—664), doubtless derived his name from Pope Deusdedit (615—618), while the West Saxon king Ceadwalla (685—688) was in all probability called after the British king of the same name, who died in 642. It is extremely likely that Hlothhere, king of Kent (673—685), obtained his name from one of the Frankish kings, Lothair II (584—628) or Lothair III (656—670), for the element *hloth-* is not used elsewhere in Anglo-Saxon names. Even in the sixth century we hear of English princes who seem to be called after Frankish or Gothic kings of the same period. Thus Tytla, the name of the father of the East Anglian king Redwald, is probably taken from the

Gothic king Totila ; it is not of an English type.   Two sons of
the Northumbrian king Ida were called Theodric and Aethelric,
perhaps after the Gothic king Theodric and his successor
Athalaric.   As the element *theod-* is somewhat rare in England,
it is not unlikely that the Northumbrian prince Theodbald, a
son of Aethelric, derived his name from the Frankish king
Theodbald.

　The occurrence of such names as Widsith and Beowulf
(*Biuulf*) in the Liber Vitae shows that names were taken not
only from contemporary persons and from books but also from
native poems and traditions.   Indeed researches which have
been made in this direction have demonstrated that names of
the latter type were extremely popular.   But it has not been
sufficiently pointed out that such names occur most frequently
in the earliest times and gradually become more rare—a fact
which is of considerable importance for our purpose.   The total
number of personal names found in the five poems Beowulf,
Finn, Waldhere, Widsith and Deor is 132[1], and of these
altogether 57 recur as names of persons mentioned in English
historical documents.   Over forty of these names belonged to
persons who appear to have lived, or at any rate to have been
born, before the end of the seventh century[2], while at least
thirteen of them are unknown after the same period.   To the
latter class belong the important names Widsith and Beowulf.

　In local nomenclature it is possible to trace at least 51 of the
132 names mentioned above.   In some cases these names may
have been taken direct from the story, e.g. when we find in Kent
two localities close together called *Hokes clif* and *Hengstes earas*
(Birch, *Cart. Sax.*, III 1000).   A similar case, very frequently
cited[3], is that of *Beowanhammes hecgan* and *Grendeles mere* in
Wiltshire (*ib.* II 677), though neither of these names is included
in our list.   But in the majority of cases it is more probable that
the place-name is taken in the first instance from that of a
previous landowner, and consequently that the connection with

---

[1] The names Grendel, Cain, Abel, Alexandreas and Casere are not included.

[2] For the figures and the method of calculation see Note I.

[3] But open to very serious objections, as has been shown by Prof. W. W. Lawrence
in the *Publications of the Modern Language Association of America*, XXIV 251 ff.

the story is only secondary.   Hence it is important to notice
that out of the 51 place-names no less than 19 contain names
which are not borne by persons in historical documents.   The
explanation of this lies doubtless in the fact that the place-names
for the most part became fixed at a very early period, and
consequently that they exhibit an earlier stratum of personal
nomenclature.

If we add the place-names to the personal names the total
number of heroic names found in England in historical
documents seems to be 76.   Out of this number only seven
apparently are limited to persons born after the end of the
seventh century, and of these again almost all occur in the course
of the eighth century.   These statistics show clearly that such
names were most popular during the sixth and seventh centuries,
especially if we bear in mind that the materials for this period
are incomparably less than those for the following three
centuries.   Hence, if we are justified in drawing any conclusions
from nomenclature, the popularity of the heroic stories was
distinctly on the wane in Alcuin's time.

The argument from nomenclature holds good of course only
for showing the popularity of the stories ; it cannot prove the
existence of the poems which we now possess.   In one case
however we may probably make an exception.   The name
Widsith is obviously fictitious[1] and based on the travels with
which the minstrel is credited.   The introduction, in which
alone the name occurs, is in all probability a later composition
than the rest of the poem[2] and designed to explain what
follows.   It is of importance therefore to note that, if we may
judge from the place in which this name occurs in the Liber
Vitae, it must have been borne by a person of the seventh
century.

[1] Compound names containing *wīd-* or *-sīþ* (*-sinþ-*) are used in other Teutonic
languages; but the latter apparently does not occur in England, while the former is
extremely rare.

[2] In contrast with the body of the poem (vv. 10—134) it is non-strophic, after the
general fashion of Anglo-Saxon poetry.   Originally when the poem was recited it may
have been introduced with a short explanation in prose, such as we find e.g. in
Rígsmál or Atlakviða.   The epilogue (vv. 135—143), which is likewise non-strophic,
may belong to the same stratum.

We must next turn to the internal evidence. The linguistic criteria are of a somewhat unsatisfactory nature and investigations in this field have led to few definite results. It is clear that the heroic poems do not exhibit any dialect in its purity—a remark which is true of Anglo-Saxon poetry in general. West Saxon forms predominate and there is no doubt that the final recension of the text is due to scribes who employed this dialect. Yet at the same time there are a sufficient number of Midland or Northumbrian characteristics[1] to render it highly probable that the poems were not only composed but also originally written down in one of these dialects. Beyond this however no safe conclusions can be attained owing to the lateness of the MSS.

In regard to syntax the heroic poems are at least as archaic as any other remains of Anglo-Saxon poetry which have come down to us. We may notice especially the use of the definite article, which in reality is still a demonstrative pronoun in the heroic poems. It occurs comparatively seldom in connection with a weak adjective followed by a substantive—a usage which is nearly universal in most of the Christian poems. Thus in Cynewulf's works the proportion of examples with and without the article varies from 7 : 1 to 9 : 1, and even in the first part of Guthlac, which is believed to date from soon after the middle of the eighth century, the proportion is 7 : 1[2]; but in Beowulf it is only 1 : 5. If the Dream of the Cross, in which the proportion is 2 : 1, is rightly attributed to the early years of the eighth century[3], it seems reasonable to date the composition of Beowulf quite half a century further back. The nearest approach to the usage of Beowulf is shown by Exodus, in which the proportion is over 2 : 3. Unfortunately we have no certain means of dating this work, though it is generally believed to be one of the earliest of the Christian poems. Its archaic character would be natural enough if it is really the work of Caedmon, who flourished while

[1] Especially the regular use of unsyncopated forms such as 3 sg. *onwindeð*, past part. *onsended*.

[2] The statistics for these poems are as follows : Juliana 27 : 3, Christ (II) 28 : 3, Elene 66 : 9, Guthlac (A) 42 : 6, Dream of the Cross 10 : 5, Exodus 10 : 14, Beowulf 13 : 65 ; see Brandl, *S.B. d. Akad. der Wiss. zu Berlin*, 1905, p. 718 f.

[3] Cf. Brandl, *l.c.* (p. 721 ff.).

Hild was abbess at Whitby (658—680) and who according to Bede[1] did compose a poem or poems on this subject.

The metrical characteristics of the heroic poems differ but little from those of Anglo-Saxon poetry in general. Cases of absence of contraction after the loss of intervocalic -*h*- (e.g. in the half-verse *hean huses*) can be paralleled in poems dating from the close of the eighth century or even later, where they are doubtless to be regarded as poetic archaisms. On the other hand importance is generally attached to the absence of any evidence for the retention of -*u* after a long syllable and to the shortening of syllables containing -*r*- which was originally followed by antevocalic -*h*-. Thus it is contended that such combinations as *to widan feore* in the latter half of a verse cannot go back to the middle of the seventh century[2], since the form in use at that time would be *feorha*, which would offend against the metre. As a matter of fact half-verses of the condemned type do occur in Anglo-Saxon poetry, Beowulf itself containing at least eight examples. But even if we were to admit all these statements and emend the offending verses the argument would be conclusive only on the assumption that the poems were written down from the very beginning[3]. Poems which are preserved by oral tradition alone are manifestly liable to small verbal changes, especially in a metre so flexible as that of the Teutonic alliterative verse. Thus in place of the expression *to widan feore* we find occasionally *widan feore* in the same sense, and even in Beowulf we meet with *widan feorh* which is not improbably the oldest form of the phrase. Before the loss of final -*u* it would be a perfectly regular half-verse, but the operation of this change would render it impossible and necessitate the substitution of a synonymous expression. In principle, it should be observed, the

---

[1] Hist. Eccl., IV 24: *canebat autem de creatione mundi et origine humani generis et tota genesis historia, de egressu Israel ex Aegypto et ingressu in terram repromissionis, de aliis plurimis sacrae scripturae historiis, de incarnatione dominica, passione, resurrectione et ascensione in caelum, de Spiritus Sancti aduentu et apostolorum doctrina. item de terrore futuri iudicii et horrore poenae gehennalis ac dulcedine regni caelestis multa carmina faciebat; sed et perplura de beneficiis et iudiciis diuinis, etc.* Prof. Brandl (*Grundr.*, II 1028) holds that the reference is to lyric poems throughout. But is this interpretation really necessary?

[2] On this date see Note II.

[3] For a brief discussion of this question see Note III.

assumption of such substitutions seems to be absolutely necessary, unless we are prepared to deny that any old poems or even verses survived the period of apocope. Yet there is a sufficient amount of resemblance between English and German poetry, not merely in the general metrical scheme but also in the construction of individual verses[1], to render such a conclusion extremely improbable. Consequently I am very much inclined to doubt whether any safe conclusions as to the date of the poems can be obtained from metrical considerations, except of course as regards their final form.

Of far greater importance is the fact that with the exception of the Finn-fragment, which consists of only fifty verses, all our poems contain passages or references of a religious (Christian) character. In Beowulf alone there are about seventy such passages of which the significance is not open to question, and seven or eight others which may belong to the same category. Out of the total number thirty-three are limited to single verses or half-verses[2], while another sixteen affect not more than two verses in each case[3]. The longest passage of all (v. 1724 ff.) contains at least 37 verses, the next longest (v. 175 ff.) fourteen. The rest vary from three to nine verses[4]. The theology which appears in these passages is of a singularly vague type. There are four distinct references to incidents in the early part of Genesis, viz. one (v. 90 ff.) to the Creation, two (vv. 107 ff., 1261 ff.) to the story of Cain and Abel and one (v. 1688 ff.) to the Flood. Apart from these there appears to be no reference to any passage in the Bible except perhaps in v. 1745 ff., which are thought by some to be based on Ephes. vi. 16, and in v. 3069, which contains the phrase 'day of judgment.' We find

---

[1] A few examples are given in the following chapter.

[2] vv. 27, 72, 101, 570, 670, 706, 711, 756 (?), 786, 788, 790, 801, 806, 811, 852, 940, 967, 975, 986 (?), 1201, 1255, 1379, 1626, 1658, 1680, 1682, 2088, 2182, 2216 (?), 2276 (?), 2469, 2650, 3083 (?).

[3] vv. 168 f. (?), 227 f., 440 f., 478 f., 588 f., 625 f., 945 f., 955 f., 1314 f., 1397 f., 1778 f., 1841 f., 1997 f., 2819 f., 2874 f., 3108 f.

[4] vv. 13—17, 90—8, 106—14, 316—8, 381—4, 665—7 (?), 685—7, 696—702, 928—31, 977—9, 1056—62, 1261—5, 1271—6, 1553—6, 1609—11, 1661—4, 1688—93, 1716—8, 2291—3, 2329—31, 2341—3 (?), 2741—3, 2794—7, 2855—9, 3054—7, 3069—73.

also a few references to rewards and punishments in a future life[1]. The word *god* is of very frequent occurrence and always used in the Christian sense. The other epithets of the Deity are 'lord' (*frea, dryhten*), 'father' (*faeder*), 'creator' (*scyppend*), 'ruler' (*waldend*), 'almighty' (*alwalda, aelmihtiga*), 'ruler of men' (*ylda* or *fira waldend*), 'ruler of glory' (*wuldres waldend*), 'shepherd of glory' (*wuldres hyrde*), 'king of glory' (*wuldurcyning*), 'guider of the heavens' (*rodera raedend*), 'helm of the heavens' (*heofena helm*), 'ruler of victories' (*sigora waldend*), 'king of victories' (*sigora soðcyning*). On the other hand there is no example of the word *gast* in a religious sense (Holy Ghost), nor of the name *Crist*, nor of any epithet denoting 'Saviour' (*nergend, haelend* etc.). Hardly less curious is the total absence of the word *engel*, for expressions such as 'lord of angels' (*engla dryhten*[2]) are among the most frequent epithets of the Deity in Anglo-Saxon religious poems. Lastly, there are no references to the saints, to the cross or to the church, nor to any Christian rites or ceremonies.

It appears then that the religious utterances of the poem are of a singularly one-sided character. Indeed it has been observed[3] that, with the exception perhaps of vv. 977—9, "their theology is covered by the Old Testament, and a pious Jew would have no difficulty in assenting to them all." Certainly the facts are such as to call for some explanation, especially since the religious poems are pervaded by a wholly different tone.

One suggestion is that Beowulf was composed under the influence of the missionaries from Iona; but it is extremely doubtful whether the influence of Irish Christianity would tend in this direction at all[4]. Another is that the poet had little direct knowledge of the Christian religion, but that he was acquainted with some religious poems. This explanation certainly seems to fit the case much better than the other. Moreover there is one piece of positive evidence in its favour.

---

[1] vv. 588 f., 977—9, 2741—3, 2819 f.

[2] It is perhaps worth noting that in v. 2186 the expression *dryhten wereda* is used of Hygelac. Elsewhere in Anglo-Saxon poetry this phrase is applied only to the Deity.

[3] Clark Hall, *Beowulf*, p. xxviii.

[4] If there is Celtic influence at all it is more probably Welsh.

In Beow. v. 89 ff. we hear of recitation to the accompaniment of the harp in Hrothgar's hall, and the subject of the recitation is the creation of the world. It appears to me highly probable that we have here an allusion to Caedmon's poem or poems on Genesis, which may very well have been among the earliest of that poet's productions. At all events it was by his hymn on the Creation that he first became known. The inference is strengthened by the rather close resemblance which the hymn bears to the phraseology of Beowulf. If the two poets were contemporary the author of Beowulf would have no other Christian poet on whom to draw, and the limitations of his theological equipment might be satisfactorily accounted for on the hypothesis that he knew only a few of Caedmon's works. As a matter of fact two or three out of the list given by Bede[1] would have been quite sufficient to provide him with all the statements and terms that he uses.

There is another question however with regard to the composition of Beowulf which has aroused more controversy than this, namely whether the Christian passages formed an original part of the poem or not. In the former case of course the poem cannot have been composed before the second quarter of the seventh century. Indeed, if we grant the use of Caedmon's poetry the earliest possible date would be about 660. On the other hand if the Christian passages are due to interpolation the upper limit for the dating of the poem vanishes into air.

As to the possibility of such interpolation in principle we need scarcely entertain any doubt. It is true that the Christian passages or references cannot as a rule be removed without breaking into the rhythm. Consequently, if interpolation has taken place we must assume it to be the work of poets or minstrels, and not of scribes. But have we any reason for doubting that the minstrels of that period were capable of such 'interpolation.' Wherever poetry—at all events anonymous narrative poetry—is preserved exclusively by oral tradition, it is usually the case that the minstrel is allowed a certain amount

[1] Cf. p. 46, note, where the passage is quoted in full.

of freedom in the presentation of his subject[1]. Now probably
no one will suggest that it was only after their conversion to
Christianity that the English began to compose poems about
'heathen kings.'   But, if we grant that such poems were already
in existence, does it really involve a greater amount of effort on
the part of the minstrels to bring these poems up to date—by
removing objectionable matter and introducing expressions in
accordance with the new religion—than to compose an entirely
new set of poems on the same subjects.   I cannot think that
such a view will be seriously maintained.   Therefore we must
consider the case of Beowulf—the only narrative poem which
has come down to us entire—without prejudice on the general
question ; and we must endeavour to see whether it bears the
stamp of a new composition or that of an old work which has
been brought into conformity with new ideas.   The probability or
improbability of the latter view will of course depend largely on
the amount of inconsistency which the poem is found to contain.

Until within the last few years the majority of scholars
believed that Beowulf was a composite work.   This theory was
most fully developed in the writings of Müllenhoff and ten
Brink.   According to the former[2] the poem was made up from
four separate lays, though in its present form nearly half of it
is the work of interpolators.   The latter[3] likewise traced the
origin of the poem to lays, but explained its inconsistencies as
being due not to extensive interpolations but to the combination
of two parallel versions.   In regard to the relative antiquity of
the various parts of the poem there was great divergence of
opinion both between these scholars and generally.   It is
perhaps partly on this account that in recent years there has
been a reaction in favour of believing that the poem as we have
it is practically the work of one man, though it is allowed that
he may have made use of earlier lays.   But those who have

---

[1] The amount of freedom differs of course greatly from case to case (cf. Note IV,
p. 101 ff.) ; but it is only in communities which have elaborated the art of minstrelsy
to a very high degree that the form of words can become absolutely stereotyped.

[2] *Beowulf* (1889), pp. 110—160.

[3] *Quellen und Forschungen*, LXII (1888) ; summarised p. 242 ff.

adopted this view seem to agree that the author, whatever his precise date, belonged to the Christian period, and consequently that the religious passages are not due to interpolation.

Now in the first place it is clear that the story of Beowulf is derived from the Baltic, and the first question which we have to settle is as to the time at which the information on which it is based became known in England. The Angli themselves were originally a Baltic people, as I have tried elsewhere to show, and there is no doubt that down to the time of the invasion of Britain they were thoroughly familiar with all the surrounding regions. But we have no evidence whatever for believing that such was the case within the historical period. By the end of the sixth century, when the first missionaries arrived in this country, they had apparently ceased to be a sea-faring people, and we have no record of any voyage made by an Englishman across the North Sea for several centuries. Again, the Danes became familiar to the west of Europe during the sixth century; but from about 580 onwards we hear no more of their presence on the North Sea for fully two centuries. During the whole of this period their name is heard of only in connection with the missionary expeditions of St Willibrord, early in the eighth century. I have suggested elsewhere[1] that their temporary disappearance was due to the maritime supremacy held by the Frisians. At all events we have archaeo-logical evidence for a considerable amount of communication between southern Norway and the Frisian coasts during this period, while for the Baltic such evidence is almost wholly wanting.

Bearing these facts in mind we can hardly doubt that the information used by Beowulf was acquired before the end of the sixth century—in all probability we may say considerably before that date[2]. Next we have to notice that we have practically no trustworthy information regarding the history of the English kingdoms before the middle of the sixth century, and I think it

---

[1] *The Origin of the English Nation*, p. 93, note.

[2] The references quoted on p. 41 ff. preclude the possibility that these stories were first acquired from the Danes, when the latter again became known in this country about the close of the eighth century.

will be the opinion of any attentive student of early English
history that even the best informed persons of Bede's time were
not much better off in this respect than we ourselves are.   How
then are we to account for the preservation of detailed information regarding the early kings of the Danes and Swedes ?
The only answer to this question, so far as I can see, is that the
doings of such persons must have become embodied in stories
which were preserved by recitation in a more or less fixed form
of words.   Such recitative pieces may have consisted of poetry
alone or of poetry mixed with prose, like some of the pieces
contained in the Older Edda.   If we may trust the analogy of
what appear to be the oldest pieces in this collection, such as
Völundarkviða or Helgakviða Hundingsbana II, the speeches
would be given in metre, while the connecting narrative might
be partly or wholly in prose and quite brief.   We have no
evidence for believing that the early Teutonic peoples ever used
entirely prose narratives, like the Icelandic and Irish sagas, for
such purposes.

At all events it seems to me that if Beowulf is no older
than the middle of the seventh century we are bound to assume
the existence of earlier poems or narratives on the same subject.
Such pieces may of course have been quite short, and it is likely
enough that our epic has made use of more than one of them.
One perhaps may have dealt with the hero's exploits at the
Danish court and another with his last adventure, while in the
scene between Beowulf and Hygelac it is possible that an older
poem has been incorporated, more or less complete, in the
text[1].

But we have yet to take account of what is perhaps the
most striking feature of the poem, namely the fact that, though
it abounds in expressions of Christian sentiment, yet the
customs and ceremonies to which it alludes are uniformly
heathen.   Among these we may mention the funeral ship in
v. 27 ff., the offerings at the shrines in v. 175 f., the observation
of the omens in v. 204 and the curious reference to hanging in
v. 2444 ff. (cf. v. 2939 ff.), probably also the use of the boar on

---

[1] A different view is taken by Schücking, *Beowulfs Rückkehr* (Studien zur engl.
Philologie, XXI), p. 65 ff.

helmets (vv. 303 f., 1111 f., 1286, 1451 ff., 2152) and the burial
of the treasure (v. 2233 ff.), together with the curse imprecated
on the person who should disturb it (v. 3069 ff.). But most
important of all are the descriptions of the disposal of the dead
by cremation in vv. 1108 ff., 2124 ff., 3137 ff. In the long account
of Beowulf's obsequies—beginning with the dying king's in-
junction (v. 2802 ff.) to construct for him a lofty barrow on the
edge of the cliff, and ending with the scene of the twelve
princes riding round the barrow, proclaiming the dead man's
exploits—we have the most detailed description of an early
Teutonic funeral which has come down to us, and one of which
the accuracy is confirmed in every point by archaeological or
contemporary literary evidence[1]. Such an account must have
been composed within living memory of a time when ceremonies
of this kind were still actually in use.

The significance of these passages seems to me to have
been altogether misapprehended by recent writers. If the poem
preserves its original form and is the work of a Christian, it
is difficult to see why the poet should go out of his way in
v. 175 ff. to represent the Danes as offering heathen sacrifices;
for not long before he has introduced a song of the Creation
at the Danish court, and in the sequel Hrothgar is constantly
giving utterance to Christian sentiments. Again why should
he lay Beowulf himself to rest with heathen obsequies, described
in all possible detail, when in his dying speeches (vv. 2739 ff.,
2794 ff.[2]) the hero has been made to express his faith and
gratitude to the Almighty? On the other hand if the poem
was originally a heathen work these inconsistencies are perfectly
natural. If it was to retain its place after the change of faith
and to be recited in the presence of bishops or clergy, all
references to actual heathen worship or belief would of necessity
have to be either accompanied by censure—as is the case in
the homiletic verses following v. 175 ff.—or else suppressed
altogether, and their place taken by expressions in accordance

---

[1] We may refer especially to the account of Attila's funeral given by Jordanes,
cap. 49 (from Priscus).

[2] Apart from certain expressions the general tone of these speeches, especially the
last words of all (v. 2813 ff.), is scarcely Christian; but they contain nothing which is
obviously opposed to Christian doctrine.

with Christian doctrine. Hence it seems to me probable that such expressions are frequently in the nature of substitutions for objectionable matter, rather than gratuitous additions; and in the same way I would account for the occasional survival of ideas which appear to be essentially heathen[1], though they are cloaked in Christian phraseology. But references to practices such as cremation which, though heathen, had long ago passed out of use, would not excite the same repugnance and consequently might be allowed to stand.

It may be urged[2] that cremation seems to have lingered on among the Old Saxons of the Continent until late in the eighth century. True: but it is quite incredible that a Christian poet should borrow from this quarter a method of funeral for his Christianised heroes. If the description of Beowulf's obsequies stood alone a bare possibility might be conceded to the suggestion that it had once formed a poem by itself, unconnected with Beowulf, and based upon a traveller's story. But cremation is clearly regarded as the normal rite throughout the poem, apart from the legendary story of Scyld. We have another description of it in the episode dealing with Finn (v. 1108 ff.), and above all there is the purely incidental reference in v. 2124 ff.: "Yet when morning came the knights of the Danes could not burn his (Aeschere's) lifeless form with fire, nor lay the man they loved on the pyre. She had carried the body away," etc. Here the poet realises the significance[3] of the rite quite clearly and consequently notes that the inability of the Danes to carry it out added materially to their sorrow. In such a case the possibility of Christian authorship seems to me to be definitely excluded.

On the hypothesis that these descriptions had come down from the days of English heathenism all is easily explicable. At the time when the poem was Christianised it may very well not have been known that the rite of cremation was still practised among the heathen of the Continent, and in later

---

[1] E.g. in the imprecation, v. 3069 ff. The imprecatory formulae of charters can scarcely be regarded as analogous

[2] Cf. Brandl, *op. cit.*, p. 1003.

[3] The same idea is frequently expressed in the Homeric poems, e.g. Il. VII 79 f., XXII 342 f., XXIII 75 f., XXIV 37 f., Od. XI 71 ff., etc.

days the verses of the old poet would be handed on in parrot fashion without their significance being generally understood. Well informed persons however, like Alcuin, who had travelled abroad, perceived clearly enough that, however much coated over with Christian phraseology, the heroic poems were in reality of an essentially heathen character.

Now cremation was widely prevalent in this country during the early days of the Saxon invasion—a fact attested by numerous cemeteries especially in the northern and midland counties, including the valley of the Thames. But it appears to have become a thing of the past when the Roman missionaries arrived here; otherwise it is difficult to account for the absence of any reference to the custom in the records which have come down to us. Indeed we may say with safety that it had passed out of general use, at least in the southern half of England, quite a generation before this time; for there are scarcely any traces of it to be found in those western districts which appear to have been conquered during the latter half of the sixth century. Consequently, if we are justified in believing that the descriptions of cremation ceremonies contained in Beowulf date from a time when the practice was still remembered, we must conclude that they were composed not later than the third or fourth decade of the seventh century[1].

But it is not contended, so far as I am aware, by any scholar that the account of Beowulf's obsequies belongs to the earlier parts of the poem. It is the final scene of the story, it is not contained in any speech, and further it is of a thoroughly epic character and would be quite out of place in a short lay. Hence, if the line of argument which we have been following is legitimate, we shall be forced to admit that though the poem has undergone a fairly thorough revision in early Christian times, it must in the main have been in existence some time before the conversion. I do not mean to suggest that the 'revision' was entirely limited to the religious element. Other changes and additions may have been made about the same

---

[1] This date does not depend in any way on the question where the poem originated. Cremation may possibly have lingered in Northumbria longer than elsewhere; but that kingdom seems to have become entirely Christian between 626 and 642.

time[1]. What I do mean is that the great bulk of the poem must have been in existence—not merely as a collection of lays or stories, but in full epic form—an appreciable time before the middle of the seventh century.

The other heroic poems do not furnish us with any similar criteria for estimating the date of their composition, but there seems to be no valid reason for doubting that they are quite as early. Two of them, Deor and Widsith, are expressed in the first person and lay claim to being of a remote antiquity. Deor says that he had been the bard of the Heodeningas and that he had been displaced by a skilful minstrel named Heorrenda. Since in old Norse literature *Hiaðningar* (i.e. *Heodeningas*) means 'Heðinn and his men,'[2] and since Heorrenda can hardly be separated from the minstrel Hôrand in Kûdrûn, it would seem that the poet claims to have been a contemporary of Heðinn and Högni, with whose story we have dealt briefly above (pp. 8 f., 16).

Widsith is still more explicit. The poet states that he visited the Gothic king Eormenric, who as we know died about 370. It is true that incidentally he mentions that he had met with a number of other princes, some of whom lived in the fifth and sixth centuries; but the visit to Eormenric is his main theme. Eormenric is of course one of the most prominent figures of the Heroic Age, and it may be for this reason—as the type of a powerful king—that he is chosen for the poet's host and patron. But then it is by no means so easy to see why he is associated with such an obscure person as Eadgils, prince of the Myrgingas. The suggestion that the poem is founded upon a tradition that this Eadgils possessed a famous minstrel breaks down upon the name *Widsith*, which is obviously fictitious as we have seen (p. 44). It appears to me that considerably less difficulty is involved in the hypothesis that the kernel of the poem[3] is really the work of an unknown bard

---

[1] E.g. possibly some of the elegiac passages (e.g. vv. 2236—2270, 2450—2464), which show a certain resemblance to such poems as the Ruin and the Wanderer.

[2] The name *Hegelinge* in Kûdrûn is probably a corruption of *Hetelinge* (i.e. *Heodeningas*).

[3] Presumably including vv. 88—108; but I am not prepared to suggest an elaborate analysis of the poem.

of the fourth century, and that successive minstrels from time to time have added the names of famous heroes with which they were acquainted[1]—a process to which the original plan of the poem may well have offered inducement.

However this may be neither of the poems shows any characteristics which suggest a later date than Beowulf. Both appear to be constructed in strophic form, a feature rare elsewhere in Anglo-Saxon poetry, while Deor also has a refrain, which is almost without parallel. Lastly, we have seen that *Widsith* occurs as a personal name, apparently in the seventh century, and that this presupposes the existence not only of the poem itself but also of the introduction, which is clearly later.

The case of Waldhere stands somewhat apart from the others, since it has been suggested that this is really a translation of a lost German poem, on which Ekkehard's Waltharius is also based. That the story came from the Continent may of course be granted; but we have also to consider when and in what form it was brought. The linguistic arguments which have been adduced in favour of the German origin of the poem are not now generally maintained. But it is further to be noticed that the poet seems to have treated his subject very differently from Ekkehard. The speeches, with which the fragments are entirely taken up, have nothing corresponding to them in the Latin poem, while the characterisation of the heroine is as unlike as it well could be. Ekkehard represents her as a timid creature, but in the fragments she displays a spirit which may fairly be called martial. It is unwise to lay stress on agreements between Ekkehard and the fragments as against the version of the story given in Thiðreks Saga af Bern. The less complicated form of the latter—in which Guthhere is omitted and Hagena represented as an officer of Attila, pursuing the fugitives—may be due either to imperfect acquaintance with the story or, perhaps more probably, to the conditions under which it had been preserved. We shall see later that for a

---

[1] These lists are perhaps derived in part from mnemonic catalogues—'inventories' of the stories known to the minstrels who composed them. Metrical catalogues of this kind are said to be in use among Servian minstrels at the present day; cf. Krauss, *Slavische Volkforschungen*, p. 186 ff., where a specimen is given.

considerable period heroic poetry appears to have been entirely neglected by the higher classes in Germany; and it may be accepted as generally true that when stories are preserved only by the peasants complex situations tend to become simplified, while all except the most prominent characters drop out. As for the date at which the story became known in England we may note that besides *Aetla* and *Hagena*, which may come from other sources, *Waldhere*, *Hildegyth* and *Hereric* were all names current during the seventh century. There seems therefore to be no adequate reason for believing Waldhere to have had a different history from the other heroic poems.

On the whole, taking all the poems, including Beowulf, together, we may conclude with probability that they assumed substantially their present form[1] in the course of the seventh century. But if our reasoning with regard to the composition of Beowulf is correct we shall have to refer the first treatment of the subject to the sixth century, i.e. almost if not quite to the Heroic Age itself. Deor and Widsith may quite possibly contain still older elements.

We may now turn to the Old Norse poems. Here the data at our disposal are of a very different character, for the metrical evidence is said to preclude the possibility that any of the extant poems date from before the ninth century. It may perhaps be questioned whether all of them are necessarily new compositions since that time—whether certain of them may not be old poems somewhat recast. To this question however we can hardly hope to obtain a satisfactory answer.

The fragmentary Ragnarsdrápa of Bragi Boddason, who seems to have lived in the first half of the ninth century, is probably the earliest extant piece which refers to stories of the Heroic Age. In this poem we find allusions both to the story of Heðinn and Högni and to the attack made upon Iörmunrekr by Hamðir and Sörli. Thiódolfr's Ynglingatal, perhaps half a century later, contains references to the story of Hagbarðr and

---

[1] Waldhere, Deor and Widsith all contain 'Christian' passages, like Beowulf. The interpolations in Widsith (e.g. vv. 15 f., 82 ff.) appear to have been made by some one who possessed a certain amount of erudition; but there is no need to attribute them to a different period.

Signý, as well as brief accounts of the Swedish kings Óttarr and
Aðils, who are mentioned in Beowulf (cf. p. 20) All these
stories, except that of Óttarr, are told also by Saxo, but in a
somewhat different form, which points to their derivation from
Danish rather than Norse sources[1].

On the other hand the stories of the Völsungar, Sigmundr
and Sigurðr, are not mentioned by any early Danish authority.
The story of Sigurðr is generally supposed to have been introduced into Norway from Germany; and in some sense or other
this would seem necessarily to be true, since in the Northern
version, as well as in the German, the scene is laid chiefly in the
Rhineland. But it is apparently impossible to determine when
and in what form the story was transmitted. We have already
noticed that there is archaeological evidence for a considerable
amount of communication between Norway (not Denmark) and
the southern (Frisian) coasts of the North Sea during the seventh
and eighth centuries, and this is clearly a factor which deserves
to be taken into account. Further, it is worth noting that, with
the exception perhaps of *Atli*[2], the names all appear in regular
Northern form[3], as if they had been known from the earliest
times, e.g. *Gunnarr, Högni, Giúki, Buðli.* This consideration, as
far as it goes, certainly favours a very early date; but it is
hardly conclusive[4].

The story of Sigmundr stands on a somewhat different
footing. In the first place Sigemund (Sigmundr) himself is
little more than a name in German tradition, while though

---

[1] Cf. Olrik, *Kilderne til Sakses Oldhistorie*, p. 132.

[2] The name appears to have been quite common in the North during the Viking
Age; yet the apparent absence of umlaut suggests derivation from a (Frisian?) form
corresponding to the Ang.-Sax. *Aetla* (cf. *Aecci, Aeddi* beside *Acca, Adda*).

[3] In contrast (e.g.) with *Kûdrûn*, which clearly shows its foreign origin
(cf. p. 34).

[4] Such names may have been current before, though their frequent occurrence is
no proof of this and may be due to the popularity of the heroic poems. It is perhaps
worth noting that alliteration is shown by certain names which are generally believed
to have been introduced into the story in Norway or Iceland, e.g. *Oddrún, Erpr,
Eitill* with *Atli, Giaflaug, Gullrönd (Guðrún?)* with *Giuki* and *Gunnarr.* If we
may judge from the genealogies in Landnámabók and elsewhere the principle of
alliteration seems to have been generally given up in family names before the ninth
century.

Welsung and *Sintarfizzilo* occur as personal names, they are not connected in any way with the story of Siegfried. Again, in the Helgi poems, which contain no reference to Sigurðr, Sigmundr is connected with the Baltic, and this is still more clearly the case with his son Helgi, who is unknown to the German story. Thirdly, in Beowulf, which knows Sigemund and Fitela, though not Sigurðr, the former is brought into juxtaposition, and apparently also into comparison, with a Danish prince named Heremod. The same two persons are brought together also in the Old Norse poem Hyndlulióð, while the Hákonarmál likewise seems to imply some connection between them, as I have tried to show elsewhere[1]. Apart from the passages specified this Hermóðr (Heremod) is apparently not mentioned in Scandinavian literature, but the facts noted seem to indicate that the two characters were connected in poetry before English and Danish tradition became separated, i.e. presumably in the sixth century.

We have seen that many of the persons mentioned in the main narrative of Beowulf were remembered also in Scandinavian tradition. But since these persons are in all probability to be regarded as historical, it is hardly safe to infer the existence of ancient Scandinavian poems, unless the same incidents are related of them, which is generally not the case. There is a rather striking verbal resemblance[2] between the first speech of Wiglaf (Beow. 2633—60) and certain passages in Biarkamál (especially Saxo's version), where Hialti is addressing Biarki; and this fact is the more noteworthy if Biarki is really to be identified with Beowulf. But the words themselves are of a somewhat general character and might have been used on other occasions. Again there is a certain affinity[3] between the account of the dragon-fight in Beowulf and that of a similar incident related of Frotho I by Saxo (p. 38 f.); and here again a connection can be traced indirectly between the two heroes. But the story of Frotho seems really rather to resemble the account given in Beowulf of Sigemund's dragon-fight; so it

---

[1] *The Cult of Othin*, p. 51 f.
[2] Cf. Bugge, *Beiträge*, XII 45 ff.
[3] Cf. Sievers, *Ges. d. Wiss. zu Leipzig, Ber.* 1895, p. 180 ff.

may be questioned whether the points of affinity between the two did not originally form part of a standard description of incidents of this kind.

A clearer case is that of the poems attributed by Saxo to Starcatherus, in which that warrior exhorts Ingellus to avenge his father. These are clearly to be connected with the speech of the old warrior to Ingeld in Beowulf (vv. 2047—2056), though there is little verbal resemblance. Moreover we have seen (p. 41 f.) that in Alcuin's time poems dealing with Ingeld were known and probably popular in England. The relationship of the passage in Beowulf to these may be compared with that of another passage (vv. 1068—1159) to the fragment dealing with Finn. The poems on Ingeld given by Saxo are traced by Prof. Olrik[1] to a Danish source; and there can be little doubt that his view is correct, as they share the characteristics exhibited by other stories which appear to come from the same quarter (cf. p. 111). Thus the queen's name is not given and her brothers are described simply as sons of Suertingus. Further, the story is cut right away from the surroundings in which we find it in Beowulf, and it may be that for a time it survived in Denmark only in ballad form. Yet, however much change it had undergone before it came under Saxo's treatment, there can be little doubt, in view of the English evidence, that its origin is ultimately to be sought in heroic poetry, or at all events heroic narrative, dating from the sixth century.

Lastly we must mention the story of Uffo's single combat, though, strictly speaking, this is probably not of Danish origin. It was certainly well known in England and there is good reason for believing that its home is to be found in the district to which it refers, i.e. the neighbourhood of Angel, Slesvig and Rendsburg. I have tried elsewhere[2] to show that this story also rests on historical foundations. But the details of the combat, as given by Saxo and Svend Aagesen, and certain legendary features, such as the dumbness or silence of the hero, which are present in both the Danish and English versions of the story, strongly favour the view that it was embodied in

---

[1] *Kilderne til Sakses Oldhistorie*, pp. 18 ff., 132.
[2] *The Origin of the English Nation*, p. 118 ff.

poetic form at a very early period. On the other hand there is nothing to show that such poems survived till Saxo's time. The story is apparently unknown to all Norse authorities.

Many of the German poems which have come down to us are known to be derived, directly or indirectly, from earlier ones, but regarding the antiquity of the latter nothing can be stated with certainty. The Hildebrandslied, which is the only extant piece of early poetry, goes back at all events to the eighth century. Further, the language[1] used by Einhard in describing the poems collected by Charlemagne (cf. p. 5 f.) would scarcely be appropriate unless they were believed to be more than a century old by that time. We may probably therefore refer them at least to the seventh century.

It seems likely that some of the lost poems of the Langobardi were of still greater antiquity. In the poem which celebrated their victory over the Vandals (cf. p. 10), a story with which we shall have to deal more fully in a later chapter, a very prominent part appears to have been played by the heathen gods. Such a piece can hardly have been composed after the end of the fifth century, at which time the Langobardi were already Christians.

Regarding the antiquity of Gothic heroic poetry there can be no question, for Jordanes, our chief authority on this subject, wrote about the middle of the sixth century, i.e. during the Heroic Age itself. We have already noticed (p. 37) that his account of Eormenric appears to be coloured by poetic tradition. But of the heroes whom he enumerates (cap. 5) as celebrated in poetry, the only one of whom we know anything, Vidigoia, is described as *Gothorum fortissimus* in a quotation (cap. 34) from Priscus, who lived about a century earlier[2]. There is good reason therefore for believing that the Goths possessed heroic poems as early as the first half of the fifth century.

---

[1] *Item barbara et antiquissima carmina, quibus ueterum regum actus et bella canebantur, scripsit memoriaeque mandauit* (Vita Caroli Magni, cap. 29).

[2] Cassiodorus (*Var.* VIII 9) states that the Gothic king Gensimundus, who according to Jordanes (cap. 48) reigned shortly after Eormenric's death, was widely celebrated in poetry (*toto orbe cantabilis*); but his name is preserved only in Gothic records.

We may now sum up briefly the results of our discussion. The heroic poetry of the Goths certainly belonged to the Heroic Age itself, and it is more than likely that certain Langobardic poems were nearly as old. Some heroic poems belonging to other German peoples may probably be referred at least to the seventh century. The chief monument of English heroic poetry must be ascribed to the first half of that century, while some of the other poems claim to be of greater antiquity. The lost heroic poetry of the Danes seems to have been occupied largely with the same subjects as the English poems, and since the stories generally refer to the Baltic we may reasonably infer that heroic poetry flourished in that region during the sixth century. On the whole then it seems probable that the development of heroic poetry began in the Heroic Age itself, not only among the Goths but throughout the greater part of the Teutonic world.

NOTE I.   THE USE OF HEROIC NAMES
IN ENGLAND.

THE distribution of heroic names in English historical documents is as follows. The Liber Vitae contains 35 (37), of which nine (eleven) are peculiar to that work[1]. Of those which occur in other documents 29[2] belong to persons born apparently before 700, six to such persons only, 14 or 15[3] to persons born between 700 and 800, two to such persons only, and 22[4] to persons born after 800, four to such persons only. It must be remembered that, apart from the Liber Vitae, the materials for the ninth and tenth centuries are much more abundant than those for earlier times.

In the Liber Vitae itself it is possible within certain limits to distinguish between persons of early and later date. Investigations in the lists of kings, queens and abbots have shown that they are arranged chronologically, and it is only reasonable therefore to expect that the same is true of the much longer lists of clerics and monks. A brief examination of the names will make it clear that such is actually the case. Some modernisms of language, such as *-ferth* for *-frith*, or of orthography, such as *-ht-* for *-ct-*, are practically confined to the last parts of the lists, which may be by later hands[5]. But even within the parts certainly written by the first scribe archaic forms such as *-iu-* for *-io-* are more frequent at the beginning of the lists than later; so also occasional *-b-* for *-f-*. Above all we may note the uncompounded names in *-i*, a type common in early Anglo-Saxon, but practically extinct after the eighth century. Fol. 24, the first in the clerics' list, contains eleven such names, while fol. 30 contains none; fol. 34, the first in the monks' list, has eight, while fol. 38 has only one. Now we shall probably be well within the mark if we assume that one fifth of the names in each list[6] belong to persons born in the seventh

---

[1] ·37 (eleven), if we admit the emendation of the corrupt forms *Vychga* and *Vurmeri* to *Wydiga* (Widia, Wudga) and *Vyrmheri* (Wyrmhere). See the Addenda.

[2] Ecglaf, Eadgils, Eomaer, *Eormenric, Frod(a), Hereric, *Hoc, *Hrothmund, Ingeld, Offa, Oslaf, Sigemund, *Aehha, Sigeferth, Aetla, *Hagena, Theodric, Waldhere, Becca, Witta, Wada, Oswine, Sigehere, *Sceafthere, Alewih, Aelfwine, Eadwine, Wulfhere, Frithuric; perhaps also Herebald. The asterisk denotes names limited to persons of the sixth and seventh centuries.

[3] Eadgils, Eanmund, Heardred, Hygelac, Ingeld, Offa, Wermund, Weohstan, Wiglaf, Wada, *Scilling, Oswine, Sigehere, *Gislhere (perhaps Eomaer).

[4] *Aelfhere, Ecglaf, Eanmund, Heremod, Offa, Sigemund, Wermund, Weohstan, Wiglaf, Wulfgar, Garwulf, *Ordlaf, Sigeferth, Waldhere, Becca, Wada, *Hun, *Hringwald, Aelfwine, Eadwine, Wulfhere, Frithuric (possibly also Deor).

[5] Only the earlier lists, those printed in Sweet's *Oldest English Texts*, p. 154 ff., are taken into account.

[6] Lines 159—192 and 332—362 in Sweet's text.

century. On this basis we find that of the 35 (37) heroic names which occur in the Liber Vitae nine (ten) are limited to persons of the seventh century[1], and twelve (thirteen) to persons of the eighth[2]. The total number of names in each century (cf. p. 43) may be obtained by comparing the evidence of the Liber Vitae with that of the other documents[3].

The fact that so many heroic names occur in the Liber Vitae has led several writers to conclude that the true home of English heroic poetry was in the north. But no such inference is really justified by the evidence. The number of personal names recorded for the south of England during the sixth and seventh centuries is very small ; yet it is only here that we meet with persons called Eormenric, Hoc and Hagena—names which belong to quite different cycles of story. Moreover out of the 37 heroic names preserved in the Liber Vitae no less than 28 occur in place-names in various parts of England. The frequence therefore of heroic names in the Liber Vitae is to be attributed in part to the great abundance of the material and in part to its comparatively early date.

Including the evidence of the Liber Vitae there are fifteen heroic names which seem to be borne only by persons of the eighth century or later times. Eight of these however occur also in place names[4]. Of the remaining seven[5] all except one or possibly two[6] make their appearance during the eighth century. On the other hand it has already been mentioned that not less than nineteen heroic names[7] occur only in local nomenclature.

We have still to mention a few heroic names which are not found in the extant remains of Anglo-Saxon poetry. Theodhere (Diether) is known only from the sixth century, Hild, Herding, Iuring, Omoling only from the

---

[1] †Beowulf, †Billing, †Folcwald, Frod, Heremod, Hereric, Oslaf, †Widsith, Alewih (†Widia?). Names marked with a dagger are confined to the Liber Vitae.

[2] Eadgils, †Hildeburg, †Hrothwulf, Wiglaf, Wulfgar, Garwulf, Aetla, Witta, †Heathuric, Sigeferth, Wulfhere, Frithuric (†Wyrmhere?). The following names are found both in the early and late parts of the lists : Eanmund, †Hama, Heardred, Hygelac, Ingeld, Offa, Sigemund, Wermund, Theodric, Wada, Aelfwine, Eadwine, †Aegelmund; perhaps also Herebald, if the abbot of this name is to be identified with the one mentioned by Bede (*H. E.* v 6).

[3] For the details see the preceding notes.

[4] Hildeburg, Hrothwulf, Wiglaf, Wulfgar, Ordlaf, Hun, Hringwald, Gislhere.

[5] Aelfhere, Weohstan, Garwulf, Scilling, Heathuric, Wyrmhere (?), Dior.

[6] Aelfhere and Dior. The latter (in the form *Diar*) occurs only once (Birch, *Cart. Sax.* 497) and may be a mistake for Diara (*ib.* 507). The name Diora need not be of heroic origin; it may be an abbreviation from such names as Diorwald, Diornoth.

[7] Breca, Finn, Fitela, Hengest, Hnaef, Hrethel, Scyld, Weland, Guthhere, Geat, Gifeca, Heoden, Helm, Wald, Beaduca, Frithla, Secca, Gifeca—to which we may add Waelse in Walsingaham. Widia is also to be added, if it is not allowed for the Liber Vitae. For the list of place-names (not the personal names) I am dependent upon Binz, *Beitr.* xx 141—223.

C.   5

seventh, Hildegyth and Blaedla from the seventh and eighth, Wulfheard from all periods, Ecga only from the eighth century, Ecgheard from the eighth and ninth, Sigesteb only from the ninth. Hild, Wulfheard and Ecga are found also in place-names. In some of these cases, e.g. in that of Hildegyth, the non-occurrence of the name in the poems is clearly due to mere accident; but it would scarcely be safe to assume that all these characters were celebrated in Anglo-Saxon poetry.

NOTE II. ON THE DATING OF CERTAIN SOUND-CHANGES IN ANGLO-SAXON.

In my *Studies in Old English*[1], published in 1899, I endeavoured to formulate a scheme for dating approximately the chief sound-changes which took place in English during the first few centuries after the invasion of Britain. In the course of these investigations I was led to the following conclusions (pp. 117, 253 ff.): i. that 'palatal umlaut' in Northumbrian and the dialect of the Vespasian Psalter took place before 650; ii. that the change from $\bar{æ}$ to $\bar{e}$ (in all dialects except West Saxon) was in operation about 650—680; iii. that the loss of intersonantal h (in all dialects) belongs to the same period or a little later; iv. that contraction through loss of intervocalic h may be dated roughly between 680—710; v. that the loss of final -u after long syllables and in words of the form ⌣⌣⌣ took place in all dialects at a time approximately contemporaneous with the operation of palatal umlaut in Northumbrian (i.e. before 650).

Prof. Morsbach in his paper *Zur Datierung des Beowulfepos*[2] has dealt with several of the same problems and come to conclusions which differ widely from those at which I arrived. The chief differences are as follows: i. that after a long syllable which bore the chief accent -u was not lost before the end of the seventh century, though after a long 'nebentonig' syllable the loss was somewhat earlier (p. 261 f.); ii. that intervocalic h was lost in Kentish by about 680, but in Mercian and Northumbrian the same change cannot be shown to have taken place before about 700 (p. 264); iii. that postconsonantal h (before vowels) was retained in Kentish in 679; its loss, at least in Mercian and Northumbrian, may be dated about 700, but after the loss of -u (p. 265). In summarising the results of his discussion (p. 273) he gives "about 700" for the loss of postconsonantal h and "shortly before 700" for the loss of -u. Incidentally he follows Bülbring (*Elementarbuch*, §§ 146, 528) in dating the origin of $\bar{e}$ (from 'West Germ.' $\bar{a}$) before the breaking, and in placing the loss of h before l (in *neolaecan*) anterior to the operation of 'palatal umlaut' (monophthongisation).

[1] *Transactions of the Cambridge Philological Society*, Vol. IV, Part II. The page-references are to the figures in the outer corners.

[2] *Nachrichten von der Königl. Gesellschaft der Wissenschaften zu Göttingen*, 1906, pp. 251—277.

The importance of this discussion for our present purpose[1] lies in the dates proposed for the loss of -*u* and of postconsonantal *h*. Prof. Morsbach concludes that Beowulf cannot have been composed before 700, since it contains a number of half-verses which would have been metrically impossible before the operation of these changes, e.g. *ofer fealone flod*(*u*), *to widan feor*(*h*)*e*. I have already expressed scepticism as to whether such inferences are really justifiable. This applies more particularly to the verses affected by the question of postconsonantal *h*, which are quite few in number. The date which Prof. Morsbach himself (p. 274) proposes for the composition of Beowulf is 700—730. He finds. no difficulty in reconciling this with the statistics (given above, p. 45) for the use of the article. This seems to me rather strange; yet the opinion of a scholar who stands in such deservedly high estimation cannot lightly be disregarded.

Now let us examine the evidence on which these conclusions are based. First it will be convenient to take the loss of *h*. Prof. Morsbach holds that in Kentish intervocalic *h* was lost before postconsonantal *h*. The evidence is derived from a single charter issued by King Hlothhere in 679 (Birch, *Cart. Sax.* 45), which contains the place-name *Vuestan ae* beside the personal name *Velhisci* (Latin Gen.). But surely conclusions of this kind are admissible only when a number of examples can be adduced. On the same principle we might argue from the name *Irminredi* (in the same charter) that the change *ǣ* > *ē* had taken place and also from the name *Aedilmaeri* (again in the same charter) that it had not. And what should we do with the earliest East Saxon charter (Birch, 81), in which the grantor is called both *Oedelraedus* and *Ho*(*di*)*lredus*? Again, it is clear that Bede wrote his own name *Baeda*; but will anyone venture to hold that this represents the current pronunciation of his name in 731—or indeed for some half a century earlier? In personal names we must clearly allow for traditional orthography. The form *Irminredi* may no doubt be used as evidence for the change *ǣ* > *ē*, and similarly the form *Vuestan ae* may be used as evidence for the loss of *h*. But forms, especially personal names, like *Velhisci* and *Aedilmaeri*, which must long have been in use, may very well show an antiquated orthography—one which correctly represented the pronunciation of thirty or forty years previously. A single instance of such a kind is totally insufficient ground for supposing that the Kentish dialect treated postconsonantal and intervocalic *h* differently.

Next we must consider the date given for the loss of *h* in Mercian and Northumbrian (p. 263 f.). I find some difficulty here in following Prof. Morsbach's line of argument. In Northumbrian there is, admittedly, no evidence at all for the preservation of *h*, while cases of its omission are numerous in Bede's History (written in 731), in addition to one or two instances in probably earlier authorities. For Mercian[2] we are dependent

---

[1] Prof. Morsbach's paper raises a number of questions besides those mentioned above. But I am obliged here to confine my attention to those which have a bearing on the dating of Beowulf.

[2] The application of this term to the Epinal and Erfurt glossaries (or the archetype) seems to me to be open to grave objection.

on the Epinal, Erfurt and Corpus glossaries, the archetype of which is placed before 700 by Prof. Morsbach. In my *Studies*, p. 232, I came to the conclusion that in this archetype the cases of retention and omission of *h* were probably about equal in number. Prof. Morsbach replies that there is no necessity for such a conclusion, since all the extant glossaries themselves date from times when *h* was already lost. He himself decides[1] against the loss of *h* in the archetype for two reasons : (1) because postconsonantal and intervocalic *h* are treated alike in the glossaries and the former was still retained in Kentish when the archetype was written[2] ; (2) because the assumption of such an early date for the loss of *h* would be incompatible with his own date for the loss of *-u*. The first of these arguments, it will be seen, rests upon the dating of the loss of postconsonantal *h* in Kentish, on which enough has been said above. The second depends upon a hypothesis which we shall have to consider presently.

My reason for concluding that the loss of *h* occurred in the archetype was that in at least eight entries (probably several more) all three glossaries agree in showing forms without *h*. It is to be remembered that in these glossaries we are dealing not with independent documents but with copies made, more or less mechanically, from one original. This remark applies of course much more to Epinal and Erfurt than to Corpus ; for in the latter the materials have been rearranged, as well as augmented from other sources, while incidentally the forms have been modernised to a considerable extent. In Epinal such modernisation is not unknown, but it is restricted within very narrow limits, as may be seen from the use of *b* and *f*[3]. Further, it is to be remarked that we have no ground for assuming the language of the archetype itself to have been consistent. The occurrence of numerous Dative forms and of expressions containing more than one word (e.g. *per anticipationem—þorch obst*) shows that the materials were derived largely from glosses in books, just as in the Leiden glossary[4]. Many of these glosses may have been written a generation or more earlier than the compilation of the archetype glossary. Whoever bears these facts in mind and at the same time compares the evidence for forms with and without *h* with that for *f* and *b* will, I think, be forced to the conclusion that the forms with *h* do not represent the pronunciation of the compiler of the archetype, but that they were taken over by him from earlier sources.

[1] If I have interpreted his meaning correctly. But I admit that I have had great difficulty in understanding the argument in paragraph 5 of p. 263 (especially the "mit -*h*-" of line 12).

[2] Prof. Morsbach seems to regard Kentish as exceptional in its treatment of intervocalic *h*, rather than in that of postconsonantal *h*. I am not quite clear as to his reason for this.

[3] Cf. *Studies in Old English*, p. 240.

[4] This text represents a more primitive type of glossary than the others and, though it is not an ancestor of theirs, it has without doubt used a considerable number of the same glosses (especially in Sweet's § XLV) which were incorporated in their archetype.

Now we may take the evidence for the proposed date of the loss of *-u*. After enumerating (p. 253 ff.) a list of cases which have been suggested by various scholars Prof. Morsbach comes to the conclusion that the only certain example of a form in which *-u* is retained[1] is the word *flodu* in the inscription on the Franks casket. As the whole theory largely depends on the value attached to this form we must consider it carefully. In my *Studies*, p. 156, I suggested that it should be regarded as an archaism and at the same time pointed out that *-u* is lost in another word (*unneg*) in the same inscription. Prof. Morsbach rejects this explanation of *unneg*, which he connects, rightly, I think now, with O. Sax. *nah*. But this form can come perfectly well from **nāh(w)u* (earlier **nēhwō*), if not from **nāhwa* (cf. Goth. *nehwa, nehw*). That Ang.-Sax. *neah, neh* has lost an *u*-sound is, I contend, shown not only by the Gothic forms, but also by *neolaecan* and *neowest* (cf. Lind. *genehwaþ*, etc.). Prof. Morsbach rejects my explanation of these forms also and adopts that of Prof. Bülbring, as stated above. But the latter is untenable; for if *ē* (from *ā*) had come into existence before the operation of breaking, we should never find forms with *ae*, which as a matter of fact are fairly common in the earliest texts of all dialects. In particular we may note that the three extant coins of the Mercian king Aethelred (675—704) all have *-ræd*. Hence the change *ǣ > ē* can hardly have taken place much before 650.

Apart from *unneg*[2], there are three forms on the recently discovered right side of the casket which may show loss of *-u*. Prof. Napier (*An English Miscellany*, p. 375 f.) is inclined to regard the forms *sær* and *dœn* (?), if not also *hos*, as Nom. sg. fem. But the interpretation of this part of the inscription is still uncertain in many details.

I confess that since the discovery of the new side I am less inclined to regard the form *flodu* as an archaism than as a mere blunder. Even in the more intelligible parts of the inscription we find a number of forms which present serious difficulty: *Romwalus, Reumwalus*[3], *gasric, Giuþeasu*. The last of these still seems to me to present the best illustration of *flodu*. If the one is due to the loss of some letters—e.g. *su* for *su(mæ)*—the same may be the case with the other[4]. At all events an inscription which presents so many difficulties cannot be regarded as a safe authority on which to base a scheme for the chronology of sound-changes.

The only other instance of *-u* on which Prof. Morsbach lays any weight

---

[1] The form *scanomodu* on the solidus need not be taken into account. It is improbable that coins of this type were minted after the sixth century.

[2] Prof. Morsbach further argues that even if my interpretation of *unneg* was correct it would prove nothing, since *-u* was probably lost after a long 'nebentonig' syllable earlier than after a long 'haupttonig' syllable. But neither the *-gar* of the Bewcastle inscription (cf. p. 70) nor the *felt* of the East Saxon charter can be admitted as evidence for this hypothesis.

[3] In spite of what is said by Prof. Morsbach (p. 264 f.) these forms are scarcely intelligible unless *h* was already lost.

[4] E.g. perhaps *flod u(þ)ahof*.

is the form *aetgaru* in the Erfurt glossary. He speaks of it as 'nicht unwahrscheinlich' (p. 257), though 'fraglich' (p. 264). Many scholars cite it as an example of -*u* without reserve. Now in order to form a just estimate of the value of any form which occurs in the glossaries it is obviously necessary to take it in connection with the forms which the other texts show in the same entry. The entry in question (*framea—aetgaru*) occurs in the Epinal and Corpus glossaries, as well as in that of Erfurt, though the two former have *aetgaeru* (*ætgaeru*) for *aetgaru*. There can be no doubt that the relationship between the three glossaries is as follows :

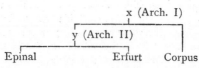

though we do not know exactly how many intermediate stages lie between the extant texts and the original archetype. It will be seen that the question at issue is whether the Erfurt glossary or the other two have kept the original form—for if the archetype had contained both forms we may assume that some trace of the double entry would have been preserved (as in other cases). Now the Erfurt glossary is the latest of the three, it is the work of a foreign scribe and it is very carelessly copied. Moreover, no letter or combination of letters has suffered more than *ae*. Most usually this combination has been reduced to *e*; but the loss of *e* is not infrequent, e.g. *smal*, *hrad*, *nacthegelae*. In view of these facts it is unintelligible to me how anyone can uphold the evidence of the Erfurt glossary against the other two. But in this case it is used to prove the existence of an archaic form for which none of the glossaries elsewhere present a parallel. Lastly, we may remark that though it is frequently assumed that the word *gar* was an *u*-stem (**gaizu-*) no evidence worth consideration has ever been adduced to prove it[1]. On all grounds therefore we are brought to the conclusion that the evidence for the preservation of -*u* in *aetgaru* is not merely open to question but entirely worthless.

We must now notice certain early documents in which -*u* is clearly lost. Prof. Morsbach mentions the form *felt* in the earliest East Saxon charter (Birch, 81), which dates from 692—3. Here then -*u* was lost before the date in question[2]. But we can get back further than this, for the place mentioned is called *Vuidmundes felt*. Some considerable time must have elapsed after the loss of -*u* before a noun, even a proper name, could change its inflection and adopt the endings of *a*-stems.

---

[1] The place-name *Wihtgarabyrg* in the Saxon Chronicle, ann. 530 (B, C), 544 (A, B, C) is more probably to be regarded as a corruption of *Wihtwara-* through the influence of the personal name *Wihtgar*.

[2] Prof. Morsbach's explanation is that *felt* here is a long nebentonig syllable. But we have no evidence that the influence of 'sentence-accent' made itself felt in this way.

Next let us take the Northumbrian evidence. The form -*gar* on the Bewcastle column can prove nothing. In the same inscription however we may find an example in *Cyniburug* ; for in view of *hnutu* etc. it is probable that consonantal stems used what was originally the Accus. sg. form also for the Nom. sg. (as in Old Norse). I cannot see any probability in the suggestion that this monument may date from some considerable time after 670[1], if it has been rightly interpreted.

More important is the fact that no example of -*u* after a long syllable is preserved in Bede's Ecclesiastical History. It is to be observed that Bede seems to have scrupulously followed the orthographical peculiarities of the documents which he used. Thus in Papal letters dating from the first half of the seventh century we find such forms as *Adilbercto*, *Audubaldi* which are not used elsewhere in the work[2]. Now in the record of the proceedings at the Council of Hertford in 673, which is quoted in IV 5, we find the forms *Herutford*, *Vilfrid*, *Vynfrid*, *Hrofaescaestir* ; and in the similar record for the Council of Hatfield in 680, quoted in IV 17, we find the form *Haethfelth*. If -*u* had not been lost by this time the forms used must have been -*fordu* or -*fordus*, *Vilfridu(s)*, etc., and it is most unlikely, in view of Bede's practice elsewhere, that he would have altered them. As a matter of fact the latter of these documents contains two forms—*Hymbronensium* (or *Humbr-*) and *Estranglorum*—which are not used elsewhere by Bede. Again, the same author almost always writes the name of the Northumbrian king Ecgfrith (r. 671—685) as *Ecgfrid* (in the Nom.). That this represents the contemporary orthography is shown by a coin of that king which bears the legend *Ecgfrid rex*.

But further, there is a whole series of names, much used in Northumbria, which have as their second element -*haeþ* from earlier -*haþu* (e.g. *Eadhaed*). At the time when -*u* was lost here the change *a* > *æ* was clearly still operative. Will anyone suggest that this was the case after the middle of the seventh century? Again, it can hardly be doubted that the form *Osuiu*, if not also *Osuald*, represents the pronunciation[3] current in the time of that king. In Bede's History, III 29, we have extracts from a Papal letter addressed to *Osuiu* (v. l. *Osuio*) *regi Saxonum*. The form *os-* can scarcely have become current in compounds before -*u* was lost in the Nom., Accus. sg.

It is surely unnecessary to enter into further details. We have seen that

---

[1] Prof. Morsbach would assign the monument to the time of Aldfrith, who reigned 685—705 (not 725, a printer's error in Vietor's book).

[2] In his own narrative of course he often uses forms which must have been antiquated in his time (e.g. *Vurtigerno*, *Aeduini*, *Aeodbaldo*) and also foreign forms in the names of persons of Continental origin (e.g. *Agilberctus*). But it may safely be assumed that all these cases are derived from earlier documents.

[3] I.e. Oswiu (Oswald) ; cf. *Baduuini*, i.e. Baduwini. I have not taken account of the possibility that -*uiu* originally contained an -*h*-. If that could be proved the present discussion would be practically superfluous.

practically the whole evidence for the proposed chronology consists of two forms, *Velhisci* and *flodu*, one of which is incapable of proving what it is meant to prove, while the other is of exceedingly doubtful value ; and on the other hand that this chronology has opposed to it a large number of forms in the glossaries, in charters and in early Northumbrian authorities of various kinds. Now let us consider the various sound-changes in relation to one another.

It is admitted, and necessarily so, that the loss of -*u* took place before the loss of *h*. For the sake of convenience we may apply the terms 'Period I' to times anterior to the loss of -*u* and 'Period II' to the interval between the two changes. From neither of these periods have we any texts surviving, unless we are to reckon the inscription on the Franks casket to Period I. Our earliest charters, and apparently also the lost archetype of the glossaries, were composed at a later time ('Period III') when *h* was no longer pronounced, though doubtless often written. But before the date of the earliest extant glossary (Epinal) a further change or changes had taken place which brought about the confusion of original *ð* and *f*. It is clear from a comparison of the glossaries that this confusion was later than the loss of *h* and also that it was almost, if not entirely, unknown to the archetype. So also in Northumbrian. In Bede's History we have no instance of *h* preserved in an English word, whereas examples of its omission are numerous. On the other hand it is clear that Bede usually retained the distinction between *b* (i.e. *ð*) and *f*, although the latter has already largely encroached on the former in the Moore MS.[1] We may therefore constitute two subdivisions of the period subsequent to the loss of *h*, namely 'Period III' prior to the confusion of *ð* and *f*, and 'Period IV' subsequent to this confusion. Now we can see clearly where to date the Franks casket, for it shows confusion of *ð* and *f* in *wylif*—according to Prof. Morsbach also in *sefu*. It belongs therefore not to Period I but to Period IV.

Any attempt to fix an absolute chronology is of course rendered difficult by the absence of very early texts. We may probably assume that Period IV begins more or less about 700. The Kentish charter of 679 falls in Period III. Now when -*u* was lost, *h* (whether intervocalic or postconsonantal) must have been a spirant—a fact which Prof. Morsbach seems to have entirely ignored. It is quite incredible that only a few years should elapse between that stage and the total loss of intervocalic *h* seen in the charter. The corresponding period in Germany lasted centuries, and I cannot conceive how the transition can have been accomplished anywhere in less than half a century. I conclude therefore that the dates which I gave in my Studies were approximately correct. If there was an error it was in putting some of the changes slightly too late. I have little hesitation now in expressing my opinion that the loss of -*u* took place not later than the second or third decade of the seventh century.

---

[1] Cf. my Studies, p. 247. It will be seen that the number of cases in which M, B and C agree in *f* (for *ð*) is very small.

NOTE III. LITERARY INFLUENCE IN BEOWULF.

I am not aware that any serious argument has been brought forward to show that Beowulf was a literary production. It is customary indeed, especially among English scholars, to use the word 'write' with reference to its composition ; but this is frequently due to mere carelessness. Nevertheless there is undoubtedly a widespread reluctance to admit that the poem came into existence without the use of writing—partly on account of its length and partly because its technique is of rather an advanced order. The first of these difficulties has now been definitely settled by the Servian poems, as we shall see in the next Note. Here we need concern ourselves only with the second.

The most definite pronouncement on this subject known to me is contained in Prof. Ker's book, *The Dark Ages*, p. 250. "*Beowulf* and *Waldere*," he says, "are the work of educated men, and they were intended, no doubt, as books to read. They are not, like the *Elder Edda*, a collection of traditional oral poems." Here we have three distinct statements. That Beowulf and Waldhere are not a collection of poems, like the Edda, is manifest. Whether they are traditional oral poems at all is a different question, the answer to which depends in the first place on our attitude to Prof. Ker's second statement—that they were intended as books to read. But this statement surely requires some evidence. The only argument brought forward is that "the *Beowulf* MS.......is intended as a book to be read, and is got up with some care. From the look of it, one places it naturally in the library of a great house or a monastic school ; and the contents of it have the same sort of association ; they do not belong to the unlearned in their present form." But, so far as the earlier part of this passage goes, the argument applies only to the tenth century. No one will deny that the earlier Anglo-Saxon poems were studied at that time ; indeed they had probably come to be regarded as, in a sense, classical. But have we any right to assume that scholars of the seventh or eighth centuries viewed these poems or their subjects in a similar light? If so how are we to account for the total absence of references to such subjects in the works of Bede? And what about Alcuin? *Quid Hinieldus cum Christo?* Is it likely that Alcuin would have regarded these *pagani et perditi reges* as suitable subjects for the attention of scholars? The natural presumption from his language is that he knew of them not from literary works, but only from street-minstrels whom he looked upon with disgust. Yet Bede and Alcuin can hardly have been ignorant of any important literary activity during their times, and it would be unfair to regard them merely as religious bigots. In view of their silence it seems to me a precarious hypothesis even that the poems were committed to writing much before the end of the eighth century.

There is no doubt of course that the writing of English was in common use during the early part of the ninth century. But the paucity of earlier evidence renders it probable that this was a recent innovation; and the orthographical characteristics of eighth century documents point to the same conclusion. Laws were written in English from the beginning; but we may safely assume that this was done by professional scribes, in all probability ecclesiastics. Otherwise there is little definite evidence for the writing of the vernacular, except of course in glosses. The more learned clergy clearly preferred to use Latin; for the less learned Bede states (*Ep. ad Ecgb.*, cap. 5) that he had himself had to make translations even of the Creed and the Lord's Prayer, for them to learn by heart. Where was a reading public to be looked for in such a period[1]?

But we have yet to discuss the statement that "*Beowulf* and *Waldere* are the work of educated men." The question here is what is meant by the word 'educated.' Nowadays the expression 'educated Chinese' is used in more than one sense. Sometimes it is applied to those who have received a good education according to the traditional standard of that nation. Sometimes however, especially in newspaper language, it is used only of those Chinese who have received a Western education. We need not doubt that the poets of Beowulf and Waldhere were among the best educated men of their day according to the traditional native standard. If they were court minstrels—a question we shall have to discuss in the next chapter—they could hardly be otherwise. But this is not what Prof. Ker means. The education which he has in view is of foreign (Roman) type, as may be seen by the latter part of the second of the quotations given above. Again (p. 252) he says: "The English epic is possibly due to Virgil and Statius; possibly to Juvencus and other Christian poets, to the authors studied by Aldhelm and Bede." If so[2], is it not remarkable that no obvious trace of such influence can be pointed out? It must not be assumed that the poets responsible for the composition or preservation of Beowulf would have any inclination to disguise their knowledge of foreign poetry. The use which they have made of incidents derived from the Bible is decisive evidence to the contrary, although their knowledge of this subject seems to have been of a most elementary description. In Widsith we actually have at least one

---

[1] The case of King Aldfrith shows that educated laymen were not entirely unknown; but it is extremely unlikely that they were common. In one charter (Birch, 99) Wihtred, king of Kent, is made to say: *signum sanctae crucis pro ignorantia litterarum expressi.* This document exists only in a late copy; but at all events it suggests that the practice of making the cross, instead of signing, was due to a widespread inability to write.

[2] I confess that I am strongly inclined to suspect that anyone imbued with Latin learning would have lacked not only the inclination but also the ability to compose such a poem as Beowulf. This however is an opinion which could only be substantiated by a wider knowledge of the history of poetry in various parts of the world than I can make any claim to possess.

reference to a classical character (v. 15 ff.). But Beowulf is entirely free from anything of the kind.

Prof. Brandl[1] has likewise been attracted by the idea that the growth of Anglo-Saxon epic poetry may have been due to Latin models. As a probable source of such influence he has fixed upon the Aeneid and even indicated a number of passages in this poem which may have suggested certain scenes and incidents in Beowulf. Thus he notes that both poems begin with the story of a wanderer (Scyld, Aeneas) who came over the sea (*feasceaft, primus et profugus*) and founded a great dynasty or empire. Then he suggests a connection between the song of Hrothgar's minstrel on the Creation (Beow. 90 ff.) and a passage (Aen. I 742 ff.) which describes how Dido's minstrel Iopas sang of the origin of men and beasts, among other cosmological subjects. Further, he compares the whole of the scene which contains the latter passage with the account of Beowulf's reception at Heorot, noting the various stages in the arrival of the two heroes from their disembarkation to the feast with which they are welcomed in the palaces. Incidentally, he remarks that at the feast Wealhtheow hands the cup to Hrothgar and then to the visitors (Beow. 615 ff.), while Dido pays the same honour to Bitias (Aen. I 738). Lastly, he compares the racing after Grendel's overthrow (Beow. 864 ff.) with the rowing contest in memory of Anchises (Aen. V 104 ff.).

I confess that, coming as they do towards the close of an admirable discussion of the subject, which no attentive student of Beowulf can fail to appreciate, the comparisons suggested by Prof. Brandl strike me as surprising beyond measure. The resemblances between the athletic contests, so far as they have any existence at all, are due to practices which are worldwide. Is there any reason for supposing that the act of courtesy ascribed to Wealhtheow was not in full accordance with early Teutonic custom? Parallels may be found, easily enough, in Old Norse literature. The arrival of the wanderer (Scyld, not Beowulf) has nothing in common with that of Aeneas. The one is a baby and probably alone ; the other is the commander of a fleet. Then, as to the resemblance between Beowulf's visit to Hrothgar and Aeneas' visit to Dido, I can only say that I fail to detect its existence. Prof. Brandl seems to lay most stress on this incident and points out certain parallelisms in the language : *corripuere uiam qua semita monstrat* (Aen. I 418) with *stig wisode gumum aetgaedere* (Beow. 320 f.), and *coram quem quaeritis adsum Troius Aeneas* (Aen. I 595 f.) with *Beowulf is min nama* (Beow. 343). But are these not purely accidental coincidences, such as one could find between almost any two narrative poems? When Prof. Brandl speaks of Aeneas' "Verhandlung mit Dido zuerst durch eine etikettegemässe Mittelsperson," I do not understand what is meant. Certainly this description applies to the entry of Beowulf. But Aeneas is present beforehand, shrouded in a cloud with which Venus has covered him. In the midst of the scene the cloud is suddenly parted and Aeneas disclosed to Dido's eyes. It seems to me that no meeting could well be more different.

---

[1] *Grundriss d. germ. Philol.*, II 1008.

There remains then only the fact that the two minstrels treat a somewhat similar theme (though in Beowulf this does not take place on the occasion of the hero's arrival). It is no doubt a curious coincidence ; but the introduction of such a subject in Beowulf may be accounted for quite satisfactorily without the hypothesis of any acquaintance with Virgil.

I cannot quit this subject without remarking how much more plausible a case could be made out for deriving Beowulf from the Homeric poems, especially the Odyssey. Here there are striking parallels both in diction and terminology, as we shall see in a later chapter. We may note especially the epithets applied to princes and the formulae with which speeches are introduced. If we wish to find a real parallel to the reception of Beowulf by Hrothgar, it is provided by the account of Telemachos' visit to Menelaos. Similar parallels are to be obtained for the minstrel's lays and many other incidents. Are we then to suppose that Beowulf is based upon the Odyssey ? That is a hypothesis which I will gladly leave for others to work out. For my own part I prefer the explanation that similar poetry is the outcome, or rather the expression, of similar social conditions. But in Beowulf and the Homeric poems, as against the Aeneid, we have additional common elements in the fact that the interest is centred in the actual characters—not in the destiny of their descendants—and in the vividness and reality of the narratives, in spite of Grendel, Scylla and the rest. The latter of these two common features seems to me to indicate that both the Greek and English poets were depicting types of life with which they were themselves familiar, whereas no one will dispute that the Aeneid is a product of the library.

Half a century ago, when the study of Teutonic antiquity was still young, there was a general eagerness to refer every institution and belief to a native origin. To-day we see the inevitable reaction—a hypercritical attitude towards every explanation of this character, coupled with a readiness to accept theories of biblical or classical influence on the slightest possible evidence. It is this intellectual atmosphere which, naturally enough, has given birth to the chimaera of a literary Beowulf—a creature which, if I am not mistaken, belongs to the same genus as certain well-known theories in Northern mythology.

CHAPTER V.

THE POETRY AND MINSTRELSY OF EARLY TIMES.

IN the preceding chapters we have seen that the persons and events celebrated in the heroic poems apparently all belonged to the fourth, fifth or sixth centuries, and further that heroic poetry was flourishing among the Goths during the same period. For the existence of English, Scandinavian or German heroic poetry at this time we have no absolutely conclusive evidence. But the materials from which our poems are formed must largely be referred to the sixth century. This may be seen most clearly in cases where the poems of two or more nations not merely treat an identical theme but also agree in the motif or in comparatively small details, as in the stories of Ingeld, Waldhere and Svanhildr. A like age is probably to be attributed to resemblances in language, such as those shown by the hortatory addresses and the accounts of dragon-fights cited in the last chapter (p. 60 f.). The fact that these resemblances sometimes occur in stories relating to entirely different characters need not prevent us from believing that they spring ultimately from a common origin.

It cannot of course be proved that the materials from which the heroic poems are derived were themselves always in poetic (metrical) form. In principle we must admit the possibility that they were transmitted from one generation to another in a more or less stereotyped form of prose narrative, such as we find later in the sagas of Iceland and Ireland. But in point of fact we have no evidence whatever for the cultivation of such traditional prose narratives among any of the early Teutonic peoples, whereas there is good reason, as we shall see shortly, for believing that narrative poetry was both ancient and widely cultivated.

In the first place we may note that English and German poetry down to the ninth century shared a common system of metre and that the Fornyrðislag, which is used in most of the Edda poems, differed but little from this type, except of course that it was always arranged in strophes. The application of this common metre to narrative purposes can scarcely be regarded as a recent innovation, for English and German poems frequently exhibit verses and half-verses of very similar construction. Thus in the Hildebrandslied speeches are generally introduced with the formula: *Hadubrant gimahalta, Hiltibrantes sunu,* which is almost identical with a formula used in Beowulf: *Wiglaf maðelode, Weohstanes sunu.* In the same German poem (v. 42) we find the verse: *dat sagetun mi seolidante* ('it has been told me by mariners'), with which we may compare Beow. 377: *þonne saegdon þaet saeliðende.* Note should also be taken of such phrases as (v. 55) *ibu dir din ellen taoc* ('if thy prowess is sufficient') and definitely poetical expressions like (v. 43) *inan wic furnam* ('war carried him off'), as compared with Beow. 572 *ðonne his ellen deah* and 1080 *wig ealle fornam Finnes þegnas.* The number of such parallels might be greatly increased if we were to take into account passages from religious poems, especially the Old Saxon Heliand.

For a very much earlier period direct evidence is furnished by the Roman historian Tacitus, who says (*Germ.* 2) that the Germani possessed ancient poems or songs (*carmina*) even in his time and adds expressly that they had no other means of preserving a historical record[1]. That these poems were partly of what may be called a 'heroic' character is clear from another passage (*Ann.* II 88), where it is stated that Arminius was still a subject of poetry among barbarian nations (*canitur…adhuc barbaras apud gentes*). In both cases the reference is in all probability to the peoples of western Germany rather than to the Goths.

On the whole then we need not doubt that the heroic

---

[1] *celebrant carminibus antiquis, quod unum apud illos memoriae et annalium genus est, etc.*

poetry which we find in England and Germany during the seventh and eighth centuries had a long history behind it. Of course as to the form of the poetry current in the first century we are entirely without information. Many scholars hold that it was exclusively choric, not only in Tacitus' time but for four or five centuries later. This is one of the questions which we shall have to bear in mind in the course of our discussion.

The earliest historical reference to the cultivation of poetry, or rather perhaps minstrelsy, in England occurs in Bede's account of the poet Caedmon (*Hist. Eccl.* IV 24). In this story we are told that it was the custom that, when the villagers met together to drink and amuse themselves, everyone should take his turn in singing to the harp. Caedmon, who had never been able to learn a song, used to leave the festivities and make his way home as soon as he saw the harp coming in his direction[1]. No information is given as to the character of these songs. Probably they would as a rule be quite short—perhaps not much longer than the hymn learned by Caedmon from the angel, which contains only nine verses. It is not unlikely that they resembled some of the metrical riddles more than any other form of Anglo-Saxon poetry which has come down to us. Longer songs, of a narrative type, may of course have been known. But it is a question whether such songs would deal with heroic themes or with folk-tales. We may think of the Scandinavian story of Svipdagr and Menglöð, which is preserved in a number of different versions, ranging in date probably from the tenth century to the seventeenth or later.

But we have already seen (p. 41 f.) that in the eighth century at least the recitation of heroic poetry was by no means unknown. Indeed we may infer from the language used by Alcuin (*ridentium turuam in plateis*) that it enjoyed a good deal of favour with the general public. Another of his letters[2] speaks

---

[1] *nil carminum aliquando didicerat. unde nonnunquam in conuiuio cum esset laetitiae causa decretum ut omnes per ordinem cantare deberent, ille ubi adpropinquare sibi citharam cernebat surgebat a media caena et egressus ad suam domum repedebat.*

[2] Mon. Germ., Epist. Carol. Aeui, II 21 (ad Hygbaldum episc. Lindisfarnensem): *lectionis studium exercete. audiantur in domibus uestris legentes, non ludentes in platea.*

to much the same effect. We may gather from the use of the word *citharista* that these recitations also were accompanied by the harp. But the language of the letters seems rather to suggest that the performers in such cases were persons who made minstrelsy more or less of a profession. A century earlier the existence of professional minstrels may be inferred from the well-known story of Aldhelm[1]—that he used to take up his position on a bridge, like a professional minstrel (*quasi artem cantitandi professum*), and sing to the people in order to call them back to church. We are not informed as to the character of the poems he recited, but clearly they were of a type calculated to attract the country people.

On the Continent we find very similar evidence. A passage in the Annals of Quedlinburg, to which we have already alluded and which dates perhaps ultimately from the tenth century, states that the country people used to sing of Dietrich von Bern[2]. From a much earlier period we have an interesting reference to a Frisian minstrel named Bernlef, who became a disciple of St Liudger. He had been blind for three years, when he was brought to the missionary, but " he was greatly loved by his neighbours because of his geniality and his skill in reciting to the accompaniment of the harp stories of the deeds of the ancients and the wars of kings[3]." This incident appears to have taken place before 785. That minstrelsy was definitely recognised as a profession among the Frisians is shown by the last clause in the Lex Frisonum, which fixes a special compensation for injury to the hand of a harpist[4].

From all this we gather that in the eighth century there existed both in England and Germany a class of minstrels whose practice it was to play the harp and recite heroic poetry

---

[1] William of Malmesbury, *Gesta Pontif.*, v § 190 (from King Alfred's *Handboc*).

[2] *Amulung Theoderic dicitur...et iste fuit Thideric de Berne de quo cantabant rustici olim* (Mon. Germ., Scr. III p. 31).

[3] *Et ecce illo discumbente cum discipulis suis oblatus est cecus uocabulo Bernlef qui a uicinis suis ualde diligebatur eo quod esset affabilis et antiquorum actus regumque certamina bene nouerat psallendo promere, etc.* Vita S. Liudgeri, II I (Mon. Germ., Scr. II p. 412).

[4] *Qui harpatorem qui cum circulo harpare potest in manum percusserit componat illud quarta parte maiore compositione quam alteri eiusdem conditionis homini, etc.* (Mon. Germ., Leg. III 699 f.).

in the village-streets or on bridges or wherever they could gather an audience. Now if we turn to the poems themselves we find that they also contain references to professional minstrels; but these appear to have been quite a different class of persons from those with whom we have been dealing.

At the close of his elegy (v. 35 ff.) Deor gives the following account of himself: "With regard to myself I will say that formerly I was the bard (*scop*) of the Heodeningas and dear to my lord. My name is Deor. For many years I have had a good office and a gracious master. But now Heorrenda, a skilful poet, has received the domain which the king had before given to me." There may be some difference of opinion as to the precise meaning of the word *londryht*[1], but it is clear enough that the poet had been a court-minstrel and that he had been supplanted in the king's favour by a rival. In Beowulf also we find mention of a person who seems to hold a similar position. The word *scop* occurs three times in this poem (vv. 90, 496, 1066)—always perhaps with reference to the same man. In each case he is represented as singing or reciting, and twice mention is made of the harp. On the last occasion, when he recites the story of Finn and Hnaef at the banquet (cf. p. 2), he is called *Hroðgares scop*, which seems to imply a sort of official position.

The case of Widsith is somewhat different. The poet is a traveller who prides himself on the large number of nations he has visited. He states also that he served under various princes by whom he had been handsomely rewarded. The poem ends with some reflections on the life of wandering minstrels; but these verses may be a later addition, like the introduction. At all events in v. 94 the poet speaks of his return home, when he presented to his lord, Eadgils prince of the Myrgingas, a valuable 'ring' which had been given him by Eormenric. This present was a reward to Eadgils for his kindness in granting the poet the land formerly held by his father. It would seem then that the poet is represented as a man of good position. Whether we describe him as a wandering

---

[1] Cf. my *Studies on Anglo-Saxon Institutions*, p. 369.

minstrel or not, his occupation is clearly to be regarded as court-minstrelsy and different therefore from that of Bernlef and the harpists mentioned by Alcuin.

Apart from these personal notices there can be little doubt that the heroic poems which have come down to us were of courtly and not of popular origin. In the first place we may note their strongly aristocratic tone. This may be appreciated from the fact that all the women mentioned in the Anglo-Saxon poems are of royal birth, while the men are either princes or persons, apparently of noble or knightly rank, attached to the retinues of princes. On the rare occasions when persons of humbler rank are referred to, their names are not mentioned. In Beowulf no name is given even to the court-minstrel. Again the poems frequently refer to details of court etiquette, with which they seem to be well acquainted. In the later German poems this feature must of course be attributed to the conditions of the twelfth and thirteenth centuries, when the poems were composed. But it is quite as marked even in Beowulf. We may note especially the long and detailed account of Beowulf's arrival at the Danish king's hall and the conversation which the chamberlain holds with the king on the one hand and the visitor on the other, before the latter is invited to enter. The chamberlain's exact position is remarked, when he approaches the king and it is added that "he knew the custom of knight-hood[1]." Other members of the court also have their position or duties described (vv. 500 f., 1161 f., 1165 f., 1794 ff.) ; but most of all the poet loves to picture the movements of the king and queen (vv. 612 ff., 920 ff., 1162 f.).

Then again it should be observed that persons of royal rank are very seldom spoken of with disrespect. The rare exceptions to this rule probably all refer to persons of a remote past, Eormenric, Thrytho and Heremod, and in the last two cases the reprobation is qualified in a very marked way. Moreover the ground of censure is invariably violence, cruelty or treachery. Of immoral or unseemly conduct we have no mention. Indeed, except in the story of Weland—which stands by itself in many

---

[1] *Cuðe he duguðe þeaw* (v. 359).

ways, as we shall see later—such subjects seem to be studiously avoided. More than this the Anglo-Saxon heroic poems are entirely free from coarseness of language, such as we frequently find in Saxo's history, and indeed from references of any kind which could offend even the most fastidious taste. In general the same remarks are true also of the German and Scandinavian heroic poems, though not in the same degree. But the gnomic and theological poems of the Edda show a wholly different tone, which at its worst (e.g. in Lokasenna) verges on bestiality.

Lastly, we must not overlook the fact that in dignity and polish of style the heroic poems far surpass any narrative works which the English language has to offer for many centuries later. It has been remarked that the composition of epic poetry requires a more or less professional training, and in the case of such poems as Beowulf this is doubtless true, not only on account of its length but also because a very large vocabulary is needed for the constant interchange of epithets which is one of its chief characteristics, while the allusions with which it abounds point to the possession of much historical or traditional lore[1]. At the time when it was produced the knowledge and leisure necessary for such composition is scarcely likely to have been found outside the entourages of kings.

On the other hand we have seen that minstrelsy of some kind was cultivated even by peasants in Caedmon's time. We can hardly doubt that such was the case to a higher degree in court circles. In Beow. 867 ff. we find a 'king's thegn' composing an account of the hero's adventure immediately after its occurrence, and utilising apparently by way of illustration the story of Sigemund. This person may be the court minstrel; but the identity of the two is scarcely certain. In a later passage (v. 2105 ff.), referring to the banquet after the fight with Grendel, we hear of the king himself taking his turn with the harp: "There we had poetry and music. The old Scylding (Hrothgar) related stories of old time out of his great store of information. Now the martial[2] hero would lay his hands on the joyous harp, the instrument that makes good cheer;

---

[1] Cf. Brandl, *op. cit.*, p. 981 f.

[2] It is generally thought that all these sentences refer to the king.

now he would recite a poem, true but sad; now a story of marvel would be related in due course by the magnanimous king. Now again, bowed with age as he was, the old warrior would begin to lament that he had lost the martial vigour of youth. His heart surged within him as he called to mind the manifold experiences of a long life." It is held that the reference here is to lyrical effusions rather than to anything in the nature of epic narrative[1]; but I am inclined to doubt if we are justified in totally excluding the latter. I would rather favour the view that the cultivation of minstrelsy, including narrative as well as lyric poetry, was a general accomplishment in royal households, and that the office of court-minstrel was an honour given to that member of the court who had attained the greatest proficiency in his art.

The statements of the poems as to the prevalence of court-minstrelsy during the Heroic Age are fully confirmed by the testimony of contemporary Roman writers. Perhaps the most important reference is a passage in Priscus' account of his visit to Attila in the year 448. After describing the banquet given by the king to his guests he proceeds as follows[2]: "When evening came on torches were lighted and two barbarians stepped forth in front of Attila and recited poems which they had composed, recounting his victories and his valiant deeds in war. The banqueters fixed their eyes upon them, some being charmed with the poems, while others were roused in spirit, as the recollection of their wars came back to them. Others again burst into tears, because their bodies were enfeebled by age and their martial ardour had perforce to remain unsatisfied."

It will be noticed that this account bears a curious resemblance to the passage from Beowulf which we have just quoted. Nothing is said as to the language in which the poems were

---

[1] Cf. Brandl, *loc. cit.*

[2] K. Müller, *Fragmenta Historicorum Graecorum*, IV p. 92. ἐπιγενομένης δὲ ἑσπέρας δᾷδες ἀνήφθησαν, δύο δὲ ἀντικρὺ τοῦ ᾿Αττήλα παρελθόντες βάρβαροι ᾄσματα πεποιημένα ἔλεγον, νίκας αὐτοῦ καὶ τὰς κατὰ πόλεμον ᾄδοντες ἀρετάς· ἐς οὓς οἱ τῆς εὐωχίας ἀπέβλεπον, καὶ οἱ μὲν ἥδοντο τοῖς ποιήμασιν, οἱ δὲ τῶν πολέμων ἀναμιμνησκόμενοι διηγείροντο τοῖς φρονήμασιν, ἄλλοι δὲ ἐχώρουν ἐς δάκρυα, ὧν ὑπὸ τοῦ χρόνου ἠσθένει τὸ σῶμα καὶ ἡσυχάζειν ὁ θυμὸς ἠναγκάζετο.

composed[1], but at all events we need hardly doubt that in this
as in other respects Attila was following Gothic custom.   For
the duet we find an interesting parallel in a passage of Widsith
(v. 103 ff.) : " Then Scilling and I began to sing with clear voices
before our victorious lord ; loudly rang out our music as we played
the harp.   Then it was openly confessed by many brave-hearted
and experienced men that they had never heard a better song."

Evidence for the cultivation of minstrelsy at Teutonic courts
in Gaul is furnished by letters of Cassiodorus (*Variarum* II, 40 f.)
and Sidonius Apollinaris (*Ep.* I, 2).   The former document is
an answer from the Ostrogothic king Theodric to a request
from Clovis, king of the Franks (d. 511), who had asked him
to send him a skilled minstrel.   Sidonius' letter is a very full
account of Theodric II, king of the Visigoths, who reigned
from 453 to 466.   He states that the king seldom admitted
jesters when he was dining, and that he took no pleasure in
music except when it encouraged manliness of spirit as well as
pleased the ear.   In neither of these cases however is it certain
that the performers were Goths.

A clearer case of Teutonic minstrelsy, dating from the same
period, occurs in one of Sidonius' poems (*Carm.* 12[2]), in which
the author complains that he has to live among troops of longhaired and greedy Burgundians, listening with polite attention,
in spite of his disgust, to their songs.   More than a century later
we hear of Frankish court-minstrelsy in a neighbouring district.
In a poem addressed to Lupus, duke of Aquitaine, about the
year 580, Venantius Fortunatus (*Carm.* VII 8. 61) says : " Let
the Roman sound your praise with his lyre and the barbarian
with his harp[3]"; and again : " Let us frame verses for you, while
barbarian poets compose their lays; thus the hero will be greeted
with like honour, though in diverse strains[4]."   In the introduction

---

[1] The performers who followed are said to have used Gothic, Hunnish and Latin.

[2] Freely translated by Hodgkin, *Italy and her Invaders*[2], Vol. II, p. 363.   That
the songs were in the national language appears from the phrases *Germanica uerba*
(v. 4), *barbaricis abacta plectris...Thalia* (v. 9 f.).

[3] *Romanusque lyra plaudat tibi barbarus harpa.*

[4] v. 67 f.   *nos tibi uersiculos, dent barbara carmina leudos :*
             sic uariante tropo laus sonet una uiro.

The word *leudos* is generally interpreted as in the next passage (Ang.-Sax. *leoð*) ;
but is it not possible that here it is an error for *leudes* (N. pl.) ?

to his poems the same author complains of the constant buzzing of the harp, as it resounds to the barbarian lays[1].

A curious case of royal minstrelsy is recorded by Procopius (*Vand.* II 6) in his account of the siege of Mount Pappua (A.D. 534). Gelimer, king of the Vandals, wrote a letter to Faras, the Herulian chief who commanded the besieging army, begging him to send him a harp, a loaf and a sponge. The explanation given by the messenger was that the king had composed a song upon his misfortunes and as he was a good minstrel he was anxious to accompany it with a mournful tune on the harp as he bewailed his fate[2]. We are again reminded of Hrothgar, but perhaps still more of Hrethel's dirge over his son (Beow. 2460 f.).

These examples are sufficient to show that minstrelsy was widely cultivated in the courts of the Teutonic princes who had established themselves in Roman territory. Taken together with the references in Anglo-Saxon poetry, which deals of course with the more northern peoples, they leave no doubt that the prevalence of court-minstrelsy was one of the characteristics of the Heroic Age. For the existence of professional minstrels the Roman evidence is not so clear, though we may regard in this light the two 'barbarians' mentioned by Priscus (p. 84). On the whole the impression which we gain from our authorities is that the cultivation of the art was more or less general as in the north.

But it must certainly not be assumed that the poems of the period were always of an ephemeral character. Jordanes (cap. 5), in a passage to which we have already referred, says that the Goths "used to sing to the strains of the harp ancient poetry dealing with the deeds of their ancestors, Eterparmara, Hanala, Fridigernus, Vidigoia and others who are very famous in this nation[3]." Again, when he mentions the migration of the Goths

---

[1] *sola saepe bombicans barbaros leudos arpa relidens* (Mon. Germ., Auct. Antiquiss. Tom. IV i p. 2).

[2] κιθαριστῇ δὲ ἀγαθῷ ὄντι ᾠδή τις αὐτῷ ἐς ξυμφορὰν τὴν παροῦσαν πεποίηται, ἣν δὴ πρὸς κιθάραν θρηνῆσαί τε καὶ ἀποκλαῦσαι ἐπείγεται.

[3] *antiquo etiam cantu maiorum facta modulationibus citharisque canebant, Respamarae, Hanalae, Fridigerni, Vidigoiae et aliorum quorum in hac gente magna opinio est, quales uix heroas fuisse miranda iactat antiquitas.*

to the Black Sea (cap. 4), he refers to "their ancient poems," where this event is commonly related in almost historical style[1]. From such expressions we must conclude that Jordanes knew, directly or indirectly, of Gothic poems which he believed to have been in existence for a considerable time.

Jordanes' language may be compared with Einhard's reference to the 'barbarous and very ancient poems' collected by Charlemagne (cf. p. 62). But in reality there appears to be an essential difference between the minstrelsy of the Heroic Age and that of Charlemagne's time. In the latter period we hear only of 'very ancient poems' or of poems dealing with 'the deeds of the ancients,' as in the story of Bernlef. The two expressions may really be more or less equivalent, for there is nothing to show that Bernlef was an original composer. For the existence in his time of court-minstrelsy, or indeed of any poetry dealing with contemporary persons and events, we have no evidence which can be called satisfactory[2].

In the Heroic Age on the other hand we have references not only to 'ancient poems' but also to original compositions, dealing with the praise or fortunes of living men. The exploits of Attila, one of the leading figures of that age, were sung in his own presence, as we know from an eye-witness. We need scarcely doubt therefore that Beowulf truly reflects the spirit of the times when it makes one of the Danish king's thegns compose a poem on the hero's exploit immediately after the event. It is to such compositions that heroic poetry—indeed in a sense we may say the Heroic Age itself—owes its origin.

The beginning of the process may be seen from a few passages in Widsith. At the end of the poem we are told that "he who wins praise (*lof*) shall have his glory (*dom*) established on high beneath the sky." The meaning of the first expression is explained by another passage (v. 70 ff.): "I have been in Italy with Alboin. No human being, as far as my knowledge goes, had a readier hand than had Audoin's son for the winning

---

[1] *quemadmodum et in priscis eorum carminibus pene historico ritu in commune recolitur.*

[2] For a passage in Saxo Poeta which seems to indicate the existence of such poems cf. p. 6, note.

of praise, nor a heart more ungrudging in the distribution of rings and shining bracelets." We may compare also what the poet says of his patroness, the princess Ealhhild (v. 99 ff.): "Her praise spread through many lands, when I set myself to declare in song where under heaven it was that I knew of a gold-adorned queen who lavished presents in the noblest fashion." The chief object which the characters of the Heroic Age set before themselves is to 'win glory'—to have their fame celebrated for all time. Thus in Beow. 1387 ff. the hero says: "Let him, who can, win for himself glory before he dies; that is the best thing which can come to a knight in after times, when he is no more." Such glory may be won by brave deeds, as when Beowulf says to Hrothgar before his second adventure (*ib.* 1490 f.): "I will win for myself glory with Hrunting (a sword), or death shall take me," or again when the queen says to Beowulf (*ib.* 1221 ff.): "Thou hast brought it about that men shall esteem thee far and near and for all eternity, wheresoever the sea encircleth its wind-swept barriers." But the same object can be attained by generosity, which will ensure one's praise being sounded from court to court.

Now perhaps we are in a better position to understand why the Heroic Age ends when it does. The latest person mentioned in the heroic poems is Alboin who died about 572. The last Roman author who mentions Teutonic court-minstrelsy is Venantius Fortunatus, who wrote apparently about ten years later. Is there a connection between these two facts? It should be remembered that we have felt some hesitation in including Alboin among the characters of the Heroic Age, for though his praises were sung among the Saxons and Bavarians, as well as in England, he does not figure in any widely known story. We may reasonably expect that such stories would as a rule—not necessarily—require a certain time in which to be elaborated. Is it possible that in Alboin's time the conditions favourable to such elaboration were no longer in existence—that court-minstrelsy was dying out or had lost its creative power?

It will perhaps be urged that the absence of reference to court-minstrelsy after Venantius' time may be due to mere accident. But a short consideration of the political position will show that there is good reason for thinking otherwise. During the period which had elapsed since the time of Priscus and Sidonius—we may say roughly about a century and a quarter—the Teutonic world had undergone great changes. Many kingdoms had disappeared, among them those of the Huns, Rugii, Heruli, Alamanni, Thuringians, Burgundians, Vandals and Ostrogoths, and probably also the Warni and Gepidae. Of the nations which survived the Visigoths and Langobardi, and to a large extent the Franks also, were settled among alien peoples and thus exposed to denationalising influences. This is partly true also of the Bavarians, and they moreover had become subject to the Franks before the middle of the sixth century. Probably the only other Teutonic kingdoms which remained on the Continent were those of the Frisians and the Danes, for there is no evidence that the Old Saxons were under kingly government at this time[1]. Moreover the Danes were almost cut off from the western peoples by the irruption of the Slavs who now occupied the greater part of ancient Germany. Hence we may conclude that even if court-minstrelsy survived in a few places the poems had now no longer any chance of obtaining a wide international circulation.

The change of faith is of course another consideration which must be taken into account. One of its effects was to cut off the Christian kingdoms from those of the Frisians and Danes. Probably also it had an adverse influence on the cultivation of court-minstrelsy, for there can be little doubt that this was originally permeated by heathen ideas. At all events we find in later times surprisingly few traces of heroic poetry in the territories of the Franks, Visigoths and Langobardi.

Of the purely Teutonic kingdoms, excluding Denmark, that of the Frisians was the last to retain both its independence and its religion. It can hardly be due to accident therefore that some of the most important of the heroic poems, such as Kûdrûn (cf. p. 34) and probably also the Norse version of the story of Sigurðr (cf. p. 59), appear to be derived from

---

[1] At all events they had no kings when we first obtain definite information about them, towards the close of the following century.

Frisian sources, though this region was not their original home. Further, we have noticed that in Frisian law a special compensation was fixed for injury done to the hand of a harpist. Still more significant is the fact that in the passage quoted above (p. 80) from the Vita Liudgeri, describing Bernlef's skill in reciting heroic poetry, one text adds the words *more gentis suae*. It would seem then that minstrelsy of this type was regarded as a distinctive characteristic of the Frisians and that heroic poetry retained its hold upon them at a time when it was little known elsewhere.

In England the conditions appear to have been quite different from those with which we have been dealing, for at the end of the sixth century this country probably contained more Teutonic kingdoms than did the whole of western and central Europe. We have seen reason for believing that Beowulf was composed within about half a century of Venantius' time and that the other heroic poems may date from the same period. From the evidence which we have discussed above we should naturally conclude that court-minstrelsy lasted somewhat longer in England than elsewhere, although it dealt entirely with stories derived from abroad. It is true that there is no external evidence for such minstrelsy; but that is fully explained by the fact that we have practically no literature of any kind before the last decades of the seventh century. Most probably its extinction was due to that wave of religious fervour which was started by the Kentish king Erconberht and which in the course of the following half century seems to have succeeded in enforcing conformity to the new faith throughout the whole country.

It will be convenient now to consider briefly the court-poetry of the Viking Age. The history of heroic poetry in the North unfortunately cannot be traced in its entire course. We have seen that there is a long gap, extending over some two centuries and a half, in Danish tradition, and also that the poems which have come down to us are probably all of Norse (Norwegian-Icelandic) origin. Yet the social conditions of the Viking Age were very different from those which prevailed on the Continent during the same period and unquestionably nearer than the latter to those of the Heroic Age. It is not unreasonable therefore to expect that the court-poetry of the Viking Age may throw light on the earlier period.

We saw in an earlier chapter (p. 15 f.) that, apart from the Edda, Old Norse literature is rich in narrative poems of the ninth and tenth centuries. These are usually the work of known authors and deal for the most part with contemporary persons and events, though they contain frequent references to characters of the Heroic Age, as well as to the ancestors of reigning princes. Many of the authors, such as Thióðolfr of Hvín, Thórbiörn Hornklofi and Goððormr Sindri, were what we may call court-minstrels—or rather court-poets, for the harp seems not to have been used by such persons, at least in the latter part of the Viking Age. But they can scarcely be regarded as professionals in any strict sense of the term. As a rule they appear to have been men of good family. Thióðolfr was a familiar friend of Harold the Fair-haired, who entrusted him with the education of one of his sons. Goððormr Sindri, who composed poems for the same king, refused to receive any reward and had sufficient influence with Harold to insist on his being reconciled with his son Halfdan Svarti. Another poet of the same period, Einarr[1], commonly called Torf-Einarr, was earl of Orkney and practically an independent prince. Eyvindr Skaldaspillir, who was attached to the service of Haakon I and Haakon, earl of Lade, was himself a descendant of Harold the Fair-haired.

It has been mentioned that from the middle of the tenth century onwards most of the poems quoted in the sagas are of Icelandic authorship. A considerable number of them may be regarded as court-poems, since they were composed in honour of princes whom the authors were visiting at the time. As an example we may take a verse quoted by Gunnlaugs Saga Ormstungu (cap. 7) from the poem composed by the hero, when he visited London in 1001 : "The whole nation reveres England's generous ruler as a god; all ranks, warrior prince

---

[1] Son of Rögnvaldr, earl of Möre, and half-brother of Gönguhrólfr (Rollo), first earl of Normandy.

and people alike, bow down to Aethelred." Such poems were often handsomely rewarded. Aethelred presented Gunnlaugr with a scarlet cloak, lined with fur and embroidered with lace, while Sigtryggr, king of Dublin, gave him a fur-lined cloak, a lace-embroidered tunic and a gold ring which weighed a mark. It happened very frequently that men like Gunnlaugr would enter a king's retinue and remain with him for months and even years. But they would seldom consent to recognise any lordship permanently, since as a rule they had lands of their own in Iceland, to which they eventually returned.

It is hardly probable that any class of persons exactly corresponding to this existed in the Heroic Age itself, for with the somewhat doubtful exception of the Old Saxons we have no evidence for independent commonwealths during that period. In Widsith, it is true, we have the case of a minstrel who claims to have wandered far and wide and to have visited many princes by whom, like Gunnlaugr, he was handsomely rewarded. But Widsith had a lord at home to whom he subsequently returned. Indeed the introduction, if we may use it as an authority, seems to make him set out at first on a definite commission from that prince. The permanent lordless state was probably altogether foreign to the conditions of the Heroic Age. The lordless man in the poems is either one who has lost his lord, as in the Wanderer, or one who has been dismissed from his lord's service, like Deor. Until he finds another lord he has neither home nor security, and his condition is pitiable in the extreme.

But it is by no means so clear how the court-minstrels of the Heroic Age differed from the Norwegian poets of the Viking Age. In Kûdrûn the minstrel Hôrant (Heorrenda) seems to hold a position quite comparable with that of Thióðolfr or Goðþormr Sindri; indeed he is even described as a relative (*mâc*) of the king[1]. Again, we may take the case of Starkaðr. He is commonly regarded as the type of a roving poet-warrior of the Viking Age. But in reality he seems to belong to the Heroic Age; for however late the poems attributed to him may be in their final form, they had their counterparts in England probably as early as the sixth century. There is no conclusive

---

[1] In the Norse form of the story Hiarrandi is the name of Heðinn's father.

evidence for denying either that he was the foster-father of Ingialdr (Ingeld) or that he entered the service of a number of different kings.

The story of Starkaðr is bound up with the history of heroic poetry in the Viking Age—a difficult problem, to which we shall have to refer again shortly. We may note here however that the poems of Thióðolfr and Hornklofi must have been preserved for some three centuries by oral tradition before they were committed to writing. There seems to be no reason therefore for denying in principle the possibility that poems may have survived even from the Heroic Age. It is to be observed that court-poets were expected to be able to recite old poems, as well as works of their own composition. Thus on the morning of the battle of Stiklestad (A.D. 1030) St Olaf ordered the Icelander Thórmóðr Kolbrúnarskald to recite the old Biarkamál. This story is interesting as it shows that the love of the heroic poems was strong enough to assert itself in an hour of supreme danger and under a most religious king.

In the course of this chapter we have seen that one of the characteristics of the Heroic Age was the prevalence of court-minstrelsy of a certain type, namely the recitation of metrical speeches accompanied by the harp. The cultivation of such minstrelsy seems to have been more or less general, and it is certain that princes had their praises and exploits celebrated in poems of this kind during their lifetime and even in their presence. But with the close of the Heroic Age the evidence for minstrelsy of this type apparently ceases altogether. In the eighth century we hear only of wandering minstrels who are invited into houses or perform in the streets. The minstrelsy of this period seems not to have been creative. At all events it deals only with characters belonging to former times, Ingeld or Alboin or ancient kings in general. Between these two periods we have to set the composition of the English heroic poems and probably also those German poems which were regarded as ancient in Charlemagne's time. Lastly, we find in Germany a series of poems dating from the twelfth and thirteenth centuries in which the old stories are treated again but in a new form.

It appears then that the history of heroic poetry falls naturally into four stages. To Stage I belong the court-poems of the Heroic Age itself; to Stage II the epic and narrative poems based on these; to Stage III the popular poetry of the eighth and following centuries; to Stage IV the German poems of the twelfth and following centuries, composed at a time when heroic subjects had again come into favour with the higher classes.

To Stage I we may assign not only laudatory poems dealing with the victories and valour of living princes, but also such compositions as Gelimer's dirge and choric songs like the funeral chant over Attila[1]. From this stage probably nothing has come down to us—though it would be difficult to point out any essential difference between Gelimer's dirge and the Elegy of Deor. We can form an idea however of these earliest poems from the poetry of the Viking Age, which seems to have been composed under very similar conditions. As instances we may cite Gunnlaugr's poem on Aethelred II (cf. p. 91 f.) and Eyvindr's poem on the death of Haakon I, which we shall have to discuss later.

Stage II is represented by the Anglo-Saxon poems, which are clearly products of court-life, as we have seen (p. 81 ff.). From its general resemblance to these it seems probable that the Hildebrandslied belongs to the same class. Some writers draw a distinction between Beowulf and Waldhere on the one hand and Finn and the Hildebrandslied on the other, classifying the former as epics and the latter as lays (Lieder). It may be granted that the style of the two latter poems appears to be more rapid and less diffuse than that of the others. Still I should prefer to speak of short and long epics, or rather perhaps of short and long narrative poems. Very probably the earliest narrative poems were comparatively short. It may be that poems on the scale of Beowulf were first composed in England— though this can hardly be proved. But the difference between the two classes seems to me to be one of degree and not of

---

[1] Jordanes, cap. 49; cf. Beow. 3170 ff.

kind. At all events no one will suggest that the Hildebrandslied
is even approximately contemporaneous with the events which
it professes to describe. One would expect it to be at least as
remote from them as is the case with Beowulf.

Stage III is directly represented only by certain ballads such
as the Seyfridslied, which in their present form date from a time
considerably later than the poems belonging to Stage IV. Much
indirect evidence however can be obtained from various sources
of earlier date, e.g. from Thiðreks Saga af Bern, which is largely
based on the popular heroic poetry of northern Germany, and
from parts of Saxo's History which seem to be derived from
Danish ballads. So far as we can judge from our authorities
the popular poems seem to have differed in many ways from
those which we have been discussing. They tended to simplify
complex stories by the loss of minor characters and to amalga-
mate stories which were originally quite unconnected. Again,
they appear to have had a preference for biographical sketches,
whereas the court poems are usually occupied with accounts of
adventures which lasted only a few days. We may add also
the absence of any detailed acquaintance with court-life and a
general approximation to the characteristics of folk-tales, e.g. in
the introduction of nameless characters and persons of humble
station.

It must be remembered of course that our authorities knew
the popular poems only as they existed in the twelfth century[1].
We cannot say with any confidence that Bernlef's poems possessed
the same characteristics. There is nothing to show that the
Hildebrandslied was written down before his time, and it may
be to persons of his type that we owe its preservation. The
Anglo-Saxon poems may not have been committed to writing
till a still later period. All that we can say is that they show
no obvious signs of popular corruption and that their diction
is much more archaic than that of poems which were composed
in the eighth century. We have seen that in Iceland poems of
a rather elaborate type could be preserved by oral tradition for
over three centuries. This however was in a community which

---

[1] Ekkehard's Waltharius of course belongs to a much earlier period, but it is not
always clear what has been added by Ekkehard himself.

was largely given up to the cultivation of poetry. A knowledge of the old poems would be a necessary part of the training of those who hoped to win rewards for their art in foreign courts. Such favourable conditions can hardly have existed either in England or Germany. The process of disintegration which the poems underwent in the latter country points to their being preserved only by village minstrels, who as time went on became less and less expert in their profession.

Stage IV is represented by the Middle High German epic poems, which both in form and spirit show all the characteristics of the age in which they were composed. In England this stage was never reached. There may have been a revival of interest in heroic poetry during the ninth and tenth centuries, but we have no evidence for the composition of new poems on these subjects.

There can be no doubt that the poems of Stage IV are derived from those of Stage III. But the question may be raised whether the latter were necessarily derived from poems of Stages I and II—whether some heroic poems may not have been entirely of popular origin. It may be freely granted that the poetry of Stage II was constantly exposed to popular influence, especially in the form of folk-tales. Most scholars indeed hold that some of the best known heroic stories, such as those of Sigurðr-Siegfried and Weland, are derived from popular mythology. With this problem we shall have to deal later. On the whole however I am inclined to doubt whether we possess a single heroic story which has not been treated in court-poetry at an earlier stage in its career.

Again, the relationship between Stage I and Stage II is not so simple as the bare statement given above might seem to imply. In the first place it is only as a class that poems of Stage I can be regarded as the earlier. Individual poems may very well be later than others which belong to Stage II. Thus it is extremely probable that Gothic princes were listening to laudatory poems about themselves at a time when other Gothic poems, of a definitely narrative type, were coming to be regarded as ancient. Then again, poems of a more or less narrative type may have been composed quite soon after the events which they

treat. Hornklofi's Hrafnsmál and the poem on the battle of
Brunanburh must be regarded as analogous to poems of Stage I,
but it is only a short step from such works to purely narrative
pieces. Indeed, in a sense, we may almost class among narrative
poems Eyvindr's Hákonarmál, which describes the fall of
Haakon I at the battle of Fitje. Yet the author was himself
present at the battle. It is by no means clear then that poems
belonging to Stage II necessarily presuppose the existence of
earlier poems or indeed of materials of any kind beyond the
author's personal knowledge and imagination.

But, more than this, we are scarcely justified in denying the
possibility that even epics may have been composed upon quite
recent events. Few will deny that the poem on the battle of
Maldon has a good claim to that title, whatever its original
length may have been. The extant portion contains nine
speeches, by seven different persons. Twenty-two warriors in
the English army are mentioned by name, and in about a dozen
cases the names of their fathers or other relatives are also given.
The poem differs from the heroic type in the fact that it does
not record the name of a single person among the enemy ; but
that need not prevent us from regarding it as an epic. Yet
there can be no reasonable doubt that it was composed within a
few years, possibly even months, of the battle[1].

It is likely enough that the author of this poem was well
acquainted with heroic poetry and that his treatment of the
subject was affected thereby. But is that any objection to
supposing that poems of this type may have been composed
within the Heroic Age itself ? We have no reason whatever for
denying that this age was capable of such compositions. Indeed
there is one piece of evidence which points very much to the
contrary.

This is a passage which occurs in Procopius' History of the
Gothic War (IV 20). After describing the embassy sent to
Justinian by the Utiguri in the year 551, the author goes on
to state that 'about this time' hostilities broke out between the
nation of the Warni and the Angli ('Αγγίλοι) who inhabit the
island of Britain (Βριττία). Not long before the Warni had

---

[1] Cf. Liebermann, *Arch.* CI, p. 15 ff.; Brandl, *Grundriss*, II p. 106.

been ruled by a king named Hermegisklos who, being anxious to establish his throne on a secure foundation, sought and obtained in marriage a sister of Theodberht, king of the Franks. By a previous wife he had an only son named Radiger, who at this time was betrothed to a sister of the king of the Angli and had paid her a large sum of money in furtherance of his suit[1]. One day, when the king was riding in a certain place with the chief men of his nation, he saw a bird sitting on a tree and croaking loudly. Now, whether it was that he really understood what the bird said, or whether he had some other source of information but pretended that the bird was uttering a prophecy which he understood—at all events he declared on the spot to his companions that he would die forty days later, for this had been clearly foretold to him by the bird[2]. Thereupon he gives advice as to what should be done after his death, namely that Radiger should marry his widow, in accordance with national custom, and dissolve his engagement with the English princess. On the fortieth day the king died, and Radiger proceeds to carry out his injunctions. But the princess, infuriated at his conduct, gathers together a fleet of four hundred vessels and invades the land of the Warni with 100,000 men. Radiger's army is completely defeated, and he takes refuge in a dense forest. The princess insists on his being taken alive at all costs, and eventually he is captured and brought before her. He expects to be put to death, but after explaining the cause of his action, he is pardoned on condition that he returns to his former engagement.

This story contains a number of features, such as the prophecy of the bird, the payment of the 'bride-fee' and Radiger's marriage with his stepmother, which show clearly that it was derived from someone who was well acquainted with the peoples of northern Europe. There is no ground for disputing that it has a historical basis; but at the same time

---

[1] χρήματα μεγάλα τῷ τῆς μνηστείας αὐτῇ δεδωκὼς λόγῳ.

[2] οὗτος ἀνὴρ ξὺν Οὐάρνων τοῖς λογιμωτάτοις ἐν χωρίῳ τῳ ἱππευόμενος ὄρνιν τινὰ ἐπὶ δένδρου τε καθημένην εἶδε καὶ πολλὰ κρώζουσαν. εἴτε δὲ τῆς ὄρνιθος τῆς φωνῆς ξυνεὶς εἴτε ἄλλο μέν τι ἐξεπιστάμενος, ξυνεῖναι δὲ τῆς ὄρνιθος μαντευομένης τερατευσάμενος, τοῖς παροῦσιν εὐθὺς ἔφασκεν ὡς τεθνήξεται τεσσαράκοντα ἡμέραις ὕστερον. τοῦτο γὰρ αὐτῷ τὴν τῆς ὄρνιθος δηλοῦν πρόρρησιν.

it is obviously much more than a mere record of facts. Apart from the incident of the bird and the gross exaggeration apparent in certain details[1], the pictorial character of the narrative, especially in its earlier part, indicates a close affinity with heroic poetry. Un-heroic features are not wanting—the introduction of nameless persons and the political reflections of Irmingisl—but they may with probability be attributed to Procopius himself. I do not mean to suggest that his source of information was an epic poem, but I do think that the intellectual atmosphere which could produce such a story must have been exactly of the kind most favourable to the growth of such compositions.

Procopius, as we have seen, places this war in or about the year 551, and we can certainly understand the course of events more easily if it took place after Theodberht's death (A.D. 548). Therefore, since Procopius' work appears to have been written within the next seven or eight years, the story had had little time to develop before it came to his ears. On the other hand we must remember that it refers to a distant region—a fact I think not without significance for the history of contemporary narrative poetry. To persons who had themselves taken part in the events poems like that on the battle of Brunanburh would appeal much more strongly than purely narrative pieces. It is for persons who were either ignorant of the events or knew them only by hearsay that the latter would seem to be primarily intended.

In this discussion we have taken no account of the heroic poems of the Edda. There can be little doubt that these poems must be assigned to Stage IV of our scheme; for though some of them are probably three or four centuries older than the German poems of this class, they bear fairly obvious marks of the disintegrating process which seems to characterise popular poetry[2]. It may be asked how such an opinion is compatible

---

[1] It is not clear whether the marvellous account of Britain which follows this story comes from the same source or not.

[2] They certainly resemble poems of Stage II both in form and spirit much more closely than their German counterparts do. But this may be due partly to the fact that Stage III was of much shorter duration in their case.

with the view that the story of Sigurðr was derived from the Continent during the seventh century (cf. p. 59). The true explanation is, I believe, that heroic poetry passed through Stage III after it became known in Norway.

We noted in an earlier chapter (pp. 30, 33) that Norway plays no part in stories of the Heroic Age. On the other hand it has what we may call a Heroic Age of its own—namely the Viking Age. We have no poems—and few stories of any kind—dealing with persons of Norwegian nationality who lived before that period. The remoteness, poverty and mountainous nature of the country doubtless retarded its development, not only politically but also in the cultivation of poetry. The strophic character of all Norse poetry is generally held to point to a choric origin, and it may very well be that this primitive type of poetry was the only one used in Norway when the heroic stories first became known there. Possibly it was to Frisian and Danish minstrels that the change was due[1]. But the conditions suitable for a flourishing court-poetry, like that of the Heroic Age, scarcely existed before the last years of the eighth century, when Norwegian princes had begun to enrich themselves with maritime enterprises.

---

[1] A reminiscence of such minstrels may perhaps be preserved in the story of the unfortunate Heimir, who fled to Norway with the child Áslaug concealed in a harp and was murdered there by a peasant from whom he had sought hospitality (*Vols. Saga*, cap. 43).

NOTE IV. ON THE HEROIC POETRY OF THE SLAVONIC PEOPLES.

THE nearest modern analogy, at least in Europe, to the types of poetry which we have been discussing is probably to be found among the various peoples of Serbo-Croatian nationality. As an example we may take the poetry current among the Mohammedan population of Bosnia[1]. Since the occupation of that province a large number of narrative poems have been collected and published, though only a few are as yet accessible in translations. These poems afford an interesting illustration of our subject, not only because they deal with similar themes—heroism in battle, single combats, love and revenge—and often in quite as full detail, but also since the events with which they are concerned and the conditions they reflect belong to a well-marked historical period, which we may regard as a kind of Heroic Age. The period in question embraces the greater part of the sixteenth and seventeenth centuries, more especially the latter, a time when the Turkish Empire was at the height of its power, and when its armies were frequently engaged in hostilities with the Austrians in Hungary and Croatia. Many of the characters mentioned in the poems are well known historical persons.

But beyond all this the value of the illustration lies largely in the fact that we have here what may be called a living heroic poetry, such as we hear of among the Teutonic peoples only through occasional notices in ancient records. As among the latter it is customary for the minstrel (*pivač*, dial. for *pjevač*) to accompany his recitation on a musical instrument, the *tambura*, a kind of guitar with only two metal strings. Among the Christian population the *gusle*, a primitive type of fiddle, is in use.

The poems vary greatly in length. Out of 320 pieces collected by Dr Marjanović thirty contained less than 100 verses, while fifteen exceeded 2000, the longest of all amounting to over 4000. The average length of the pieces described as epic is given at 873 verses; a hundred and three vary from 600 to 1000, and sixty-two from 1000 to 1500. These figures are especially important in view of their bearing on certain prevalent ideas as to the limits of oral poetry. It is to be observed that the ordinary Servian metre is decasyllabic, the verse not being appreciably shorter than the average Teutonic alliterative verse. The minstrel begins his recitation quite slowly, but after about a hundred verses he attains such a speed that not even a shorthand writer can keep pace with him. Such recitations are extremely fatiguing, and in the longer poems it is customary to allow intervals of rest for refreshments, questions and criticism. It will be seen

---

[1] The first part of this note is mainly derived from an interesting paper by Prof. M. Murko in the *Zeitschrift des Vereins für Volkskunde* (Berlin), 1909, p. 13 ff., to which the reader is referred for further information and authorities. The collections of poems published by Marjanović and Hörmann have not been accessible to me.

that if carried out on these principles the recitation of a Teutonic poem of 2000, or even 3000, verses would be nothing impossible in the course of a long evening's entertainment.

In the 'recitation' great freedom is allowed. A minstrel need only hear a poem two or three times (once, if it is sung) in order to reproduce it; but the reproduction is by no means given in the same words. To a certain degree, says Prof. Murko, every minstrel is a more or less creative poet ('Nachdichter'). But even by the same man a poem is never repeated in exactly the same words. In the course of years changes may be introduced which apparently render it almost unrecognisable. Some minstrels are experts in particular lines, special popularity being enjoyed by those who know best how to describe a girl's dress or the trappings of a horse. The faculty for expansion and compression is also very marked. Cases are known of minstrels who have doubled and even trebled the length of poems which they had heard. In one instance two variants of a poem are known, of which one contains 1284 verses, the other barely 300. Such cases, as Prof. Murko remarks, supply interesting evidence for the origin of different recensions of epic poems—particularly, we may add, for the relationship of lays and epics.

From what has been said it will be clear enough that the poems are preserved by oral tradition. Vague rumours of written texts are heard of from time to time and, though none have yet been discovered, it seems probable that some poems have been committed to writing in the past. But the minstrels of the present day are invariably unable to read or write. As to the age and origin of the poems nothing is known for certain, though most of them are believed to be about two centuries old. Four minstrels knew of an authoress—a certain 'pale-cheeked Ajka' from the Lika (in Croatia); but regarding her little or no information seems to have been obtained. The other minstrels could only give the names of those from whom they had themselves heard the poems.

The minstrels belong to various stations of life. Some are men of good family, but the majority are peasant proprietors or workmen. Not many carry on minstrelsy as a regular profession, except when they have fallen on bad times. The recitations are given in coffee-houses or at any holiday gathering. Very often too the minstrels are invited to the residences of the Begs[1]. The case is recorded of one minstrel who recited over a hundred

---

[1] Some interesting remarks relating to the prevalence of minstrelsy—apparently among the Christian population—during the eighteenth century are to be found in Fortis' *Travels into Dalmatia* (London, 1778). "A Morlacco travels along the desert mountains singing, especially in the night time, the actions of ancient *Slavi* kings and barons or some tragic event.......Although the Morlacchi usually sing their ancient songs, yet other poetry is not altogether extinguished among them; and their musicians, after singing an ancient piece, accompanied with the *guzla*, sometimes finish it with some extempore verses, in praise of the personage by whom they are employed" (*ib.*, p. 85).

poems for a certain Beg within six weeks. The Mohammedan ladies are especially fond of such recitations. For his services the minstrel receives payment, sometimes in money, sometimes in corn or livestock, sometimes only in coffee and cigarettes.

It will not escape notice that a good deal of what is said here might be applied with considerable probability to the Frisian minstrel Bernlef or the English minstrels mentioned by Alcuin. Indeed, apart from the coffee and cigarettes, there is scarcely a single feature in the description given above for which we should not expect to find parallels in Teutonic minstrelsy towards the close of the eighth century. We may therefore reasonably look for traces of those characteristics which distinguish Stage III in the history of Teutonic heroic poetry, and in point of fact there seems to be abundant evidence in this direction[1]. The action is usually spread over a considerable time. The characters mentioned by name are few in number and recur again and again in different stories, each district apparently having a favourite hero who is introduced as its representative on many different occasions[2]. Geographical indications are very frequently erroneous, while historical persons figure in quite unhistorical relationships. The unsympathetic characters are often guilty of atrocious brutality. Moreover, we constantly find repetitions of the same words or formulae in consecutive verses after the manner of ballads. Indeed the characteristics of the poems generally—their merits as well as their faults—are to a large extent those of popular rather than court poetry.

But, though the poems show the characteristics which we associate with Stage III, it is questionable whether we are justified in including them in this category; for there is no evidence that they have passed through anything corresponding to Stages I and II. Practically the only court which they know at all is that of Stamboul, and of this their knowledge is naturally slight and remote. The highest personages with whom they are really acquainted are the Begs. It is not unlikely that in the days of Turkish supremacy—the sixteenth and seventeenth centuries—the provincial nobility were much more wealthy and influential than they now are; and it may be that some Begs then had minstrels attached to their own personal following. But their position can never have been comparable with that of even petty Teutonic princes. Hence, if we are entitled to suggest the previous existence of court-poetry at all, it can only be in a very restricted sense—so far at least as the extant poems are concerned.

On the other hand Servian poetry has without doubt had a long history, and even heroic poems are by no means the exclusive property of the Mohammedan population. Indeed some of the Christian poems[3] seem

---

[1] The following observations are based on the poems published in Krauss' *Slavische Volkforschungen*.

[2] Thus in a number of poems the Beg Ljubović appears as the representative of Hercegovina.

[3] Especially several of those dealing with the battle of Kossovo 1389), to which we shall have to refer in a later note.

to exhibit the characteristics of Stage III to a far less degree than the Mohammedan ones; and they frequently deal with much earlier events. It is likely enough that the beginnings of heroic poetry go back to the fourteenth or fifteenth centuries[1], at which time its growth may have been fostered by conditions much more similar to those of the Teutonic Heroic Age. To this question we shall have to refer again. The subject as a whole however is one which must be left to experts. In order to form a sound opinion one would have to take account of the history of narrative poetry among the neighbouring peoples, more especially the Bulgarians and Slovenians[2]. The total change of subjects in the Mohammedan poems would be a necessary consequence of the change of faith; that heroic poetry survived such a change at all is probably to be attributed to the fact that a large proportion of the nobility in Bosnia embraced Islam.

Before we leave the subject however note must be taken of one more important feature in the poems. The Mohammedan Bosnians were religious fanatics, and the spirit of religious war is generally present. It is not absolutely universal; some poems even represent Moslems and Christians in sworn brotherhood. As a rule however the world is regarded as divided into two hostile camps, one under the Sultan (Car), the other under the Emperor (César). In this respect, as in several others, Bosnian poetry shows affinity with the Old French epics, whereas in early Teutonic poetry differences of creed, and even nationality, are scarcely recognised.

In the north of Russia numerous ballads are still current which seem to be based on events much more remote than anything treated in Servian poetry. Many of them deal with stories relating to the time of Vladimir I, who ruled over Kiev about 980–1015, and their antiquity is rendered highly probable by the fact that the same king, together with his chief hero, Ilja of Murom, figures in Thiðreks Saga af Bern. In their present form these ballads show the characteristics of popular poetry to such an extent that they are scarcely distinguishable from folk-tales. Yet it is possible that they are in part descended from poems which might fairly be brought under Stages I and II of our scheme.

At all events there is some reason for suspecting that in early times court-poetry was not unknown in Russia. Evidence to this effect is supplied by the Slovo o polku Igorevě ('Story of Igor's expedition'), which may be

---

[1] There are references to the existence of heroic poetry in the neighbourhood of Spalato and Sebenico as far back as the sixteenth century; cf. Murko, *Arch. f. slav. Philol.*, XXVIII 378. A much earlier reference has been traced in Nicephorus Gregoras' account (*Hist. Byz.*, VIII 14) of his mission to the court of Stephan Uroš in the year 1326, where it is stated of his followers: φωναῖς ἐχρῶντο καὶ μέλεσι τραγικοῖς· ᾖδον δ' ἄρα κλέα ἀνδρῶν ὧν οἷον κλέος ἀκούομεν οὐδέ τοι ἴδμεν. But it is extremely doubtful whether these persons were Servians.

[2] In the middle of the sixteenth century the Slovenians of Tolmino used to sing "di Mattia re d' Ungheria e di altri celebri personaggi di quella nazione" (Murko, *Zeitschr. d. Vereins f. Volksk.*, 1909, p. 14, note). Matthias Hunyadi died in 1490.

described as an epic, though it has no fixed metrical form. The subject is a disastrous expedition undertaken by Igor, the son of Svjatoslav, against the Polovtses on the Don in the year 1185. It is believed to be an absolutely contemporary work, composed within two years of the event. Both in language and spirit it shows rather a striking resemblance to Anglo-Saxon heroic poetry. "Igor leads his soldiers to the Don : the birds in the thicket forebode his misfortune; the wolves bristle up and howl a storm in the mountain clefts; the eagles screech and call the beasts to a feast of bones; the foxes bark for the crimson shields.......The Russians bar the long fields with their crimson shields, seeking honour for themselves and glory for the Prince[1]." There are frequent references also to mythical beings. It is held by many that this work was composed by a bard who belonged to the družina or military following of the prince and that it is the last relic of what may once have been a considerable body of poetry. Certainly we may note that the author repeatedly refers to a certain 'Bojan the Wise, nightingale of ancient time,' a poet who is unknown from other sources, but who apparently lived nearly a century before the composition of the Slovo. This carries us back practically to what we may call the Russian Heroic Age, for Bojan is represented as singing the praises of the sons of Vladimir I. In their time the Russian courts still maintained intimate relations with the Scandinavian kingdoms. Vladimir indeed appears to have had Norwegians in his service, and Olafr Tryggvason is said to have been brought up at his court. It is scarcely impossible therefore that this early poetry may have been due, in part at least, to Scandinavian influence.

NOTE V. THE HEROIC POETRY OF THE CELTIC PEOPLES.

In the history of the various Celtic peoples there is evidence for the existence of more than one Heroic Age. In the first place we have some traces of heroic poetry among the ancient Gauls, though unfortunately it has entirely perished, together with all their vernacular records. Then again Ireland has preserved a great body of heroic literature, referring to a remote period. But, whatever may have been their original form, these stories have come down to us for the most part only in prose. Moreover, the subject is beset with so many difficulties, both historical and linguistic, that it cannot be approached with safety except by an expert. We shall have to confine our attention therefore to the heroic poetry of the Cymry.

Even here the difficulties to be encountered are sufficiently serious. Yet it is fairly clear that many of these poems deal with events which are referred by the chronicles to the sixth century and the first half of the seventh. We may note especially four groups of poems: (1) a few concerned

---

[1] Wiener, *Anthology of Russian Literature*, I p. 84.

with the exploits of Arthur and his heroes ; (2) a somewhat larger number referring to princes named Gwallawg, Urien and Rhydderch ; (3) certain poems dealing with *Gododin* and *Catraeth* ; (4) a few relating to Cadwallon. There are also two or three others, such as the elegy over Cynddylan, which seem to refer to the same period, though they cannot be classed under any of these headings. A number of the above poems, especially those included in the second and third groups, are attributed to two poets named Taliessin and Aneirin.

There is no doubt that Cadwallon is the well known Welsh king who overthrew the Northumbrian king Edwin in 633 and was himself destroyed by Oswald in the following year. But the poems of the second group seem also to have a historical basis. In the Historia Brittonum (Harleian text), § 63, we hear of four kings, *Urbgen et Riderch Hen et Guallanc et Morcant*, who fought against the Northumbrian king Theodric and his successors, Frithuwald and Hussa. Urbgen is said to have besieged his opponents for three days in Lindisfarne (*Metcaud*), and to have perished eventually through the jealousy of Morcant. In another passage (§ 62) we hear of *Neirin et Taliessin* among other poets who composed British poetry in the time of a king named Dutigirn[1], who is made contemporary with Ida, the father of Theodric. The origin of these entries is unfortunately obscure. They are incorporated with an English genealogical document, dating apparently from the end of the eighth century ; but they may quite possibly be derived from earlier sources. In any case they cannot well be later than the first quarter of the ninth century.

All the four kings mentioned in § 63 are known to us also from genealogies of the tenth century. But one of them, Riderch Hen, is named in Adamnan's Life of St Columba, which is of course altogether independent of Welsh tradition. It is there stated (I 15[2]) that Rodercus, king of Dumbarton, consulted St Columba as to his fate and received the answer that he would die a peaceful death in his house—a prophecy which was subsequently fulfilled. As St Columba died probably in 597, the date given for Riderch Hen agrees well enough with what is stated in the Historia Brittonum ; for according to the most trustworthy records Theodric and his two immediate successors reigned from about 572 to 592 or 593. We have no ground for doubting that the references to Urbgen and the rest are based on equally good tradition.

For the characters mentioned in the Gododin poems no such evidence is available. The poems themselves however contain references to the death of *Dyvynwal Vrych*—doubtless the Dalriadic king Domnall Brecc, who according to the Irish annals was killed by the Britons three years after the fall of Oswald, i.e. about the year 645. Unfortunately it is not made clear

---

[1] *Tunc Dutigirn in illo tempore fortiter dimicabat contra gentem Anglorum. tunc Talhaern Tataguen in poemate claruit, et Neirin et Taliessin et Bluchbard et Cian, qui uocatur Gueinth Guaut, simul uno tempore in poemate Britannico claruerunt.*

[2] *De rege Roderco, filio Tothail, qui in Petra Cloithe regnauit.*

in what relationship this event stands to the main action of the poems[1]. The few identifications which can be made from the genealogies seem to be compatible with a date somewhere about this time.

There can scarcely be any doubt that we are justified in regarding the period covered by the poems as a kind of Heroic Age. The story of Arthur was the one most elaborated in later times—a process which must have begun before the ninth century, when it was incorporated in the Historia Brittonum (§ 56). How much historical truth this story contains we do not know, though the chronicles refer Arthur to the early part of the sixth century, i.e. the beginning of our period. To a certain extent however the other stories have experienced the same process; for, apart from the question when the poems under discussion were composed, there are others of undoubtedly later date, such as the Englynion y Beddau, in which the same heroes are mentioned. Moreover it must not be assumed that these were the only persons of the same period whose praises were celebrated in poetry. Maelgwn, king of Gwynedd, who died about 548, figures prominently in traditions of later times, and it is likely enough that the beginnings of these stories were due to a similar cause. On the other hand there is apparently no evidence for the composition of poems dealing with the exploits of princes who lived in the latter part of the seventh century or for several centuries later.

As to the origin of the poems discussed above we have no evidence which can be called conclusive. Some of the poems themselves claim to be the work of the poets Aneirin and Taliessin. At the present time however it seems to be generally held[2] that they are scholastic products of a later age, based upon chronicles and composed with the intention of glorifying the ancestry of some distinguished Welsh families. In support of this view it is contended that the language of the poems cannot possibly represent the form of Welsh spoken in the sixth or seventh centuries. But this argument is scarcely decisive; for it is clear that parts of the poems have undergone a certain amount of modernisation, and it is by no means incredible that the same process may have been in operation for centuries. I find it difficult to believe that in order to celebrate the ancestry of certain families poems would be composed recording an action which is represented as an overwhelming disaster for the British forces, such as that described in the Gododin poems. And can it really be proved that many of the heroes celebrated in these poems were claimed as ancestors by families in Wales?

At all events it is clear that the author of the entries in the Historia Brittonum knew of ancient British poets. *Neirin* and *Taliessin* are only two out of five names recorded by him, the rest apparently being altogether

---

[1] It is possibly worth noting that the Irish annals record a battle between Oswio and the Britons in the same year as Domnall Brecc's death; cf. Skene, *Chronicles of the Picts and Scots*, pp. 70, 348.

[2] This view is favoured by Prof. Anwyl in his *Prolegomena to the Study of Old Welsh Poetry* (Trans. of the Hon. Soc. of Cymmrodorion, 1903–4), p. 7 f.

unknown from other sources[1]. It is true that he places all these persons about a generation before Urien and Rhydderch Hen, but chronological accuracy is hardly to be expected in references to such a remote period. Certainly we should note that the last British king mentioned in these entries is a certain Cadafael (*Catgabail Catguommed*), who is said to have escaped alone from the battle in which Penda was killed (A.D. 655). The wording of this passage (§ 65) seems rather to suggest acquaintance with a poem on the subject.

We have seen now that the persons and events celebrated in the poems belong to a period extending roughly from 500 to 650 and that there are ancient records of famous British poets, who are referred to the earlier part of this period and of whom two are traditionally associated with the poems. Next we must notice that the poems themselves, even in the corrupt and often unintelligible form in which they are preserved, plainly show all the marks of Stage I of our scheme. Their characteristics are those of court-poetry, but they never attain to true narrative. For analogies to the poems which deal with Urien we can hardly do better than turn to the court-poetry of the Viking Age (cf. pp. 15 f., 91); for the Gododin poems perhaps the best parallels are to be found in the Battle of Maldon and the Story of Igor's Expedition, though in both the latter the narrative element is much more fully developed. Taking all the evidence into account, it seems to me that the choice lies between two alternatives : either the poems really are works of Stage I, which have survived from the Heroic Age itself, or they are exceedingly clever imitations of such works, composed at a time when the latter were still in existence. The decision between these two alternatives must of course be left to experts. In the meantime we shall be ready to admit that the poems are extremely corrupt, and that in some cases perhaps we have nothing more than disjecta membra of earlier pieces. But until conclusive evidence is brought forward it seems to me highly improbable that the original poems have been entirely lost[2].

The history of Cumbrian heroic poetry is easily intelligible when taken in connection with the national history. It is probable enough that on the withdrawal of the legions large portions of the country were occupied by northern Britons from beyond the Wall—who are represented in tradition by Cunedda and his sons[3]. These were doubtless affected by Roman

---

[1] It has been suggested that *Bluchbard* (cf. p. 106, note) may be a corruption of the name *Llywarch*. Certainly the form *Neirin* (which is thought to be due to a misunderstanding of *aneirin* as *et neirin*) seems to show that the scribe himself had no knowledge of Aneirin.

[2] The question of the antiquity of the poems must of course be distinguished from that of their authorship. If they are, even in part, the work of Taliessin and Aneirin, we must conclude that these poets are wrongly dated in the Historia Brittonum.

[3] In dealing with such traditions it is essential to remember that our authorities date from times when (apart from Strathclyde) the Cymry had long been confined to Wales and that they represent the point of view of writers living in Wales. If the

influence to a very much less degree than the inhabitants of the province ; and the growth of heroic poetry during the sixth century may be satisfactorily accounted for by the wealth and prosperity which would naturally accrue to their princely families during the early days of their dominion. It was probably not until the time of Aethelfrith that their power was really broken. But the following half century was a most disastrous period, ending in the permanent obliteration of their nationality—in a political sense—throughout the whole region between the Dee and the Clyde. Any records which survived must owe their preservation, ultimately at least, to refugees who escaped into the Welsh highlands.

Now we can see why so many place-names (Reged, Catraeth and dozens of others) are incapable of identification. But further, the conditions in Wales, the poorest and probably the most backward part of the province, were doubtless highly unfavourable to the development of heroic poetry. Under such conditions we should expect that narrative poems would rapidly disintegrate into the semblance of folk-tales ; and it may be that here we have the explanation of the medieval stories of Arthur. At all events they show a certain resemblance to the Russian stories of Vladimir and his heroes. But Arthur, as we have seen, belongs to the beginning of the Heroic Age. We have no evidence for the composition of poems, which can properly be called narrative, dealing with the later heroes. Here the original type of poem seems to have become stereotyped—presumably because conditions favourable to development were no longer present. The only marvel is that so much has been preserved.

kings of Gwynedd were really descended from the 'men of the north' their settlement in that region is probably to be regarded as part of a much larger movement, of which the traces elsewhere were obliterated by the English conquest.

CHAPTER VI.

SUPERNATURAL ELEMENTS IN THE HEROIC STORIES.

MOST of the heroic poems and stories which have come down to us contain elements generally comprehended under the term 'folk-tale' (Märchen), and it will be convenient at once to distinguish tales of this class from popular tales in general. Under the latter term we may include all stories which are frequently repeated without being committed to writing. It is on such foundations probably that all the surviving heroic poems are built. The lapse of time between the events narrated and the composition of the poem may amount to weeks or to generations; in certain cases the story may be wholly fictitious—but this does not affect our definition. When a story is put into metrical form by a skilful poet it becomes more or less crystallised and has a good chance of being preserved. In fact the result is somewhat similar to that of committing it to writing. Stories which are not put into poetic form are more liable to become obscured and forgotten.

The term 'folk-tale[1]' is of less wide application. Probably different scholars would define it in different ways; but in this book it is applied only to stories dealing with anonymous characters. The hero or heroine (villain etc.) is described either (1) as 'the man,' 'the girl,' etc., or (2) by some common name such as Jack or Hans, which conveys no means of identification, or (3) by a name which is obviously made to suit his or her special circumstances or characteristics, such as Aschenbrödel

---

[1] Under this heading we may include metrical compositions. The term 'folk-song' cannot conveniently be used here, as it has acquired a wider signification.

or Sneewitchen. It will be seen that this limitation would not prevent us from regarding stories about the gods as folktales in origin; for most of the gods bear descriptive names, e.g. Thunor, Frig, Balder, Frey. Yet by the time of our earliest authorities these names had come to denote definite personalities; and consequently we must classify such stories in a separate category, namely as myths. On the other hand it must not be assumed that the presence of supernatural features, in some form or other, is a necessary characteristic of folk-tales. Such features do indeed occur very frequently; but that is due merely to the fact that in illiterate societies the marvellous has a special attraction for men's minds.

Into the origin of folk-tales in general we need not enter here. Some apparently spring from attempts to account for natural phenomena, social customs or religious rites. Others are probably founded on adventures, real or fictitious, of individuals whose names have been forgotten. Thus, to take an instance, the story of Alfred and the cakes is not a folk-tale according to our standard; but if the king's name had been forgotten we should have no hesitation in regarding it as such. Again, there can be no doubt that many modern folk-tales are derived ultimately from literary sources. In the same way we must regard it as possible that in earlier times many folk-tales were descended from heroic poems.

Prof. Olrik[1] has pointed out that it is possible very often to distinguish between the Danish and Norse sources followed by Saxo in his History. One of the safest criteria is the presence or absence of characters whose names are not given. In stories of Norse origin, as in Old Norse literature generally, it is customary for every character to have a name—a characteristic which also distinguishes the old heroic poetry. In stories derived from Danish sources on the other hand the characters mentioned by name are few in number. A good instance is to be found in the story of Ingellus (Ingeld), which in consequence of the loss of proper names has been torn right away from its true connections—as may be seen by a comparison with Beowulf. Yet there can be little doubt, as we have seen, that this story is

---

[1] *Kilderne til Sakses Oldhistorie*, p. 18 ff.

ultimately derived from heroic poems. It would appear then that Danish tradition tended to approximate to the folk-tale.

If heroic stories sometimes passed into folk-tales it is still clearer that the latter tended to make their way into heroic stories. We shall see shortly that even the early heroic poems relate a number of incidents which seem to be derived from folk-tales, while in the later forms of the stories such incidents become more and more frequent, most commonly in connection with the childhood or ancestry of the hero. The same phenomenon occurs of course in stories of famous men which have nothing to do with heroic poetry. Thus there is a widely spread folk-tale (told of the god Thor in Old Norse literature), which relates how some animal, a goat, reindeer or calf, is killed and eaten, but care is taken not to break any of its bones. Then on the following day the hero restores the animal to life. In the Historia Brittonum (cap. 32) this story is related of St Germain, the well known bishop of Auxerre.

It is a more difficult question and one which we shall have to discuss later whether any of the heroic stories are wholly derived from folk-tales. The story of Balder bears the stamp of a folk-tale, for the chief characters (Balder, Höðr, Nanna) have names with an obvious meaning. But it is only in Saxo's History that this story appears in a heroic setting; and though his account seems to be more primitive in several respects than that given by the Norse authorities, there is some reason for suspecting that either he himself or one of his (comparatively recent) predecessors was responsible for the setting. It should be observed however that the occurrence of one or more names with obvious meanings does not in itself prove that a story is derived from a folk-tale. Thus in the story of Heðinn and Högni the fact that the heroine (in contrast with the other characters) bears a name which means 'war,' does not of necessity involve her origin in a folk-tale any more than that of her namesake, the abbess of Whitby.

Apart from the distinguishing feature with which we have been dealing folk-tales as a class have certain general characteristics which may be appreciated by a comparison with those of heroic poetry. In the last chapter (p. 82 f.) we gave a short list of the characteristics by which the latter is specially distinguished. To all these the typical folk-tale presents a marked contrast. Some of the leading characters, including either the hero or the heroine or both, are usually persons of humble birth. The opponents of the hero or heroine tend to be represented as monsters of cruelty or vice, even when they are of royal rank, as is often the case. There is no inclination to avoid horrible or coarse subjects. Above all we miss those detailed descriptions of court life upon which the heroic poems are so fond of dwelling. The life and thought which we find reflected in folk-tales is that not of the court but of the village.

It would of course be rash to assume that folk-tales formed the sole intellectual pabulum of the peasantry in early times. No doubt we have to add 'popular tales,' similar to those which formed the foundation of the heroic poems. But since these tales were not put into poetic form—i.e. not into such poetic form as would ensure their preservation[1]—they were always liable to disintegration and thus were constantly approximating to folk-tales. Hence, though we must make allowance for influence of the one upon the other, it is probably not so very far from the truth that what heroic stories were to the courts folk-tales were to the rest of the population.

In Norway court poetry flourished down to Christian times, though in the generation before the conversion it had come mainly into the hands of Icelanders. But practically nothing is known as to the existence of court poets in Denmark; and here we have, I think, the explanation of the peculiar character of the Danish sources used by Saxo. The old heroic poems had been largely forgotten, and what remained was preserved only in the form of ballads and popular tales—which in some cases practically amounted to folk-tales.

Lastly, we must note that the existence of a folk-tale may sometimes be inferred when we have no knowledge of it in its uncontaminated form. Such is the case (e.g.) when we find the same adventure, especially if it be of a supernatural character, related of several different and unconnected persons, whose historical existence may be quite satisfactorily authenti-

---

[1] Ballads on heroic subjects may of course have begun quite early.

cated.   But such inferences must be used with caution, for it is
not necessary to suppose that supernatural incidents in heroic
stories are always due to the influence of folk-tales.   They may
often truly reflect the belief of an age which did not clearly
distinguish between natural and supernatural.   That the supernatural is less prominent in heroic poetry than in folk-tales is
due doubtless to the fact that the courts of that period possessed
a far higher degree of culture than the rest of the population.
The same phenomenon is still more noticeable in Welsh
literature than in Teutonic.   In the early court poems the
supernatural is comparatively little in evidence, whereas in the
Mabinogion, which are largely made up of folk-tales, it is
developed to a most astounding degree.

Various kinds of supernatural beings are brought before
our notice in heroic stories.   In the Northern versions the god
Othin is introduced not unfrequently.   Thus, to give a few
instances, the Völsunga Saga brings him into contact with
Sigmundr on two occasions : first when he enters Völsungr's
hall at the wedding feast and plants in the tree a sword which
Sigmundr alone is able to draw out (cap. 3), and again in his
last battle when the hero's sword is shattered at the touch of
Othin's javelin (cap. 11).   Twice also the same saga makes him
meet with Sigurör : first when he chooses for him the horse
Grani (cap. 13), and later when he accompanies him on his way
to attack the sons of Hundingr (cap. 17 ; cf. also cap. 18).   In
all these cases alike the god's identity is not suspected, at least
until after his departure.   In the poem Reginsmál, from which
the last of these incidents is taken, we find also a story of quite
a different character and laid wholly in the realm of the supernatural, namely the adventures of the gods Othin, Hoenir and
Loki with the otter and the dwarf Andvari.   Of other divine
or semi-divine beings we may mention Hlióð, the daughter of
Hrímnir and adopted daughter of Frigg, who became the wife
of Völsungr and mother of Sigmundr.   As a last instance
reference may be made to a passage from the lost Biarkamál
(Saxo, p. 66), where the hero suspects that Othin is present
among the enemy and expresses his desire to attack him.

In the German heroic poems, which are entirely Christian, we find no mention of the gods. Note should be taken however of an incident in the Rabenschlacht (v. 964 ff.), where Witege in his flight from Dietrich gallops into the sea and is rescued by the mermaid Wâchilt. If we were dealing with a Greek story we should regard this person as a goddess without hesitation.

In much earlier times a very good instance is furnished by the legendary history of the Langobardi. According to the story (cf. p. 9 f.) the Langobardi, who were then called Winniles, soon after their emigration from Scandinavia came into conflict with the Vandals. The Origo Gentis Langobardorum, an anonymous tract dating from the latter part of the seventh century, gives the following account of what happened : Ambri and Assi, the leaders of the Vandals, asked Wodan (*Godan*) that he should give them victory over the Winniles. Wodan replied, saying : "Whomsoever I shall first look upon, when the sun rises, to them will I give victory." Then Gambara with her two sons Ibor and Aio, who were chiefs over the Winniles, asked Fria (*Frea*), the wife of Wodan, that she should be gracious to the Winniles. Fria then gave counsel that the Winniles should come when the sun rose and that their women should let down their hair about their faces after the fashion of a beard and should come with their husbands. Then, as it became light, while the sun was rising, Fria turned the bed, on which Wodan lay, and put his face to the east and wakened him. And he looked and saw the Winniles and their women with their hair let down about their faces and said : "Who are those long-beards?" And Fria said to Wodan : "As thou hast given them a name, give them also victory." And he gave them victory, etc.

Woden is mentioned also in the Anglo-Saxon poem on the magic herbs, and Ing in the Runic poem. In strictly heroic pieces however the only possible case is the reference to the passionate love of Geat in the Elegy of Deor (v. 15)[1]. Indeed, were it not for the Langobardic story we might perhaps suspect that the introduction of the gods in heroic poetry was a Scandi-

---

[1] Elsewhere this name occurs only in the genealogies, where it is borne by an ancestor of Woden. It is possible however that in the Elegy some unknown hero of the Geatas may be meant (cf. Beow. 640, 1785 etc.).

navian innovation.   But as the case stands, although this story
cannot properly be regarded as heroic, it is more likely that
their non-appearance in the English heroic poems is due to
a process of expurgation or elimination.   From such passages as
Beow. 175 ff. we may infer with probability that no definite
reference to the gods would be tolerated after the courts had
become Christian (cf. p. 53 f.).

In the poems which have come down to us the supernatural
element is represented chiefly by what we may call monsters.
This is especially the case in Beowulf, the main part of which is
devoted to encounters with such beings.   We can hardly obtain
a better example than the hero's adventures in the first part of
the poem.   But it will be well at the outset to guard against the
assumption that the story of Beowulf was in any way typical of
early heroic poetry.   Thus we have no satisfactory evidence that
either the story of Waldhere or that of Finn contained supernatural elements of any kind, while even in that of Siegfried
they are comparatively unimportant.

The story of Beowulf's adventures with the monsters seems
to be derived from a folk-tale.   In the Icelandic Grettis Saga,
cap. 64—66, the famous outlaw Grettir, who died in 1031, is
credited with performing almost the same exploits.   The resemblance between the two stories indeed descends in some
cases even to small points of detail.   These, as well as the
points of difference, may best be seen by giving an analysis of
the two side by side.

Beowulf learns that King Hroth-gar's hall has been attacked by night for twelve years and many of his warriors carried off and devoured by the monster Grendel. He comes and offers his services.	Grettir learns that Steinvör has lost her husband and a trusted servant at two successive Christ-mases through mysterious nightly attacks on her house. He comes to her and claims hospitality at the third Christmas.
He is left in charge of the hall at night with his fourteen companions.	He is left alone in charge of the hall at night.
Grendel (a male monster) attacks the hall, devours one warrior and engages in a desperate wrestling struggle with Beowulf.	He is attacked by a huge female monster and a desperate wrestling struggle takes place.

Grendel finds Beowulf too strong and eventually escapes, but with the loss of an arm which Beowulf tears off.

Grendel's mother attacks the hall and carries off a Danish knight. Beowulf goes to the lake where the monsters were believed to dwell, in order to exact punishment.

Beowulf dives into the lake and is seized by Grendel's mother who drags him into her cave, where there is a bright fire. Beowulf's followers and the Danes remain above on the bank.

The monster overthrows Beowulf and attacks him with a dirk (*seax*); but he succeeds in chopping her asunder with a huge sword which he finds in the cave. After slaying her he comes upon the dead Grendel and cuts off his head. He also sees a quantity of treasure.

The lake is stained with the monster's blood. All think that Beowulf has perished, and the Danes return home; but Beowulf's followers remain on the bank.

Grettir is dragged out of the house to a precipice over the river, where he eventually succeeds in chopping off one of the monsters arms. She falls over the edge.

There is no further attack, but Grettir determines to examine the river from curiosity.

Grettir dives off the cliff into the river, just below a waterfall. He climbs up beneath the waterfall and finds a cave there with a fire in it. The priest Steinn waits for him on the cliff.

Grettir on reaching the cave is attacked by a huge male monster armed with a *heptisax*[1]. This snaps at the first thrust; and as the monster reaches back for a sword which is hanging behind him, Grettir slashes him down the front. Afterwards he finds the remains of the two missing men in the cave.

The river is stained with the monster's blood, and Steinn, thinking that Grettir has perished, leaves the cliff.

There can scarcely be any doubt that these two stories are connected in some way. Some scholars indeed hold that the Icelandic story is derived from the other; but the discrepancies seem to me to be too great for this to be probable. Moreover there is another Scandinavian story which has to be taken into account. This is contained in Orms Tháttr Storolfssonar[2], a document which dates from the fourteenth century, and also in later ballads from Sweden and the Faroes. According to the

[1] This word is said to occur only here and in a following verse. From the description the weapon seems to have been a kind of dirk with a long wooden shaft.

[2] Fornmanna Sögur, III p. 204 ff. (especially p. 223 ff.)

story Ormr was an Icelander who lived towards the end of the
tenth century. Like Beowulf and Grettir he had a reputation
for laziness in his youth. In his time an island called Sauðey
off the coast of Norway was inhabited by the monster Brusi
and his mother who had the form of a black cat. One of
Ormr's friends, a Dane named Asbiörn, lost his life in an
attack upon them. Ormr then set out to avenge him. When
he reached the monster's den the cat assailed him fiercely with
her claws, but he ultimately succeeded in destroying her.
Then he had an encounter with Brusi, whose head he tore
open with his hands, afterwards cutting the 'blood-eagle' upon
his back. In the den he found a large amount of gold and
silver. The later forms of the story add several features which
recall the adventures of Beowulf, especially in regard to the
situation of the den and the cannibalistic propensities of the
monsters.

Here again we have in all probability only another form of
the same story. But it is to be observed that there is no special
affinity between the two Scandinavian versions, while the setting
and the names of the characters are entirely different in all three.
Yet if one version was really the source of the others it is difficult
to believe that every trace of its original connections could have
vanished. With far more probability we may conclude that the
story once existed independently, i.e. in the form of a folk-tale,
and as a matter of fact we possess an Icelandic folk-tale which
contains most of the principal features, though the hero has been
split up into five brothers[1]. In its original form the tale was
probably only a specialised variety of the type familiar to us
through Jack the Giant-killer. Stories of this kind seem to
have been particularly popular in Norway—a fact due perhaps
in part to the survival of isolated savage communities among
whom cannibalism may not have been entirely unknown[2]. We
meet with them sometimes in quite unexpected places. Thus
in the account of Thóroddr Snorrason's mission to Jemtland in

---

[1] Cf. Brandl, *Grundriss d. germ. Philol.*[2], II p. 993 f. The following pages
(995 f.) contain an admirable summary of the whole question.

[2] Cf. Hansen, *Landnám i Norge*, p. 160. For stories of monsters which suggest
savages, cf. Ketils S. Haengs, cap. 2 f., and Gríms S. Loðinkinna, cap. 1.

St Olaf's Saga (Heimskr.), cap. 151, we find a graphic and circumstantial story of a female monster who killed and devoured eleven merchants in the inn where the envoy was resting. Thor too, the chief Norwegian deity, came to be regarded essentially as a giant-killer, his origin in the thunder being entirely, or almost entirely, forgotten.

It is no serious objection to our view that Grettir seems to be a perfectly historical character; for no one will contend that the story of his doings at Sandhaugar is true, any more than a number of other exploits with which he is credited. The same remark applies to the story of Thóroddr, whose father, the magistrate Snorri (Grettir's contemporary), was perhaps the best known and most influential man in Iceland. We have seen that in the true folk-tale the hero is nameless; but his adventures are liable to become linked with the names of historical characters—just as in our own day everyone knows of remarkable persons who have had associated with them stories which really were in existence before their time. In Grettir's case exceptionally favourable conditions for such association were provided by the man's great strength, by the unruly disposition which he showed from his childhood and by the many thrilling adventures which he doubtless did experience during his long outlawry. Indeed, though the saga in its present form was not composed until nearly three centuries after his time, we might naturally expect that many untrue stories about such a person would be in circulation even before his death.

Just as the folk-tale became attached to the historical Grettir, so it may have been associated with another person in earlier times. Now the only character in Northern tradition who has been identified with Beowulf is a certain Boðvarr Biarki, a warrior in the service of Hrólfr Kraki. The identification is denied by many scholars, but there are two points in the story of Biarki which seem to me to lend great probability to it. In the first place as Beowulf goes from the land of the Geatas (Gautar), where his uncle is king, to the court of the Danish king Hrothgar, so Biarki goes from the land of the Gautar, where his brother is king, to the court of Hrólfr Kraki, i.e. Hrothwulf, Hrothgar's nephew and colleague. Secondly, at

a later time Biarki, like Beowulf, assists the Swedish prince
Aðils (Eadgils) in his victorious campaign against Áli (Onela),
though he is represented not as king of the Gautar but as Hrólfr
Kraki's emissary.

On the other hand it is true that no resemblance to the story
of Beowulf is shown by the Scandinavian accounts of Biarki's
origin and death. In Hrólfs Saga Kraka[1], which dates only
from the fourteenth century, Biarki is said to have been born
in Norway. His father was called Biörn ('bear') and his mother
Bera ('she-bear'). The former indeed was actually turned into
a bear by witchcraft. Further, from the time of his arrival in
Denmark Biarki remained in the service of Hrólfr till the end
and lost his life in the final attack made upon that king. A
reminiscence of his ursine antecedents appears in the last scene.
When the enemy are attacking the king's hall Biarki cannot be
roused out of slumber, but a huge bear (the warrior's spirit) is
seen fighting among the king's knights.

Saxo says nothing about Biarki's origin and it may be that
the story given in the saga was unknown in his time. At all
events it is doubtless derived from a folk-tale. In the twelfth
century Vita et Passio Waldevi[2] almost the same story is told
of the father of Siward, the famous earl of Northumbria, who
died in 1055, while a further parallel is to be found in the
De Gestis Herwardi Saxonis[3], another work of the same period.
Both stories contain indications of Scandinavian origin and we
can hardly doubt that the motif was a popular one in the folk-
tales of the North. Indeed for the version of the story found
in Hrólfs Saga, transformation into animal form through the

---

[1] A somewhat similar account of Biarki's origin is given in the (fifteenth century)
Biarkarímur.

[2] *Tradunt relaciones antiquorum quod uir quidam nobilis, quem Dominus permisit,
contra solitum ordinem humane propaginis, ex quodam albo urso patre, muliere generosa
matre, procreari, Ursus genuit Spratlingum; Spratlingus Ulsium; Ulsius Beorn,
cognomento Beresune, hoc est filius ursi. Hic Beorn Dacus fuit natione, comes
egregius et miles illustris. In signum autem illius diversitatis speciei ex parte generan-
tium produxerat ei natura paternas auriculas, sive ursi etc.* Michel, *Chroniques
Anglo-normandes*, p. 104.

[3] *Illum maximum ursum......cuius pater in silvis fertur puellam rapuisse et ex ea
Biernum regem Norweye genuisse.* ib. p. 7 f. A similar story is told by Saxo (p. 345 f.)
of the ancestry of Svend Estrithson.

agency of a wicked stepmother, analogies are to be found in many parts of the world.

In his account of the last fight Saxo quotes at great length from the lost Biarkamál; but here again no reference is made to the bear motif[1]. We may note however that in this version no explanation is given of Biarki's behaviour in refusing to rise from his bed in response to the exhortations of his colleague[2]. It is scarcely safe therefore, I think, to assume that Saxo's account—apart from the quotations which consist entirely of speeches—necessarily represents an earlier form of the story than that given in the saga; for in the latter Biarki's conduct is quite satisfactorily explained. There is surely at least as much to be said for supposing that the incident of the bear— or something which gave rise to it—has been ignored or forgotten by Saxo.

Now Beowulf is represented as an enormously strong man, but his strength is not altogether of a natural order. We are told that he was fated not to gain victory with the sword. It is not only the struggle with Grendel which he wins by wrestling; in v. 2506 f. we hear that he hugged or crushed to death the Frisian champion Daeghrefn—a method of warfare appropriate to a bear rather than to a man. The explanation is perhaps to be found in the curious phenomenon called *berserksgangr*[3], which is so frequently mentioned in sagas and even in legal works. It is to be remembered that in popular belief this form of madness was connected with the werwolf idea, of which the bear form was a common variety. The transition therefore to the story found in Hrólfs Saga is nothing very strange.

In conclusion mention must be made of an incident which

---

[1] Yet Hialti's third speech (p. 61) contains the words *igne ursos arcere licet*, the significance of which is obscure. It is curious, as Prof. Olrik (*Danmarks Heltedigtning*, p. 51) has pointed out, that Hrólfs Saga (cap. 33) refers to bears in a corresponding place, though the context is quite different.

[2] Prof. Olrik (*op. cit.*, p. 45) says that Biarki's sleep is certainly of a supernatural character and suggests that it is due to magical arts on the part of the enemy.

[3] Cf. especially Yngl. S. 6 : Othin's men went to battle without mail-coats and were frenzied like dogs or wolves. They bit into their shields and were as strong as bears or bulls. They made slaughter of other men ; but neither fire nor iron took effect upon them. This is called *berserksgangr*.

has been brought into connection with the fight between Beowulf and Grendel. In Hrólfs Saga, cap. 23, it is stated that shortly after his arrival at the Danish court Biarki encountered and slew an animal demon which at two successive Yules had ravaged the live-stock in the king's farm. Saxo alludes clearly to the same story when he states that Biarki won great fame by killing a huge bear[1]. Now it should be observed that the representation of Grendel is by no means clearly anthropomorphic, though the human element is much more apparent in the cave scene. The various accounts may, I think, be satisfactorily reconciled on the hypothesis that in the original story the hero killed a monster or demon (*iötunn*) in the form of a bear (*biarnar hamr*). In England this story must have been expanded and modified by the influence of the folk-tale of the two cannibal monsters which we have discussed above. In Scandinavian tradition however no such intrusion took place, though a totally different folk-tale became attached to the early history of the same hero.

Two adventures with dragons are recorded in Beowulf. The first, that of Sigemund, is related quite briefly (vv. 884—900), but the second forms the subject of the latter part of the poem. The Older Edda (Fáfnismál), followed by the prose Edda and Völsunga Saga, gives an account of the killing of Fáfnir by Sigurðr; and in the late Seyfridslied two adventures of the same kind are narrated in connection with the same hero. Dragons figure also occasionally in the German epics, especially in the story of Wolfdietrich. Here too we must mention Saxo's accounts of the dragons slain by the Danish kings Frotho I and Fridleuus II. The two stories are almost identical, but the former (p. 38) contains a description of the dragon and of the means to be used in attacking him, which is given in Latin verse and may very well be derived from an old poem.

There are certain resemblances between Saxo's stories and the great dragon fight in Beowulf, and many scholars are

[1] The identity of the two stories is shown by the fact that in both cases Hialti is made to drink the creature's blood—a custom known in Norway in comparatively recent times (cf. Olrik, *op. cit.*, p. 118). The Biarkarímur tell of two encounters, the first with a she-wolf, the second between Hialti and a bear.

inclined to the view that they have a common origin. The former however in both cases ended successfully. Moreover in two points at least they agree rather with the adventure ascribed to Sigemund in Beowulf, namely (i) that the hero attacks and kills the dragon alone and (ii) that he carries away the treasure in a boat. On the other hand it is generally agreed that the stories of Sigemund and Sigurðr must be connected, though opinion is divided as to whether the adventure was first ascribed to the father or the son. Beowulf is at all events by far the earliest of the authorities. Against this stands the fact that both Scandinavian and German tradition names Sigurðr (Siegfried) as the hero. But this argument could have weight only if there was reason for thinking that the story was known in the North before the composition of Beowulf.

Fáfnir is called *dreki* in Völsunga Saga, but he seems always to be represented rather as a reptile than a dragon. It is not at all clear that he is a being of the same kind as the dragon encountered by Beowulf, which is said to fly and breathe fire. This is perhaps to be noticed, since the flying dragon is also known in the North ; we find it mentioned even in old poems such as Völuspá. The description of Sigemund's dragon is too brief to enable us to determine its character. It is once called *draca* and thrice *wyrm* ; but the latter word is used also of the flying dragon. On the other hand it is not certain that the word *draca* always denotes a supernatural being. The *saedracan* and *niceras* mentioned in Beowulf 1425 ff. would seem from the description to be animals of the seal-class.

One feature however is common to all the English and Northern dragons, namely that they are represented as guarding hoards of gold. In the North this idea must have been very widespread, since expressions such as 'bed of the dragon' (or 'snake') are among the commonest terms for gold in Old Norse poetry. In Anglo-Saxon poetry also it is generally recognised[1].

It has been mentioned above that many scholars connect the story of Beowulf's dragon-fight with that related of Frotho I by Saxo. To me the affinities of the latter seem rather to lie with

---

[1] Cf. the Cott. Gnomic Verses, 26 f.: *draca sceal on hlaewe frod fraetwum wlanc.*

Sigemund's dragon; but the truth may be that for adventures of this kind there was a standard poetic description which could be applied to any number of cases. More important perhaps is the fact that genealogically Saxo's Frotho I corresponds to Beowulf the son of Scyld[1]. In common with practically all Scandinavian genealogical texts Saxo has the series Frotho[2] —Haldanus—Ro (Hróarr) and Helgo corresponding to the Beowulf—Healfdene—Hrothgar and Halga of the poem[3]. Quite possibly therefore it is not without significance that this person is credited with having killed a dragon.

We have seen that the two stories differ essentially in regard to the outcome of the adventure. Frotho's death is recorded by Saxo in quite a different connection and apparently long afterwards. But here we may turn to the story of the other Frotho, Saxo's Frotho III (the Peaceful), for there can be little doubt that the two characters were originally identical. According to Saxo this latter king was killed in his old age by a sorceress who had taken the form of a 'sea-cow' (*marituma bos*), though the author does not make clear what kind of creature he means by that term. It is at least a question whether this story does not belong to the same class as the others; for whatever differences there may be in other respects between a 'sea-cow' and a dragon, it may be observed that nearly all the dragons of Northern legends make their home by the sea.

If there is a connection between the two stories—the dragon-fight of Frotho I and the death of Frotho III—their origin must surely be sought in myth. Fróði the Peaceful (Frotho III) is

---

[1] It is generally held that this person's original name was Beowa or Beaw. The latter is the form given in the genealogy in the Chronicle (*ad ann.* 855); but in view of the many corruptions which this genealogy has suffered it may very well be due to a scribal error for *Beowa*. This again may be a hypocoristic form for *Beowulf*, though on the other hand it is by no means impossible that the name of the son of Scyld has been assimilated to that of the hero of the poem. But in any case there does not seem to be any adequate ground for the commonly accepted view that the adventure with Gre del originally belonged to this person.

[2] In Skiöldunga Saga, Langfeðgatal etc. Halfdan's father is not Friðfróði (Saxo's Frotho I) but Fróði hinn froekni (Saxo's Frotho IV), the Froda of Beowulf.

[3] As regards Frotho's parentage—Saxo makes him son of Hadingus, son of Gram, son of Scioldus. In Skiöldunga Saga, Langfeðgatal etc. Friðfróði is son of Friðleifr, son of Skiöldr; while Fróði hinn froekni is son of Friðleifr, son of Danr.

the central figure of Danish legend and his fame became proverbial even in Germany. Moreover, though there is no evidence that he was regarded as a god, it is clear that he was the Danish counterpart of the god Frey.

It may not be out of place here to cite one more of Saxo's stories (p. 29 f.). Hadingus, the father of Frotho I, while bathing in the sea off the coast of Helsingland encountered and killed a sea-monster of unknown species. As he was having it carried to his camp he met a woman who uttered a prophecy of dire woe, saying that he had killed one of the deities who was wandering about in a form not his own[1]. In order to propitiate the gods he instituted a sacrifice to Frey, which was to be repeated at regular intervals and which the Swedes call Fröblod. This story seems to take us back to the days of theriomorphic religion—or perhaps one should say to a time when certain marine animals were regarded as divine. But is it not also connected somehow with the story of Frotho's death?

We need not enter here into a discussion of these mythical stories, though it may be remarked in passing that theriomorphism plays a very prominent part in the religious practices and conceptions of primitive peoples, and, what is more, that we hear not unfrequently of a struggle between a god or national hero and some theriomorphic being whose sanctuary or attributes he appears to have taken over[2]. But it is perhaps worth noting that in Beowulf also the hero is repeatedly involved in adventures with water-monsters. This feature is entirely absent from the story of Biarki and can hardly have a historical

---

[1]

Tantum pene uis celica pensat.
quippe unum e superis alieno corpore tectum
sacrilege necuere manus : sic numinis almi
interfector ades.

[2] We may compare the case of Apollo and the Python at Delphi, and possibly the story of Thor (Miðgarðs véurr) and Miðgarðsormr. Note should also be taken of the existence of a local tradition—going back apparently to the Middle Ages—to the effect that the Isefjord was formerly haunted by a monster which demanded a human victim from every ship that passed. It was finally expelled by the arrival of the relics of St Lucius, to whom Roeskilde cathedral is dedicated (cf. Sarrazin, *Beowulf-Studien*, p. 10 fi.). The traditional burial-place of Fróði the Peaceful is on the shore of the Roeskilde Fjord ; but the two fjords have a common entrance.

basis. What I would suggest is that it is derived, in part at least, from the same group of legends which in Danish tradition are centred round the names Hadingus and Frotho. But in that case there is considerable probability that these stories have been transferred to the hero from his namesake, the son of Scyld, who belongs genealogically to the same group of persons.

This explanation will at all events account for the discrepancy between the English and Scandinavian accounts of the hero's death[1]. Only the latter properly comes into consideration for Beowulf the son of Ecgtheow. For the suggested transference we have a certain analogy in the various incidents which are connected sometimes with one Frotho, sometimes with the other. A much better case however occurs in an English work of later date, the Vitae Duorum Offarum. In that work Drida, the wife of Offa II (the Mercian king), is represented as a most desperate character, and incidents are related of her which seem to be totally incompatible with what we know of this queen—whose real name was Cynethryth—from contemporary sources. On the other hand they agree very well with the brief account given in Beowulf of Thrytho the wife of Offa I (king of Angel). We may compare too the hopeless confusion which prevails in the chronicles with regard to Anlaf the son of Sihtric (Olafr Kvaran) and Anlaf the son of Guthfrith. It can scarcely be doubted that heroic poetry was liable to mistakes of the same character, although the question has scarcely received as much attention as it deserves.

In the explanation put forward above I do not mean of course to suggest that the dragon of northern heroic poetry is always a distorted form of some marine animal. My view is that this is one of the elements which have contributed to the

---

[1] It does not of course remove all difficulties. The chief of these perhaps is the presence of Wiglaf, who seems clearly to belong to Beowulf, the son of Ecgtheow. The discrepancy between the names Beowulf and Fróði is of minor account, since the latter may very well have originated in a title (cf. Beow. v. 2928). On the other hand if this person is really a mythical national hero the name *Beowa* (perhaps for an earlier form *Biowi*) would seem more natural than *Beowulf*. Yet there may have been intermediate stages between the original hero and the person finally credited with the exploit.

formation of the stories—playing a part similar to that of the
crocodile in the legends of southern lands[1]. Dragons endowed
with supernatural or at least unnatural characteristics figure in
the folk-tales of many nations throughout the world ; and such
stories are by no means restricted to maritime populations.
Very frequently no doubt they are handed on from one people
to another, and their currency is perhaps assisted by works of
art.　We have to remember that the word *draca* is derived
from Latin.　Yet the conception itself is probably much older ;
at all events the association of such monsters with hoards of
gold can be traced back in northern regions to a very remote
antiquity[2].

As regards the origin of this association—which is clearly
unnatural and not due in any way to the influence of marine
animals—it may be noted that the dragon's lair is often a tomb
or barrow[3], as in the case of the one encountered by Beowulf.
An explanation of this phenomenon seems to be afforded by
a story relating to the tomb of Charles Martel, which is found
in a number of medieval chronicles.　St Eucherius, bishop of
Orleans, in a vision saw Charles in hell, and on coming to
himself begged St Boniface and others to go and inspect the
prince's burial place.　On opening the tomb they saw a dragon
dart out suddenly and found the grave all blackened as though
it had been burnt up.　Here it would seem that the dragon—a
fiery dragon, like the one in Beowulf—was nothing else than the
spirit of the dead prince, and it is permissible to suspect that
such was the case elsewhere.　At all events the fact that dragons
are represented as inhabiting tombs is clearly to be taken in
connection with their character as guardians of gold ; for in early
times it was customary to bury with the dead a considerable
amount of treasure.

But there is another feature which deserves notice in the

---

[1] Thus upon some of these legends a good deal of light seems to be thrown by
certain usages cited by Mr Frazer in his *Lectures on the Early History of the Kingship*,
p. 180.

[2] Herodotus (III 116, IV 13, 27) speaks of a region in the extreme north of Europe
or Asia which was said to be inhabited by gold-guarding griffins ($\chi\rho\upsilon\sigma\text{o}\phi\acute{\upsilon}\lambda\alpha\kappa\epsilon\varsigma$ $\gamma\rho\acute{\upsilon}\pi\epsilon\varsigma$,
cf. *goldweard*, Beow. 3082).

[3] Cf. the reference to the Gnomic verses quoted on p. 123, note.

story of Charles Martel's grave.   The earliest document[1] in
which it is found dates from the year 858, i.e. about a century
after the incident is said to have taken place.   But the closing
words of the account[2] state quite definitely that the writer or
writers had known persons who were present at the opening of
the tomb.   We have thus to deal with evidence which is strictly
second-hand, as in the case of more than one remarkable story
told by Bede.   The explanation lies no doubt in the fact that
the men of that age did not clearly distinguish between the
supernatural and that which is merely unusual.   At such a time
if a person asserted that he had seen a fiery dragon, his statement would be received doubtless with wonder but not necessarily with incredulity.   As a matter of fact we find it stated in
the Saxon Chronicle[3], *sub anno* 793, that in that year fiery
dragons were seen flying in the air.   It cannot therefore be
assumed with safety either that the killer of a dragon must be a
fictitious person or that the adventure itself must have been
invented long after the hero's time.

In conclusion we have to take account of supernatural
properties possessed by beings which in themselves are natural.
As an instance we may take the speeches of the birds (nut-
hatches) which in Fáfnismál 32 ff. warn Sigurðr of the treachery
prepared for him by Reginn.   Similar stories occur elsewhere in
Old Norse literature.   Absurd as this belief may seem we have
good contemporary evidence for its existence in Procopius'
account of the Warni, which we discussed in the last chapter
(p. 97 f.).

Under the same head may be mentioned the faculty ascribed
to various persons of being able to change into wolves or bears.
As instances we may mention the case of Sigmundr and
Sinfiötli given in Völsunga Saga, cap. 8, and the story of Biarki

[1] Epistola Synodi Carisiacensis ad Hludowicum regem Germaniae directa (Mon.
Germ., Legum Sect. II, Capit. Reg. Franc., Tom. II, p. 432 f.).

[2] *nos autem illos uidimus qui usque ad nostram aetatem durauerunt, qui huic rei
interfuerunt et nobis uiua uoce ueraciter sunt testati quae audierunt atque uiderunt.*

[3] Texts D, E, F.   This entry seems to come from the Northumbrian *Gesta*, which
were probably composed not very long afterwards.   The last entry which we can trace
is for the year 806.

discussed above. For the latter we have already suggested an explanation. But though the motif may not have been a common one in heroic poetry—as compared with sagas relating to the Viking Age—there can be no doubt that the belief in shape-changing goes back to a remote antiquity. It is of frequent occurrence in poems and stories dealing with the gods, while similar ideas are widely prevalent among primitive peoples at the present day.

Among other supernatural characteristics may be mentioned that of invulnerability, through the use of magic which rendered all weapons harmless—a feature found in Beowulf (in the case of Grendel) as well as in later works. Often too heroes are capable of superhuman powers of strength or endurance, as in Beow. 377 ff., 544 ff.[1], though many of these cases may be set down to mere exaggeration. On the whole however such characteristics are scarcely as prominent as they are in the heroic stories of other nations.

The love of the marvellous is more strikingly displayed in Procopius' account of Britain (*Goth.* IV 20) than in any of the poems which have come down to us. In the first place he says that the whole country beyond the great wall (i.e. the Roman Wall) was inhabited only by snakes and wild beasts, and that if any man ventured there he would die at once from the pestilential atmosphere. Then he goes on to say that Britain was the dwelling place of the spirits of the dead, and describes in detail how certain people who dwelt on the Frankish coast ferried the souls across. As to the truth of this story Procopius himself expresses scepticism; yet he states that he had heard it from numerous witnesses. It is scarcely permissible therefore to suppose that he had been victimised by a humorist. More probably he is reporting stories actually current among the Teutonic soldiery in the Roman army, which doubtless contained adventurers from many distant lands. In short we have here to

---

[1] A curious light on the enormous strength ascribed to Beowulf is thrown by a passage in the Liber Monstrorum (cf. p. 24). It is there stated that Hygelac (Beowulf's uncle) was of such immense size that no horse could carry him after he reached the age of twelve. His bones were shown as a marvel to visitors.

do with folk-tales[1] which had been localised in Britain and were
believed to represent its condition truly at the very time when
Procopius was writing. It is exceedingly remarkable that such
stories should obtain credence at a time when, as we know from
more than one source, there was quite a considerable amount of
communication between Britain and the Continent. Indeed
Procopius himself says that large numbers of English emigrants
had recently settled within the Frankish dominions.

In the course of this chapter we have seen that many of the
heroic stories contain elements derived from myth and folk-tale.
The distinction which we have drawn between the two categories
is that only the former deals with definite—though unhistorical—
personalities[2]. It is commonly held that myth is a necessary
element in heroic stories; but this is a question which we must
reserve for discussion in the next chapter. Further, we have seen
that the presence of supernatural elements does not necessarily
mean that the stories in which they occur were composed or
modified long after the events which they relate; that, on the
contrary, such elements are to be found in contemporary or
almost contemporary narratives. They must be taken as faithful
reflections of the beliefs and ideas of an uncritical age. But it
is scarcely correct to regard these elements as the distinctive
characteristics of heroic poetry. Their chief domain in reality
is the folk-tale, a far more primitive form of composition, which
without doubt was in existence during the same period. The
truly distinctive characteristics of heroic poetry are rather those
which differentiate it from the folk-tale.

---

[1] The folk-tale represented by the second story may of course be derived ultimately from some ancient custom; cf. Beow. 26—52.

[2] Not, of course, personalities consciously invented by an individual brain; these
must be classed under fiction. On the other hand myth must be held to include personifications of the heavenly bodies and natural phenomena—as (e.g.) in Gylfaginning,
cap. 10 ff. (from Vafþrúðnismál, etc.), and certain Lithuanian folk-songs ('Dainos')—
in so far at least as such personifications are of popular origin.

CHAPTER VII.

MYTHICAL ELEMENTS IN THE HEROIC POEMS.

WE have now to consider the question whether myth is a necessary element in the formation of heroic poetry. It has been noticed that historical persons figure in many stories of the Heroic Age, while others do not contain a single character whose historical existence can be authenticated. These latter stories are believed to be wholly mythical in origin, though they may not show any supernatural features in their final form. But even in stories of the former type it is held that some of the characters are almost always of mythical origin, and that their association with historical characters is a secondary development —due to confusion or to poetic imagination.

In the last chapter we put forward the view that Beowulf, the hero of the poem, has been confused with a mythical character of the same name, and that the adventure with the dragon originally belonged to the latter. It can scarcely be doubted that Scyld Scefing, the father of this earlier Beowulf, was also a mythical character. The only element in his story common to English and Scandinavian tradition is that he is regarded as the ancestor of the Scyldungas or Skiöldungar, the Danish royal family, and all analogies suggest that he came into existence as their eponymus. The brief account of him given in the poem might, except in two particulars, be applied to almost any successful king of the Heroic Age. One exception relates to the story of the funeral ship, on which the dead king's body is sent out to sea. In spite of Prof. Olrik's doubts[1]

---

[1] *Danmarks Heltedigtning*, p. 248 ff. With this subject I have already dealt in *The Origin of the English Nation*, p. 287 f.

I cannot but think that this is a reminiscence of ancient custom. The other is the reference to his arrival as an infant, likewise by sea—a story told more fully of Sceaf in certain English chronicles. The only question here is between myth and folktale. The story may fairly be classed under the latter head, though I think its origin is ultimately to be sought in a ritual myth. Scandinavian authorities, apart from Saxo[1], record nothing distinctive of Skiöldr, except that he was a son of Othin and the husband of the goddess Gefion[2]—which again points to myth.

In Scyld-Skiöldr we have the case of an eponymous ancestor appearing in the introduction to a poem which deals largely with the fortunes of his descendants. But there is no evidence that his own deeds ever formed the subject of an independent heroic poem. It would be somewhat hasty therefore to use this case as an argument for the origin of characters who are brought before us in the main action of heroic poems.

Next we may take the story of Weland, as to the mythical origin of which nearly all scholars seem to be agreed. It has indeed a historical or semi-historical connection in the fact that Weland is represented as the father of Widia (Wudga), i.e. the early Gothic hero Vidigoia mentioned by Jordanes (cf. p. 27); but this is held to be a secondary element in the story. In its original form the story is believed to have dealt only with the incidents related in Völundarkviða, viz. (i) the adventure with the swan-maidens, (ii) Weland's imprisonment by Nithhad and his revenge[3]. Behind the story itself however there lies a widespread belief in the existence of a supernatural smith of this name. Several places in Germany (Westphalia and Holstein) are reputed to be the scene of his operations, while in this

---

[1] Saxo (p. 11 f.) records several incidents of which we know nothing from other sources. He represents Skiöldr (*Scioldus*) as a reformer of the laws, but not as the first king.

[2] This is stated only in Ynglinga Saga (cap. 5); but the question to be asked is whether it is likely that such a combination would be invented in late times.

[3] From Deor's Elegy and the picture on the Franks casket in the British Museum it is clear that almost all the main features of the second part of the story were known in England. Reminiscences of the first part occur in the medieval German poem *Herzog Friedrich von Schwaben*.

country he is connected with the cromlech called Wayland Smith, near Ashdown in Berkshire. In its ultimate origin this belief is traced to the myth of a fire-demon. Certainly it is to be noted that the name *Weland* is of a very exceptional type— apparently participial in form. One can hardly help suspecting that it once had a definite meaning, though this cannot now be determined with certainty[1].

Now there can be little doubt that the adventure with the swan-maidens is derived from a folk-tale. In this part of the story there is no indication of a fire-demon, or even of a smith, while analogies for the incident are fairly common both in Teutonic lands and much farther afield. We may confine our attention therefore to the second and better known part—that which deals with Weland's imprisonment and revenge.

It is manifest that this story departs very decidedly from the ordinary standard of heroic poetry—firstly in the fact that the hero is here clearly represented as a smith, and secondly in the cruelty, treachery and vindictiveness ascribed to the chief characters. These are features which would be in place either in myth or folk-tale. But we may note further that there are analogies for part of this story, just as much as for the incident of the swan-maidens. As an example we may take Saxo's account of the robbing of Mimingus by Hotherus (p. 70 f.). Mimingus is a *satyrus*, i.e. clearly either an elf or dwarf, who dwells in a cave in an almost inaccessible forest. Hotherus surprises and binds him and then takes away his sword and a magical ring. A connection between the two stories is shown even in the name, for Weland's most famous sword is called Mimming[2]. For a more remote parallel we may compare the story of Loki and Andvari. Indeed the spoiling of a dwarf is quite a common motif in Northern tales, while at the same time such beings are constantly credited with extraordinary skill in metallurgy. The distinctive feature in the story of Weland, apart from the revenge, is that sympathy is on the side of the smith.

It is the end of the story—where Weland (Völundr) rises into the air and flies away—that is supposed to point most

---

[1] It is usually connected with O. Norse *vél*, 'contrivance,' 'artifice.'

[2] Waldhere, I 2 f.; Thiðreks Saga, cap. 23 etc.

clearly to a fire-myth. But this feature cannot be traced except in the Norse version[1]. Moreover here we have also the adventure with the flying swan-maidens, in whose case there is no suspicion of such a myth. Setting aside this incident the story is perfectly explicable as a folk-tale founded on actual experience. There can be no doubt that in the Heroic Age—and indeed in much earlier times—princes were especially anxious to obtain slaves, whether foreigners or not, who were skilled in metallurgy. And it is by no means incredible that such slaves were sometimes lamed in order to prevent any attempt at escape —although, quite apart from this explanation, smith's work may be regarded as a vocation natural to the lame man, just as minstrelsy to the blind. Further, it is likely enough that servile smiths, when cruelly treated, would take any opportunity that presented itself of avenging themselves on their masters. For the murder of Nithhad's sons we have a somewhat striking historical parallel in Eugippus' Life of St Severinus (cap. 8). Feletheus, king of the Rugii, who were settled on the Danube in the time of Odoacer, had a young son who one day was entrapped by some goldsmiths in the queen's service. They threatened to take his life; but the saint intervened and rescued the boy on condition of the smiths obtaining their freedom[2].

What seems to me to be really the most remarkable feature in the story is that a person in this position should come to be made the subject of heroic or semi-heroic poetry; for it is plain enough from many sources, especially Saxo's History, that smiths were generally regarded with deep aversion. In Deor's Elegy Weland is said to be a more distinguished man than Nithhad; in Völundarkviða he is called a chief of the elves, while the introduction makes him the son of a king of the Finns. Yet, except in the late Thiðreks Saga, his father's name is never given, and none of our authorities credit him with possessing a following of his own.

---

[1] In Thiðreks Saga, cap. 30, Weland flies away in a garment which he has made from feathers collected for him by his brother Egill. It is thought by some that the engraver of the Franks casket had the same story in mind, since a figure catching birds is represented behind the form of Beaduhild.

[2] It is commonly held that this account has been influenced somehow by the story of Weland. If so it is a valuable illustration of the process discussed in p. 119 ff. above. But the view seems to me somewhat far-fetched.

Now is there any real necessity for the assumption that Weland's relationship to Widia is a secondary development? It is found in two of the three national versions of the story[1], and hence dates back in all probability at least to the sixth century. It is not found in the Völundarkviða; but then Widia is altogether forgotten or unknown in Northern tradition. Moreover there is a distinct reference to offspring of Weland and Beaduhild at the end of the poem. Once grant that the relationship is old and the reason for the heroic treatment of the story becomes obvious. It is merely the reflection of the son's fame upon the father. As Widia is never said to be the son of anyone else the probability is that he was supposed to be illegitimate, and that a story was soon current as to his being the offspring of a union between a princess and a bondsmith. In such a case there would be a natural tendency to the accumulation of material from folk-tales about his parentage.

If this view is correct the story must of course come originally from the Goths or some neighbouring people. I cannot see that the Westphalian traditions are any more conclusive than the Berkshire cromlech as to its original home. If Weland was a character of folk-tale and his name had at one time a definite meaning, these local traditions may have been quite independent of the heroic story. The real difficulty seems to me to lie in determining the amount of material from folk-tale contained in the latter. We need not entertain any doubt as to the adventure with the swan-maidens. But what about Nithhad and Beaduhild? The latter name is not obviously framed to suit the character or circumstances of the unfortunate princess. *Nithhad* might be explained more easily in this way; yet a Gothic prince of that name is recorded by Jordanes (cap. 22). At all events there is no conclusive evidence in either case that these characters did not originally belong to the story of Widia.

Another story which is believed to be of wholly mythical origin is that of Heðinn and Högni. In Kûdrûn it appears as

---

[1] Waldhere is the only English poem which mentions Weland as the father of Widia; but I cannot admit that there is any ground for supposing this poem to have had a different origin from the rest (cf. p. 57 f.). The variant forms *Widia—Wudga* may be explained by English sound-laws, while *Niðhad*, whatever its explanation, occurs also in Deor's Elegy.

the introduction to a much longer story, from which point of view it bears a superficial resemblance to the story of Scyld and possibly to that of Weland.   But since this feature is peculiar to the German poem and the second story seems to be entirely unknown from other sources, we can hardly do otherwise than treat the story of Heðinn and Högni as an independent narrative.

This must have been one of the most popular stories of the Heroic Age, since it can be traced in England, as well as in Germany and the North.   None of the characters however can be traced in any historical work[1], and the time to which it refers is quite uncertain.   The Northern version of the story contains a supernatural element in the endless battle which forms its conclusion.   It is generally held that this is the oldest element in the story and that Hild, whose name means 'war,' was really a valkyrie.   The whole story then is to be regarded as a myth of 'unceasing strife between conflicting powers[2].'   But we may naturally ask whether it is truly scientific, when dealing with a story known from three separate national traditions, to regard as the original element a feature found in only one of the three. It may be urged of course that the reconciliation, which in Kûdrûn[3] takes the place of the tragic ending found in the Northern version, rendered it necessary to drop the mythical element; and again that we have extremely little information

---

[1] Saxo (p. 158 ff.) connects the story with the reign of Frotho III (Fróði the Peaceful), and this may be an ancient feature, as Fruote von Tenemarke appears as one of Hetel's chief men in Kûdrûn.

[2] "Ein Bild des unaufhörlichen, allgemeinen, aber nie entschiedenen Kampfes entgegengesetzter Mächte, des Aufgangs und des Niedergangs, des Entstehens und Vergehens, des Seins und Nichtseins" (Müllenhoff, ZfdA. XXX 229).   Prof. Sijmons (Grundriss, III 711, where this interpretation is quoted with approval) regards the story as 'tiefsinnig.'   I confess the interpretation is too deep for my comprehension. A totally different view is taken in Panzer's Hilde-Gudrun, where the origin of the story is traced to a folk-tale (p. 250 ff.).   It seems to me that this theory is open to somewhat the same objection as the other, namely that it is founded too much upon features peculiar to one or other version.   At the same time I doubt whether Wate's original connection with the story can be properly inferred from Wids. 21 f.   The influence of folk-tales is clear enough in both versions of the story, but I think it is secondary.

[3] From a passage in Lamprecht's Alexander (v. 1321), a work of the twelfth century, it appears that Hagen (Högni) was killed in the earlier German version of the story.

about the English form of the story.   The latter remark is certainly true; but the little that we do know practically precludes the possibility of a mythical interpretation.   Strictly speaking the passage in Deor's Elegy (cf. p. 56) is not a reference to the story at all, but a matter of fact statement by the poet that he had been in the service of the Heodeningas.   Hence in view of the fact that this passage—together with Widsith, v. 21—is probably by far the earliest reference to the story which we possess, I cannot regard the mythical interpretation as anything more than an extremely doubtful hypothesis[1].

Thus far we have been dealing with stories which are supposed to be of entirely mythical origin.   Now we have to consider certain cases in which elements undoubtedly historical are believed to be blended with myth.   As examples of this type we may take the stories of Waldhere and Sigurðr.   In both cases the historical elements are practically the same.

In the former case it should be mentioned that the mythical theory is by no means universally accepted.   Those scholars however who do adopt this interpretation base their view upon a supposed connection between the story of Waldhere and that of Heðinn and Högni.   The chief points of resemblance between the two are as follows: (i) The heroine is called in the one case Hiltgund (Hildegyth), in the other Hildr (Hild).   (ii) Both stories deal with abduction (so-called) and then with fighting. (iii) The man (Waldhere, Heðinn) who carries off the girl has in both cases to fight with a man called Hagen or Högni. (iv) In both cases the combatants have previously been friends— though strictly this feature applies only to the Northern version of the Heðinn story.   Now the first consideration carries no weight at all; for half the feminine names which occur in Anglo-Saxon heroic poetry contain the element -hild- (e.g. Beaduhild, Hildeburg), while in the Continental and Scandinavian authorities also they are extremely common.   Again, the last consideration obviously has little validity, except when taken in conjunction with the other two.   But these (the second and

[1] For the endless battle there are a number of parallels; cf. Panzer, op. cit., p. 327 ff. (also Pausanias, I 32. 3, with Mr Frazer's note).

third) points of resemblance are, it seems to me, altogether misleading. To begin with it is hardly correct to apply the term 'abduction' to an escape of hostages, such as the story of Waldhere relates; at all events the conditions have nothing in common. Then the fight which follows is not, as in the case of Heðinn and Högni, with an aggrieved father, or indeed with a pursuing force of any kind; it is an unprovoked attack made by a third party in the hope of plunder. Lastly, the part played by the person called Hagen (Högni) is quite different in the two cases. In one he is the injured father who is wholly responsible for the fight; in the other he is a vassal of Gunther (Guthhere), who is only drawn into it, with great reluctance, through the obligation of avenging his nephew (Patufrit), who has already been slain.

It is true that a different version of the story appears in Thiðreks Saga af Bern[1]. Here Högni (Hagen) is represented as pursuing the fugitives on behalf of Attila, while Guthhere does not appear. Now it has been widely assumed that this version is an independent and more original form of the story than that contained in Ekkehard's work, in spite of the fact that it does not make its appearance till nearly three centuries after the latter—and probably nearly six centuries after the composition of the Anglo-Saxon poem. But the lapse of time in itself provides a perfectly adequate explanation of such divergencies, especially if we bear in mind the unfavourable conditions under which the heroic stories were preserved in Germany during the early Middle Ages. As the stories gradually became forgotten two tendencies are constantly observable: (i) to connect stories or incidents which originally were quite distinct, (ii) within the individual story to lose sight of all except the outstanding characters and incidents. Hence it is only in accordance with what we might expect that two different sets of opponents of the hero should be confused. For a parallel we may compare the late North German ballad on Eormenric's death (cf. p. 9), which describes how Theodric with eleven companions broke into the king's castle and slew him. It is generally agreed that

---

[1] There is also a Polish version which has several peculiarities of its own but shows no special affinity with the form of the story found in Thiðreks Saga.

this ballad is due to confusion of some kind with the story of Hamðir and Sörli[1], who were likewise enemies of Eormenric, though not connected in any way with Theodric.

The saga itself really contains evidence which points to an earlier form of the story agreeing with that given by Ekkehard. For the hero is called Valtari af Vaskasteini[2], and there can be no doubt that this expression is to be explained by the rocky defile mentioned by Ekkehard (v. 490 ff.) in the Vosges (*saltus Vosagus*)—on the confines of Guthhere's dominions. Further it is to be noted that the story is introduced as an episode in the relations of Theodric and Eormenric, and that the hero is represented as a nephew of the last named. All scholars are agreed that this is due to late combination—and no doubt rightly. Yet Waldhere is associated with Theodric and Eormenric also in a number of German poems which are quite independent of the saga, and consequently it is by no means improbable that these combinations both preceded and helped to bring about the disappearance of Guthhere from the story.

In its earlier form the affinities of the story with that of Heðinn and Högni are, as we have seen, scarcely worth consideration. Yet apart from this supposed connection there is no case for believing it to have a mythical foundation—except the assumption that myth is a necessary ingredient in every heroic story. Whether it is to be regarded as history or fiction is of course quite a different question and one which we shall have to consider later.

Of all the stories of the Heroic Age probably none has been more frequently referred to a mythical origin than that which deals with Sigurðr (Siegfried). It is held by the great majority of scholars that the Nibelungenlied and the corresponding Edda poems—or rather the earlier poems or legends on which both were based—came into existence through the

---

[1] The early North German version of this story, represented by the Annals of Quedlinburg (cf. p. 37, note), apparently made Eormenric perish in the fight.

[2] It is held by many that this name was originally connected with *Wascono lant*, an early German name for Aquitaine (Gascony) and that the introduction of the Vosges (*Wasgunberg*) was later and due to the confusion of two similar names. But, if there has been any such confusion at all, chronological considerations render it far more probable that the transference was in the reverse direction.

amalgamation of an essentially mythical story with historical traditions of Attila and the fall of the Burgundian kingdom[1]. The original elements of the former are believed to have been as follows: A young prince is brought up by a cunning smith in a forest, away from his father's home. On reaching manhood he gains an immense treasure by killing a dragon; also he releases a maiden by overcoming difficulties and dangers, by fire or water, which were insurmountable to any other person. These two adventures are connected by many scholars. Later, the hero falls into the hands of foes, who slay him and take for themselves his wife and treasure.

It is held that this story was originally a myth of light and darkness—applying however to the course of the year as well as to that of the day. Sigurðr himself is a 'light-hero' and Brynhildr a 'sun-maiden' whom he releases at the dawn, while the treasure represents the blossoms of summer which the light-hero likewise wins by destroying the dragon of winter. Then, in the evening or autumn, he has to yield to the powers of darkness or winter. The original name of these powers was Niflungar or Nibelunge, a name connected with Old Norse *nifl*, 'mist,' *Niflheimr*, 'Hades.' Their chief representative is Högni or Hagen, who, like Sigurðr and Brynhildr, belongs to the mythical elements of the story. Many scholars also hold that the powers which destroyed the hero and appropriated his wife and treasure were originally identical with those from which he had won them at the beginning; and this view seems to be more or less involved by the interpretation given above, since day and night, winter and summer are constantly alternating with one another.

Now it will be obvious at once that the story as thus reconstructed differs greatly from both the forms in which it has come down to us. Indeed the only original feature preserved in both versions is the slaying of the dragon by Sigurðr. But it is only in the Norse version that the hero gains the treasure thereby; in the Nibelungenlied this is obtained by a different encounter, with two princes named Schilbung and Nibelung, while in the Seyfridslied it really belonged to certain dwarfs,

---

[1] Among the exceptions mention may be made especially of an interesting paper by Prof. Mogk in *Neue Jahrbücher*, 1 pp. 68—80.

the sons of Nybling[1]. Again, only the Norse version records that Sigurðr released Brynhildr—from a perpetual sleep with which she had been punished; the incident is not connected with the dragon adventure. The Seyfridslied does relate that the hero rescued a maiden from a dragon; but here the maiden is Kriemhild, whom the dragon has carried off from her home. Further, it is only in the German version that Hagen kills the hero. In the Norse version the actual perpetrator of the deed is Gutthormr, but the instigator is Brynhildr herself. Lastly, neither version of the story makes Brynhildr or the treasure return to their former owners, although—in the German version only—the first owners of the treasure bear the same name as those into whose possession it comes after the hero's death.

It appears then that the original form of this story has been greatly obscured in both versions. The explanation given is that, through confusion with a historical tradition, the Burgundian kings, Gunnarr (Gunther) and his brothers, have taken the place (as well as the name) of the Niflungar. Hence, in order to form a just estimate of the theory it is necessary to examine the various mythical characters separately. These are—in addition to the dragon—Brynhildr, Sigurðr and the Niflungar, including Högni.

The evidence for believing that Brynhildr was originally a mythical character lies chiefly[2] in the identification of her with the valkyrie Sigrdrífa (cf. p. 13), who is mentioned only in the Norse version. The identity of the two characters is clearly recognised in the Helreið Brynhildar and also in the prose authorities. On the other hand it is not recognised in Grípisspá, which is supposed to be a late work, while the other poems leave it uncertain. The evidence therefore on the whole is not very strong.

---

[1] It is stated however that Seyfrid thought that it belonged to the dragon. Hence this story is often connected with the Norse version.

[2] The only German evidence worth consideration is the fact that certain rocks in the Taunus and the Palatinate are called the 'bed' or 'chair of Brynhildr' (*lectulus Brunnihilde, Brinholdestul*) in medieval documents. But I do not see how these names can prove anything more than the popularity of the story. In all lands it is customary to adopt such names from remarkable characters, whatever their origin may be. We may think of the cave of Frederic Barbarossa at Berchtesgaden or the numerous places called after Robin Hood in England.

In the case of Sigurðr the evidence, apart from the valkyrie incident, rests upon his being the slayer of the dragon. But it is agreed that this part of the story must be connected with the similar adventure attributed by Beowulf to Sigemund (Sigmundr); so that the question at issue is whether the exploit was first related of the father or the son. We have already seen (p. 123) that the argument in favour of the latter based on the agreement of the Norse and German authorities is in reality misleading. Hence the balance of probability is in favour of believing that the incident has been transferred to Sigurðr from Sigemund.

In the case of the Niflungar the evidence depends upon the interpretation of the name. The use of the name is certainly somewhat curious. In the Seyfridslied (Part II) the dwarfs are called sons of Nybling. In the first half of the Nibelungenlied Nibelung is the name of one of the brothers slain by Siegfried in his youth, while the people who become subject to him, together with the treasure, on the death of the brothers, are collectively called Nibelunge. In the latter half of the poem however the same name is applied to the Burgundians. In the Norse version *Niflungar* always means Gunnarr and his people (i.e. the Burgundians), except perhaps in the expressions *arfi Niflunga, hodd Niflunga* (in Atlakviða), by which the prose authorities at all events understood the treasure which Sigurðr had taken from Fáfnir. The explanation given for this double use of the name is as follows. Originally it belonged to the mythical enemies of Sigurðr, i.e. Högni and his people—whether these were identical with the former owners of the treasure or not. Later, when Högni became associated with the historical Burgundian kings (Gunnarr etc.), the use of the term was extended so as to embrace them also. But it is to be observed that the interpretation of the name *Niflungar* as 'children of mist' or 'darkness' is not free from difficulty. In the Edda it is twice written *Hniflung*-[1], and on both occasions the *H*-alliterates, whereas alliteration with *n*- is never found. This

---

[1] Helgakv. Hund. I 48, Atlamál 88. In the former case the name is used quite generally, like *Ylfingar* in the same poem. In the latter *Hniflungr* is the name of Högni's son.

fact suggests that the original form of the name was *Hniflungar*
and that the form without *H-* is due to later influence—presumably on the part of scribes—from German sources, where
of course the *H-* (before *-n-*) would regularly be lost at a much
earlier date. If so the name cannot originally have had any
connection with O. Norse *nifl*, etc.

In all these three cases then the evidence for the mythological interpretation of the story seems to be at best inconclusive.
But we have yet to consider the case of Högni; and here it
must be remarked that the demonic character of Högni is quite
essential to the mythological theory. In the Norse version
Gutthormr is a mere instrument and the person really responsible for the murder is Brynhildr herself—a feature obviously
incompatible with the interpretation which we are discussing.
Högni's mythical origin is as necessary for this interpretation
as that of Sigurðr or Brynhildr. In order to maintain the
theory the mythical character must be vindicated in all three
cases alike.

Now it has been remarked that Hagen (*Haguno, Hagano*
etc.) is not uncommon as a personal name even in quite early
times. This is a curious fact if the name had such associations[1].
But there is a much more serious difficulty. It is altogether
contrary to reason or probability to separate Hagen the vassal
of Gunther in the Nibelungenlied from Hagen the vassal of the
same Gunther in the story of Waldhere. His character in the
two cases is certainly quite different. He is brave in both ; but
in the former he is both faithless and cruel, whereas in the
latter he is an honourable man who is reluctantly drawn by
circumstances into a course of action of which he heartily
disapproves. But this is precisely the character borne by Högni
in the Norse version of the story of Sigurðr—a fact which is the
more remarkable since this type of character is extremely rare
in heroic poetry. The agreement between the story of Waldhere
and the Norse version seem to me to render it overwhelmingly
probable that the character which they ascribe to Högni was
that which he originally bore.

---

[1] There was of course another heroic character of the same name; but this does
not meet the objection.

I am not arguing now to prove that Högni was a historical person. He may be of fictitious origin or even mythical (though the latter seems to me extremely improbable). But if so clearly he must have been taken either from the story of Sigurðr into that of Waldhere, or from the story of Waldhere into that of Sigurðr. Which of the two he belonged to originally is a question of minor importance. The essential point is that an earlier German form of the story of Sigurðr must be the link between the Norse version and the story of Waldhere; for there is no evidence that the story of Waldhere itself was ever known in the North. The conclusion to which we are naturally brought is that in this earlier German form of the story Högni bore the same character which is attributed to him in the Norse version. This character however is of course totally incompatible with a demonic origin ; and here, it seems to me, the interpretation which we are discussing hopelessly breaks down.

I cannot help thinking that the investigation of the whole story has been greatly prejudiced by the application of wrong methods. There can be no doubt that a story of some kind— in which the adventures of Sigurðr were already combined with those of the historical Burgundian princes—was in existence long before the date of the earliest extant records, and that from this story, whether it was embodied in a single poem or consisted only of a mass of lays or legends, both the Norse and German versions are ultimately derived. It seems to me that, before trying to ascertain the origin of the various elements contained in the story, the object should be to determine the main features of this common foundation. The way to achieve this end is surely not by arbitrarily selecting one feature from the Norse version and another from the German, but by bringing together all the various features which the two have in common. To carry out such a process systematically would be quite beyond the scope of this book, but a brief outline of the scheme may not be out of place here.

First then we will take the part of the story relating to the hero's early adventures, which is preserved mainly in a different set of authorities from the rest. The chief German authority is the late Seyfridslied which, as we have seen, is really made up of two different ballads, inconsistent with one another.   The Nibelungenlied contains only allusions to this part of the story, the action proper beginning shortly before the hero's arrival at Worms.   The Norse version is given in the trilogy, Reginsmál, Fáfnismál and Sigrdrífumál, as well as in Völsunga Saga, which is derived from these poems.   The account given in Thiðreks Saga is mainly a combination of the German and Norse versions, though it has one or two features peculiar to itself.

In this part of the story the common elements are very few in number.   (1) Sigurðr kills a dragon; (2) Sigurðr gains a great treasure.   In the Norse version the two adventures are combined, but in the Nibelungenlied the treasure belonged to Nibelung and his brother who had quarrelled and who are both killed by the hero.   It may be noticed that Reginn and Fáfnir are also brothers who have quarrelled over a treasure, and they too are both killed by Sigurðr; but Fáfnir has become a dragon—or perhaps a reptile.   The Seyfridslied, Part I mentions only the killing of a dragon (serpent), while Part II unites the acquisition of the treasure with the killing of a dragon—a fiery dragon— but states that the hero erroneously thought that the treasure belonged to the dragon.   Really it belonged to the three sons of the dwarf-king Nybling, who are friendly to the hero and not killed by him.   As a further common element we may mention (3) that Sigurðr is brought up by a smith.   This story is found in the Seyfridslied, Part I, and in Thiðreks Saga— practically also in the Edda, since Reginn is represented as a smith.   Again, (4) both in the ballad and in Norse prose authorities Sigurðr breaks the smith's anvil, though the circumstances are quite different.   It is doubtful whether we should connect the eating of Fáfnir's heart, which enabled the hero to understand the birds, with the German story that he became invulnerable by bathing in the dragon's blood.   Further, we have seen that the awakening of the valkyrie in Sigrdrífumál has practically nothing in common with the rescue of the maiden (Kriemhild) from the dragon related in the ballad (Part II).   Lastly, it is to be observed that though the hero's father has the same name (Sigemund) in all authorities, there is great discrepancy as to his childhood.   In the Edda he is posthumous but knows his parentage, in the Nibelungenlied he is brought up at his father's court, in the ballad, Part I, he leaves his home and goes to the smithy, in Part II and Thiðreks Saga he does not know his parentage—in the latter indeed he is a foundling and suckled by a hind. It will be seen that this part of the story is permeated throughout by the supernatural and marvellous.

From the time of the hero's arrival at the Burgundian court we may take the Nibelungenlied for the German version, while the Norse one is best represented by the poems from the fragmentary Sigurðarkviða I to Atlamál. For the earlier portion we have also to use Völsunga Saga and the prose Edda in place of certain poems which are lost (cf. p. 13). In this part of the story the elements common to the two versions are far more numerous and striking. (1) Sigurðr comes to the Rhineland (Worms in the German version) and marries a sister (Guðrún, Kriemhild) of King Gunnarr (Gunther). (2) Sigurðr in supernatural disguise wins Brynhildr for Gunnarr. (3) Sigurðr again in supernatural disguise sleeps with Brynhildr and takes from her a ring[1]. (4) Brynhildr quarrels with Sigurðr's wife, and the latter shows her the ring[1]. (5) Brynhildr bitterly resents the treatment she has received and devises the hero's death. (6) Sigurðr is killed by treachery; but the versions differ in regard to the perpetrator of the deed. (7) The hero's widow is for a long time irreconcilable, but eventually is married to Atli (Etzel). (8) Gunnarr with Högni and many others are invited to Atli's home. (9) The gold is sunk in the Rhine. (10) Gunnarr and Högni are captured alive and the rest killed in Atli's land. (11) A demand for the gold is made and refused. (12) Gunnarr and Högni are killed.

It will be seen that the supernatural is here confined to (2) and (3); indeed these are almost the only incidents in which it occurs in this part of the story. There is a difference between the two versions in regard to the character of the supernatural disguise. In the Norse version, where the two incidents are combined, Sigurðr and Gunnarr have exchanged forms; in the German Gunther is present in both cases, though Siegfried, who

---

[1] On both these occasions the Nibelungenlied mentions also a girdle.

has rendered himself invisible, is the real actor. Several other important differences between the two versions have already been noted (p. 13 f.). In addition to these each version has of course many characters and incidents peculiar to itself.

Of the discrepancies enumerated on p. 13 f. the fifth is by far the most important, since Kriemhild's revenge for Siegfried forms the central motif of the second half of the Nibelungenlied. In the Norse version no such central motif is to be found. In the prose piece Dráp Niflunga Atli's conduct is attributed to revenge for the death of Brynhildr, while in Völsunga Saga it is ascribed to his lust for Sigurðr's gold. But in the poems themselves no real explanation is given, and the connection between this part of the story and that relating to Sigurðr is scarcely more than a personal one—viz. that Guðrún, Gunnarr and Högni figure in both. This however is a phenomenon for which parallels are to be found in other heroic stories, e.g. those of Beowulf and Weland. It is now held—and doubtless rightly—by the majority of scholars that the unity of interest imparted to the Nibelungenlied by the motif of Kriemhild's revenge is a later improvement on the somewhat disconnected story given in the Edda. For our present purpose however the question is immaterial, since it is not contended that this part of the story is of mythical origin.

In spite of the discrepancies noted above it cannot be denied that the two versions contain a remarkable number of identical features in this part of the story—a fact which renders all the more striking the very slight amount of agreement in the part dealing with the hero's early adventures. Unless all analogies are misleading the conclusion to which we are driven is that the original story began more or less where the Nibelungenlied begins, and that the hero's youthful adventures are later accretions, such as we see gathering round the childhood or ancestry of other heroes, e.g. Biarki (cf. p. 120). We may add also the cases of Starkaðr, Hagen in Kûdrûn and perhaps Witege (cf. p. 135). They appear to be derived, in part at least, from folk-tales. One of these—affecting probably only the Norse version—may be identified with the Scandinavian story of Svipdagr and Menglöð (cf. p. 12), a variety perhaps of that of the Sleeping Beauty. Another is that of the forest dwarf who forges or preserves a magical sword. We may note that in Thiðreks Saga the smith is called Mimir, a name which recalls Saxo's Mimingus (cf. p. 133)[1]. The story of the treasure-guarding dragon may also be included in this category, though strictly perhaps it belongs rather to popular belief than to folk-tale. From the fact that some of these elements are common to both versions we may probably infer that the process of accretion had begun before the story reached the North. Yet there do seem to be some indications of a reflex influence[2]—from the North or some region exposed to Northern influence—upon the development of the story in Germany.

In addition to folk-tales we must take into consideration also a tendency which is often associated with them—the desire to account for an obscure name. This seems to be the most reasonable explanation of the names *Nibelung* and *Nibelunge* in the first part of the German epic and *Nybling* in the ballad—all denoting the original owners of the treasure. We have seen that in the Norse version, as well as in the latter half of the Nibelungenlied, *Niflungar* means the Burgundians. May we not suppose that it was really a dynastic name[3] like *Scyldungas*, *Uffingas, Merewioingas*? In that case of course *hodd Niflunga* (*hort der Nibelunge*) ought to mean the family treasure of the Burgundian kings. But is it quite certain that Atlakviða does not use it in this sense? That it is identified with Fáfnir's treasure in later authorities may be due to subsequent German influence. As for the fact that the name *Nibelunge* is used for the Burgundians only in the second half of the German epic, may not this spring from some stylistic peculiarities of the 'common foundation'? It is not necessary to suppose that the latter was all the work of one author or even of one generation.

In dealing with questions such as these we cannot hope to get beyond a reasonable hypothesis, since the paucity of common

---

[1] It seems likely that Mímir was the dwarf's original name and that Saxo has given him a name which properly belonged to his sword; cf. the phrase *Hoddmímis holt* (Vafðr. 45), etc.

[2] E.g. the name Schilbung and the references to Norway. The story of Sigemund and the dragon also belongs to a maritime region.

[3] Cf. Skaldsk. 42: "Gunnarr and Högni are called Niflungar and Giúkungar."

features between the two versions admits of few definite conclusions.   But from the time when the hero arrives at the
Burgundian court the case is quite different.   In spite of certain
discrepancies there is no difficulty in determining the main outline of the story.   Even in the most important point of all—the
true cause of the hero's death—the two versions are really in full
agreement.   Gutthormr does the deed in one version, Hagen in
the other; but in both alike it arises out of the bitter resentment
cherished by Brynhildr, owing to the deception which has been
practised upon her.   We have seen that this motif is incompatible with the current mythological interpretation of the story.
But more than this, it is plainly not a motif derived from
mythology at all, but from real life.

It must not be overlooked that the Brynhildr and Högni of
the Norse version are in the nature of character-studies.   Both
appeal to our sympathies, though we do not approve of the
actions which they commit or allow.   Here we are in a region
of thought as alien as possible to that of the folk-tale.   But it is
also alien to that period of thought, which was most open to the
influence of folk-tales, the period which we have called Stage III
in the history of German poetry.   In such a period the person
who destroyed the hero must necessarily be a villain as black as
Hell.   Between the instigator of the deed and the perpetrator,
who by this time was Hagen—whether this was so originally
or not is immaterial—the choice was made, not unnaturally in
the circumstances, in favour of the latter, while the former was
allowed, awkwardly enough, to drop out of the story.   Thus the
peculiarities of the German version may be explained quite
naturally as modifications of an earlier form similar to the other
—modifications necessitated by the conditions under which
heroic poetry was preserved in Germany.   The effect produced
is somewhat similar to that which would be obtained by con-
verting a modern problem play into a popular melodrama.

The conclusion then to which we are brought is that the
supposed traces of myth, so far as they have any foundation at
all, are due to late accretions to the story, while the central
motif in both versions alike is by no means of a mythical
character, but essentially human.   Consequently the story of

Sigurðr stands quite on a line with the other stories of the Heroic Age. Most of them contain elements which may be interpreted as mythical ; but these elements are always most prominent in the latest forms of the story. It must not escape notice that those scholars who most strongly uphold the mythical interpretation base their arguments chiefly on such works as the Seyfridslied and Thiðreks Saga af Bern. The explanation is that myth is a growth which requires time to develop. Even Beowulf is no real exception to the general rule, for in the latter part the hero is probably confused with a namesake whose story may have been of considerable antiquity, while the only character in the poem who is quite clearly of mythical origin is the first ancestor of the Danish royal family[1].

---

[1] Cf. Schütte, *Oldsagn om Godtjod*, pp. 35—38, where it is well pointed out that all the clearest cases of myth in early Teutonic records belong to stories dealing with the origin of nations or dynasties. "Den eneste udtrykkelige Myte, der udenfor specielt religiøse Gøremål har været episk frugtbar i Folkevandringstiden er Ophavs-myten."

CHAPTER VIII.

THE USE OF FICTION IN THE HEROIC POEMS.

THE question how far the use of fiction was permitted in heroic poetry is of course one to which we cannot possibly hope to give a definite answer. All poetry which deserves the name claims to do something more than provide a bare record of facts. According to the ancient definition[1] its proper function is to express the universal rather than the particular—what may happen or may have happened rather than what has happened. Some freedom of play for the imagination is therefore essential. These remarks hold good for early Teutonic poetry just as much as for Greek. If we could recover the poems recited in Attila's presence (cf. p. 84) we should doubtless find that they contained far more than a mere statement of facts. In the works which have come down to us however the degree to which freedom is allowed to the imagination varies very greatly from case to case. Thus in the poem on the battle of Brunanburh it is restricted within comparatively narrow limits, while in the almost contemporaneous Hákonarmál the historical fact on which the poem is based is very largely obscured by a wholly fictitious narrative. We may naturally expect that the authors of heroic poems likewise differed in the treatment of their subjects, though not necessarily to the same degree.

As an instance of a poem which obviously contains a large amount of fiction we can hardly do better than take the Anglo-Saxon Widsith. The greater part of this poem consists, as we

---

[1] Aristotle, *Poet.* IX: ὁ γὰρ ἱστορικὸς καὶ ὁ ποιητὴς...διαφέρουσιν...τῷ τὸν μὲν τὰ γενόμενα λέγειν, τὸν δὲ οἷα ἂν γένοιτο. διὸ καὶ φιλοσοφώτερον καὶ σπουδαιότερον ποίησις ἱστορίας ἐστίν· ἡ μὲν γὰρ ποίησις μᾶλλον τὰ καθόλου, ἡ δ' ἱστορία τὰ καθ' ἕκαστον λέγει.

have seen, of a speech by a minstrel enumerating the various peoples and princes with whom he was acquainted. Amongst others he states that he had visited the Gothic king Eormenric (who died before 375), the Burgundian king Guthhere (who died about 437) and the Langobardic king Aelfwine (who died about 572). Now it is commonly held that the poem is of composite formation, and there can be little doubt that additions have been made to it from time to time. This will account for statements such as those given above and, though it does not prevent them from being fictitious, it may enable us to form some idea as to how fiction was used. Poets of the seventh century probably possessed no chronological tables, and consequently they may not have been aware that the foreign princes of whom they were speaking belonged to quite different ages. Yet without such knowledge the visits of the minstrel may clearly be placed among the 'things which may have happened.' What these poets certainly did know was that Eormenric was a prominent figure in some traditional stories, Guthhere in others. It did no violence to the story ($\mu\hat{v}\theta o\varsigma$) itself to bring an anonymous character into contact both with Eormenric and Guthhere, although doubtless no one would have done this while either of the two was alive or indeed for some time after their death. But we must not in such cases apply the principle that, since A comes into contact with both B and C, therefore B may come into contact with C—and conclude from it that poets of the seventh century thought it right to bring Eormenric and Guthhere together in the same story. That is a more advanced stage and one for which we have no satisfactory evidence in Anglo-Saxon poetry[1].

Now, if we turn to the Old Norse poems, which date of course from a much later period, we certainly find this stage reached. Here Guðrún, the sister of Gunnarr (Guthhere), is represented as the mother of Svanhildr, the wife of Iörmunrekr (Eormenric), as well as of Hamðir and Sörli who attacked that king. It is to be observed that there is no hint of a connection between this

---

[1] In Wids., v. 112 ff. we find a list of Gothic heroes belonging to various ages introduced by the expression *innweorud Earmanrices* ('Eormenric's household-troop'); but this expression need not be interpreted literally with reference to the whole list.

story and that of the Burgundian family except in Norse literature. Even here Guðrún is the sole connecting link between the
two stories, and there can be little doubt that the confusion is
due to a mistaken identification of two different women. In the
account of Iörmunrekr given by Saxo, who apparently knows
nothing of the Norse version of the story of Sigurðr, Guðrún is
the name given not indeed to the mother of Hamðir and Sörli
but to a sorceress consulted by them. If the wife of Sigurðr had
originally the same name the difficulty would be capable of
explanation; and it is to be remembered that the evidence for
believing that she was originally called Grímhildr (Kriemhilt) is
by no means of a conclusive character. For the identification
of persons bearing the same name we may compare the confusion which pervades Scandinavian tradition in regard to the
various kings called Fróði[1].

In other cases where we find two stories which seem to be
wholly irreconcilable with one another, the difficulty can be
traced to the misinterpretation of an epithet. Thus the relationships and adventures of the Swedish kings mentioned in
Beowulf differ a good deal from what is recorded of the same
persons in Norse literature. In Beowulf the Swedish king
Ongentheow has two sons Onela and Ohthere, the former of
whom is married to a sister of the Danish kings Hrothgar and
Halga[2]. Strife breaks out between Onela and his two nephews,
Eanmund and Eadgils, the sons of Ohthere (who is perhaps dead);
Eanmund is slain, but Eadgils with the help of Beowulf succeeds
in defeating and killing his uncle and gaining for himself the
throne. In Norse tradition Aðils (Eadgils) is the son and
successor of Óttarr (Ohthere), but the grandfather is called Egill
and there is no mention of Eanmund. Aðils again is married to
Yrsa, who is both the wife and daughter of Helgi (Halga)—
which is hardly compatible with the account given in Beowulf.
He engages in war with a king Áli (Onela) whom he defeats
and kills with the help of Biarki (Beowulf) and other warriors

---

[1] Frotho I and Frotho III were no doubt originally identical; but the confusion
extends also (especially in Skiöldunga Saga) to Frotho IV (the Froda of Beowulf),
who cannot reasonably be connected with the others (cf. p. 124, note).

[2] The MS. here (v. 62) is defective, but no other interpretation is probable.

sent to him by his stepson Hrólfr Kraki.   But Áli is said to be
a Norwegian, and there is no hint of any relationship on his
part to either the Swedish or the Danish royal family.

In this story it seems clear that the Norse tradition has been
led astray by a misinterpretation of the expression *hinn Upplenzki*
('the man of the Uplands'), which is applied to Áli.   There was
a district called Upplönd in Norway, but it was also the name
of the Swedish province in which the capital (Upsala) was
situated.   Since, according to Beowulf, Onela was the actual
king of the Swedes, there can be no doubt that it was the latter
to which the title originally referred.   The erroneous identification with the Norwegian district—natural enough in Norse
tradition—led to the idea that Áli was an invader, and hence to
further dislocations in the story.

In the group of stories which cluster round Dietrich von Bern
we find a number of unhistorical situations, which may largely
be due to similar mistakes rather than to deliberate invention.
Thus when Dietrich appears at Etzel's court, as in all German
authorities, including Thiðreks Saga af Bern, it is probable that
the hero has been confused with his father (Theodemir), who,
as we know from Jordanes, was really subject to Attila.   This
situation cannot be traced in Anglo-Saxon poetry, while in Old
Norse literature (apart from Thiðreks Saga) it is limited to Guðrúnarkviða III[1] and the prose introduction to Guðrúnarkviða II,
which is believed to be derived from the other poem.   The
association of Dietrich with Siegfried occurs only in Thiðreks
Saga and some of the later German poems, which seem to invent
combinations quite freely[2].

But a much larger number of authorities, including the Annals
of Quedlinburg, bring Dietrich into connection with Ermanrich
and the early Gothic hero Wittich; and this combination is
believed to be of much greater antiquity, as the names Theodric
and Widia are associated also in the Anglo-Saxon poem
Waldhere.   Here we are confronted with a question of great

---

[1] The MS. once has Thióðmar, as against two examples of Thióðrekr in the verses
and one in the introduction.   Is it really impossible that the name has been altered
by a scribe familiar with Thiðreks Saga?   Cf. Jónsson, *Oldn. Litteraturs Historie*, I 295.

[2] This tendency is doubtless due largely to the influence of romantic poetry.

difficulty. The association of Theodric and Eormenric is unknown to all the early Scandinavian authorities, and even in
Germany it cannot be traced back beyond the end of the tenth
century; in the old Hildebrandslied Dietrich's enemy is called
Otachar, i.e. Odoacer. Further, apart from the passage in
Waldhere, there is little or no decisive evidence for a knowledge
of the story of Dietrich von Bern in England[1]; for the statement
in Deor that Theodric possessed the *Maeringa burg* for thirty
years may just as probably be applied to the exile of Wolfdietrich
with Berchtung of Meran[2]. Now Dietrich and Wolfdietrich must
be confused to some extent in German tradition, since they are
both credited with an exile of thirty years. Perhaps this confusion goes deeper than is generally recognised. The true
explanation may be that a considerable portion of Wolfdietrich's
story has been transferred to his namesake. I cannot admit
that the identification of Wolfdietrich with the Frankish king
Theodberht is anything more than a very doubtful hypothesis;
he may really have been an early Gothic prince[3]. Certainly the
name was extremely common in that nation, for we meet with
four Gothic kings called Theodric within half a century of one
another.

So far we have been dealing with stories which have been
distorted—apparently in quite late times—either by mistaken
identifications or by an erroneous interpretation of some title
or incident. The lapse of time in itself will account for some
of these changes, especially if we bear in mind the influence of
Stage III (cf. p. 94 ff.), through which the stories have passed both
in Germany and in the North. Fiction of a type however,
especially the tendency towards combination, is certainly not

[1] Prof. Brandl, *Grundriss*, II 953, calls attention to the fact that the Bernician
king Ida is said to have had two sons called Theodric and Theodhere. But is not the
date rather early? The occurrence of the name *Sigesteb* in the council of Ecgberht,
king of Wessex (Birch, 395), is perhaps stronger evidence. The name *Omulung*
which is found more than a century earlier (Birch, 76, 116) scarcely necessitates
acquaintance with the story of Dietrich von Bern.

[2] The case would be different if it could be proved that the person described as
skati Marika (*Maringa*) in the inscription of Rök was Dietrich von Bern.

[3] It is worth noting that in Widsith, v. 115, Seafola and Theodric (i.e. Saben and
Wolfdietrich) appear among the Gothic heroes.

wanting   In the medieval German poems indeed it is widely
used and on a scale far more ambitious than what we have
observed in Widsith.   Here however we have to take into
account the influence of romantic poetry.   The nature of the
use of fiction in the North is not so clear.   If it could be proved
that such stories as those of Oddrún and the ordeal of Guðrún
originated in the North we should certainly have to grant that
it was of a fairly advanced type.

Now we must consider certain cases which seem to have
originated in much earlier times.   As an instance we may take
the Norse story that Atli was murdered by Guðrún.   Now this
story conflicts with what appear to be the true facts in two
distinct points : (i) that Attila was murdered at all; (ii) that the
person who was present with him when he died was anyone
whom we can identify with Guðrún.   The story that Attila was
murdered by a woman is, as we have seen, one of great antiquity;
but there is nothing to show that this woman was Guðrún.   It is
true that Norse and German tradition agree in stating that
Attila married a sister of Guthhere.   This is a statement which
cannot be proved, though there is nothing intrinsically improbable in such a marriage.   But both traditions represent Attila
and his Burgundian wife as married for a number of years, and
both speak of their children.   Yet there can be little doubt that
according to the original story Attila was murdered by his bride
(Ildico) on the night of the wedding.   Hence we must surely
trace the origin of the Norse story to a combination between
two much earlier traditions : (1) that Attila married a sister of
Guthhere ; (2) that Attila was murdered by his wife.   In view
of the story of Guthhere's death—which is common to both
traditions and undoubtedly ancient—it required but little poetic
imagination to identify the two women and to represent the
murder as an act of vengeance.   I see no ground for supposing
that this combination took place before the Viking Age.   The
other story is of course much older ; but the evidence seems to
me to point to an origin in common report rather than in poetic
fiction.

The story of Hamðir and Sörli is a somewhat different case.
Here again, as we have already seen, Guthhere's sister was drawn

into the story only in the Norse version and probably quite late. But even before this time it contained features which cannot be regarded as historical. In the Danish (Saxo's) version also Svanhildr appears as the wife of Iörmunrekr; but there is no satisfactory evidence for this except in the North, and it is clearly contrary to Jordanes' account. Again, the North German form of the story[1] agreed with the Northern versions in stating that the king lost both his hands and both his feet in the encounter. Consequently this feature may be regarded as at least comparatively ancient; but it seems not to be known to Jordanes. As in the last case, therefore, we can trace the gradual development of the story more or less clearly. In its earliest known form, as given by Jordanes, Svanhildr is said to have been the wife of a man (apparently the prince of a dependent tribe) who deserted Eormenric (perhaps by joining the Huns). To punish his disloyalty the king had her tied to wild horses and thus torn to pieces. In an attempt to avenge this outrage her brothers gave him a serious wound, which was partly the cause of his death[2]. In the last point Jordanes may have been trying to combine the tradition with another account of Eormenric's death which he knew from historical sources. Otherwise the story contains nothing incredible[3]. Yet the element of fiction was probably present from the beginning. In the earlier stages its influence may be detected at least in the elaboration of the incident and in exaggeration of its effects, whereas in later times it shows itself in the invention of relationships and in false combinations.

[1] This version (represented by the Ann. Quedl., cf. p. 37, note), like the Norse, added a third brother, though he bears a different name. But the person killed, whose name is not given, is said to have been the father of the brothers, not their sister.

[2] *Hermanaricus rex Gothorum...de Hunorum...aduentu dum cogitat, Rosomonorum gens infida, quae tunc inter alias illi famulatum exhibebat, tali eum nanciscitur occasione decipere. dum enim quandam mulierem, Sunildam nomine, ex gente memorata, pro mariti fraudulento discessu rex furore commotus equis ferocibus inligatam incitatisque cursibus per diuersa diuelli praecepisset, fratres eius Sarus et Ammius germanae obitum uindicantes, Hermanarici latus ferro petierunt; quo uulnere saucius, aegram uitam corporis imbecillitate contraxit... inter haec Hermanaricus tam uulneris dolorem, quam etiam Hunorum incursiones non ferens...defunctus est* (cap. 24).

[3] The Frankish queen Brunhild was put to death in a similar way in the year 613. We may also compare the Thuringian atrocities described by Gregory of Tours (III 7).

Next we will take the story of Beowulf's death, which has the great advantage of being preserved in an early form. This story may be regarded in a sense as pure fiction. Strictly speaking however it consists of at least three distinct elements: (i) Beowulf's encounter with the dragon, (ii) the hero's funeral, (iii) incidental references to the past history of the Geatas. The last element is in part, and probably to a very large extent, founded on fact; so we will confine our attention to the other two. The account of the hero's funeral is a good illustration of Aristotle's dictum as to the true function of poetry—to express the universal rather than the particular. We have no reason for supposing that the poet had any information regarding Beowulf's real funeral. The description which he composed is that of such a funeral as might reasonably be expected for a man of Beowulf's rank and reputation. But the same remark is largely true also of the first element. Grant that the latter part of Beowulf's career was really unknown and that, through confusion with an earlier hero, it had come to be said that he perished in an encounter with a dragon—nearly all the rest[1] can be attributed to the same faculty for elaboration which we find in the funeral scene. More imagination perhaps was required in this case; but it must not be supposed that our author was the first to describe an encounter of this kind. Far more probably he was working upon a theme which in his time was already well worn.

We have now seen that fiction in early times shows itself especially in the way of elaboration, or perhaps we may say in the structure of the story[2]. The subject itself (the $\mu\hat{v}\theta os$) may be based upon fact or upon common report or rumour which was clearly false or even totally incredible, as in the last instance. But I know of no story, dealing with historical characters, which can be shown to be the product of deliberate and conscious invention. We have still however to consider the most important question of all. Did the use of fiction include the invention of characters?

---

[1] The chief exception is the part played by Wiglaf; possibly also the incident of the cowardly knights.

[2] ἡ τῶν πραγμάτων σύστασις (Aristotle, *Poet.* VI 9).

It is not safe to assume this. We know that some of the characters are historical in most of the heroic stories. On the other hand it is not obvious that a single one of the characters mentioned in the primary authorities is fictitious[1]. This being so it is unreasonable to take the view that characters should be regarded as fictitious, unless they can be proved to be historical[2]. On the contrary, until the use of fictitious characters is proved there is a decided presumption in favour of believing any given character to be historical—unless of course his name or some other special circumstance gives clear ground for suspicion.

Wiglaf is a character known to us only in connection with the story of Beowulf and the dragon. Consequently he may be regarded with a certain amount of suspicion. But in one passage it is stated that his father, Weoxtan, had served under the Swedish king Onela and slain Eanmund, the brother of Eadgils. Now in the Kalfsvísa (cf. p. 20) we find a Vésteinn mentioned among those who accompanied Áli (Onela) to the 'ice,' i.e. to the battle on the frozen lake Vener, in which that king lost his life. This can hardly be a different person. But if we grant the identity chronological considerations render it highly improbable that he is a fictitious character.

A somewhat different case is presented by another of the characters which figure in Beowulf, namely Unferth, the Danish king's 'spokesman.' The name does not occur elsewhere in English works, and it is of an unusual, though by no means unknown, type[3]. According to the current explanation name

---

[1] For the case of Widsith see p. 56 f. Supernatural beings, such as Grendel, and mythical personages of the past, such as Scyld, cannot fairly be regarded as exceptions, since it is not at all likely that they were invented by the poet himself. They figure largely in skaldic poems of the Viking Age (e.g. Hákonarmál) which probably never introduce fictitious contemporary characters. On the other hand some of the characters in the Edda poems may have been invented in the North.

[2] This must be emphasized because one constantly finds theories of fictitious origin introduced with some sentence such as the following: 'It has not yet been proved that this story has any historical foundation.' Such an attitude seems to me not only unreasonable but wrong in principle.

[3] Cf. *Unwona*, the name of a bishop of Leicester who died about the beginning of the ninth century, and *Unwine* (*Unwenes*, Gen.), the name of Eastgota's son (Wids. 114). The name *Unfrid* itself occurs in Germany during the eighth and ninth centuries.

and character are alike fictitious, the former being framed to express the man's malevolent disposition. He is said (vv. 587 f., 1167 f.) to have killed his brothers, and on Beowulf's arrival he soon proceeds to wrangle with him[1]. But against this stands the fact that his father is called Ecglaf, an ordinary unsymbolical name, while his quarrel with Beowulf is afterwards amicably settled. It seems to me therefore that the hypothesis is at best uncertain. We may note that Hrothgar's other retainers (Wulfgar, Aeschere, Yrmenlaf) bear names which betray no special significance.

A somewhat similar interpretation, though on a more ambitious scale, is applied to the story of Hamðir and Sörli[2]. The name *Sunilda* (for *Sōnahildi* or *Sōnihilds*) is supposed to have been chosen for Eormenric's victim in order to express the fact that her death was an 'expiation' (O. High Germ. *suona*) of the offence committed by her husband, while Hamðir and Sörli themselves have got their names from their armour (O. Norse *hamr*, A.-S. *hama*, etc.; Goth. *sarwa*, A.-S. *searu*). Now an interpretation of this kind deserves careful consideration when it provides a reasonable and more or less simple explanation of the names involved; but not otherwise. In this case it is held, contrary to all analogies, that the name *Hamðir* (for *Hama-þius*[3]) is extended from an earlier Gothic form *Hamjis* (Jordanes' *Ammius*). But even then the etymology is hardly rendered any more probable; for *ham-* by itself can only mean 'dress,' 'covering.' It is only when compounded with words meaning 'war' (as in A.-S. *guð-hama*) that it can be used in the sense of 'mail-coat.' Again, *Sörli* is regarded—and this is probably correct—as a diminutive of *Sarus*, which is held to represent Goth. *sarws*, though no such word is known (in any Teutonic language) except as a proper name. What is important

---

[1] Prof. Olrik (*Danmarks Heltedigtning*, p. 25 ff.) suggests further that he was the instigator of a quarrel between Hrothwulf and Hrothgar or his sons. But I cannot help thinking that his interpretation of vv. 1166 ff., ingenious as it undoubtedly is, goes a good deal beyond what the passage actually warrants.

[2] Cf. Jiriczek, *Deutsche Heldensagen*, I 63 f., Sijmons, *Grundriss*, III[2] 683.

[3] The true form is probably *Hami-*. It is surely far more probable that *Ammius* is a shortened (hypocoristic) form from the compound name (cf. A.-S. *Hemma*, *Hemmi*). But in that case of course we shall have to conclude that the name had been familiar for some time before it came to Jordanes' knowledge.

to notice however is that a Gothic prince of this name was fighting in Italy in the year 405, i.e. little more than thirty years after Eormenric's death.   Lastly, we may note that there appears to be no satisfactory evidence for regarding *Svan-* (in *Svanhildr*) as a transformation ('Umformung') of *Sōn-*[1].   Such a change would be intelligible enough if the name had become known through a document written in Latin letters; but that is a hypothesis which we need not discuss.   As the evidence stands, considering the extremely corrupt state of the proper names given by Jordanes, it is far more probable that his form has lost an -*a*-, than that the Northern name has been changed. The conclusion therefore to which we are brought is that, whether the story be fictitious or not, its interpretation must be considered without regard to such etymological speculations as these[2].

I am far from denying of course that the etymological interpretation is applicable in its proper sphere. We have a reasonably safe instance in the name *Widsith* (cf. p. 44), as well as in the case of characters derived from folk-tale or myth. In particular we have the eponymous ancestors of families and even nations. But these are not characters invented by the poet himself. Further they are always referred to a more or less distant past, and their occurrence in heroic poetry is not very common.

Next we will take the stories of Waldhere and Sigurðr. Here again the etymological interpretation is often brought forward, especially in connection with the women's names; but on the whole it is of minor importance. Now we have seen that several of the chief characters, Guthhere, Hagena and Attila, are common to both these stories. There is no question of course that Guthhere and Attila are historical persons; but

[1] No argument can be based upon the name *Suanailta* which is found in a document at St Gall dating from 786 (in conjunction with other names which show a knowledge of the story of Eormenric), for it may contain either *swan-* or *sōn-*. It is admitted that the name *Swanahilt* was in use.

[2] With how much greater plausibility could the name *Eormenric* be accounted for! Had it not been for the incidental reference to this king in Ammianus Marcellinus' history, nothing could possibly have saved him from being regarded as a purely fictitious personage.

for Hagena this cannot be proved. If he is fictitious, then one of the two stories necessarily presupposes the other. But it is by no means clear to which of them we should assign the priority. There is no valid reason for doubting that both of them go back to the Heroic Age.

The story of Waldhere contains no feature which can be regarded as intrinsically improbable if allowance be made firstly for poetic elaboration, and secondly for the influence of Stage III (cf. p. 94 ff.). To the first we may perhaps assign the account of the single combats; to the second probably the somewhat grotesque conclusion of the last fight, as given by Ekkehard, and certainly the discrepancy which prevails in regard to the hero's origin. Ekkehard[1] says that his father (Alpharius) was king of Aquitaine, while the medieval German poems speak both of Spanie (Spain) and Lengers (Langres) as his home. Now the name *Aquitani* cannot be taken from an old native poem, and the same remark is probably true of *Spanie*. Moreover, if we were to suppose that the hero belonged to either of these regions we should have to conclude that he was a Visigoth. As a matter of fact this conclusion is generally accepted; but it involves, obviously enough, many difficulties. Langres however is scarcely open to any such objection, and it further has the advantage of proximity to Chalon-sur-Saône, which according to Ekkehard was the home of Hiltgund. These districts must have been occupied at some time by settlers from the lower Rhine, as appears from the names *Pagus Attoariorum* and *Pagus Amauorum*, the former of which lies directly between Chalon and Langres. We have no definite evidence as to when the occupation took place, but probably it was considerably anterior to the time of Clovis[2]. Small Teutonic communities of this kind were doubtless too insignificant to be mentioned in the scanty chronicles of that age; but there is nothing unlikely in the story that children belonging to their princely families were given as hostages to the Huns.

---

[1] In Ekkehard's case the influence of Stage III is supplemented or amended by erudition. The national names which he gives (*Franci*, *Burgundia*, etc.) are accommodated to the political divisions of his own time.

[2] Cf. Zeuss, *Die Deutschen und die Nachbarstämme*, p. 582 ff., where a much earlier date is suggested.

The case of Sigurðr must be considered independently of
the hero's youthful adventures, which, as we have seen, are
probably to be regarded as later accretions to the story. Hence
it is practically only in connection with the Burgundian royal
house that the hero is known[1], and as soon as we lose sight
of this we drift at once into fruitless speculation. The story
represents Sigurðr as wealthy, brave and personally attractive;
but it does not credit him with achievements which changed the
destiny of nations. Consequently he is not the type of person
whom we could reasonably expect to find mentioned in the
chronicles of that period. Guðrún (Kriemhild) again is unknown
to history; we do not even know that Guthhere had a sister.
But we are certainly not justified in assuming either that such
a person never existed or that she could not have married a
prince from the Netherlands. The same remarks, mutatis
mutandis, apply to the case of Brynhildr, the king's wife.

From the analysis given on p. 146 it will be seen that the
original story appears to have contained two features which
we may more or less safely regard as fictitious. One of course
is the disguise; the other is the incident of the ring. In the
former case the two versions differ—from which we may perhaps
infer that this feature was not very clearly indicated in the
original form of the story. The incident of the ring also is
introduced in quite different circumstances. But at the same
time it is really the central feature of the plot; for the ring is
the instrument chosen to bring about the ἀναγνώρισις—the
recognition by Brynhildr of the deception which has been
played upon her. This is an incident such as we frequently
find in modern works of fiction. Yet it cannot by itself be
held to prove the fictitious origin either of the characters or
of the story as a whole. It may equally well be regarded as
a device for explaining the subsequent course of events, in
which case we may set it down as an instance of poetic
elaboration.

Perhaps the objection may be raised that the sequel—

---

[1] It is impossible here to enter into a criticism of theories such as those brought
forward in Boer's *Untersuchungen über den Ursprung und die Entwickelung der
Nibelungensage*.

Brynhildr's resentment against Sigurðr—necessarily presupposes
the deception practised upon her and that this deception is in
both versions of a supernatural character.   That is doubtless
true ; but the explanation is not far to seek.   Both versions
of the story are really aware of a previous acquaintance between
Sigurðr and Brynhildr.   In the Völsunga Saga[1] we hear of
two distinct meetings, firstly when he awakens her from the
enchanted sleep (cap. 20 f.) and again when he woos her
on his visit to Heimir (cap. 24).   If Brynhildr is really to be
identified with the sleeping valkyrie, these two accounts may
be regarded as variants of one original story.   On the other
hand the Grípisspá treats the two events separately, like the
saga, though unlike the saga it does not identify Brynhildr with
the valkyrie.   Both forms of the story however agree that there
had been some meeting, through which Brynhildr had been led
to expect marriage with Sigurðr.   Now the Nibelungenlied says
nothing of a relationship of this kind.   But at the same time it
states more than once—without any explanation—that Siegfried
had known Brünhild and her dwelling.   There is some ground
therefore for suspecting that a portion of the story has been
suppressed or lost in the German version.   If so, then the
explanation of the supernatural disguise becomes clear enough.
It is a device, doubtless an ancient device[2], for saving the hero's
character.   Then also we obtain a much stronger motive for
Brynhildr's resentment.   It was a case not merely of deception
but of faithlessness.   There is nothing incredible in that, though
in real life the ἀναγνώρισις would probably come about in a
different way.

     If the story is fictitious—i.e. if Sigurðr, Brynhildr, Högni,
Guðrún (Kriemhild) and all their doings are creations of fancy—
one conclusion at all events must, I think, be accepted.   Such a
story must be the product of the brain of one gifted poet ; it

---

[1] Owing to the great lacuna in the MS. of the Edda (cf. p. 13) the poems which
dealt with this part of the story are lost.

[2] The story may have come to the North in two different forms, one of which
related the wooing of Brynhildr by Sigurðr, while the other, a later form, contained
the incident of the supernatural disguise.   But it is also possible that even the original
poem or poems on the subject dealt with this incident, though without altogether
suppressing the previous relations between Sigurðr and Brynhildr.

cannot be the result of a fortuitous concourse of lays by different
authors. The analysis shows that the strength of the story lies
chiefly in that element which is common to both versions. Here
we have the character-studies of Brynhildr and Högni; for even
in the Nibelungenlied, greatly defaced as they are, the original
outlines can still be traced. The plot too conforms to the
highest standard of tragic art. It has complete unity in itself[1];
all the characters are more or less sympathetic; and the hero's
downfall is due not to any villainy ($\mu o\chi\theta\eta\rho i a$) on his own part,
but to a great error ($\dot{a}\mu a\rho\tau i a$). Lastly, whatever view may be
taken as to the fate of Brynhildr—a point in which the versions
differ—nothing could be more tragic than the grief of Guðrún
(Kriemhild), which is common to both. For the creation of a
story possessing all these features—a story too which lived in
different parts of Europe for many centuries under somewhat
unfavourable conditions—we must surely assume not only a
talented poet but also a poem of some considerable length.

　　I do not of course regard this as a conclusive argument for
believing that the story is based on fact. For even in that case
its presentation would require epic form, as well as poetic talent.
The decision between the two interpretations rests ultimately
on the question whether such a story is more likely to have
been invented or drawn from life. It seems probable that some
of the characters added in the Norse version are products of
fiction. But here we have to deal with a period removed by
many ages from the times to which the story relates, and with
a people who had developed the cultivation of imaginative
poetry to a very high standard. The origin of the story however must surely date from a period when Guthhere and the
Burgundian kingdom on the Rhine were still remembered. In
that period we have no positive evidence for the composition
of fiction at all, much less for fiction of this extremely elaborate
type. On the other hand we have in Procopius' account of
Irmingisl and Radiger (cf. p. 97 ff.), written within six or seven
years of the events, practically all the materials for the composition of an epic poem on a very similar subject. Indeed

---

[1] There is no need to assume that the story of Guthhere's death was embodied in
the same poem, though the two were doubtless connected from quite early times.

they can hardly be called merely crude materials; for certain incidents are depicted, in poetic fashion, rather than related, and even the supernatural element is not wanting. The evidence of this passage seems to me to tell decidedly in favour of the view that the story of Sigurðr is founded on fact[1].

In the course of this chapter we have examined a number of heroic stories with a view to determining how and to what extent fiction has been employed in their composition. We have seen that in early times its influence was shown chiefly in the imaginative presentation or structure of stories, some of which were founded on fact, others on popular report or rumour which frequently introduced elements from folk-tales, occasionally even from myth. All such cases however may be included among the 'things that may have happened,' if we take into account the spirit of the times. On the other hand for the composition of wholly fictitious narratives—narratives which the author himself knew to be fictitious—and more especially for the deliberate invention of characters there seems to be no conclusive evidence in the stories which we have considered; and I am not aware of any others for which a stronger case could be made out. I am not prepared of course to state dogmatically that such fiction was not known. The case is far too uncertain for such a statement as that; there is no question here of such gross improbabilities as those which beset the hypothesis of 'rationalised myth.' One is certainly entitled to doubt whether all the characters even in early poems, such as Beowulf, are taken from life. But if we grant, as I think we must, the existence of earlier poems dealing with the Danish court, there is nothing incredible in the supposition.

These remarks apply of course only to poems belonging to Stage I and Stage II. The effect of Stage III was to disintegrate the stories and to introduce unhistorical elements of all kinds.

---

[1] It would be difficult to doubt its historical origin if it could be proved that the hero's father was originally identical with Sigemund the son of Waelse (Völsungr), who figures in Beowulf; for the two stories are almost entirely independent of each other and refer to quite different regions. The adventure with the dragon, which is related both of Sigurðr and Sigemund, shows that they were connected in very early times. Still I know no real proof of original identity.

Hence in poems of Stage IV we meet with numerous situations which are quite incompatible either with history or with the older forms of the traditions. In the same period we find also many fictitious characters, not only in the German poems, where they may be ascribed to romantic influence, but also probably in those of the North.

There is one type of fiction which we have not taken into account in our discussion. Various scholars from time to time have put forward the theory that some of the chief characters of the Heroic Age are really well-known historical persons under fictitious names. Thus Sigurðr has been identified with a number of famous princes from Arminius to Sigebert. It cannot be said that any one of these identifications is of a nature to carry conviction; in no case indeed have they gained wide acceptance. But I cannot help thinking that an error in principle underlies the whole theory. It was scarcely through the greatness of their power, much less through the effects of their achievements on after generations, that the characters of the Heroic Age acquired celebrity; it was far more through the impression made upon their neighbours and contemporaries by their magnificence and generosity, by their personality, and perhaps above all by the adventures and vicissitudes of fortune which fell to their lot. This is a question to which we shall have to return in a later chapter.

CHAPTER IX.

THE HEROIC AGE OF GREECE.

THE literary records of the Heroic Age of Greece resemble those of the northern Heroic Age in several respects. Both literatures alike begin with heroic poems which, as we shall see later, possess many common characteristics. Then, at a much later date, we find in both literatures a new series of narrative works dealing again with the old stories. Lastly, in both cases works of all periods, both poetic and prose, contain frequent incidental references to the same stories, testifying thereby to their popularity. In Greek literature indeed such references occur more frequently than in that of the Teutonic peoples—a fact doubtless due to the preservation of great poems of the former period, which at an early date came to be regarded as classics or something more. Among the northern peoples, as we have seen, it was only in England that any considerable amount of the early heroic poetry was preserved; but here the continuity of literary development was broken through political causes, and consequently all memory of the Heroic Age was practically lost.

On the other hand we have no evidence for the Heroic Age of Greece in any way comparable with those more or less contemporary Roman works which enable us to identify many of the characters and incidents of the northern Heroic Age. In Greece the Heroic Age had passed away long before the date of the earliest historical documents which have come down to us; while though inscriptions of a remote antiquity are still in existence, none prior to the seventh, or possibly the eighth century, have as yet been deciphered. Further, the monuments of the surrounding countries, such as Egypt or Assyria, make no reference to Greece beyond the occasional bare mention of a geographical or tribal name. Hence it comes about that we cannot with certainty pronounce any single person or event of the Heroic Age to be historical. All that it has been possible as yet to verify is the existence of ancient centres of civilisation in certain localities which figure prominently in stories of the Heroic Age. Archaeological investigation has shown that some of these places possessed at one time an extraordinary amount of wealth and splendour, though within the historical period they were inconsiderable or even uninhabited.

Of the early heroic poetry very little has come down to us except the two great epics, the Iliad and the Odyssey, which between them contain nearly 28,000 verses. These poems are, strictly speaking, anonymous, though from very ancient times, at least from the seventh century, the name Homer has been associated with them. In the Alexandrian age there were critics who believed that the Iliad and Odyssey were the work of different authors ; but it is only within modern times that they have been considered to be of composite formation. At present it is probably the most prevalent view that the Iliad was formed gradually in the course of the ninth century and that it attained substantially its present form about the middle of the eighth century. The Odyssey is generally thought to be a later work. Its date is set by many as late as the seventh century, though it is believed to have used and probably incorporated earlier poems, of the ninth or eighth century. There are however still a number of scholars who both deny the composite authorship of the poems and also believe them to be of greater antiquity than the dates here given.

Apart from the Iliad and Odyssey the only early heroic poem which has come down to us is the Shield of Heracles, a work containing 480 verses and giving an account of the single combat between Heracles and Cycnos. It has been attributed to Hesiod by various writers, at least since the Alexandrian period; indeed the Argument cites Stesichoros as authority for this belief. At the present time however most scholars regard it as the work of an unknown poet of the seventh century[1].

In ancient times there were a considerable number of other early epic poems, of which only a few insignificant fragments now remain. Some of these, the Cypria, Aithiopis, Little Iliad (Ἰλιὰς μικρά), Iliu Persis and Nostoi, dealt with the same cycle of story as the Iliad and Odyssey. They seem however to have been of much smaller compass and to have treated their subjects in a far less detailed manner. It is thought by many that the Cypria was composed as an introduction to the Iliad and the others as continuations of it—the Nostoi connecting on to the Odyssey. At all events they were utilised by the authors of the prose κύκλοι, in Alexandrian and Roman times, for the purpose of presenting a connected account of the whole story[2].

The authorship of these poems is attributed in late writings to a number of persons—Stasinos of Cyprus, Arctinos of Miletos, Lesches of Lesbos and Agias of Troizen—of whom nothing definite is known, but who are believed to have lived either in the eighth century or in the early part of the seventh. In early times however—indeed probably down to the fourth century—it seems to have been the general belief that several, possibly all, of them were by Homer. Herodotus (II 117) expresses his disbelief in Homer's authorship of the Cypria; but his words imply that he was contesting a commonly accepted view. On the other hand Hellanicos[3], who was approximately contemporary with Herodotus, is said to have attributed the Little Iliad (including possibly the Iliu Persis) not to Lesches or Arctinos but to a certain Cinaithon of Lacedaemon, who is said to have lived before the middle of the eighth century. Lastly we must mention the Telegoneia, a sequel to the Odyssey, which is said to have been composed by Eugammon of Cyrene[4], probably in the sixth century.

---

[1] Chiefly because the description of the shield (vv. 139—320) appears to correspond to the art of that period.

[2] The κύκλοι embraced much more than the story of Troy; cf. *W. v. Christs Geschichte d. griech. Litteratur*[5], § 47 f. The relationship of these works to the poems may be compared with that of Völsunga Saga to the heroic poems of the Edda.

[3] Schol. to Euripides, *Troades*, 822.

[4] Eusebius, *Chron.*, ad Olymp. 53. The same authority however also attributes it to Cinaithon of Lacedaemon (ad Olymp. 4).

Apart from the series of poems dealing with the siege of Troy the most famous of the early epics was the Thebais, which gave the story of the legendary kings of Thebes. This poem was attributed to Homer by Callinos of Ephesus[1] who lived early in the seventh century—which probably implies that it was not of recent composition even then. It had a sequel called Epigonoi, which likewise seems to have been attributed to Homer, though Herodotus (IV 32) again apparently felt doubtful. In addition to these mention may be made of the Oidipodeia, which also dealt with the Theban story, and of the Oichalias Halosis and Phocais, which were concerned with adventures of Heracles.

All the poems mentioned above were probably composed in quite early times, though we have practically no trustworthy data as to their age or authorship. A number of other epics bore the names of persons who were attributed to the eighth or seventh centuries, such as Cinaithon (see above), Eumelos of Corinth and Asios of Samos. These however seem to have been rather of a genealogical than heroic character. Peisandros of Rhodes, the author of an epic on Heracles, is also referred, though on rather doubtful authority, to the close of this period. But the other epic poets whose names have survived seem to have belonged to a considerably later time. The didactic epos began, under Hesiod, apparently before the end of the eighth century, while early in the following century there arose new types of poetry, elegiac and iambic, concerned chiefly with present topics and the personal interests of the poets, and seldom even referring to the Heroic Age. The last remark is true also, though to a less extent, of the early lyric poetry. But in the early part of the sixth century Stesichoros of Himera began to utilise it for presenting stories of the Heroic Age in a new form In Pindar's odes too, nearly a century later, the allusions to heroic stories are very frequent and often of considerable length. One ode indeed contains almost an epos.

In the fifth century however the Heroic Age figures most prominently in Athenian tragedy. Of the seven extant plays of Aeschylus four or five[2] deal with the Heroic Age and one with

---

[1] Fragm. 6 (Bergk), from Pausanias, IX 9. 5.

[2] The Suppliants is hardly to be reckoned as a heroic play. It is referred to

contemporary history, while the last is concerned exclusively with supernatural beings. Of the two later dramatists, Sophocles and Euripides, all the surviving plays[1] take their subjects from the Heroic Age. Further, we know the names of a large number of lost plays, both by these and other authors, and from them it appears that the surviving pieces are fairly representative, so far as choice of subjects is concerned. During the same period we hear of a few epic poets whose works are now lost. Some of these, such as Panyasis and Antimachos, dealt with stories of the Heroic Age and some, as Choirilos, with contemporary history. About two centuries later heroic epic poetry was cultivated at Alexandria, especially by Apollonius Rhodius.

Among incidental references to the Heroic Age one of the most interesting occurs in Hesiod's Works and Days (vv. 156—170), where an age of the heroes[2] who fell at Thebes and Troy is introduced between the bronze age and the iron age. Herodotus'

a time many generations before the siege of Troy and all the characters appear to be personifications of nationalities. Regarding the epic Danais little information seems to be obtainable.

[1] The Ion and Bacchai are perhaps rather to be regarded as pre-heroic; the former deals with a story which apparently belongs to the same type as Aeschylus' Suppliants.

[2]

> αὐτὰρ ἐπεὶ καὶ τοῦτο γένος κατὰ γαῖα κάλυψεν,
> αὖτις ἔτ' ἄλλο τέταρτον ἐπὶ χθονὶ πουλυβοτείρῃ
> Ζεὺς Κρονίδης ποίησε δικαιότερον καὶ ἄρειον,
> ἀνδρῶν ἡρώων θεῖον γένος, οἳ καλέονται
> ἡμίθεοι, προτέρη γενέη κατ' ἀπείρονα γαῖαν.
> καὶ τοὺς μὲν πόλεμός τε κακὸς καὶ φύλοπις αἰνὴ
> τοὺς μὲν ὑφ' ἑπταπύλῳ Θήβῃ, Καδμηΐδι γαίῃ,
> ὤλεσε μαρναμένους μήλων ἕνεκ' Οἰδιπόδαο,
> τοὺς δὲ καὶ ἐν νήεσσιν ὑπὲρ μέγα λαῖτμα θαλάσσης
> ἐς Τροίην ἀγαγὼν Ἑλένης ἕνεκ' ἠϋκόμοιο. κ.τ.λ.

In this passage the word ἥρως seems to have already begun to acquire its later meaning, viz. a distinguished man of the past (generally of the Heroic Age) who was honoured with worship, though not as a god. For such worship Teutonic records naturally furnish few parallels, since most of the Teutonic peoples became Christian either during the Heroic Age itself or soon after. We may compare however what Jordanes (cap. 13) says of the Goths : *proceres suos, quorum quasi fortuna uincebant, non puros homines sed semideos, id est Ansis, uocauerunt.* In Old Norse the name *æsir* (*ansir*) is applied only to the gods (Othin, Thor, etc.) ; but we do hear occasionally of worship paid to heroes of the Heroic Age, as well as to distinguished persons of later times. An instance of the former (in the case of Hrólfr Kraki) occurs in Yngl. S. 41.

history abounds with references to the Heroic Age, and even Thucydides refers to it not unfrequently, though in a more critical spirit. In later times we have to notice especially antiquarian writers such as Strabo and above all Pausanias. The last-named derived his information very largely from local tradition and consequently the stories which he gives may often be independent of the poems.

We may now consider briefly the chronological aspect of the Greek Heroic Age. It has already been mentioned that a passage in Hesiod's Works and Days speaks of an age of heroes intermediate between the bronze and iron ages, and that it further defines these heroes as those who fought at Thebes and Troy. To the latter number belong no doubt the various characters of the Iliad and Odyssey and the other poems (Cypria, etc.) which dealt with the Trojan cycle of legend, while the deeds of the former must have been treated in the Thebais and the Epigonoi. In the surviving Attic dramas which deal with the Heroic Age the distribution of subjects is as follows. Sixteen plays (three by Aeschylus, three by Sophocles and ten by Euripides, including the Cyclops and Rhesos) treat of the heroes of the Trojan war or their children; six plays (one by Aeschylus, three by Sophocles and two by Euripides) deal with the Theban story; and six plays (one by Sophocles and five by Euripides) are concerned with the doings of Heracles, Theseus or Iason. It is to be observed that the heroes of the Theban story are always represented as belonging to the generation immediately preceding that of the heroes of Troy, while Heracles, Theseus and Iason are all loosely connected with one another and made roughly contemporary with the Theban heroes. The remaining three plays (Aeschylus' Suppliants and Euripides' Ion and Bacchai), if we are justified in regarding them as heroic at all, refer to persons much farther back in the genealogies.

It appears then that the characters who figure most prominently in stories of the Heroic Age were, with few exceptions, ascribed to a period covering not more than three or four generations. There are, it is true, a number of stories referring to much earlier generations—in addition to those treated in the three plays mentioned above—but they seem to have been distinctly less popular than the others. On the other hand there is scarcely any reference to persons later than the children of the heroes who fought at Troy.

With the evidence at our disposal it is impossible to fix any absolute dates for the Heroic Age. All that we can say is that the end of that age appears to coincide with the movement or series of movements, traditionally known as the Return of the Heracleidai, to which the Dorian states in the Peloponnesos were believed to owe their origin. According to the story, the Return took place in the second generation after the siege of Troy, and the grandsons of Agamemnon, the Achaean leader at the siege, were killed or expelled by the Dorians. Certainly it is to be noted that the scheme of tribal or political geography presented to us in the Homeric poems seems to show no trace either of Dorians in the Peloponnesos or of Ionic settlements in the eastern Aegean—another series of movements which are said to have been brought about by the Dorian conquest.

The great majority of scholars apparently regard the story of the conquest as containing at least a nucleus of truth, though it refers to times long anterior to what we should call the historical period. The ancients themselves dated the events in question back to the twelfth or eleventh century (B.C.). But the evidence on which their conclusions were based is not of a very satisfactory character and will require careful consideration.

Before entering upon this question it will be convenient to notice briefly the scenes of the stories and the localities and peoples to which the various characters belong. The scene of the Iliad is laid in the north-west corner of Asia Minor, a short distance south of the Dardanelles. But the stories introduced incidentally refer for the most part to places on the mainland of Greece, less frequently to localities in Asia Minor or Thrace. The distribution of the principal heroes is as follows: Agamemnon's territories, according to the Catalogue of Ships (Il. II 569 ff.), lie in the north-east of the Peloponnesos, including the north-western part of what was later called Argolis and at least the eastern half of Achaia. Elsewhere (Il. IX 149 ff., 291 ff.) he appears to have possessions in Messenia. His brother, Menelaos, rules over Sparta and other places in Laconia. Nestor's kingdom is on the western side of the Peloponnesos, to the south of Elis. Idomeneus belongs to Crete, Achilles to southern Thessaly (Phthiotis), Aias, the son of Telamon, to Salamis, his namesake to the eastern Locris, Diomedes to the eastern and southern parts of Argolis and Odysseus to the Ionian Isles. It must not be overlooked that most of these districts were of little or no political importance during the historical period and, further, that the territories of the kingdoms appear not to have coincided as a rule with the political divisions which we find in later times.

The scene of the Odyssey is laid chiefly in the Ionian Isles, to a much smaller extent in the Peloponnesos. The wanderings of the hero himself appear to lie chiefly in regions to the west of Greece, though there may be reminiscences of the Black Sea. Some scholars relegate them largely or altogether to the realm of fairyland. Incidental references occur to Thesprotis (Epeiros) and the Aegean, as well as to more distant lands such as Egypt.

Thebes was doubtless the scene of the lost Thebais and Epigonoi. The story of Pelops seems to have been connected chiefly with Elis and that of Perseus with Mycenae and Tiryns, while Minos belonged to Crete and Theseus to Athens. Iason's home was in eastern Thessaly, but his story is largely taken up with journeys in the Black Sea and other distant regions. Heracles' adventures are spread over the greater part of Greece and many other lands, though Boeotia and Malis are perhaps the districts most prominent in his story. The scene of the Shield of Heracles is laid in Phthiotis.

It appears then that the heroic stories are distributed over the greater part of the ancient Greek world. Certain districts however are excepted, and to these special attention should be given. In the first place we have practically no reference to Greek cities in Italy or Sicily or to heroes belonging to them, though we do hear occasionally of travellers' acquaintance with these countries. More important is the absence of any mention of Greek cities in Asia Minor[1] and the adjacent islands, except

---

[1] In the Nostoi after the departure from Troy some of the Achaeans (Calchas,

those off the coast of Caria. The legends which speak of colonies led to Lesbos by Penthilos the son of Orestes or to Miletos and elsewhere by the sons of Codros are hardly to be reckoned among heroic traditions. The names indeed, at least in the first case, are taken from this source, but they form the subject of no connected story. Miletos is mentioned in the Trojan catalogue (Il. II 868), but it is said to be in the possession of the Carians. To Chios there is only a geographical reference (Od. III 170 ff.), and though Lesbos is mentioned more frequently its inhabitants are treated as enemies by the Achaeans. The only real exceptions are the southern islands, several of which, such as Rhodes and Cos, send contingents to Agamemnon's army. Cyprus too seems to be fairly well known and its princes, though they take no part in the expedition, are on friendly terms with the Achaeans—a fact which renders the absence of reference to the Ionic cities all the more striking. In Greece itself nearly every district has a story connected with it. Attica however is one of the least prominent and possesses no hero of much note except Theseus.

For the tribal distinctions which figure so prominently in later Greek history there is extremely little evidence in stories of the Heroic Age. The name Αἰολέες is not mentioned in the Homeric poems, while Δωριέες occurs only once, as the name of one of the five peoples of Crete, and Ἰάονες once as that of a people (perhaps the Athenians) associated with the Locrians and Boeotians. On the other hand the most frequently used of all national designations is Ἀχαιοί, a name which in later times was borne only by the inhabitants of two comparatively unimportant districts, Phthiotis and the north coast of the Peloponnesos. In the Homeric poems it appears to be a collective term for the inhabitants of Greece and the surrounding islands. In the same sense we find also Δαναοί, a name which later is used only in archaistic poetry. Ἀργεῖοι and Ἕλληνες seem properly to be geographical terms, though the former occurs frequently (the latter only once[1], in the form Πανέλληνες) as a synonym

---

Leonteus and Polypoites) were made to arrive at Colophon. The story of Calchas' contest with Mopsos perhaps comes from the same source.

[1] Once also, together with Ἀχαιοί (Il. II 684), as a name for the subjects of

for Ἀχαιοί. Names of peoples, such as Ἄβαντες, Ἐπειοί, Αἰτωλοί, are of course frequently used; but they denote comparatively small sections of the nation.

Though the term Ἀχαιοί is used for the inhabitants of Greece collectively, it may of course really be the name of a tribe or people which was regarded as dominant at the time. At all events in Od. XIX 176 we find the Achaeans mentioned as merely one of five peoples which inhabit Crete. As an instance of a people who were apparently never included among the Achaeans we may take the Pelasgoi mentioned in the same passage. Here however we are faced with a question of nationality, for Herodotus speaks of the Pelasgoi of his own time as a barbarous people[1], though at the same time he holds that several Greek peoples, especially the Ionians and Athenians, were sprung from them. No indication is given in the Homeric poems that the Pelasgoi spoke a foreign language; but this remark is true also of many Asiatic peoples, including the Trojans.

On the question of Greek nationality there is unfortunately very little evidence either in the Homeric poems or in other stories relating to the Heroic Age. We cannot even tell whether the population of the Greek mainland was believed to be homogeneous. Only in the case of Crete is detailed ethnographical information given. In a passage cited above we

Achilles, or rather Peleus. Ἑλλάς is used sometimes for a place or district in Peleus' kingdom, sometimes apparently in a wider sense.

[1] He states (I 57) that in his time they inhabited Placia and Scylace, on the south coast of the Sea of Marmara, and Κρηστῶνα πόλιν, probably in the Chalcidian peninsula (though some scholars emend this name to Κρότωνα, i.e. Cortona in Tuscany). Down to the fifth century they are said to have also occupied Lemnos and Imbros (IV 145, V 26, VI 138 ff.), and in early times Samothrace (II 51), while their name was preserved at Antandros, in the Gulf of Adramyttion (VII 42). Later writers speak of the Pelasgoi as having formerly inhabited many other regions. Into the difficult problems connected with this name we need not enter here; for the most recent and perhaps fullest discussion of the subject reference may be made to Prof. Myres' paper in the *Journ. Hell. St.* 1907, p. 170 ff. As regards the etymology analogies indicate that Πελασγοί represents an earlier form *Pelag-skoi*. If this is a Greek word the most probable meaning is 'people of the sea' (though another explanation has been proposed; cf. Kretschmer, *Glotta* I 16 f.). But it may really be a national name (cf. Πελάγονες). In that case we may note that the use of the suffix -sko- in national names is Indo-European, though not Greek.

C. 12

are told that this island contained five peoples, namely the Achaeans, Eteocretes, Cydones, Dorians and Pelasgoi. The first and fourth of these are well-known sections of the Greek nation, but we have no satisfactory evidence as to the nationality of the others. Herodotus (I 173) says that the Lycians came originally from Crete and adds that the whole of the island was once possessed by barbarians. Interesting light on the latter statement has been thrown by the recent discovery of certain inscriptions at Praisos, in what is said to have been the Eteocretan part of the island. These inscriptions are written in forms of the Greek alphabet which were current in the sixth and fourth centuries (B.C.) respectively, but the language is not Greek. Besides these numerous inscriptions dating from much earlier times have been found at Cnossos and elsewhere; but they have not yet been deciphered. All that can be said at present is that we have no reason for discrediting Herodotus' statement.

In Greece itself we have not such clear evidence for the prevalence of a non-Greek language. Here we are dependent on somewhat doubtful inferences from place-names. Yet the majority of scholars would not admit that the language was indigenous. Indeed the tendency at present is to believe that Greece and the Aegean islands were originally inhabited by peoples of one stock, the existence of which can be traced back in Crete for many thousands of years, and that these peoples were ultimately overwhelmed and absorbed—perhaps in the course of the second millennium—by invaders from the north. Asia Minor is supposed to have had a somewhat similar history. Originally it is believed to have been occupied by various kindred peoples, of which the most prominent were the Hittites of Cappadocia. Eventually—about 1200 B.C. according to the most recent view[1]—there took place a great irruption of Thraco-Phrygian peoples from the north-west, who became dominant throughout the larger part of the peninsula[2].

[1] Meyer, S.-B. d. Akad. zu Berlin, 1908, p. 18.

[2] Into the linguistic affinities of these various peoples we need not enter here. It will be sufficient to notice that the Thracian and Phrygian languages are commonly believed to have belonged to the eastern division of the Indo-European group. Certainly this is the case with the language of the Armenians, who according to Herodotus (VII 73) were an offshoot (ἄποικοι) of the Phrygians. The evidence of the

In the Iliad the forces ranged in defence of Troy are drawn from a wide area, extending from the Axios (Vardar) on the west to Paphlagonia on the east and Lycia on the south. The nationalities represented seem to be chiefly of Thraco-Phrygian stock, though a few, such as the Lycians and perhaps the Carians, belong to the indigenous population. On the other hand there is no reason for supposing that any of the peoples represented in Agamemnon's army were of other than Greek nationality. The story may therefore be regarded as one of national conflict. Yet it cannot be said that this feature is ever emphasised in the poems themselves, although the point of view throughout is that of an Achaean.

For local or tribal patriotism the Homeric poems furnish us with little or no evidence. No Greek communities and few even of their princes are described otherwise than in terms of respect. We may point also to the old controversy regarding Homer's birthplace—a controversy which owes its very existence to the absence of any local patriotism in the poems. In this respect it will be seen that Greek heroic poetry agrees with Teutonic.

We must now return to the consideration of the chronological problem. In ancient times, especially during the Alexandrian period, various attempts were made to calculate the exact date of the siege of Troy. Of these the most generally accepted was that of Eratosthenes, which was based on the length of the reigns ascribed to the kings of Sparta. This calculation brought the foundation of the Dorian kingdom at Sparta to the year 1104–3, and eighty years were added to obtain the date of the fall of Troy. But it has long been pointed out that the figures given for the reigns of the early kings are so greatly above the average that they cannot be regarded with any confidence.

Phrygian inscriptions themselves is unfortunately somewhat ambiguous. To the same eastern division belonged the ancient Illyrian languages, if the present dialects of Albania are descended from them. On the other hand the languages of the indigenous peoples throughout Asia Minor and the Aegean area are commonly believed to have been non-Indo-European. Yet Prof. Conway (*British School at Athens*, Ann. VIII, p. 141 ff.) holds that the inscriptions of Praisos belonged to a language of this group. If this should turn out to be the case with the earlier Cretan inscriptions current views as to the early history of the Indo-European languages would require considerable modification.

Thus the first Olympiad (B.C. 776–5) was made to coincide with the tenth (or eleventh) year of Alcamenes and Theopompos. Alcamenes was the ninth in succession from Eurysthenes and Theopompos the eighth from Procles, and the number of years ascribed to the previous reigns amounts on the average to over thirty-five years for one dynasty and over thirty-nine for the other. But in kingdoms for which we have reliable information extending over a long period of time the usual average length is apparently between twenty and twenty-five years[1]. Hence, if the lists of kings themselves are to be trusted—and even this is very doubtful in view of the fact that they are almost identical with the genealogies—it is difficult to avoid suspecting that the total period ascribed to their reigns collectively is more than a century too long.

More reliance is perhaps to be placed on the genealogies of the two royal families given by Herodotus (VII 204, VIII 131). Leonidas (r. 488—480) and Leotychidas (r. 491—469), with whom we are on sure historical ground, are represented as fifteenth in descent from Eurysthenes and Procles respectively. According to all analogies therefore we should expect that the two latter flourished not very long before the middle of the tenth century. In other words the date given by Eratosthenes for the 'Return of the Heracleidai' would seem to be from a century to a century and a half too early. A very reasonable explanation of the difficulty has been suggested by Prof. Meyer who points out that several passages in Herodotus' history seem to imply the reckoning of a generation at forty years[2]. Among the figures given we find (II 145) Heracles dated about 1330. Cleomenes, his descendant in the twentieth generation, was born about 530, or at all events not much later. For Eurysthenes and Procles, in the fifth generation from Heracles, this would give about 1130, which is not very far from the date fixed by Eratosthenes.

[1] For England from its unification under Alfred the Great to the present time the average is about twenty years; for France from 840 to 1793 it is between twenty-three and twenty-four years.

[2] *Forsch. z. alten Geschichte*, p. 170 f. The reckoning is not due to Herodotus himself but taken over by him from an earlier writer. Prof. Meyer suggests as its author Hecataeus, who was a contemporary of Cleomenes.

It is to be remembered in the first place that the date fixed for Eurysthenes and Procles is apparently that of their birth, and, secondly, that Eratosthenes' scheme is probably only a modification of a previously existing system, other varieties of which are quoted by Prof. Meyer[1]. Indeed it would not require any great exercise of ingenuity to point out traces of a more or less symmetrical distribution of the period covered by the reigns of the early Spartan kings[2]. But, apart from any such speculations, we can hardly doubt, in the light of Prof. Meyer's showing, that the date for Eurysthenes and Procles is derived ultimately from a calculation based on the genealogies rather than from any contemporary written record or tradition. The genealogies themselves of course may represent tradition, so far as they are not interpolated[3], but they point, as we have seen, to a much later date than that which we have been discussing[4]. If we substitute 32×15 for 40×15, starting from the birth of Cleomenes, we are brought to about the year 1000. That must be regarded as the date really indicated by Spartan tradition for the birth of Eurysthenes and Procles.

We may now turn for a moment to the genealogies of the other Heraclid families, namely those of Argos, Messenia and Corinth. The first of these places Pheidon in the sixth generation, according to one version, in the ninth according to another,

---

[1] *Op. cit.* p. 178 ff.

[2] Eratosthenes reckons nearly 320 years from the accession (birth) of Eurysthenes to that of Alcamenes in the ninth generation, while the reigns of the father, grandfather, great-grandfather and great-great-grandfather of the latter make up 159 years. Sosibius, who reckoned by the Eurypontid dynasty, appears to have had a similar period of 320 years from Procles to Theopompos, although his dates were different from those of Eratosthenes—1091/0 to 771/0 according to Prof. Meyer (*op. cit.* p. 179 f.). The accession of Theopompos was equated with that of Alcamenes by Eratosthenes. Possibly these periods were originally sub-divisions of a longer period of 640 years, reckoned from the fortieth year of Cleomenes (or Leonidas?).

[3] Two names (Prytanis and Eunomos) in the Eurypontid list are generally regarded with doubt, but none of the Agiad names is really of a suspicious character. The fact that Agis and Eurypon are not the first names in the genealogies ought not to be used as an argument against the trustworthiness of the tradition. In many Teutonic genealogies—e.g. the Gothic, Frankish (Merovingian), Kentish, East Anglian and Mercian—the name which performs patronymic function is not that which stands first in the list.

[4] Prof. Meyer's view is not that the chronologists fixed too early a date for the Dorian invasion, but that the early parts of the genealogies themselves are unhistorical.

from Temenos, the uncle of Eurysthenes and Procles. Unfortunately different dates are assigned for Pheidon. The earliest, which is not generally accepted, places his reign about the middle of the eighth century. But even this, taking the longer form of the genealogy, does not carry us appreciably farther back than the Agiad list. The Corinthian genealogy places the last king, who is said to have been killed in 747, in the thirteenth generation from Heracles. This would agree with the longer form of the Argive genealogy; several of the names however are generally regarded as suspicious. The Messenian genealogy is materially shorter.

Apart from these Dorian genealogies there are some notices relating to the ancestry of persons belonging to other parts of Greece, which must not be ignored. Herodotus (II 143) states that Hecataeus, who was a prominent man at the beginning of the fifth century, claimed to be descended in the sixteenth (i.e. fifteenth) generation from a god. This probably takes us back to the Heroic Age, when divine parentage is common, whereas later it appears to be almost, if not entirely, unknown[1]. Again, it is believed that the genealogy of the Philaidai at Athens, which actually survives, though only in a corrupt form[2], placed Philaios, the son of Aias, in the twelfth generation above Hippocleides, who was archon in 566. Further, according to Pausanias (I 11), Tharypas, king of the Molossoi, who was born soon after the middle of the fifth century, claimed to be descended in the fifteenth or sixteenth generation from Pyrrhos the son of Achilles. It will be seen that, though these genealogies do not agree exactly, the discrepancy is not very great. They seem to indicate the existence of a belief that persons who flourished in the first half of the fifth century were removed by about fifteen generations from the Heroic Age.

On the other hand Pindar (*Pyth.* IV 9 ff.) in an ode written in 466 and addressed to Arcesilaos IV, king of Cyrene, places that king's seventh ancestor, Battos I, in the sixteenth generation

---

[1] Prof. Meyer (*op. cit.* p. 173 and note) cites the case of Telamon the son of Poseidon, ancestor of the priests of Poseidon at Halicarnassos, whom he places after the Return of the Heracleidai. But the question is a complicated one. The genealogy cannot be used for our purpose, as we do not know where it ends.

[2] Cf. Töpffer, *Attische Genealogie*, p. 278 f. ; Meyer, *op. cit.* p. 174, note.

from Euphemos the Argonaut, a contemporary of Heracles. This exceeds even the Agiad reckoning, for Pleistarchos, the representative of that family reigning in 466, was only in the twenty-first generation from Heracles. From the other non-Heraclid genealogies we should have expected that the number of generations to Arcesilaos would be about what is recorded for Battos I[1].

Whatever may be the explanation of this case, it will be seen that the other non-Heraclid genealogies are shorter than that of the Agidai by at least three generations—if we equate Philaios, Pyrrhos (Neoptolemos) and the grandson of Hecataeus' god with Aristomachos the grandfather of Eurysthenes. The dates which they indicate for the 'floruit' of these persons are in no case earlier than the middle of the tenth century. As to the relative value of the two traditions we have nothing to guide us, and the same remark applies to the Greek genealogical evidence in general. Two points however must be insisted upon: (i) that the calculations of scholars of the Alexandrian age, or even earlier times, are not to be interpreted as evidence of tradition; (ii) that the evidence of tradition, whatever be its value, brings the end of the Heroic Age at least towards the close of the eleventh century.

Apart from the evidence discussed above, unsatisfactory as it doubtless is, chronological data for the Heroic Age itself seem to be entirely wanting. We know however that a highly advanced civilisation flourished in the Aegean in early times, and that it was succeeded by a long period in which both art and general culture were at a very low ebb. This latter period, which is commonly known as 'geometrical' from the type of art which prevailed in it, lasted, so far as one can judge, until about the end of the eighth century, at which time oriental influence began to make its appearance. The 'orientalising' period again continued down to the beginning of the classical age. It is a common and natural hypothesis to equate the low-watermark of culture early in the geometrical period with the generations

---

[1] Battos I is believed to have founded Cyrene about 630. It may be observed that the interval between that date and 466 is surprisingly short for the lapse of seven generations.

immediately following the Dorian conquest of the Peloponnesos. But unfortunately we cannot thereby obtain any certain date for the latter, since Greece appears to have had little contact with the outside world during the geometrical period.

In recent years some advance has been made through the operations carried out by the British School at Sparta, which is perhaps the most important site for our purpose. From the stratification of the deposits Mr Dawkins, the director, has come to the conclusion that the earliest temple and altar at the sanctuary of Artemis Orthia date from the ninth or even the tenth century[1]. The temple, which must have been one of the earliest known, appears to have been a narrow and unpretentious structure of crude brick and timber. Some geometrical sherds were found beneath the floor, a fact which shows that the sanctuary had been in use somewhat earlier. If the sanctuary was founded at the beginning of the Dorian settlement at Sparta it is obvious that this result agrees well enough with the date indicated for the conquest by tradition. No relics of pre-geometrical times appear to have been found.

When we turn back to the times of the earlier civilisation it is much easier to establish chronological equations; for the presence of Egyptian objects among Aegean remains and of Aegean objects or representations of Aegean objects in Egypt shows that there was frequent communication between the two areas. Thus there is little doubt that certain Cretan remains date from periods contemporaneous with the twelfth and Hyksos dynasties. Others again clearly belong to the period of the eighteenth dynasty—at all events the earlier part of it. As to the date of the destruction of the Cretan palaces opinions still differ considerably; the most recent statement by Dr Evans is in favour of about 1350[2]. But this catastrophe did not bring the Aegean civilisation to an end. We find inscriptions dating from the subsequent period (Late Minoan III) apparently quite

---

[1] *British School at Athens*, Ann. XIV, pp. 3, 18 f.

[2] Cf. Hawes, *Crete the Fore-runner of Greece*, p. 18. A much later date is favoured by Dr Dörpfeld (*Ath. Mitteilungen*, XXXII 602), whose views on Cretan chronology differ greatly from those of English archaeologists. To this question we shall have to refer again in a later chapter.

similar to those discovered in the earlier stratum, and the various artistic types, though decadent, show no breach of continuity. Indeed 'Mycenean' influence seems to have been more widespread (e.g. in Thessaly and Italy) at this time than in any earlier period. In Egypt vases of the same type are depicted in the wall-paintings on the tomb of Rameses III, who died about 1170. After this time however traces of Mycenean influence are rarely found in that country.

Within the last few years it has come to be noticed that the deposits dating from the last Mycenean period fall into two well-marked groups. The remarks made above, as to the art of Late Minoan III being a continuation of that of the preceding period, apply properly only to the first of these groups—represented by the cemeteries of Zafer Papoura (Cnossos) and Phaistos, the late Mycenean megaron at Hagia Triada (also in Crete) and the late palace at Phylakopi in Melos. Other deposits, represented by the tombs found at Mouliana, Milatos, Kavousi and Erganos (all in Crete), though they have certain features in common with the former group, yet at the same time show a number of characteristics which are entirely new. Of these the most important are the practice of cremation and the use of fibulae and iron weapons, all of which are unknown in the Aegean before this time. From a careful study of the pottery found in these deposits Dr D. Mackenzie[1] has come to the conclusion that it belongs to the same period as the famous 'Warrior Vase' from Mycenae. This again is obviously contemporary with a painted stele, likewise representing warriors, which was found in one of the latest graves in the lower town at the same place. Fibulae also were found here in the same group of graves. The importance of these observations lies in the fact that the armature of the warriors depicted on the vase and the stele corresponds in all essentials to what is described in the Homeric poems. This had already been pointed out by Prof. Ridgeway[2]; but many scholars have attributed both objects to a much later period. Now however in view of the sequence

---

[1] *British School at Athens*, Ann. XIII, p. 423 ff.

[2] *Early Age of Greece*, p. 317. Representations of both the Vase and the Stele are given in the same work (p. 313 f.).

which Dr Mackenzie has succeeded in tracing, in Cretan pottery and other articles, from the time of the destruction of the palaces onwards, it appears that the latter view can hardly be maintained. Lastly, Dr Mackenzie has pointed out that all the above deposits differ radically from those of the strict geo-metrical period found in cemeteries at Cnossos and Courtes and in the 'beehive' tomb near Kavousi (all in Crete). There are clear indications that all the latter belong to a subsequent time.

As a result of his investigations then Dr Mackenzie has come to the conclusion that three well-marked periods can be distinguished in Cretan history, after the destruction of the palaces. But further, he believes that each of these periods coincides with a new settlement in the island—the true geo-metrical period with the Dorian settlement, the 'sub-Mycenean' with that of the Achaeans, and the last true Mycenean period (Late Minoan III) with a settlement of Pelasgoi. The evidence of the deposits found at Sparta and elsewhere tends distinctly to favour the first of these identifications. For, though geo-metrical art was by no means confined to the Dorians, it may be presumed that their settlement was the latest of those which took place in Crete. Some scholars hold that they came there from the Peloponnesos, while others place their settlement in the island prior to the invasion of the peninsula—and ancient authority can be obtained for both views. But in either case it is improbable that the two events were separated by a long interval. Again, the identification of the second or sub-Mycenean period with that of Achaean settlement is rendered extremely probable by the resemblance which deposits of this period show to objects and customs described in the Homeric poems, e.g. in regard to armature and the use of fibulae and cremation. In the poems the Achaeans are clearly represented as dominant even in Crete, while in Greece itself, as we have seen, the exist-ence of other nationalities is practically ignored.

In regard to the earliest of the three settlements Dr Mac-kenzie's theory may be open to more serious question. The ethnical affinities of the Pelasgoi are still quite obscure. Again, although new types, apparently derived from the mainland, do occur at this time, the break of continuity with the preceding age does not seem to be anything like so marked as in the subsequent periods. It is scarcely impossible that the destruction of the palaces may be due to naval warfare or piracy on a large scale, or even to commotions within the island itself. For our purpose however this part of Dr Mackenzie's theory is of minor importance[1].

In other respects at all events the theory seems to provide a very satisfactory explanation of the phenomena. We have seen that the Spartan evidence, whether traditional or archaeological, affords no justification for dating the Dorian invasion very long before—or after—1000 B.C. Now we find very good evidence for two distinct periods of culture between that event and the destruction of the Cretan palaces, which took place probably in the fourteenth century. The later of these periods is the one with which we are chiefly concerned; for Greek tradition universally places the Heroic Age in times immediately preceding the Dorian invasion. It is therefore a fact of great significance that the deposits of this age agree in so striking a manner with the evidence of the Homeric poems. As to the relative duration of the two periods (Late Minoan III and sub-Mycenean or Achaean) archaeologists apparently have not as yet ventured to express an opinion. But it may be observed that the poems themselves give no indication that the Achaean dominion was believed to be of recent growth. The Cretan king Idomeneus is one of the oldest leaders at Troy, and his grandfather is said to have reigned at Cnossos before him. The evidence of the poems then favours the idea that even in Crete Achaean dominion lasted at least a century.

This brings us back nearly to times when, fortunately, historical evidence is available once more, namely from the Egyptian monuments. During the thirteenth and twelfth centuries Egypt was threatened on several occasions by formidable armies. During the reign of Merenptah, probably about 1220,

---

[1] Dr Mackenzie's theory would certainly gain in probability if it could be shown that the Pelasgoi were identical with the Pulesatha or Philistines (cf. p. 188). The arguments in favour of such an identification are obvious enough; but they are scarcely of such a nature as to carry conviction. The appearance of -st- for -gsk- in the name is perhaps hardly to be regarded as an insuperable difficulty; for we know nothing of the languages involved or of the sound-changes to which they were subject.

it was attacked by a host of Libyans and "foreign soldiers of the Libyans" whom "the miserable Libyan had led hither[1]." The names given to the confederates are Akaiuasha, Thuirsha (Turusha), Shakalesha (Shakarusha) and Shardina. Very early in the next century, during the reign of Rameses III, a fresh attack was made from the same quarter. A few years later Rameses encountered both by land and sea a great host coming from the north. "The Isles were restless, disturbed among themselves at one and the same time. No land stood before them, beginning from Kheta (Cappadocia and Cilicia), Kedi (the 'circling' of the Syrian coast at the Gulf of Iskanderun), Carchemish, Arvad and Alashiya. They destroyed them, and assembled in their camp in the midst of Amar (*Amurru*; Palestine)[2]." The invaders here are called Shardina, Pulesatha (or Purusatha), Vashasha, Tchakaray (Zakar) and Danaau (or Danauna)[3]. Other Shardina appear to have been fighting on the side of the Egyptians. About a century earlier the Hittites brought a great confederacy against Rameses II. Among the names given here are Luka, Pidasa, Kalakisha, Dardenui and Masa[4]. On this occasion also we find Shardina in the Egyptian army. In the Tell-el-Amarna tablets, which date from shortly before the middle of the fourteenth century, we hear of Sirdana (apparently the same people) serving under the Egyptians in Palestine, and of attacks made upon the coast by Lukki, who are believed to be identical with the Luka[5].

Unfortunately scholars have not yet been able to come to any general agreement as to the identification of most of these names. It is commonly held that Pulesatha and Luka denote the Philistines and Lycians respectively. Many writers also identify the Shardina with the Sardinians and the Shakalesha with the Siceloi, but others connect these names with Sardis

---

[1] Cf. Hall, *The Oldest Civilization of Greece*, p. 180 f.; *Ann. of the Brit. School at Athens*, VIII, p. 180; Petrie, *History of Egypt*, p. 108 ff.

[2] Hall, *Ann. of the Brit. School*, VIII 183; cf. also Breasted, *Ancient Records of Egypt*, IV, p. 37 f.

[3] Prof. Breasted (*l.c.*) gives these names as *Peleset*, *Thekel* (i.e. Zakar), *Shekelesh* (omitted above), *Denyen* and *Weshesh*.

[4] Cf. Hall, *op. cit.* p. 177 f.

[5] Cf. Breasted, *History of Egypt*, pp. 336, 386; Hall, *op. cit.* p. 176 f.

and Sagalassos in Asia Minor. Other identifications which
have received more or less assent are those of Akaiuasha,
Thuirsha, Danaau, Dardenui and Masa with the Achaeans,
Tyrrhenians, Danaoi, Dardanoi and Mysians, and of Vashasha
and Pidasa with the inhabitants of Oaxos (in Crete) and Pedasos
(in Caria) respectively. It has been supposed also that the
Tchakaray, who are mentioned occasionally as mariners in later
times, likewise belonged to Crete.

In spite of the large element of doubt attaching to most of
these identifications one important conclusion may be drawn with
safety, namely that several of the nations mentioned had come
from a considerable distance. Even those scholars who deny
the references to Sicily and Sardinia hold that nearly all parts
of the Aegean are represented in the lists. The inscriptions
frequently speak of the invaders as coming from the sea or from
islands. Thus the Pulesatha are said to be " in the midst of the
sea." Again the king " slaughtered the Danauna in their isles[1]."
We find also the expressions " Vashasha of the sea," " Shardina
of the sea," " Thuirsha of the sea[2]." Such terms are said to be
often used loosely; but under the eighteenth and nineteenth
dynasties the territories of the Hittite kingdom in Syria and
Cappadocia had become so well known to the Egyptians that it
is incredible that any of the peoples of that region can be
meant. The appearance too and the armature of the Shardina,
as portrayed on the monuments, are quite incompatible with the
supposition that they belonged to any of the countries round
the south-east of the Mediterranean.

We have seen that the northern invasion repelled by
Rameses III was preceded by 'disturbances in the isles,' while
the lands of the Hittites and their neighbours had apparently
been overrun by the invaders before the attack upon Egypt.
Now it has been noted that the great Hittite kingdom (in
Cappadocia) appears to have been destroyed about the same
time. In explanation of this the theory has recently been put
forward[3] that the invasion repelled by Rameses III was closely

---

[1] Cf. W. M. Müller, *Asien und Europa*, pp. 361, 363; Petrie, *History of Egypt*,
III, p. 150.

[2] Cf. W. M. Müller, *op. cit.* pp. 361, 371 ; Petrie, *op. cit.* pp. 151, 162.

[3] Cf. Meyer, *S.-B. der Akad. zu Berlin*, 1908, p. 18 f.

connected with that irruption of Thraco-Phrygian peoples into Asia Minor to which we have already referred (p. 178). It will be seen that this theory has an important bearing on the Homeric question ; for in the Iliad we find the Thraco-Phrygian peoples already fully established in Asia Minor, and no hint is given that their settlement there was believed to be in any sense recent.

But it is by no means impossible that the 'disturbances in the isles' may refer to a displacement of population in a different quarter—which may or may not be connected with the Phrygian settlement in Asia Minor.   The movement against Egypt was, in part at least, a maritime one, and when Rameses is said to have slaughtered the invaders in their islands the reference can hardly be to the old Hittite kingdom, which had long been known to the Egyptians.   Surely it is more natural to connect the 'disturbances' with those national movements in the southern Aegean which eventually brought the Mycenean civilisation to an end.   We have seen that the last period of this civilisation is believed to have begun in the fourteenth century and to have lasted some considerable time.   The convulsions of Rameses' time (the early years of the twelfth century) may therefore mark a stage in the movements which brought about its destruction.

In any case it is from the Egyptian monuments of this period that we obtain the clearest evidence for contact between the true Mycenean civilisation and that ' sub-Mycenean' or ' Achaean' type which followed it.   The warriors of the invading forces[1] are represented as armed with swords of the regular Mycenean pattern or with spears of no very great length.   Some of them —the Pulesatha and Tchakaray—wear a peculiar head-dress, apparently made of feathers[2], which recalls the type used in later times by the Lycians according to Herodotus (VII 92).   On the other hand the Shardina are depicted with very elaborate

---

[1] A considerable number of the figures are reproduced in W. M. Müller's *Asien und Europa* (cap. 27, 28) ; many also in the Histories of Egypt by Meyer and Petrie.

[2] This head-dress is figured on a discus recently found at Phaistos (Crete) among deposits dating from 'Middle Minoan III' (cent. XVII ?).   The discus, if not actually of Cretan origin, is said to come clearly from some district under the influence of Cretan civilisation.   Cf. Meyer, *S.-B. d. Akad. zu Berlin*, 1910, p. 1022 ff.

helmets[1], which, except that they have no plumes, are almost identical with those borne by the figures on the Warrior Vase (cf. p. 185). The Shardina and many of the Pulesatha also carry round shields, held in one hand, as in the case of the warriors represented on the Vase[2] and the Stele. This fact is especially noteworthy, since the round shield seems to have been totally foreign not only to the Egyptians themselves, but also to the Hittites and all neighbouring peoples[3], while even in the Aegean area it was apparently not used in centres of Mycenean civilisation[4]. On the other hand both these features correspond to the type of armature described in the Homeric poems. It would not be correct of course to say that the portraits of the Shardina might be taken as faithful representations of Homeric warriors. We find no trace of greaves, while the body-armour is of a less elaborate type than that described in the poems[5]. The Homeric type of armature—represented by the Warrior Vase as well as in the poems—belongs clearly to a later stage of development than the Shardina type, and therefore probably to a later age than the early part of the twelfth century. Yet there is sufficient resemblance between the two to render it more than likely that the one is descended from the other.

Whatever may have been the causes which brought about the movement encountered by Rameses III, some of the other references point distinctly to bands of mercenary soldiers, rather than to national migrations. This is especially clear in the case

---

[1] They are said to be white; but it is difficult to believe that they are not metal—possibly bronze overlaid with tin (cf. Il. xxiii 560 ff.).

[2] The shields figured on the Vase (apparently also those on the Stele) seem to have a section cut out of them; but they can hardly be regarded otherwise than as round shields. Cf. Lippold, *Münchener Arch. Studien*, p. 406.

[3] Except the Assyrians (cf. p. 203, note); but there the evidence comes from much later times.

[4] It occurs probably on the discus from Phaistos (cf. Meyer *l. c.*) and on a porcelain fragment from the third shaft-grave at Mycenae (cf. Reichel, *über hom. Waffen*, p. 58) —both times in conjunction with head-dresses of the Pulesatha or Shardina types—as well as on ivory objects from Enkomi in Cyprus (cf. Evans, *Journ. Anthr. Inst.*, xxx 209), here also in conjunction with similar armature, though only the lower part of the helmet is visible.

[5] Many of the figures, both Shardina and Pulesatha, wear body-armour of some kind. Greaves are first found at Enkomi.

of the Shardina, who are mentioned for the first time as serving
under the Egyptians in Palestine. But the earliest reference—
in the Tell-el-Amarna letters—carries us back to the destruction
of the Cretan palaces, if Dr Evans' date for this catastrophe is
correct. It has been remarked that, in striking contrast with
Mycenae and other early centres of civilisation in Greece, the
Cretan palaces were almost entirely unfortified ; and the explanation commonly given of this fact is that their owners ruled
the seas. If this is true we must conclude that the earliest
maritime expeditions of the Shardina and their confederates did
not take place without their consent.

In the course of this discussion we have seen that, though
historical evidence for the Greek Heroic Age is entirely wanting,
later tradition points to the eleventh century as the time to
which the poems and legends refer; and further, that, unsatisfactory as it doubtless is, this evidence is corroborated to a
considerable extent by the results of archaeological investigation.
In much earlier times various parts of the Greek world possessed
a high civilisation, which has left remains of magnificent palaces
and many elaborate works of art.   The evidence of these remains
does not correspond at all to the state of society revealed in the
poems. But at the close of this earlier period many new objects
—belonging, it would seem, to a new population—make their
appearance ; and these latter do fulfil the conditions required.
Lastly, it is of interest to note that from the fourteenth to the
twelfth century Egypt and the Levant were frequently visited
by bands of soldiers, who seem to have come from the Aegean
or neighbouring regions and who outwardly bear a somewhat
striking resemblance to the warriors described in the poems.   It
would appear that at this time the East must have been more
familiar to the Greek world than Greek records would lead us
to expect.   This is the more noteworthy since during the
following centuries the Greeks seem to have had but little
contact with foreign nations.

CHAPTER X.

THE HOMERIC POEMS.

It has been mentioned that, according to the theory now most commonly accepted, the Homeric poems were not the work of one author or even of one generation—that on the contrary they grew up gradually in the course of several hundred years, reaching their final form (in the case of the Odyssey) perhaps not before the middle of the seventh century. We must now review briefly the evidence on which this theory is based.

The earliest historical references to the poems reach back only to the beginning of the sixth century, and even these are not altogether satisfactory. Cleisthenes, tyrant of Sicyon, according to Herodotus (V 67) prohibited rhapsodists from reciting the Homeric poems, because they were full of the praises of Argos and its people. But the reference here is perhaps rather to the Thebais or Epigonoi than the Iliad. Again, it is said that when Athens and Megara were disputing about the possession of Salamis, both parties appealed to the authority of Homer in support of their contentions. If this story may be trusted it is of importance as showing that the poems were generally venerated at such an early date. And though all the evidence is late[1], the form in which the passage in question (Il. II 557 f.) has survived does clearly suggest Athenian influence.

References in the works of other poets carry us back to a considerably earlier period. It has already been mentioned that Callinos is said to have attributed the Thebais to Homer, from which we may infer that poems under this name were already

---

[1] Plutarch, *Solon*, cap. 10; Diogenes Laertius, *Solon*, cap. 48, etc. In some form or other the story was known to Aristotle (*Rhet.* I 15).

known. Archilochos, who likewise flourished before the middle of the seventh century, seems to have attributed the Margites to Homer[1]. The extant fragments of his works also contain several passages which apparently show Homeric influence[2]. Terpandros, probably an older contemporary of Archilochos, is said to have invented a musical accompaniment for the Homeric poems[3]. In Hesiodic poetry we find a number of references to heroic subjects. The Catalogue appears to have dealt with certain adventures of Odysseus, which were probably derived from the Odyssey[4].

This evidence, vague and somewhat uncertain as it is, renders it probable that Homeric poetry was in existence before the seventh century. Further than this we cannot hope for any direct external evidence, for the authors cited are the earliest of whom we know anything worth mention. Indeed the age of the various Hesiodic poems themselves is very problematical. It is customary now to attribute the Theogony and the Works and Days to the close of the eighth century and the other poems to the seventh. But Herodotus (II 53) referred Hesiod, as well as Homer, to a period about 400 years before his own time, i.e. to about the middle of the ninth century.

Turning now to the internal evidence, we may at all events regard one fact as established, namely that the subject-matter was determined at a period considerably anterior to those of which we have been speaking. It is not merely that the persons mentioned are uniformly referred to the Heroic Age, for we have yet to discuss the possibility that all the characters of this age are fictitious. But we have also to take into account the ethnographical indications contained in the poems. There is no hint of the presence of Dorians in the Peloponnesos, nor of the existence of Ionic states in Asia Minor or even in the Cyclades[5]; indeed the scheme of tribal or political geography which they present is far removed from anything we find even in the earliest

---

[1] Archilochos, Fragm. 153 (in Bergk's *Poetae Lyrici Graeci*).
[2] Cf. Croisset, *Rev. des deux Mondes*, 1907, 5, p. 605.
[3] Plutarch, *De Musica*, III 9.
[4] Hesiod, Fragm. 65 f. (in Rzach's edition, 1902).
[5] In Od. VI 162 ff. there is a reference to the sanctuary of Apollo in Delos.

records of the historical period. We shall see later that the same remark holds good with regard to the system of government depicted in the poems, e.g. in the universal prevalence of kingship, and so also with their indications as to social organisation, religion and even ethical standards. Then there is the fact that in references to weapons bronze is far more frequently mentioned than iron; yet it is generally agreed that iron must have been in common use by the tenth century, while some scholars would refer its introduction to a much earlier date. Lastly, we may take note of certain passages and expressions which seem to contain reminiscences of the prehistoric civilisation of the Aegean —a civilisation which, as we have seen, had passed its zenith in the fourteenth century and which was probably altogether submerged in the convulsions which accompanied the Dorian and Ionic migrations. Among such reminiscences we may probably count the descriptions of the palaces of Menelaos and Alcinoos and the use of such terms as κύανος. Of course it is not to be supposed that any part of the poems goes back to the period of the early civilisation. Yet the features noted above seem to me to point quite clearly to a time when some of the ancient palaces were still known and perhaps still inhabited. Hence it is not merely the case that the poems are concerned exclusively with characters of the Heroic Age. We are bound to conclude further that the environment in which these characters are placed is in general such as belonged to the same period. This of course involves the existence of a verbal tradition practically from the Heroic Age itself. Indeed, we may say that it probably involves a poetic tradition, for we have no evidence for the existence of traditional prose narratives, whereas references to the cultivation of poetry in early times are fairly numerous.

Now it is generally agreed that the Heroic Age—or perhaps we should say the type of civilisation and the ethnographical conditions with which this age is associated—cannot have lasted much beyond the close of the eleventh century. Hence the date accepted by many scholars for the completion of the Odyssey (cf. p. 169) involves a period of more than three centuries, during which the Homeric poems were in process of formation. That is a long period for continued composition in one subject, and it

13—2

will be well now to review briefly the evidence on which this theory rests.

Kirchhoff[1] dated the 'later redaction' of the Odyssey between Ol. 30 and Ol. 50, or at all events not much before Ol. 30 (B.C. 656). To this conclusion he was led primarily by the reference to the voyage of the Argo in XII 59—72. It is probable enough that this passage implies acquaintance with a poem dealing with Iason's adventures; but the same can hardly be said of Kirchhoff's further suggestion, viz. that this lost poem must have been composed some considerable time after the colonisation of Cyzicos[2]. The accounts which we have of the travels and adventures of the Argonauts can scarcely be said to indicate that the earliest poems on this subject were composed at a time when the Black Sea was already familiar to the Greeks; on the other hand travellers from time to time may have penetrated into that region centuries before the foundation of Cyzicos[3].

Others have sought to show that the later parts of the poem betray an intimate acquaintance with the western seas, such as would be possible only after the development of Corinthian maritime enterprise about the close of the eighth century, whereas the knowledge of the same regions shown by the earlier parts is of the vaguest description[4]. Here the evidence is derived chiefly from the references to Sicily (Σικανίη) and the

---

[1] *Die Composition der Odyssee*, p. 85 f.; *Die hom. Odyssee*[2], p. 287 ff.

[2] The references to the spring Ἀρτακίη (cf. Od. X 107 f.) cannot be regarded as conclusive, since such connections are capable of more than one explanation—even if we bear in mind the name of the adjacent mountain (Ἀρτάκη). The mountain itself may have been known to the Greeks from early times.

[3] In view of the evidence pointed out at the close of the last chapter one will do well to hesitate before denying the possibility of such distant expeditions in early times. But any communication which may have existed must have been interrupted by the invasions of the Bithynoi and Treres, probably in the ninth and eighth centuries. Note may also be taken here of what is said about the Cimmerioi in Od. XI 14—19; cf. Meyer, *Geschichte des Alterthums*, II, pp. 367 f., 445 f.

[4] Cf. especially Wilamowitz-Möllendorff, *Hom. Unt.* p. 24 ff. The theory that the Ephyre of II 328 must be a different place from the Ephyre of I 259 seems to me very problematical if the author of the second book had only a vague knowledge of the geography of western Greece. Again, if Ilos Mermerides (I 259) is taken from the story of the Argo, is it really necessary that the source should be a different one from that referred to in XII 69 ff.?

Siceloi, Alybas (traditionally placed in the Gulf of Otranto, but perhaps rather a coined name) and Temesa, which is identified with Tempsa in Calabria. This theory seems to me to be open to much the same objections as the other. It is clear now that in prehistoric times the south of Italy was intimately connected with the eastern coast of the Adriatic, and we have no ground for denying that the former may have been known to Greek traders or pirates long before the date of the earliest colonies.

A third argument, and one which has exercised a much wider influence, is based on the relationship of certain portions of the poems to the lost Cyclic poems (Cypria, etc.). It is held for instance that the Catalogues in Il. II, at all events the Trojan catalogue, were taken from the Cypria, and again that in the Nekyia (Od. XI) and elsewhere use has been made of the Little Iliad and the Nostoi, as well as the Cypria. But, granting the correctness of these hypotheses, no conclusions as to date can be drawn from them unless the dates of the lost poems themselves are established. We have seen however that such is not really the case; it is admitted that the attribution of these poems to Arctinos, Lesches and others does not occur until very late times. All that can be said is that they appear to have contained certain 'post-Homeric' features, such as purification for manslaughter (in the Aithiopis). With these we shall have to deal later. There is no need however to suppose that the lost poems were any more homogeneous than the Iliad and Odyssey.

Again it is thought that certain passages betray the influence of Hesiodic poetry, while others indicate genealogies or relationships which are at variance with statements contained in the latter[1]. Among the former we may note especially the list of women in the Nekyia (Od. XI 235—327[2]), which is compared with the Hesiodic Catalogue of heroines. This evidence would be useful for chronological purposes if we knew (i) when Hesiod lived, (ii) that he was the first to compose catalogues of this kind.

---

[1] From this it has been argued that the 'Odyssey' known to Hesiod must have differed greatly from the poem which has come down to us. But it is to be remembered that there are quite as noticeable discrepancies between the Odyssey and the Iliad.

[2] We shall have occasion later to notice more than one point in which this passage departs from the customary Homeric standards.

But unfortunately neither of these propositions can be admitted. To the first we have already referred. The majority of scholars hold that Hesiod cannot have lived much after the end of the eighth century. But there is nothing to show that he did not live before that time; for no sound argument can be founded on the last verses of the Theogony. As for the Catalogue it belongs to a class of poetry of which the beginnings may go back to a remote antiquity. The presumption is that it originated in times when descent was still traced through the mother.

On internal grounds many arguments have been brought forward for the purpose of showing that the poems in their present form have undergone a long process of development. With discrepancies in the narrative itself we need not concern ourselves. They are doubtless of importance for determining the question of single or composite authorship, but they do not necessarily point to authorship of quite different ages. For instance, one poet may have conceived of the Achaean camp as fortified, another as without fortifications. But that does not prove that the two poets were not contemporary, for it will not be disputed that the people of the Heroic Age were capable of building fortifications. Again, it may be that the original poem on the ‘Wrath of Achilles’ did not originally contain Books II— VII. But, apart from one or two details which we shall discuss presently, there is nothing to suggest that these books are the product of an entirely different period.

We may even take what is perhaps the most extreme case, that of the Doloneia. This book is joined on very loosely to what precedes, and its contents are practically disregarded in the rest of the Iliad[1]. Some critics even in ancient times seem to have believed that it did not originally belong to the poem. Moreover it contains a number of features peculiar to itself and several expressions which are regarded as indications of lateness. In particular there are some striking parallels to the passages in

---

[1] Except probably in XIV 9 ff., as has been ingeniously pointed out by Mr Lang (*Homer and his Age*, p. 276 ff.). In the same chapter Mr Lang shows that several features in the Doloneia which have been interpreted as marks of lateness may very well be due to the peculiar circumstances of the situation.

the Odyssey, and it is held that in certain cases they are due to direct influence from the latter[1]. But, granting all this, we are still not in a position to decide whether the chronological difference between the Doloneia and the earlier parts of the Iliad is to be reckoned at three centuries or two or one[2].

As no definite results can be attained from such considerations as these we will now confine our attention to arguments which are founded upon real or supposed differences of culture. The most important class of evidence for our purpose is that which relates to the use of the metals. Both bronze and iron are frequently mentioned and there can be no doubt that both were well known. But it has been observed that weapons are nearly always said to be of bronze ($\chi a\lambda\kappa\acute{o}s$, $\chi\acute{a}\lambda\kappa\epsilon o\nu$ $\check{\epsilon}\gamma\chi o s$, etc.[3]), whereas iron is usually mentioned either as a substance or in reference to tools, especially hatchets[4]. Only in seven verses do we hear of iron weapons, even if we include in this category the knives mentioned in Il. XVIII 34 and XXIII 30. Two verses (ib. VII 141, 143 f.) speak of an iron club and one (ib. IV 123) of an arrowhead, while the other two (Od. XVI 294, XIX 13) refer to the arms in Odysseus' house collectively.

The obvious inference from the statistics is that iron tools came into use before iron weapons, and though this was long thought incredible it has recently been shown that there is some

---

[1] Gemöll, *Hermes*, XV 557 ff. (cf. XVIII 308 ff.). Cf. also Shewan, *Class. Quarterly*, IV 73 ff., where this view is rejected.

[2] Mr Lang (*Homer and his Age*, p. 265 ff.) has called attention to the fact that in v. 261 ff. Odysseus is represented as wearing a cap of a type which appears to have been in use during the Mycenean age. If it could be shown that the article in question was peculiar to that period, the lateness of the book would certainly be open to serious question.

[3] Bronze is mentioned 279 times in the Iliad and 80 times in the Odyssey. In a large proportion of these cases the reference is to weapons. Cf. Helbig, *Das homerische Epos*, p. 329 ff.

[4] Iron is mentioned altogether 48 times. In nine cases it is spoken of merely as a substance—a possession or article of trade. To these we may add fifteen more in which the word is used metaphorically as a standard of hardness, etc., and one (Od. IX 393) which refers to the testing of iron in water. Iron tools or implements are mentioned thirteen times, apart from the two references to knives given above. We hear also of iron chains (Od. I 204), the iron axle-tree of a (divine) chariot-wheel (Il. V 723), and the iron door of Tartarus (ib. VIII 15); cf. Cauer, *Grundfragen der Homer-kritik*[2], p. 281 ff.

evidence for the prevalence of such conditions in Palestine[1]. Moreover a somewhat striking confirmation of the Homeric evidence was furnished by the excavations at Troy, where a small lump of unwrought iron was found among deposits belonging apparently to the fifth stratum[2]. It has been compared, and doubtless rightly, with the lump mentioned in Il. XXIII 826 ff., though the latter must have been much larger. The presumption is that, like this, it was intended for some tool or agricultural implement; for all the weapons found at Troy—few as they were unfortunately—up to the seventh stratum were of bronze. It is probable therefore that the use of the metals not only in the fifth stratum but also in the sixth—the great Mycenean fortress— was similar to that which is indicated in the Homeric poems.

For those who believe that these poems are the work of a single author the words "Iron does of itself attract a man[3]" (Od. XVI 294, XIX 13) present a serious difficulty. I cannot believe in view of the evidence given above that iron weapons were regularly employed in the Heroic Age[4] and that the use of the word χαλκός is a piece of traditional poetic archaism. Otherwise however there is no alternative but to regard the Odyssey verse as an interpolation[5]. But in reality it is no great step from iron knives and arrow-heads to the use of the same metal for spears or even swords. If we were to adopt the view that the age of the composition of the Homeric poems coincides with the period of transition between the first use of iron for cutting and piercing instruments to its general employment for weapons of all kinds, we should not necessarily require much more than a century for their development. Indeed the presence of iron

---

[1] Cf. Macalister, *Palestine Expl. Fund, Quart. Rep.*, 1903, p. 199; Lang, *Class. Rev.* XXII, p. 47.

[2] Cf. Dörpfeld, *Troja und Ilion*, p. 368.

[3] αὐτὸς γὰρ ἐφέλκεται ἄνδρα σίδηρος. Cf. Burrows, *The Discoveries in Crete*, p. 214 ff.

[4] Cf. Ridgeway, *The Early Age of Greece*, p. 294 f. Prof. Ridgeway allows the occasional use of bronze swords, e.g. in the case of Euryalos the Phaeacian (Od. VIII 403—6). But the swords of Paris, Patroclos, Achilles and Odysseus (Il. III 334 f., XVI 135 f., XIX 372 f., Od. X 261 f.) are described in very similar terms (ξίφος ἀργυρόηλον χάλκεον). Further, the tendency of bronze swords to snap off short at the hilt is well illustrated by the case of Lycon in Il. XVI 338 f.

[5] Cf. Lang, *Homer and his Age*, p. 192 f.

swords in graves of the sub-Mycenean period in Crete (cf. p. 185) would seem to show that the transition had begun within what may be regarded practically as the Heroic Age itself.

Again, it is held that many anachronisms or chronological inconsistencies appear in the battle scenes of the Iliad. Sometimes we find descriptions of armour and tactics which are thought to be copied from those of Ionic hoplites in early historical times and to be irreconcilable with the type of warfare depicted in other passages. Many of the chief men are represented as armed with breastplates, for which, it is said, there is no evidence in the Mycenean age[1]—though this statement is more than doubtful[2]. In regard to the form of the shield also there is a discrepancy. Sometimes it is described as being of great length, 'like a tower' or 'reaching to the feet'—terms which would suit the long shields often depicted on objects of the Mycenean age. Sometimes on the other hand we hear of 'round' shields, which suggest the comparatively small circular shield of the historical period.

These inconsistencies only concern us in so far as they are supposed to point to widely different ages. Unfortunately our information regarding the geometrical period is still very defective, and we do not know how far its characteristics were the same in all parts of Greece. The same remarks apply with still greater force to the preceding or sub-Mycenean age. Hence, though it may be true that the round shield does not make its appearance in Attica till the close of the eighth century, we cannot argue from this that it was unknown in other parts of Greece[3]. In the more northern parts of Europe it appears to be the earliest form of shield which has been found. More important however is the fact that the Shardina and their confederates used the round shield as far back as the thirteenth century, while the shields represented on the Warrior Vase and the Stele from Mycenae (cf. p. 185) can hardly be regarded otherwise than as a variety of the same type. Hence, whatever may be the connection between

---

[1] Cf. Reichel, *Über homerische Waffen* (Abh. d. arch.-epigr. Seminares d. Univ. Wien, Heft xi), p. 79 ff.

[2] Cf. p. 191 and Evans, *Journal of the Anthropological Institute*, xxx 213 f.

[3] Cf. Ridgeway, *op. cit.* pp. 324 f., 475.

the disappearance of the long shield and the growing use of
body armour, there is not the slightest justification for supposing that the round variety was not used in the Heroic Age
itself.

The commonest type of Mycenean shield, the oval type contracted in the middle, belongs to a class of shields which occur in
various parts of the world. It is probably akin to the Zulu shield,
though in this the lateral contraction has lost its meaning and
almost disappeared. The primary purpose of the whole class
appears to be for defence against missile weapons (ἕρκος ἀκόντων),
whether light javelins or arrows. But the special characteristic
of the Mycenean variety is the use of a suspending strap
(τελαμών[1]) in place of a handle. The object of this was to leave
both hands free for the use of a long spear in fighting at close
quarters—as we see in the representation of a lion-hunt engraved
on a dagger-blade found at Mycenae. But it is to be observed
that the method of fighting most commonly employed by
Homeric warriors is of quite a different character. First the
spear was hurled—apparently with one hand (cf. Il. XXII 320)—
and then an attack was made with the sword. For both these
movements the Mycenean shield was obviously ill adapted.
Indeed for the second, which required agility above everything,
it would be more of an encumbrance than a protection. But
even when the spear was used for thrusting there is nothing to
show that it was usually held in both hands[2]. Hence we can
hardly avoid concluding that the Homeric tactics were due to
the use of a different type of armature, which included a comparatively small and mobile shield. We need not suppose of
course that the Mycenean shield was unknown or even uncommon. It seems fairly clear that Aias the son of Telamon
uses one of this type[3], and so also Periphetes the Mycenean

---

[1] This strap seems to have been used for carrying even comparatively small
shields down to a much later period. It is not found apparently in the representations of the Shardina, though they have an arm-strap as well as a handle.

[2] The Shardina on the temple of Medinet Habu and the warriors represented on
the Stele hold their spears poised in their right hands, precisely at the same angle.
But it is not quite clear to me whether a cast or thrust is intended.

[3] φέρων σάκος ἠΰτε πύργον (Il. XII 219, etc.). There is a reference no doubt to
the hero's great stature.

whose shield reached to his feet and caused him to stumble
(Il. xv 645 ff.)[1].

A further suggestion is that the Homeric use of the chariot
was due to the long shield[2]. The argument in this case is that
such shields could not be carried on horseback, while their weight
was too great to allow them to be borne for any distance on foot.
This is an extremely dubious theory for two reasons. In the
first place the Homeric use of the chariot is a problem which
concerns not Greece alone but a considerable part of Europe,
including countries where there is no evidence for the Mycenean
shield[3]. Secondly, it may be regarded as a general rule that

[1] Very recently the history of Greek shields has been treated at length by
Dr G. Lippold (*Münchener Archäologische Studien*, pp. 399—504). This work is
largely taken up with a criticism of Reichel's theories, and in the course of the
discussion it is pointed out that the latter are in many points insufficiently supported
by evidence. Dr Lippold (pp. 406, 474) seems to have no hesitation in assigning the
Warrior Vase and its congeners to the late Mycenean age—he does not distinguish
between 'Mycenean' and 'sub-Mycenean'—and he also recognises (p. 461 ff.) that
two kinds of shields figure in the Homeric poems. The 'tower' shield however
is identified by him with the Dipylon shield, from which he believes the 'Boeotian'
shield to be descended. He holds that the round shield was of Oriental origin, since
it was used by the Assyrians in the ninth century, and that it was first introduced into
Greece towards the end of the Mycenean period; then, after being banished for
a while from the Greek mainland by the Dipylon shield, it was re-introduced, in
a somewhat modified form, towards the end of the Dipylon (Geometrical) period.
The Homeric poems are held to reflect the time of transition when it was re-introduced; but no date appears to be given except that it was before the eighth century
(p. 468). This explanation seems to me to be open to a serious objection, namely
that the Homeric shields will then have to reflect a different age from that indicated
by the Homeric evidence on the use of the metals; for the latter clearly belongs to
the close of the Mycenean—or rather 'sub-Mycenean'—period. So far as I can see,
it is only by Dr Mackenzie's equation of the Homeric poems with the Warrior Vase
and certain East Cretan graves (cf. p. 185) that we can obtain a consistent and
intelligible sequence. Of course it may very well be that the round shield was
banished for a time from the Greek mainland by the Dipylon type. On the other
hand the suggestion that the former was of Assyrian origin surely requires evidence
earlier than the ninth century; for we find it used by the Shardina, who cannot
properly be regarded as Oriental, as far back as the thirteenth century. I have to
thank Mr A. B. Cook for calling my attention to Dr Lippold's work.

[2] Cf. Reichel, *op. cit.* p. 53 f.

[3] Long shields were regularly used during the La Tène period by the Celtic
peoples, and also by many of the Teutonic peoples probably much later. But they
seem to have been of a totally different type from the Mycenean. In late times they
were certainly of great length (cf. Diodorus, v 30, and the figures on the bowl of

those peoples which use the long shield not only fight but also
go to battle on foot.   Moreover the evidence of the poems themselves does not really bear out the suggested connection.   Thus
there is no instance of the long shield more clear than that
belonging to Aias the son of Telamon, and this hero is one of
the few leading men who are never said to wear breast-plates.
But he is also apparently one of the very few who do not possess
chariots.   Indeed a better case could probably be made out for
connecting the chariot with the breast-plate.

The Homeric use of the chariot gives rise to another question
which probably deserves more careful consideration.   In the
action itself driving appears to be universal; at most we have
only one doubtful case of riding (Il. X 513).   But there are at
least two incidental references (Il. XV 679 ff., Od. V 371) which
betray acquaintance with the latter art.   It is quite possible
therefore that the knowledge of riding was a comparatively
recent accomplishment which the poet or poets knew to have
been foreign to the Heroic Age.   Unfortunately the history of
equitation is a very obscure subject.   In more eastern countries
the use of chariots—which here were war-chariots in the true
sense—continued until quite late times.   In Cyprus we hear of
them at the beginning of the fifth century; and in Italy they
were introduced, or re-introduced, still later.   But we do not
know when riding began.   In the wall-sculptures at Karnak[1]
which commemorate the victories of Sety I and date from
towards the close of the fourteenth century several Hittites are
shown on horseback.   The scene represents a battle, and it may
have been the artist's intention to depict what was not a normal
custom but the last resource of fugitives whose chariots had
broken down.   But even then the possibility remains that in
emergencies or under special conditions riding may have been
practised by the Greeks long before it was in regular use.   The
whole subject however requires further investigation, in particular

Gundestrup); but the earliest examples (e.g. the oval shields depicted on the
Hallstatt sword-sheath) may really be modifications of the round shield.

[1] Cf. Ridgeway, *The Origin and Influence of the Thoroughbred Horse*, p. 510.   A
similar case occurs in a painting representing the victory of Rameses II over the
Hittites, figured in Meyer's *Geschichte des alten Aegyptens* (plate following p. 290).

the question whether there is reason for supposing the Hittites to have been more skilled in horsemanship than other nations.

Another series of inconsistencies has been pointed out in references to marriage customs, particularly in regard to the use of the word ἔεδνα (ἔδνα). In several passages this word evidently denotes the sum paid by the bridegroom to the bride's guardian; but in others it seems to mean presents given to the bride at marriage by her own relatives. We can scarcely doubt that a difference of custom is involved in these usages; but it does not necessarily follow that the second group of passages belong to a later period than the first. Account must be taken of local divergencies, for there is hardly any subject in which early Teutonic custom varied so much as in this, even from the time of our oldest records. Again, it has been suggested[1] with considerable probability that the inconsistencies of the Odyssey are to be attributed to a change of custom—not in the sense that the earlier parts of the poem reflect one form and the later parts another, but that the poem as a whole belongs to an age of transition when different forms of matrimonial arrangements were in vogue. This is a question with which we shall have to deal more fully in a later chapter.

We have yet to consider certain inconsistencies in regard to religious observances Once only (Il. VI 303) is mention made of the figure—a seated figure—of a deity, and consequently it is held that the passage in question must be late. Recent discoveries however have tended to throw doubt on this view; for a number of statuettes, apparently representing deities, have come to light in deposits belonging both to the Mycenean and Geometrical periods, while primitive female figures, often in a sitting position, are quite common. The finding of a larger image would now scarcely call forth much surprise, though it cannot be supposed that such statues were of frequent occurrence.

In references to sanctuaries we sometimes hear of temples (νηοί), but more frequently only of shrines or sacred groves. The most certain examples[2] of the former are those of Apollo and

---

[1] Cauer, *Grundfragen d. Homer-kritik*[2], p. 294 ff.

[2] It is uncertain whether the sanctuaries of Apollo at Pytho (Delphoi) and of

Athene at Troy (Il. V 446, VI 88, VII 83, etc.) and another of
Athene at Athens (Il. II 549, Od. VII 81). The sanctuary of
Apollo at Chryse is also once described as a temple (Il. I 39),
though the account of the sacrifice (*ib.* 440 ff.) suggests an open-
air shrine. Besides these we have a general reference to temples
among the Phaeacians (Od. VI 10) and a vow made by Odysseus'
followers to construct a temple to Helios on their return home
(*ib.* XII 346). Now it is held that all these passages belong to a
late stage in the growth of the poems and that in their original
form temples were unknown. Sanctuaries of the earlier period
are described only by such terms as ἄλσος or τέμενος βωμός τε
θυήεις. There can be little doubt that the grove and the open-
air shrine represent more primitive types of sanctuary than the
temple. But the advocates of this theory seem to have overlooked the fact that among many peoples the more primitive
and the more developed forms of sanctuary are found existing
side by side[1]. Thus beside the great temple at Upsala, the chief
sanctuary of the North, there stood a grove which appears to
have been regarded with still greater veneration, even down to
the very end of heathen times. Close by was a spring in which
human victims were sacrificed[2]. This case shows how entirely
unjustifiable it is to assume the non-existence of a temple, when
only a shrine or sacred grove happens to be mentioned. We
may cite as an example the proposed sacrifice to Spercheios in
Il. XXIII 145 ff.[3] In general however the Homeric evidence

Poseidon at Scheria (Il. IX 404 f., Od. VIII 79 ff., VI 266 f.) are regarded as temples ;
cf. Cauer, *op. cit.* p. 301 f. In the former case however it is decidedly probable.

[1] Many well-known survivals of such usage occur in Greece itself.

[2] Adam Brem. IV 27 : *corpora autem suspenduntur in lucum qui proximus est
templo. is enim lucus tam sacer est gentilibus ut singulae arbores eius ex morte uel
tabo immolatorum diuinae credantur.* Cf. also the (contemporary) schol. 134 : *prope
illud templum est arbor maxima late ramos extendens, semper uiridis in hieme et
aestate, cuius illa generis sit nemo scit. ibi etiam est fons ubi sacrificia paganorum
solent exerceri et homo uiuus immergi. qui dum non inuenitur ratum erit uotum
populi.*

[3]
Σπερχεί', ἄλλως σοί γε πατὴρ ἠρήσατο Πηλεὺς
κεῖσέ με νοστήσαντα φίλην ἐς πατρίδα γαῖαν
σοί τε κόμην κερέειν ῥέξειν θ' ἱερὴν ἑκατόμβην,
πεντήκοντα δ' ἔνορχα παρ' αὐτόθι μῆλ' ἱερεύσειν
ἐς πηγὰς ὅθι τοι τέμενος βωμός τε θυήεις.

clearly suggests that temples—and the same may possibly be the case with images—were chiefly to be found in cities, while the more primitive forms of sanctuary remained in less populous places.

I cannot but think that to any student of comparative religion the argument derived from the references to sanctuaries will appear entirely worthless. The argument against the antiquity of the round shield also can hardly be maintained. Of the rest all except the one based on the use of the metals contain a certain element of doubt. But even if we grant their validity in every case it cannot be said that either individually or collectively they necessitate the lapse of a long interval between the earlier and later portions of the poems. If the interval had amounted to anything like three centuries discrepancies of a far more striking character must have come to light.

As yet we have taken no account of linguistic inconsistencies. The poems as we have them present a medley of forms belonging to different ages and different dialects. But these inconsistencies appear everywhere; it is not the case that certain portions of the poems contain only early forms and others only late ones. The Odyssey is said to contain a certain number of apparently late usages, especially of prepositions and conjunctions, which are wanting or only occur rarely in the Iliad. It is held also that within the poems themselves earlier and later portions can be distinguished to a certain extent by similar differences of usage. But the evidence on the whole is slight and generally somewhat ambiguous[1]; and consequently linguistic criteria have as a rule played only a subordinate part in the attempts which have been made to determine the stratification of the poems. We must conclude then either that the later parts were composed in an artificial type of language, thoroughly permeated with archaisms, or that the earlier parts have undergone a very considerable amount of modernisation. Indeed the latter explanation must be admitted to some extent in any case; for relatively modern forms occur frequently in what are usually regarded as the very

[1] The Appendices in Miss Stawell's *Homer and the Iliad* (pp. 238—326) suggest that many of the instances commonly cited are due to insufficient consideration.

earliest parts of the poems. But if the preservation of the poems
was dependent on oral tradition for any considerable length of
time it is very difficult to set a limit to the operations of such a
process. In Anglo-Saxon poems—even in those which were not
entirely dependent on oral tradition—modernisation prevailed to
such an extent that archaic forms disappeared practically everywhere, while substitutions of one word for another were very
frequent. The more elaborate character of Greek metre doubtless
acted as a check on this tendency to change, but at the same
time I cannot help thinking that its importance in the history of
Homeric poetry has been greatly underrated.

On the question of dialect something more must be said. It
is true no doubt that the language of the poems as we have them
must be regarded as Ionic—but only with certain reservations.
In the first place we have to note the regular preservation of *h-*,
which in strict Ionic—the language of the Asiatic coast—was lost
in the seventh century, if not earlier. Again, we find a considerable number of forms which cannot be assigned to any
Ionic dialect, e.g. such as contain -ᾱ- (λαός, Ἀτρείδαο, αἰχμητάων).
Special attention must be paid to forms which are definitely
Aeolic, such as πίσυρες, ἄμμε, ἐρεβεννός. Whatever may be the
explanation of the preservation of *h-*, it is universally agreed that
the Aeolic element is deeply rooted in the history of Homeric
poetry. Some scholars indeed hold that the poems were
originally composed in Aeolic and that their present form is
practically an Ionic translation. The more general view however is that Ionic was the language of epic composition from the
beginning and that such forms as πίσυρες and ἄμμε are derived
from early Aeolic lays on which the epics were for the most part
based.

The legends as to Homer's birthplace are perhaps not without significance for this question. In ancient times, from Pindar[1]
downwards, Smyrna's claim to this honour was the one most
generally recognised, and the majority of modern scholars are
inclined to the view that the birthplace of Homeric poetry is to
be sought in or around that city. Now Smyrna was originally

---

[1] Fragm. 189, Boeckh.

an Aeolic state, but was captured by the Ionians of Colophon[1], apparently towards the close of the eighth century, from which time onwards it appears as Ionic. The mixture of dialect found in the poems—an older stratum of Aeolic underlying a later stratum of Ionic—would therefore be perfectly in accord with what we know of the history of the city, although unfortunately no early inscriptions are extant[2].

The most serious competitor of Smyrna was Chios, the claim of which found favour with several of our earliest authorities. Especially important is the fact that in a fragment published among the remains of Simonides of Ceos (fragm. 85, Bergk), but now frequently attributed to Semonides of Samos, who lived about the middle of the seventh century, a verse of the Iliad (VI 146) is ascribed to the 'man of Chios.' In this island also there dwelt in later times a clan called Ὁμηρίδαι[3] who claimed descent from the poet. But here again there is a tradition that the population was at least in part Aeolic[4]. Moreover, though the language of the earliest extant inscriptions is Ionic in its main features, it possesses certain Aeolic characteristics, especially the change of ὅν to ὅι[5] before s (e.g. πρήξοισι, λάβωισι against Ion. πρήξουσι, λάβωσι). There is no record of an Ionic conquest of the island, as in the case of Smyrna, but we know that it did not enter the Ionic confederation until a comparatively late period, probably the seventh century[6].

It appears then that the peculiarities of Homeric language can be satisfactorily accounted for by the history of either Smyrna or Chios[7]. But now we are confronted with a very

---

[1] Cf. Mimnermos, fragm. 9. 5 f. (Bergk), Herodotus, I 150, etc. According to Pausanias (v 8. 7) Smyrna had become Ionic before the year 688 ; cf. Wilamowitz-Möllendorff, S.-B. der Akad. der Wiss. zu Berlin, 1906, p. 52, note.

[2] Acquaintance with the district round Smyrna is shown by the reference to the figure of 'Niobe' on Mt Sipylos in Il. XXIV 614 ff., although the identification of this figure is still disputed.

[3] On the problems connected with this name see Allen, Classical Quarterly, I 135 ff.

[4] Stephanus Byzant. s. v. Βολισσός.

[5] But not the corresponding change of an to ai (cf. τάς, πᾶσα).

[6] Cf. Wilamowitz-Möllendorff, op. cit. p. 52 f.

[7] The Ionic states of Clazomenai and Phocaia, to the west and north-west of Smyrna, seem to have been founded at a comparatively late period, though probably

grave difficulty. The same scholars who hold that Smyrna was the birthplace of Homeric poetry yet insist that the language of the epics themselves was never anything else than Ionic, although they allow that the Iliad was nearly complete some considerable time before the conquest of Smyrna. This position is quite incomprehensible to me. The only explanation offered, so far as I am aware, is that the language of this district may have been of a mixed character[1]. It is no doubt true that when the coast was first occupied settlers may have come from many different quarters. But when Mimnermos speaks of the capture of 'Aeolic Smyrna' we are surely not justified in assuming that the city had become Ionicised before that time. On the other hand the supposition that the two dialects were not yet differentiated to any considerable extent appears to me to be irreconcilable with the evidence of the poems themselves as well as with all that we know of the history of the Greek dialects.

The question which we are discussing is one which concerns not only the Iliad and Odyssey, together perhaps with certain Hymns and other Homeric poems, but also the various works attributed to Hesiod. In particular we may note the Works and Days and the Theogony, both of which claim to be of Boeotian origin. Whether by chance or not they contain few forms[2] which are peculiar to Aeolic proper, i.e. the dialect of Asiatic Aeolis. But in all other respects their language is of the Homeric type, i.e. generally speaking Ionic, though with certain reservations, notably that $\digamma$ is generally kept and $\bar{a}$ frequently occurs before o, ω. Now it cannot be contended seriously that this extraordinary mixed dialect sprang up naturally on both sides of the Aegean. The only alternative however is to suppose that Boeotian poets borrowed it from Asia. But is this really probable at such a time?

Before leaving this subject we must notice briefly the

---

in the eighth century. Since the promontory of Ἀργεννον, opposite Chios and to the south-west of Erythrai, has an Aeolic name, it is possible that the whole of the coast north of Teos was once occupied by Aeolians.

[1] Cf. Wilamowitz-Möllendorff, op. cit. p. 75 and (for a criticism) Cauer, Grund-fragen[2], p. 181 ff.

[2] The Shield of Heracles contains a number of clearly Aeolic forms (ἄμμες, ὔμμι, etc.).

alternative theory that the Homeric poems were originally composed in Aeolic. According to the form in which this theory has
become most widely known they were translated into Ionic at a
comparatively late date—towards the close of the sixth century[1].
It is rather a serious objection to this hypothesis that the poems
contain no trace of late Aeolic characteristics, such as the change
of n to i before s (e.g. τοίς, παῖσα). Further, if the poems had
been known so long in Aeolic, though doubt might have prevailed as to Homer's birthplace, the fact that he was an Aeolian
could never have been called in question. Above all it is difficult to see how the need of a translation could have arisen at
such a date, for the Aeolic dialect was then well known throughout the Greek world through the poems of Alcaeus and Sappho.

On the other hand there can be no possible objection in principle to the idea that the poems have undergone a change of
dialect. We have seen that a large proportion of Anglo-Saxon
poetry has passed through a similar process, generally from one
English dialect to another, but occasionally, as in the case of
Genesis (vv. 235—851), from a continental to an English dialect.
In some few cases we still have parallel texts preserved in
different dialects[2]. Indeed, when the poetry of one community
becomes current in another community, it would seem that
under certain conditions such changes were not merely possible
but even inevitable. This is a question to which we shall
have to return in the course of the next few pages.

There is still one vexed question which we have not as yet
touched upon, namely the relationship of the Homeric poems
to the art of writing. Wolf and his immediate successors held
that the art was unknown when these poems came into existence.

---

[1] Cf. Fick, *Die homerische Odyssee* (1883), and *Die homerische Ilias* (1886), where
the poems are reconstructed in their original Aeolic form.

[2] E.g. the two texts of Riddle XXXVI (both printed in Sweet's *Oldest English
Texts*, p. 150 f.) and the texts of Caedmon's Hymn from the Moore MS. of Bede's
Eccles. History (*ib.* p. 149) and the Anglo-Saxon version (IV 24). Reference may
also be made to the Dream of the Cross and the extracts given in the inscription on
the Ruthwell Cross. A portion of the Old Saxon Genesis is printed, together with
the Anglo-Saxon version, in Cook and Tinker's *Translations from Old English Poetry*,
p. 184

Among more recent scholars however the general tendency has been to regard this view as mistaken. Some leading authorities even hold that considerable portions of the poems were written down from the time of their composition.

The poems themselves contain only one reference to writing, namely in Il. VI 168 ff., where it is stated that Proitos sent Bellerophon to Lycia "and gave him baneful tokens, writing many deadly things in a folded tablet, which he bade him show to his (Proitos') father-in-law, with a view to his own destruction[1]." So long as no further evidence was forthcoming there was a natural inclination either to regard this passage as an interpolation or to interpret it as denoting something which could not properly be called writing. But of late years archaeological investigation has brought to light, especially in Crete, numerous inscriptions dating from very remote times, and there cannot now be any question as to the antiquity of writing in the southern Aegean. Moreover the Homeric poets themselves can hardly have been ignorant of the existence of such an art, for rock-hewn figures with inscriptions dating from pre-Homeric times—including one which has been identified with the figure of 'Niobe' mentioned in Il. XXIV 614 ff.—are to be found quite close to the Asiatic coast.

Yet in spite of all this it is a very remarkable fact that the whole 28,000 verses of the Iliad and Odyssey contain only one reference to writing. The significance of this may be appreciated by turning to modern Servian poetry, which abounds with allusions to letters and written orders, although the minstrels themselves are quite ignorant both of reading and writing. It is true that in Beowulf we find only one direct reference to writing. But the Iliad and Odyssey together contain nearly nine times as many verses as Beowulf.

On the whole it seems to me that the evidence for the antiquity of writing given above does not prove exactly what it is commonly supposed to do. The inscriptions on the rock-hewn figures are Hittite. The ancient Cretan inscriptions have not

1   πέμπε δέ μιν Λυκίηνδε πόρεν δ' ὅ γε σήματα λυγρὰ,
     γράψας ἐν πίνακι πτυκτῷ θυμοφθόρα πολλά,
     δεῖξαι δ' ἠνώγειν ᾧ πενθερῷ ὄφρ' ἀπόλοιτο.

yet been deciphered, and in view of the later inscriptions found at Praisos the probability as yet is distinctly against their being in the Greek language. But in any case they date from ages long anterior to Homeric times, and there is nothing to prove their continuity with the writing of the historical period. With regard to the passage in Il. VI 168 ff. it is to be observed firstly that Proitos is one of the very earliest persons mentioned in the poems—some three generations removed from the characters of the Trojan story—and secondly that the curious phraseology seems rather to suggest that the poet was speaking of something which he did not clearly understand. On the whole then it is much to be doubted whether writing was a current and native practice during the period when the poems were composed.

A reservation should perhaps be made with regard to the latest elements in the poems. Although definite evidence is wanting, the beginnings of the Greek alphabet may quite probably go back to the ninth century, and it may very well be that the poems had not then attained their final form. But it should not be assumed that the alphabet was introduced simultaneously throughout the Greek world. Some districts may have acquired it generations before others, and Aeolis (including even Chios and Smyrna) was probably not one of the more advanced. Further, we must admit that in all probability its use was at first very limited. From all analogies we should expect that it was employed for inscriptions, correspondence, etc. for a very long time before it was made to serve any literary purpose. Such apparently was the case with the alphabet of ancient Rome and with the Runic alphabet almost throughout its history. Unless the conditions in Greece were quite exceptional we should not expect the alphabet to come into contact with heroic poetry for a considerable time.

The theory that certain portions of the poems were written down from the beginning presupposes of course a use of writing quite different from that which is brought before us in the story of Bellerophon. This theory[1] is, and necessarily must be, bound

---

[1] The analysis of the Odyssey given by Prof. v. Wilamowitz-Möllendorff admittedly postulates a written text (*Hom. Untersuch.* p. 293). But I cannot assent to the

up with another theory, which we have already discussed, that these portions date from a period not earlier than the seventh century. Our discussion has led us to the conclusion that the evidence for the latter theory is unsatisfactory. But, apart from this, it is inconceivable that the 'literary' portions, which are said to amount to several thousand verses, should contain no reference, direct or indirect, to the use of writing. In Beowulf we find only one direct reference to writing (v. 1694 f.)—an inscription in Runic letters such as had long been in use. But in the Christian additions or 'interpolations' we meet with three examples of the verb *scrifan* (*forscrifan, gescrifan*—from Lat. *scribere*), which of course is indirect evidence for the use of writing, though in a different language[1]. If large portions of the Homeric poems were really of literary origin the authors could scarcely have failed to betray themselves by usages of this kind, even though they deliberately avoided all mention of writing.

In addition to this general consideration we have to take account of the linguistic difficulties discussed above. We have seen that Hesiod's works show almost the same form of language as the Homeric poems, although the Boeotian dialect was quite different from anything spoken on the other side of the Aegean. Did Hesiod, who lived in the eighth century, probably before the Ionian conquest of Smyrna, really employ the 'impure Ionic' in which his poems have come down to us? He himself says (W. and D. 650 ff.) that he had never crossed the sea except (once apparently) to Chalcis. Presumably then his knowledge of heroic poetry was derived either from Boeotia, where he lived, or from Cyme in Aeolis, from whence his father had emigrated. But Cyme never came into Ionian hands. Are we to suppose then that either here or in Boeotia poets were already employing as their vehicle a form of language which according to the theory under discussion owed its existence (whether in

___

proposition that the Catalogue of Ships in itself must come from a written source. This list scarcely differs in principle from the catalogues of Widsith.

[1] Further indirect evidence, of native origin, is supplied by the word *facenstafas* (O. Norse *feiknstafir*) in v. 1018, if the original meaning of this compound was 'harmful runes' (used magically). Cf. also vv. 317, 382, 458, 1753.

ordinary speech or only in poetry) to certain political changes
in a third district—changes too which had hardly begun much
before the time of Hesiod? This hypothesis seems to me quite
incredible[1].

On the other hand if Hesiod's poems have undergone a
change of dialect since their original composition may not the
Homeric poems have passed through the same process? In
this case of course such a change would come about quite
naturally if Smyrna or Chios was the original home of the
poems. But here we must notice a curious feature in the
'epic dialect' to which we have already referred. Except in
Aeolic forms—and this exception deserves to be remarked—
the poems almost always preserve initial h-[2]. This is a characteristic which the 'epic dialect' shares with western or European Ionic but not with the language of the Asiatic coast[3]. Its
presence raises a distinct difficulty in the way of supposing that
the poems were Ionicised in their original home.

Now if the Homeric poems had been written down in Aeolic
and preserved in literary form we can hardly doubt that they
would have retained their original dialect, just like the works
of Alcman, Alcaeus, and Sappho. It must not be argued that
Ionic was the proper language of the epic, Doric and Aeolic
of the lyric; for if the Homeric poems had become generally
known in Aeolic nothing could have prevented this dialect
from becoming the language of the epic also. We may assume
then that they were not transmitted in written Aeolic. But the
same argument really militates against the theory that they were
written in Asiatic Ionic[4], though in this case the difference of
dialect is less striking.

---

[1] It may be added that we really know nothing of the Ionic of Hesiod's time.
It is quite uncertain how far it had already developed those characteristics which we
find in our texts.

[2] The few exceptional forms such as (τ') οὖλον (Od. XVII 343) may be due to fairly
late scribes familiar with (eastern) Ionic texts.

[3] We may note also the absence of the literary Ionic forms κότε, κῶς, etc.

[4] It is true that we do not know exactly when h- was lost. But before that
change took place H cannot have been used for $\bar{e}$; consequently a wholesale
μεταγραμματισμός would be involved (doubtless also affecting the representation of $\bar{o}$),
just as in the case of Athens.

A form of language practically identical with that of the epics appears in the remains of several poets of the seventh and sixth centuries, such as Archilochos and Solon. The only noticeable difference is in the proportion of non-Ionic forms which they use. Now since these authors belonged to quite different districts we must, if we are to trust our evidence, infer the existence of a kind of literary language at this time. Its difference from Asiatic Ionic is of course comparatively slight, and in the texts which have come down to us it is not always carefully observed[1]. Still there is a sufficient amount of regularity to show that it was generally recognised.

The true home of this literary language must not be sought in Athens, but rather in Euboea or the Cyclades; and we may probably attribute its spread, in part at least, to the influence of the poems of Archilochos. But it certainly affected the writing of Attic for some two centuries, and there can be little doubt that it was thoroughly domiciled in Athens at quite an early date—probably in the seventh century. I cannot see any objection therefore to supposing that it was in Athens that both the Homeric and Hesiodic poems acquired those peculiar linguistic characteristics which we comprehend under the term 'epic dialect.' This of course brings us back to the story that the poems were collected or written down by order of Peisistratos. The evidence for the story is late, and its truth is hotly contested by many scholars. But at all events it has the merit of providing a satisfactory explanation of the linguistic phenomena.

Certainly, if we may judge from the analogy of other peoples, heroic poetry would not by any means be among the first species of literature to get committed to writing. There is no reason whatever for supposing that anything of this kind was written down in England before the eighth century, i.e. at least a century after the language was first applied to literary purposes, in Aethelberht's time. The same remark seems to be true of Ireland, Germany and the North, while Bosnian heroic poetry is being written down only in our own generation, and not by natives of the country. It is only natural therefore to expect

---

[1] Cf. Hoffmann, *Griech. Dial.* III, p. 549 f. ; Fick, *Neue Jahrbücher*, I 504 ff.

that the Homeric poems would be written down according to an orthography which was already well established.

This orthography no doubt represents more or less truly the form in which the poems were recited in Athens at the time. But does it also represent the form in which they were recited at (let us say) Sicyon? That is a question upon which we have no direct evidence. But it is worth noting that in Doric and other non-Ionic states we find a number of ancient inscriptions in hexameters or elegiacs which contain epic words and forms. We may note especially the Gen. sg. ending -οιο, e.g. κασιγνετοιο, οδοιο, Αραθθοιο, and above all false imitations of epic forms, such as Τλασκιαϝο[1]. But in all these inscriptions Ionic characteristics are conspicuously absent[2]. Does this mean that wherever the heroic poems were introduced the rhapsodists tried to accommodate them, as far as possible, to the language of the district? But if so, is it possible that the Ionic element in our texts is wholly due to the rhapsodists? A Chalcidian or Naxian or Athenian audience would certainly experience at least as much difficulty in following a purely Aeolic Iliad as a southern English audience would have in listening to a purely Northumbrian or Mercian Beowulf. On the other hand an Iliad Ionicised in Chalcis or Naxos would be easily intelligible in Athens[3].

---

[1] Cauer, *Delectus Inscr. Graec.* 83, 84, 91. We may compare also such epic expressions as ευρυχορο, γαιας απο πατριδος, πολυμελο, κλεϝος απθιτον (*ib.* 54, 83, 445, 202), and, more particularly, an inscription on a bronze discus from Cephallenia (cf. Cook, *Class. Review*, XIII 77 f.) :

Εχσοιδα μ ανεθεκε Διϝος φοροιν μεγαλοιο
χαλκεον ηοι νικασε Κεφαλανας μεγαθυμος

(cf. Hom. Hymn. XXXIII 9 ; Il. II 631).

[2] The same remark is true of heroic names occurring in Doric inscriptions, e.g. ϝεκαβα, Κεβριονας, Δαιφοβος on a vase (Cauer, *op. cit.* 78) found near Caere. So also with the heroic names used by Pindar and other non-Ionic poets—not to mention the Latin forms. Yet these poets use the Ionic forms of foreign names, such as Μῆδοι (Cypr. *Ma-to-i*), which had come to them presumably through Ionic channels. On the other hand we find in inscriptions on Chalcidian vases more purely Ionic forms, e.g. Αινεϵς (*ib.* 545), than those preserved in our text. These seem to count against any place except Athens as the home of the final form of the 'epic dialect.'

[3] From the fact that Pindar and other non-Ionic authors use what is apparently an Ionic form—indeed, strictly speaking, a western Ionic form—in the poet's name

At all events we have seen that there is a very serious objection on chronological grounds to the view that Hesiod's poems were composed in a form of 'impure Ionic' borrowed from the Asiatic coast. In this case it is surely far more probable that the Ionic element is due to the rhapsodists, whether in Chalcis or Athens. But is there any real reason for denying that the Homeric poems may have had a similar experience? This is a question which I do not feel qualified to answer. But it seems to me to deserve more attention from scholars than it has received as yet.

In this chapter we have seen that the Homeric poems contain elements of great antiquity. Although we have no means of fixing an exact date for these elements, we can hardly doubt that they originated at a time before iron had come into general use for weapons. According to the prevailing opinion of archaeologists this innovation cannot have taken place after the tenth century. We need not suppose that any considerable portions of the poems in their present form date from such an early period. But the 'type' must have been fixed by that time, and to a considerable extent also the subject-matter.

Still more clearly we have seen that there is no ground for supposing that the earlier and later elements are separated from one another by a wide interval. For the idea that the earlier elements reflect the conditions of the last age of Mycenean splendour—probably about the thirteenth century—while the later elements betray acquaintance with conditions of the seventh century, we have not been able to find any justification. The period intervening between the Mycenean age and the beginning

("Ομηρος), while they give the names of the heroes themselves in non-Ionic form, we are justified in concluding that they had acquired the former from a different (presumably literary) source. Certainly the earliest references to the poet come from Ionic authors. Again, Thucydides (III 104) is clearly recording a generally accepted opinion when he quotes the Hymn to the Delian Apollo under Homer's name; and I can see no reason for doubting the identity of Semonides' Χῖος ἀνήρ (cf. p. 209) with the author of this poem (v. 172: τυφλὸς ἀνήρ, οἰκεῖ δὲ Χίῳ ἔνι παιπαλοέσσῃ). The Hymn dates probably from the period when Chios was in process of becoming Ionicised. At such a time the repertoire of a Chian minstrel would have an exceptionally favourable opportunity of gaining currency (naturally under his own name) in Ionic circles—in the Cyclades probably as well as in Ionia itself.

of the classical age is certainly one which has as yet yielded comparatively little to archaeological research. But our discussion
has led us to infer that the conditions of life reflected in the
poems throughout belong to some part of this period, rather
than that they are due to a combination taken from the preceding and following ages[1] with a more or less blank interval
of some five or six centuries.

I have spoken advisedly of earlier and later 'elements'
rather than of earlier and later 'portions' in the poems. Elaborate analyses, such as that proposed for the Odyssey by
Prof. von Wilamowitz-Möllendorff, are admittedly hopeless
unless we assent to the hypothesis that the person responsible
for the final form of the poem possessed a written text; and
we have seen that this hypothesis is open to grave objections.
The existence of different strata in the work must doubtless be
conceded. We may even allow that it is built up out of shorter
epics. But I cannot admit that such a poem as the Odyssey
can be successfully constructed out of shorter ones by stringing
the latter together, even if we do grant that the additions made
by the editor amount to a sixth part of the whole[2]. It is questionable therefore whether we are justified in regarding the last
stratum as the work of an 'editor'—whether we ought not rather
to regard this person as the 'author' of our poem. He must
have used earlier pieces, and he may have incorporated them
in large mass in his work. But we have no guarantee that he
did not greatly expand his materials as well as provide connecting links between them.

In the Iliad we are confronted to a certain extent with the
same problems. But the process of unification does not appear
to have been carried out so thoroughly and the proportion of
early matter incorporated is probably much greater. The point
however which I would especially emphasise in both cases alike

[1] Cf. Reichel, *op. cit* p. 59: "Das Epos schildert, wie in allen Dingen, auch hier
die ältere Prachtzeit," and pp. 63, 102 f., where the first appearance of the round
shield (of which the knowledge is granted, p. 55 ff.) is referred to the middle of the
eighth century, and that of breast-plates to about the beginning of the seventh century.

[2] Prof. v. Wilamowitz-Möllendorff holds that the editor was a person of inferior
ability and that the poem as a whole is not a success; but this view is scarcely
in accordance with the generally received opinion.

is that the unification process cannot be used as an argument for lateness of date. If we bear in mind the undoubtedly archaic character of both poems, the paucity of inconsistencies points to an entirely opposite conclusion. The greater the amount of matter which we attribute to the last strata, the shorter must be the period during which the poems grew until they reached their final form.

Lastly we have seen that though the linguistic evidence agrees very well with the tradition that 'Homer' belonged to Smyrna (or Chios), there are very serious objections to the view that the poems were originally composed in the Ionic dialect[1]. They may have been subsequently Ionicised in their original home, but even that is scarcely certain. The form in which they have come down to us belongs properly to the western Ionic of the islands, which in early times was used as a literary language in Athens.

---

[1] It is worth noting that these objections apply even to what are commonly regarded as among the latest parts of the poems. Thus in Od. XXIV 305, where Odysseus describes himself as υἱὸς Ἀφείδαντος Πολυπημονίδαο ἄνακτος, the point is entirely spoilt by the Ionic form. That the true form should be Aeolic (-παμμον-) is rendered more than probable by such names as Ἀλιθέρσης, Πολυθερσείδη—of which at least the second likewise belongs to the 'later' portions of the poem.

CHAPTER XI.

EARLY GREEK POETRY AND MINSTRELSY.

In Chapter V we saw that four well-marked stages may be distinguished in the history of Teutonic heroic poetry. The first is that of strictly contemporary court poetry, dealing with the praises or the adventures of living men. The second is that of epic or narrative court poetry, which celebrates the deeds of heroes of the past, though not of a very remote past. The third is the popular stage, during which the same stories were handled by village minstrels. The last stage is that in which the old subjects again found favour with the nobility in Germany and were treated in a new form which reflected the conditions of the age of chivalry. We must now see whether any such stages can be traced in the history of Greek heroic poetry.

For the first stage plenty of evidence is supplied by the Homeric poems. In the Odyssey we meet with several persons who seem to be professional court minstrels. Such are Demodocos at the court of Alcinoos and Phemios at that of Odysseus, while others are mentioned at the courts of Agamemnon and Menelaos. Both Demodocos and Phemios are represented as singing of recent events, namely the adventures of the Achaeans on their return from Troy, though the former also produces one song upon a mythical subject. The song or recitation is invariably accompanied upon a lyre, probably much in the same way as the Teutonic minstrel used his harp[1].

As among the Teutonic peoples, we hear also occasionally

---

[1] In Od. IV 17 ff. two acrobats give a performance while Menelaos' minstrel is singing, and in VIII 261 ff. Demodocos' song on the love of Ares and Aphrodite is both accompanied and followed by dancing. More usually however the minstrel's song and music is the only form of entertainment.

of royal minstrels.   Paris appears to be a skilful musician (Il. III 54), while Achilles is amusing himself by singing the 'glories of heroes' (κλέα ἀνδρῶν) when he is visited by Aias and Odysseus (*ib.* IX 189).   But the status of even the professional minstrel was, sometimes at least, one of considerable importance.   Agamemnon, on his departure to Troy, is said to have entrusted his queen to the care of a certain minstrel (Od. III 267 f.)—a case which may be compared with several Teutonic stories relating both to the Heroic Age and the Viking Age.   The Phaeacian minstrel Demodocos is blind, like the Frisian Bernlef; but, unlike the latter, he seems to have a recognised position at Alcinoos' court.   He is evidently regarded as a person of distinction; in VIII 483 we find him described as ἥρως, a term frequently applied to princes.   For minstrels of Bernlef's type we have no clear evidence in the Homeric poems.   In Od. XVII 382 ff. we hear of invitations given to minstrels; but the reference may be to persons of Widsith's class.   The same seems to be true of the Thracian minstrel Thamyris mentioned in Il. II 595 ff.; for it is stated that he was coming from Eurytos of Oichalia when disaster befell him.

On the whole then the court minstrelsy of the Homeric poems bears a striking resemblance to that of the Teutonic Heroic Age.   We cannot, it is true, obtain any corroborative evidence for its existence from contemporary historical documents.   But the negative evidence is almost as decisive.   Even in the earliest times of which we have record no trace of such an institution is to be found in Greece   We hear of rhapsodists at Sicyon as early as the beginning of the sixth century; but they are clearly persons of Bernlef's type, reciting 'Homeric' poems, i.e. stories of ancient times.   Moreover they were viewed with disfavour by the ruler.   Another type of professional poet may be seen in such persons as Alcman.   These were what may be called 'state-poets'; sometimes they were trainers of the state choruses.   But there is nothing to show that they were court poets.   We hear also of poets, sometimes men of noble birth, like Eumelos, who composed hymns for festal occasions. But these too worked for the glorification of the state, or indeed for that of any state which employed them, and their position was essentially different from that of the court minstrel who composes for his lord's gratification. Minstrelsy of the Homeric type is conceivable only in an age of real kingship, and it is incredible that such a type could have been invented after that institution had ceased to exist. Indeed the nearest Greek analogy to it is probably to be found in such poets as Anacreon who flourished at the courts of the later tyrants. Their poems however dealt with an entirely different class of subjects.

It is true that minstrels are mentioned beside kings in a passage in Hesiod's Theogony (v. 94 ff.), both being said to derive their endowment from divine sources[1]. But there is nothing to show that these were court minstrels. At all events it is clear enough from another passage in the same poem (v. 22 ff.), as well as from the Works and Days, that Hesiod himself was not a man of this type. Moreover, the subjects with which the minstrels are said to deal are the 'famous deeds (glories) of men of old' (κλέεα προτέρων ἀνθρώπων). The reference then is to heroic poetry, but in a stage not earlier than Stage II of our scheme. The passage however is undoubtedly interesting as showing a stage intermediate between Homeric minstrels and the later rhapsodists. From the word κιθαρισταί we may perhaps infer that the musical accompaniment, which the latter seem to have discarded, was still in use.

Probably no one will suggest that the Homeric poems themselves are products of the type of minstrelsy (Stage I) which we have been considering. Now therefore we must try to ascertain which of the other three stages they correspond to. Curiously enough no such question as this appears to have been discussed in any of the numerous Homeric researches which the last half century has produced. Nearly all writers have completely ignored the existence of the Anglo-Saxon heroic poems. On the other hand medieval German poems, such as the Nibelungenlied, have been ireely used in illustration of Homeric

---

[1]   ἐκ γὰρ Μουσάων καὶ ἐκηβόλου Ἀπόλλωνος
        ἄνδρες ἀοιδοὶ ἔασιν ἐπὶ χθόνα καὶ κιθαρισταί·
        ἐκ δὲ Διὸς βασιλῆες· ὁ δ' ὄλβιος ὅντινα Μοῦσαι
        φίλωνται· γλυκερή οἱ ἀπὸ στόματος ῥέει αὐδή.

problems, and there can be no question that in many respects the supposed analogy has had far-reaching influence on their interpretation. In the application of these illustrations as a rule no account whatever has been taken of what we may call the stratification of Teutonic heroic poetry.

Let us now consider briefly the history of the Nibelungenlied. We have seen that the origin of the story is to be sought in poems composed probably within memory of certain events with which it deals, and that the subject appears to have been worked up into a somewhat elaborate form within the next two centuries. It can scarcely be doubted that these early poems were products of court-minstrelsy and that their form was that of the old Teutonic alliterative verse. Later however there came a time when all heroic poetry passed out of fashion among the higher classes, and when this story, like the rest, must have been preserved only by village minstrels. Then, after a lapse of several centuries, it appears again in an entirely different metrical form, and permeated through and through with the ideas and customs of the age of chivalry. Little beyond the bare outlines of the story can have been inherited from the original poems, and even these appear to have undergone considerable modification.

Now if the history of Homeric poetry is really parallel to this, we shall have to suppose that the stories were first treated in court poetry about the close of the pre-migration period; that after flourishing for a while they fell out of favour in royal circles and were preserved only by village minstrels, at whose hands they underwent a long process of disintegration; and that finally they formed the basis of new aristocratic poems some six or seven centuries after they first saw the light. In order to present a complete parallel the later poems must use a new metrical form, of foreign derivation, which will preclude the possibility of their containing a single verse of the original poems. The customs and ideas too which they reflect must be wholly, or almost wholly, those of their own period, and not those of the Heroic Age.

But it is manifest that this description will not fit the Homeric poems in any way. According to the opinion held by the majority of scholars the customs and ideas reflected by the Homeric poems are inconsistent—sometimes they are those of the Heroic Age, sometimes those of the poets' own age. Indeed many scholars hold that the former type predominates. Personally I am not ready to admit that the difference between the two ages was anything like so great as is commonly assumed. But in any case it must be granted that in some respects, e.g. in regard to political geography and the use of the metals, the conditions of the Heroic Age are truly reflected almost everywhere. Further it is commonly held that considerable portions of the poems go back, more or less in their present form, not perhaps to the Heroic Age itself, but at all events a long distance in that direction. We must conclude therefore that, unless modern criticism has gone hopelessly astray, the Nibelungenlied presents no true analogy to the history of the Homeric poems.

Now let us take the Anglo-Saxon heroic poems. It is obvious enough that here there is at all events a superficial resemblance between the two cases, although the Greek poems are on a much larger scale. Both sets of poems are the work of colonists who had crossed the sea, and both equally suppress all reference to the existence of such settlements. It is true that the scene of the Iliad is laid in a district not far from that in which it appears to have been composed. But this district is represented as being in possession of an alien people. The compatriots of the poets—who clearly speak from the Achaean side—are uniformly represented as dwelling on the west of the Aegean. But these after all are merely accidental coincidences. Far more important for us is the fact, which we have already noted, that both sets of poems carry the history of heroic poetry back to court minstrels who are represented as living in the Heroic Age itself. The question which we have to face is whether or not the Iliad and Odyssey likewise resemble the Anglo-Saxon poems in being themselves products of court-minstrelsy in direct continuation of that which they depict as existing in the Heroic Age.

If this question is incapable of being answered we must, I think, conclude that the historical study of early Greek poetry is futile. No impartial observer can fail to have been struck by the immense strides made within the last generation by Greek archaeology, as compared with the very small amount of progress made from the literary side—at least if progress is to be judged by the attainment of any general consensus of opinion. Experienced archaeologists can now very soon determine whether the remains which they find are those of a village or a palace, and whether they belong to (let us say) the classical or the geometrical or the Mycenean period. Again, in the case of sites long occupied they can easily detect the existence of different strata—especially if a palace has been built on the site of an earlier village, or if a village settlement has intervened between two 'palace-periods.' Is it really impossible to distinguish such strata in the history of poetry, or is the absence of progress which we have noted to be attributed to other causes—perhaps that the criticism has been of too subjective a character?

Now it is almost universally agreed that the Homeric poems are considerably older than any other form of Greek literature which has come down to us. Some scholars indeed hold that the latest portions of the Odyssey belong to the seventh century; but we have seen that the evidence for this view is by no means satisfactory. Certainly by the middle of the seventh century, and probably somewhat earlier, we meet with totally different types of poetry. In the first place we find a number of new metrical forms, elegiac, iambic and trochaic, not to speak of the numerous varieties of lyric metre. In matter and in spirit too the difference is just as marked as it is in form. The new poets are primarily concerned with the affairs of their own day. Callinos and Tyrtaios are inspired by national patriotism. Their fragments may be compared with the poem on the battle of Brunanburh, though even this is nearer to the heroic spirit. Archilochos again is almost entirely taken up with his own experiences and passions. A good analogy for his case is to be found in the Icelandic adventurer Egill Skallagrímsson. In all respects then the poetry of this age is as far removed as possible from the heroic type of poetry.

Yet traces of an intermediate or transitional stage are not

altogether wanting. From the fragments of the Hesiodic Catalogue and other works which are attributed to the close of the
eighth and the early part of the seventh centuries it is clear that
—apart from hymns—the old hexameter metre was retained for
a time in a class of poetry which appears to have been largely
genealogical in character. In matter also, as well as in form,
this class had certain elements in common with Homeric poetry,
since both were concerned with the far past. But in spirit its
affinities were rather with the poetry of the following age; for
its object seems clearly to have been the glorification of the
state.

These observations lead us to conclude that a sequence can
be traced in the history of poetry, as in that of art. It is at
least a natural hypothesis that the great development of original
poetry in the age of Callinos and Archilochos was connected in
some way with those political and social movements which so
greatly affected the Greek world during the eighth and seventh
centuries—changing almost every kingdom into a republic.
Moreover the existence of the transitional (genealogical) type
of poetry which we have noted is altogether favourable to this
idea; for the form of government which took the place of
kingship was at first that of a strictly limited aristocracy. But
have we any ground for believing that heroic poetry was the
poetry of the age of kingship? How far is such an equation in
accord with the chronological data at our disposal? In Greece
itself kingship generally seems to have come to an end about
the middle of the eighth century. In Aeolis however, with which
we are primarily concerned, the change was in all probability
somewhat later; for the Phrygian king Midas (Mita of Muski),
who perished in the Cimmerian invasion about the beginning of
the seventh century, is said to have married a daughter of
Agamemnon, king of Cyme. But few will deny that the great
bulk of Homeric poetry was in existence by this time. The
equation therefore seems to be fully justified. Survivals and
imitations may occur in later times, as in the case of art; but,
broadly speaking, it appears that heroic poetry is properly the
poetry of the age of kingship.

We must not assume forthwith however that it was the only

type of poetry which existed during this age. Certain passages in Hesiod's poems (Theog. 80 ff., W. and D. 38 f.) render it clear that kingship in some form or other still existed when they were composed; yet they differ very greatly from the Homeric type. Our next object therefore must be to try to ascertain the true provenance of Homeric poetry. Was it court poetry or popular poetry, or are we to trace its origin to conditions which cannot well be brought under either of these categories?

It cannot seriously be contended, I think, that the Homeric poems are of popular origin. In the first place their length is scarcely compatible with such a hypothesis[1]. Their metrical form also is clearly the product of a long artistic development; it is inconceivable that popular poetry could be capable of creating anything so elaborate. Again they are by no means in the nature of biographical sketches (cf. p. 95); in spite of their great length the action in both cases extends over quite a brief period of time. Further, there is little or no definite evidence—certainly none which can be called conclusive—for that confusion of different stories which characterises popular poetry. The heroes who figure in the Homeric poems are scarcely the most famous representatives of their states. Most of them are little known elsewhere. Popular poetry could hardly have failed to introduce into the action such persons as Heracles, Theseus, Peirithoos, Minos, Iason or Adrastos. Then again we may note the presence of nearly all those features which distinguish the heroic poetry of the Teutonic peoples (cf. p. 82 f.). The characters brought before us in the Iliad are almost invariably either princes or persons attached to the retinues of princes, and themselves apparently of what we may call knightly rank. The chief exception (Thersites) is described in a way which only proves the rule. It is true that this principle is not so strictly observed in the latter part of the Odyssey.

[1] Cf. Breal, *Pour mieux connaître Homer*, p. 24 : "Attribuer à la poesie populaire une composition en vingt-quatre chants, quelle folie !" But one must bear in mind the length sometimes attained by Bosnian poems (cf. p. 101). I may remark here that this work—like many others dealing with the Homeric poems—frequently uses arguments which would not have been put forward if attention had been paid to the heroic poetry of other European peoples.

Several persons of humble rank are introduced here, though it is to be noted that the most prominent of them (Eumaios, the swine-herd) is said to be of princely birth.   In other respects however the Odyssey conforms to the rules of Teutonic court poetry just as much as the Iliad.   Thus it is fond of describing in detail the movements of kings and queens in their palaces and the conventions observed in the reception of strangers. Again, persons of princely rank are seldom spoken of with disrespect in either poem.   Dialogues must of course be excepted, and also references (especially in the Nekyia) to persons of the far past—precisely as in Teutonic poetry.   But in general there is a noteworthy absence of any display of feeling against the opponents of the poet's heroes—as much in the case of Penelope's suitors as in that of the Trojans.   Perhaps the most striking instance is the semi-apologetic account of Clytaimnestra's conduct given by Nestor (Od. III 263—272), a passage which may be compared with the story of Offa's wife in Beowulf. We may note also the surprisingly lenient treatment of Paris in the Iliad.   Indeed the characters represented in the most unfavourable light are gods—a phenomenon for which we have analogies in Old Norse poetry.   Lastly, we must observe the strict avoidance of coarseness and of things not mentioned in polite society.

Before we proceed further it will be convenient to turn for a moment to Hesiod's poems.   For these also early Teutonic literature presents a number of fairly close parallels.   In particular the proverbial part of the Works and Days has many analogies in gnomic poetry, both English and Scandinavian.   As an example we may cite the first and last portions of Hávamál. Again the precepts on husbandry and the calendar resemble several Anglo-Saxon works both in prose and verse.   For the Theogony the closest Teutonic parallel—and it is very close— is the prose Gylfaginning; but earlier poetical works, such as Völuspá and Hyndlulióð, run on somewhat similar lines.   There is evidence too that subjects of the same kind were once popular in England[1].   Lastly, the verses (22 ff.) which relate how the

---

[1] Cf. especially a letter from Daniel, bishop of Winchester, to St Boniface, written about the year 720 (Jaffé, *Bibliotheca Rerum Germanicarum*, III 71 ff.).

poet received his inspiration may be compared with the story of Caedmon.

Now if we compare the characteristics of Hesiodic and Homeric poetry we cannot fail to notice that they present a very striking contrast in several respects, even apart from the absence of a common theme. In the first place Hesiod takes no pains to conceal his personality. Again, his poems contain little in the way of detailed description, except where the occupations of a farmer's life are discussed. Thirdly, they show no tendency to avoid indelicate subjects. Lastly, they betray no acquaintance with court life. Kings are occasionally mentioned, though not by name, but all the references are to their public appearances, as judges or mediators. We may notice too that though in the Theogony (v. 80 ff.) they are spoken of with respect, in the Works and Days (v. 38 f.) the title is coupled with an opprobrious epithet (δωροφάγους). No one can fail to observe that in nearly all these respects[1] Hesiod shows the characteristics which commonly distinguish popular poetry.

But we have to remember that in spite of all these differences Hesiod uses the same metrical form and to a large extent the same style of language as the Homeric poems. There can be little doubt that priority lies with the latter; indeed Hesiod frequently betrays acquaintance with Homeric poetry. But it must not be assumed that his themes were new; they are far more primitive than anything of the heroic type. If Hesiod was the founder of a new era in poetry we must conclude that his innovation consisted in the application of the forms of heroic poetry to purposes for which they had not previously been used. The heroic hexameter is the only form of metre which can be traced back beyond the seventh century, and we can hardly doubt that it is the oldest form of cultivated Greek poetry. But less elaborate forms of verse—perhaps rude precursors of the iambic and lyric metres—must also have been in popular use for ages in ballads, songs and hymns. We may infer then that what Hesiod did was to turn to popular use the form of poetry which represented the highest standard of art in his day.

[1] The suppression of the poet's personality is not a mark of heroic poetry as such, but of epic or narrative heroic poetry.

But what were the conditions which produced this elaborate and highly artificial type of poetry? The characteristics of Homeric poetry enumerated above are conclusive evidence that it was not of popular origin. Some of them are extremely difficult to account for unless its true home was in the king's courts. It may be objected that Hesiod was familiar with Homeric poetry, though he knew nothing of court life. But Hesiod probably belonged to the last days of the kingly period, when that institution was losing its power and popularity. It is only in accordance with what we might expect that in such an age court poets—in view of Theog. 94 f. we should perhaps say minstrels—would frequently try to get a hearing from a wider circle. Hesiod's own activity falls in with this explanation perfectly well. His popularity was due to the fact that he pre-served the artistic form of court poetry, while at the same time he discarded its conventions and turned to subjects which were more in accordance with the tastes and interests of his own class.

Apart from the courts it is difficult to see where conditions favourable to the growth of Homeric poetry could have existed. Aeolis in the eighth century must have differed very greatly from the city states of the sixth and fifth centuries. Hesiod himself belonged to a family which was possessed of some property. His father was a merchant; but we can hardly suppose that this class was either numerous or wealthy, in a land which consisted essentially of agricultural communities. We shall hardly go astray, I think, in believing that the conditions here at the time of which we are speaking bore far more resem-blance to those which prevailed in Teutonic kingdoms some twelve or thirteen centuries later than to those of cities like Miletos or Athens at their prime. There as here the wealth was probably to a large extent in the possession of the kings. Indeed from the story of Midas' relations with Agamemnon of Cyme (cf. p. 227) we may perhaps infer that the kings retained a certain amount of influence even in the latter part of the eighth century. On the other hand the name of this king may certainly be taken as evidence that the courts were interested in heroic poetry[1].

[1] Unfortunately there seems to be hardly any material which might enable us to

We have now seen that Homeric poetry goes back to the age of kingship and that it is not of popular origin (Stage III), but in all probability a product of court life. Our next object must be to consider whether this poetry was a direct continuation of the court-minstrelsy of the Heroic Age (Stage I), represented by Demodocos and Phemios—in which case of course it will correspond to Stage II of our scheme—or whether it is rather a secondary outgrowth from popular poetry (Stage IV). The problem, it will be seen, is essentially one of stratification. If we may, in archaeological language, speak of the Homeric poems as a 'palace-structure'—it ought surely to be possible to determine whether traces of a 'village settlement' lie immediately beneath it.

It has been pointed out above (p. 224 f.) that the Nibelungenlied cannot furnish any true analogy to the history of Homeric poetry. The other type of Stage IV which we have considered (p. 99 f.) is that of the Edda poems. But I do not think that anyone will seriously expect to find a strict parallel here. In that case we should have to suppose that heroic poetry was originally unknown to the Aeolians, whether in Asia or Thessaly. But the Thessalian element—including as it does such striking conceptions as the location of the gods on Mount Olympos—is too deeply engrained in this class of poetry to render such a hypothesis probable. We shall see shortly that a better analogy for the history of the Edda poems is perhaps to be found in quite a different quarter.

The theory which obtains most currency at the present time is that Homeric poetry grew up in the Greek settlements on the Asiatic coast on the basis of ballads derived from Thessaly—perhaps also from other parts of Greece. This theory does not exactly answer to our definition of Stage IV; but we may treat it under the same heading, as it likewise involves the development of heroic poetry out of popular poetry. According to any explanation of this kind we must of course assume that the court-minstrelsy depicted in the poems is a reflection of court

estimate the popularity of heroic names in Greece in early times (cf. pp. 42 ff., 64 ff.). Note however may be taken of the existence of a prince named Hector in Chios, perhaps shortly after the time of Agamemnon of Cyme.

life in the Asiatic settlements. This is conceivable enough in itself, provided that the requisite conditions are carried back at least to the ninth century. But is the theory probable? No one will suggest, I suppose, that the wealth or culture of the Aeolic settlements during the tenth and ninth centuries was superior to that of the Greek kingdoms in general towards the close of the Achaean period. Briefly stated then the current theory comes to this : the wealthier and more cultured period produced nothing but popular ballads, while the poorer and ruder period produced a most elaborate and magnificent court poetry.

We have seen that Homeric poetry possesses certain characteristics which are incompatible with the idea that it is itself of popular origin. But a closer inspection will show that some of these characteristics are almost as difficult to account for on the hypothesis that it was a recent outgrowth from popular poetry. In particular this is true of their metrical form, if we are justified in believing that the Homeric type of verse presupposes a long artistic development. Again, the confusion of different stories which characterises popular poetry (Stage III) will not be removed in its more cultivated successor (Stage IV); Dietrich von Bern (Theodric) remains by the side of Etzel (Attila) in the Nibelungenlied. The same remark too applies to those changes of character which popular poetry is apt to produce. In the Nibelungenlied Hagen remains as cruel and Kriemhild as passionately vindictive as popular fancy had painted them. The poets of a later age will not trouble themselves to save the characters of persons who lived long ago. We shall see shortly that this is true of Greek poetry just as much as of German. But the Homeric poems—except perhaps in the Nekyia—will not supply us with examples.

Finally, we must bear in mind those reminiscences of Mycenean—or rather 'sub-Mycenean'—splendour which the poems contain and their almost invariable use of bronze as the material for weapons—not to mention the fact that the political and national boundaries which they record are totally different from those which existed in the ninth century. Will anyone seriously maintain that such traditions could be preserved through the medium of popular ballads alone? I confess that such a hypothesis is altogether incredible to me.

Now let us take the alternative explanation, suggested by the Anglo-Saxon poems. It is generally agreed that the Aeolic settlements are older than the Ionic in Asia; but since even the former are ignored in the poems it is hardly probable that they came into existence until towards the close of the Achaean period. When the storms broke upon Greece crowds of refugees, not only from Thessaly but also from many other parts of the country, fled to the new Aeolic settlements across the Aegean. Among them, according to the suggested analogy, were many court minstrels, of the type represented by Demodocos and Phemios, who brought with them not only a poetic technique matured by long experience but also a number of poems, of which the newest would probably be the most in favour. This poetry was developed and expanded by the court minstrels of subsequent generations; but the subject-matter became stereotyped and—precisely as in England—everything relating to the new settlements was completely ignored. This is the conclusion to which all the evidence at our disposal seems to me to point.

We must now turn for a moment to the Cyclic poems. And here it is to be remembered in the first place that our information is very defective, if not actually misleading. Herodotus (II 117) doubted Homer's authorship of the Cypria on the ground that it contained a statement in direct contradiction with the Iliad, namely that Alexandros arrived at Troy with Helen on the third day after leaving Sparta, whereas it is stated in the Iliad (VI 290 ff.) that he wandered out of his course (to Sidon) when he brought her. But the epitome of the Cypria which has come down to us states expressly that Alexandros did go to Sidon. Hence we can only conclude that its trustworthiness as an authority for the contents of the poem is open to serious doubt.

Taking the evidence as it stands we can detect at once an important difference between the Cypria and the Nostoi on the one hand and the Iliad and the Odyssey on the other. In the two former poems the action seems to have been spread over a considerable number of years, while in the latter it was limited to a few days or weeks. Again, as far as we can judge, the two former treated a much larger number of events, in proportion to their length—events too which were not so closely connected with one another. Indeed they seem to have been almost in the nature of chronicles. These however are characteristics of popular rather than court poetry.

The story of the Cypria, as we know it, bears a curious resemblance to the Edda trilogy Reginsmál—Fáfnismál—Sigrdrífumál (cf. p. 13). Both the Cyclic poem and the trilogy served as introductions to famous stories. Both stories were essentially concerned with the adventures and passions of human beings; but in both cases the introduction begins with the gods, and the origin of the tragic events which follow is traced ultimately to irresponsible, not to say mischievous, conduct on the part of certain deities. There can be no doubt that the whole theme of the Northern poems is a late addition to the story of Sigurðr, and that the poems themselves were composed as an introduction to this story. Is it not possible that the Cypria was of somewhat similar origin? The latter part of the poem, if we are to trust the epitome, contained some extraordinary features. The story of Odysseus' pretended madness and how he was eventually compelled to join the expedition is difficult to reconcile with the general tone of Homeric poetry. Again, the army is represented as assembling twice at Aulis and twice starting for Troy. The account of the first of these incidents agrees with what is stated in the Iliad (II 303 ff.), while the second contains the story of the sacrifice of Iphigeneia, according to the version in which she was rescued by Artemis. On the other hand it is worth bearing in mind that the poem is said to have ended with a catalogue of the Trojan allies, presumably the same list which we find in the Iliad (II 816 ff., or perhaps 840 ff.) —and this can hardly be regarded as a late composition.

The chief characteristic of the Nostoi seems to have been absence of unity. Beginning with the departure of the Achaeans from Troy, it narrated the adventures which befell various heroes on their return. These formed, as far as we can tell, a number of quite distinct stories, unconnected with one another except at the beginning. If we may judge from the number of books

contained in the poem—five as against eleven in the Cypria—
these stories must have been very short, and consequently it is
perhaps questionable whether we are justified in regarding the
Nostoi as an epic at all, except in the same sense in which that
term is applied to Hesiodic poetry. Indeed it seems to have
had an affinity with the latter in more than one respect; for the
stories of the various heroes were probably not uninfluenced by
genealogical interests. In the same light we may perhaps
regard the fact that one scene is laid in an Ionic city (Colophon).
All these features suggest that the poem came into existence at a
fairly late period. If the Cypria was designed as an introduction
to the story of the siege of Troy there can be little doubt that
the Nostoi was composed as an epilogue to the same. On the
other hand many scholars hold that it has been used by the
Odyssey. But it is at least questionable whether the references
in question do not come from the sources of the poem rather
than the work itself[1].

The other poems of the Trojan series—the Aithiopis, Little
Iliad and Iliu Persis—resembled the Cypria and the Nostoi in
the fact that they dealt with a considerable number of separate
episodes[2]. But the resemblance was perhaps only superficial;
for these episodes were apparently represented as following one
another in regular sequence. If we had only a fragmentary
epitome of the Iliad we might gather from it much the same
impression. All these poems were on a small scale, eleven
books in all; but, unlike the Cypria and the Nostoi, the action
covered only a short interval of time. Several incidents which
they related are referred to or even told at length in the
Odyssey; but we have not sufficient information to enable us
to determine whether the references are taken from the poems
themselves. The chief argument to the contrary is that these
poems seem to have contained certain 'post-Homeric' features,
notably the rite of purification from bloodshed, in the Aithiopis,

[1] Athenaeus (281 b, 395 d) mentions a poem called Κάθοδος Ἀτρειδῶν, of which
nothing seems to be known elsewhere. As it contained at least three books it can
hardly have formed part of the Nostoi.

[2] Cf. Aristotle, *Poet*. XXIII 4, where it is stated that the Iliad and Odyssey
provide material for only one or two tragedies each, the Cypria for many and the
Little Iliad for eight.

and the sacrifice of a virgin (Polyxene), in the Iliu Persis. The former case is especially significant, because—in striking contrast with the spirit of later Greek poetry—the ideas of pollution and purification seem to be entirely ignored in the Iliad and Odyssey[1].

These so-called post-Homeric features are of course really characteristics of a more primitive religion, and it would be better to describe them as 'non-Homeric' or 'non-heroic.' But the fact that such practices are ignored in the Iliad and Odyssey, while later poets had a special affection for them, renders it probable that their presence in the Cyclic poems is due to popular influence. Are we then justified in assigning these poems to Stage IV of our scheme? That is a question which, considering the evidence at our disposal, I feel a good deal of hesitation in answering. Certainly they cannot have differed from the Iliad and Odyssey in anything like the same degree that the medieval German poems or even the heroic poems of the Edda differ from Beowulf. They may actually have incorporated a good deal of ancient matter. On the whole the balance of probability seems to me to incline towards the view that the Cyclic poems are derived ultimately from the same body of early heroic court poetry upon which the Iliad and Odyssey themselves are based; but that their composition took place in later times, when the 'Homeric' standard was no longer preserved in its purity.

Whatever may be the case with the Cyclic poems there are other poetic works which may be assigned to Stage IV without hesitation. For our purpose it will perhaps be best to take an illustration from the drama; for, though such works are only secondary authorities, they are on the whole less open to objection than lost poems on which our information may be misleading. A good example is furnished by Aeschylus' Oresteia, a series of plays which deals with a subject treated at some length in the Odyssey. The chief incidents are the murder of Agamemnon by his wife Clytaimnestra, the vengeance taken upon her by her son Orestes, the persecution of the

---

[1] The 'purification' of the house of Odysseus (Od. XXII 437 ff.) is of an essentially different character: cf. Harrison, *Prolegomena to the Study of Greek Religion*, p. 24 f.

matricide by the Erinyes, his purification by Apollo, and his
trial by Athene and the citizens of Athens.   In the Odyssey
the first of these incidents, the murder, is ascribed to Aigisthos,
Clytaimnestra's paramour.   As regards the second we have
nothing but a passing reference to Clytaimnestra's funeral.
The other incidents are not mentioned at all.   Again, in
Aeschylus' work prominence is given to an attempt on Clytaimnestra's part to placate the dead Agamemnon, to an
invocation of him for vengeance by his children, and to the
instigation of the Erinyes by Clytaimnestra's ghost.   These
features too are unknown in the Odyssey; indeed they are
directly opposed to all that we know of Homeric religion.
Then again we find frequent and detailed allusions to tragic
events which had occurred previously in the history of Agamemnon's family—especially the 'banquet of Thyestes' and
the sacrifice of Iphigeneia.   On these matters too both the
Iliad and the Odyssey are completely silent.   Yet in the latter
case this silence cannot be due to accident.   Either the poets
were ignorant of the story, or they deliberately suppressed it.

Few modern readers can fail to appreciate the Oresteia as
an almost unrivalled masterpiece of poetic art, in spite of the
fact that the ideas with which it is permeated are largely strange
and unreal to us.   But what would have been the effect if such
a work had been recited at one of those courts in which Homeric
poetry was patronised in early times ?   There can scarcely be
any doubt, I think, that the recitation would not have been
tolerated.   To such an audience the poet's religious conceptions
would have been intelligible enough, but only as products of a
degraded and baneful superstition, while his skilful presentation
of various painful incidents in the history of a royal house—the
most distinguished in Greece—would have appeared not merely
an offence against good manners but rather a wanton insult to
the kingly class in general.

The social conditions and the ethical standard of Aeschylus'
time differed no doubt very greatly from those of the Homeric
age.   This is a subject with which we shall have to deal later.
It should be observed however that nearly all the special features
which characterise Aeschylus' treatment of this story can be

paralleled from Scandinavian works which we may assign to
Stage IV. A very close analogy for the 'banquet of Thyestes'
is furnished by the story of Guðrún, Atli and their children;
and it is to be remembered that, though Atli at least was a
historical character, this story cannot possibly have any foundation in fact. The persecution of Orestes by the Erinyes may
be compared with Saxo's story (p. 246) of the curse inflicted
upon Haldanus[1], likewise as a result of the shedding of 'kindred
blood.' With the sacrifice of Iphigeneia we may compare that
of Vikarr in Gautreks Saga (cap. 7), which was also brought
about by the prevalence of contrary winds. Invocation of the
dead is not uncommon in such works. On the other hand it is
extremely doubtful whether any of those features would have
been permissible in early heroic poetry. They do not occur in
the extant poems of Stage II.

There is sufficient evidence that most of the characteristic
features of Aeschylus' story were not invented by him, though
as to his sources our information is not very satisfactory. The
lost Oresteia of Stesichoros was doubtless one of his chief
authorities, and there is some reason for believing that the
version given in this work differed from the Homeric account
quite as much as that of Aeschylus. Beyond Stesichoros we
may perhaps think of the Cyclic poems, especially the Nostoi;
but it is very doubtful if they would have furnished such a very
markedly divergent form of the story. Stesichoros himself is
said to have treated his authorities with great freedom. But
some of the non-Homeric features can hardly be due to
deliberate alteration. We may notice especially the differences
in the personal relations of Agamemnon's family. In the
Iliad he is the son of Atreus; Stesichoros and others call him
son of Pleisthenes. In the Iliad he has three daughters, Lao-
dice, Chrysothemis and Iphianassa; Aeschylus gives him two,
Electra and Iphigeneia, the latter of whom seems to have figured
also in the Cypria[2]. There is also a good deal of discrepancy

---

[1] This incident may also be compared with a passage in the Iliad (IX 453 ff.).
Phoinix' speech (perhaps designedly) shows a nearer approximation to this type of
religion (cf. also v. 568 ff.) than any other part of the Homeric poems.

[2] The version of the sacrifice given in the Cypria (cf. p. 235) is probably to be

in regard to the scene of the events. In the Iliad and Odyssey Agamemnon belongs to Mycenae; in Aeschylus' account this place is forgotten and the story transferred to Argos, while Pindar, apparently also Stesichoros and Simonides[1], placed it at Amyclai (close to Sparta). Now these are just the kind of corruptions and discrepancies which characterise popular poetry everywhere. Taken together with the other non-Homeric features discussed above they seem to me to afford ground for suspecting that Stesichoros and his followers drew upon a popular and perhaps Doric or Peloponnesian version of the story[2] which was independent of Homeric poetry. Their work then would be similar in more than one respect to that of those Norse poets who rehabilitated the old story of Sigurðr and Guðrún after the (strophic) type of their own national poetry.

The course of our discussion has led us to conclude that the Homeric poems are products of court poetry or minstrelsy in direct continuation of that type of minstrelsy which we considered at the beginning of the chapter. As yet however we have expressed no definite opinion as to the length of time involved in their development, although we have noticed that the evidence commonly adduced in favour of a long interval between the earliest and latest portions of the poems is highly unsatisfactory. It must be admitted that beyond a certain point the evidence at our disposal does not admit of anything more than an estimation of probability.

We have seen that there is good reason for believing that the history of heroic poetry in Aeolis and in England proceeded on similar lines in several respects, and also that the chief monument of English heroic poetry was probably composed within ⋅ not much more than a century after certain events which it

---

regarded as later than the other, although it occurred in what was doubtless a much earlier poem.

[1] Cf. Pindar, *Pyth.* XI 32; Stesichoros (Bergk), fragm. 39.

[2] The Spartans possessed a tomb of Agamemnon at Amyclai (cf. Pausanias, III 19. 6). Indeed, from Herodotus, VII 159, it would seem that they claimed him as one of their own kings as far back as the time of Xerxes. It has been suggested that a similar version of the story is implied in Od. IV 514 f.; but the inference is doubtful. Aigisthos rules Mycenae (after Agamemnon's death in III 305).

records. Now in any comparison between English and Greek
heroic poetry we must of course leave out of account the frequent
Christian allusions which occur in the former (cf. p. 47 ff.); for
there is no reason whatever for supposing that any change
comparable with the introduction of Christianity came over the
Greek world during the times which saw the development of
Homeric poetry. Apart from this element anachronisms are
not very numerous or marked; but they do occur. Thus the
road which leads to the Danish king's dwelling is described
as a Roman road (*straet*), paved with stone (Beow. 320), while
the members of the same king's court (*ib*. 768) are termed
'inhabitants of a chester' (*ceasterbuendum*). Such cases may be
compared with the Homeric inconsistencies discussed in the
last chapter—e.g. perhaps the occasional use of iron for weapons.
It can hardly be maintained, I think, that the latter are of greater
significance than the anachronisms in English heroic poetry.

This absence of striking anachronisms decidedly favours the
view that the period involved in the development of Homeric
poetry was not very long. Against such a conclusion it may
of course be urged that there is a constantly recurring phrase
(οἷοι νῦν βροτοί εἰσι) which contrasts the 'men of the present
day,' i.e. the men of the poet's own time, with the heroes of the
siege of Troy, emphasizing the superior strength of the latter.
But it is quite unnecessary to suppose that a long interval of
time is intended here. The old Nestor uses almost the same
expression in Il. I 272 (τῶν οἳ νῦν βροτοί εἰσιν ἐπιχθόνιοι),
when he compares the men among whom he was then living
with those he had known in his youth. Again, in Od. VIII 122f.,
Odysseus contrasts the 'men of the present day' (ὅσσοι νῦν
βροτοί εἰσιν ἐπὶ χθονὶ) with the 'men of old' (ἀνδράσι προτέ-
ροισιν); but by the latter phrase he means persons belonging
to the generation next above his own (Heracles and Eurytos).
The same usage occurs elsewhere. Thus in Il. IX 524 Phoinix
speaks oı the 'glories of those heroes that were of old' (τῶν
πρόσθεν ἐπευθόμεθα κλέα ἀνδρῶν ἡρώων); but the story which
he proceeds to relate is of Meleagros, the uncle of Diomedes.
Indeed persons of more than two generations back are seldom
mentioned in the Homeric poems.

C.   16

An expression very similar to the one last quoted is used by Hesiod (Theog. 99 ff.) when he speaks of the minstrel as singing the "glories of men of old and the blessed gods who hold Olympos[1]." Here of course the reference is not to persons of the last generation, but to the heroes of Homeric poetry. In the Works and Days, vv. 156 ff., 174 ff., the Heroic Age is distinguished with all possible clearness from the period in which the poet himself lived. It is not to be overlooked that antiquarian interest forms a prominent feature in all Hesiodic poetry. Even in the Works and Days it is obvious enough, although such topics have little in common with the main theme of the poem. In the Catalogue we meet with such characters as Hellen and Doros, who owe their existence to speculations in tribal origins. The poetry of the following period seems to have been essentially of a genealogical character.

For such antiquarian interest the Homeric poems furnish no evidence, except perhaps in the Nekyia. Not only are the genealogies of the heroes seldom carried back more than two generations, but—what is more important—there is scarcely any reference to their descendants, beyond the first generation. Again, Achilles is said to have been singing the 'glories of heroes' ($\kappa\lambda\acute{\epsilon}\alpha$ $\acute{\alpha}\nu\delta\rho\hat{\omega}\nu$) when he received the embassy (Il. IX 189); but it is not stated that these were heroes of former times. The songs of Demodocos and Phemios deal with the adventures of the Achaeans at Troy and on their return home. That this is no accident is shown by Od. I 351 f., where Telemachos pleads in excuse for Phemios that "men always prize that song the most which rings newest in their ears." No sentiment could well be more foreign to the tone of Hesiodic or post-Hesiodic poetry than this. If any poet of that school had interested himself in contemporary history our knowledge of the eighth century would not be the blank which unfortunately it is. Clearly the only heroic poetry known to them was the $\kappa\lambda\acute{\epsilon}\epsilon\alpha$ $\pi\rho\sigma\tau\acute{\epsilon}\rho\omega\nu$ $\acute{\alpha}\nu\theta\rho\acute{\omega}\pi\omega\nu$. That means very much the same thing

$\epsilon\grave{\iota}$ $\gamma\acute{\alpha}\rho$ $\tau\iota\varsigma$ $\kappa\alpha\grave{\iota}$ $\pi\acute{\epsilon}\nu\theta\sigma\varsigma$ $\check{\epsilon}\chi\omega\nu$ $\nu\epsilon\sigma\kappa\eta\delta\acute{\epsilon}\iota$ $\theta\nu\mu\hat{\omega}$
$\check{\alpha}\zeta\eta\tau\alpha\iota$ $\kappa\rho\alpha\delta\acute{\iota}\eta\nu$ $\acute{\alpha}\kappa\alpha\chi\acute{\eta}\mu\epsilon\nu\sigma\varsigma$, $\alpha\grave{\upsilon}\tau\grave{\alpha}\rho$ $\acute{\alpha}\sigma\iota\delta\grave{\sigma}\varsigma$
$M\sigma\upsilon\sigma\acute{\alpha}\omega\nu$ $\theta\epsilon\rho\acute{\alpha}\pi\omega\nu$ $\kappa\lambda\acute{\epsilon}\epsilon\alpha$ $\pi\rho\sigma\tau\acute{\epsilon}\rho\omega\nu$ $\acute{\alpha}\nu\theta\rho\acute{\omega}\pi\omega\nu$
$\acute{\upsilon}\mu\nu\acute{\eta}\sigma\eta$ $\mu\acute{\alpha}\kappa\alpha\rho\acute{\alpha}\varsigma$ $\tau\epsilon$ $\theta\epsilon\sigma\grave{\upsilon}\varsigma$ $\sigma\ddot{\iota}$ $\H{O}\lambda\upsilon\mu\pi\sigma\nu$ $\check{\epsilon}\chi\sigma\upsilon\sigma\iota\nu$, $\kappa.\tau.\lambda.$

as Einhard's *ueterum regum actus et bella* or the *antiquorum actus regumque certamina* sung by Bernlef (cf. pp. 80, 87). At such a time if anyone was composing a heroic poem it would probably have seemed natural enough to use the formulae with which several of the Edda poems begin : "It was long ago," or "It was in early times that," etc. On the other hand Telemachos' remark would be perfectly appropriate in the earlier stages of Teutonic poetry. We have seen (p. 85) that in Beowulf one of the Danish king's knights begins to compose a poem on the hero's adventure within a few hours of the event. Procopius' account of Hermegisklos and Radiger (p. 97 ff.) must also be borne in mind, although this story may not have attained the form of an epic poem.

The conclusion then to which the Teutonic evidence leads us is that at all events the type of narrative was fixed very early. The growth of the Homeric poems may or may not have taken longer than that of their Teutonic counterparts. Records of the eighth century B.C. speak of κλέεα προτέρων ἀνθρώπων; records of the eighth century A.D. speak of *antiquorum actus*. But in neither case do the poems themselves give expression to a consciousness of the antiquity of the events which they relate.

NOTE VI. THE TROJAN CATALOGUE.

In the last chapter we have endeavoured to estimate in general terms the position of the Homeric poems relatively to the poetry of the Heroic Age itself on the one hand and to Hesiod and genealogical poetry on the other. I have avoided entering into details in regard to the relationship between the extant poems and the lost Cyclic poems because I did not wish to load the discussion with matter which, owing to the fragmentary nature of the evidence, must largely be of a hypothetical character. At the same time I am inclined to think that the Trojan Catalogue (Il. II 816 ff.) does contain some indications which may permit the date of its composition to be determined with a fair amount of probability.

According to Proclus' Chrestomathy[1] the Cypria contained (apparently at the end) a κατάλογος τῶν τοῖς Τρωσὶ συμμαχησάντων, and it is commonly believed[2] that this is the list which has been incorporated in our text of the Iliad. Proclus' words, taken literally, would seem to indicate that the list did not include the Trojans themselves. The 'allies' proper begin perhaps at v. 840, and consequently it has been held that vv. 816—839 are a later addition. Considering the nature of the evidence, this view can scarcely be regarded as beyond question. But there certainly are noticeable differences between the first and second portions of the list, apart from the fact that the former contains no national names except Τρῶες and Δαρδάνιοι. The first part is much more dependent on the Iliad than is the second. Thus all the personal names which occur in it are to be found in other parts of the poem, while several passages (eight verses[3] out of the twenty-four) have been borrowed practically verbatim. On the other hand, out of the twenty-five persons mentioned in the second part of the list eleven are not met with elsewhere in the Iliad, while four of the others are not elsewhere associated with the nations (Mysians, Phrygians and Meiones) to which they belong here. Again, though several verses show acquaintance with other passages in the Iliad, there is apparently no single verse which has been borrowed entire. The most striking fact however is that in two cases we have references to heroes who are said to have been slain by Achilles in the river. Neither of these persons is mentioned in the account of the river fight given in the Iliad. In explanation of this it has been suggested that another scene of this kind occurred in the Aithiopis; but we have no evidence to his effect, and it is surely at least as probable that they are derived from a different version of the river fight described in the Iliad.

[1] Cf. Kinkel, *Epicorum Graec. Fragmenta*, p. 20.   [2] See the Addenda.

[3] v. 822 f. from XII 99 f., vv. 831—4 from XI 329—332, v. 838 f. from XII 96 f. The borrowing of vv. 831—4 can hardly be ascribed to the same man who took Amphios (the son of Selagos) from V 612. Ignorance of the contents of the poem such as we find here is very rare; its occurrence therefore in what is probably a very late addition to the text deserves to be noticed.

In both parts of the list we meet with a considerable number of geographical names—of cities, rivers and mountains—many of which (five in the first part and twelve in the second) do not occur elsewhere in the Iliad. The majority of the names mentioned belong to the immediate neighbourhood of the coast, and it is a fact worth noting that these almost all fall into three distinct groups—in Paphlagonia, the Troad and Caria respectively. There is a great gap covering apparently the whole of the Bithynian coast and another embracing the coast of the Aegean from Troy itself to Mycale. In explanation of this fact it has been suggested[1] that the names in the coast-districts are derived from an early poem or poems on the voyage of the Argo. This hypothesis might certainly account for the mention of the Paphlagonian names in v. 852 ff. But they are the only names in the second part of the list for which it gives any explanation ; for the suggestion that the references to the Carian localities in v. 868 f. are connected in any way with the story of the Argo can hardly be taken seriously. Hence, if we are to trust the hypothesis in any form, it is more probable that v. 853 ff. are a subsequent addition to the list. But even in the first part the evidence in its favour is of the most slender description[2]. Of the thirteen place-names which occur in this section eight are found elsewhere in the Iliad ; of the rest only two apparently are mentioned in the accounts of the voyage of the Argo which have come down to us. What is more important however is that these accounts do mention a considerable number of Bithynian localities[3], both on the coast of the Sea of Marmara and on that of the Black Sea, as well as several peoples who do not appear in the Catalogue. We must conclude then that this hypothesis in no way accounts for the peculiarities of the Catalogue.

The true explanation is not far to seek. It was well known to the ancients that the Bithynians were an intrusive Thracian people who had crossed over from Europe. Again, the Aegean coast, at all events from the Gulf of Adramyttion southwards[4], was covered with Aeolic and Ionic settlements. Greek tradition unanimously held that these settlements were planted subsequently to the Trojan War, and we have no reason for supposing that the author of the Catalogue thought differently. At the same time we may infer from his silence that he did not claim to know what peoples had occupied these regions previously. On the other hand he did

---

[1] Cf. Niese, *Der homerische Schiffskatalog*, p. 53 ff.

[2] The argument that Abydos and Sestos cannot have been connected except in a περίπλους (cf. Niese, *op. cit.* p. 54) is one which will appeal probably to no student of early Teutonic history.

[3] Cf. Apollon. Rhod. I 1164 ff., II 649 ff., 720 ff., 901 ff., etc.

[4] It is held that the Aeolic settlements in the south of the Troad were established at quite a late period, probably in the seventh century. But we are not justified in assuming that no such settlements existed previously. It is highly probable that the whole of this district was devastated by the barbarians whose remains have been found at Troy (cf. p. 295, note).

claim such knowledge of the previous occupants not only of the Troad but also of the Carian coast.

This fact surely furnishes the means of dating the composition of the Catalogue with a fair amount of probability. It is generally agreed that the Ionic settlements were later than the Aeolic; but probably no one will contend that the Greek occupation of Miletos and Mycale began appreciably later than the end of the tenth century. It is not necessary of course to suppose that these places were still in Carian hands when the Catalogue was composed. But at the same time the memory of their former possessors is not likely to have been perpetuated in an incidental reference like this much more than a century after they became Greek settlements. The more northern part of the list contains at all events nothing incompatible with the view that it was drawn up in the first half of the eighth century. The excavations in the Troad have certainly brought to light the fact that that district was overrun by barbarians. But there is nothing to show that this took place at the time of the Bithynian invasion, whether the two movements were connected in any way or not. The evidence on the whole seems to indicate that the barbarian occupation occurred not very long before the foundation of the Ionic colonies on the Hellespont. There is nothing very remarkable in the fact that the places mentioned in the Catalogue lie chiefly on the coast; for such places would naturally be the most familiar to the Asiatic Greeks, who must have been a seafaring people to some extent from the beginning.

Now in other parts of the Iliad we find mention of several peoples which apparently occupied the districts left blank in the Catalogue. Thus in X 429, XX 329 we hear of the Caucones, who seem to have belonged to Bithynia[1]. In XXI 86 f., VI 396 f. (cf. II 691, etc.) we meet with peoples called Leleges and Cilices, the positions of which are quite definitely stated. The former are said to have dwelt in the valley of the Satnioeis, in the south of the Troad, the latter somewhat further to the east, about the Gulf of Adramyttion. Again, in Od. XI 519 ff. we hear of a certain Eurypylos the son of Telephos, chief of the Ceteioi. Telephos and his son figured in the Cypria and the Little Iliad; and Greek tradition placed their home (Teuthrania) in the region between the Gulf of Adramyttion and the Hermos. The name Κήτειοι has been connected with that of the Hittites (Kheta); but without going into this question we may probably follow Strabo (XIII 1. 70) in tracing a reminiscence of them in the name of a stream called Ceteios, a tributary of the Caicos. The Catalogue contains no reference to any of these peoples, presumably because their names were not familiar to the author. In later times we hear no more of the Ceteioi, while Cilices are found only in Cilicia. The Leleges indeed are mentioned frequently and on both sides of the Aegean, but only as a people of the past.

It is an easy and popular method of interpretation to discredit evidence for which no obvious explanation is forthcoming; and following this method

---

[1] Cf. especially Strabo XII 3. 5.

many scholars have regarded the names under discussion as phantoms. The point against which adverse criticism has chiefly been directed is the location of the Cilices in the Gulf of Adramyttion. It is to be remembered however that we have no evidence earlier than the seventh century for the presence of a people called Cilices in the land which ultimately bore their name. In the eighth century this people apparently dwelt to the north of the Taurus. In earlier times we hear of them, so far as I am aware, only in the 'Poem of Pentaur,' a work which celebrates the battle fought at Kadesh early in the thirteenth century, between Rameses II and the Hittites. It is there stated that the "chief of Kheta had come, having gathered together all countries from the ends of the sea to the land of Kheta, which came entire[1]." In addition to a number of Syrian names which occur in the accounts of earlier wars the poem contains a group of new names of peoples, consisting of *Pidasa, Dardenui, Masa, Kalakisha* and *Luka*, with two others[2]. The last two of these names are almost universally identified with the Cilices and Lycians, and the first is usually connected with the name Πήδασος or Πήδασα, while many scholars accept the identification of the second and third with the Dardanoi and Mysians respectively. If the names *Pidasa* and Πήδασος are connected we are brought to the Aegean, where we find both Pedasos on the Satnioeis and Pedasa[3] in Caria. Evidence to the same effect is furnished by the procession of ten warriors depicted on one of the monuments[4]. Of these five are of the Hittite type and two Semitic; but the other three are of Aegean physiognomy and wear different varieties of that feather headdress which is known in Crete from much earlier times[5]. When we find that this earliest reference to the Cilices associates them with a group of peoples[6], of whom some clearly belong to the west of Asia Minor, and some quite probably to the north-west corner of the peninsula, it must be admitted that we have no valid ground for discrediting the evidence of the Iliad as to their presence around the Gulf of Adramyttion.

---

[1] Cf. Breasted, *Ancient Records, Egypt*, III p. 138.

[2] One of these names has been variously read as *Maunna* or *Ariunna* (*Arwena*) and identified with the Μῄονες and Ἴλιον of the Iliad, as well as with Oroanda and other places. The other, *Keshkesh*, seems to bear the same relationship to the cuneiform *Kasku* which the Eg. *Kalakisha* (*Kelekesh* in Breasted's orthography) bears to the cuneiform *Hilakku* (beside *Hilak*). If *-ku* is a suffix *Kasku* may possibly be connected with Κᾶρες (which seems to represent an earlier *Ka(s)-ar-*).

[3] Perhaps also called Pedasos (cf. Herod. V 121). According to Strabo (XIII 1. 59) this place also belonged to the Leleges who, he says, once possessed a considerable part of Caria and Pisidia.

[4] Reproduced in W. Max Müller's *Asien u. Europa*, p. 361.

[5] Cf. p. 190, note 2.

[6] There is no question here of a national migration on the part of these peoples. They were mercenaries hired by the Hittite king, who "left not silver nor gold in his land (but) he plundered it of all his possessions and gave to every country, in order to bring them with him to battle." (Cf. Breasted, *op. cit.*, pp. 129, note, 138.)

On the other hand it must not be overlooked that later authorities know nothing of Cilices in this region ; neither do they mention Leleges in the south of the Troad or Ceteioi anywhere. If these peoples had survived the Aeolic invasion it is difficult to believe that they could have perished subsequently without leaving some trace of their existence in Greek tradition. The Pelasgoi of Larissa in the valley of the Hermos[1] appear to have been remembered in tradition, although their territories were occupied by the Aeolians—probably at quite an early date. The presumption then is that the other peoples had already been destroyed by Greek raids—as is stated in the Iliad—or else that they had been expelled or absorbed by the surrounding nations before the Greek colonies were fully established. In either case we shall have to carry back the poetic traditions relating to them practically to the beginning of the first millennium.

We have seen that it is difficult to date the composition of the Trojan Catalogue—at all events the latter part of it—after about the middle of the eighth century. I am not aware of any valid reason for denying that the Cypria as a whole may have been composed about this time or for supposing that the Catalogue ever existed independently. It is in the preceding period—presumably between the eleventh and eighth centuries— that we must place the composition of the Iliad, though its form may not have been finally settled when the Cypria came into existence. Any more definite conclusion is rendered difficult by the unsatisfactory nature of our information regarding the Cypria. But the general impression conveyed by the epitome is that an appreciable portion of the poem was derived from incidental references in the Iliad, and that as a whole it possessed to a considerable degree the characteristics of popular poetry. If this impression is correct we must conclude that heroic court-poetry was in its decadence when the Cypria was composed ; and consequently we shall do well to place the flourishing period, which produced the great epics, at least a century earlier.

---

[1] Cf. Strabo XIII 3. 3 f. I see no reason for doubting the existence of traditions relating to the presence of Pelasgoi in this region. The identification of Larissa Phriconis with the Larissa of the Iliad (II 841, XVII 301) seems to be at least as likely as any of the others which have been proposed.

CHAPTER XII.

SUPERNATURAL ELEMENTS IN THE HOMERIC POEMS.

In Chapter VI we saw that the heroic poetry of the Teutonic peoples was very largely affected by folk-tales; that supernatural beings were frequently introduced, while ordinary human beings or animals were credited with supernatural properties—in short that the distinction between natural and supernatural was not clearly drawn. We saw further that these features were by no means confined to the later stages of heroic poetry—that on the contrary some of them were prominent even in the Anglo-Saxon poems, while the others appeared to be of equal antiquity.

The same phenomena appear in Greek heroic poetry. Mythical beings and features obviously derived from folk-tales figure quite as frequently as in the Teutonic poems. Their presence is often regarded as a proof that the stories into which they enter and the persons with whom they are brought into contact are themselves products of myth or fiction. This is a question with which we shall have to deal in the following chapters. For the present it will be sufficient to quote what may be regarded as a typical expression of the attitude of more cautious scholars towards the problem of the story of Troy[1]: "It is fantastic to treat the siege of Troy as merely a solar myth —to explain the abduction of Helen by Paris as the extinction of the sunlight in the West, and Troy as the region of the dawn beset and possessed by the sunrise. It is equally fantastic, and more illogical, to follow the rationalising method—to deduct the supernatural element, and claim the whole residuum as historical

---

[1] Jebb, *Introduction to Homer*, p. 147.

fact.   Homer says that Achilles slew Hector with the aid of Athene.   We are not entitled to omit Athene, and still to affirm that Achilles slew Hector."

It may be observed that the gods are introduced in the Homeric poems in many different ways.   The incident just cited—where Athene takes the form of Deiphobos (Il. XXII 226 ff.)—belongs to one of the commonest types, and one which requires comparatively little imagination, if we are prepared to grant the existence of a belief that the gods were capable of disguising themselves in human form.   Sometimes again deities render themselves visible only to certain individuals out of a crowd, as in Il. I 194 ff., where Athene intervenes in order to stay Achilles from drawing his sword upon Agamemnon.   Another type is the disguise of gods as birds, as when we find Athene and Apollo sitting upon an oak in the form of vultures, before the combat of Hector and Aias (ib. VII 58 ff.).   On other occasions birds are sent by a god as a sign of his favour or protection, as in Il. XXIV 315 ff. and many other passages.   Somewhat akin to this type is the dream sent by Zeus to Agamemnon in Il. II 5 ff.

It has been remarked that in such cases as these a sceptical person might have accounted for everything that passed without reference to any intervention on the part of a deity.   But there are a number of other cases where the action is affected by gods in ways which could not be accounted for on any rationalistic hypothesis.   We may refer to Il. III 380 ff., where Aphrodite snatches Paris away from Menelaos and conveys him to his own house in Troy.   Or again to several passages in the Diomedeia where deities show themselves almost or quite without disguise and even take an active part in the fighting.   A still greater amount of imagination perhaps is required for the scenes which depict the quarrels and amusements of the gods in Olympos, and their schemes for helping or destroying the combatants. It has been held that all such passages as these belong to a later period than those of the less imaginative types described above.

In Teutonic stories of the Heroic Age, as we have already seen, very few notices relating to the gods have been preserved.

The appearances of Othin in Völsunga Saga (cf. p. 114) may be compared with those of Apollo in the Iliad or Athene in the Odyssey ; for his divinity is not recognised at once, though he does not take the form of a person known to his favourites. Again, though I know no exact Homeric parallel to the incident in Sigmundr's last battle, when the hero's sword is shattered at the touch of Othin's javelin, the idea is in complete harmony with several passages in the Diomedeia (e.g. v 129 ff., 438 ff., VI 128 ff., 306 f.). It is true that we do not know whether these incidents in Völsunga Saga are based on old tradition or not. But a good parallel for the last of the Homeric types is furnished by the Langobardic story of Wodan and Fria and the victory granted by them to the Winniles (cf. p. 115). The similarity between this story and the incident related of Zeus and Hera in Il. XIV 153—353 gives us some ground for suspecting that the heathen poetry of the Teutonic Heroic Age may have possessed decided 'Homeric' characteristics in its treatment of the gods.

As the case stands however we shall have to take our illustrations from stories of the Viking Age. A somewhat curious parallel to the incident of Athene and Hector in Il. XXII 226 ff. is to be found in the story of Haraldr Hilditönn, as told in Saxo's History, pp. 255, 263. Haraldr had a confidential servant named Bruno, whom he employed to drive his chariot and to carry messages to his nephew Ringo (Sigurðr Hringr). This man eventually was drowned ; but Othin took his place and form, and exerted himself to sow discord between the two kings. It was not until the battle at Bravalla had begun that Haraldr had any suspicion of the treachery which had been played upon him. Then suddenly recognising the identity of his charioteer he begged him to grant him victory. But Othin threw him out of the chariot and slew him.

The story of Haraldr Hilditönn refers, it is true, to times for which we have no historical records. But a still more graphic story of intervention on the part of divine beings occurs in connection with a well-known event—the expedition made against Norway by the Jómsvíkingar. In the latter part of the tenth century a number of Scandinavian adventurers had established and fortified a settlement at Jómsborg on the island of Wollin at the mouth of the Oder. About the year 994 their leaders, Sigvaldi and Búi, made a vow to attack Haakon, earl of Lade, who then ruled Norway. The earl was taken by surprise and had not been able to muster all his forces when he encountered the hostile fleet at Hiörungavágr, near the mouth of the Romsdal Fjord. The battle at first went against him ; and, according to the story, he took advantage of a respite in the fighting to retire to one of the islands and pray to Thórgerðr Hölgabrúðr. He was not able to obtain her assistance until he had sacrificed to her his youngest son. When he resumed the fight, the weather, which had been hot, underwent a complete change. A snow-storm came from the north and beat in the faces of the pirates, so that they were numbed with the cold and could neither move nor see. But worse was to come. "It is said that Hávarðr, one of Búi's companions, was the first to see Thórgerðr in Haakon's fleet ; but soon she was seen by many, both those who had second sight and those who had not. When the snow abated a little they saw also that arrows were flying, as it seemed, from every one of the demon's fingers, and each arrow brought about a man's death." Then they tell Sigvaldi, who says : "It seems to me that we have got to fight to-day not against men, but against the worst of devils." Still he continues the fight. When Haakon saw that the snow was abating he cried with all his might to Thórgerðr and her sister Irpa, reminding them how much he had given up to them in sacrificing his son. Then the storm began again, and soon Hávarðr saw two female figures on Haakon's ship, both acting as the one had done previously. Then Sigvaldi said that he would now take to flight and that all his men were to do likewise, for they had made no vow to fight against devils[1].

Here also we may cite a story connected with another historical event, which took place about ten years before the battle of Hiörungavágr. Eric the Victorious, king of Sweden, expelled his nephew Styrbiörn from the kingdom ; and the latter

---

[1] Jómsvíkinga Saga, cap. 44 (Fornmanna Sögur, XI p. 136 ff.) ; Flateyiarbók, I 191 f. Snorri gives a different account of the battle in the Heimskringla (Olafs S. Tryggv. 43 ff.) ; but he was acquainted with at least part of the story given above.

invaded the country with the help of the Danish king Harold Blue-tooth. On the eve of the battle Eric went into Othin's temple and in order to obtain victory promised to give himself up dead at the end of ten years. Soon afterwards he saw a big man with a long hood, who put a cane into his hand and told him to throw it over Styrbiörn's army saying : " You all belong to Othin." When he threw the cane it seemed to turn into a javelin and brought blindness upon Styrbiörn and all his host. On the same occasion Thor was seen in Styrbiörn's camp[1]. Such cases are by no means isolated. Olafr Tryggvason, who reigned over Norway from 995 to 1000, is said to have been visited both by Othin and Thor[2].

Of dreams perhaps the most interesting case is a story told of an Icelander named Glúmr, a contemporary of Earl Haakon of Lade. A certain Thórkell possessed an estate which he was compelled to sell to Glúmr. Before leaving he went to Frey's temple, sacrificed an ox and prayed that Glúmr likewise might be forced to give up the estate. This actually came to pass. But before he left, Glúmr dreamed that he saw a great crowd on the river banks coming to see Frey, who was seated on a chair. In his dream he asked who they were. They replied that they were his departed relatives and that they were praying Frey that he (Glúmr) should not be driven from his estate. But it was of no use ; Frey answered curtly and angrily, remembering the ox which Thórkell had given him[3].

For the action of Homeric deities in sending birds as a mark of favour or omen of success a good parallel is to be found in another incident in the life of Earl Haakon of Lade. When Jutland was invaded by the Emperor Otto II in 974 Harold Blue-tooth summoned Haakon to his assistance. After the campaign the Danish king adopted Christianity and compelled Haakon to do likewise. But the latter set off with his fleet as soon as possible and, landing on the coast of Östergötland, proceeded to offer a great sacrifice. Thereupon there came two

---

[1] Styrbiarnar Tháttr, cap. 2 (Fornm. Sög., V p. 250).

[2] Olafs S. Tryggv. A (Heimskr.), cap. 71; Olafs S. Tryggv. B, cap. 213 (Fornm. Sög., II p. 182 ł.).

[3] Víga-Glúms Saga, cap. 9, 26.

ravens flying by and screaming loud.   The earl interpreted this as a sign that Othin had accepted the sacrifice and that he would have a favourable time for battle[1].

The importance of the last case is enhanced by the fact that it is derived from a contemporary poem, the Vellekla (cf. p. 16), in which the ravens are mentioned.   In the other cases given above no such early authority is extant, and our texts themselves are separated by a period of from two to three centuries from the events which they relate.   But there is no reason for doubting that the stories had long been in existence.   It is questionable indeed whether the account of the battle of Hiörungavágr could have been invented after all recollection of Haakon and his religious observances had died away.   The earl's devotion to the worship of Thórgerðr Hölgabrúðr is known from other sources ; but she seems not to have been a generally recognised member of the Northern Pantheon.

However that may be, no doubt can be entertained with regard to the poem Hákonarmál, which deals with the death of King Haakon I at the battle of Fitje in 961 (cf. p. 15).   The author, Eyvindr Skaldaspillir, was himself present at the battle. The poem relates how Göndul and Skögul were sent by Othin to select a prince of Yngvi's line, who should go and dwell with him in Valhöll.   Then, after a short account of the battle, we are told that " the princes sat with their swords drawn, with scarred shields and mail-coats pierced ; in no cheerful mood was the host which had to make its way to Valhöll.   Then said Göndul, as she leaned upon her spear : 'Now will the forces of the gods be increased, since they have summoned Haakon to their abodes with a great host.'   The prince heard what the noble Valkyries were saying.   Thoughtful was their mien, as they sat on their steeds, with helmets upon their heads and holding their shields before them.   'Why hast thou thus decided the battle, Skögul ? Surely we have deserved success from the gods.'   'We have brought it about that thou hast won the day and that thy foes have fled.   Now,' said the mighty Skögul, 'we must ride to the green homes of the gods, to tell Othin that a monarch is coming

[1] Olafs S. Tryggv. (Heimskr.), cap. 27 f.

to enter his presence.'" Then the scene changes to Valhöll; and Othin sends Hermóðr and Bragi out to meet the king and bid him welcome[1].

Such poems as Hákonarmál and Eiríksmál must be regarded as products of vivid poetic imagination. They are clearly in the nature of conscious fiction, though it should not be assumed that the pictures of the gods and their abode which they present were conceptions altogether unreal to the poets' audiences. I suppose that ultimately this type of composition is derived from visions or dreams, such as the story of Glúmr given above. For, though the latter in its present form dates from a period at least two centuries later than Hákonarmál—both referring to persons who lived more or less about the same time—it will probably be agreed that the conception there is far more primitive.

Now we have good evidence that visions which took the form of visits to the home of the gods did really obtain credence in the Viking Age. When St Ansgar visited Sweden for the second time, not long after 850, he found that the success of his mission was seriously endangered. A man had come to Birca (Biörkö, on the Mälar), where the king, Olaf, was residing, and stated that he had been present at an assembly of the gods, who had sent him to deliver a message to the king and nation. This was to the effect that the gods had long been gracious to the Swedes and had preserved their land in peace and prosperity. Yet now the Swedes were abandoning their accustomed sacrifices and introducing a strange god. If they wished to retain their favour the sacrifices must be resumed on a larger scale, and the new god must be refused admittance. "But if you desire to have more gods, and we are not sufficient for you, we unanimously enrol in our body Eric who was formerly your king, so that he shall be counted among the gods." This story created a profound impression among the inhabitants. "They founded a temple in honour of the above-mentioned king, who had

---

[1] This latter part of the poem is copied from Eiríksmál (cf. p. 15), in which Othin sends out Sigmundr and Sinfiötli to meet Eiríkr. We do not know either the date or the author of Eiríksmál; but it would seem from the Saxon Chronicle that Eiríkr was still alive about the year 954.

long been dead, and began to offer prayers and sacrifices to him as a god[1]."

The Life of St Ansgar, from which this story is taken, is practically a contemporary authority. It was written by St Rembert, one of Ansgar's disciples, who succeeded him as Archbishop of Hamburg in 865 and died in 888. In face of such evidence we have no reason for doubting that stories such as that of Glúmr would readily obtain credence. Indeed it seems scarcely impossible that the doings of Thórgerðr Hölgabrúðr at Hiörungavágr may have been believed by persons who were alive at the time. Yet credulity was no special characteristic of the Northern peoples. We learn from inscriptions that Asclepios was in the habit of showing himself to pilgrims in his temple at Epidauros. Still more striking evidence is furnished by Herodotus' story (I 60) that Peisistratos recovered the tyranny at Athens by dressing up a woman to personate Athene and accompanying her in a chariot to the city. Herodotus himself remarks that this took place at a time when the Greek race had long been distinguished from the rest of mankind by its superior sagacity and freedom from silly credulity—and in a state too which was held to be intellectually supreme among the Greeks. Whatever doubt may be entertained as to the truth of the story it is significant enough that Herodotus should record it, apparently without any hesitation, in less than a century after Peisistratos' death. Some four centuries earlier men may well have been ready to hear that the gods took an active part in the battles of their fathers or grandfathers, while the latter themselves may have been quite as ready to attribute their success or failure to the disguised agency of the same powers.

It is clear at all events that the Scandinavian evidence fails to provide any justification for the view that poems which introduce the gods must date from times far removed from the events which they claim to commemorate. In the contemporary

---

[1] *Porro, si etiam plures deos habere desideratis, et uobis non sufficimus, Ericum, quondam regem uestrum, nos unanimes in collegium nostrum asciscimus, ut sit unus de numero deorum............ Nam et templum in honore supradicti regis dudum defuncti statuerunt, et ipsi tanquam deo uota et sacrificia offerre coeperunt.* Rembertus, *Vita S. Anscharii*, cap. 23.

Hákonarmál we find two of the most advanced Homeric types. First, we have deities participating without disguise in battle ; then a change of scene carries us to the actual home of the gods. The second scene in Hákonarmál—which is likewise the scene of Eiríksmál—may be compared both with the various 'Olympic' episodes and also with the two Nekyiai. For, since Othin is a god of the dead, his abode corresponds in a sense both to Olympos and the home of Hades. On the whole perhaps the nearest affinities of the two Norwegian poems are with the second Nekyia (Od. XXIV 1—204), which is commonly regarded as one of the latest portions of the Odyssey.

Lastly, the Scandinavian evidence gives no support to the belief that the more imaginative types of divine intervention necessarily belong to a later date than the others. In principle of course it may be admitted that they are less primitive. But in Old Norse literature it so happens that they occur in both earlier and more nearly contemporary works. The explanation lies doubtless in the fact that the theological apparatus of Norse poetry was fully developed before the time of our earliest authorities. So far as I can see, there is no good reason for denying that the same remark holds good for the Homeric poems. But if so it is futile to use evidence of this kind as a criterion for determining the date of the various portions.

Monsters and theriomorphic demons are by no means unknown in Greek heroic stories, though in the poems which have come down to us they figure prominently only in episodes dealing with past events. The nearest Homeric analogies to Beowulf's adventures are perhaps to be found in the stories of Bellerophon and Meleagros[1] (Il. VI 178 ff.; IX 538 ff.). It may be that these stories and others, such as that of Perseus, them-selves once formed the main themes of heroic poems, and that the backward position which they ultimately came to occupy, as compared with stories of anthropomorphic deities, is due to the growth of poetic art and humanistic tendencies. But on the

---

[1] The first stage in the growth of such a story as this may be illustrated from the message of the Mysians given by Herodotus, I 36. The development which it may ultimately attain can be seen from the story of Kilhwch and Olwen.

other hand we have to remember that heroic poetry is always liable to the intrusion of folk-tales, in which adventures with monsters form one of the favourite themes.

The chief store-house of folk-tales in the Homeric poems is the narrative of his adventures given by Odysseus to the Phaeacians (Od. IX—XII). This narrative contains a considerable number of incidents, of which ten may be regarded as more or less distinct: (i) the encounter with the Cicones, (ii) the visit to the land of the Lotus-eaters, (iii) the adventure with Polyphemos, (iv) the two visits to Aiolos, (v) the disaster in the land of the Laistrygones, (vi) the two visits to Circe, (vii) the journey to the home of Hades, (viii) the singing of the Sirens, (ix) the adventure with Scylla and Charybdis, (x) the slaughter of the cattle of Helios.

The first of these incidents bears no obvious traces of derivation or influence from a folk-tale; but it is the only one of the series of which this can be stated with any confidence. The adventures with the Lotus-eaters and the Laistrygones should perhaps be regarded rather as travellers' stories—founded possibly on actual experience of foreign peoples—yet the latter at least contains certain distorted features which may fairly bring it within our category. As to the origin of the adventure with Polyphemos there can be little doubt. It appears to be found with slight variants in many different parts of the world[1].

The last incident of the series is perhaps the one least widely known; but a parallel may be cited from one of Saxo's stories (p. 286 f.). A certain Danish king named Gormo[2] was an ardent explorer. Above all he desired to visit the abode of Geruthus (Geirröðr), which lay beyond the ocean in a land of perpetual darkness. Taking with him as guide an experienced traveller, named Thorkillus, he set sail with three ships and made his way beyond Halogaland (the north of Norway). There, having lost its way in a storm, the expedition came to be

---

[1] Cf. Macculloch, *The Childhood of Fiction*, p. 279 ff.

[2] The historical connections of this story are somewhat obscure. But this is immaterial for our purpose, as the part with which we are dealing is clearly derived from folk-tales.

in want of food.   Eventually they arrived at an island which contained herds of extremely tame cattle.   Against the advice of Thorkillus the mariners slaughtered a large number of these. The following night they were attacked by monsters, one of whom declared that they would not be allowed to sail away until they made compensation for the losses they had inflicted on the herd of the gods.   In order to save themselves they had to give up one man from each ship.

It will be seen that this incident bears a general resemblance to the slaughtering of the cattle of Helios, and we need scarcely hesitate to regard both stories as variant forms of a folk-tale. As to its origin we are not altogether without evidence in the Northern case.   In Alcuin's *Vita Willebrordi*, I cap. 10, it is stated that a certain island (now Heligoland) was entirely sacred to a god named Fosite.   So great was the sanctity with which it was regarded that no one ventured to touch any of the animals which grazed upon the island.   The violation of the sanctuary, in this and other respects, cost one of St Willebrord's companions his life.   Hence there is no need to doubt that a basis of fact underlies the stories of islands in which animal life was held sacred—just as in holy woods throughout the north of Europe.   It is scarcely impossible that similar island sanctuaries may once have been known in the Mediterranean.

The subsequent course of the story has a certain affinity with that of Circe.   After leaving the island Gormo and his men sailed in safety to the farther part of Permland, where they were met by a giant named Guthmundus[1], the brother of Geruthus, who invited them to his house.   Thorkillus strictly enjoined his companions to abstain from all food and drink offered them, even from the fruits which grew in the garden, and to avoid contact with members of the household.   Those who yielded to temptation, as a few eventually did, would have to spend the rest of their lives among monsters.   There is no actual transformation as in the story of Circe; but this in itself is a widely known incident in folk-tales.

When the travellers at length reach the abode of Geruthus

---

[1] Guðmundr of Glæsisvellir is a well-known figure in the unhistorical parts of sagas.

the scene, though horrible in every way, seems to be a variety of
the Enchanted Castle rather than a parallel to the home of
Hades[1]. We have seen above that the poems Hákonarmál and
Eiríksmál may in a sense be compared with the two Nekyiai ;
for Valhöll is the abode not only of the chief god but also
of the spirits of fallen warriors. But here we have to deal with
elaborate conceptions of court poetry which are further removed
from the spirit of the true folk-tale than either of the passages
in the Odyssey[2]. A better parallel to the first Nekyia is perhaps
to be found in another of Saxo's stories (p. 31). Once upon
a time, when King Hadingus was feasting, there appeared to him
a woman who was carrying hemlocks. She wrapped him in her
mantle and took him with her underground in order to show
him where the hemlocks grew. On the way they passed through
a dark cloud and then along a well-worn path, where they saw
many men richly attired. After viewing the sunny regions
where the hemlocks grew, they crossed a rapid river and then
saw two armies engaged in desperate conflict. The woman told
Hadingus that these were men who had been slain by the sword
and continually rehearsed the manner of their death. They are
obviously to be connected with the *einheriar* of Old Norse
poetry—the slain warriors who dwell in Valhöll and spend their
days in combat—though possibly this passage represents a more
primitive form of the idea   It is to be observed that Saxo himself
explicitly interprets the story as a visit to the region of the dead.

Stories of this kind are to be found in many parts of the
world—among peoples as widely apart as the Algonquins, the
Zulus and the Maoris[3]. There can be little doubt that to a large
extent the first Nekyia belongs to the same category. At the
same time of course I do not mean to imply that it is wholly to
be regarded as a folk-tale. In the interview with Agamemnon
and his companions (vv. 385—564) we find ourselves in much
the same world of ideas as is presented to us in Eiríksmál and

[1] A better parallel is perhaps furnished by Thorkillus' subsequent visit to the
abode of Ugarthilocus (p. 292 ff.). The description of this place recalls that of
Náströnd in Völuspá 39, Gylfaginning, cap. 52.

[2] The home of Hades resembles the abode of Hel rather than Valhöll. To this
also we have a visit (by the god Hermóðr) in Gylf. 49.

[3] Cf. Tylor, *Primitive Culture*[1], I p. 346, II p. 50 ff.

Hákonarmál.   Again, it is to be remembered that the object of
Odysseus' journey was to consult the spirit of Teiresias, and
this is perhaps the original kernel of the story.   Such an idea
however may be derived from ancient religious observances
rather than from a folk-tale.   Herodotus (V 92) records that
Periandros, tyrant of Corinth, about the close of the sixth
century, sent an embassy to the oracle of the dead (νεκυο-
μαντήϊον) on the river Acheron in Thesprotis, in order to consult
the spirit of his wife Melissa.   After making all allowance for
antiquarian and etymological speculation[1] it seems probable
that this oracle did influence the conceptions of the home of the
dead current in Greek poetry.

It would appear then that in the composition of the first
Nekyia we have to take account of the influence of at least
three different elements—court poetry, folk-tale and religious
(necromantic) observances.   If we are right in supposing that
Aeolis was the true home of all Homeric poetry, the absence of
any precise geographical indications is easily accounted for.
During the centuries which intervened between the end of the
Heroic Age and the beginning of the historical period there is
extremely little evidence, whether traditional or archaeological,
for communication with distant lands; and it is likely enough
that at that time Thesprotis was as unfamiliar as Egypt to
the inhabitants of Aeolis.   Few scholars will dispute that the
geographical indications throughout the story of Odysseus'
wanderings are both vague and contradictory.   Sometimes he
appears to be in the west; sometimes again he is following the
track of the Argo—presumably in the Black Sea.   That is after
all the kind of confusion which might reasonably be expected
from poets who were dealing with traditions of voyages made
long before in regions now altogether forgotten.

The ascription of supernatural properties to men or animals
is not a very striking feature in Homeric poetry—unless we

---

[1] As seen (e.g.) in the application of the name Κωκυτός to a tributary of the
Acheron.   The presumption is that this name was originally a creation of poetic
fancy, just as much as Πυριφλεγέθων.   The diffusion of the names Acheron and
Acherusia in other regions (Italy, the Black Sea, etc.) is doubtless due to the influence
of poetry or tradition.

include under this head stories of exaggerated prowess.   As an example we may cite Il. XIX 404 ff., where one of Achilles' horses speaks and prophesies his master's death.   Incidents such as the flame on the same hero's head in Il. XVIII 205 ff. and the changes in Odysseus' appearance (Od. XIII 429 ff., etc.) are attributed to the direct action of deities.   On the other hand exaggeration is common and often carried out systematically. Among such cases we must include the feats of valour performed by some of the combatants, and also presumably the numbers of the forces stated in the catalogues, if we admit that the story of the siege of Troy has any historical foundation.

On the whole it appears that those elements in the Homeric poems which may quite safely be derived from myth or folk-tale resemble the corresponding elements in Teutonic heroic poetry very closely.   We may perhaps doubt whether the gods ever figured so conspicuously in Teutonic poetry as they do in the Iliad and Odyssey ; but the difference between the two cases is one of degree only.   In the use made of folk-tales the difference is very slight.   It remains for us now to consider whether the remaining elements in the poems—their main groundwork in fact—should be regarded as of similar origin in both cases.

CHAPTER XIII.

MYTH IN THE HOMERIC POEMS.

IT is commonly held that history, myth and fiction have all contributed to the formation of the Greek heroic stories; but opinions differ widely as to the relative importance to be attributed to the three elements. Among modern scholars the general tendency has been to assign the chief weight to myth. By many indeed the heroes of the Trojan War are believed to be as mythical in origin as the gods themselves.

One conclusion may safely be drawn from the Northern evidence discussed in the last chapter: we must definitely dismiss the argument that the Homeric heroes cannot have been men of flesh and blood because they are brought into contact with the gods. No one will be so hardy as to suggest that King Haakon or his namesake, the famous earl of Lade, were products of myth or poetic imagination. Yet Göndul is as much responsible for the death of King Haakon as Athene is for that of Hector. There is certainly this difference between the two cases, that we have no historical evidence for the existence of the Homeric heroes. But the fact that deities participate in their destruction does not in itself prove that they are themselves products of myth or fiction.

There was a time, not so very long ago, when most of the characters of the Greek Heroic Age were believed to owe their origin to nature-myth—personifications of light, darkness and so forth. At the present time however it is only in some few cases that this view is generally maintained. Its chief stronghold is the case of Achilles; and here we are invariably referred for proof to the story of Sigurðr. The two characters have of

course a good deal in common.   Both are more or less idealised
types of youthful strength and valour, and both die prematurely.
But it would be pure folly to regard these features as in themselves proofs of mythical origin.   In order to prove this it is
necessary to point to features which can only be mythical, and
to show that such features formed an original element in the
stories.

Now we have seen (p. 140 ff.) that the current explanation
with regard to Siguror is open to the most serious—in my
opinion fatal—objections.   On the other hand there certainly
was a tendency for myth to grow up in later times round this
hero.   As an instance we may take his invulnerability, a feature
which is peculiar to the German version of the story.   Achilles
possesses the same characteristic—but not in the Iliad or Odyssey.
It is as much unknown in the Homeric account of Achilles as
in the Norse account of Siguror.   Indeed the only essentially
mythical feature which the poems themselves record in the case
of Achilles—and it is by no means peculiar to his case—is that
he is the son of a deity[1].   But divine descent was claimed also
by many Teutonic princes, though the heroes of our stories are
usually separated from their divine ancestors by two or three
generations[2].   Whatever may be the explanation of this
phenomenon it is doubtless to be connected with the stories
of conjugal relations between human and divine beings which
we find both in Greece and in northern Europe.   This is a
subject to which we shall have to return in a later chapter.
Above all, however, we have to take account of the influence
of folk-tales[3] and popular beliefs, which, as we have seen from

---

[1] Achilles himself was worshipped as a deity in certain localities; and the same is
true of some other heroes.   We may refer to the story of St Ansgar, quoted above
(p. 255 f.).   With such cases as that of 'Zeus Agamemnon' we shall have to deal later.

[2] According to Völsunga Saga, cap. 2, Sigmundr, the father of Siguror, had a
divine mother (cf. p. 114).

[3] Some resemblance to the case of Peleus and Thetis is shown by a story in Hrólfs
S. Kraka, cap. 15, where an elf-woman bears a daughter to Helgi, the father of
Hrólfr Kraki.   Such incidents are not uncommon in folk-tales.   We may note
especially those cases in which the supernatural bride is a mermaid, perhaps representing the Swan-maiden of earlier times.   Thetis has a good deal in common
with the latter class of beings.

the Teutonic evidence, may make itself felt even in the description of very recent events.

The story of the abduction of Helen is another case for which many scholars still claim a mythical origin. It is perfectly true that stories of (e.g.) the abduction of the sun or the incontinence of the moon[1] do occur, though examples of this type are by no means so common or widespread as many writers have assumed[2]. But what is apt to be overlooked is that these stories arise from a personification of the sun or moon, and that it is in consequence of this personification that the heavenly bodies are believed to be exposed to perils and passions such as affect human beings. It is surely nothing less than an inversion of the natural order of things to suppose that the numerous class of folk-tales which deal with the abduction of a girl or wife originated in the type—a comparatively rare type—in which this motif is applied to the sun. There can be no reasonable doubt that the prevalence of such folk-tales is due to the innumerable occurrences of abduction in real life. But the theory we are discussing involves not merely the personification of heavenly bodies and natural phenomena but their complete anthropomorphisation[3]—a very doubtful process in the best of cases—whereas the story which it seeks to explain bears no trace even of derivation from a folk-tale. In other words we are asked to assume a most complex and precarious hypothesis

---

[1] Cf. Aeneas Sylvius, *Hist. de Eur.*, cap. 26, and the first Daina in Schleicher's *Handb. d. litau. Sprache*. Night and day or dawn are also frequently personified—the last especially where, as in Greece, the sun is regarded as a male. But none of these lend themselves so readily as the sun and moon to the development of mythical stories. The personification of light, darkness, etc. in the abstract seems to belong to a much more advanced stage of thought.

[2] Eclipse-myths (usually of a simple character) are widespread and fairly common. A probable example is to be found in Gylfaginning, cap. 12 (cf. also Tylor, *Primitive Culture*[4], I p. 328 ff.). But a good deal of scepticism is justifiable in regard to the interpretation of stories which are supposed to have originated in myths of sunrise and sunset. This remark applies even to those Polynesian and Red Indian stories which are commonly regarded as among the best examples of their class.

[3] The personification of the sun and the dawn in the Homeric poems is very similar to what we find in the north of Europe, e.g. in Gylfaginning, cap. 10 f., and the first four Dainos in Schleicher's *Handbuch*. The most important difference is that the Dawn-goddess, like other deities, has sexual relations with mortals (see the Addenda). But her true character is not for a moment forgotten.

in order to account for a story for which parallels are to be found very frequently in almost all stages of human society.

Of course I do not mean to say that the story of Helen is entirely devoid of mythical elements. On the contrary, it is a most instructive example of the growth of myth, and as such it furnishes an interesting parallel to the history of similar stories in the north of Europe. In the Iliad Helen possesses no mythical characteristics, except that she is the offspring of a divine father. In the Cypria she had apparently also acquired a divine mother (Nemesis). By the seventh century we find her figuring in quite a different story of abduction—a story which seems to have been treated by Alcman and Stesichoros, as well as on the 'Chest of Cypselos.' This time she is carried off by Theseus, with the help of Peirithoos, and rescued by her brothers, the Dioscoroi[1]. Somewhat later we find a new version of the story of her abduction by Paris. Now it is said to be only her εἴδωλον which is carried off by Paris; Helen herself is taken by Hermes to Egypt[2]. There seems to be little reason for doubting that the εἴδωλον was a deliberate invention of Stesichoros, though in other respects this version of the story may well have been influenced by the Egyptian version, recorded by Herodotus (II 112 ff.). The latter again comes in all probability from Greek settlers in Egypt, who connected the narrative of Helen's sojourn in Egypt, related in the Odyssey (IV 125 ff., 351 ff.), with a cult which they found existing in that country. This version of the story then should perhaps be regarded as a product of fiction rather than myth. The other story however—that of Theseus, Peirithoos and the Dioscoroi—is doubtless of popular origin. It is important to notice that both these pairs of heroes are

---

[1] There is probably an allusion to this story in Il. III 144, although a different explanation is quoted by Plutarch (*Theseus*, cap. 34) from Istros. But the verse in question was condemned by some ancient, as well as modern, scholars. It is 'inorganic' (cf. Od. II 331) and due in all probability to the same process as Il. II 831 ff. (cf. p. 244, note).

[2] This list is by no means exhaustive. We may mention also the story of Helen and Achilles in the 'White Isle' (cf. Pausanias III 19. 11) and that of Ariston's wife, related by Herodotus (VI 61). The Rhodian story (cf. Paus. III 19. 10) is obviously due in part to the influence of the Homeric poems; but it is at least questionable whether this Ἑλένη Δενδρῖτις was originally identical with the other Helen.

connected with other stories of abduction[1]. Moreover in both cases these stories have certain elements in common with that of Persephone. There can be little doubt therefore that we have to deal with a folk-tale. The introduction of Helen into the story may be due partly to her kinship with the Dioscoroi and partly to the influence of the story of her abduction by Paris.

At the present time it appears to be the more general opinion that the Homeric heroes originated mainly not in personifications of natural phenomena, but in tribal divinities or personified conceptions of peoples ('hypostasierte Volks-individualitäten'). Now we have seen (p. 131 f.) that in Teutonic heroic poetry we occasionally meet with the mythical eponymous ancestors of families, though such persons are referred to the past and not introduced into the main action of the stories. Similar characters are to be found in the Homeric poems. Perhaps the best example occurs in a speech of Aineias (Il. XX 200 ff.), where the names Δάρδανος, Τρῶς and Ἶλος are included in the hero's genealogy. The Cadmos of Od. V 333 is probably to be regarded, in some sense or other, as the eponymous ancestor of the Cadmeioi, though he is not mentioned in connection with Thebes. Again, in Od. XVII 207 we have a reference to eponymous heroes of places, Ithacos and Neritos. They are perhaps creatures of the poet's own imagination, i.e. fictitious rather than mythical beings; but it is probable that they were modelled upon existing types. Other examples of both types may be found elsewhere in the poems[2]. Yet it cannot be said that they are common. In Greece, as in northern Europe, the true home of eponymous ancestors (Hellen, Doros, Achaios, etc.[3]) is to be found in post-heroic, or at least non-heroic, literature.

In recent years however several scholars have put forward the theory that the characters who figure in the main action of

---

[1] Attention should be paid not only to the case of the Leucippides but also to the story of Phormion (Paus. III 16. 3).

[2] In Il. II 828 ff. (if the name Ἄδρηστος is taken from VI 37 ff. or XVI 694) we have apparently the case of an already existing character being turned to account as an eponymous hero.

[3] Αἰολίδης occurs occasionally as a patronymic for individuals. The 'keeper of the winds' seems to have no connection with these characters.

the Iliad are tribal heroes in disguise. For a simple example of this theory we may refer to the interpretation put upon Il. v 43 ff., where the Cretan leader Idomeneus is represented as slaying a man named Phaistos (Φαῖστος). Now there was in Crete a well-known city called Phaistos (Φαιστός). According to Prof. E. Bethe (*Neue Jahrbücher*, VII 669) it cannot be disputed that the man Phaistos is the 'eponym' of the city and that we have here the remains of an ancient Cretan heroic lay. But the origin of the man is stated explicitly enough in the poem (*l.c.*): he is the son of Boros the Maeonian and had come from a place called Tarne. Before we can assume that he was the 'eponym' of a Cretan city we must surely ask how he came to be represented as a Maeonian (Lydian). Is it inconceivable that a name identical with that of a city should be borne by anyone except the eponymous hero of the city?

This is not the only case of the kind which has been brought forward. In Il. v 706 we hear of an Aetolian named Trechos slain by Hector and in Il. xx 455 of a Trojan named Dryops slain by Achilles. Here we are said to have 'eponyms' of Trachis and the Dryopes. In England during the centuries immediately following the Heroic Age we find mention in historical documents of princes or ecclesiastics called Walh, Cumbra, Seaxa, Dene, Fronca, etc. Are we to suppose that these persons are the eponymous heroes of the Welsh or Cymry, the Saxons, Danes and Franks? But national names of this type seem to have been just as frequently used by the Greeks, at least in historical times. We may mention Achaios of Eretria, Ion of Chios and Dorieus the brother of Leonidas. Is there any reason for denying their use in earlier times[1]?

The evidence of these names has been brought forward in support of a far-reaching theory—that the conflicts which we find described in the Iliad are echoes of tribal struggles which once took place in Greece, and that the warriors, Trojans as well as Greeks, are in reality mythical heroes in whom the various

---

[1] In the Homeric poems it is in the case of minor characters among the Trojans and their allies that names of this type are most common. In this case the use of such names may be accounted for with considerable probability under the head of fiction (cf. p. 300, note).

contending tribes have become personified. If this theory is
sound it will be obvious that the resemblance between Greek
and Teutonic heroic poetry must be merely superficial—that
the two groups of poems spring from essentially different sources.
It will be well then to examine somewhat carefully the evidence
on which the theory is based.

The first argument in its favour is derived from a story
quoted by Plutarch (*Theseus*, cap. 34) from Istros, a writer of
the third century, to the effect that Alexandros (Paris) was
overcome by Achilles and Patroclos on the banks of the
Spercheios. In confirmation of this story it is pointed out
that the warriors with whom Paris fights in the Iliad mostly
belong to Thessaly, while his sister Alexandra (Cassandra)
was worshipped by the Locrians. Another argument rests
on a story derived from the Little Iliad, that Andromache
was brought to Pharsalos after the fall of Troy. The inference
that she belonged originally to this region is supported by the
proposed identification of Thebe Hypoplacie, her home in the
Iliad, with the Phthiotic Thebes, to the east of Pharsalos. Yet
a further argument relates to Hector. It is noted that he was
worshipped as a hero at Thebes in Boeotia, and that most of
the persons associated with him, either as friends or foes, are
connected with Boeotia, Thessaly and the intervening districts.
In Prof. Bethe's words " Hector's tracks lead from southern
Thessaly, through Phocis and Boeotia, to the Cadmean Thebes."
" In other words Hector, or rather the tribe which honoured
Hector as their hero, migrated by this road. More accurately,
the tribe gradually, in how many centuries none can tell, moved
in a south-easterly direction, driven by a pressure which was no
doubt exerted by the Aeolic tribe represented in the Epos by
Achilles[1]."

Now it is manifest that the argument derived from Istros'
story can have validity only if it can be shown that there is
reason for believing it to be based on genuine native tradition,
independent of the Homeric poems. For everyone who has
studied the history of Teutonic heroic poetry knows that in the
later forms of the stories the scene is liable to be changed to

---

[1] Murray, *Rise of the Greek Epic*, p. 197 (from Bethe, *N. Jahrb.*, VII 672).

entirely different countries.   Thus the fight of Heðinn and
Högni is located in the Orkneys in the Norse version of their
story, while in Kûdrûn Hagen is made a king in Ireland.   Again,
in the Vitae Duorum Offarum the whole story of Offa and his
single combat is transplanted to the English Mercia, the home
of the hero's descendants.   Yet in the case of Istros' story the
requisite evidence seems to be altogether wanting.   If the story
really comes from local tradition it may very well be due to
an imperfect acquaintance with the Homeric poems.   But the
context, which mentions Hector as well as Paris, suggests
rather that Istros was referring not to the story of the Iliad
at all but to an early adventure of the two brothers[1]—presumably one of those accretions to the old heroic cycles, for which
so many parallels can be found in late Teutonic authorities like
Thiðreks Saga af Bern.

The argument relating to the Locrian cult of Alexandra
(Cassandra) need scarcely be considered at length; for, however
ancient this cult may have been, it was always connected with
the sanctuary of Athene at Troy[2].   The cult of Hector at
Thebes likewise seems to have been derived from the same
quarter, perhaps in comparatively late times[3].   Again, the
identification of Andromache's home with Thebes in Phthiotis is
admittedly nothing more than a conjecture.

One argument still remains for consideration, namely that
the persons brought into contact with Hector come chiefly from
the north-eastern parts of Greece and those encountered by
Paris chiefly from Thessaly.   Now it is to be observed that
several of the persons whose names figure in Prof. Bethe's
lists (*op. cit.*, p. 670 ff.) are not said to come from Thessaly,
Boeotia, etc. in the Iliad itself.   That they were derived from
this quarter is merely an inference from the fact that other
persons belonging to Thessaly, Boeotia, etc. bear the same
names.   It cannot for a moment be suspected that in v. 705,
XV. 547 ff. the poets themselves were thinking of Orestes the
son of Agamemnon or of Melanippos the famous Theban hero.

---

[1] Cf. Crusius, *S.-B. d. k. bayer. Akad.*, 1905, p. 774 f.

[2] Cf. Brückner, *Troja und Ilion*, p. 557 ff.

[3] Cf. Crusius, *op. cit.*, p. 761 ff.

But surely nothing can be more absurd than the proposition that persons who bear the same name must necessarily be identical in origin. In the Teutonic Heroic Age we know from historical sources of five kings named Theodric, all of whom were living within half a century of one another. Have we any reason for supposing that the ancient Greeks were more careful to avoid the use of names which had already been appropriated?[1]

Again, the lists given by Prof. Bethe contain merely a selection of the warriors encountered by Paris and Hector. The former fights in the Iliad not only with the Thessalian heroes Machaon, Eurypylos and Menesthios, but also with Menelaos from Sparta, Diomedes from Argos and Euchenor from Corinth. Hector's antagonists include, among others, Aias from Salamis, Stichios from Athens, Periphetes from Mycenae, Lycophron from Cythera and Amphimachos from Elis. On the other hand Melanippos is merely one, and by no means the most conspicuous, of the same hero's supporters. Considering the evidence as a whole therefore I fail to see that this argument is worth any more than the others.

It appears then that the evidence adduced in favour of the theory which we are discussing is open to serious objection at every point[2]. But, leaving questions of detail, we have yet to notice that the theory as a whole consists of two main propositions. The first of these is that the warriors of the Iliad are really 'tribal heroes,' i.e. in some sense or other personifications of tribes. In other words the contests described in the poem were originally conflicts of tribes and not of individuals. The second proposition is that these conflicts must have taken place between neighbouring tribes. It will be seen that this proposition

---

[1] As a matter of fact the name Melanippos is borne by three Trojans and one Achaean in the Iliad. Nothing is stated regarding the home of the Achaean. The name Orestes is borne by one Trojan and one Achaean, besides the son of Agamemnon.

[2] I have dealt with only one of the groups of names treated by Pror. Bethe; but it is the one which he has discussed most fully. A second (Laconian) group is treated by him on p. 672 f. On this it will be sufficient here to refer to Crusius, *op. cit.*, p. 771 ff., where it is pointed out that the chief argument rests apparently on a mistranslation.

depends very largely upon the first. If the conflicts of the
Iliad really took place, as the poem states, between individual
warriors or bands of soldiers, there is no occasion for supposing
that the combatants were necessarily neighbours. As far back
as the twelfth and thirteenth centuries Egyptian monuments
testify, as we have seen, to enterprises far more distant than
the expedition against Troy.

Now the first proposition is of course nothing new in itself.
On the contrary, Prof. Bethe's theory is an outgrowth from a
view which has been long and widely current—that the conflicts
recorded in the Iliad are a reflection of the Aeolic settlement of
the Asiatic coast. His purpose has been to show that only a
comparatively small portion of the story comes from this source[1],
and that the bulk is derived from reminiscences of earlier tribal
struggles in Greece, which have become embedded in the story
of Troy. The two theories differ very greatly in the explanations
which they give of the origin of various incidents and characters.
But it is not to be overlooked that the principle of interpretation
is the same in both cases.

No one will deny that the personification of tribes and
nationalities is to be found in both the poetry and the prose
literature of many peoples. In certain passages of the Old
Testament this principle of interpretation has been recognised
from ancient times. But the authorities in which these passages
occur cannot be described as heroic poems. Again Greek
literature itself also yields plenty of obvious examples, such as
the stories of Hellen and his sons and Danaos, several of which
can be traced back to quite early poems. But these poems
appear to have been of the Hesiodic, and not of the Homeric
school. If we turn to the Teutonic peoples, evidence for such
personification is abundant, and some of it belongs to our very
earliest records. But, except in genealogical references such as
we have dealt with above (p. 267), examples are not to be found
in heroic poetry. The idea that the characters who are brought
before us in the poems—let us say Beowulf or Sigurðr or Witege
—are themselves personifications of tribes is one which probably
no scholar would entertain.

[1] Cf. *Neue Jahrb.*, VII 662—9; XIII 2 ff.

Now in the Homeric poems, as we have them, just as much as in Teutonic heroic poetry, the interest of the poets lies in the fortunes of individual heroes, not in those of the communities to which they belong. Even in those Teutonic stories which have the least claim to be regarded as historical there is no reason for doubting that such was the case from the very beginning. On the other hand the current hypothesis with regard to the origin of the Greek heroic stories postulates what can only be described as a complete revolution in the interests of the poets and their audiences. This however is a postulate which ought not to be accepted, unless decisive evidence is forthcoming in its favour.

In the first place it must be observed that the existence of a poem or story which deals with reminiscences of tribal conflicts necessarily presupposes an absorbing interest in tribal history. It will probably be admitted by everyone that this interest can hardly have been of an academic character; indeed, we may assume, I think, that it must be inspired by patriotic motives. If so, the foremost place will naturally be taken by that tribe or community with which the story originated. Now it is generally agreed that the Homeric poems contain both Aeolic and Ionic elements. Further, though opinions differ widely as to the relative importance of the two, there is a practical unanimity in believing that the Aeolic element is the earlier one. The tribal interest then, at least in the earlier elements in the poems, should be essentially Aeolic. For 'Aeolic' we may practically say Thessalian (using the term of course in a geographical sense); for the Aeolic settlements, mainly at least, had proceeded from Thessaly. But Achilles, the chief hero of the Iliad, himself belongs to Thessaly; and so all is well. Further, many scholars hold that the later or Ionic elements in the poem are marked by the introduction of Nestor. There was, apparently, a tradition current in Colophon that the inhabitants of that city had originally come from Pylos. Nestor therefore may be regarded as typifying the later or Ionic interests of the Iliad, just as Achilles typifies its earlier or Aeolic interests. This opinion however is by no means so widely entertained as the other.

So much for the Iliad; now let us turn to the Odyssey. Here we are confronted with a serious difficulty. Odysseus is at least as much the hero of the Odyssey as Achilles is of the Iliad. But Odysseus belongs to the Ionian Isles ; and there is no trace of either an Aeolic or an Ionic population in these islands. It is not surprising then that the Odyssey is put aside by the advocates of the theory which we are discussing. The tendency is to regard it as a later work—originating perhaps at a time when tribal interests had become forgotten. We must confine our attention therefore to the Iliad.

As applied to the Iliad the theory was long ago seen to be open to one serious objection. Achilles is the only one of the chief Achaean leaders who can be referred to Thessaly. His nearest neighbour is the Locrian Aias ; but the Locrians, in spite of their connection with Troy, cannot be regarded as an Aeolic people. All the other Achaean leaders who may be termed 'heroes of the first rank' belong to the southern and western parts of Greece. Their positions geographically cannot be reconciled with the theory of Aeolic tribal wars. In order to obviate this difficulty various suggestions have been put forward. On the one hand we have Prof. Bethe's hypothesis which brings the Trojan leaders, Hector and Paris, to the north-eastern parts of Greece. Upon this enough has been said above. On the other hand there is an older and still very popular hypothesis, according to which some of the southern leaders, Agamemnon in particular, originally belonged to the northern parts of the country. It is to this that we must now turn our attention.

In the Iliad Mycenae is represented as being the home of Agamemnon. But it has been observed that this place is comparatively seldom mentioned, and that sometimes Agamemnon is said to rule over 'Argos.' Unfortunately there is a considerable amount of ambiguity in the use of the latter name. Occasionally it denotes the well-known city in Argolis ; but more often it is clearly used in a much wider sense, for the Peloponnesos or the whole of Greece. Once however (II 681) we find the expression τὸ Πελασγικὸν Ἄργος as a name for the home of Achilles. In ancient times the meaning of this expression was not known. Some authorities believed it to be the name of a city, while others understood it as a designation for the plain of Thessaly. Many modern scholars have adopted the latter interpretation. But further, they hold that this was the original Argos, and that the application of that name to the Peloponnesos or any part of it is due to a misunderstanding on the part of later (Ionic) poets, by whose time the northern Argos had been forgotten.

In favour of this view Prof. Cauer[1] brings forward the following arguments. "If Agamemnon, as well as Achilles, belongs to the oldest elements in the story, he also must come from a land in which Aeolic was spoken ; and indeed not Aeolic in the extended sense which the ancients gave the term—where the name includes Elean and Arcadian—but Lesbian-Aeolic. This was, as inscriptions show, the language of the original inhabitants of Thessaly." Again "Agamemnon started with his fleet from Aulis....He was associated with Achilles in the story from the beginning. His Argeioi are the companions of the Achaeans led by Achilles. The two tribal names are used for one another indifferently, and either of them can be employed as a designation for the forces which fought at Troy. Consequently the Argeioi and the Achaeans must have been neighbours." Further, it is urged by Prof. Cauer that the epithet ἱππόβοτον as applied to the Peloponnesian Argos is inappropriate. This state possessed no cavalry in the fifth century, and none of consequence at any time. On the other hand it is a very suitable epithet for the plain of the Peneios ; Thessalian cavalry were famous. Lastly, it is argued that the expression καθ' (ἀν') Ἑλλάδα καὶ μέσον Ἄργος, which occurs four times in the Odyssey, must originally have denoted two neighbouring districts, though in the passages in question it is used in a very wide sense—perhaps for all Greece.

The last argument does not seem to me to have any decisive bearing upon the question under discussion. If we admit, as I think we must, that Homeric poetry is essentially Aeolic and that Aeolis was settled mainly from Thessaly, it is only natural that the poems should preserve traces of traditional Thessalian phraseology, just as they preserve poetic conceptions which must have originated in the same country. But, though we grant that the phrases in question may possibly have been used

[1] *Grundfragen der Homerkritik*[2], p. 223 ff.

originally of the Thessalian Argos mentioned in II 681, we are
not bound thereby to conclude that this was the only Argos
known to the earliest poems on the siege of Troy.   Again, it is
scarcely inconceivable that the traditional epithet ἱππόβοτον
may have been transferred from one Argos to the other, though
on the other hand there seems to be good reason for doubting
whether the application of this term to the Peloponnesian Argos
is as much out of place as has been alleged[1].   Still less cogent
is the argument relating to Aulis.   For the assembling of such a
fleet as the story describes the choice of a convenient central
position in sheltered waters would be suggested by the most
elementary notions of strategy.

All these however are comparatively minor considerations.
I doubt if they would have been seriously brought forward
except as reinforcements to the main contention—viz. that
Agamemnon, like Achilles, must have come from an Aeolic
district, if he belongs to the oldest elements in the story.   It is
surprising to see how this principle appears to have commanded
the assent of Homeric scholars.   To anyone who has made a
study of Teutonic heroic poetry such an argument seems nothing
less than absurd.   Out of 132 personal names which occur in
the Anglo-Saxon heroic poems only three or four, so far as we
know, belong to persons of English nationality (cf. p. 32 ff.).
Beowulf is concerned almost exclusively with the doings of
princes of the Danes, Götar and Swedes.   In Waldhere, another
English poem, the characters are Burgundians and (perhaps)
Franks; in the German Hildebrandslied they are apparently
Goths.   The Norse poems of the Older Edda are occupied
chiefly with the adventures of Huns, Burgundians and Goths.
What need then is there for supposing that Agamemnon must
have belonged to the same branch of the Greek race as Achilles?
And what need is there for supposing that an Aeolic poem must
contain any Aeolic characters at all?   In the Odyssey it is not
the case.   In the Iliad, as we have it, only a small proportion
of the characters at most can be regarded as Aeolic[2].

---

[1] Cf. Crusius, S.-B. der k. bayer. Akad., 1905, p. 755 ff.

[2] It must be clearly understood that I am using the term 'Aeolic' in the modern
(linguistic) sense.   I am under the impression that Prof. Cauer uses the term in the

The reason why Agamemnon must belong to an Aeolic
district is clearly to be found in the assumption that both he and
Achilles were originally not individuals but personifications of
tribes. Starting from this assumption we become involved in a
series of hypotheses each of which is dependent upon the preceding one. i. The sources of the Iliad were concerned only,
or at least chiefly, with the fortunes of tribes (though in point of
fact the Iliad, as it stands, is concerned only with the fortunes of
individuals). ii. These tribes belonged to adjacent districts
(though in fact the heroes of the Iliad are represented as coming
from nearly all parts of Greece). iii. Since Achilles belongs to
an Aeolic district, Agamemnon and the Argos over which he
rules must be located in the same quarter. But the third
hypothesis is by no means the only one which is dependent
upon the second. Menelaos must have been transferred from
the north, i.e. from Thessaly, with his brother. Again, Pylos
lies far away from any Aeolic district. Here we have a choice
between two hypotheses. Some hold that Nestor, like
Agamemnon, belonged originally to Thessaly (the district of
the river Enipeus); others that he is a late and Ionic addition

---

same sense. The only difference, so far as I can see, between his terminology and
mine is that—in accordance, I think, with general usage—I would include Boeotian
as well as Thessalian and Lesbian-Aeolic in this category. Some ancient writers of
course use the terms Αἰολεῖς and Αἰολίς in a totally different sense. Thus Thucydides
(III 102) applies the name Αἰολίς to the district about Pleuron and Calydon, and
again (IV 42) he speaks of the ancient inhabitants of Corinth as Αἰολῆς. There may
be some difference of opinion as to whether the use of these names in such cases is
due to the influence of genealogies—in the former case through Aethlios and
Endymion, in the latter through Sisyphos—or whether the genealogies themselves are
due to a current use of the names Αἰολεῖς, Αἰολίς, etc. The form Αἰολίδης in Il. VI 154,
Od. XI 237 rather suggests that these names may have belonged to a family (or
possibly a clan) before they came to be applied to a people; but into this question
we need not enter. The term 'Aeolic' (in its linguistic sense) belongs properly to
the Asiatic Aeolis, and this name itself is derived in all probability from the Thessalian
Aeolis (cf. Herod. VII 176), the fatherland of the Asiatic Aeolians. There may
possibly have been some connection between the reigning families of the Thessalian
Aeolis and those at Calydon, Corinth and elsewhere which claimed descent from
Aiolos; but there is not the slightest evidence that an Aeolic dialect (in the modern
sense) was ever spoken at either Calydon or Corinth. It may be added that nothing
but confusion of thought can arise from introducing into this discussion the terminology
of writers of the Roman age (cf. especially Strabo VIII 1. 2), who apply the name
'Aeolic' to every dialect which is not Attic, Ionic or Doric.

to the story. With Diomedes the case is somewhat similar. He cannot have ruled over Argos even in the second stage of the story; for then, before Mycenae was introduced, Argos belonged to Agamemnon. Either then he has been transferred from Aetolia, the home of his ancestors; or he is a late addition, due to Ionic poets. Again, Idomeneus' case is due to 'attraction'; originally he belonged to quite a different cycle of story, like Tlepolemos. Aias, the son of Telamon, is clearly a 'doublet' of the Locrian Aias; and so forth. By this process we are enabled to dispose satisfactorily of all the southern Greek heroes.

It will be seen that according to some scholars only a few of the leading heroes belonged to the original form of the story, and that their number has grown by gradual accretions. According to others the majority were there from the beginning; but they belonged originally to the northern parts of Greece, more especially the Aeolic districts. With reference to this latter view it may be observed that the Aeolic districts are by no means unrepresented in the Iliad as we have it. On the contrary we find a considerable number of leaders both from Thessaly and Boeotia; but they are all what we may term 'heroes of the second rank.' Are we to suppose that these are 'Ionic' substitutions for the original heroes, when the latter were transferred to the southern parts of Greece?

But we have yet to consider a more important question than this. In the Iliad itself only two of the leading heroes, namely Achilles and the Locrian Aias, are represented as coming from the northern parts of Greece. But the Locrians cannot be regarded as an Aeolic people. Achilles then is the only leading hero whose Aeolic nationality rests on any solid evidence, and it is, as we have seen, chiefly owing to their association with him that the same nationality is claimed by hypothesis for Agamemnon and the rest. But before we bring our discussion to a close it will be well to ask whether Achilles' nationality really is established beyond question by the evidence.

It has been mentioned above that 'the Pelasgian Argos' is said to be the home of Achilles, though unfortunately neither ancient nor modern scholars have been able to determine with

certainty what is meant by that name.   Of the other places
recorded in the same context (Il. II 681 ff.[1])—viz. Alos, Alope,
Trechis, Phthia and Hellas—all except the third are involved
in somewhat similar obscurity.   Phthia—whether it be a city or
a district—was generally located between Mt Othrys and the
Malian Gulf.   Hellas was believed to be in the same neighbourhood, if not actually identical with Phthia; some placed it on
the north side of Othrys, a short distance away.   The names
Ἄλος and Ἀλόπη were borne in historical times by places in
Locris, and also by other places in Phthiotis, on the Pagasean
Gulf and the Malian Gulf respectively.   Opinion was divided
as to which of these were the places mentioned in the Iliad.
Trechis (Trachis) lay on the south of the Spercheios.

It must not be overlooked that, except the indefinite Hellas
and Phthia, all these places, including 'the Pelasgian Argos,' are
mentioned only in the Catalogue of Ships, a section of the poem
which is commonly regarded with very little respect.   Indeed
the same scholars who lay so much stress upon the Pelasgian
Argos as the home of Achilles have no hesitation about rejecting
the evidence of the Catalogue as to the homes of Agamemnon,
Menelaos, Nestor, Diomedes and others.   Yet the Thessalian
section of the Catalogue is admittedly far more difficult to
understand than any other.   It is scarcely credible that the poet
responsible for it can have been personally acquainted with the
places he was enumerating.   Now in other parts of the poem
Achilles and his followers are associated with the Spercheios or
Ellada; from XVI 173 ff., XXIII 144 ff. it is quite clear that his
home was supposed to be in the immediate neighbourhood of
that river.   According to IX 484 his vassal Phoinix rules over
the Dolopes, a people who, at least in historical times, inhabited
the mountainous country to the north-west[2].   These indications,
it will be seen, agree perfectly well with the only place in

---

[1]   νῦν αὖ τοὺς, ὅσσοι τὸ Πελασγικὸν Ἄργος ἔναιον,
        οἵ τ' Ἄλον οἵ τ' Ἀλόπην οἵ τε Τρηχῖν' ἐνέμοντο,
        οἵ τ' εἶχον Φθίην ἠδ' Ἑλλάδα καλλιγύναικα, κ.τ.λ.

In v. 681 Zenodotos read:
        οἳ δ' Ἄργος τ' εἶχον τὸ Πελασγικὸν, οὖθαρ ἀρούρης.

[2] This passage seems to indicate that the poet included the basin of the Spercheios
in Phthia.

the Catalogue which can be identified with certainty, namely
Trechis. On the whole also they favour the view that
'Alope' is the Phthiotic Alope. Achilles' country then is the
basin of the Spercheios, together probably with the coast lands
on the Malian Gulf between the mountains of Oite and Othrys.
It may have included the northern slopes of the latter, in the
territory of the Dolopes ; but neither the evidence of the
Catalogue itself nor references in other parts of the Iliad give
us any warrant for supposing that it extended into the plain of
Larissa[1].

Now there is not a particle of evidence that an Aeolic dialect
was ever spoken either in the basin of the Spercheios or in the
districts bordering on the coasts of the Malian Gulf. A form
(Μαχαειος) which may be an Aeolic patronymic occurs in an
inscription from Melitaia[2]; but the inscription in other respects
is definitely non-Aeolic, although Melitaia lies to the north of
Othrys. A similar form (Ευβιοτεια) occurs in an inscription
found near Pteleon[3], which is too short for us to determine its
character ; but Pteleon lies in the extreme east of Phthiotis,
outside the Malian Gulf, and according to the Catalogue belonged
to Protesilaos. The only inscription of definitely Aeolic (Thessalian) character as yet found in Phthiotis comes from near
Eretria, just inside the boundary. This place is not mentioned
in the Catalogue, or elsewhere in the Iliad ; but Strabo (IX 5. 10)
conjectured that it belonged to Achilles' territories. If we are
to follow the indications given by the Catalogue the question
would seem to lie between the territories of Protesilaos and

---

[1] So far as I can see, the identification of 'the Pelasgian Argos' with the plain
of Larissa rests merely on a conjecture, of the truth of which even Strabo himself
(IX 5. 5) was not confident. It may very well have been suggested by the name
(Pelasgiotis) borne by this district in later times. The oracle quoted by Prof. Meyer
(*Forsch.*, p. 30, note 1) proves nothing, and there is no evidence that the name was
used in historical times. On the other hand the fact that the citadel of the Peloponnesian Argos was called Λάρισα (cf. Pausanias II 24. 1) does suggest a connection
between this name and Ἄργος. But if so, it is more natural to think of Larissa
Cremaste, which according to Strabo (IX 5. 13, 19) was also called Pelasgia. This
place is much nearer to the Spercheios than the northern Larissa, and in spite of
Strabo (IX 5. 14) may quite possibly have been included within the same territory.

[2] Cauer, *Delectus*[2], No. 388.

[3] *ib.*, No. 390.

those of Eurypylos; there is nothing to show that Achilles'
country was believed to extend so far. It is most surprising
therefore to find Prof. Cauer[1] concluding from such evidence as
this that "we are justified in claiming the valley of the
Spercheios also as an Aeolic district and Achilles as a hero
of Aeolic nationality."

For the language of Achilles' country itself we are by no
means without evidence. Fairly long inscriptions have been
found at Hypate in the valley of the Spercheios and at Lamia,
to the north of the Malian Gulf—to which may be added an
inscription, apparently of the Oitaioi, at Drymaia in Phocis.
All these show the form of language usually known as 'north-
west Greek,' and the same is true of other inscriptions found
in the north and east of Phthiotis. Although they are all late,
there is no valid reason for doubting that this language is
indigenous[2]. Only two inscriptions[3], so far as I know, contain
references to Aetolian magistrates. The dialect is almost
identical not only with that of the Aetolian inscriptions, but also
with those of the Locrians and Phocians, the former of which is
well known from much earlier times. Greek communities as
a general rule were slow to change their language, and the
influence of the Aetolian League was scarcely of such a
character as to favour the permanent extension of its dialect[4].

---

[1] *Grundfragen der Homerkritik*[2], p. 214.

[2] By this of course I do not mean that the inscriptions give an absolutely faithful
reproduction of the local pronunciation, any more than do those of the Aetolians.
From the fourth century onwards 'phonetic spelling' appears to have been superseded
in most parts of Greece. No earlier inscriptions, representing the Achaean dialect
in its purity, have been found as yet. From Thetonion however, near Cierion in
Thessaliotis, about twenty miles north of the border, we have an inscription of the
fifth century (*C. I. G.*, XII ii 257) in a curious mixed dialect, which combines north-
western Greek and Thessalian (Aeolic) characteristics in the proportion of about 7 : 3
(or 4). The evidence of this inscription seems to me to dispose definitely of the
hypothesis that the introduction of north-western Greek into this region was due
to the influence of the Aetolian League. Even the dialect of Pharsalos is not quite
pure Thessalian.

[3] Cauer, *Delectus*[2], Nos. 239, 386. The former is included by Prof. Cauer, no
doubt rightly, among the Aetolian inscriptions.

[4] The extension of the Dat. pl. ending -ois to consonant-stems etc. has often been
quoted as a mark of Aetolian influence. But in reality it is common to all the
dialects of western Greece. The earliest examples apparently occur in Elean and
Locrian inscriptions.

If we are to trust all the evidence which we possess Othrys, and not Oite, was the southern limit of the Aeolic (Thessalian) dialect. The communities of Phthiotis were politically dependent upon Thessaly, but they seem never to have been subjugated in the same way as the Aeolic population north of the mountains[1]. They had their own troops and sent a separate contingent to Xerxes' army.   Indeed Herodotus (VII 173, 196 ff.) clearly distinguishes between 'Thessaly' and 'Achaia' (i.e. Phthiotis). Moreover it appears to have been the general opinion among the Greeks themselves that this district was the original home of the Achaeans of the Peloponnesos.   Pausanias (VII 1. 6) traces the Peloponnesian Achaeans to Archandros and Architeles, the sons of Achaios, who had come from Phthiotis[2].   Herodotus (II 98) was evidently familiar with some form of this story, though he calls Archandros son of Phthios and grandson of Achaios.   The supposed connection therefore goes back at least to the fifth century.   How far these genealogies were constructed upon linguistic affinities is a question which needs some discussion.   We may remark in passing however that the dialect of the Peloponnesian Achaia, so far as it is known to us[3], shows but little difference from the dialects north of the Gulf of Corinth.   It is commonly included in the list of 'north-west Greek' dialects.

In the meantime we may notice an argument which has

---

[1] According to the generally accepted view, which there seems to be no reason for doubting, the language of the Thessalian (Aeolic or 'North-Thessalian') inscriptions belonged originally to the indigenous population.   The name 'Thessalian' however, properly speaking, belonged to the invaders, regarding whose language we have no information.

[2] Strabo (VIII 5. 5) likewise connects the Peloponnesian Achaeans with Phthiotis; but he attributes their settlement in the Peloponnesos to an invasion by Pelops.   In this passage (as in many others) it is greatly to be questioned whether Strabo (or the authority whom he followed) was recording genuine tradition—whether he was not rather endeavouring to provide an explanation of the traditions.

[3] The inscriptions are late; but their evidence as to the general character of the dialect is confirmed by some short but early inscriptions from the Achaean settlements in Italy.   It is assumed by many scholars that Arcadian was the original language of the Peloponnesian Achaeans; but I am not aware that any evidence worth consideration has been adduced in support of this view.   No ancient authorities, so far as I know, connect the Arcadians with the Achaeans, nor do the Arcadians themselves appear to have claimed such a connection.

sometimes been brought forward in support of the hypothesis
that Aeolic was once spoken much further south. This is the
presence of an Aeolic or semi-Aeolic form of language in
Boeotia. The ancients themselves believed that the Boeotians
were not indigenous. Thucydides (I 12) states that they had
been expelled by the Thessalians from 'Arne' after the Trojan
War; but this was not the only form of the story. On the
other hand many modern scholars have adopted the view that
the 'north-western' dialects of Locris and Phocis were intrusive[1],
and that the non-Aeolic characteristics of the Boeotian dialect
itself were due to an extension of the same movement—in short
that Aeolic was the earliest form of Greek spoken throughout
the whole region from Thessaly down to the borders of Attica.
For such a displacement of population[2] no evidence is to be found
either in history or tradition. Moreover this hypothesis has
opposed to it the evidence of what may be called linguistic
geography. The Ionic dialects of Euboea and Attica have
much more in common with the 'north-western' dialects of
Locris and Phocis than they have with Boeotian. The latter
indeed stands quite isolated in many respects among the dialects
of this part of Greece. It will be sufficient here to notice the
close pronunciation of $\bar{e}$ (e.g. in Gen. sg. $\mu\epsilon\iota\nu\acute{o}s$) and the open
pronunciation of $\breve{o}$ (e.g. in Acc. pl. $\tau\acute{\omega}s$)—both of which are
probably to be regarded as Aeolic characteristics—the use of
Aeolic patronymics in -ios (e.g. $\H{I}\pi\pi\omega\nu$ $\mathrm{A}\theta\alpha\nu\sigma\delta\acute{\omega}\rho\iota\sigma s$) and more
especially the Aeolic tendency to change labiovelar explosives
into labials before $\breve{e}$, which we find exemplified at both ex-
tremities of the Boeotian area ($\mathrm{B}\epsilon\lambda\phi o\acute{\iota}$, $\Pi\epsilon\upsilon\mu\alpha\tau\tau\acute{o}s$). The last

---

[1] This theory is of course quite distinct from the theory which traces the language
of the Phthiotic inscriptions to the influence of the Aetolian League. The two are
scarcely reconcilable if it be held that the Locrians and Phocians came from the
north-west; for in that case their route must have lain through the valley of
the Spercheios, a district which would not readily be neglected by peoples seeking
new territories.

[2] I.e. in times subsequent to the Heroic Age. I do not mean of course to suggest
that the north-west Greek dialects belonged originally to these districts; but I see no
reason for supposing that the previous language was Aeolic. The Ainianes may have
moved southwards later. But the language of their inscriptions (at Hypate) is indis-
tinguishable from that of the surrounding peoples. It is to be remembered also that,
according to the common tradition, the Dorians themselves had come from a district
within this area.

peculiarity is doubtless one of the earliest cases of dialectal variation which can be traced in the Greek language; but it is impossible to date. All this evidence tends to show that Aeolic was the intrusive element—in other words, to confirm the tradition that Boeotia was at some time invaded by settlers from an Aeolic-speaking district[1].

In recent years there has been a tendency to classify the Greek dialects in two main groups—'East Greek' and 'West Greek.' In the former are included Arcadian, Cypriot, Ionic (with Attic) and the Aeolic dialects, i.e. Thessalian and Lesbian-Aeolic, together with the Aeolic element in Boeotian. To the latter are referred the remaining dialects, i.e. the Doric dialects and all the dialects of the mainland of Greece except Arcadian, Attic, Thessalian and Boeotian, so far as Boeotian can be regarded as Aeolic. It may be doubted whether this classification is altogether satisfactory, since the affinities of Aeolic with Ionic and Arcadian are by no means close; as much perhaps might be said for a division into 'North Greek' (Aeolic) and 'South Greek' (non-Aeolic). But there can be no doubt that the 'West Greek' dialects, i.e. Doric and north-western Greek, except perhaps Elean, do really form a homogeneous group. Indeed it can hardly be maintained that the Doric dialects as a whole show any divergence from the other members of the group[2], though there are marked differences between one Doric dialect and another. It is this West Greek group which specially requires our attention, for according to all the evidence we possess it included the dialects of both the Phthiotic Achaeans and the Peloponnesian Achaeans.

[1] It may be added that the fertile plains of Boeotia are more likely to have attracted invaders than the mountainous lands to the north-west.

[2] Cf. Meister, *Sächs. Ges. d. Wiss. Abhandl.* 1906, Nr. 3, summarised p. 96 ff., where it is pointed out that the characteristics commonly described as Dorian belong in reality also to Achaean and that in general they are rather to be ascribed to the latter. At the same time it is to be noted that some of the characteristics here claimed as specifically Dorian are shared also by Cypriot, a fact which rather suggests that they may be indigenous to the south-east of the Peloponnesos. If the Dorians came from the same quarter as the Achaeans—and not very many generations later— it is intelligible enough that the two groups of dialects should be difficult to distinguish, even apart from the fact that an Achaean stratum—however insignificant numerically —underlies the Dorian practically everywhere.

Now let us return to the genealogical problem. We have seen that Herodotus was familiar with a story which traced the descent of the Peloponnesian Achaeans from Phthios the son of Achaios. The same writer elsewhere (I 56, etc.) draws a distinction between 'Hellenic' and 'Pelasgian' peoples. Among the former he includes the Dorians; among the latter the Athenians (I 56, VIII 44), the Ionians (VII 94), the Arcadians (I 146) and the Aeolians (VII 95). By Αἰολέες he means here the inhabitants of the Asiatic Aeolis. But in view of other passages (I 57, VII 176) it can scarcely be doubted that he would have included the earlier population of Thessaly in the same category.

Now Herodotus himself believed the Pelasgoi to have been a barbarous nation. The peoples of whom he is speaking here were regarded by him as 'Hellenized' Pelasgoi. Some modern writers think that he was mistaken in this view, and that the Pelasgoi were a Greek people from the beginning[1]. Some hold also that the term Πελασγοί in most of these cases is due simply to the influence of genealogies[2]. It is a serious objection to this latter view that the well-known genealogy in which the descent of Ion, as well as Aiolos, is traced from Hellen, goes back at least two or three centuries before the time of Herodotus. But we are not primarily concerned here with Herodotus' opinions; for it is clear from the expressions which he uses (e.g. VII 95 : τὸ πάλαι καλεόμενοι Πελασγοί, ὡς Ἑλλήνων λόγος) that the distinction between Πελασγοί and Ἕλληνες was one which was generally recognised in his time. Some of his contemporaries may have regarded the Pelasgoi as Greeks, others as barbarians. What was generally agreed was that the term

---

[1] Cf. especially Meyer, *Geschichte des Alterthums*, II p. 55 f., *Forsch. zur alten Geschichte*, I p. 112 ff.; Ridgeway, *Early Age of Greece*, p. 659 ff., etc.; Kretschmer, *Glotta*, I 17 ff. Prof. Meyer has subsequently abandoned this view (*Gesch. d. Alt.*[2], I p. 687).

[2] Cf. Meyer, *Forsch.* I (*passim*). The genealogical explanation seems to me to be pressed too far here. The case of the Arcadians is the one in which it is most probable, since apart from genealogies there is no real evidence that this people was connected with the Pelasgoi in any way. Yet even here the cause assigned (*ib.*, p. 53 ff.) is scarcely adequate. One might rather suspect a confusion or identification of the names Λυκάων and Λυκαῖος; but I have no inclination to propound a theory on the subject.

"Ελληνες was originally applied only to a portion of the inhabitants of Greece.   We may refer to Thucydides (I 3¹): " The
different tribes, of which the Pelasgian was the most widely
spread, gave their own names to different districts. But when
Hellen and his sons became powerful in Phthiotis, their aid was
invoked by other cities, and those who were associated with
them gradually began to be called Hellenes, though a long
time elapsed before the name prevailed over the whole country.
Of this Homer affords the best evidence ; for he, although he
lived long after the Trojan War, nowhere uses this name
collectively, but confines it to the followers of Achilles from
Phthiotis, who were the original Hellenes."   In a certain sense
therefore we may regard Πελασγοί as a term of negative value,
i.e. ' non-Hellenic.'

Herodotus does not expressly describe any people as
' Hellenic,' in the narrower sense, except the Dorians.   But we
are surely not justified in concluding from this that he regarded
the Dorians as the only true Hellenes². He is interested in
pointing out that certain Greek (Hellenic) peoples were believed
to be of Pelasgian origin.   Doubtless he considered it unnecessary to say that those for whom no such origin was claimed
were really Hellenes, except in such a passage as I 56, where
a ' Hellenic ' and a ' Pelasgian ' people are specially contrasted
with each other.   In general then the presumption is rather
that a people was believed to be truly Hellenic, unless we have
a statement to the contrary. In particular however it is incredible
that the Achaeans were regarded as Pelasgian, for it was in the
Achaean Phthiotis—more properly perhaps in ' Phthia '—that
traditional belief located the eponymous Hellen.   Thucydides,
as we have seen, observes that this belief was confirmed by the
evidence of the Homeric poems.   The term ' Hellenic ' belongs
essentially to the followers of Achilles (οὕπερ καὶ πρῶτοι
"Ελληνες ἦσαν).

It can hardly be contended either that the story of Hellen is
derived from the Homeric usage, or that the Homeric usage is

---

¹ Quoted from Jowett's translation.

² Cf. Meyer, Forsch., I p. 115; yet in another passage (ib., p. 111, note) considerations are pointed out which can hardly have been unfamiliar to Herodotus.

derived from the story of Hellen. Both alike are based on the
common knowledge or belief that the names "Ελληνες and
'Ελλάς belonged originally to Phthia. It is not difficult to see
why names from such a district, obscure and remote as it was,
should come to be applied to the whole nation. The valley of
the Spercheios was regarded as the gate of Greece. Certain
peoples, such as the Boeotians and Eleans, may have come into
possession of their territories by maritime invasions. But there
can be little doubt that in pre-historic, as in historical times—
we may refer to the Persians and the Gauls—great invasions
usually made their way through the pass of Thermopylai. That
is true probably not only of the later invasions of the 'West
Greek' peoples (the Achaeans, Locrians, Dorians, etc.) but also
of those much earlier movements by which the first Greek
populations—the ancestors of the Ionians and Arcadians—were
introduced into the peninsula. But if we are to trust all the
evidence at our disposal it was with the later movements that
the names 'Ελλάς[1] and "Ελληνες[2] were originally connected.

The results of our discussion may now be summarised as
follows: (i) According to current hypotheses the language of
the Achaeans of Phthiotis was Aeolic, while that of the Peloponnesian Achaeans was perhaps Arcadian ; but in point of
fact all the linguistic evidence which we have from both districts
(including the colonies of the Peloponnesian Achaeans) is
definitely West Greek. In all probability the valley of the
Spercheios was one of the first, if not actually the very first,
of the districts occupied by the West Greeks in the eastern and
southern parts of the peninsula. (ii) According to a belief current
in the fifth century certain Greek peoples were truly 'Hellenic,'
while others were of 'Pelasgian' origin. The former category
coincided, at least to a large extent, with the 'West Greek'
linguistic division, the latter with the 'East Greek' division, or
—to speak more accurately—with the northern, eastern and

---

[1] It is to be remembered that the name ἡ μεγάλη 'Ελλάς appears to have come
from the Achaean colonies in Italy.

[2] It is worth noting that stems in -ān-, as names of peoples, seem to have been
specially characteristic of north-western Greek ; e.g. Αἰνιᾶνες, 'Αθαμᾶνες, Εὐρυτᾶνες,
Κεφαλλᾶνες, 'Ακαρνᾶνες.

southern groups of dialects.   In certain cases, owing to the
silence of our authorities, it may be permissible to doubt whether
a people was regarded as 'Hellenic' or 'Pelasgian'; but no such
doubt applies to the followers of Achilles, 'who were the original
Hellenes.'   It was in Phthia that much earlier tradition located
the eponymous Hellen ; and from the same district came
Archandros and Architeles, the legendary progenitors of the
Peloponnesian Achaeans, several generations before the Trojan
War.   It is clear then that the 'West Greek' language of the
extant inscriptions is in perfect agreement with the belief of
the fifth century Greeks that this community was essentially
Hellenic.   We may dismiss therefore as totally without foundation the hypothesis that Achilles was an Aeolic (or Pelasgian)
hero[1].

Now let us drop hypotheses and consider briefly the evidence
actually furnished by the Iliad.   The poem leaves us in no doubt
as to who are regarded as the principal persons in the Achaean
army.   In II 404 ff. Agamemnon is represented as calling
together "the elders, the chiefs of the whole Achaean host"
(γέροντας ἀριστῆας Παναχαιῶν).   They are Nestor, Idomeneus,
Aias the son of Telamon and his Locrian namesake, Diomedes,
Odysseus and Menelaos.   In another council (X 194 ff.) we find
the same party together with three additional persons, Thrasymedes, Meriones and Meges.   In the debates, which occur so
frequently, the leading speakers are almost always Agamemnon,
Nestor, Diomedes, Odysseus and Menelaos.   In the battle
scenes the aged Nestor naturally does not play an active part.
The other four heroes however, together with Idomeneus, Aias
the son of Telamon and (to a somewhat less extent) the Locrian
Aias, are by far the most conspicuous figures in the army.   In
response to Hector's challenge, from which Menelaos has been
forced to retire, all the other six come forward, together with
Meriones, Eurypylos and Thoas.   There can be no doubt then

---

[1] It is scarcely necessary to notice the subsidiary arguments which have been
adduced in favour of the hypothesis—e.g. that Achilles had been instructed by the
Centaur Cheiron and that his spear had come from Pelion.   They are sufficiently
accounted for by the fact that the poems are of Aeolic origin.   The suggestion that
Peleus himself is the eponymus of Pelion belongs to a class which has been sufficiently
discussed above (p. 267 ff.).

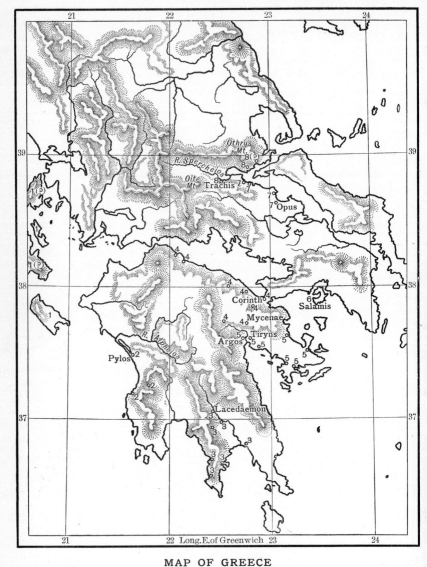

MAP OF GREECE

illustrating the 'Catalogue of Ships'

The numerals denote cities or territories belonging to the
chief leaders of the Achaeans.

1	possessions of	Odysseus	5	possessions of	Diomedes, etc.
2	,,	Nestor	6	,,	Aias son of Telamon
3	,,	Menelaos	7	,,	Aias son of Oileus
4	,,	Agamemnon	8	,,	Achilles

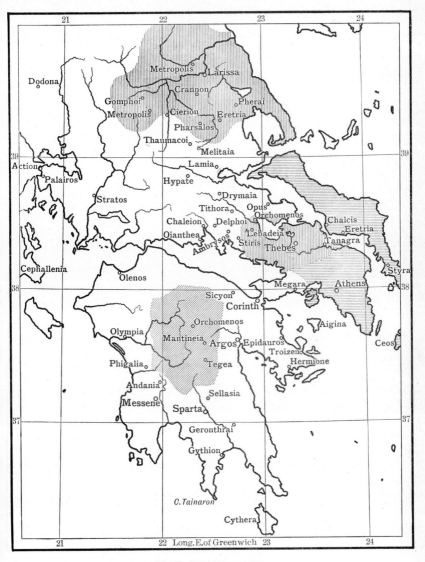

MAP OF GREECE

showing the distribution of the dialects in historical times

Aeolic (Thessalian and Boeotian)

Ionic (with Attic)

Arcadian

West Greek dialects not shaded.

that the eight leading men are Agamemnon and his brother,
Nestor, Idomeneus, the two Aiantes, Diomedes and Odysseus.
To these we must certainly add Achilles, who is in retirement
throughout the greater part of the poem.

Hypothesis after hypothesis has been tried in order to claim
an Aeolic or Ionic origin for most of these heroes. The plain
fact is that all except one[1] belong to communities which in the
fifth century were regarded as truly 'Hellenic'—or at all events
to districts where dialects of the West Greek type prevailed
in historical times. The leading Aeolic hero is Eurypylos; but
he ranks only with Meriones, the Cretan second-in-command,
Thoas the Aetolian and Nestor's sons. The other Aeolic and
Ionic leaders are distinctly less prominent.

From the evidence at our disposal it seems to me that, if the
poets of the Iliad, or rather their predecessors, were interested
in any nationality at all, that nationality must have been West
Greek or 'Hellenic.' Of the two chief leaders one belongs to
Achaia Phthiotis, the other to the Peloponnesian Achaeans;
the Catalogue of Ships (Il. II 569 ff.) assigns to him territories
which in the main coincide with the later Achaia, though they
cover a somewhat larger area. We have scarcely any evidence
worth consideration that either Achaia Phthiotis or the Peloponnesian Achaia was ever held by a different nationality within the
period embraced by history and tradition[2]. The territories of
the other chief Peloponnesian leaders were occupied in historical
times by the Dorians. But it was the unanimous belief of the
ancient world that the Dorian period had been preceded by an
age of Achaean domination in the east, south and west of the
peninsula. Lastly, the Odyssey (XIX 175), in a passage which
is commonly believed to preserve a true ethnographical record,

---

[1] The exceptional case is that of Aias the son of Telamon. But we have no
information relating to Salamis before its conquest by the Athenians in the sixth
century. It may have been under Achaean rule in early times.

[2] In the case of the Peloponnesian Achaia it is conceivable that a genuine tradition
of a conquest of earlier (Ionic) inhabitants may be preserved in Herod. I 145. But
the story that this conquest was connected with the Dorian invasion can hardly be
due to anything but 'combination'; and traces of such a process can be distinguished
plainly enough in Herodotus' account. The important fact is that the author of the
Catalogue of Ships evidently knew nothing of the story.

speaks of the presence of Achaeans in Crete. Thus at least six[1]
of the nine principal leaders come from regions with an Achaean
population. In view of this fact is it any wonder that Ἀχαιοί
is by far the commonest term applied in the poems to the Greeks
collectively[2]? This then must be the nationality in which the
poets were interested. But the Achaeans of historical times, as
we have seen, everywhere used a form of language which is West
Greek. Moreover, it is to the northern Achaeans that we first
find the name Ἕλληνες applied (Il. II 684). The facts noted
seem to indicate that the Achaeans were the dominant people
of the West Greeks—indeed, we may say, of the Greeks generally
—during the Heroic Age, a position in which they were
eventually succeeded by the Dorians.

But the poems themselves are of Aeolic origin. It is this
fact—supported by speculations of writers of the Roman period,
who included under the term 'Aeolic' every dialect not obviously
Doric, Ionic or Attic[3]—which has led to the unfortunate equation
'Achaean' = 'Aeolic.' In reality the heroes and the poems
belong to two entirely different sections of the Greek nation.
Shall we then set up another hypothesis—that the original
poems were Achaean? But then we should only be repeating
the old error of building hypothesis upon hypothesis. For it is
a hypothesis, and nothing more, that the original poems were
concerned with tribal or national interests; the poems which
have come down to us deal with the fortunes of individuals.
Moreover we should not thereby save the theory that the Iliad
is a reflection of the Greek settlement of the north-western coast
of Asia Minor; for that settlement was not Achaean but Aeolic.
The truth is that the initial hypothesis is entirely unjustified.
We have no more reason for supposing that the heroes must be

[1] We may probably add Odysseus. In the Odyssey the hero's subjects are
regularly described as Ἀχαιοί. They are not called Ἀργεῖοι or Δαναοί, although the
three names are used interchangeably as collective terms for the Greek army before
Troy. Regarding the national affinities of the inhabitants of the Ionian Isles in later
times we have little information; but the language was clearly of the 'north-west
Greek' type. Indeed Aias the son of Oileus is the only one of the nine heroes in
whose case Achaean nationality is distinctly improbable.

[2] The figures for the Iliad are: Ἀχαιοί 605, Ἀργεῖοι 176, Δαναοί 146; cf. Cauer,
Grundfragen[2], p. 220.

[3] Cf. especially Strabo, VIII 1. 2.

Aeolic if the poems are Aeolic—or that the poems must be Achaean if the heroes are Achaean—than we have for assuming that the Anglo-Saxon poems were of Danish or Gothic origin because Danes and Goths figure in them more prominently than persons of English nationality. It is likely enough that poems once existed dealing with Aeolic heroes, such as Iason, perhaps also Peirithoos and others. But the reason for the prominence assigned to Achaean heroes, at all events in the poems which have survived, is to be found not in the national sympathies or interests of the poets, but in the fact that during the Heroic Age the Achaeans were the dominant people in Greece.

CHAPTER XIV.

FICTION IN THE HOMERIC POEMS.

WE have now to consider briefly how far the use of fiction, i.e. of conscious, deliberate invention, was permitted in the composition of Greek heroic poetry. This question gave us considerable difficulty when we were discussing the Teutonic poems. It is assuredly not less difficult here. The higher artistic level of the Greek poems cannot but pre-dispose us in favour of the view that their use of fiction is of a more advanced type. This expectation is fully realised in the elaborate presentation of many of the scenes, whether the actors be human beings who may or may not have taken part in the events described, or divine beings whose mythical origin no one will dispute. In the σύστασις τῶν πραγμάτων the art of poetic invention is developed to a high degree of perfection.

The chief difference between our present problem and the one which we had to consider in Chapter VIII lies in the fact that here we are entirely without that contemporary historical evidence which enables us to recognise some characters or events in nearly all the Teutonic poems. The way lies open therefore for regarding the whole story of the siege of Troy as a product of fiction ; and this is a view which many modern scholars have adopted. For an example we can scarcely do better than quote the words of the late Sir R. C. Jebb (*Introduction to Homer*, p. 147) : "The tale of Troy, as we have it in Homer, is essentially a poetic creation ; and the poet is the sole witness." The same scholar was prepared to grant that " some memorable capture of a town in the Troad had probably been made by Greek warriors"; but, he adds, "beyond this we cannot safely go." This attitude is doubtless perfectly correct from the historian's point of view. But if we approach the problem from the ethnologist's side we cannot rest satisfied with an attitude of scepticism owing to the absence of historical evidence. Our duty includes the question how far we are justi- fied in admitting the use of fiction. The Iliad would still be a great monument of human genius even if all the characters and events in it could be proved to be historical. But if it is wholly, or almost wholly, a work of fiction we shall have to conclude that the Homeric poets had developed the inventive faculty to a degree which has scarcely been equalled even in our own days. That is a conclusion which we shall do well to adopt only after careful consideration, seeing that we are dealing with the earliest monument of European literature. Scepticism is required in this direction therefore just as much as in the other.

At the outset we are confronted by two considerations which amply justify this attitude. The first is the evidence of the Teutonic poems. Here, as we have seen, myth and folk-tale both play their parts, the latter often a very important part. But we have no proof that any one of the stories is a product of conscious fiction. Wherever we can put it to the test, the setting is found to be historical, at least in the earlier forms of the stories. In medieval poetry we meet with many fictitious stories of wars waged by imaginary kings of, let us say, Byzan- tium or Britain. But in poetry which is entirely free from scholastic influence, such as the old heroic poems or the poems of the Viking Age, we shall look in vain for trustworthy examples. The same remark is probably true of Slavonic and Cumbrian heroic poetry.

The other consideration is still more serious. It is the opinion of the ancient Greeks themselves. Here again we may quote Sir R. C. Jebb's work (p. 84) : " They held that his events and his persons were, in the main, real....Thucydides differs from Herodotus in bringing down the Homeric heroes more nearly to the level of common men. But the basis of fact in Homer is fully as real to Thucydides as to Herodotus." The current hypothesis assumes that both were deceived, and with them the universal consensus of educated Greek opinion. But is not this a strange assumption? Those who hold that the Homeric poems are wholly the work of one author may cherish the belief that this person was so gifted as to be able to perpetrate a hoax upon his countrymen which in their most enlightened days they never succeeded in detecting. But I do not see how any such idea can be reconciled with the theory of evolution. The story was invented, we must presume, by the first poet and elaborated by his successors. Were these latter persons cognisant of the deception? If not, we must regard their contributions as negligible ; and consequently we are brought back virtually to the theory of single authorship. And yet no one will suggest that the poets of several generations were accomplices in such a deception. The only alternative then, which remains, is that the poets invented and elaborated a romance, which they did not intend to be taken seriously. How greatly then has the history of Greek thought been misunderstood! It appears now that the period between the ninth and the fifth centuries was characterised not by intellectual emancipation but by the growth of credulity.

In view of these considerations the burden of proof must be held to lie with those who hold that the story is fictitious. Until such proof is forthcoming it seems to me that the only reasonable course is to follow the opinion of the ancients, except in so far as we have good reason for believing that they were mistaken. The ancients not only accepted the siege of Troy as a historical fact; they were prepared also to point out the site of the city. The correctness of this identification was indeed disputed by Demetrios of Scepsis, a native antiquary of the second century, who fixed upon another site, some four miles away ; while modern scholars until recently believed that both were wrong. This is why in the passage quoted above Sir R. C. Jebb used the expression "a city in the Troad." But about five or six years after the publication of his book the traditional site was fully vindicated by the excavations of Dr Dörpfeld, which brought to light the remains of a fortress dating, approximately at least, from the period indicated by the story. It was made clear also that this fortress had been destroyed, presumably by enemies. That the destroyers were Greeks could not of course be proved by the excavations. But the evidence of the poems in this respect is confirmed by the fact that the district was inhabited by Greeks in later times[1].

It is held by many scholars that the story of the siege of Troy is a reflection of the Aeolic colonisation of the Asiatic coast. We have already discussed the principle underlying this theory and found no evidence in its favour. But it does not follow from this that the two events were unconnected. One of the most famous stories[2] recorded by Scandinavian tradition is that of the expedition to England which was undertaken by the sons of Lothbrok for the purpose of exacting vengeance for their father's death. Now we have an account of this invasion from a contemporary historical work (the Saxon Chronicle), which gives the names of two of the princes (Inwaer and Healfdene), as well as that of the Northumbrian king Aella against whom the expedition was directed. We know also that Lothbrok's sons were by no means contented with the overthrow of Aella; that on the contrary they ravaged the greater part of England. Long after they were all dead or departed the eastern half of the country remained Scandinavian territory. According to the Iliad Achilles did not confine his energies to Troy; he is said to have ravaged Lesbos and several places in the country round the Gulf of Adramyttion. Is there any valid reason for denying that the Greek occupation of these lands may have originated in such events? We need not suppose of course that the conquered lands were fully occupied at once. But the first settlers may well have secured enough to serve as a refuge for those of

---

[1] It has been held that the Aeolic settlements in the Troad itself date only from the seventh century (cf. Meyer, *Geschichte des Alterthums*, II pp. 203, 463 f.), and there is some evidence that movements of this kind were in operation about that time. But the excavations at Troy brought to light the fact that the district had been occupied, in times long subsequent to the destruction of the fortress, by a semi-barbarous people, apparently from the region of the Danube. The evidence at our disposal seems to indicate that there were Greek settlements in existence before this time, but that they were temporarily overthrown by the barbarians (cf. Brückner, *Troja und Ilion*, p. 567 ff.). At all events it is clear that the Homeric poets were familiar with the district.

[2] For a full account of this story see Mawer, *Ragnar Lothbrók and his sons* (published in the Saga-Book of the Viking Club, Jan. 1909).

their countrymen who fled from the Thessalian invasion, probably no long time afterwards. A good parallel is furnished by the Scandinavian settlements in the British Isles, which served as a retreat for many Norwegians who refused to bow to the encroachments of Harold the Fair-haired.

The Greek settlements in this region were Aeolic, a fact due probably, as we have said, to the Thessalian invasion. But Achilles was an Achaean, and the same is true of most of the other chief heroes. The Iliad does not represent Troy as being attacked merely 'by Greeks,' but by an army gathered together from nearly all parts of Greece. This is one of the features in the story to which objection has been taken most generally. We may grant freely that no parallel for such an undertaking is to be found in historical times. Indeed, the objection itself contains a weak point here; for from all that we know of the earliest historical period it is scarcely credible that such an idea could have suggested itself, even in a work of fiction. On the other hand in the thirteenth and twelfth centuries the monuments of Rameses II, Merenptah and Rameses III give us information of expeditions which were on at least as large a scale and covered much greater distances. We have no reason for doubting that such an undertaking was possible also in the eleventh century.

But if the expedition itself is nothing incredible in such a period, what shall we say with regard to its motive? The reason assigned by the poem—that it was brought about by Paris' escapade—is one of those features which have been put aside by modern scholars as unworthy of consideration. This attitude is due partly to the application of modern political theories to a state of society in which they are quite out of place. With this question we shall have to deal in the following chapter. But it is due still more to the absurd hallucination that a story of abduction must have originated in the 'hypostasis' of natural phenomena. According to Scandinavian tradition the expedition of Lothbrok's sons was inspired by a purely personal motive— the desire to exact vengeance for their father's death. But in the Heroic Age itself we have from a strictly contemporary authority (cf. p. 97 f.) the story of the great expedition of the

Angli against the Warni, which was caused by a breach of promise of marriage.

It appears then on examination that the central feature of the story, namely the destruction of Troy, rests upon fact, while the other main features gain in probability the more one takes into account the conditions of the age and the analogies furnished by similar stories elsewhere. These considerations tend to support the view that the employment of fiction is to be seen rather in the presentation than in the conception of the story. But the term 'presentation' here, just as in Chapter VIII, must be interpreted in a very liberal sense.

What has been said above applies of course properly only to the Iliad. With the Odyssey the case is quite otherwise. In the first place we have to note that the ancients themselves took a different view with regard to this poem—at all events that part of it which relates to the hero's wanderings. The credibility of the various incidents was frequently and warmly debated; but many of them were defended only by an allegorical interpretation. Then again the conditions are similar to those in which we find the most pronounced use of fiction in early Teutonic poetry. Sigemund is expressly said to have been alone when he attacked the dragon, and most of Beowulf's marvellous exploits are performed when he is either alone or with a single companion. The motif of the lonely wanderer in distant lands is not prominent in the remains of our poetry, but from what is said of Sigemund in Beow. 876 ff. we can scarcely doubt that it would have been utilised for the exercise of the inventive faculty.

Now we have seen (p. 258 ff.) that the hero's narrative in Od. IX—XII is evidently derived from an accumulation of folk-tales. Here the art of fiction is shown chiefly in the poet's adaptation of this material to his own purpose. But there are other parts of the poem—notably the preceding three books (VI—VIII)—which obviously require a different explanation. It is frequently assumed that the Phaeacians are wholly a creation of the poet's fancy. Without going so far as this[1] we may seriously doubt

---

[1] Cf. Βαιάκη. πόλις τῆς Χαονίας. Ἑκαταῖος. κ.τ.λ. (Steph. Byz., s.v.) From this notice we gather that at the beginning of the fifth century (or earlier) the Greeks

whether they were a Greek people and whether there was any foundation in history or tradition for the account given here—with a quite exceptional amount of detail—of their princes, their city and institutions. If this part of the story is to be regarded as fiction it is certainly a more elaborate type of fiction than anything which we meet with in the early heroic poetry of the Teutonic peoples. But the false stories told by Odysseus in the latter part of the poem at all events go far towards showing that such fiction was not beyond the power of Homeric poets.

According to our explanation the extensive use of fiction in the story of Odysseus is due to the fact that in this case the poet or poets had a free hand, whereas elsewhere, more particularly in the Iliad, they were bound down by tradition. It is not to be overlooked however that the Iliad itself contains many incidents which may similarly be regarded as products of invention—additions to the story which did not conflict with anything that had been 'handed down.' As a likely instance of this kind we may cite the Doloneia. But since we can seldom or never get beyond a hypothesis with such cases, it will be more profitable, I think, now to turn our attention to another question, namely whether the use of fiction also included the invention of characters—and if so to what extent.

In our consideration of the Teutonic stories we came to the conclusion that there was no really satisfactory evidence for such invention. In the Homeric poems the evidence is much stronger. We will first take the case of names which appear to have been coined with an obvious meaning. A good example

knew of a city or state called Baiace in Chaonia, i.e. opposite the island of Corfu, which was usually identified with Scheria in ancient times. It has been remarked by several scholars that the name Βαιάκη is obviously independent of Homeric poetry. We may infer also (i) that it was derived from a non-Greek source and (ii) that if Βαιακ- and Φαιηκ- are identical the latter name must have become known to the Greeks in very early times. It is not impossible that in the Heroic Age the Greeks may have been familiar with more than the name of this people; but there is no evidence, so far as I am aware, for the existence of a prehistoric civilisation on the Albanian coast—such as we find depicted in Od. VI—VIII. Until such evidence is forthcoming probability is in favour of the view that the picture drawn of the Phaeacian community in the Odyssey is derived from a different region—most likely from the Aegean.

occurs in Od. VIII III ff., where the Phaeacian athletes are enumerated:

ὦρτο μὲν ᾿Ακρόνεώς τε καὶ ᾿Ωκύαλος καὶ ᾿Ελατρεὺς
Ναυτεύς τε Πρυμνεύς τε καὶ ᾿Αγχίαλος καὶ ᾿Ερετμεὺς
Ποντεύς τε Πρωρεύς τε, Θόων ᾿Αναβησίνεώς τε
᾿Αμφίαλός θ᾽ υἱὸς Πολυνήου Τεκτονίδαο·
ἂν δὲ καὶ Εὐρύαλος βροτολοιγῷ ἶσος ῎Αρηι,
Ναυβολίδης θ᾽, κ.τ.λ.

Other Phaeacians have names of the same type, e.g. Ναυσίθοος, Ναυσικάα, ῎Αλιος, Κλυτόνηος, ᾿Εχένηος, Ποντόνοος. In such a case as this the poet can scarcely have intended to deceive his audience. Indeed the principle is clearly admitted in another passage (XXIV 305), where Odysseus in a false story describes himself as υἱὸς ᾿Αφείδαντος Πολυπημονίδαο ἄνακτος. We need not doubt then that other names are constructed on the same plan, e.g. that of the minstrel, Φήμιος Τερπιάδης, perhaps also those of the shipowner, Νοήμων son of Φρόνιος, and Menelaos' pilot, Φρόντις ᾿Ονητορίδης. Similar cases may be found also in the Iliad[1], e.g. (V 59 ff.) Φέρεκλον...Τέκτονος υἱὸν ῾Αρμονίδεω, ὃς χερσὶν ἐπίστατο δαίδαλα πάντα τεύχειν, or the name of a Trojan herald (XVII 323 f.) Περίφαντι ᾿Ηπυτίδῃ, probably also the spy Δόλων Εὐμήδεος υἱός (X 314). This list of course makes no claim to be exhaustive. But on the whole it can hardly be said that the type is really common in either poem, except the section dealing with the Phaeacians.

It is far more difficult to form an opinion with regard to the origin of characters whose names bear no such obvious mark. Few probably would be inclined to doubt that the names of Helen's handmaidens (Od. IV 123 ff.) were coined by the poet.

---

[1] Possibly Θερσίτης is another example of this type. It seems to me more probable however that it is a nickname, similar to ῎Ιρος (Od. XVIII 6 f.). It has been well connected with Θηρίτας, a Laconian name for Ares or Enyalios (cf. Usener, S.-B. d. Akad. zu Wien, CXXXVII, p. 53). But I cannot see any justification for the hypothesis (ib., p. 57) that the practices described by Pausanias (III 14. 8 f.; XIX 7 f.; XX 2. 8) represent a contest between Enyalios and Achilles, or for connecting them in any way with the story of the killing of Thersites by Achilles in the Aithiopis. Achilles was worshipped elsewhere in connection with athletic practices (cf. Pausanias, VI 23. 3; also the Δρόμος ᾿Αχιλλέως mentioned by Arrian, Peripl. 21. 1), probably for the same reason that worship was paid to famous athletes of the past (cf. Pindar, Isth. VII 37, 59 ff.).

But what shall we say with regard to the suitors of Penelope[1]? The argument may not be a sound one, but it is not easy to see under what conditions historical names could have been preserved in such a connection. And again, what about the numerous names which figure in the ἀνδρο-κτασίαι? Even though many of the names do recur again and again, their number is surprising[2]. It is difficult to doubt that the poets gave free rein to their inventive faculties in such scenes.

But what limits are we to set to this process? If we regard the chief heroes themselves as products of fiction we shall be involved in much the same difficulties as if we interpreted the story as a whole in this way. In a sense indeed the difficulties will be increased; for it is scarcely conceivable that a heroic story should come into existence without heroes[3]. No one can reasonably doubt that the list of Phaeacian athletes is the

---

[1] Curiously enough the most suspicious names are those of the two chief characters, Εὐρύμαχος son of Πόλυβος, and Ἀντίνοος son of Εὐπείθης.

[2] Under the head of fiction I think we may probably include many national names and names derived from cities, rivers, etc. It has been remarked above (p. 268, note) that these names occur chiefly among the Trojans and their allies, e.g. Τρώς (son of Alastor), Δάρδανος (son of Bias), Μύγδων, Ἀσκάνιος, Δρύοψ, Δόλοψ, Τεύθρας, Πήδαιος, Ἴμβριος, Ἰδαῖος, Σκαμάνδριος, Θηβαῖος, Θυμβραῖος. I do not mean of course to suggest that all such names are necessarily fictitious. The type doubtless was ancient, but it possessed obvious facilities for the formation of names for fictitious characters of foreign nationality.

[3] This point seems to me to be of fundamental importance; but it is apparently not always recognised. Prof. Meyer (*Geschichte des Alterthums*, II p. 207) holds, rightly as I think, that there is no valid reason for doubting that Troy actually was destroyed by a king of Mycenae. Yet elsewhere (*ib.*, p. 186 f., etc.) he regards Agamemnon himself as a Spartan deity and most of the other chief Achaean heroes as mythical or fictitious or at least unconnected originally with the story of Troy. According to my view the interest in heroic poetry, Greek as well as Teutonic, Welsh or Servian, was from the beginning essentially bound up with individual characters, e.g. not with a (nameless) king of Mycenae—which is comparatively seldom mentioned (cf. p. 274)—but with King Agamemnon. It is true that under certain conditions one name occasionally does displace another in heroic stories; but we have seen no reason for believing that the conditions favourable to such changes ever prevailed in the history of Greek heroic poetry. Neither the name Ἀγαμέμνων nor the later references to Ζεύς Ἀγαμέμνων seem to me to afford any valid ground for doubting that Agamemnon was the king of Mycenae originally concerned in the story.

invention of one man[1]. In the case of Penelope's suitors this is
not so clear. Yet personally I cannot understand the Odyssey
if it is not, in its present form, largely the work of an individual
brain, however much it may have utilised and even incorporated
older matter. This 'redactor' or 'author' or whatever he may
be called may well have invented the names of most of the
suitors; they are not essential to the story. But how can any
such explanation be applied to the heroes of the siege of Troy?
These were not obscure chieftains in a distant group of islands
without external connections. Many of them are represented
as rulers of what were once certainly the chief states in Greece,
and they were universally recognised as historical persons from
the earliest times of which we have any record. In some cases
they were even honoured with worship, and distinguished
families claimed to be descended from them. Mythical characters, such as Scyld or Dardanos, may come to be regarded
as historical. But these are products of many minds rather than
of one, and of reflection rather than imagination. Their personification is a gradual process, and even when it is accomplished
they figure only in the background of heroic stories, without any
definite individual characterisation. The hypothesis which we
are now testing has no relation to such figures as these—for
Agamemnon, Achilles and their companions are not eponymous
heroes. If they are creations of one man's imagination we
must ask how this person, however gifted he may have been,
succeeded in passing off his romance as history. On the other
hand if they were gradually 'evolved' by a succession of poets
we must ask at what stage and by what process so great a
misunderstanding of their real character originated.

It is a great assumption that every local record relating to
the heroes of the Trojan War owes its origin, directly or indirectly, to the influence of Homeric poetry; and yet that is
what is involved by the hypothesis under discussion. There

---

[1] Note should be taken also of the fact that the peculiar type of nomenclature
which we find among the Phaeacians (cf. p. 299) is not confined to the list of athletes
but spread over the whole of this section of the poem. It is quite possible of course
that the few exceptional names, such as Ἀλκίνοος, may be derived from tradition or
from an earlier poet.

is no doubt that heroic poetry can influence local tradition in
an age given to antiquarian speculation ; but where shall we
find any parallel for such a result as this ?   Pausanias (II 16. 5)
states that the tombs of Agamemnon and his household were
to be seen at Mycenae.   It is likely enough that in this case
the local belief was derived ultimately from the poems, although
it seems to have contained some unorthodox features.   But in
Pindar, Aeschylus and other early poets we find forms of the
story which differ much more widely from the Homeric
account.   These authorities also give us a good deal of information regarding other members of the family, Pelops, Atreus
and Orestes—persons who seem not to have figured prominently
in any Homeric poems that we know of.   Particularly we should
notice that according to Pausanias (III 19. 5) the Spartans also
possessed a tomb of Agamemnon (at Amyclai), and that in
early times they appear to have claimed him as one of their
own kings.   To this we have already referred (p. 240).   The
problem as a whole is surely one which requires considerably
more investigation than it has yet received.   But I should be
much surprised if such investigations, carried out in an impartial
spirit, did not bring to light many traces of stories relating to
the Heroic Age, which were independent of anything that we
may fairly call 'Homeric' poetry.

Perhaps it may be said that we can safely claim a fictitious
origin for some of the leading characters without committing
ourselves to the view that all of them were sprung from this
source.   The case of Agamemnon, which we have mentioned
above, is scarcely one of the most promising.   We will now
take what is generally regarded as the most certain case, namely
that of Aias[1].   There are two heroes of this name, of whom one
is a Locrian, while the other belongs to Salamis.   The theory
now most usually held is that one of the two—preferably the
latter—is a fictitious character, derived from the other.   This
theory rests on the following arguments: (i) that the two heroes
are often found together, (ii) that Salamis is only mentioned
in two passages, (iii) that, apart from his brother Teucros, the

---

[1] Cf. Robert, *Studien zur Ilias*, p. 406 ff.; Bethe, *N. Jahrb.*, XIII p. 1 ff.; Cauer,
Grundfragen[2], p. 197 ff.

connections of Aias of Salamis are themselves obviously
fictitious. The distinctive characteristic of this Aias is his
enormous shield; and this gave birth both to the name of
his father Τελαμών ('Strap'), and to that of his son, Εὐρυσάκης
('Broad-shield'). The appropriateness of the latter name is
evident enough; but it does not occur in the Homeric poems.
The evidence seems to indicate that this person is a genealogical creation of much later times—possibly due to the
misunderstanding of an epithet. On the other hand the force
of the name Τελαμών does not strike me as particularly obvious.
Aias' distinguishing characteristic was not his shield-strap, but
the shield itself. Several heroes, Agamemnon, Diomedes and
others, are said to have shield-straps; indeed from Il. II 388 f.
we may infer that they were commonly, if not generally, used.
Moreover the word τελαμών does not necessarily mean 'shield-
strap'; we find it used also, in several passages, for 'sword-strap.'
Its original meaning appears to have been 'supporter'; and we
have no reason for supposing that such a word was inadmissible
as a proper name[1]. Again, the argument that Salamis is only
mentioned twice loses its force when the general usage of the
Iliad is taken into account. Except in three cases—due largely
to certain stereotyped formulae—it is not customary to refer to
the home or nationality of the Achaean leaders[2]. Even if the
genuineness of Il. VII 199 be doubted, there can scarcely be any
question that Aias was localised at Salamis by the time when
the Homeric poems first obtained general currency in Greece;
for the post-Homeric (or non-Homeric) genealogy of the
Aiacidai and their connection with Aegina go back probably
beyond the seventh century. There remains then only the fact
that two friends and colleagues have the same name. That is

---

[1] It is to be remembered that as a patronymic Τελαμώνιος is an Aeolic formation.
The rareness of forms of this type renders it highly improbable that a nickname thus
formed should have been misinterpreted as a patronymic. As a nickname too should
we not rather have expected Τελαμωνεύς?

[2] Two passages mention Λοκροί in connection with the other Aias; three mention
Ἰθάκη or Κεφαλλῆνες in connection with Odysseus. Σπάρτη and Λακεδαίμων are mentioned in connection with Menelaos only in the Catalogue. References to Eurybates
and Helen are of course not included here. The only leading Achaean heroes whose
home or nationality is frequently mentioned are Achilles, Nestor and Idomeneus.

doubtless a curious coincidence; but not more curious than many such cases which occur in real life. On the whole I cannot help thinking that the readiness with which this theory has been received is due to the prevalent enthusiasm for such hypotheses. When soberly considered the evidence in its favour is of the slightest.

In conclusion we must take account of another hypothesis, which seems to be particularly popular at present—namely that many characters have been attracted into the Trojan cycle from different quarters, some from other cycles of heroic poetry, and some from local tradition. Strictly speaking we have here to do with two different hypotheses; but they may conveniently be taken together. Both are credible enough under certain conditions. In the first place we must assume the existence of a nucleus of original matter sufficient to provide the 'attractive' force. Secondly, the poets' audience must not have such knowledge either of the original or the subsidiary stories as would check their readiness to allow the amalgamation. Thus no audience of the fifth century would have consented to see Heracles introduced into a drama dealing with Orestes. But medieval German poems do bring Dietrich von Bern into association both with Attila and Eormenric, although we know that the three heroes belonged originally to quite distinct stories. This parallel has frequently been urged in support of the contention that Agamemnon or Nestor or Idomeneus may once have belonged to separate stories before they were associated with Achilles or Aias the Locrian or whoever it was who was first connected with the siege of Troy.

In Chapter XI we discussed the supposed analogy between Homeric and medieval German poetry and came to the conclusion that it had no foundation. The roots of the latter doubtless go back to court-poetry. But for centuries it was preserved only by popular minstrels; and during this period it underwent not only a process of disintegration in regard to subject-matter, but also a complete change both in spirit and metrical form. Our discussion led us to conclude that there was no ground for supposing the Homeric poems to have passed through such a stage as this—that on the contrary they appear to have been preserved by court poets until they attained their final form. But heroic court-poetry is everywhere bound by convention. The poet must be a master of traditional lore as well as of form; but he must not be a revolutionary. He may borrow descriptions, incidents, probably also minor characters, from other stories and even from folk-tales—especially when he is dealing with the adventures of a solitary wanderer in unknown lands[1]. But, since his audience likewise consists of persons who are more or less trained in the same kind of lore, he will find considerable difficulty in transferring a well-known hero from one story to another—more difficulty indeed than in inventing the hero outright. He would probably have just about as much chance of success as a modern dramatist who wished to introduce Cromwell into a serious play dealing with Napoleon Bonaparte. We must have good evidence before we can believe that the court poets of ancient Greece were able to indulge in such flights of imagination.

But no such evidence appears to be forthcoming[2]. One of the cases most commonly cited is the fight of Tlepolemos and Sarpedon. This case rests partly on the fact that the two combatants are represented as coming from districts, both remote from Troy but not very distant from one another, and partly on the groundless assumption that opponents must be near neighbours. Unfortunately Sarpedon himself is killed by Patroclos, a hero from Phthiotis. To meet this difficulty we find a further hypothesis, which need not be discussed here. I do not say that it is impossible that Tlepolemos and Sarpedon have been taken from a different story. My view is that until it

---

[1] For folk-tales cf. p. 258 ff. The same conditions are probably favourable both to transference and invention. The latter faculty is perhaps first displayed in lists of supernatural beings, such as those of the Nereids in Il. XVIII 39 ff. and Theog. 242 ff. (which differ a good deal). We may compare the list of dwarfs given in Völuspá.

[2] We need not discuss the identification of the Adrestos and Amphios of Il. II 830 with the famous Adrastos and Amphiaraos of the Theban story (cf. Usener, *S.-B. der Akad. zu Wien*, 1898, p. 37 ff.). The strangest feature in this 'discovery' is the fascination which, in spite of its obvious untenability, it seems to have exercised on subsequent writers.

is supported by evidence[1] such a conjecture does not deserve serious consideration. The same remark applies to the case of Idomeneus which has likewise been cited in this connection. Indeed it is surely a fatal objection to this hypothesis as a whole that, with one exception[2], the heroes of the Iliad are persons who are known practically only in connection with the siege of Troy. The force of this objection may be appreciated by the fact that both poems contain many incidental allusions to heroes who are well known to us from other sources, as well as to persons of whom we know little or nothing at all. If the personnel of the Iliad has really grown up through a process of attraction how is it that Heracles, Iason, Peirithoos, Theseus, Minos and Adrastos have not been drawn into the net? Some of them certainly have sons or grandsons who figure in the Iliad; but it deserves to be remarked that, with the exception of Idomeneus, these are all persons of little importance. On the other hand the fathers of the principal heroes are themselves in no case—unless we count Tydeus—'heroes of the first rank.' Can any one seriously argue that such a result as this would be produced by an artificial scheme—a scheme, that is to say, in the framing of which poets had a free command of their material? On the contrary the only conclusion, I think, to

[1] The evidence of the grave-mound in Lycia, cited by Prof. Murray (*Rise of the Greek Epic*, p. 191, note), can hardly be taken seriously. Indeed Prof. Murray himself seems to consider Sarpedon's Lycian connections at least as illusory as his connection with Troy.

[2] Diomedes no doubt figured in the story of the second attack upon Thebes. It has been suggested that this hero was also originally identical with the Bistonian Diomedes, who fed his mares with human flesh and was killed by Heracles. The value of this identification depends largely upon the question whether the Doloneia formed an original part of the story of the Iliad. That is a view which would probably gain the assent of few scholars—even of those who believe that the Doloneia is not much later than the rest of the Iliad in its final form. The other arguments are of little consequence. Diomedes displays a propensity for capturing chariots—a feature which perhaps gave rise to the adventure with Rhesos; but the same remark is true of Antilochos. He fights also with the 'Thracian' god Ares, as well as with Aphrodite. But it is clear that the feud with these deities really belongs to Athene, Diomedes' hereditary guardian. In later stories, relating to the east of Italy, there may have been a confusion between the two heroes; and it is scarcely impossible that here and there Diomedes of Argos took over a cult belonging to his namesake. If so we shall have to suppose that the Bistonian Diomedes was originally an Illyrian rather than a Thracian hero.

which an unbiassed study of the evidence can lead, is that the poets never enjoyed such freedom; that the later poets were bound by the work of their predecessors, and these again by something which bears a suspicious resemblance to facts of real life.

In the course of this and the preceding chapters we have reviewed briefly a number of hypotheses which have been brought forward from time to time with the object of explaining the origin of the characters and events treated in the Homeric poems. These hypotheses may be grouped summarily under four headings: (i) nature-myths, (ii) tribal heroes, (iii) fiction, (iv) transference. In dealing with the first group we have restricted ourselves to the consideration of two cases which appear as yet not to have fallen into the same discredit as the rest. Our conclusion however is that they rest on equally unsubstantial foundations. The second group is more popular just now, and this we have examined at length. We find that—apart from some genealogical names—this group of hypotheses rests upon a number of assumptions, some of which are incapable of proof, while others are demonstrably incorrect. The third group has a much better case. We find that the use of fiction appears to be shown not only in the presentation of the stories (as in Teutonic poetry) but also in the invention of minor characters. The extent to which it is used is a problem which requires further investigation. The last remark applies also to the fourth group. In principle it is only reasonable to expect that both characters and incidents may have been transferred from one story to another. But the instances which have been suggested are tainted with the 'tribal hero' hypothesis and the evidence on which they rest is altogether inconclusive. Lastly, we have noted that, if our view of the history of Homeric poetry is correct, the use of both fiction (invention) and 'transference' must have been confined within certain limits[1].

---

[1] The most highly developed use of fiction occurs probably when the poets are dealing with unknown regions or peoples, as in the story of Odysseus (cf. p. 297 f.). But I am not aware that there is any evidence for the existence of poems on wholly fictitious subjects.

It may perhaps be said that these conclusions show an inadequate recognition of the results attained by modern investigations in the history of Greek heroic tradition. But we may fairly ask how many definite results have been attained in this field—results, I mean, which command the unanimous approval, or anything like the unanimous approval, of present-day scholars. It is a common opinion, at least in this country, that the general effect has been rather to obscure than to solve the real problems presented by the poems. If we put aside the opinions of more conservative scholars we may indeed find a common element—namely the belief that the attitude of the ancients themselves to stories of the Heroic Age was mistaken. But this belief cannot be regarded as a result established by the investigations; it is rather their starting point.

By 'the ancients' I do not mean merely the poets and mythographers of antiquity. It is admitted that "the basis of fact in Homer is fully as real to Thucydides as to Herodotus." Now the work undertaken by Thucydides was not a history of the Trojan War; but he had evidently considered that story. Apparently it did not occur to him to doubt that the war had taken place, or even that the expedition had been commanded by Agamemnon, king of Mycenae. What he had reflected on was the question whether the expedition was really on so large a scale as is stated in the Iliad; and the result to which his reflections brought him was that there was not a sufficient case for scepticism (οὔκουν ἀπιστεῖν εἰκός). We are at liberty to form a different opinion. Yet Thucydides was a man no whit inferior intellectually to the best of modern scholars. Moreover he had the advantage of being a native; and he was separated from the Heroic Age by some six centuries, whereas we are separated from it by nearly thirty. There can be little doubt that many sources of information were open to him—traditions, poems and even monuments—which are entirely lost to us. It seems to me therefore that before we disregard the opinions of such persons we shall do well to consider carefully in what respects we are better qualified for forming a judgment.

So far as I can see we have the advantage in two respects only. Firstly, there is the evidence of the Egyptian monuments

and of that pre-historic Aegean civilisation which has been revealed to us by the discoveries of Schliemann, Dörpfeld, Evans,
Halbherr and many others. It is at least improbable that
Thucydides was as well acquainted with either of these sources
of information as we are. If he had seen Dr Dörpfeld's excavations at Troy he might perhaps have modified his opinion
about the numbers of the Achaean army, although he had
noted the dimensions of Mycenae. But that after all is a
trifle. Can it be said that the general effect of the new evidence
has been to discredit the tradition? The records of Rameses II
and his successors have definitely disposed of the idea that
Agamemnon's expedition was anything impossible, while the
discoveries in Crete have shown once for all that 'early' does
not mean the same thing as 'primitive.' It is a significant fact
therefore that in many investigations of the type we are discussing little or no use has been made of this new evidence.
The evidence on which they rely is evidence which was at least
as accessible to Thucydides as it is to us.

Secondly, it is in our power, probably far more than it was
in that of Thucydides and his contemporaries, to compare the
Homeric stories with others of the same type. It is here that
our great advantage lies. But can it be said that this advantage
has been turned to account by modern writers? Many works
contain no reference to any poetry other than Greek and Latin—
the latter of which, owing to its dependence upon Greek, is of
little value for our purpose. Many others, it is true, have used
the evidence of Teutonic heroic poetry. But only by taking
a single poem belonging to the latest stratum, without reference
to its history or its connections in the poetry of other Teutonic
peoples, and by using precarious hypotheses as to the origin of
the story as a foundation for similar hypotheses in relation to the
Homeric stories. The earlier strata of Teutonic heroic poetry
have been ignored as much as the heroic poetry of other European
peoples.

I have no doubt that much which is obscure in Homeric
poetry and tradition may be illuminated by a historical study
of heroic poetry elsewhere—not merely Teutonic but also Celtic,
Slavonic and even non-European. For the story of the Iliad in

particular I suspect that a fairly close parallel—perhaps the closest of all—is to be found in those Servian poems which deal with the battle of Kossovo[1]. My object however in this book is to bring to light the relations of Greek and Teutonic heroic poetry—or rather to make a start in that direction, for the object is by no means one which can be accomplished in a single attempt. So much however may be said with confidence even now: all that we know, apart from hypotheses, with regard to the origin of the Teutonic heroic stories corresponds to the views held by Thucydides and his contemporaries.

With the affinities between Homeric poetry and the old Teutonic court-poetry we shall have to deal in the next chapter. I do not think that any true analogy to the medieval German poems is to be found in Greek literature; but I have ventured to suggest (p. 239 f.) that the poems of the Edda have something in common with those of Stesichoros and his followers. Apart from the poems however, Greek literature preserves numerous records of the Heroic Age, frequently, though not always, in the form of local traditions. Some of these are doubtless due to the influence of Homeric or 'Stesichoric' poetry; but we have no right to assume that this is universally true. There are a number which appear to be of popular origin, whether they come from poems of Stage III (cf. p. 94 ff.) or from poems which were 'popular' from the beginning or from stories which never were clothed in poetic form.

As an example we will take the story of Minos. So far as I know, there is no evidence that this hero figured prominently in any early poems of which we have record, though incidental allusions to him occur both in the Iliad and the Odyssey. Yet there is no doubt that the Greeks regarded him as one of the very greatest figures of the far past. The most striking tradition recorded of him is that he possessed a powerful fleet, which enabled him to subdue the islands, to put down piracy and thus to secure safety for navigation. This thalassocracy is mentioned both by Herodotus (I 171, III 122) and Thucydides (I 4, 8); and the former adds that no such attempt to command the sea was made again until the time of Polycrates of Samos, in the latter

---

[1] On this subject see Note VII.

part of the sixth century. Later writers relate the famous story of the Minotaur; they represent Minos also as the founder of cities, including Cnossos and Phaistos, the great prehistoric palaces lately excavated, and as a legislator or judge. In what is commonly regarded as one of the latest additions to the Odyssey (XI 568 ff.) we find him giving judgments among the dead.

It is obvious enough that the story of Minos contains many mythical features. But do these features constitute the original kernel of the story, or are they accretions, due to folk-tales or popular belief? We need not enter here into the story of the Minotaur, upon which Dr Evans' discoveries have thrown such a curious light. But there are other features in the story which may be illustrated from medieval beliefs regarding Dietrich von Bern. Sometimes we find this hero represented as the leader of the 'Wild Hunt,' the army of ghosts[1]—a position elsewhere occupied by Wodan or other mythical beings. In medieval German homilies and other religious works he is credited with having been the founder of several famous Roman buildings, such as the Amphitheatre at Verona and the Castle of St Angelo at Rome[2]. In such beliefs we have a close enough parallel to the traditions of Minos. There is no reason for supposing that the Greeks were better acquainted with the prehistoric Cretans than the Germans were with the ancient Romans. In both cases doubtless it seemed natural to attribute the foundation of venerable buildings to a prominent hero of their own race[3]

---

[1] Cf. J. Grimm, *Teutonic Mythology*[4] (Engl. Transl.), p. 936 f.

[2] Cf. W. Grimm, *Deutsche Heldensage*, p. 40 (and passim); J. Grimm, *op. cit.*, p. 1183.

[3] Prof. Meyer (*Gesch. d. Alt.*[2], 1 p. 680 ff.) has pointed out that, while Thucydides seems to have regarded Minos as a Greek, Herodotus apparently held a different view. Such is certainly the natural inference to be drawn from the language of the two historians, though the evidence is perhaps not quite conclusive in either case. But Herodotus, at all events in VII 171, clearly derived his information from the people of Praisos—a community which cannot have been wholly Greek even in his time. Their account seems to have been due to an attempt to reconcile Greek and native traditions, Homeric influence being shown by the sentence τρίτῃ δὲ γενεῇ μετὰ Μίνωα τελευτήσαντα γενέσθαι τὰ Τρωϊκά, κ.τ.λ. We may compare the Egyptian story of Helen (cf. p. 266). In the Homeric poems themselves Idomeneus is descended from Minos, and no hint is given that either of them was regarded as non-Greek. The same remark appears to be true of Greek tradition elsewhere.

But Dietrich von Bern (Theodric, king of the Ostrogoths) was not originally a mythical being.

Nor need the tradition of Minos' thalassocracy be regarded as altogether incredible. We have seen that in the reigns of Merenptah and Rameses III Egypt and the neighbouring lands were invaded by large forces from the Aegean or even more remote regions. After the time of Rameses III we hear little of these peoples, though it is clear that they had formed settlements on the coast of Palestine. From the following centuries we have apparently only one detailed piece of information relating to the Mediterranean, namely the story of a certain Unuamen (or Wenamon), an official belonging to the temple of Amen at Thebes, who had been sent to the Lebanon to buy timber[1]. From this story we may infer with some probability that the eastern end of the Mediterranean was policed or controlled by the fleets of some Aegean nation[2]. The time to which the story refers is either the reign of Herhor or that of his predecessor Rameses XII[3]—about the beginning of the eleventh century. That seems to be approximately the time indicated for Minos by Greek tradition; for according to Il. XIII 451 f. and Od. XIX 178 ff. he was the grandfather of Idomeneus. It is scarcely impossible that an ambitious Greek prince of this age may have been animated by the desire of regaining the supremacy of the ancient Cretans, just as Theodric was inspired by the idea of restoring under Gothic rule the power formerly held by the Roman emperors.

[1] Cf. Petrie, *History of Egypt*, III 197 ff.; Breasted, *Ancient Records (Egypt)*, IV 274 ff. Prof. Breasted believes that this document is Wenamon's authentic report of his expedition.

[2] In the course of an adventurous journey the envoy was intercepted by some ships of the Zakar (Tchakaray), a people mentioned among the Aegean confederates who fought against Rameses III (cf. p. 188 ff.). These Zakar brought him before the prince of Byblos and demanded that he should be arrested. Prof. Petrie speaks of them as Cretan 'pirates,' but neither their own behaviour nor that of the prince seems to me to be reconcilable with such a view. According to Prof. Breasted's reconstruction of the story—where the papyrus is defective—the envoy had himself been guilty of lawless conduct previously. Incidentally it appears from the story that a considerable amount of traffic was being carried on at this time both in Egyptian and Syrian ships.

[3] Herhor is mentioned in the story, but not as king.

NOTE VII. THE BATTLE OF KOSSOVO
IN SERVIAN POETRY.

IT has been mentioned above (p. 310) that for the story of the Iliad a fairly close parallel is to be found in those Servian poems which deal with the battle of Kossovo[1]. This parallelism has long been noticed, but unfortunately it has given rise to an unnecessary controversy. Servian writers, inspired by patriotic zeal, have sought to make an 'Iliad' by stringing their national poems together, while scholars of other nations have denied that the Servians possess anything which deserves to be called epic poetry. We need not concern ourselves here with a discussion about terms. It is clear enough that Servian heroic poetry bears little resemblance to the Homeric poems as we have them. But we may strongly suspect that at an earlier stage in the history of Homeric poetry the resemblance would be much closer, although the art of heroic poetry in Greece had doubtless been elaborated for centuries to a far higher degree than was ever attained by Servian poets.

It is to the treatment of the story however, and not to the qualities of the poetry, that I wish to call attention. Beowulf, Finn, Waldhere and the Hildebrandslied all deal with fighting of various kinds, but we do not know how early Teutonic poetry treated a story of actual war. The Servian poems resemble the Iliad chiefly in the comparatively large number of prominent characters which they introduce and in the fact that they deal with a series of more or less distinct episodes, in which various heroes from time to time play the leading part. Lazar's council or court furnishes an interesting parallel to that of Agamemnon—the more instructive because we can here check the evidence of the poems by historical records, some of which are practically contemporary, while many date from within a century of the battle.

King Lazar himself and his opponent, Sultan Murad I, are of course well-known historical persons. There is no doubt also with regard to Vuk Branković, the chief of Lazar's followers or allies. In the poems he is represented as the husband of Mara (Maria), the king's daughter ; but in this case there may be some confusion. According to Ducas (p. 17[2]) Lazar had

[1] My object in this note is to call attention to a subject which appears to have been strangely neglected by English Homeric students. I cannot claim to possess the requisite qualifications, linguistic and historical, for an independent investigation of the subject. English translations of many of the poems are to be found, together with a historical introduction, in Mme Mijatovich's *Kossovo* (London, 1881). For a more critical study the reader may be referred to the introduction to Pasić's *Narodne Pjesme o boju na Kosovu godine 1389* (Agram, 1877), to which I am much indebted.

[2] The references to Laonicos' and Ducas' histories, as well as to the translation of the latter, are to the pages in Niebuhr's edition. It may be that Ducas was mistaken with regard to the name of Bajazet's wife ; cf. Engel, *Geschichte von Serwien*, p. 332.

a daughter of this name who was married to Bajazet, the son and successor of Murad, after the conclusion of the war. Vuk Branković was however a son-in-law of Lazar according to Laonicos Chalcocondylas (p. 53). Again, Jug Bogdan, represented in the poems as Lazar's father-in-law[1], is believed to be identical with a certain prince named Μπόγδανος (Πόγδανος), who, according to Laonicos (p. 28), was granted by Dušan the territories between Pherrai and the Axios (Vardar), and who about 1372 submitted to Murad together with the other Servian princes in this region. To these we may add the vojvoda Vladeta ; for there can be little doubt that this person is to be identified with that Vlathico Vlagenichio who, according to the anonymous translation of Ducas' history (p. 352), was sent by his uncle Iuathco (Tvrtko), king of Bosnia, to support Lazar with 20,000 men.

On the other hand some doubt has been expressed with regard to Miloš Obilić (or Kobilović) the chief Servian hero of the story. He is not mentioned apparently by any strictly contemporary authority. Yet the traditional account of Murad's death is known to the two Greek historians Ducas and Laonicos, both of whom are believed to have written within about three quarters of a century after the battle. The latter (p. 54) states that according to the Greek version of the story a Servian nobleman named Μήλοις rode fully armed into the Turkish camp, representing himself to be a deserter. Murad gave orders that he was to be allowed to come near and say what he wished. But when he reached the door of the Sultan's tent he threw his spear and slew Murad, meeting with his own death immediately afterwards. Laonicos however also says that the Turks gave quite a different account of the affair—namely that as Murad was pursuing the enemy a Servian (ἄνδρα Τριβαλλόν), who was on foot, turned and transfixed him with a javelin. Ducas' version of the story (p. 15) resembles that given by the poems in the fact that the assassin uses a dagger. His name is not given, but he is said to have been a young and distinguished Servian and to have asked to see Murad as a deserter with important information.

Closer affinity with the poems is shown by the anonymous translation of Ducas' history (p. 352 ff.), which contains much additional matter. Indeed it is scarcely possible to doubt that the additions are partly derived from poems, though these may not have been exactly identical with any which are now extant. When Miloš ('Milos Cobilichio, capetanio de Lazaro') reaches the Sultan's tent we are told, as in the poems[2], that he is bidden to

---

[1] I do not know whether this is historically correct. There seem to be a number of historical references to Milica, Lazar's queen; cf. Engel, *op. cit.*, pp. 311, 331, 346 f.

[2] Cf. Pasić, *op. cit.*, VI v. 13 ff. (p. 92). This passage is taken from a Croatian poem (Nr 6, v. 166 ff.) published by Miklosich, *Denkschriften d. k. Akademie d. Wissenschaften* (Vienna), XIX p. 73 ff., from a MS. collection at Ragusa dating from about 1728. Mme Mijatovich's poem on the same subject (p. 120 ff.) differs a good deal from this and bears a closer resemblance to the Italian in one or two points.

kiss Murad's foot 'according to the usage of his kingdom[1].' Far more
striking however is the account of the banquet on the preceding day, which
in places appears to be little more than a free translation of a fragmentary
poem published in Karadžić's collection[2]: "El zorno precedente a quello
che seguì la iniqua et infelice bataglia, Lazaro convocati tutti i signori et
principali del suo imperio[3], comandò che se aparechiasse una sdraviza
secondo la usanza dela sua corte; in laquale, come gratioso et benigno
signore, a tutti porse la sdraviza con sua mano. Quando la volta toccò a
Milos, se fè dar una grande taza d' oro piena de pretioso vino[4]; la qual
porzendoli disse a Milos : 'Excellentissimo cavalier, prendi questa sdraviza,
che con la taza te dono...sdravize per amor mio. Ma molto mi doglio che
ho inteso una mala novella, che al tuo dispoto sei facto ribello'[5]. Al qual
Milos, reverentemente presa la taza con chiara faza, disse : 'Signor dispoto,
molto te ringratio della sdraviza et taza d' oro che m' ai donata. Ma molto
mi doglio dela mia dubitata fede[6]. Doman de matina, se dio darà effecto al'
alto pensier mio, se cognoscerà se io son fidele o ribello dela tua Signoria."

This translation is believed to be of Dalmatian origin[7] and, according to
Prof. Bury[8], itself dates from the fifteenth century. We are bound to conclude therefore that Miloš' exploit was treated in poems—from which some
of the extant pieces are ultimately descended—within a century of the battle.
The earliest direct reference to poems dealing with *Khobilouitz* (i.e. Miloš

[1] 'Secondo la usanza del suo imperio' (cf. Miklosich, 6. 167 : 'Ovaki su zakoni,
Milošu, u zemlji mojoj,' etc.).

[2] Vuk Stef. Karadžić, *Srpske Narodne Pjesme*, Vol. II (Vienna, 1875), 50 iii
(p. 310 ff.). This is translated, with a few slight changes, in Mme Mijatovich's
piece 'The Banquet before Battle' (p. 116 ff.). A somewhat different account of the
same incident—and showing less resemblance to the Italian—occurs in Miklosich,
6. 116 ff., a passage which is not used by Pasić or Mijatovich.

[3] Cf. Karadžić, II 50 iii, v. 3 f. :
Svu gospodu za sofru sjedao (*scil.* Lazare),
svu gospodu i gospodičiće.

[4] *Ibid.*, v. 13 :
Car uzima zlatan pehar vina, etc.

[5] *Ibid.*, v. 31 ff. :
Zdrav Milošu, vjero i nevjero !
prva vjero, potonja nevjero !
Sjutra ceš me izdat' na Kosovu,
i odbjeći Turskom car-Muratu ;
zdrav mi budi ! i zdravicu popij :
vino popij, a na čast ti pehar.

[6] *Ibid.*, v. 39 ff. :
Vala tebe, slavni knez-Lazare !
Vala tebe na tvojoj zdravici,
na zdravici i na daru tvome ;
al' ne vala na takoj besjedi ; etc.

[7] Cf. Pasič, *op. cit.*, p. 26.

[8] Gibbon's *Decline and Fall of the Roman Empire*, VII p. 327.

Kobilović) goes back to the first half of the sixteenth century, at which time they are said to have been numerous[1]. It may be however that the accounts given by Ducas himself and by Laonicos are also derived ultimately from poems[2]. But if so the poetic treatment of the subject must have begun within living memory of the battle; for it is clear from the evidence of these authors that by the middle of the fifteenth century the story had come to the Greeks in more than one form and that it had even attained great celebrity among them[3].

The Kossovo poems certainly give us some evidence for the phenomenon which we have above (p. 307) called 'transference.' In one poem (Karadžić, II 46, v. 59 ff.) we find it stated that King Vukašin entered into the battle and met with his death. In reality he was killed at (or shortly after) the battle of the Marica in 1371. The same poem also, immediately afterwards (v. 71 ff.), introduces Erceg Stepan, who lived nearly a century later. But this poem[4] is of a very peculiar type—distinctly non-heroic—and it is not legitimate to draw conclusions from it as to the poems in general. It would be of far more importance for our purpose if we knew that Jug Bogdan was attracted into the story. He must certainly have been an old man in 1389, since he had his territories granted to him by Dušan, who died in 1356. But he is regularly described as 'the old' (*stari*) in the poems. The fact also that he had been a vassal of Murad from 1372 onwards is hardly conclusive; for it is clear that a great effort was made in 1389 to unite the various Servian princes. On the whole the evidence, so far as it is known to me, does not seem to indicate that attraction or transference has played an important part in the story.

For the invention of characters there is, so far as I know, no absolutely decisive evidence. But probably few would be inclined to regard such a person as Vaistina, the servant or squire (*sluga*) of Musić Stefan[5] (Karadžić,

[1] Cf. Murko, *Geschichte der älteren südslaw. Litteraturen*, p. 205.

[2] This is perhaps rather suggested by one or two of Laonicos' sentences, e.g. (Μήλοιν φασίν) ὡπλισμένον ἐλαύνειν σὺν τῷ ἵππῳ ἐπὶ τὸ Ἀμουράτεω στρατόπεδον, ὡς ἂν αὐτομολοῦντα ἀπὸ τῶν ἐναντίων (p. 54); and more especially by the speech which Ducas (p. 15) attributes to Miloš: "Βούλομαι τοῦτον ἰδεῖν καὶ λόγους τινὰς ὑποψιθυρίσαι ὡς ἐγκρατὴς γενέσθαι τουτουΐ τοῦ πολέμου· ἔνεκα γὰρ τούτου αὐτόμολος ἐλήλυθα." With the last sentence we may compare Miklosich, 6. 164:

Ja sam ti se odvrg'o od vojske Lazara kneza.

[3] Cf. Laonicos, l.c.: Ἕλληνες...λέγουσιν ἄνδρα γενναιότατον ἐθελῆσαι ἑκόντα ὑποστῆναι ἀγῶνα κάλλιστον δὴ τῶν πώποτε γενομένων, and again, below: ὁρμὴν πασῶν δὴ καλλίστην ὧν ἡμεῖς ἴσμεν.

[4] The first part of this poem (vv. 1—44) corresponds to Mijatovich, p. 104 ff.; the second part (v. 47 ff.) to Mijatovich, p. 126 ff. In such cases as this it is much to be regretted that Mme Mijatovich did not adhere to Karadžić's text. If the explanation be that her version is derived from a different source—and not due to arbitrary transposition—this should have been made clear.

[5] In Miklosich, 6. 1—58, which deals with the same story the squire is called Oliver, while his master's name appears as Bušić Stjepane.

II 47), otherwise than as a product of fiction; and the same remark applies
to the squire Milutin who brings the news of Lazar's death to the queen
(*ib.* 45. 146 ff.). It is a more difficult matter to form an opinion as to whether
any of the more important characters are fictitious. Several of them appear
to be unknown from contemporary historical works. Among these we may
mention Musić Stefan himself and more especially Banović Strahinja, the
hero of the longest poem in the cycle (*ib.* 44). So far as I know, the earliest
reference to the latter is in the Chronicle of Tronoša, which mentions incidentally the destruction of his palace[1]. Again, according to the poems
Miloš was accompanied on his errand to Murad by two of his friends, Milan
Toplica and Ivan Kosančić. Both these persons are mentioned in the same
connection by the Chronicle of Tronoša, which adds that at the banquet on
the preceding night they, as well as Miloš, had been charged with disloyalty
by the king. This chronicle is believed to be derived from a MS. of the
sixteenth century; but there is practically no doubt that it has drawn largely
from poetic sources. Our earliest authorities, Laonicos and Ducas, together
with the translation of the latter, seem to imply distinctly that Miloš carried
out his exploit alone. That however does not prove that the characters
themselves are fictitious. On the whole, considering the limited amount of
information which early records furnish, it would probably be wise to hesitate
before adopting the view that any of the more important characters are
invented—at all events those which can be traced back to within two centuries of the battle.

There seems to be no evidence for the introduction of what can properly
be called mythical beings in poems of the Kossovo cycle[2]. But sometimes
we certainly find supernatural incidents. In Karadžić, II 45. 119 ff. two
crows from the field of Kossovo bring to the queen the first news of the
battle and of Lazar's death. A more extravagant case occurs in the opening
verses of (*ibid.*) II 46—a poem to which we have already referred. Lazar is
here made to receive a letter dropped by a swallow (which is carried by a
falcon) offering him the choice between the heavenly and earthly kingdoms.
In another (Croatian) poem (Karadžić, II 48[3]) the mother of the Jugovići
prays that she may receive the eyes of a falcon and the wings of a swan.
Her prayer is answered, and she flies to the field of Kossovo and sees the
dead bodies of her sons and husband. This poem is largely taken up with
the marvellous throughout and has little in common with heroic poetry.

But it is from the point of view of their presentation of the story that the
Kossovo poems chiefly merit our attention. This presentation contains
many features which may be included under the head of fiction. Yet in

---

[1] Quoted by Pasić, *op. cit.*, p. 30.

[2] Other poems, both Christian and Mohammedan, frequently introduce Vile,
i.e. nymphs or elf-women.

[3] Not included in the collections of Pasić and Mijatovich. A slightly variant form
(apparently of Montenegrin origin) is published, together with a translation, in Krauss'
Slavische Volkforschungen, p. 289 f.

certain cases it is a question whether we have not rather what may be called a growth of myth. By this I mean the introduction and development of motives which, though incorrect historically, can hardly be regarded, at least in their entirety, as conscious inventions of an individual. They would seem rather to have originated in rumour and popular misconceptions. As examples we may take what are perhaps the two most salient features in the story—the exploit of Miloš and his confederates and the treachery of Vuk Branković.

We have already dealt with the first of these incidents. The poems make Miloš and his companions perform prodigies of valour before they are overcome. But our earliest authorities state that Miloš was killed almost immediately; and they imply that he was alone. Indeed we know that the Turks gave quite a different account of Murad's death. It is not at all clear that between the two the Servian account possesses the greater probability. But it may very well have been believed among the Servians from the very beginning, whether its origin is to be traced to genuine information derived from the Turkish camp or merely to idle rumour.

Again, the treachery of Vuk Branković is proclaimed again and again in the poems. But there is no evidence earlier than the sixteenth century to substantiate the charge[1]. The first reference to treachery in Lazar's army occurs in the translation of Ducas' history (p. 354); but here the traitor is called 'Dragossavo Probiscio, capitaneo del campo del dispoto.' It has been suggested that Vuk's unenviable celebrity in the poems is due to the unpopularity of his son, George Branković, who ruled over Servia from 1427 to 1457[2].

The above brief sketch will probably be sufficient to show that these poems are capable of throwing a good deal of light upon the origin and development of a heroic story. The period is one for which, comparatively speaking, a fair amount of information is available; and quite possibly more might be obtained by a careful investigation of the documents of that age. It is to be remembered of course that after the middle of the fifteenth century nothing like court poetry can have existed in Servia. We should expect then that from this time onwards the poems would become more and more permeated by those characteristics which we have assigned to Stage III of our scheme. As a matter of fact some of the poems show these characteristics only to a comparatively slight degree. This is especially the case with the poem on the banquet (Karadžić, II 50 iii); but part of this poem, as we have seen, can be traced back to the fifteenth century. On the other

---

[1] Prof. Murko (*op. cit.*, p. 202) states that Vuk "in der Schlacht in hervorragender Weise seine Pflicht erfüllt und sich dann mit den Türken gar nicht ausgesöhnt hat wie Lazar's Sohn Stefan." I do not know the authority for the first part of this statement; but according to the Turkish account (cf. Engel, *Geschichte von Serwien*, p. 346) the (right) wing of the Servian army which was commanded by Vuk was successful.

[2] Cf. Pasić, *op. cit.*, p. 42.

hand the characteristics of Stage III are very strongly marked in Karadžić II 46 and 48. I should expect that these poems are late compositions.

So far as I have been able to deal with the subject the result of the discussion has been that there is little or no definite evidence for the invention of characters. That is a result which can scarcely be regarded as surprising, in view of the history of Servian poetry. On the other hand the conditions were such as we should expect to be exceptionally favourable to the development of transference or attraction. Yet there is but little satisfactory evidence in this direction. I am inclined therefore to think that the force of this principle has been considerably overestimated by recent writers. What the Kossovo poems do seem to suggest is—not that the characters of the Iliad were invented or attracted from other quarters, but that their exploits and their relations with one another may in reality have been very different from what we find depicted in the poem.

CHAPTER XV.

THE COMMON CHARACTERISTICS OF TEUTONIC AND GREEK HEROIC POETRY.

OUR review of the Homeric poems has led us to conclude that their origin and early history was in many respects analogous to that of the English heroic poems ; and further, that there is no valid reason for regarding the stories with which they deal as mythical or fictitious, although we cannot, as in the case of the English poems, actually prove that they rest upon a historical basis. We must now endeavour to see what common elements the two series of poems contain in regard to style and spirit. This will enable us to determine whether the term 'Heroic Age,' as applied to the two cases in common, can be held to mean anything more than an age of 'heroes,' whose deeds were celebrated in poetry.

The most cursory glance at the two groups of poems will be sufficient to show that they contain many common features in regard to style. In both we find the constant repetition of the same formulae, e.g. in the introduction of speeches. Thus in the first part of Beowulf eight speeches out of thirteen by the hero himself are introduced by the formula : *Beowulf maþelode bearn Ecgþeowes,* while three of Hrothgar's seven speeches follow the words : *Hroðgar maþelode helm Scyldinga.* In the Iliad we may compare the constant repetition of such formulae as: τὸν δ' ἀπαμειβόμενος προσέφη κρείων Ἀγαμέμνων or : τὸν δ' ἠμείβετ' ἔπειτα Γερήνιος ἱππότα Νέστωρ. The explanation of such formulae is probably to be found in the fact that both sets of poems were designed for preservation by oral tradition. In literary poems such as the Aeneid they seem to be avoided.

Indeed the words introducing a speech are here seldom allowed to occupy a whole verse.

Another feature common to the two groups of poems is the love of describing somewhat minutely the details of a transaction which in itself is nothing unusual. Often in such cases they use very similar language. Thus in Od. IV 778 ff. Antinoos' preparations are described as follows: "With these words he picked out twenty men who were the best, and they went on their way to the swift ship and the sea-shore. First of all they pushed out the ship into deep water; and they placed the mast and the sails in the black ship and made ready the oars in the leathern rowlocks, each in its proper place, and spread out the white sails. And high-hearted squires carried their arms. The ship they moored afloat in the roadstead; but they themselves disembarked. There they took their supper and waited for the approach of evening." With this passage we may compare Beow. 205 ff.: "The hero had with him picked champions of the men of the Geatas, the bravest he could find; so with fourteen companions he made his way to the vessel. A skilful pilot was the man who pointed out the features of the coast. When due time had elapsed the ship was afloat beneath the lee of the cliff, and the warriors all prepared ascended the prow, where the waves of the sea were playing upon the sand. Into the bosom of the craft men bore their bright treasures, even their resplendent armour. The company pushed off their timbered craft and started on the adventure of their choice."

Again the movements of royal personages in their palaces are sometimes rather carefully noted. In Od. I 328 ff. we are told that " Icarios' daughter, thoughtful Penelope, became conscious of the glorious song in her upper chamber; and she descended the lofty staircase of her dwelling, but not alone, for two attendant maidens accompanied her. Now when the noble lady drew near the suitors she stood beside the pillar of the well built house, holding her shining veil before her face; and one of her trusty attendants stood by her on either side." With this we may compare Beow. 921 ff.: "As for the king himself, the guardian of the ring-hoards, famed for his sterling qualities—he likewise strode majestically from his bedchamber with a great following; and with him his queen traversed the ascent to the mead-hall, accompanied by a band of maidens. When Hrothgar arrived at the hall he stood by the pillar (?), gazing on the lofty roof, adorned with gold, and on Grendel's arm."

Both poems also elaborate the various stages in the arrival and reception of visitors. As an example we may take the account of Telemachos' arrival at Menelaos' palace in Od. IV. 20 ff.: "At this time the hero Telemachos and Nestor's distinguished son had drawn up with their horses in the vestibule of the palace. Now the lord Eteoneus, renowned Menelaos' active squire, came forward and saw them. And he went on his way through the building to give the news to the shepherd of the people; and standing beside him addressed him with winged words." Menelaos replies that the strangers are to be brought in at once. The arrival of Beowulf at the Danish king's palace is described at much greater length. First, he is greeted by Wulfgar, the king's herald and henchman. Then he replies, and Wulfgar promises to take his message. "Quickly then he sped to where Hrothgar was sitting, aged and grey-haired, among his retinue of nobles. Exulting in his prowess he passed on until he took his stand at the side of the prince of the Danes; for he knew the usage of chivalry." After this we have still three more speeches—first by Wulfgar to the king, then the latter's reply and finally Wulfgar's answer to Beowulf—before the visitors enter.

We may compare also the formulae used in greetings to strangers. Thus in Od. I 169 ff. Telemachos addresses the disguised Athene as follows: "Now come, tell me this and declare it plainly: Who of men art thou, and whence? Where are thy city and thy parents? And (tell me) upon what sort of a ship thou hast come"—with several other questions. Another case occurs in III 71 ff., where Nestor is greeting Telemachos: "Sirs, who are ye, and whence do ye sail the watery paths? Is it upon some enterprise, or do ye wander over the sea at random, like pirates who rove, risking their lives and bringing evil to men of other lands?" Beowulf receives a somewhat similar greeting from the Danish coast-guard, when he lands (v. 237 ff.): "What warriors are ye that thus have come clad in coats of mail, bringing hither your lofty ship over the waters along the high road of the sea?" And again, shortly afterwards (v. 251 ff.): "Now must I know your origin, before ye start hence and proceed further as spies into the land of the Danes. Ye dwellers afar, ye who traverse the sea, hear now my fixed resolve. Best is it with speed to make known whence ye are come."

Again, both poems like to dwell upon the emotions felt in greeting or bidding farewell to friends. Thus in Od. XVI 14 ff. it is stated that Eumaios "came up to his lord and kissed his head and both his fair eyes and both his hands, and the hot tears fell from him. As an affectionate father greets his son when he returns from a distant land after nine years absence— an only son and well loved (?), for whose sake he has endured many hardships—even so then did the noble swineherd kiss god-like Telemachos all over and embrace him as one escaped from death." With this we may compare the account of Hrothgar's farewell to Beowulf (v. 1870 ff.): "Then did the king of noble lineage, the prince of the Scyldingas, kiss that best of squires and clasp him round the neck. Tears fell from him, as he stood there with his grey hair. Aged and venerable as he was, he felt uncertain, indeed he thought it unlikely, that they would ever meet again in spirited converse. So dear was this man to him that he could not restrain his heart's emotion; but in his breast, fast bound within his heart, a secret longing for the beloved man burnt in his blood."

The frequent use of similes, as in the last passage from the Odyssey, is one of the chief features in which Greek heroic poetry differs from Teutonic. Sometimes however the same kind of picture is brought before us in a different way. Thus among the commonest Homeric similes are those derived from hunting scenes. A typical example occurs in Il. XV 271 ff.: "As when hounds and men of the country chase a horned stag or a wild goat, and it is saved by a precipitous rock or dense wood, and they cannot succeed in finding it," etc. With this may be compared a passage in Beowulf describing the pool in which the demons had made their lair (v. 1369 ff.): "Though the heath-ranger, the stag of mighty horns, may make his way to the forest when beset by hounds after a long chase, he will yield up his spirit and his life on the brink before he will be willing to shelter his head therein."

Occasionally we meet with similes of a more ambitious, not to say extravagant, character, as in Il. II 455 ff., where the gleam arising from the bronze armour of the Achaean army is compared to the blaze produced by a forest fire. For this also we find parallels in Teutonic poetry, e.g. Finn 35 f.: "A gleam arose from the swords, as though Finn's fortress were all on fire."

In the use of epithets and poetical expressions many remarkable parallels are to be found. Some of these are merely of a descriptive character, e.g. ἄκριας ἠνεμοέσσας (Od. XVI 365) beside *windige naessas* (Beow. 1359), and some are little more than circumlocutions, e.g. υἶες Ἀχαιῶν, *Geata bearn*, for Ἀχαιοί, *Geatas*. In other cases however a distinct metaphor is involved, as when ships are called ἁλὸς ἵπποι (Od. IV 708), corresponding to the Anglo-Saxon *brimhengest*, which is probably an epic word, though it does not occur in the extant fragments. In particular note should be taken of the metaphorical terms applied to kings, e.g. ποιμὴν λαῶν which may be compared with *folces hyrde*, ἕρκος Ἀχαιῶν with *eodur Scyldinga*, and perhaps also οὖρος Ἀχαιῶν with the very common expression *eorla hleo*.

The characteristics which we have been discussing up till now affect only the language and style of the two groups of poems. But it is to be observed that they possess also certain common features which appear to be of deeper significance. Thus such expressions as ὄλβον ἐπέκλωσαν or *wigspeda gewiofu* ('the webs of success in war') are probably to be traced to a primitive religious conception, which may be seen more clearly in Od. VII 196 ff.: "There he shall experience afterwards whatever Fate and the stern Κλῶθες ('spinning women') spun for him when he was born[1]." For the prevalence of similar ideas among the Teutonic peoples we may refer to Helgakviða Hundingsbana, I 3 f., Gylfaginning cap. 15, Niáls Saga, cap. 157, and above all to the Saga af Nornagesti (cap. 11), which

[1] We may compare such expressions as *me þaet wyrd gewaef* in the Anglo-Saxon Rhyming Poem (Cod. Exon.), v. 70.

presents such a remarkable parallel to the story of Althaia and Meleagros.

Somewhat clearer evidence of a common religious conception is furnished by Beow. 2124 ff., a passage which we have already quoted (p. 54). The rite of 'paying the due of fire' (λελάχωσι πυρός) to a dead man is often mentioned in the Iliad (e.g. VII 79 f., XXII 342 f., XXIII 76; cf. XXIV 37 f.) and undoubtedly had a religious significance. This may be seen especially from the speech of Elpenor in Od. XI 71 ff.: "There I exhort thee then, my lord, to be mindful of me and not to leave me behind unlamented and unburied, abandoning me when thou goest away, lest I bring down wrath from the gods upon thee. But burn me up with my arms, all that I possess, and construct for me a barrow upon the shore of the grey sea, the memorial of an unfortunate man, so that I may be known even to those who shall be hereafter."

It will be observed that this passage, apart from its religious bearing, expresses a desire on the part of the speaker that his memory may not be forgotten. Here we are brought to one of the most striking characteristics of heroic poetry, both Greek and Teutonic, namely the constantly expressed thirst for fame, both during one's own life and in after times. As a typical example we may take a passage from Hector's speech before his combat with Aias (Il. VII 85 ff.): "I will give up his body to the longhaired Achaeans, so that they may take him to the well-decked ships for burial and construct for him a memorial barrow by the broad Hellespont. So shall it be said in time to come by some one who lives in after days, when he sails his many-oared ship over the dark sea: 'This is the memorial of a man who died long ago, who once upon a time was slain in his prowess by glorious Hector.' So shall it be said in time to come; and my fame shall never perish." In Od. XXIV 80 ff. Agamemnon's spirit describes how such honours had been paid to the remains of Achilles: "Then over them our sacred host of warriors from Argos constructed a great and splendid grave-mound, upon a projecting headland above the broad Hellespont —so that it might be conspicuous to men upon the sea, both those who are now alive and those who shall be hereafter." With both

these passages we may compare the dying words of Beowulf
(v. 2802 ff.): "After the pyre is consumed command my famous
warriors to construct a splendid grave-chamber where the headland juts into the sea.   It shall tower aloft on Hrones Naes as
a memorial for my people—so that in after days the name of
'Beowulf's Barrow' shall be familiar to mariners who ply their
tall ships from afar over the dark waters."

The summit of a hero's ambition is to have his glory celebrated everywhere and for all time.   Odysseus himself says
(Od. IX 20) that his glory reaches to heaven.   His wife bewails
her troubles in the following words (*ib.* IV 724): "Before this I
lost my brave lion-hearted husband who was preeminent among
the Danaoi for every kind of excellence.   Far and wide was that
brave man's glory spread, throughout Hellas and mid Argos."
The extent of Beowulf's fame is proclaimed in more extravagant
terms.   One passage (v. 1221 ff.) has already been quoted (p. 88).
We may compare also v. 856 ff.: "There was Beowulf's fame
celebrated.   Frequently and by many was it declared that
whether to the south or north, between the two seas, on earth's
broad expanse and beneath the canopy of heaven, there existed
no nobler warrior nor one more worthy to govern."

This love of glory is held up as an incitement to bravery in
critical situations, as in Wald. 1 8 ff., where Hildegyth encourages
the hero as follows : "O son of Aelfhere, a day is come which
without doubt has in store for thee one or other of two issues—
either to lose thy life or to possess lasting glory among mortals."
For the alternative form of expression, though used from a
different point of view, we may compare Socos' speech in Il. XI
430 ff.: "O far-famed Odysseus, today thou shalt either be able
to boast over two sons of Hippasos—that thou hast slain such
men as we are and robbed us of our arms—or smitten beneath
my spear thou shalt lose thy life."

The last passage introduces us to another prominent characteristic of heroic poetry, namely the boasting of warriors over
their own personal prowess and the deeds they have performed
or are going to perform.   Sometimes this is represented as
taking place in the banqueting hall, as in Il. XX 83 ff., where the
disguised Apollo thus taunts Aineias: 'Aineias, thou counseller

of the Trojans, where now is thy boasting, in which thou didst vow to the princes of the Trojans, when quaffing thy wine, that thou wouldst try thy strength in open battle against Achilles son of Peleus!" We may compare Beow. 480 ff.: "Often enough have scions of combat vowed over the ale-cup, when drunken with beer, that they would abide Grendel's onset in the hall with their terrible swords." Beowulf himself indulges in a similar boast (v. 636 ff.): "I am resolved to perform a deed of knightly prowess or to meet with my life's end in this mead-hall."

Again, it is by boasting of much the same kind that warriors make themselves known to one another when they meet in battle. A typical example occurs in Finn 24 ff.: "Sigeferth is my name. I am a prince of the Secgan and a rover known far and wide. Many hardships and stern encounters have I endured. Here too thou shalt have for certain (i.e. I shall not draw back from) whichever course (i.e. war or peace) thou dost prefer to take with me." We may compare Il. XIII 448 ff., where Idomeneus makes himself known to Deiphobos: "Now stand forth thyself to face me, that thou mayest see what sort of a scion of Zeus is come here. First Zeus begat Minos to be ruler of Crete, and Minos again begat the blameless Deucalion; and Deucalion begat me to be lord over many men in broad Crete. But now have ships brought me hither with consequences evil to thee and to thy father and the rest of the Trojans."

It will be seen that in this passage Idomeneus prides himself as much on his ancestry[1] as on his own prowess. The idea of inherited valour finds expression again in Il. V 252 ff., where Diomedes says to Sthenelos: "Exhort me not to flight, for I am sure thou wilt not persuade me. Nowise inbred in me is it to fight a runaway battle, neither to cower in fear. My courage is steadfast still." Practically the same idea appears in Beow.

---

[1] We may compare a passage from the poem on the battle of Maldon, which largely follows heroic poetry (cf. pp. 3, 97). In v. 216 ff. Aelfwine, one of Byrhtnoth's knights, boasts as follows: "I will make my lineage known to all, that I come of a great Mercian house. My grandfather, Ealhhelm by name, was a wise earl and blessed with worldly prosperity. Not against me shall knights bring public reproach, that I am willing to leave this army and make my way home, now that my prince lies slain in battle." Ealhhelm held office in the reign of Edmund I.

2694 ff.: " Then, as I have been told, in the national king's dire need the knight stood upright and showed forth his prowess—strength and valour such as was inbred in him."

The feeling of pride in a noble family becomes clearly noticeable also on occasions when the family is threatened with extinction. Beowulf's farewell words to Wiglaf are (v. 2814 ff.): " Thou art the last remnant of our house, even of Waegmund's line. All my kinsmen in their knightly prowess has Fate swept off to their doom. I myself must follow them." We may compare Od. XIV 180 f., though here the speaker, Eumaios, is only a dependent of the house : " On his return home the illustrious suitors are lying in wait for him, in order that the seed of godlike Arceisios may vanish nameless from Ithaca."

Lastly, the heroic spirit shows itself in the exhortations of princes to their followers. As an instance we may quote a verse which occurs several times, in speeches of Hector and Patroclos: " Be men, my friends, and set your minds upon impetuous valour." The same exhortation, though in a more elaborate form, occurs in Finn 10 ff.: " But awake now, my warriors, have your hands ready (or 'take your mail-coats'), be mindful of your prowess, leap forth in the forefront (?), be stout of heart."

It is true that these last two passages would in themselves be appropriate in any martial poetry. But we must take the context into account. Patroclos immediately (XVI 271 f.) adds the words "in order that we may do honour to the son of Peleus, who is by far the best of the men of Argos." So in Finn 40 f. we are told that " never was a nobler recompense paid for sweet mead than was (then) rendered to Hnaef by his bachelors." The same thought occurs elsewhere in the English poems, e.g. in Beow. 2634 ff., where Wiglaf is exhorting his comrades : " I remember the time when we were receiving mead, when in the beer-hall we pledged ourselves to our lord who gave us these bracelets, that if need like this befell him we would repay the battle-harness, the helmets and sharp swords." And again, shortly afterwards (v. 2646 ff.): " Now is the day come that our liege-lord needs the strength of brave warriors. Let us draw near to help our war-chief, so long as the heat of the fierce and terrible flames shall last."

The underlying idea is clearly that which is described by
Tacitus (*Germ.* 14) in his account of the comitatus of the ancient
Germans : "The *principes* fight for victory, but the *comites* fight
for their *princeps*[1]." And this description is probably true of the
Homeric Greeks just as much as of the Teutonic heroes. The
terms used in the two sets of poems (θεράπων—*þegn*, i.e. *comes* ;
ἄναξ—*dryhten*, i.e. *princeps*), seem to correspond to one another
almost exactly, though it is not easy to find a satisfactory rendering for them in modern English. For kings too, especially such
as are of preeminent position, we find in each case a very similar
expression (ἄναξ ἀνδρῶν—*eorla dryhten*), which properly denotes
the relationship of liege-lord.

In both cases alike the leading idea of the Heroic Age may
be fittingly summed up in the phrase κλέα ἀνδρῶν. This is
practically equivalent to the Anglo-Saxon *dom*, with which we
have dealt above (p. 87 f.). It is essential to notice that the
object so much prized is personal glory. In Hector's speech
before his combat with Aias (cf. p. 325) the glory which would
result from the combat to the hero or his opponent is the only
subject touched upon. No consideration is taken of any effect
which might be produced thereby upon the fortunes of the war.

The same characteristic appears throughout the passages
which we have quoted and countless others. Occasionally we
hear also of pride of family, but scarcely ever of any truly
national feeling. Patroclos exhorts his men to bravery (Il. XVI
270 ff.) in order that they may win glory not for the Achaean
nation but for their own personal lord ; and he adds further that
by so doing they will bring shame upon the national leader.
Achilles himself retires from the conflict owing to a personal
wrong, and only returns to it in order to avenge his friend. The
same phenomena appear in the English poems. That Wiglaf
whose bravery is said to be 'inbred' (cf. p. 328) was the son of a
certain Weohstan, whose great achievement was the slaying of
the Swedish prince Eanmund. Yet Eanmund was at this time
apparently under the protection of Heardred, king of the Geatas,

---

[1] *iam uero infame in omnem uitam ac probrosum superstitem principi suo ex acie
recessisse. illum defendere, tueri, sua quoque fortia facta gloriae eius assignare praecipuum sacramentum est. principes pro uictoria pugnant, comites pro principe.*

who also lost his life in the same war. Weohstan however, though he belonged to the Geatas, was in the service of Onela, their enemy. It would seem then that he was fighting against his own nation. Such cases appear to have been by no means uncommon in the Teutonic Heroic Age. For it was customary at that time for young noblemen to take service under foreign princes; and the obligations which personal service imposed were held to be superior to all others.

Love of home and zeal in its defence are of course frequently mentioned in both groups of poems. We may refer to the common phrase φίλην ἐς πατρίδα γαῖαν. Most frequently however, as we might expect, these features appear in connection with the Trojans. In Il. XII 243, when Pulydamas has urged retreat in consequence of an omen, Hector replies: "The best of all omens is to fight in defence of our country." Priam uses the same expression (*ib.*, XXIV 499 f.) when he comes to plead with Achilles for his son's body: "He preserved my city and its inhabitants, even Hector whom thou hast now slain as he fought in defence of his country." These feelings may be regarded as forms of patriotism; but it is patriotism of a distinctly practical kind, as may be seen from Il. XV 494 ff., where Hector is addressing his followers: "Now fight in close formation at the ships. Whosoever of you through shot or blow meets with death and fate, let him die. Not unseemly is it for him to die fighting in defence of this country. He will leave his wife and children in safety, his house also and his estate unharmed, if the Achaeans depart with their ships to their own dear fatherland." Much the same feelings are expressed in the English poems. As an example we may take Beow. 520 ff., where Unferth is describing the return of Breca after his swimming contest: "Welcome to his subjects was he when he made his way to his own dear home, the land of the Brondingas and his beautiful sacred city[1] where people, city and treasures belonged to him." We may refer also to Widsith, v. 119 ff.: "I have visited Wulfhere and Wyrmhere. Often enough did they wage war unceasing, when

---

[1] *freoðoburh*, lit. 'city of peace.' The expression probably springs from the sacred peace attaching to the king's dwelling, to which we find frequent allusions in the laws (Ine, § 6, Alfred, § 7, etc.).

around the forest of the Vistula the Gothic army with their sharp swords had to defend their ancient domain[1] from Attila's subjects." And again (*ib.*, v. 127 ff.) : "Often enough did the spear fly whistling and shrieking, from that troop into a hostile army, when Wudga and Hama guarded their golden treasures and (the lives of) their men and women."

Such passages as these afford abundant evidence for patriotism of the practical kind. But this is not the same thing as national pride. We shall best be able to appreciate the special characteristics of heroic poetry in this respect by comparing it with other martial poems, dating from later times. An excellent example of national pride is furnished by the well-known epitaph on Leonidas and the Spartans who perished at Thermopylai. We may also quote the 'Laconian Embaterion' commonly included among the fragments of Tyrtaios : "O ye youths, whose fathers have been citizens of Sparta, the home of heroes, come, hold forth the shield in your left hand and cast the spear with good courage. Regard not your life, for so to do is not Sparta's ancestral custom." Other good examples may be found in the works of the early elegiac poets.

What perhaps deserves notice above all in poetry of this type is the use of the first person plural with reference to exploits performed by the poet's nation in bygone times—a form of speech which seems to be quite foreign to heroic poetry. An example occurs in Tyrtaios' Eunomia (fragm. 2): "This city has been given to the Heracleidai by Zeus himself, the son of Cronos and husband of fair-crowned Hera. Together with them we forsook breezy Erineos and made our way to Pelops' broad island." Here the reference is to the first arrival of the Dorians in the Peloponnesos. Another case may be found in the poem on the Messenian war (fragm. 5): "...our king Theopompos dear to the gods, by whose help we captured spacious Messene ...Round about it (or 'for its sake') war was waged for nineteen

---

[1] *ealdne eþelstol.* If this expression is to be interpreted in a local sense ('seat of authority') it is possible to read the idea of patriotism as a sentiment into it ; but my impression is that the poet means no more than defence of home. A different interpretation of the passage is given by Prof. Heusler (*S.-B. d. Akad. d. Wiss. zu Berlin*, 1909, p. 926), according to whom it means "Verteidigung des *eald eþelstol*, des alten Erbthrones (nicht Stammsitzes)."

years, ever without ceasing, by the fathers of our fathers, warriors who possessed the spirit of endurance." A similar usage appears in Mimnermos, fragm. 9: "On quitting steep Pylos, the town of Neleus, we came in ships to the pleasant land of Asia, and at fair Colophon with overmastering strength we took up our abode, beginning the arduous assault. Thence in turn, starting from the river Aleis, by the will of the gods we took Aeolian Smyrna[1]." Both the foundation of Colophon and the capture of Smyrna took place long before the poet's time.

The same patriotic sentiment is to be found in the martial poetry of later times in England. Thus in the poem on the battle of Brunanburh (v. 20 ff.) we are told that "throughout the whole day the West Saxons with troops of horse pressed on in pursuit of the enemy's forces. Fiercely they cut down the fugitives from behind with swords sharpened on the grindstone. Nor did the Mercians refuse stern hand-to-hand combat to any of the warriors who in the ship's bosom had followed Anlaf over the rolling waters to our land, to meet their doom in battle. On the field of action lay five young kings stretched lifeless by the sword ; and with them seven of Anlaf's earls, and a countless host both of the seamen and the Scots." And again (v. 65 ff.) : "Never in this island before now, so far as the books of our ancient historians can tell us, has greater slaughter been made of an army by the edge of the sword—since the time when the Angles and Saxons made their way hither from the east over the wide seas, invading Britain, when warriors eager for glory, proud forgers of war, overcame the Welsh and won for themselves a country."

We need not hesitate to interpret the last part of this quotation as an expression of national consciousness, just as much as in the poem of Mimnermos given above, although it does not use the first person with reference to the achievements of the Saxon invaders. But the poem as a whole differs essentially from the heroic type owing to the fact that—though the princes are mentioned incidentally—it is permeated throughout by the sense of national rather than individual glory.

[1] For the translation of this fragment I am indebted to the kindness of Mr A. B. Cook.

Thus far we have been dealing with individual passages in the poems. Now we must consider briefly the motives of the stories and the characteristics for which the heroes are celebrated. The story of Beowulf consists of a series of adventures in which the hero seeks to display his prowess in encounters with monsters. The story of Finn, if we may form an opinion from the fragmentary evidence at our disposal, dealt with a fatal quarrel between two brothers-in-law, followed by revenge. The theme of Waldhere's story is the elopement, or rather escape, of lovers and the bravery shown by the hero in defence of his bride. The term elopement may more properly be applied to the story of Heðinn and Högni, whatever was the original form of its ending. A counterpart to this is furnished by the story of Hagbarðr and Signý, which ended tragically in the death of the lovers. The story of Sigurðr deals with a woman's revenge, brought about by disappointed love. The theme of the story of Hamðir and Sörli is the revenge undertaken by them for the death of their sister. Revenge is likewise the theme of Ingeld's story—in this case for the death of a father. The story of Offa is an instance of heroism in single combat. In the various stories connected with Dietrich von Bern attention is centred chiefly on the bravery, loyalty and resourcefulness of the hero and his knights.

It will be seen that throughout the heroic poetry of the Teutonic peoples, in episodes as well as in the main stories, the chief motif is almost invariably love or revenge or personal bravery. The same remark applies obviously enough to Greek heroic poetry—to the Iliad and Odyssey, as well as to the stories of Heracles, Iason and the rest. The characteristics too for which the heroes are distinguished are on the whole very much the same in both cases—strength, courage, resourcefulness, generosity, hospitality. The characters of Beowulf and Hrothgar may appeal to us more than those of Achilles and Nestor, but the main outlines are very similar. If there is any difference worth noting in this respect between the two sets of poems it is that the Greek attach more importance to personal beauty—a feature which only becomes prominent in the later forms of the Teutonic stories.

Now let us turn for a moment to the heroes of 'post-heroic'

times. During the centuries which immediately followed the
Heroic Age we hear of many princes and other persons who
rose to fame both in England and on the Continent. Sometimes
this fame was acquired through successful warfare; but it is as
generals rather than as warriors that such persons are celebrated.
More frequently they are known to us as legislators, founders
of institutions, promoters of religion and protectors of the public
peace. In this country we may think of such persons as the
Kentish king Aethelberht, the Northumbrian kings Edwin and
Oswald, the Mercian king Offa, and, above all, of Alfred the
Great—not to mention numerous prominent ecclesiastics. In
Greece the number of names known to us during the corresponding period is extremely small. Yet the most prominent names
which we meet with at the dawn of the historical period are
those of legislators and public benefactors, such as Zaleucos and
Solon. In earlier times by far the best known name is that of
the Spartan legislator Lycurgos, whether he was really a historical
person or a character of mythical origin. We may perhaps
compare him with that Wiger Spa, 'a heathen in the heathen
age,' whose authority is referred to in King Byrger's preamble
to the Law of the Uppland Swedes.

A similar character is borne by the traditional heroes of
nations which have no Heroic Age. We may instance Bruteno
and Widowuto the legendary founders and legislators of the
state of the ancient Prussians. The same is true of the early
kings of Rome, Romulus, Numa, Servius Tullius and the
founders of the Republic. The essential feature which distinguishes these characters from those of the Heroic Age is the
fact that they are known chiefly, not for what they performed or
experienced during their lives, but for the effects of their doings
upon later generations.

The explanation of this difference is no doubt to be sought
largely in the nature of the records. For a modern analogy to
the stories of Sigurðr or Achilles we should turn naturally to a
romance or novel; for those of Offa or Lycurgos analogy would
be sought rather in the biography of a statesman[1]. But it must

---

[1] This analogy applies perhaps also to the objects aimed at in the two sets of
records. Within certain limitations it may be said that the object of the heroic stories

be clearly recognised that the difference here does not lie between historical and unhistorical.   Attila was a man of flesh and
blood, no less certainly than Offa, while the historical existence
of Lycurgos is as much debated as that of Achilles.   And what
shall we say with regard to such a character as Romulus?   The
difference lies rather between political and non-political, or—to
speak more accurately—between national and non-national.
Offa's fame is inseparably bound up with the aggrandisement
and reorganisation of the Mercian kingdom.   Lycurgos and
Romulus are scarcely conceivable without Sparta or Rome.
But Sigurðr and Achilles might belong to any Teutonic or Greek
community; in the former case indeed the hero's nationality is
not known for certain.   We have seen that the heroic poetry of
the Teutonic peoples had what may be called an international
circulation from the beginning; and we have no reason for
doubting that in the Heroic Age itself the same was the case in
Greece.   On the other hand the memory of the later heroes and
their achievements was preserved only, or almost only, in the
records and traditions of individual states.   The interest to which
stories of this latter group appeal is in general limited to the
hero's own state; we have no evidence that such stories were

is to entertain and that of unheroic records to instruct.   The latter remark holds good
not only for historical works but also for tribal traditions and tribal law.   It is likely
that opportunity was taken to impart instruction of this type at festal gatherings.   We
may quote a passage from Praetorius' *Deliciae Prussicae* (ed. Pierson, p. 24) relating
to a festal gathering of young people at a time when the Prussian Lithuanians had not
yet been entirely converted.   "Darauf haben sie sich um die Eiche und Stein
niedergesetzt, der Weydulut aber uf den Stein das Fell gelegt, sich darauf gesetzet,
einen Sermon gehalten von ihrem Herkommen und alten Gebräuchen, Glauben p. p.,
den Zemyna, den Perkuns und andere mehr genennet."   There is abundant evidence
for the existence of similar traditions among the Teutonic peoples from the earliest
times—for which the reader may be referred to Dr Schütte's interesting book *Oldsagn
om Godtjod* (especially pp. 118—197).   But in heroic poetry, whether Teutonic or
Greek, references to the early traditions of a nation are extremely rare and practically
limited to the ancestors of the royal family, while 'law' is the will of the ruler.   For
Greek parallels we must turn to works of the Hesiodic school and the elegiac poets.

    With regard to historical works we have to remember that all records dating from
the Heroic Age are of foreign origin.   But it is certainly to be noted that the interest
of the stories given by Gregory of Tours and other writers of the sixth century—in so
far as they relate to persons of Teutonic blood—is essentially personal, and similar to
that which characterises the poems.   This is the more noteworthy since these stories
are related from a totally different point of view (cf. p. 338 f.).

international property[1]. It is the fact that the interest of the heroic stories was both individual and universal—i.e. that it lay in individuals not essentially bound up with a given community —which fitted them for international circulation.

But this difference of interest is itself a matter which calls for explanation. If we are to trust the evidence of the records it is due to differences in the ideas which animated heroic and non-heroic society[2]. Among these we may note especially an essential difference in the conception of the state. With this question we shall have to deal more fully in a later chapter. It may be indicated here however that in the Heroic Age the state appears to have been regarded as little more than the property of an individual—or rather perhaps of a family, which itself was intimately connected with a number of other families in similar

[1] Except in so far as (in the case of Teutonic stories) they are connected with the Church.

[2] I would call attention here to an interesting paper by Prof. Heusler (*S.-B. d Akad. d. Wiss. zu Berlin*, 1909, p. 920 ff.), in which he seeks to show that the historical element in Teutonic heroic poetry has been exaggerated. The evidence adduced in favour of this view consists in the first place of unhistorical situations, chronological dislocations, etc. Most of the examples are taken from the later forms of the stories (Stage IV of our scheme). We have already discussed these phenomena (p. 152 ff.), and here I would only add that the observation quoted from Prof. Murko's paper on p. 936, note, may be applied, *mutatis mutandis*, to chronological as well as geographical relations. What interests us here however is the second piece of evidence brought forward by Prof. Heusler (p. 924 f.). He fully recognises and admirably expresses the individualistic, non-national spirit of Teutonic heroic poetry—as contrasted with that of the Old French epics: "Es herrschen in unsrer Sage die persönlichen Ideen"......"Die germanische Sage kennt keinen Nationalfeind," etc. Yet apparently he regards this phenomenon ('die persönliche Fabel') as a characteristic of the poetry only, and not of the society which produced it. Now in order to prove that this is an 'unhistorical' element evidence must be brought to show that the attitude of the poems—the early poems (Stage II)—does not faithfully reflect the spirit of the age. I know of no evidence to justify so startling a conclusion; on the contrary we shall see in the following chapters that contemporary historical works frequently testify to the prevalence of the same ideas which we find expressed in the poems. Even the statement that Teutonic heroic poetry is 'unpolitical' seems to me to require some reservation. Certainly it knows nothing of modern ideas of politics. But have we any ground for disputing that it represents the politics current in the courts in which it grew up? Lastly, objection must be taken to the contrast drawn on p. 933 between Teutonic and Greek heroic poetry. So far as the Homeric evidence is concerned the observations made here apply not to the poems as we have them but to certain hypotheses regarding their 'pre-history,' with which we have dealt above (p. 267 ff.).

positions. The decline and disappearance of kingship in Greece
during the eighth century presupposes of course that such a
conception had long ceased to retain its vitality. And even
among the Teutonic peoples, which usually preserved the institution of kingship, we find abundant evidence for a similar
change of view. Among the Franks kingship had long been a
mere shadow when the non-royal Pippin took the throne in 752.
In England we do not meet with non-royal kings until more
than a century later; but even by Bede's time it is clear that the
kingdom had come to be looked upon as something more than
the property of the royal family.

When once the characteristics of the spirit of the Heroic Age
have been fully recognised they will be found to explain several
features in the stories which have often been regarded as incredible. One of these is the fact that wars are generally
represented as arising out of the personal quarrels or jealousies
of princes, or out of wrongs perpetrated by one prince upon
another. Thus it has been assumed by many scholars that the
story of the abduction of Helen is of mythical origin, not on
account of any intrinsic improbability contained in it, but because
it is founded on a motif which is extremely common in folktales.
But it has been pointed out above (p. 265) that the reason why
the abduction motif is common in folktales lies in the fact that
under unsettled social conditions such occurrences were common
in real life. The conditions of the Heroic Age, whether Greek
or Teutonic, were doubtless not normally so unsettled that the
abduction of a queen or princess could fail to attract attention.
In the case of the wife of a distinguished king it can scarcely be
doubted that such an event would produce a profound sensation;
and it is to this, we may presume, that the story in the first
place owed its celebrity. But the part played by women in
international quarrels during the Teutonic Heroic Age must not
be overlooked. In addition to the stories of which love adventures form the main theme (cf. p. 333) we may allude to such
cases as Beow. 2930 ff., where Haethcyn is said to have carried
off the Swedish queen with consequences disastrous to himself.
Above all however it is well to bear in mind the story of the

C.   22

war between the Angli and the Warni (cf. p. 97 f.), a war which owed its origin to Radiger's repudiation of his marriage contract with the English king's sister. We have seen that this story comes not from a poem, but from the work of a strictly contemporary Roman historian.

Nor can it be said that this case stands alone. According to Gregory of Tours (III 6) the overthrow of the Burgundian kingdom was due to the instigation of Hrothhild, who implored her sons to exact vengeance for the murder of her parents—a case not unlike the Norse version of the story of Hamðir and Sörli. Hildeberht's invasion of Spain was undertaken in answer to messages from his sister Hlothhild, who had been illtreated by her husband, the Visigothic king Amalaric (*ib.*, III 10). The dissensions which eventually brought about the downfall of the Thuringian kingdom had their origin in the proud and jealous character of Amalaberga, the wife of Irminfrith (*ib.*, III 4). Unless we are prepared to shut our eyes to the plain evidence of history we are bound to recognise that the personal feelings of queens and princesses were among the very strongest of the factors by which the politics of the Heroic Age were governed.

There has undoubtedly been a tendency among modern historians to neglect the personal element in early Teutonic history and to concentrate attention upon the movements of peoples and upon 'constitutional' changes. The feature with which we have just been dealing is only one of several which owing to this neglect have been regarded as essentially 'poetic' motives, the origin of which must be sought in myth or fiction. Decisive evidence to the contrary is furnished by writers of the sixth century. Certainly the picture of Teutonic court life which they give produces a different impression from that which we gain from the poems. The atmosphere suggested by the latter is one of adventure and romance, whereas the former convey an idea of reckless brutality. Yet it is only necessary to place the two sets of records side by side in order to see that the one is complementary to the other—that the difference lies not in the subjects treated but in the point of view from which they are regarded. Gregory (II 28) records without comment or explanation that the Burgundian king Gundobad slew his brother

Hilperic (Hrothhild's father) with the sword and drowned his wife with a stone tied to her neck.   If this incident had been treated in heroic poetry we should doubtless gain a very different impression.   Different too would be the impression conveyed by the story of Sigurðr, if we had it from a Roman historian.   But when the two stories are compared it cannot be said that the picture which the poems present of the Burgundian kingdom under Guthhere is incompatible with the picture which history gives us of the Burgundian kingdom under Gundobad, some fifty years later.   No true impression of the Heroic Age can be obtained by crediting the youthful kings of unlearned communities with a knowledge of political principles which we have acquired from long study of the history of many nations; and it is equally futile to seek for grounds of policy in actions which very frequently were dictated solely by passion.   Ambition was no doubt a factor, as in all stages of society.   But the form which it seems to have taken as a rule was purely personal and directed towards the acquisition of wealth or glory rather than with any view of establishing the kingdom upon a permanent basis[1].

Another feature to which exception has been taken is the fact that in battle scenes the fighting is generally represented as a series of single combats between the various leading men. Here again the objection seems to be based on a misunderstanding of the conditions of heroic warfare.   In the first place we have no reason for doubting that in both the periods with which we are dealing the leaders were far better armed than the rank and file of the forces.   In hand to hand fighting the possession of defensive armour, helmet and mail-coat, constitutes an overwhelming advantage.   Secondly, the passion for personal glory, which is so prominent in the poems, must have prompted the ambitious man to pick out the most distinguished opponents. If he was a 'squire' success would bring rich rewards[2].   But

---

[1] As a typical case we may cite the story of the Frankish prince Hlothric (Greg. Tur., II 40), who at Clovis' suggestion caused his own father to be murdered.   He offered Clovis a share of the treasures, but was himself killed by the envoys of the latter while he was bending over his father's treasure-chest.

[2] In Beow. 2991 ff. we are told that Eofor, who slew the Swedish king Ongentheo, was rewarded by Hygelac with the hand of his only daughter and an enormous grant of land and treasure.

even the leaders themselves, as among the Germans of Tacitus' time[1], were doubtless expected to distinguish themselves by preeminence in bravery, rather than by skilful generalship. Thirdly, and this is the most important point, the general object aimed at in a battle was not to gain a strategic advantage but to kill the leaders. Very often this meant the destruction of the enemy's organisation. At times indeed it appears that the death or capture of a king led forthwith to the end of hostilities. Thus in the battle of Strassburg in 357, when the Romans captured the Alamannic king Chonodomarius, his personal retinue, to the number of two hundred, gave themselves up voluntarily to share his captivity[2]. And in Beowulf we see from more than one passage that when the king was slain the heart of the resistance was broken. Under such conditions we may well believe that the direction to 'fight neither with small nor great, save only with the king,' was a piece of perfectly sound policy.

We have to take account moreover of another element, somewhat strange to modern ideas, namely the intense eagerness to get possession of a fallen enemy's arms. In the battle scenes of the Iliad this feature is constantly to the fore; indeed the most severe conflicts usually take place over the bodies of warriors. In the English poems it is much the same. We may quote Beow. 2985 ff.: "Thereupon the warrior (Eofor) despoiled his opponent. He took from Ongentheo his iron mail-coat and his sharp and hilted sword, together with his helmet, and brought the old man's accoutrements to Hygelac." And again v. 2613 ff.: "To him (Eanmund) Weohstan brought death in combat by the

---

[1] Cf. *Germ.* 14: *cum uentum in aciem turpe principi uirtute uinci, turpe comitatui uirtutem principis non adaequare.* It is not to be doubted that princes of the Heroic Age did seek to display their prowess in single combats. The story of Theodric's combat with an Avar champion named Xerxer (Fredegar, *Chron.* II 57) appears to be based on an exploit for which we have contemporary evidence in Ennodius' Panegyric (p. 266 in Hartel's edition; cf. Jiriczek, *Deutsche Heldensagen,* I p. 140 f.), where the defeated warrior is called *Bulgarum ductor.* It is well known also that the princes of the ancient Gauls were in the habit of engaging their enemies in single combat. There is satisfactory historical evidence for two cases in which distinguished Romans proved victorious in such encounters (cf. D'Arbois de Jubainville, *La Civilisation des Celtes,* p. 17 ff.). The period to which these notices refer may be described as a Gaulish Heroic Age (cf. p. 427 ff.).

[2] Cf. Ammianus Marcellinus, XVI 12. 60.

sword's edge; and to his kinsmen he presented the burnished
helmet, the ring-formed mail-coat and the ancient sword of
giant workmanship—though the latter was returned to him
by Onela." It will be seen that the Teutonic warriors, who
in both these cases are 'squires,' render up the spoils to their
lords, whereas the Greek princes keep them for themselves;
but we need not doubt that they expected an equivalent reward.

The article chiefly coveted seems to have been the coat of
mail. In Wald. II 16 ff. the hero says to Guthhere: "Take from
me the grey mail-coat, if thou dare; for thou seest how I am
worn out with battle. Upon my shoulders here stands an
heirloom from Aelfhere; good it is and..., adorned with gold, a
superb garment for a prince to possess, when his hand is defending
life's treasure from his foes." Such articles were doubtless very
costly, and often, as in this case, they were handed on from
generation to generation. Beowulf's coat of mail had belonged
to his grandfather, and was believed to be the workmanship of
Weland. Before his encounter with Grendel he charges the
king of the Danes to send it back to Hygelac in the event of his
death. A coat of mail which was found intact at Vi in Fyn
contains about twenty thousand rings, and it has been calculated
that such an article would take a single workman nearly a whole
year to make[1].

It is to be remembered further that wealthy princes, prompted
no doubt by love of display, were in the habit of carrying about
their persons a considerable amount of gold. Glaucos indeed is
said to have gone to battle in golden armour worth a hundred
oxen (Il. VI 235 f.). Hygelac, when he was slain, was wearing
the magnificent necklet which Wealhtheo had given to Beowulf
(v. 1195 ff.). Historical records give evidence to the same effect[2];
and there can be little doubt that the spoils of such kings often
amounted to a considerable fortune. If, in addition to spoils of
this kind, account is taken of the chances of booty and ransoms,

---

[1] Cf. S. Müller, *Nordische Altertumskunde*, II p. 128.

[2] Cf. especially Procopius' description of Totila at his last battle (*Goth.* IV 31):
τήν τε γὰρ τῶν ὅπλων σκευὴν κατακόρως τῷ χρυσῷ κατειλημμένην ἠμπίσχετο καὶ τῶν οἱ
φαλάρων κόσμος ἔκ τε τοῦ πίλου καὶ τοῦ δόρατος ἀλουργός τε καὶ ἄλλως βασιλεῖ πρέπων
ἐκρέματο θαυμαστὸς ὅσος.

not only after a general victory but also in incidental and more or less private forays[1], it will be seen that warfare of the heroic type offered very substantial inducements, apart from the acquisition of glory.

It is not to be supposed that such warfare was really of an effective character. Even in the Iliad itself (VI 67 ff.) a warning is raised against it by the old Nestor, who is represented (*ib.* II 555) as an exceptionally skilful general, but his advice seems to be unheeded. Between two armies of the heroic type the issue had to be decided, if at all, by a pitched battle. Sheltered behind fortifications, even an inferior army had not much to fear. In that case the people most exposed to danger were what we should call non-combatants—not only the women and children and unwarlike dependents of the combatants themselves[2], but also any neighbouring communities who might be caught unawares by bands of hungry warriors.

On the other hand against organised forces, like those of the later Spartans or the Romans, at all events if commanded by generals who followed a definite plan of campaign, the Homeric Achaeans would have had no chance after the first encounter. This may be seen especially from the history of the campaigns against the Italian Gauls, who appear to have employed a very similar method of warfare. The Saxons and other northern peoples owed their successes largely to the rapidity of their movements, combined with the fact that they had command of the sea. But, so far as we know, they seldom or never had to deal with any considerable Roman army. In Britain their procedure was probably similar to that followed by the Scandinavian invaders in the Viking Age; but the latter were unable to cope

---

[1] Even in time of peace merchants might turn into freebooters (cf. Od. XIV 262 ff.). Piracy indeed was scarcely regarded as disreputable (*ib.* III 72 ff.; cf. p. 322). The same conditions prevailed during the Viking Age and doubtless also during the Teutonic Heroic Age.

[2] As illustrations of the barbarities associated with warfare of this type we may refer to the speech of Theodric, king of the Franks, given by Gregory, III 7, and to the behaviour of Theodberht's army in Italy, recorded by Procopius (*Goth.* II 25). At such a time the atrocities which Greek tradition relates in connection with the fall of Troy would have caused little comment. Yet the early heroic poems give less evidence even than the Homeric poems for cruelty of this kind.

with prolonged and organised resistance, such as was offered by Alfred the Great. The armies of the Goths at the height of their power were doubtless more formidable; but they had probably learnt much from long experience of the Romans, both as foes and allies. It is not to be forgotten however that supremacy came ultimately to the Franks, who of all the Teutonic peoples seem to have been least affected by the spirit of the Heroic Age.

CHAPTER XVI.

SOCIETY IN THE HEROIC AGE.

THE evidence of the German poems for the social and political conditions of the Heroic Age cannot be regarded as trustworthy owing to the lateness of the period in which they were composed. In principle the same is true also of the Norse poems. These reflect the conditions of the Viking Age rather than those of the Heroic Age, though, as we have already noted, the difference here is less marked. On the other hand, in addition to the Anglo-Saxon poems and the works of contemporary Roman historians, such as Ammianus Marcellinus, Jordanes and Procopius, we have valuable evidence from the early Teutonic codes of law. Some of these, such as the Lex Salica and the Lex Burgundionum, date from the first half of the sixth century or earlier, i.e. from the Heroic Age itself, while a number of others—in particular we may note the earliest English laws— belong to the following two centuries and show probably little deviation from the custom of the Heroic Age. All the codes of course contain certain Roman or Christian elements; but this influence in some cases goes back to the fifth century or even further.

The chief forces which governed the social system of that age were the bonds of kinship and allegiance. The influence of the former extended not merely, as with us, to rights of succession and duties of guardianship over children and women. It was also the power by which the security of the property and person of each member of the community was guaranteed. If a man received injury or insult, his kindred were bound to assist him to obtain redress. If he were slain they had to exact vengeance or compensation from the slayer. On the other hand not only the slayer himself but every member of his kindred became liable to vengeance, and each had to pay his quota towards the compensation (wergeld), just as it was divided among the kindred of the slain—the proportion varying in both cases according to the degree of relationship. In case of bloodshed a certain sum had also to be paid to the king, even in the earliest times of which we have record; but this sum seldom exceeded half the wergeld, and as a rule amounted to considerably less.

The character and size of the kindred appear to have varied in different nations. Some laws speak of claims to succession as remote as the seventh degree, while the rights and duties connected with the payment and receipt of wergelds seem generally to have extended as far as third cousins, i.e. the descendants of great-great-grandparents. Again, we hear sometimes of royal or noble families which bore a common name derived from some ancestor, real or mythical, from whom their power or prerogatives were believed to be inherited. Such were the Oescingas, the Wuffingas and the Icelingas, the royal families of Kent, East Anglia and Mercia respectively; so also the Scyldungas (Skiöldungar) among the Danes, the Merovingi among the Franks, and the Agilolfinga and other noble families among the Bavarians. Persons belonging to these families had probably— in some cases certainly—special wergelds; and the throne or principality seems to have been regarded as in some sense family property. Some writers believe that kindreds in general were permanent organisations of this kind, and that originally they held land, and possibly other property also, in common. But this view goes a good deal beyond what the facts warrant, at all events for the period with which we are dealing. It is clear that at this time kinship on both sides was recognised everywhere; maternal relatives shared in the payment and receipt of wergelds with those on the father's side, though not always in the same proportion. Moreover the idea that the inclusion of the maternal relatives was due to an innovation cannot be maintained. Thus, in spite of the fact that the Frankish kings claimed the throne by direct descent in the male line from Merovechus, there are clear indications that Frankish law in its earliest form gave priority to the mother's side. No doubt on the whole the agnatic system of relationship had become predominant almost everywhere in the Heroic Age; but sufficient traces of the opposite system remain to render it probable that a change had taken place not so very far back[1].

Any such change of course involves—or rather perhaps implies—a weakening in the force of the bonds of kinship; and of this we have very clear evidence in the Heroic Age. Now it has often been pointed out that early Teutonic custom seems to have made no provision for the case of homicide within the kindred. In such a case the persons on whom vengeance devolved would be identical, in part at least, with those against whom it would be directed—and so also with the compensation. It is generally held that homicide of this kind was extremely rare and that, when it did occur, the slayer was outlawed. That would no doubt be in accordance with primitive custom. Indeed in a state of society based on blood-relationship the life of a kinsman must be sacred above all else. Further, it is clear enough that the shedding of kindred blood was regarded with abhorrence in the Heroic Age. Thus Procopius (*Goth.* II 14), describing the euthanasia practised by the Heruli, states that when the dying man has been laid upon the top of the pyre, one of his countrymen goes up with a dagger and stabs him; but he adds explicitly that this man must not be related to his victim[2]. Again, to take another point of view, perhaps the saddest passage in Beowulf is that which relates how Herebald was accidentally killed by his brother Haethcyn. But the aspect of the case which first strikes the poet is not one which would appeal to a man of modern times. "That was a slaughter without compensation," he says (v. 2441 ff.), "the prince had to lose his life unavenged."

Yet, in spite of all this, instances of the slaying of kinsmen seem to have been by no means uncommon in the Heroic Age.

---

[1] Cf. *The Origin of the English Nation*, p. 327 ff.

[2] ξυγγενῆ γὰρ αὐτῷ τὸν φονέα εἶναι οὐ θέμις. Cf. Greg. Tur., II 40, where Clovis says: *nec enim possum sanguinem parentum meorum effundere, quod fieri nefas est.* But this is represented as mere hypocrisy; cf. II 41, *ad fin.*

In Beowulf the spokesman of the Danish kings, Unferth, is said
to have killed his brothers, and though the fact was a reproach to
him, it apparently did not prevent him from holding an important office at court. In the same poem we hear of dissensions
within the Swedish royal family, which ended in death for both
Onela and Eanmund. According to the legends preserved in
Ynglingatal this family had had a very bad record for such
quarrels in the past. Among the Goths we have the case of
Eormenric, who put his nephews Embrica and Fritla to death.
And it is by no means only in poetry or tradition that we meet
with such cases; historians also furnish numerous examples.
Thus according to Gregory of Tours (II 28) the Burgundian
king Hilperic was killed by his brother Gundobad, while Sigismund, son of the latter, had his own son, Sigiric, put to death
(III 5). The Thuringian king Irminfrith slew his brother Berht-
hari (III 4); the Frankish king Sigiberht was murdered by the
orders of his son Hlothric (II 40). Clovis is said to have put to
death a number of his relatives, while his sons and grandsons
were repeatedly involved in deadly strife[1].

In view of such evidence we must conclude that the primitive
sanctity of the family was giving way in the Heroic Age. For
the change of feeling which was taking place one passage in
Beowulf is particularly instructive. In the struggle between
Onela and Eanmund the latter was slain by one of the king's
knights named Weohstan. He stripped the dead man of his
arms and brought them to Onela who presented them to him
and "said nothing about that deed of guilt although it was
his brother's son whom he (Weohstan) had laid low[2]." To the
modern reader the poet's reflection seems strange; for Onela
had been relieved of a dangerous foe, who was trying to deprive
him of the kingdom. Yet there can be no doubt that according

[1] In some cases the deed was certainly done by the relative's own hand. Such
was the case with Lothair and the sons of Chlodomer (Greg. Tur., III 18).

[2] Beow. 2618 f.:

> no ymb ða faehðe spraec,
> þeah ðe he his broðor bearn abredwade.

Many scholars here understand ða faehðe to mean not the encounter between Eanmund
and Weohstan, but the hostility (vendetta) which devolved upon Onela as Eanmund's
kinsman; but I think the idea is rather that of 'bloodguiltiness' (towards Onela)
incurred by Weohstan. Eanmund was the son of Ohthere, Onela's brother.

to primitive tribal custom he ought to have taken vengeance upon his knight.

It is clear then that primitive custom was breaking down even in countries far removed from contact with Christianity and Roman civilisation. We cannot tell indeed how far the change was general, since our knowledge is practically limited to the princely families. It is by no means unlikely that the lower strata of society were more conservative in many respects.

The principle which had now become dominant, at least in the higher ranks, was that of personal allegiance. This principle was of course by no means new. Even in Tacitus' works we hear of the *comites* who lived and fought in their lord's service and thought it a disgrace to survive his death. In the Heroic Age however it is probable that among the more northern peoples every man, except the king himself, had a lord. In the Anglo-Saxon laws the lord shares with the kindred the duty of protecting his men, and when one of them is slain he receives a special payment (the *manbot*) when the wergeld was paid to the relatives. Also, when any of his men die, at all events a man of the higher classes, he is entitled to the heriot, i.e. the arms of the dead man, which in theory at least the latter had originally received from him[1].

But in the poems, as is natural, we hear most frequently of the knights who formed the courts and retinues of kings and princes. As a summary of the services rendered by such persons to their lord, Tacitus' brief description (*Germ.* 13) still holds good : their presence gave him dignity in time of peace and protection in war. They dwelt and served him at his court and joined him in hunting and other amusements, while he rewarded their services with gifts of treasure and arms. In the descriptions of kings which we meet with in the poems there is no characteristic—not even personal bravery—which receives more commendation than that of generosity to their followers. In return the knight was expected to give up to his lord whatever

---

[1] It may be observed that in Beow. 452 ff. the hero requests the Danish king to send his mail-coat to Hygelac, if he should be killed by Grendel. This mail-coat (described as Weland's handiwork) is said to have belonged formerly to Hrethel, Hygelac's father (Beowulf's grandfather).

he gained by his own exploits—just as Beowulf renders up to
Hygelac and his queen the valuable gifts which he had received
from the king of the Danes.   As an instance of personal devotion in time of war we may cite the surrender of Chonodomarius'
retinue at the battle of Strassburg—an incident to which we
have already referred (p. 340).   So also in the various accounts
of the fall of Hrólfr Kraki given by Scandinavian authorities
the king's knights are said to have perished to a man.   The
same spirit survived in England in later times, as we see from
the story of Cynewulf's death, when in each of the two encounters only one member of the defeated party was left alive.
It was also thoroughly in the spirit of the Heroic Age that
Edwin's knight, Lilla, acted when he threw himself between the
king and the assassin and received a mortal wound in so doing.

It was customary for the sons of noblemen to enter the
king's service at an early age.   Beowulf went to Hrethel's court
when he was only seven years old; but this case may have been
exceptional, as he was the king's grandson.   When they reached
manhood[1] the king was expected to provide them with estates
or jurisdiction over land, which would enable them to marry
and support a household of their own.   Thus Beowulf, after
proving his prowess at the Danish court, is presented by Hygelac
on his return with seven thousand hides—a considerable province—together with a residence and a prince's authority.   The
grant is accompanied by the gift of a sword, signifying that the
bond of personal allegiance was still preserved.   Beowulf in
turn presents his young relative Wiglaf with the dwelling-place
of their family and the public rights appertaining thereto.   The
court minstrels Widsith and Deor receive grants of land from
their lords.   In two of these cases (those of Wiglaf and Widsith)
we are told that the estate had previously been in the possession
of the recipient's father; and we may probably assume that such
cases were not uncommon.   Yet it is plain that such practices
must very largely have destroyed the tribal custom of succession—at least in the higher ranks of society.

---

[1] In the seventh century it appears to have been customary to make these grants
when the recipient was about twenty-four or twenty-five years old; cf. Bede, *Hist.*
Abb., §§ 1, 8; *Ep. ad Ecgb.*, § 11.

Those who had received grants of land or jurisdiction did not thereupon cease to attend the court.   In the English courts of the seventh century Bede distinguishes between the *comites*, who already held office, and the *ministri* or *milites*, who seem in general to have been young knights without such official positions.   The Anglo-Saxon version of the Ecclesiastical History translates *comes* by *gesið* and *minister* or *miles* by *þegn*.   In poetry both these words are of frequent occurrence, though they appear to be used more or less indiscriminately.   It should be observed that the word *þegn* means properly no more than 'servant[1]' though (like *knight* in later times) it came to be specialised, while *gesið* is almost an exact equivalent of *comes*[2]. In Beowulf however we meet with the same classes under the collective terms *geogoð* and *duguð*, i.e. youths and men of tried valour respectively.   To the latter may be assigned such persons as Aeschere, Hrothgar's "confidant and counsellor," who had stood by his side on the battlefield; but the former class were probably as a rule in the majority.

Another characteristic of these retinues, which deserves notice, is the fact that they were not always composed of born subjects of the king.   Bede (*H. E.* III 14) says that Oswine, the popular king of Deira, attracted young noblemen to his service from all sides; and in the Heroic Age such cases appear to have been frequent.   Perhaps the most striking case in the poems is that of Weohstan, who took service under the Swedish king Onela and consequently became involved in hostilities against his own nation.   It is probably due to the same custom that we find so many Teutonic chieftains serving under the Romans during the Heroic Age.   Among them we may mention Arbogastes, Stilicho, Ricimer and Odoacer.   Most frequently perhaps the men who sought service abroad were those who had either lost their lords or had had to leave their homes through vendetta.   Such cases occur frequently in the Anglo-Saxon poems; we may refer especially to the Wanderer and the

---

[1] We may compare the use of the word *sluga* in Servian heroic poetry (cf. p. 316); its ordinary meaning is 'servant.'

[2] The same word is used in a similar sense in the Langobardic laws; *gasindus* (or *gasindius*), 'Gefolgsmann,' and so also *gasindium*, 'Gefolgschaft'; cf. Bruckner, *Quellen und Forschungen*, LXXV p. 205.

Husband's Message. Further, it appears from the story of Waldhere and Hagena that even hostages were expected to fight for the prince to whom they had been given. In later times we may compare the case of the British hostage who was wounded in the fight following Cynewulf's murder. But there are a number of other stories which seem to indicate that it was at one time a regular custom for young princes to set out from their homes, on reaching manhood, and to seek the court of some foreign king with a view to marrying his daughter and thereby acquiring a share in the sovereignty. Such incidents are of the commonest occurrence in folktales; and we find them also in works, such as Hervarar Saga and Ynglinga Saga, which claim to be based on genuine tradition. It is in this light too that all northern authorities represent the position of Sigurðr at the home of Guðrún.

What has been said above applies primarily of course to the more northern peoples. The Goths were early exposed to Christian and Roman influence, and the same is true also of the Burgundians, especially after their settlement in Gaul. The Franks were no doubt less affected at first; but their customs seem from the beginning to have differed a good deal from those which we have been considering. They too had retinues of warriors (*antrustiones* or *homines in truste regis*) attached to the kings by personal service; but the prevalence of lordship in the lower ranks of society is by no means so clear. The possession of land also seems to have been governed at first by tribal principles and later by that of succession in the male line—without reference to the will of a superior. These differences are doubtless connected with certain features which distinguished the social organisation of the Franks from that of the other Teutonic peoples.

Every one of the early Teutonic nations possessed a more or less elaborate social system, with various class gradations. These gradations may be seen most clearly in the sums of money fixed for wergelds, for the compensations fixed for various injuries and insults and for fines; in some cases also they show themselves in the relative value attached to oaths. Apart from slaves, who do not come into consideration in these matters, the classes usually met with are those of nobles, freemen and freedmen. Sometimes however a class is subdivided; sometimes again one class is wanting altogether. Thus in the Anglo-Saxon king-doms, except Kent, there were two grades of nobility, apparently landowning and landless, while freedmen did not form a distinct class. Among the Franks on the other hand we find no noble class. In general the freeman's wergeld is about double that of the freedman, while that of the noble is twice or thrice as great as the former; and the other payments usually follow more or less the same proportion. The actual sums fixed in the various laws differ greatly in each case, owing to the employment of different systems of currency. But it may be regarded as extremely probable that the normal wergeld of the freeman was originally a hundred head of cattle. Some nations, further, had special wergelds for certain high officials. Among the Franks persons *in truste regis* had threefold wergelds, and the same applied to the ordinary freeman when engaged in military service. In England the existence of special official wergelds is uncertain, at least before the great Danish invasion, though such persons were entitled to higher compensations in other respects. But in this country members of the royal families had wergelds six times as great as those of the higher class of nobles.

All the above classes (excluding officials of course) seem to have been as a rule hereditary. In some nations indeed the descendants of freedmen did become freemen. But it is scarcely probable that this class everywhere consisted only of manu-mitted slaves or their offspring. Sometimes we find the terms *litus, latus, lazzus* (*laet* in the Kentish laws) in place of *libertus*; and there is good reason for believing that this class was largely derived from subject populations. Its numbers seem to have been very large. As to the numbers of the nobility there was apparently great difference between one nation and another. Among the Bavarians it consisted only of six families, including that of the duke, whereas in England it appears to have formed a considerable element in the population. The term applied to it here was *gesiðcund*, i.e. of *gesið* origin (cf. p. 350), which indi-cates clearly a hereditary official or rather military class. Indeed the evidence seems to show that the population consisted of two clearly defined classes, which we may describe as military and agricultural, and that all serious fighting was left to the former. This is another feature in which Anglo-Saxon custom differed from that of the Franks, whose armies in the sixth century appear to have been of a more truly national or even tribal character. With regard to the other nations we have less information; but it is probable that the military organisation of the Danes and other Baltic peoples approximated more nearly to the English type.

In Homeric society we find the same forces operative as in that of the Teutonic Heroic Age. The duty of protecting or avenging one's relatives is frequently mentioned. Thus in Od. XVI 97 f. the disguised Odysseus says to Telemachos: "Hast thou fault to find with thy brethren, for it is in them that a man trusts to do battle, even if a great quarrel takes place?" Telemachos replies (v. 115 ff.): "Nor have I fault to find with my brethren, in whom a man trusts to do battle, even if a great quarrel takes place. For our family has been reduced to one man by the son of Cronos, as I will tell thee. Arceisios begat one only son Laertes, and Odysseus again was the only son begotten by his father; but Odysseus begat me only and left me in his palace without profit to himself. Hence there are now innumerable enemies in our house."

The duty of vengeance is clearly recognised by Nestor in Od. III 196 ff.: "How good a thing it is for even a dead man's child to survive! For he (Orestes) also took vengeance on his father's slayer, the crafty Aigisthos, who killed his famous father." It was in order to escape such a fate that Theoclymenos besought Telemachos to take him on his ship (*ib.* XV 272 ff.): "I also have left my country, having killed a man of my own tribe (or 'people'). And in Argos, the pastureland of horses, he had many brethren and kinsmen who hold great authority among the Achaeans. I have taken to flight and so evaded death and black fate at their hands; for it is still my lot to wander among men. Now take me on thy ship, since I have come to thee as a fugitive and suppliant, lest they kill me outright; for I am sure they are in pursuit." We are reminded here of the story of Ecgtheo, the father of Beowulf, who fled for protection to the Danish king Hrothgar owing to a similar cause (Beow. 459 ff.). Another case of such exile occurs in Il. XIII 695 ff. (XV 334 ff.): "He (Medon) dwelt in Phylace, away from his own fatherland; for he had slain a man, the kinsman of his stepmother Eriopis, whom Oileus had to wife." We may compare also Il. XV 430 ff. where Hector slays "Lycophron, the son of Mastor, the Cytherian squire of Aias, who dwelt with him; for he had slain a man in divine Cythera."

Among the Homeric Greeks, as in northern Europe, compensation for manslaughter could be made to the dead man's relatives. Thus in Il. IX 632 ff. Aias says to Achilles: "And yet one accepts compensation from a man who has slain one's brother or for the death of a son. Hence it comes to pass that the one, when he has paid a large compensation, remains in his own land, while the other, after he has accepted the compensation, restrains his feelings and his proud spirit." Again, in the description of Achilles' shield we find a scene (*ib.* XVIII 497 ff.) representing a dispute over the payment of a wergeld. "The folk were gathered in the assembly place; for there a strife was arisen, two men striving about the blood-price of a man slain; the one claimed to pay full atonement, expounding to the people, but the other denied him and would take naught; and both were fain to receive arbitrament at the hand of a daysman[1]." In this case the transaction takes place before certain elders, one of whom is to receive a payment of two talents, apparently as a reward for bringing about an agreement. There is no mention of any payment to the king[2].

From the passage relating to Theoclymenos quoted above (v. 273: πολλοὶ κασίγνητοί τε ἔται τε) we may probably infer that the duty of vengeance extended beyond the brothers of the slain man; and evidence to the same effect is given by the story of Tlepolemos (Il. II 661 ff.). But it is not at all clear how many degrees of relationship were either involved in this duty or entitled to compensation. Indeed the poems give us very little

---

[1] Quoted from the translation by Lang, Leaf and Myers.
[2] The interpretation of Hesiod, *W. and D.* 38 f., need not be discussed here.

information regarding the character of the kindred. Patronymic forms such as Ἀτρείδης[1] are very common and correspond in use to Anglo-Saxon forms such as *Hreðling, Wonreding.* But they are almost always used of individuals or of a pair of brothers (Ἀτρείδα, δοιοὶ Ἱππασίδαι). Collective names for families, such as Ἡρακλείδαι, Πελοπίδαι, seem not to occur in the Homeric poems[2]. Indeed the patronymic is nearly always derived from the name of the father. Cases where they are taken from the grandfather's name, e.g. Αἰακίδης for Achilles, appear to be quite exceptional. This is a feature in which Homeric usage differs not only from Teutonic but also, still more, from that of later times in Greece, where we frequently find families or kindreds bearing patronymic names derived from a remote ancestor. As examples we may mention the Aigeidai at Sparta and the Philaidai at Athens.

But the difference between Homeric and later usage in this respect does not seem to be one of nomenclature only. At Athens we find later an elaborate system of 'tribes' (φυλαί), phratries or 'clans' (φράτραι) and 'kindreds' (γένη), of which the last at all events were supposed to rest on a basis of blood-relationship, involving common religious rites. Divisions of a more or less similar type seem to have existed in the other Greek states. In the Homeric poems however we find extremely little evidence for anything of this kind. The clearest case is in Il. II 362 f., where Nestor instructs Agamemnon as follows: "Divide thy men according to tribes and clans, Agamemnon, that clan may render succour to clan and tribe to tribe[3]." In the battle scenes we hear little of any such organisation, though this may be due to the fact that attention is entirely concentrated upon the leaders. But it is worth noting that the word

---

[1] The other types (e.g. Πηλείων, Τελαμώνιος) are less frequent.

[2] Καδμεῖοι, Καδμείωνες are at best very dubious examples, for Cadmos is probably to be regarded as an eponymous national hero, like Dardanos.

[3]
      κρῖν᾽ ἄνδρας κατὰ φῦλα, κατὰ φρήτρας, Ἀγάμεμνον,
      ὡς φρήτρη φρήτρηφιν ἀρήγῃ, φῦλα δὲ φύλοις.

Cf. Tacitus, *Germ.* 7: *quodque praecipuum fortitudinis incitamentum est, non casus nec fortuita conglobatio turmam aut cuneum facit sed familiae et propinquitates.* But the context shows that the conditions here are of a totally different character from those in the Iliad.

φρήτρη occurs only in this passage[1]. Again, φυλή does not occur at all, except possibly in the form καταφυλαδόν (Il. II 668), while φῦλον is a word of very vague significance, ranging from φῦλα ἀνθρώπων etc. to the φῦλον Ἀρκεισίου, i.e. the descendants of a man whose son is still alive[2]. The same is true also of γένος. Lastly, there is no evidence for any religious rites peculiar to certain families or clans.

It would be rash of course to conclude from this that the clan and family system of later times was unknown in the age of the poems; for in itself it bears every mark of antiquity. But there must be some reason for the neglect with which it is treated in the poems. If we examine individual cases we find that scarcely any heroes claim an ancestry of more than three generations. The Achaean families with the longest history are those of Agamemnon and Odysseus; but, if we are to believe post-Homeric tradition, the former changed its territories after the time of Pelops.

This brings us to the question of succession. In Ithaca the throne seems to pass in the regular paternal line; and, though there is really no king after the retirement of Laertes, it is generally expected that the young Telemachos will eventually take his place (Od. I 386 f., II 14). Similarly Nestor has succeeded his father Neleus, while Idomeneus apparently occupies the throne formerly held by his father's father, Minos. On the other hand, according to the story told by Glaucos (Il. VI 192 f.), Bellerophon, a stranger, received half the kingly rights in Lycia with the hand of the king's daughter. Moreover all post-Homeric authorities agree that Menelaos received the throne of Sparta by marriage, from his father-in-law Tyndareos. Similar stories are told of Tydeus, Telamon, Peleus, Teucros and many others[3]. It is to be observed that, though these stories do not occur in the Iliad and Odyssey, they do not conflict with any evidence to be found there. Many of them

---

[1] But cf. Il. IX 63, where the word ἀφρήτωρ occurs, apparently with reference to the same institution.

[2] The meaning of the word ἔμφυλον in Od. XV 273 seems to be quite ambiguous.

[3] Cf. Frazer, *Lectures on the Early History of the Kingship*, p. 238 ff. The story of Peleus and Eurytion bears rather a close resemblance to that of Bellerophon.

can be traced back to the seventh century, indeed probably to the eighth.

If we are to trust post-Homeric authorities it would seem that the wife remained in her parents' home quite as often as she went to that of her husband. This state of things however points to the prevalence of a cognatic organisation of society. In the case of Bellerophon indeed there can scarcely be any doubt; for the Lycians reckoned descent through the mother down to the time of Herodotus. The historian himself (I 173) remarks on the custom as strange and without parallel elsewhere —from which we may probably infer that it had disappeared altogether from Greece before his time. Yet in one Greek community we have evidence almost as explicit. According to Polybius, XII 5, the Epizephyrian Locrians stated that with them all ancestral honours were derived from women and not from men, and that even then (i.e. in the second century) their nobility traced their descent from certain women of 'the hundred families,' who had taken part in the foundation of the colony. 'The hundred families' were those which before this time had been selected by the Locrians (i.e. the Hypocnemidian Locrians) as the families from which they were to choose the virgins who were to be sent to Ilion. This story seems to imply that cognatic organisation survived in Locris down to the beginning of the seventh century[1]. In other states[2], so far as I am aware, we find only traces of the former existence of such an institution. Some of these however suggest that the change may not have been of any very great antiquity[3].

The Homeric poems themselves contain some further evidence, which points in the same direction. We may note that a number of heroes are said to be sons of gods. But it can hardly be without significance that the Lycian prince Sarpedon (daughter's son of Bellerophon) is the only son of Zeus, who belongs to the story of the Trojan war, whereas in the earlier

---

[1] It is to be borne in mind that the Epizephyrian Locrians were one of the first, if not the very first, of all Greek communities to obtain a codification of their laws—probably indeed within half a century of the establishment of the colony. This fact may perhaps account for the survival of primitive institutions among them.

[2] Except perhaps in Cos; but the evidence here is ambiguous.

[3] Cf. Ridgeway, *The Origin of Tragedy*, p. 190 ff.

generations examples are comparatively common. In post-Homeric genealogies the succession of son to father seems to become less frequent the farther one goes back.

In regard to marriage customs the poems show a remarkable absence of uniformity. The story of Bellerophon is by no means the only case in which the wife remains at home, even if we leave out of account such marriages as those of Menelaos and Tydeus, upon which the poems themselves are silent. Alcinoos proposes a union of this kind to Odysseus (Od. VII 311 ff.)[1], and the wife of Iphidamas the son of Antenor appears to remain with her father (Il. XI 225 f.). On the whole however the other type seems to be decidedly more common. Then we have to take into account the use of the word ἔεδνα. It is commonly held that this originally denoted the 'bride-price,' paid by the bride-groom to the relatives of the bride; and there is no doubt that the word is so used in several passages. In others however it may at least equally well denote presents made to the bride herself; occasionally indeed it appears to mean presents (i.e. a dowry) given by the bride's parents. By far the most prominent case of course is that of Penelope; and here the question is com-plicated apparently by a doubt as to the proper person entitled to bestow the bride—who is presumed to be a widow. Some-times the decision seems to rest with her son, Telemachos, sometimes with her father—never with Laertes; but in the end she takes the matter into her own hands, after exacting presents for herself from all the suitors. It has been well suggested[2] that the ambiguity in the situation is due to a real change of custom. But I am by no means convinced that the ancient custom, now being superseded, was one of real purchase. It is made fairly clear (Od. I 396 ff., XV 518 ff., XXII 49 ff., etc.) that at least some of the suitors have ulterior objects in view. That the throne should be conveyed through Penelope seems to us no doubt il-logical; for Odysseus himself had not acquired it by his marriage.

---

[1] The nature of Agamemnon's proposal to Achilles in Il. IX 144 ff. (286 ff.) is not quite clear. Achilles is to choose one of Agamemnon's daughters and take her to Peleus' home. But with her Agamemnon is to give seven cities, situated apparently in Messenia, which in future are to be subject to Achilles. Possibly v. 149 is to be understood as introducing a new (alternative) proposal.

[2] Cf. Cauer, *Grundfragen d. Homerkritik*[2], p. 292 ff.

But, if we are right in believing that the type of marriage represented in the story of Bellerophon is earlier than the other, the situation depicted in the Odyssey is one for which ancient custom could not have made provision; indeed in such a situation traditional feeling might very well incline towards regarding the queen, even though a stranger, as the proper channel for conveying the succession. Add to this the practical consideration that Penelope is apparently the person actually in command of the treasury; and we have no reason, so far as I am aware, for doubting that treasury and kingdom were as closely bound up together in Heroic Greece as they were in the Heroic Age of the northern peoples[1]. It has often been remarked that the position of women in the Homeric poems appears to be one of greater influence and responsibility than anything we find in later times. But nowhere is this responsibility made so clear as in the absence of all evidence for the constitution of a regency when the king is away from home.

If the view put forward above is correct we must conclude that a change had been taking place in the organisation of society, and indeed that it was as yet by no means complete[2]. We have noticed that the conditions seem to have been somewhat similar in the Heroic Age of the Teutonic peoples. But we saw also that there the change was apparently accompanied by a relaxation in the bonds of kinship, which shows itself especially in fatal strife between relatives. The same phenomenon

[1] We may compare Beow. 2369 ff., where—in a situation somewhat analogous to that of the Odyssey—Hygelac's widowed queen offers both treasury and kingdom to the chief surviving prince, distrusting the ability of her young son to hold his own.

[2] That the type of organisation which prevailed during the growth of Homeric poetry was agnatic may be inferred from the regular use of the word πάτρη and the (probably older) expression πατρὶς γαῖα, which perhaps originally denoted 'land of one's father' (the *faeder eðel* of Widsith, v. 96). But according to Plato (*Republic*, 575 D) the Cretans used μητρίς for πατρίς. Evidence for the prevalence of cognatic organisation in early times is furnished by certain words denoting relationship, especially ἀδελφός (originally 'uterine brother'), and a relic of the feeling that this form of relationship was closer seems to be preserved in Il. XXI 95. We may also take into account the formation of patronymics in -ιδᾱ, which appear to be extended from the feminine suffix -ιδ- by another suffix (-ᾱ-) also properly feminine. In the north-western dialects these names were declined as feminines (e.g. N. sg. Εχσοιδα, G. sg. Προκλειδας). One can hardly help suspecting that these names belonged originally to genealogies of the Lycian type.

appears in the Homeric poems.   Thus according to Il. II 662 f.
Tlepolemos slew his father's mother's brother, Licymnios, and
had to leave his country in consequence.   Among Achilles'
followers (*ib.* XVI 570 ff.) was a certain Epeigeus who had taken
refuge with Peleus because he had killed a cousin or kinsman
(ἀνεψιός) in his own city.   Again in Il. IX 566 f. it is at least
implied that Meleagros slew his mother's brothers (in accordance
with the story found later).   In the same speech (V 458 ff.)
Phoinix confesses that he had been on the point of killing his
own father.   Then there is the tragic history of the house of
Pelops.   The facts stated in the Odyssey are that Aigisthos
slew Agamemnon, his father's brother's son, and that Orestes,
the son of Agamemnon, eventually slew Aigisthos.   The most
important feature in this story is that here we have not only
homicide but also vengeance within the kindred.   It is not
actually stated that Orestes slew his mother; but from Od. III
310 we may infer at least that she perished at the same time
as Aigisthos.   This is one of the cases in which I suspect that
disagreeable incidents connected with royal families have been
suppressed (cf. p. 238).   Later authorities add many more instances of homicide within the kindred.   Some of these, such as
the 'banquet of Thyestes,' bear a close resemblance to Teutonic
stories which we know to be unhistorical.   Others again may
have been invented to account for the presence of heroes in
districts far from their native place.   Yet from the fact that this
motive is so frequently employed we may conclude that the
murder of relatives was nothing very rare.

In this respect then the Greek evidence agrees entirely with
the Teutonic.   In both cases alike the bonds of kinship seem to
have lost their force to a great extent[1].   But it is to be remembered that among the Teutonic peoples we have in general
no evidence except for the families of kings and royal officials;
in other ranks of society the kindred may have retained much

---

[1] It is possibly due to the same cause that we meet with some curious marriages.
Thus Alcinoos is married to his brother's daughter, and Iphidamas to his mother's
sister.   The former case offends against the principle of agnatic organisation, the latter
against the cognatic.   Some other heroes (e.g. Diomedes) seem to be in somewhat
similar positions.

more vitality—as indeed the laws seem to imply. Such may also have been the case in Greece; for the Homeric poems are concerned almost exclusively with persons of princely rank. Certainly the strength and sanctity possessed by the kindred in early historical times is most easily to be explained on the supposition that the tendency which we have been discussing affected only a limited element in society[1].

The second of the two principles which we find dominant in early Teutonic society, namely that of personal allegiance, seems at first sight to play by no means so important a part in the life of heroic Greece. But for the lack of prominence assigned to it there are special reasons—a different reason in the case of each poem. In the Iliad, which deals with campaign life, the stage is so crowded with kings that there is little room left for persons of humbler station. The only force indeed of which we have any account at all is that of Achilles. This was divided into five troops, each under a leader of its own, in addition to Patroclos and Automedon. We saw in the last chapter that the speech in which Patroclos exhorts his men to battle is entirely in the spirit of the Teutonic *comitatus*. The appeal which he makes to them is not to any feeling of patriotism, but entirely to the effect that they should show their devotion to their own lord. We may note that several of the chief men, at all events Patroclos, Automedon and Phoinix, seem to share Achilles' hut. The passionate friendship of Achilles and Patroclos appears to be a stronger bond than any other relationship that we meet with in the Homeric poems. But even if we set this on one side as something exceptional, the devotion shown to Achilles by Phoinix is quite in accordance with the best traditions of Teutonic thegnship.

The Odyssey presents us with the picture of a king's house in time of peace. But, though Penelope has not less than fifty women in the house, the only men apparently, besides the suitors and their followers, are Telemachos himself, the herald Medon and the minstrel Phemios, together with the swineherd, neatherd and goatherd who come with provisions each day from a distance.

---

[1] The Locrian case quoted above (p. 357) suggests that the kindreds may, sometimes at least, have been organised on a cognatic basis.

But the conditions here are abnormal; the king himself has been away from home for many years, and his son is only just reaching manhood. It is scarcely credible that a Teutonic *comitatus* could have existed under such conditions. Menelaos appears to have something of a retinue at his court. In IV 22 f. we hear of a θεράπων named Eteoneus, who seems to be a person of some rank, as he is called κρείων. In V. 216 f. another θεράπων, Asphalion, is mentioned, while v. 37 f. speak of several of such persons, though their number is not stated. All that is said of them seems to indicate that their position was much the same as that of the thegns in early Teutonic courts. The picture of the Phaeacian court also bears a general resemblance to that of the Danish court as described in Beowulf.

The use of the word θεράπων appears to correspond almost exactly to that of *þegn*[1]. In both cases the general meaning is 'servant'; but, just as we find Beowulf described as *Hygelaces þegn*, so in the Iliad the term θεράπων is applied to such distinguished persons as Meriones and Patroclos. The converse term ἄναξ also seems to correspond almost as closely to the English *dryhten*. Like the latter it is used for the master of a slave (e.g. Od. XV 557), while on the other hand it is applied, again like *dryhten*, to the most important kings—and even deities— in relation to all who recognise their authority. We have already noticed (p. 329) that the phrase ἄναξ ἀνδρῶν seems to correspond very closely to the English phrase *eorla dryhten*.

There is little or no evidence to show whether it was customary for the sons of leading men to be brought up at the king's court. Patroclos was declared to be the θεράπων of Achilles at an early age (Il. XXIII 89 f.); but the circumstances were exceptional. Certainly the θεράποντες often came from beyond the king's dominions. Thus Patroclos had come from Opus (*ib.* XXIII 85 ff.) and Lycophron, Aias' squire, from Cythera (*ib.* XV 430 f.). It is true that both these persons had had to leave their homes owing to homicides which they had committed; and no doubt many such cases were due to circumstances which rendered a change of abode advisable. Thus

[1] There is a certain amount of parallelism also between ἑταῖρος and *gesið* (cf. p. 350). But the former has scarcely the same technical significance as the latter.

Phoinix had sought the protection of Peleus owing to a deadly quarrel with his father. Yet apart from such emergencies the protection and friendship of a wealthy and powerful king probably offered considerable attractions. We may refer to a somewhat remarkable passage in the Odyssey (IV 174 ff.), where Menelaos says that it had been his wish to bring Odysseus to his own country, with his son and his followers and possessions, adding that in order to make a home for him he would have ejected the inhabitants from one of the neighbouring cities which were under his lordship.

Menelaos' intention seems to have been to put Odysseus in the position of a dependent prince. We have seen that Teutonic kings were in the habit of rewarding their knights with grants of jurisdiction; and the same appears to have been the case with the kings of Homeric times. Thus in Il. IX 483 f. Phoinix says that Peleus had made him rich and granted him many followers, and that he had made his dwelling in a frontier district as lord over the Dolopes. This passage seems to furnish almost an exact parallel to the treatment of Beowulf by Hygelac (cf. p. 349). A similar case perhaps was that of Medon, the son of Oileus, who according to Il. II 727 commanded the forces from Methone and the adjacent districts, in the absence of Philoctetes, and who, like Phoinix, was a fugitive from his native land (cf. XIII 695 ff.). Here too we may mention the case of Phyleus, who had left his own country and gone to Dulichion owing to a quarrel with his father (ib. II 629), and whose son Meges commanded the forces from that island. In many such cases of course there may have been a marriage with a princess of the native royal family; but it is hardly necessary to assume that this was universal. In the case of Phoinix indeed such an assumption is improbable.

There seems to be no actual record of a Homeric hero who left his home except under stress of circumstances; and hence, after making all deductions, we are bound, I think, to conclude that the system of the *comitatus* was not so highly developed as in the north of Europe. This is in full conformity with the fact that kingly families were apparently much more numerous. Among the suitors of Penelope twelve princes belong to Ithaca alone, an island of no great size and probably never thickly populated[1].

For a class of nobility distinct from the princely families we have no clear evidence[2]. Persons like Eteoneus, the squire of Menelaos, may belong to such a class; but it is quite possible that they are princes. We may refer also to the false story told by Odysseus in Od. XIII 256 ff., from which it appears that chiefs with small followings might be expected to place themselves in the position of θεράποντες to more powerful chiefs. But Odysseus does not here make clear what rank he claims to have possessed in Crete. Quite possibly the practice referred to might be somewhat analogous to what we find in the Saga of Harold the Fair-haired, where a number of petty kings submit to Harold and take the rank of earls.

The same want of definiteness occurs in regard to the humbler ranks of society. Even the slave's status is not made particularly clear, while there is no reference to the existence of freedmen or to the practice of manumission[3]. Slaves are apparently able to buy other slaves on their own account (cf. Od. XIV 449 ff.). In other respects however their position seems to be very similar to that of slaves in early Teutonic society[4]. Still less do we hear of differences of rank or status within the free population[5]. But it should be observed that the Anglo-Saxon poems give us no more information on such matters. Were it not for the early laws and foreign authorities

---

[1] Assuming the Homeric Ithaca to be identical with the Ithaca of later times. If 'Same' is the later Ithaca, the number of suitors furnished by this island is twenty-four.

[2] Cf. Fanta, *Der Staat in der Ilias und Odyssee*, p. 26 f., where a distinction is drawn between higher and lower nobility—the βασιλῆες being only a portion of the ἀριστῆες; but the evidence seems to me inconclusive.

[3] Yet the promise made by Odysseus to the herdsmen in Od. XXI 213 ff. may perhaps be analogous to the change of status involved when a Teutonic slave was made a freedman.

[4] In both cases the household slaves seem to have been almost entirely women, who were occupied for the most part in grinding corn.

[5] From Od. IV 644 and VI 489 f. it seems probable on the whole that there existed a class of landless freemen corresponding to the Ang.-Sax. *geburas*. But no information apparently is given with regard to the κλῆρος—whether it corresponded at all to the hide of the *gafolgelda* (roughly comparable with the Athenian ζευγίτης) or whether it represented normally a much larger estate.

we should know nothing of the distinction between land-holding and landless peasants, nor even of the great classes of noble, freeman, slave, etc. The true explanation seems to be that both sets of poems alike are interested only in persons of royal rank.

No light is thrown on the social system by the passages which mention the payment of wergelds; for we are not informed whether these were fixed by custom or whether they formed the subject of bargaining in each individual case. In Il. XXI 79 f. Lycaon says that Achilles had sold him into Lemnos for a hundred oxen and that he had been ransomed from thence for three hundred. Even the smaller of these sums is of course much too great for an ordinary slave's price. In the light of Teutonic custom it is possible that both represent standard wergelds, regarded as man-values in general; but one can hardly say that it is more than a possibility. The silence of the poems upon this subject is nothing surprising, for the Teutonic poems yield us no more information.

We may now briefly summarise the results of this discussion. The salient characteristic of the Heroic Age, both in Greece and in northern Europe, appears to be the disintegration of the bonds of kinship, a process which shows itself chiefly in the prevalence of strife between relatives, and which in both cases is probably connected with a change in the organisation of the kindred—agnatic relationship having come gradually to take the place of cognatic. How far this process affected society as a whole we cannot tell, since our evidence is generally limited to the royal families. The binding force formerly possessed by kinship was now largely transferred to the relationship between 'lord' and 'man' (*dryhten—þegn, ἄναξ—θεράπων*), between whom no bond of blood-relationship was necessary. The *comitatus* was probably not developed in Greece to the same extent as it was in northern Europe; indeed in regard to social development generally the conditions in Greece seem to have been more primitive. Yet in individual cases the bond between lord and man was apparently the strongest force of which we know.

CHAPTER XVII.

GOVERNMENT IN THE HEROIC AGE.

DURING the Heroic Age of the Teutonic peoples kingship appears to have been practically universal. The Old Saxons may have formed a solitary exception to the general rule; but our knowledge of this people really begins only towards the close of the seventh century.

Much has been written about the various powers possessed by the kings, but it is still by no means clear what they could not do, so long as they had a powerful and contented body of personal followers. If they forfeited the allegiance of their retinues by violence or outrage their power of course was gone at once. In the course of the eighth century several English kings were killed or expelled by their retinues; and in Beowulf (v. 902 ff.; cf. v. 1709 ff.) we hear that a former king of the Danes named Heremod had met with a similar fate. But in early times such cases do not seem to have been common. Again, the numbers of the retinue might decrease through want of generosity or excessive love of peace on the king's part, and he would then be exposed to the attack of any aggressive neighbour or of some member of his own family whom he had offended. The only definite statement however which we possess regarding a limitation of the king's authority is a passage in Ammianus Marcellinus' history (XXVIII 5. 14) referring to the Burgundians — before their conversion — according to which kings were regularly deposed as a consequence of unsuccessful war or famine. The context, though not plainly expressed, seems to suggest that this deposition was carried out by the decision or through the agency of a high-priest whose authority was permanent.

The statement that the kings of the Burgundians were deposed on account of famine points to the survival of a primitive idea of kingship, which credited the ruler with superhuman powers. The kings of the Swedes also, according to Ynglinga Saga, cap. 47, were believed to have control over the seasons[1], like the god Frey from whom they claimed descent; and it is said that two of them were sacrificed in times of famine. In the same saga, cap. 20, it is stated that the members of this dynasty individually were called Yngvi, a name of the ancestral god[2]—which seems to indicate that they were regarded as his representatives. How far such ideas were general during the Heroic Age it is impossible to say, owing to the fact that we have few records dating in their present form from heathen times. Note may be taken however of the peculiar position occupied by the later Merovingian kings[3]. During the last century of their existence as a dynasty their power was entirely taken from them and transferred to a viceroy (commonly known as *maior domus*)—whose office became practically hereditary in one family. The only duties which were retained by the kings were certain ceremonial functions, which point to a more or less sacral character, so far as was possible in a Christian community. We may note further that in the North there is no evidence for a specifically priestly class; temporal and spiritual power were apparently united in the same person. Among the Angli on the other hand there was such a class, though, in contrast with the Burgundians, the high-priest seems to have been subordinate to the king[4].

---

[1] For analogies to this belief cf. Frazer, *Lectures on the Early History of the Kingship*, p. 112 ff. Especially interesting parallels are to be found in the region of the Congo; cf. Pinkerton, *Voyages and Travels*, Vol. XVI. pp. 330, 577.

[2] Frequently used in poetry. The god's full name seems to have been Yngvifreyr or Ingunarfreyr, both of which occur occasionally (cf. *The Origin of the English Nation*, p. 231).

[3] We may compare Ibn Fadhlan's account of the king of the (Scandinavian) Russians, who never put his foot to the ground. His duties also were discharged by a viceroy. Cf. Frähn, *Ibn Foszlan's und anderer Araber Berichte über die Russen älterer Zeit*, pp. 21, 23.

[4] The priesthood figures very prominently in Tacitus' *Germania*. But it is not safe to assume that the conditions described there are necessarily more primitive than those which we find in much later times in the North.

In Sweden there was a form of election for kings, which may have had a religious significance. The electors (the lawman and twelve others from each province) stood on huge stones (Morastenar), fixed in the earth, which may still be seen at Hammarby near Upsala. Saxo (p. 10 f.) records the former existence of a similar custom in Denmark. On the other hand the Frankish custom of hoisting a new king on a shield probably meant no more than a proclamation of lordship, as may be seen from the first recorded instance[1]. Whatever the formalities employed, it appears that in practice the reigning king was usually able to secure the succession for his son; but failing such the nearest male relative acceptable to the court would normally be chosen[2]. It was not an unknown thing even for minors to succeed[3]. Frequently we find the kingdom shared by two or more brothers, just like any other property; and on the death of one of them his son was sometimes allowed to take his place, as in the well-known case of Hrothgar and Hrothwulf. On the other hand the survivor might, and apparently often did, refuse any such concession; and consequently struggles between relatives for the possession of the throne were of not infrequent occurrence.

National or tribal assemblies figure prominently in Tacitus' account of the ancient Germans, and among several of the Continental Teutonic peoples they survived down to the seventh or eighth century. At this time they were generally held in the early spring—whence the name *Campus Martius* applied to the assembly of the Franks. After the adoption of Christianity however they had come to be little more than military reviews for the most part, though at the same time a meeting of dignitaries, lay and ecclesiastical, was held for the transaction of business. In much later times we meet with national assemblies

---

[1] Tacitus, *Hist.*, IV 15.

[2] Among the Ostrogoths during their war with the Romans (from 535 onwards) we meet with several kings of non-royal birth; but the conditions were altogether abnormal. One king (Eraric) was a Rugian and appointed apparently by his own followers.

[3] E.g. Athalaric the grandson of Theodric and Walthari the son of Waccho, king of the Langobardi. Aethelberht, king of Kent, must have succeeded as a child. Heardred, the son of Hygelac, is represented as very young.

in the North also, especially in Sweden, and there can be little
doubt that these had long been in existence. They were used
by the kings for the purpose of publishing proclamations, and
at the same time they presented an opportunity for coercing or
overthrowing a king who had aroused popular resentment in
any way. But they appear to have been primarily religious
gatherings, for the great annual sacrifices at the chief national
sanctuary. It is more than probable however that such was the
case also with the assemblies of the ancient Germans[1]. At all
events there is nothing to show that, apart from special emergencies, they met more than once, or possibly twice, in the year.
In England evidence seems to be altogether wanting for any
assemblies which could properly be called national; nor do we
find any reference to such an institution in the poems.

It is true that we hear not unfrequently of discussions and
deliberations in works dating from the Heroic Age. But
although precise information as to the size and constitution of
these meetings is seldom given, they appear to be those of
comparatively small bodies, similar to the royal councils of the
Anglo-Saxon kingdoms. The latter however were nothing more
than meetings of the court from the earliest times to which our
records go back. When important questions were discussed
care may have been taken to summon all the leading men; and
no doubt age and high rank ensured priority of hearing, as in
the assemblies of Tacitus' day. But still they remained essentially
meetings of the king's personal dependents. So far as I am
aware, there is no reason for supposing that gatherings like that
described by Procopius (*Vand.* I 22), when Genseric received the
embassy from his compatriots in Europe, differed in any way
from the meeting called by Edwin in 625 to discuss the adoption
of Christianity. Often indeed the persons present are described
as οἱ λόγιμοι or λογιμώτατοι. Again, in Beowulf we hear more
than once of Danish councillors (*witan Scyldinga*), but there
is nothing to show that these were a different body from the
members of the court who entertained Beowulf; and it is clear
from vv. 778 ff., 936 ff. that their meetings were held in the same
building. The old and distinguished councillor who persuaded

---

[1] Cf. especially Tacitus, *Germ.* 39; *Ann.* I 51.

Genseric to reject the petition of the envoys would seem to have been just such another person as Aeschere, Hrothgar's trusted adviser (cf. p. 350). In the story of Hermegisklos and Radiger also (cf. p. 97 f.) it is clear that the same 'distinguished men of the nation' (οἱ λόγιμοι, λογιμώτατοι) act both as companions of the old king and advisers of his young successor.

In spite of what has been said above there is some evidence for the existence of councils consisting of a fixed number of men, namely twelve, whose position may have differed somewhat from that of the ordinary members of the court[1]. The Old Saxons had a council of twelve which met annually at a place called Marklo, on the Weser; but this case stands by itself, as the Old Saxons had no king. In Sweden however we meet with such councils both in tradition and in historical times, and what we know of them indicates that they were composed of the chief men. Moreover councils of twelve for judicial purposes occur both in provinces and small districts in various parts of the Scandinavian peninsula, as well as in the Scandinavian settlements in the British Isles. The gods too were credited with possessing a council of twelve which had both judicial and sacrificial duties[2]—a fact which is interesting as it points to a connection between the councils of which we have been speaking and bodies of twelve with sacrificial duties, of which we hear in stories relating to heathen times. If we take into account the legend of the twelve Frisian judges (*asegen*) and the fact that councils of twelve are known to have existed among the Celts and other European peoples, we can scarcely doubt that this type is of great antiquity. Yet there is nothing to show that such councils were at all general during the Heroic Age; in England they seem to be entirely unknown before the period of Scandinavian influence. It is probable therefore that in this, as in other respects, the Swedes had preserved an institution which other kingdoms had discarded.

From the stories quoted above we see that it was customary for the king to consult his council or court when any question involving difficulty or danger arose; and there can be little doubt

---

[1] For references see *Folk-Lore*, XI, pp. 280, 282 f., 300.
[2] Cf. especially Gylf. 14, Yngl. S. 2, Gautreks S. 7.

that he would feel his position strengthened by so doing. But we have no reason for supposing that the opinion of the council possessed anything more than moral force; and consequently it would depend upon the king's strength of character or the security of his position whether he felt himself bound to follow their advice or not. Procopius (*Goth.* I 2) states that Amalaswintha was coerced by the leading men of the Goths with regard to her son's education; but she was only a regent at this time. Again, in another passage (*ib.* IV 27) he relates how Hildigisl, a claimant to the Langobardic throne, fled for refuge to Thorisin (Turisindus), king of the Gepidae. Audoin, king of the Langobardi, demanded that he should be given up; and his request was supported by Justinian. Thorisin consulted his distinguished men (οἱ λόγιμοι), but they replied that it would be better for the whole nation of the Gepidae to perish than to commit such an act of sacrilege. The king now, says Procopius, felt himself to be in a great difficulty. For he could not carry out what was demanded against the will of his subjects, and at the same time he was afraid to go to war against the Romans and Langobardi. So he contrived to get the fugitive murdered secretly, obtaining a *quid pro quo* in the murder of one of his own rivals. It must be observed that Thorisin himself had obtained the throne by violence. So the young Radiger, when he was captured and brought before the English princess, pleaded that he had been forced to renounce his promise to her by his father's commands and the insistence of the leading men (τὴν τῶν ἀρχόντων σπουδήν). Genseric on the other hand dismissed the envoys in accordance with the old councillor's advice; but we are told that both of them were ridiculed by the rest of the Vandals for so doing. Plainly then there was no question of having to follow the opinion of the majority.

It might naturally be expected that the authority of the council would make itself felt most on the occasion of the king's death; and the story of Radiger seems to bear this out. Yet it is worth noticing what is recorded in Beowulf on an occasion of great emergency. Hygelac, king of the Geatas, lost his life in the disastrous expedition against the Frisians and left an only son, Heardred, who seems to have been scarcely more than a

child. Beowulf escaped from the slaughter, and on his return
(v. 2369 ff.) " Hygd offered him the treasury and the government,
the rings and the throne. She trusted not that her child would
be able to hold his patrimony against foreign nations, now that
Hygelac was dead." There is no reference to any action on
the part of the council or court; but the queen offers the throne
to the late king's nephew. The whole passage seems to indicate
that the throne with all its rights was regarded very much like
any ordinary family property. Its disposition is arranged by
the family itself, without any notion of responsibility to others;
and the members of the court are not taken into account any
more than the servants in a private household.

It may perhaps be argued that court poets would be apt to
exaggerate the power of the royal family and consequently
that the picture of its authority given here is misleading. Yet
Amalaswintha, who was a contemporary of Hygelac, appears to
have acted on her own authority when she associated Theodahath,
the nephew of Theodric, in the sovereignty with herself after her
son's death. There is other evidence also which goes to show
that this passage truly reflects the spirit of the times. In the
story of Radiger we see how a young princess was able to gather
together a huge army and bring about a sanguinary struggle
between two nations on account of an insult offered to her by
a neighbouring king. Again, Paulus Diaconus (*Hist. Lang.* I 20)
states that the war between the Heruli and the Langobardi was
due to the murder of the Herulian king's brother by a Langobardic princess. Even if this story is untrue, it is significant
enough that it should obtain credit. To the prominent part
played by women in determining the destinies of nations we
have already alluded (p. 337 f.). In particular we may call
attention to the position of Fredegond and Brunhild, who after
the deaths of their husbands practically ruled the kingdom of
the Franks. In the seventh century Hygd's action in disposing
of the kingdom is easily outdone by Sexburg, the widow of the
West Saxon king Coenwalh, who is said to have kept the throne
for herself.

There is no doubt of course that the ease with which kings
and princes were able to draw their nations into war was due

largely to the restless spirit which animated their retinues. Sometimes indeed they appear to have been drawn into war against their own inclination. Procopius (*Goth.* II 14) differs from Paulus Diaconus in the cause which he assigns for the outbreak of the war between the Heruli and Langobardi. According to him it was due entirely to the fact that the Heruli could not endure a peace of more than three years duration, and consequently forced their king into hostilities. The Frankish king Lothair I is said by Gregory (IV 14) to have been driven into a disastrous campaign against the Saxons from the same cause. In this direction then we may certainly recognise the influence of the court; but the pressure probably came not from the old councillors, but from the younger men who hoped to gain riches and glory thereby.

This brings us to the question of international relations. What is said in the opening verses of Beowulf regarding Scyld Scefing, the eponymous ancestor of the Danish royal family, may probably be taken as a standard description of a typical successful king of the Heroic Age: " He deprived many dynasties of their banqueting halls...and gained glory after glory, until every one of his neighbours across the whale's road had to obey him and pay him tribute." With increasing wealth however the love of peace frequently reasserted itself, especially perhaps towards the end of the period, by which time the kingdoms had materially decreased in number and consequently increased in size. We now see alliances more and more taking the place of conquest. Theodric organised an alliance not only with the Visigoths but also with the kings of the Thuringians, Heruli and Warni, which extended his influence from the Mediterranean to the North Sea; and his name seems to have carried weight as far as the eastern part of the Baltic. In Beowulf too we see the nations of the Baltic dealing with one another for the most part on friendly terms.

That such alliances were primarily of a personal rather than a national character is shown in two ways. In the first place they were often cemented by marriage. Thus two of Theodric's daughters were married to Alaric, king of the Visigoths, and Sigismund, king of the Burgundians, respectively, his sister to

Thrasamund, king of the Vandals, and his niece to Irminfrith, king of the Thuringians, while Theodric himself married a sister of Clovis. We have seen (p. 98) that similar marriages were contracted by the kings of the Warni, while the Frankish royal family was intermarried with those of practically all the surrounding nations. In the North the same custom seems to have prevailed, for in Beowulf one of the Swedish kings, probably Onela, is married to a sister of the Danish king Hrothgar. The term *friðuwebbe* (usually interpreted as 'weaver of peace'), which we find applied to ladies of royal rank in Anglo-Saxon poetry, probably owes its origin to this bond of union between kingly families. Such marriages seem to have sometimes taken place after a war, as in the case of Ingeld and Freawaru in Beowulf.

Secondly, we hear of kings entering into a relationship called 'fatherhood' and 'sonship' with other kings. For an example we may cite one of Cassiodorus' letters (*Var.* IV 2), addressed to a king of the Heruli and informing him that Theodric creates him his 'son in arms' (*filius per arma*), which is a great honour[1]. The letter is accompanied by a valuable present of arms and horses. Parallels are to be found in much later times. We may refer to the Saxon Chronicle, ann. 924, where the Scottish king (Constantine II) and several other princes in northern Britain accept Edward the Elder as 'father and lord.' It is scarcely to be doubted that in such cases the 'son' is expected to render assistance to the 'father' when required. The king of the Heruli appears to have been in alliance with Theodric[2], while Malcolm I, the successor of Constantine II, was under an engagement with Edmund to be his "cooperator both by sea and by land[3]." The *imperium* which Bede (*H. E.* II 5) ascribes to several English kings in all probability involved somewhat similar obligations; and it rested without doubt upon an acceptance of lordship, if not of fatherhood.

---

[1] In Beow. 946 ff. (cf. 1175 f.) Hrothgar pays a similar compliment to the hero, who is not a king at this time. Probably the intention is to do Beowulf a quite exceptional honour.

[2] Cf. Cassiodorus, *Var.* III 3.

[3] Cf. Chron., ann. 945. For the form of agreement entered into upon such occasions reference may be made to ann. 874, 921 (ad fin.) etc. The terms probably varied from case to case.

After the establishment of overlordship the next stage is that in which the smaller kingdoms are annexed and incorporated by the larger ones—generally in consequence of a revolt. The place of the native king or kings is often taken at first by a member of the victorious dynasty; but such arrangements were seldom lasting, and before long the national organisation was abolished. The completion of this process on the Continent belongs of course to times subsequent to the Heroic Age, while in this country it took place still later. But we can see such changes going on within the Heroic Age itself. At the end of the period the number of Teutonic kingdoms on the Continent was quite small. Several however, such as those of the Alamanni, the Burgundians and the Thuringians, had disappeared within the last half century; in the fourth century they were probably far more numerous. Many of them may have been quite insignificant, like the petty kingdoms which are said to have existed in Norway—eight apparently in the district of Trondhjem alone—down to the time of Harold the Fair-haired. Several of the nations which figure prominently in Tacitus' works had perhaps disappeared still earlier. At all events they are never mentioned either in historical works or traditions referring to the Heroic Age.

The reverse process cannot be traced so clearly. The division of a kingdom between brothers or other relatives does not seem as a rule to have led to a permanent partition. Very often indeed it was apparently no more than a temporary distribution of estates and spheres of jurisdiction, not necessarily in solid blocks[1]. In such cases the kingdom was still regarded as one property, of which the kings were joint possessors. But there can be no question that many kingdoms established on alien soil, e.g. in Britain, were offshoots from other kingdoms.

This consideration brings us to the much debated question of the relationship between kingdom and nation. It has been assumed by many scholars that among the Teutonic peoples the kingdom was a comparatively late outgrowth from the nation or tribe. It reality this problem seems to me to have

---

[1] For the case of the Frankish kingdom see Waitz, *Deutsche Verfassungsgeschichte*, II, p. 145 ff.; Brunner, *Deutsche Rechtsgeschichte*, II, p. 25 f.

much in common with that of the hen and the egg. With the earliest kingdoms of all we are not concerned here; it will be enough to mention that our earliest historical notices testify to the prevalence of kingship, though not always to monarchy in the strict sense of the term. In the Heroic Age however we certainly find kingdoms springing up where no nation or tribe, properly speaking, can be said to have existed previously. We may cite the case of Odoacer, who in 476 made himself king in Italy with the help of his troops. In principle we may regard him as the *princeps* of a *comitatus*. Then we have to consider the various Anglo-Saxon kingdoms. The Mercian royal family traced their descent from Offa, the ancient king of Angel, while the West Saxon dynasty claimed to be sprung from that Wig, the son of Freawine, who was earl of Slesvig under Offa's father, according to the story preserved by Saxo. But to the origin of the rest the genealogies give us no clue. If they were all of royal origin—and apparently they did claim divine descent—the Angli must have possessed a numerous royal class; and we are scarcely justified in denying that this may have been the case[1]. On the other hand it is by no means impossible that some of them were sprung from foreign peoples, such as the Danes, Swedes or Warni. But what we may regard as practically certain is that the individual kingdoms did not rest upon a national or tribal foundation. There is not the slightest ground for supposing that (e.g.) the East Anglians as a people belonged to a different nation or tribe from the Northumbrians. It is scarcely credible that the first kings were anything else than *principes* in command of *comitatus*, whether they set out from the homeland in this position or established themselves at a later date by severing their allegiance from other kings in Britain itself.

Nor is there any reason for supposing that this phenomenon was peculiar to Britain. The story of Waldhere tells of the presence of small Teutonic communities in eastern Gaul, each

---

[1] In the account of Wulfstan's voyage given in King Alfred's translation of Orosius (p. 20 in Sweet's edition) it is stated that the land of the Este (in East Prussia) contains very many fortified places (*burh*, i.e. probably stockaded villages) and that in each of these there is a king. But it is scarcely probable that such primitive conditions survived among the Angli even four or five centuries before Alfred's time (cf. p. 380, note).

under a royal family of its own. And not only heroic stories but also historical works relating to the earlier part of the Heroic Age frequently refer to comparatively small bands of warriors— such as that led by the Goth Sarus in Stilicho's time—in various parts of the Roman empire, and even beyond its borders[1]. Such bands may very well have produced communities like the one ruled by Waldhere's father[2]; but it would be absurd to speak of them as nations or tribes. They have clearly far more in common with the military kingship established by Odoacer. The peculiarity of his position indeed lies only in the magnitude of the power to which he attained.

In brief we have to distinguish between two classes of kingdoms in the Heroic Age. In the new kingdoms, settled on foreign soil, we find an essentially military kingship, an *imperium* vested in a particular family. These kings either established themselves in Roman cities, such as Ravenna, Langres or York, or moved about from one royal estate to another. Of national assemblies we have frequently no trace at all, while the council is identical with the *comitatus* and consists of relatives and nominees of the king. Such kingdoms often rest on no national or tribal foundations ; the king and his *comitatus* form the nucleus of the organism. On the other hand the older kingdoms, especially in the North, retained many features of a more primitive constitution. The king's position had a religious significance, and his capital, e.g. at Leire or Gamla Upsala, was the chief national sanctuary, at which assemblies, primarily religious but possessing considerable political influence, took place from time to time. It is likely too that the councils here were originally permanent bodies with more or less fixed prerogatives—essentially religious, but

[1] It is only in this way that we can account for the more or less simultaneous appearance of Heruli in Gaul and on the Black Sea in the latter part of the third century. In the fifth century this nation had a powerful kingdom in Central Europe. We may refer also to the traces of various peoples (Angli, Warni, etc.) which we find in the basin of the Saale, as well as to the kingdom of the Suabi in Spain, the Goths in the Crimea, etc. Abundant parallels are to be found in the history of the Viking Age.

[2] It is quite possible that many of the leading characters in the heroic stories may belong to such communities, e.g. Hnaef, Sigmundr and Sigurðr, Heðinn, Hamðir and Sörli, Haki and Hagbarðr.

yet by no means without political power. Between these two types of kingdoms we find others of an intermediate character, especially in nations which had migrated *en masse*; and there can be little doubt that during the Heroic Age even the most conservative of the older kingdoms were influenced by the newer type. It is the newer type of course which we must regard as truly characteristic of the Heroic Age.

In post-heroic times again we find a reversion to the national idea of a kingdom, though on a much larger scale. In English history this tendency can be traced from the seventh century onwards. In Bede's works it is clear that such an expression as *Merciorum gens* (*Myrcna maegþ*) had come to mean something more than the royal family of the Mercians with their property and dependents. By the ninth and tenth centuries however this feeling is much more clearly perceptible. We may cite King Alfred's will, where it is clearly recognised that the kingdom should not be divided up as a family property. But it is not until the time of Aethelred II that the full sense of the king's responsibility to the nation finds expression in definite terms.

The form of government which we find depicted in the Homeric poems seems to be not unlike that which we have discussed above. Here too kingship is universal—apparently also without any recognised constitutional limitations to the royal authority. The murder or expulsion of a prince is not unknown; but such cases are due to strife within the royal family. Any differences which we can detect between the authority of Homeric kings and that wielded by early Teutonic rulers may be ascribed partly to the much smaller size of the kingdoms and partly to a social feature noted in the last chapter (p. 363 f.), namely that in many Greek communities kingly or princely rank seems to have been claimed by a number of different families.

The last consideration is especially prominent in the Odyssey[1]. The throne of Ithaca has been in the possession of one family

---

[1] In explanation of this phenomenon the view has been put forward (cf. Finsler, *N. Jahrb.* XIII 319 ff., 396 ff.; summarised 410 ff.) that the form of government depicted in the Odyssey is really an aristocracy, whereas the evidence of the Iliad is inconsistent owing to traditional reminiscences of a time of real kingship. Thus in

for three generations. Yet in I. 394 ff. Telemachos says that there are many kings of the Achaeans, both young and old, in the island, and he expects that one of them will take the sovreignty, now that Odysseus is dead. In Scheria also we hear of twelve sceptre-bearing kings under Alcinoos; but to this case we shall have to return shortly. That a king was not necessarily a person of great magnificence may be inferred also from one of the scenes depicted on Achilles' shield (Il. XVIII 556 ff.), where we find a king in the harvest-field watching the work of the reapers and feasting on the spot. We are reminded here of the story of the Norwegian king Sigurðr Sýr who was summoned from the harvest-field to greet his step-son, St Olaf, and whose state-robes had to be sent to him there in order to enable him to make a suitable appearance[1].

In this connection it is perhaps worth noting that according to the Catalogue of Ships the contingents supplied by several communities were under a number of different princes. Thus the Epeioi have four leaders and the Boeotians five, without counting those from Orchomenos and Aspledon. The troops from Argolis (exclusive of Agamemnon's dominions) are led by three princes, all of whom according to later authorities were related—two of them, Diomedes and Sthenelos, being sons of

the latter poem βασιλεύς (in the singular) is generally used only of Agamemnon, though there are exceptions, e.g. I 331, where it is applied to "Achilleus, dem der Titel, streng genommen, nicht zukommt, da Peleus noch lebt" (p. 404 f.). I do not think that this explanation is likely to carry conviction to anyone who has studied early Teutonic history. It is clear that in early times throughout the Teutonic area —in England down to the end of the seventh century and in the North much later— the title of king was applied to sons and other relatives of kings, as well as to dependent princes. The only qualifications for the title were (i) royal birth, (ii) the possession of some kind of authority or 'lordship' (τιμή). How small this authority might be can be seen from St Olaf's Saga (Heimskr.), cap. 4, where we are told that Olaf had the title of king given to him by his followers; "for it was customary that *herkonungar* (i.e. Viking chiefs) who were engaged in piracy should take the title of king at once, if they were of royal birth, although they governed no territories." The qualification of royal birth however was essential. The title was not taken even by so great a man as Earl Haakon of Lade, who had kings practically dependent on him. I see no reason for regarding the conditions depicted in either of the Homeric poems as different from what we find in the North, although, owing presumably to the smallness of the kingdoms, all the important characters appear to be persons of royal birth.

[1] St Olaf's Saga (Heimskr.), cap. 30 ff.

Adrastos' daughters, while the third, Euryalos, was his brother's
son[1] Diomedes is said to be the commander-in-chief, but as
Sthenelos is his charioteer the relations between them are
evidently of an intimate character. It is not stated whether
all these princes were actually reigning kings, or merely leaders
selected for the expedition; but Diomedes and Sthenelos at
least have no fathers living.

There is no evidence, so far as I am aware, for any form of
election for kings. In the case of Bellerophon we are told that
"the Lycians apportioned him a demesne" ($\tau\acute{\epsilon}\mu\epsilon\nu o\varsigma$ $\tau\acute{a}\mu o\nu$); but
it was the king who granted him half the royal rights. And
similarly in all other cases the kingly power seems to have been
obtained from some relative by blood or marriage. This renders
it more easily intelligible that the plural kingship—if such it
was—of which we have spoken above, may be due ultimately
to family arrangements. It is scarcely necessary to suppose
that in such cases the kingdom was always divided into geographical halves and quarters. As to the relationship between
the various kings under such an arrangement—e.g. whether the
phrase $\sigma\upsilon\mu\pi\acute{a}\nu\tau\omega\nu$ $\dot{\eta}\gamma\epsilon\hat{\iota}\tau o$ applied to Diomedes in Il. II 567
means a formal recognition of lordship on the part of his
colleagues—we have apparently no precise information.

The religious aspect of kingship is not very prominent in
the Homeric poems. When the armies are gathered together
to perform a sacrifice Agamemnon acts as priest (Il. III 271 ff.)
with the cooperation of Priam, and Nestor seems to take the
chief part in sacrifices at Pylos (Od. III 444 ff.). There is no
reason for supposing that such cases are exceptional; as in the
North (cf. p. 367) the king or chief person seems likewise to have
acted as priest. We do occasionally hear of priests of sanctuaries,
such as Chryseus at the opening of the Iliad; but no mention is
made of state-priests or tribal priests. In historical times the

---

[1] This passage offers at least a partial explanation of the phenomenon which we
have been discussing. If royal rank is traced both on the male and female sides the
kingly class will inevitably be numerous. Such may have been the case among the
Angli also at one time. But it is not unlikely that at least in the remoter parts of
Greece each ' city ' or small district may have retained a royal family of its own, like
the communities visited by Wulfstan (cf. p. 376, note). We may refer to such a
passage as Il. IX 395 f., if $\dot{a}\rho\iota\sigma\tau\acute{\eta}\omega\nu$ here means dependent princes.

case was otherwise. Thus Athens possessed a state-priest known as βασιλεύς. The name of the office itself shows that it was a relic of the kingship which had been gradually stripped of all except its religious duties. Political power here was transferred at first to an official called ὁ ἄρχων, whose origin may have been similar to that of the Frankish *maior domus*. We may note also that at Sparta, where the institution of kingship was preserved in a modified form, priestly functions were among the chief duties preserved by the kings.

The poems themselves do not make it clear that the religious aspect of kingship amounts to more than priestly position, for such phrases as θεὸς ὣς τίετο δήμῳ are scarcely free from ambiguity. But later authorities give us much more information in this respect. In the first place we may notice certain legends, such as that of the impious king Salmoneus, who aspired to the functions of Zeus—a story which is now thought by many scholars to have arisen from a misunderstanding. More than one of the early Attic kings also seem to have been regarded as at least partly divine[1]. But above all we have to take into account the statement of Clement of Alexandria (*Protr.* II 38) that the Spartans worshipped a certain Ζεὺς Ἀγαμέμνων, which has led some writers to assume that Agamemnon was originally a god. In all probability the true explanation is furnished by Tzetzes[2], who says that in early times kings regularly bore the name Ζεύς. We have an interesting parallel here to the usage of the ancient Swedes[3], whose kings are said to have been called Yngvi (cf. p. 367). In both cases we may probably infer that the king was regarded in some sense as the god's representative;

---

[1] Cf. especially Cook, *Folk-Lore*, XV 385 f.

[2] *Chil.* I 474 (τοὺς βασιλεῖς δ' ἀνέκαθε Δίας ἐκάλουν πάντας) and elsewhere. On this subject see Cook, *Class. Rev.* XVII 409, and *Folk-Lore*, XV 303 f. (cf. 301), where full references are given.

[3] The parallel must not be pressed too far of course. According to Tzetzes all kings were called Ζεύς. But apparently not all kings were descended from Zeus; Nestor, for example, was sprung from Poseidon according to Od. XI 254 ff. We may refer however to Hesiod, *Theog.* 96, where kings are said to derive their authority from Zeus, and to the Homeric epithet διοτρεφής (possibly also διογενής) which is commonly applied to kings. Frey on the other hand was an ancestral god but not the chief of the gods, though he is sometimes in poetry called *jolkvaldi goða*, which Saxo translates by *satrapa deorum*.

possibly he personated him on certain occasions. Yet it must
be remembered that this aspect of kingship is not brought
forward in the poems[1]. If our sketch of the history of Homeric
poetry is correct in its main outlines, we must conclude that the
divinity of kings was not a doctrine to which supreme importance
was attached in the courts themselves.

National or tribal assemblies are not often mentioned. In
Od. VIII 26 ff. Alcinoos addresses the Phaeacians in their
assembly (ἀγορή) and declares to them his resolve to assist
Odysseus. Again, in II 6 ff. Telemachos calls an assembly
in Ithaca. But on this occasion the first speaker, Aigyptios,
says that the assembly has not met since the departure of
Odysseus, some twenty years before, and further that he wonders
who it is who has called them together now. The former
statement seems to indicate that such meetings were not held
regularly, while the latter at first sight suggests that it was open
to anyone to call them, and consequently that they were of a
quite informal character—in spite of certain rules of procedure
which seem to have been usually followed. But the conditions
here are abnormal. The king has disappeared and no one has
yet taken his place; Aigyptios is perhaps scarcely prepared to
expect that the young Telemachos would summon the assembly.
It is true that in Il. I 54 ff. the Achaeans are called together by
Achilles, not Agamemnon; but here we have to deal with a
confederate army in the field[2], and with a prince who shortly
afterwards sets Agamemnon's authority at open defiance. There
is scarcely sufficient ground for supposing that a similar course
would have been possible at home, when the king was on the spot.
Further, it is to be noted that on all the above occasions the
notice served is so short that only those in the immediate neighbourhood could attend. On the whole then we are probably
justified in doubting whether any definite rules existed as to

---

[1] A trace of the belief that kings had power over the seasons (cf. p. 367) may
perhaps be found in Od. XIX 109 ff.

[2] I cannot help thinking that evidence derived from the Achaean gatherings in
the Iliad is somewhat precarious ground on which to build up a theory regarding
the constitutional rights possessed by the ἀγορή at home. The same remark applies
to such a passage as Od. XII 297, where an important constitutional change (cf. Fanta,
op. cit., p. 91) has been inferred from the mutinous behaviour of a ship's crew.

when the assembly should be called, and indeed whether this body had much in common with the constitutionally regulated assemblies of historical times[1]. It seems rather to be a more or less fortuitous gathering called together on the spot by criers when the king wishes to bring something before the notice of the public[2].

In Od. III 5 ff. we certainly do hear of a great public gathering —indeed we may probably say a national gathering—of a kind which can only have taken place at definitely fixed times. But it is clear that this was essentially a religious festival[3]. Such gatherings may of course have been used for political purposes, as in the North ; but we have no information on this subject.

The Achaean 'council of elders' ($\beta o \upsilon \lambda \grave{\eta}$ $\gamma \epsilon \rho \acute{o} \nu \tau \omega \nu$) in the Iliad seems to be a body of quite as informal character as the assembly. On several occasions Agamemnon calls together a small number of princes, namely Nestor, Idomeneus, the two Aiantes, Diomedes and Odysseus, together with his brother Menelaos. This number of course forms only a small proportion of the leading men in the army. Occasionally however we find

---

[1] It cannot fairly be argued from Od. II 192 f. that the assembly (apart from the king) has a right to impose fines, for the suitors here are relying not upon any 'constitutional' rights but on force majeure. It is to be remembered too that Eurymachos appears to have designs upon the throne (cf. p. 358 f.).

[2] It has been suggested that the true name for such a gathering was $\theta \acute{o} \omega \kappa o \varsigma$ ($\theta \hat{\omega} \kappa o \varsigma$) and that this was something different from the $\dot{\alpha} \gamma o \rho \acute{\eta}$ (cf. Fanta, op. cit., p. 77) ; but the evidence for such a distinction is very far from convincing. We may refer to such passages as Od. XII 318 and, more especially, to V 3 ($\theta \hat{\omega} \kappa \acute{o} \nu \delta \epsilon$), which is clearly parallel to Il. XX 4 ($\dot{\alpha} \gamma o \rho \acute{\eta} \nu \delta \epsilon$). Cf. Finsler, N. Jahrb., XIII 327.

[3] In the Hymn to the Delian Apollo, v. 146 ff., mention is made of a festal gathering of Ionians at Delos, apparently on a considerable scale. Similar gatherings may have been in existence quite as early, or even earlier, in other parts of Greece. For the festival at Pylos however much better parallels are to be found in the great religious gatherings which took place every nine years at Leire and Upsala, the old Danish and Swedish capitals. Cf. Thietmar of Merseburg, Chron. I 9 : est unus in his partibus locus...Lederun nomine...ubi post nouem annos, mense Ianuario...omnes conuenerunt et ibi diis suismet XCIX homines et totidem equos cum canibus et gallis pro accipitribus oblatis immolant. And Adam of Bremen, IV 27 : solet quoque post nouem annos communis omnium Sueoniae prouintiarum sollempnitas in Ubsola celebrari. ad quam uidelicet sollempnitatem nulli praestatur immunitas. reges et populi omnes et singuli sua dona transmittunt ad Ubsolam. It does not appear however that on these occasions—in contrast with the festival at Pylos—any of the victims were eaten. In this respect they are probably to be compared rather with the great quadrennial sacrifices of the Gauls ; cf. Diodoros, v. 32.

others summoned, such as Meges and even Thrasymedes and Meriones, who are not the chiefs of contingents. The council of an expeditionary army however is an exceptional case. On the Trojan side we hear of a number of δημογέροντες with Priam (Il. III 146 ff.), seven of whom are named. Three of them are brothers of the king, while others are fathers of the most distinguished Trojan warriors. They are described as eloquent orators, but no account is given of their deliberations. In the Odyssey references to councils are very rare. No mention is made of such a body in Ithaca. In Scheria however Alcinoos has twelve kings under him (VIII 390 f.), who clearly form his council and are to be identified with the 'leaders and rulers of the Phaeacians' (Φαιήκων ἡγήτορες ἠδὲ μέδοντες) who feasted in his hall (VII 98 f., 186; VIII 26, 41, 46 f.), though on Odysseus' arrival they were apparently not all present (VII 189). It may be observed that in the account of the Phaeacian assembly Alcinoos uses the same formula as when he is addressing the princes in his hall: "Hearken, ye leaders and rulers of the Phaeacians." His speech then is directed primarily to the princes—a fact which seems to indicate that council and assembly were not very clearly distinguished. In this connection we may note that in the assemblies of the Iliad, as in those of the ancient Germans, the speaking is almost invariably left to the princes.

So far as the councils of the Iliad are concerned little can be said against the view that Agamemnon calls together from time to time those of the leaders in whom he has most confidence. The same may be true of Alcinoos' council[1]. But on the whole it seems more probable that this is a permanent institution, with definitely fixed numbers and privileges. The 'sceptre-bearing' under-kings are twelve in number, like the councils of so many European peoples in ancient times. The agora where they meet, with its polished stones, is clearly a place specially constructed for such functions and similar apparently

[1] It is scarcely capable of proof that the picture of the Phaeacian community in the Odyssey is derived from a Greek model (cf. p. 297 f. and note); but I believe I am following the generally accepted view in assuming this to be the case. The features noted here are such as we might expect to find in a Greek community if we take into account the evidence of later times.

to the one described in the trial scene depicted on Achilles'
shield (Il. XVIII 497 ff.), where the elders are seated on polished
stones 'in a sacred circle.' We are reminded here of the Northern
council of the gods—especially as described in Gautreks Saga,
cap. 7[1]—and of the 'circle of judgement' (*domhringr*), which
we find at 'chief-places' (i.e. centres of jurisdiction) in Iceland.
Possibly too we should refer to the stones used in the election
of Scandinavian kings (cf. p. 368). If we take the evidence as
a whole it can hardly be denied that the Phaeacian council does
seem to show the characteristics of a primitive communal organisation[2]. But it would be unwise to assume that councils of this
type were universal in the Heroic Age.

The actual power possessed by the council, whatever its
constitution, does not seem to amount to much. Agamemnon
is often ready to take advice from some of his colleagues,
especially Nestor; and in Od. VII 167 ff. Alcinoos acts on
the suggestion of the old Echeneos. Both these cases may
be compared with the story of Genseric (cf. p. 369 f.[3]). But it
is clearly as individuals that the councillors have influence. In
the Iliad Achilles acts on his own initiative and withdraws from
the war in open defiance of Agamemnon. But even in the case
of home councils—I mean councils of the kingdoms—we never
hear of organised action. In Ithaca, where the king is away, no
council seems to exist. Nor is any mention made of a council
in the story of Agamemnon's death and Orestes' vengeance.
This fact deserves to be remarked all the more because we find

---

[1] We may refer also to the rökstólar (judgement-seats) on which the gods sit
when they gather in session (Völuspá, str. 9, 23, 25).

[2] For a true analogy we must of course turn to councils which were attached to
the king's court. Such appears to have been the case with the twelve chiefs of the
Uppland Swedes who, according to St Olaf's Saga (Heimskr.), cap. 96, constantly
attended the Swedish king, sitting in judgement with him and giving him advice in
matters of difficulty. If the meaning of Od. XIII 130 is that the Phaeacians in general
are descended from Poseidon, we have a further analogy with the same community,
who appear to have claimed descent from the god Frey. Cf. Saxo, p. 260 (in the
catalogue of Ringo's warriors at Bravalla) : *At Sueonum fortissimi hi fuere...qui
quidem Frø dei necessarii erant et fidissimi numinum arbitri...iidem quoque ad Frø
deum generis sui principium referebant.*

[3] For Genseric's disregard of the general opinion of those present a parallel is
presented by Agamemnon's conduct in Il. I 22 ff.

apparently just the same phenomenon in Anglo-Saxon poetry, e.g. in Beowulf where the proceedings after Hygelac's death are related.   The natural inference to be drawn from the evidence is that the councillors were essentially advisers to the king and that after his death or disappearance their standing was gone. But here again caution is necessary.   It is difficult to believe that such a description can be true of a council like that of the Phaeacians, however ready they may seem to follow the king in ordinary circumstances.

The cases of emergency arising out of the misfortunes of Odysseus and Agamemnon bring to our attention another curious feature, again possibly analogous to the conditions described in Beowulf, namely that the king does not seem to appoint a regent in his absence[1]. Odysseus has entrusted his household to Mentor (Od. II 226 f.), and Agamemnon has put his wife in charge of a minstrel (*ib.* III 267 f.); but nothing is said of the kingdom in either case.   Are we to suppose that the queen is the person in authority?   Presumably, like Hygd, she has command over the treasury; for (as also perhaps in the North) the treasury seems to be connected with the queen's chamber.   If it be objected that the absence of any national control apart from the king's (or queen's) personal authority must have been productive of strife, we have only to refer to the stories to see that dissensions, especially between members of the same family, were by no means of rare occurrence.

With regard to international relations warfare between different kingdoms does not seem to be particularly common. Apart from the siege of Troy we hear incidentally of a number of struggles, such as the two expeditions against Thebes, the war of the Aetolians against the Curetes, and those of the Arcadians and the Epeioi against Pylos, while references to buccaneering exploits are frequent.   But on the whole the normal state of relations between the various kingdoms is one of peace.

As in the Teutonic Heroic Age, we hear frequently of marriages between different royal families.   Agamemnon's offer of one of his daughters to Achilles is part of his attempt at

[1] Cf. Seymour, *Life in the Homeric Age*, p. 81.

reconciliation and may be compared with the marriage of Ingeld
and Freawaru.   Menelaos marries his daughter to Achilles' son.
Both these cases show that such marriages were not limited to
neighbouring families.   So also Penelope the daughter of Icarios
(whose home is not stated in the poems) has married the king
of Ithaca, while her sister is the wife of Eumelos at Pherai in
Thessaly (Od. IV 795 ff.).   Such marriages would doubtless do
much towards promoting friendly relations between the various
royal families.   Indeed visits paid by one prince to another
seem to be nothing very unusual[1].   Autolycos visits his son-in-
law Laertes in Ithaca, and Odysseus later goes to stay with
Autolycos in the neighbourhood of Parnassos.   Helen recognises
several of the Achaean princes from the walls of Troy and
remarks (Il. III 232 f.) that Idomeneus had frequently been
entertained by Menelaos in her old home.

Again, it can scarcely be doubted that the expedition against
Troy involves the existence of relations of some kind between
Agamemnon and the other kings.   But the character of
Agamemnon's position in Greece itself is never clearly defined
in the poems.   According to Od. XXIV 115 ff. he has considerable difficulty in persuading Odysseus to take part in the
expedition.   On the other hand in Il. XIII 669 we hear of
a fine ($\theta\omega\eta$) for those who refused to serve[2].   This passage
however refers to a native of Corinth, who was doubtless a
much nearer neighbour.   Indeed the Catalogue of Ships (Il. II
569 ff.) represents the Corinthian contingent as under Agamemnon's immediate command.   According to this section of
the poem Agamemnon's own territories consist of the north-
western part of Argolis, together with at least the eastern half
of Achaia, while the rest of Argolis belongs to Diomedes and
his colleagues.   But in IX 149 ff (291 ff.) it is clear that

[1] It may be observed here that we often hear also of journeys for trade and other
purposes, as in Od. III 366 ff., where Athene, disguised as Mentor, says she is going
to the land of the Caucones to collect a debt.   Voyages even to countries as distant
as Egypt and Phoenicia are not unknown.

[2] Cf. XXIII 296 ff., where a certain Echepolos (presumably a fictitious character)
is said to have given Agamemnon a mare in order that he might be excused from
the expedition.   This person belongs to Sicyon, another adjacent city and likewise
included in Agamemnon's domain in the Catalogue of Ships.

Agamemnon possesses part of Messenia, bordering apparently on Pylos (the territory of Nestor). Further, we have to take into account that, apart from the Catalogue neither poem gives evidence for the existence of anything which can fairly be called a kingdom in the Peloponnesos, except Pylos, Elis and the territories of the two brothers[1]. Taking the positive and negative evidence together it seems probable that Agamemnon and his brother were regarded as ruling over the greater part of the peninsula, though certain cities and districts remained in possession of native princes, perhaps in a dependent position. Again, I am not aware that there is any evidence apart from the Catalogue for supposing that the territories of the two brothers were regarded as definitely marked off from one another. From Il. IX 149 ff., taken together with the references to Sparta and Mycenae, we may infer the contrary. On the whole it seems more probable that we have here to do with a case of divided kingship, as so frequently among the Teutonic peoples, rather than with two separate kingdoms. In that case too we shall obtain a satisfactory explanation of the later tradition (cf. p. 240) which claimed Agamemnon for Sparta or Amyclai.

Beyond his own territories Agamemnon's authority does not seem to be represented as anything more than a somewhat indefinite hegemony—comparable probably with the relationship of Theodric the Ostrogoth to his northern allies (cf. p. 373 f.). The army which he leads against Troy is furnished partly by his own subjects and partly by a number of princes whose positions may have varied from complete dependence to something which may best be described as alliance. A good parallel is to be found in the army led by the Mercian king Penda against Oswio, which according to Bede (*H. E.* III 24) consisted of thirty *legiones* under *regii duces*. Among these were the king of East Anglia and several Welsh kings.

---

[1] The evidence of the Catalogue as to the dimensions of Diomedes' dominions is not corroborated elsewhere in the Iliad. The author may of course have derived his information from other sources, e.g. from poems dealing with the story of Adrastos and the expedition against Thebes. But it is at least equally possible that he was influenced by the desire of providing each king with dominions comprised in a compact geographical area.

How Agamemnon acquired his imperial position we are not told; for scarcely anything is recorded of his doings before the Trojan war. From Il. II 104 ff. we may perhaps infer that his family had held a preeminent position before him[1], although Pelops was located by later tradition in a different part of the peninsula[2]. Nor again is it made clear whether the hegemony remained with the family after Agamemnon's death. All that can be said is that the Odyssey represents Menelaos as a very wealthy king and that neither the poems nor later tradition give any hint of the rise of a new power in the Peloponnesos before the 'Return of the Heracleidai.' What may be regarded as certain is that no individual Greek prince attained to such a supremacy again, for many centuries after the close of the Heroic Age.

In conclusion we must consider briefly the question how far the Homeric kingdoms rested upon a national or tribal basis (cf. p. 375 ff.). Upon this question the nomenclature of the poems seems to throw some light. In the north of Greece, except the plain of Thessaly, the inhabitants of the various kingdoms bear what are apparently national or tribal names, e.g. Βοιωτοί, Λοκροί, Δόλοπες, Ἐνιῆνες, Μάγνητες, Αἰτωλοί, Ἄβαντες— probably also Φωκῆες and Μυρμιδόνες (Ἕλληνες). The same is true of kingdoms outside Greece, e.g. Φαίηκες, Τρῶες and the various Trojan allies. But in the Peloponnesos the only names of this type are Ἐπειοί, Ἀρκάδες and Καύκωνες; for Πύλιοι and Ἀργεῖοι are not primary national names but derivatives of Πύλος and Ἄργος, while Ἀχαιοί is a name, like *Engle*, applied to the inhabitants of many kingdoms. This evidence, so far as it goes, tends to indicate that the southern kingdoms rested on a political or military rather than a tribal basis—which is natural enough

---

[1] The passage suggests that the σκῆπτρον is regarded as a symbol of authority. Thyestes here appears between Atreus and Agamemnon. In Od. IV 517 f. Aigisthos is said to have dwelt where Thyestes had formerly dwelt, though unfortunately the locality is not stated. The two passages however are not necessarily inconsistent, for it does not follow that Agamemnon, when he took the *imperium*, would deprive his relative of the estate on which he lived. For the method of succession—which was of course extremely liable to produce strife—many Teutonic parallels might be cited. We may refer to the events which took place on the death of Alfred the Great.

[2] Thucydides (I 9) relates how Atreus acquired the sovereignty at Mycenae; but his account seems to be largely in the nature of a conjecture.

if we are right in believing that the Peloponnesian Achaeans were an offshoot from the Achaeans of northern Greece. It would seem then that these kingdoms are to be compared with the newer kingdoms of the Teutonic Heroic Age, the nucleus of which consisted of the kings with their military followings; and I am not aware of the existence of any evidence inconsistent with this view. I do not mean of course that these kingdoms were necessarily areas carved out by the sword, like the Anglo-Saxon kingdoms. What I mean is that we have no reason for supposing that Agamemnon's subjects believed themselves to be of a different nationality from Nestor's subjects or the rest of the Achaeans and that each of these kingdoms had a separate tribal organisation and tradition of its own.

If our observation is correct it is important to notice that several of the chief Achaean leaders belong to kingdoms which apparently rest on a non-national basis. Among them we have to include not only Agamemnon, Menelaos and Nestor, but also probably Idomeneus; for the name Κρῆτες in the Homeric poems can scarcely mean anything else than inhabitants of Crete. The followers of Diomedes and of Aias, the son of Telamon, likewise appear to bear no national names. The case of Odysseus is doubtful, since his subjects are described both as 'Αχαιοί and Κεφαλλῆνες. The question is whether he is king of the Cephallenes in general or only king of Ithaca, with a temporary lordship over the rest of the nation. The only 'heroes of the first rank' who clearly represent national kingdoms are Achilles and Aias the son of Oileus.

In the course of this chapter we have noticed many remarkable resemblances between the Homeric and the early Teutonic systems of government. Not all of these however can be regarded as characteristic of the Heroic Age; some have been inherited in all probability from an earlier stage of development. Such are the religious type of kingship, the council of twelve and the national gathering for religious (sacrificial) purposes[1]. The form

---

[1] Among the Teutonic peoples we have records of such gatherings from the first century (cf. p. 369, note) to the eleventh (at Upsala; cf. p. 383, note). There is evidence also for similar festivals among the Lithuanians and Prussians; cf. Matthias

of government truly characteristic of the Heroic Age in both areas alike is an irresponsible type of kingship, resting not upon tribal or national law—which is of little account—but upon military prestige. Such kingdoms are often of recent origin and without roots in any national organisation. The assembly here, so far as it exists at all, is a gathering summoned at the king's pleasure, while the council consists of an indefinite number of his trusted followers, whose advice he may wish to have from time to time. Lastly, we may observe in both cases a very strong tendency to develop intercourse between one kingdom and another—partly by royal marriages and partly by the cultivation of personal relations between the kings, which generally take the form of a recognition of overlordship, though in varying degree. The general effect of this intercourse must have been to produce something in the nature of an international royal caste, and to break down tribal and local prejudices, at least in the highest ranks of society.

With the end of the Heroic Age the lines followed by Teutonic and Greek political history part company. In both cases, it is true, we find a revival of national feeling. Among the Teutonic peoples however the kingdoms constantly tend to decrease in number and increase in size—partly by the process sketched above (p. 375) and partly by pressure from without. In Greece on the other hand this tendency was brought to an abrupt end[1] by the Thessalian and Dorian conquests, by which the richest parts of the country were brought into the power of populations in a lower stage of civilisation and governed largely

a Michov, *De Sarm. Europ.*, Lib. II (in Grynaeus' *Novus Orbis Terrarum*, etc., Basel 1537, p. 519): *insuper prima Octobris die maxima per Samagittas in syluis praefatis celebritas agebatur, et ex omni regione uniuersus utriusque sexus conueniens illuc populus cibos et potus quilibet iuxta suae conditionis qualificationem deferebat; quibus aliquot diebus epulati diis suis falsis, praecipue deo lingua eorum appellato Perkuno, id est tonitru, ad focos quisque suos offerebat libamina.*

[1] It is important to notice that the tendency appears to have been by no means so far developed as in the Teutonic Heroic Age. We cannot tell, it is true, how far the various dependent cities and districts remained in the hands of native royal families and how far they were governed by officials. In the latter category we may include such a person as Phoinix (Il. IX 483 f.). But it is clear that the royal families form a much larger proportion of the population than was the case among the Teutonic peoples of the fifth century.

by tribal principles and prejudices.   The general effect of these
movements was to isolate the various communities—not only
in the conquered provinces but also in those districts, such as
Attica, which remained entirely or comparatively untouched.
This isolation in turn was probably favourable to the growth
of internal dissensions.   In the end at all events no king succeeded in maintaining a personal lordship over the rest of his
class[1], even within the smallest communities.   The title came
to denote an official with constantly diminishing powers, often
indeed of an exclusively religious character, while the allegiance
formerly owed to an individual was now transferred to the state
and its constitution[2].   At a later date, it is true, most of the
Greek states again came for a time into the power of individual
rulers.   But it is not until the days of Philip II, king of the
Macedonians, that we find any single man holding an authority
over the Greek world such as the poems attribute to Agamemnon.

---

[1] Teutonic analogies occur, though they are not common.   We may instance
Bede's account (*H. E.* IV 12) of what took place after the death of Coenwalh, king
of Wessex (about 673): *acceperunt subreguli regnum gentis et diuisum inter se tenuerunt
annis circiter* x, after which *deuictis atque amotis subregulis Caedualla suscepit imperium*.
The Saxon Chronicle certainly gives a different impression; and from Eddius, *Vita
Wilfridi*, cap. 40, it appears that Centwine's authority was recognised at least to
some extent.   Reference may also be made to Procopius' statement (*Goth.* II 14)
that—early in Justinian's reign—the Heruli slew their king, ἄλλο οὐδὲν ἐπενεγκότες
ἢ ὅτι ἀβασίλευτοι τὸ λοιπὸν βούλονται εἶναι; but the interregnum was of short duration.
Earlier cases may be found among the Cherusci and other peoples of western Germany
during the first century—where it is to be noted that Tacitus' *principes* and *regnum*
correspond to Bede's *subreguli* and *imperium* respectively.   I cannot help thinking
that much confusion has been introduced into early Greek history through failure to
distinguish between kingship and lordship.

[2] This is true even of Sparta.   We may quote Herodotus' account (VII 104) of
Demaratos' speech to Xerxes: ἐλεύθεροι γὰρ ἐόντες (sc. οἱ Λακεδαιμόνιοι) οὐ πάντα
ἐλεύθεροί εἰσι· ἔπεστι γάρ σφι δεσπότης νόμος, τὸν ὑποδειμαίνουσι πολλῷ ἔτι μᾶλλον
ἢ οἱ σοὶ σέ.   It is the recognition of this impersonal force—not of course any sense
of universal right, but the 'law' of the community—which perhaps most clearly
distinguishes post-heroic and pre-heroic society from that of the Heroic Age.   The
existence of such a force—operating, under religious sanction (cf. p. 366), as a restraint
upon the king's freedom of action—is implied by Tacitus, *Germ.* 7, 11.   But it is
a strange misunderstanding which has led several scholars to compare the former of
these passages with Beow. 73, where the limitations stated are those of Hrothgar's
generosity, not of his power.

CHAPTER XVIII.

RELIGION IN THE HEROIC AGE.

IN the course of the Heroic Age many of the Teutonic peoples were converted to Christianity. The change of faith began among the Goths soon after the middle of the fourth century and must have spread very quickly to the Vandals. The Gepidae and Langobardi seem to have followed the example of these peoples in the course of the following century. At the time of Justinian's accession the Heruli were probably the only Teutonic people in eastern central Europe who remained heathen. In the west the Burgundians accepted Christianity apparently about the beginning of the fifth century, and the Franks before its close. The conversion of England took place in the seventh century; that of the Frisians and Old Saxons for the most part in the eighth. The Northern Kingdoms in general were little affected by the change until towards the close of the tenth century, though the first missionary efforts in Denmark and Sweden began before the middle of the ninth. In parts of Sweden the heathen religion lingered on until late in the eleventh century.

In the Nibelungenlied it is clearly recognised, perhaps through scholastic influence, that the multitude assembled at Attila's court included both Christians and heathens; but no such distinction is drawn in the English and Norse poems. In the former all the characters are made to speak as Christians, though they observe heathen rites; in the latter no indication is given that any of the characters were Christians. In point of fact there can be little doubt that most of the persons who figure in the heroic stories were heathens In all probability such was the case with the earlier Goths, Eormenric and his contemporaries, as well as with all the characters of the Danish cycles. On the other hand the later Goths, Theodric and his contemporaries, were certainly Christians, and so also were the Burgundians, Guthhere and his brothers, as well as Alboin, king of the Langobardi.

With the Christian religion we are not concerned here; for, greatly as it influenced the Teutonic peoples, it was in no sense native. It is to the religion which Christianity displaced that we must give our attention. Unfortunately however the records which have come down to us from the Heroic Age itself are entirely of foreign authorship, and on the whole they give us extremely little information on this subject. We are bound therefore to base our account of Teutonic religion upon the comparatively abundant evidence preserved in Scandinavian literature, though we must not assume that the religion of the Heroic Age possessed the characteristics which we find in the North some five centuries later. When we have given a brief summary of the chief features of this later religion we shall have to discuss in somewhat more detail the small amount of information available for the earlier period. This is rendered all the more necessary by the fact that in works dealing with the subject the religion of the Heroic Age has not generally been distinguished from that of the Germans of Tacitus' time.

Now the feature which will probably strike any one most forcibly from a careful study of Northern religion is an extraordinary discrepancy between the mythical stories contained in the Edda and elsewhere on the one hand and references to actual religious observances on the other. In the former we find the gods grouped together in an organised community, of which Othin is the recognised head. Frigg is his wife, Thor and many of the other gods his sons. Most of the mythical stories deal with Othin's exploits and adventures, and serve to illustrate his power and wisdom. On the other hand the references to religious rites point in quite a different direction. In Iceland, for which our records are most full, there is practically no evidence for the worship of Othin. Thor is by far the most prominent figure, and after him Frey; occasionally also

we hear of Niörðr[1]. References to the worship of other supernatural beings, elves and landvættir (*genii locorum*), are not
unfrequent. In notices referring to Norway the evidence is
not very different. We do indeed sometimes hear of worship
paid to Othin, especially in legendary stories, relating to early
times; but in references to what may be called the historical
period—the tenth and eleventh centuries—Thor and Frey are
distinctly more prominent.

Two explanations have been given of this curious pheno-
menon. One is that the cult of Othin was introduced into the
North at a comparatively late period and that it had not yet
obtained a real hold at the time when Iceland was settled.
This explanation has no foundation in tradition. Indeed the
evidence of the stories points to an entirely opposite conclusion.
Moreover it is worth noting that according to Procopius (*Goth.*
II 15) the inhabitants of 'Thule' (i.e. Scandinavia) worshipped
'Ares' more than any other god. Since Othin is essentially
a god of war it is natural to suppose that he is the deity meant,
rather than the somewhat obscure Týr.

The other explanation is that the cults of Othin and Thor
belonged to two different classes of the community, the former
to princely families and their retinues, the latter to the country
people, more especially the (non-official) landowners. This
explanation seems to be in complete accordance with the facts.
There is no evidence for the worship of Othin either in early or
late times except by princes or persons attached to their courts,
while there are very few instances of the worship of Thor by
such persons. Further we may note that while names compounded with *Thór-* (e.g. *Thórkell, Thórolfr*) are about the
commonest type of all among the ordinary free population, both
in Norway and Iceland—and such names are significant since
they denote that the persons who bore them were dedicated
to the god—they are practically unknown in royal families.

[1] These are the three gods mentioned in the solemn oath which, according to
Landnámabók, IV 7 (Hauksbók), had to be sworn on the sacred bracelet at all legal
proceedings: *hialpi mér svá Freyr ok Niörðr ok hinn almáttki Áss*, etc. In the later
Melabók (a compilation of the seventeenth century) it is suggested that *Áss* here
means Othin; but I do not think this explanation is generally accepted. It is scarcely
credible that Thor should be ignored on such an occasion.

It will be convenient now to give a short sketch of the two deities and their cults.

Thor is represented as a middle-aged man of immense bodily strength. He is well disposed towards the human race and looked upon as their protector against harmful demons, to whom he is an implacable foe. In the poems Thrymskviða and Hýmiskviða and in a number of prose stories we have descriptions of Thor's adventures with giants, in which he is generally represented as breaking their skulls with his hammer. He uses no weapon except the hammer, and when he travels he either walks or drives in a car drawn by goats. When he comes to the assembly of the gods he is said to wade through certain rivers on the way. His escort never consists of more than three persons; very often he goes alone. The picture which the stories give us is clearly that of an idealised Norwegian countryman of primitive times. There are scarcely any traces of his original connection with the thunder, though in Sweden it was clearly remembered.

The portraiture of Othin offers the greatest possible contrast to that of Thor. He is represented as an old man, generally with one eye, and he gains his ends not by bravery or physical strength but by wisdom and cunning. Sometimes we find him coming, usually in disguise, to giants or witches, in order to gain from them some magical power or knowledge of the future; sometimes he imparts his knowledge, again generally magical, to men. He presents his favourites with weapons and instructs them in the art of war. Above all he is the god who gives victory in battle.

Othin's chief dwelling is called Valhöll (the 'hall of the slain'), and all persons who fall in battle were believed to go to him there. Hence we find such expressions as 'to go to lodge with Othin' or 'to go to Valhalla' used as euphemisms for 'to be killed.' Before joining battle it is said to have been customary to throw a javelin over the enemy with the words 'Othin has you all.' After a battle prisoners were commonly sacrificed to Othin, and on such occasions, and indeed at all human sacrifices, the formula regularly used was: 'I give thee to Othin.' The usual method of sacrifice was by hanging or stabbing or a combination

of both.   With this practice we may probably connect a somewhat obscure myth recorded in Hávamál, str. 138, according to
which Othin was sacrificed to himself, by hanging and stabbing,
on the world-tree.   Certainly it is to be noted that the sacrifices
to Othin seem to have been invariably human.   They were
clearly rites of quite a different character from the sacrificial
feasts frequently mentioned in the sagas, where the victims
consisted of horses, oxen and other edible animals, part of which
was offered to the gods, while the rest was consumed by the
worshippers.   We do sometimes hear of horses being sacrificed
with men, but on such occasions dogs and hawks are also
mentioned, and there is no evidence that any of the victims
were eaten.   There are very few records of human sacrifices
to any god except Othin.

The picture of Valhalla presented to us in the poems is a
glorified copy of a military king's court[1].   The vast number of
slain warriors assembled there in Othin's service spend their
days in single combats and their evenings in feasting.   Beside
them we find the Valkyriur ('choosers of the slain'), Othin's
adopted daughters, who distribute ale to the feasters.   These
also are sent out by Othin to decide the issue of battles and
to select warriors for Valhalla.   It is noteworthy that the term
Valkyriur seems to be applied both to supernatural beings—
what may perhaps be called minor divinities—and also to living
women endowed with supernatural powers, such as that of
flying.   Thus both Brynhildr and Sigrún, the wife of Helgi
Hundingsbani, are called Valkyries; and it was for deciding
a fight contrary to Othin's command that the former was
punished with perpetual sleep.

In Ynglinga Saga, cap. 8, Othin is said to have ordained
"that all dead men should be burnt and brought on to the pyre
with their property.   He said that every dead man should come
to Valhöll with such property as he had on the pyre....But the
ashes were to be cast out into the sea or buried down in the

---

[1] The description in Grímnismál, str. 23, curiously recalls what is said of Egyptian
Thebes in Il. IX 383 f.   The nearest approach to Valhalla to be found among
Northern kingdoms is Ibn Fadhlan's account of the Russian court; cf. Frähn, *l.c.*
(p. 367, note).

earth." Valhalla seems to be represented as a spirit world, somewhat far away and not connected at all with the burial-place. This observation brings us to another remarkable discrepancy between the traditions and the customs which we find actually prevailing in the North. We know both from descriptions in the sagas and from discoveries made in modern times that in the last few centuries before the adoption of Christianity it was customary to bury the dead in their ships or in elaborately constructed wooden chambers—the whole being covered with a barrow of considerable size. In the Prologue to Snorri's Heimskringla this custom is said to be of later date than the one attributed to Othin; first was the age of burning, then the age of barrows. Now there is evidence both from the discoveries and from the sagas themselves that the barrows were regarded as sacred and that the spirits of the dead were believed to dwell either within them or in the immediate neighbourhood. Not unfrequently we hear of persons coming to a barrow to consult the spirit. Sometimes the ghost, embodied in the corpse, even defends his property against grave-robbers. The activities of the dead are often represented as injurious; but this is by no means always the case. On one occasion we hear of a dispute between several different districts for the possession of the body of a king whose reign had been distinguished by great prosperity.

On the whole then it is clear that the cult of the dead was practised in the North very much as in most other parts of the world. Yet modern discoveries have brought to light abundant evidence for cremation in the early iron age—sometimes in spots which are marked by no external monument—so that the statements of Ynglinga Saga may be regarded as based on good tradition. We are driven to conclude therefore that in their conception of immortality, as in their theology, the inhabitants of the North held two wholly inconsistent views—or, perhaps it would be more correct to say, two entirely opposite views as to the desirability of retaining the souls of the dead. In Iceland the practice of cremation seems to have been extremely rare, but when it was resorted to the object is said to have been to get rid of a troublesome ghost. The one view of immortality was by no means so closely bound up with the cult of Thor as the other was with that of Othin.   But it certainly prevailed among Thor's worshippers.

The next most important deity after Othin and Thor was Frey. His cult was widely spread in Norway and Iceland; yet according to tradition its true home was Sweden[1].   The Swedish royal family and nobility traced their descent from Frey, and Upsala, their capital and the chief sanctuary of the North, was believed to have been founded by him.   In Ynglinga Saga, cap. 12 f., we have an account of him which is worth quoting as an illustration of Northern manes-worship.   Frey is here represented as a prince whose reign was characterised by unparalleled prosperity. His death was concealed for three years.   But when it became known, the Swedes would not burn him; for they believed that prosperity and peace would last as long as Frey was in Sweden. They made a great barrow for him therefore and poured into it the tribute which they had been wont to pay him; and they worshipped him for prosperity and peace ever afterwards. A very similar account is given of the Danish king Fróði the Peaceful—from which we may infer that in Frey we have to deal not with a deified man but with a mythical character —a 'king of the golden age.'   His name originally seems to have meant 'prince' or 'lord' (Ang.-Sax. *frea*, cf. $\check{a}\nu a\xi$); very probably it was at one time a title of the Swedish kings[2].

Frey appears to be regarded as a youthful god.   The blessings for which he was worshipped were peace and fertility, both of the crops and livestock, as well as of the human race. His power of controlling the weather may be accounted for by his association with the Swedish kings (cf. p. 367); but it is clear that his character contains elements drawn from more than one source.   His father Niörðr, who is sometimes associated with him, possesses much the same characteristics, though he appears to be more particularly connected with the sea.   There can be little doubt however that both he and his son have inherited the attributes of an ancient earth-goddess.   Although there has

---

[1] Frey's connection with Sweden appears in Saxo's History (frequently) as well as in sagas, but not in the Edda.

[2] The full form, *Yngvifreyr* or *Ingunarfreyr*, is clearly connected with *Ingwina frea*, a title borne by the king of the Danes in Beowulf; cf. p. 367 and note.

been a change of sex, Niörðr's name is identical with that of Nerthus (*id est Terra Mater*), a deity who according to Tacitus, *Germ.* 40, was worshipped on 'an island in the ocean'—in all probability Sjælland. Niörðr also has a daughter called Freyia (i.e. ἄνασσα, Δέσποινα), who is represented as a female counterpart of Frey. It is worth noting that she is sometimes associated with the next world. According to Grímnismál, str. 14, she shares the slain equally with Othin.

The deities with which we have just been dealing were collectively known as Vanir. They were held to be of a quite different stock from the Aesir, to whom Othin and Thor belonged, and according to the mythology had been given to the latter as hostages. Of the other deities those who figure most prominently in mythical stories are Frigg (Othin's wife), Ullr, Hoenir, Týr, Heimdallr, Iðun, Gefion and Balder; but we seldom hear of worship paid to any of these.

In the Edda all the gods together form a regularly organised community. Their home is called Ásgarðr, and they hold their meetings beside the 'world-tree,' Yggdrasill's Ash. It is to be observed that Ásgarðr is a totally different conception from Valhalla[1]; it is not an abode of the slain. Indeed in this connection Othin himself does not appear to be represented as a god of the dead. But apart from Ásgarðr each god has a special abode of his own—Thor at Thrúðheimr, Ullr at Ýdalir, Niörðr at Noatún, Balder at Breiðablik, etc. All these localities are mythical—or at all events incapable of identification. It is a striking characteristic of Northern mythology that the gods are not associated with any known localities. Practically the only exceptions are Frey and Gefion, who are connected by tradition with Upsala and Sjælland respectively; and neither of these connections is preserved in the poems of the Edda. In order to understand this feature we must of course bear in mind the fact that our mythological records are almost entirely derived from Iceland, which lies far away from the old national sanctuaries.

---

[1] The two conceptions are sometimes confused, e.g. in Völuspá, str. 34. But the eschatological conception involved by the story of Balder is that of the 'house of Hel'; and there can be no doubt that this conception itself is ancient, although the description of Hel in Gylf. 34 is probably quite late.

It is probably due to the same cause that we hear but little
of special cults.   In Iceland the only noteworthy exception is
that, beside the more usually prevailing cult of Thor, we find a
number of persons who are devoted to the service of Frey.
Certain chiefs bear the title *Freysgoði* (' priest of Frey ') ; in one
case a whole family bore the surname *Freysgyðlingar*.   Temples
apparently sometimes contained the figures of a number of gods,
though Thor's or Frey's is usually the only one mentioned by
name.   In Norway however the case is somewhat different.   We
hear frequently of temples and statues of Thor, occasionally
also of those of Frey.   But in addition to these there are notices
of sanctuaries belonging to other deities—though not to Othin.
In Friðþiófs Saga, cap. 1 (and passim), mention is made of a
temple and image of Balder in the district of Sogn.   It is the
fashion to treat this incident as a product of antiquarian speculation ; but there is little in the story itself to justify such a view,
and the fact that the worship of Balder is not found elsewhere
proves nothing.   More important however is the fact that in a
number of records we hear of statues and temples of Thórgerðr
Hölgabrúðr, with whom her sister Irpa is sometimes associated.
There can be no doubt that under the rule of Earl Haakon of
Lade the cult of Thórgerðr was more prominent than that of
any other deity, at least in the district of Trondhjem.   This fact
is the more remarkable because Thórgerðr and Irpa are never
associated in any way with the rest of the gods ; in the poems
of the Edda and even in Gylfaginning their existence is ignored.

A very interesting illustration of the practice of special cults
occurs in Niáls Saga, cap. 88, which describes a temple owned
in common by Earl Haakon and Guðbrandr, a powerful *hersir*
(hereditary local chief) in the highlands.   This temple contained
figures of Thórgerðr and Irpa and also of Thor in his car[1].   We
know from other sources that the cult of Thor was hereditary in

---

[1] The text does not say (as is stated in several works on Northern mythology) that
Thor occupied the central position, but merely that he was robbed after Thórgerðr
and before Irpa.   This is the only mention, so far as I am aware, of a cult figure of
Thor in his car—a feature which occurs in Hýmiskviða and Gylfaginning and may
possibly have some ethnological significance.   It is somewhat remarkable that in the
tract Frá Fornióti (in Hrafn's *Fornaldar Sögur*, II p. 6 f.) the ancestry of Guðbrandr
is traced to the giant Thrymr, Thor's antagonist.

the family of Guðbrandr. Indeed it appears to be generally true that families adhered to the same cult from generation to generation[1], though in one case we do hear of an Icelander bearing the title Freysgoði, who belonged to a family distinguished for its service to Thor.

The relations between the worshipper and his deity were of a personal and intimate character; he regarded the latter as friend, counsellor and protector. Where the two are of different sexes the relationship is apt to take a conjugal form. Thus in the Flateyiarbók, I p. 107 f., Olafr Tryggvason, after robbing one of Earl Haakon's temples, and carrying off the image, calls out in derision: "Who wants to buy a wife? I think Thórkell and I are now responsible for this woman, since she has had the misfortune to lose her husband who was exceedingly dear to her." One of the bystanders then addresses the image: "How is it, Thórgerðr, that thou art now so humiliated and stripped in unseemly wise of the splendid apparel wherewith Earl Haakon had thee clothed when he loved thee?" So in the poem Hyndlulióð Freyia speaks of her devoted worshipper, Óttarr the son of Innsteinn, as her husband. We may compare with this the fact that in the Flateyiarbók, I 337 f., the priestess in charge of Frey's temple in Sweden is said to have been called his wife. I see no reason therefore for supposing that Snorri was giving rein to his imagination when he stated (Yngl. Saga, cap. 5) that Gefion was the wife of Skiöldr who, though a mythical character (cf. p. 131 f.), was not a god.

Sometimes again we meet with a definitely hostile attitude towards a deity—generally Othin—and it must not be supposed that such ideas first arose after the introduction of Christianity. In Saxo's translation of the lost Biarkamál the hero suspects that Othin is among the enemy and expresses his eagerness to attack him. If once he can catch sight of him, he says, the god

---

[1] Cults peculiar to certain families appear to have been common among the Lithuanians and kindred peoples; cf. Lasicius, *De diis Samogitarum* (Respublica... Poloniae, etc.; Leyden, 1642, p. 280): *sunt etiam quaedam ueteres nobilium familiae, quae peculiares colunt deos, ut Mikutiana Simonaitem, Micheloviciana Sidzium, Schemietiana et Kiesgaliana Ventis Rekicziovum, aliae alios.*

will not escape from Leire unharmed[1].   Such ideas can only be explained by a vivid anthropomorphic conception of the deities.

The same attitude appears elsewhere.   In Gautreks Saga, cap. 7—a story which contains many archaic features—we find the destiny of a man being determined by Othin and Thor, the former of whom is friendly to him, the latter hostile.   In the introduction to Grímnismál as the result of a disagreement with Othin Frigg plays a trick upon him which leads him into serious trouble.   Nor is the married life of Niörðr and Skaði as happy as might be wished.   But the chief cause of discord among the gods is the malicious Loki.   In the poem Lokasenna he charges most of the chief goddesses with unfaithfulness or unchastity, while at the same time he reproaches the gods with unseemly conduct or with being involved in humiliating positions. The picture of the divine community which the poem presents to us is anything but pleasant.   No doubt Loki is representing every circumstance in the most unfavourable light possible ; but there appears to be a definite mythical foundation for most of his charges.

Loki serves as a connecting link between the gods and the iötnar ('giants'), a class of beings who are represented as generally hostile to both gods and men.   Yet there are exceptions to this rule ; and some of the gods, e.g. Niörðr and Frey, have wives from the iötnar.   Next to them we must mention the dwarfs, who are distinguished for their cunning and skill in metallurgy. Neither of these classes however can properly be regarded as objects of worship.   Elves were certainly worshipped, but only collectively, as far as we know.   In early records they are scarcely ever spoken of as individuals.   Most probably their origin is to be sought in animistic conceptions, connected with the cult of the dead.   On this last subject enough has been said

---

[1] p. 66:   *Et nunc ille ubi sit qui uulgo dicitur Othin*
armipotens, uno semper contentus ocello,
dic mihi, Ruta, precor, usquam si conspicis illum.

....

si potero horrendum Frigge spectare maritum,
quantumcunque albo clypeo sit tectus et altum
flectat equum, Lethra nequaquam sospes abibit.
fas est belligerum bello prosternere diuum.

above; we need only add that the formal deification of dead
men was not unknown[1]. Sacred trees and groves also figure
as prominently as in other parts of Europe.

Thus far we have been dealing with the religion of the Viking
Age, primarily as we know of it in Iceland and Norway. But
we have seen that the actual records of religion in Iceland agree
in no way with the theology of the Edda. Nor can it truly be
said that the evidence for Norway shows a better case. Here
too we find the worship of Thor and Frey. But for the worship
of Othin, Niörðr, Freyia and Balder the evidence is slight and
generally doubtful. For that of the rest of the gods there is no
evidence at all. On the other hand we find that the deity who
after Thor figures most prominently of all in these records is one
who is entirely unknown to the theology of the Edda. The only
conclusion which it seems to me legitimate to draw from these
facts is that the mythology of the Edda is not a true reflection
of Norwegian religion, at all events as it existed in the Viking Age.

Now let us consider the various deities individually. It will
be convenient to begin with those whom we know to have been
worshipped in Norway or Iceland. There is no question that
Thor was known not only in Sweden and Denmark but also
in Germany and England, under the forms *Donar* and *Thunor*
respectively. Apart from local nomenclature and the use of his
name (as a translation of *dies Iouis*) in the fifth day of the
week, there are a few direct references to worship of him—e.g.
in the inscription on a brooch found at Nordendorf in Bavaria
and in a Low German renunciation formula for the use of
converts. His cult goes back without doubt to the Heroic Age
and probably much earlier, though he is apparently not mentioned
by Tacitus.

The cult of Frey was believed to have come from Sweden,
as we have seen. How old it was there we do not know; but

---

[1] Cf. Adam of Bremen, IV 26: *colunt et deos ex hominibus factos*, etc. (with reference to the passage from the Vita Anscharii quoted on p. 255 f.). It is not clear
whether Grímr Kambann, the great-great-grandfather of Thórsteinn Sölmundarson
who settled in Iceland (cf. Landnámabók, I 14), was deified; but the worship paid to
him is evidently regarded as something exceptional. Some scholars hold that Bragi,
the god of poetry, is no other than the poet Bragi Boddason.

there is some reason for believing that it was not originally confined to that country. The Slavonic inhabitants of eastern Holstein worshipped a deity of the same name[1]; and the presumption is that they found the cult in existence when they occupied that district—not later than the seventh century. But the name *Yngvi* has a much longer history and can be traced in various records back to the time of Tacitus. From what is said of Ing in the Anglo-Saxon Runic Poem it is clear that he was a perfectly definite, though doubtless mythical, personality[2].

We have already noticed that Niörðr can be traced back to a goddess Nerthus, who was worshipped in the first century by the Angli and other peoples in the south-western part of the Baltic. When the change of sex took place we do not know. The feminine form of the deity is probably preserved in Freyia, who under the name *Skialf* seems to have her roots in early Swedish tradition.

With Othin we shall have to deal presently. There is abundant evidence that he was known not only in Sweden and Denmark but also in England and at least the greater part of Germany. In the two latter countries he bore the names *Woden* and *Wodan* respectively. Even in Tacitus' time he appears (under the name *Mercurius*) as the chief god.

Balder's history is not so clear. From Saxo's account (p. 70 ff.) there can be little doubt that he was known in Denmark. The question whether he was recognised in Germany[3] depends practically upon the interpretation of the (second) Merseburg charm, to which we shall have to refer again shortly.

Now let us take the deities who are known to us only from the mythology. Both Frigg and Týr were certainly known in England and Germany. Their names are preserved in the sixth and third days of the week. Frigg (*Frea*) also figures, as the wife of Wodan, in the Langobardic story quoted above

---

[1] *Proue(n)* ; cf. Helmoldus, *Chron. Slavorum*, I 53, 70, 84.

[2] I have discussed this subject (also Niörðr and Freyia) in detail in *The Origin of the English Nation*, chapters IX–XI.

[3] I do not think that Aethelweard's substitution of *Balder* for *Baeldaeg* (the first part of which is certainly *bǣl-*) in the genealogy of King Aethelwulf (III 3) can be held to prove the existence of the cult of Balder in England. The theory that the word *baldor*, 'prince,' arose out of the god's name is open to still more serious question.

(p. 115), while Týr (*Mars*) is mentioned more than once by Tacitus.

Of Ullr traces are preserved in local nomenclature both in Denmark and Sweden. From Saxo (p. 81 f.) it appears that he was remembered in Danish tradition. Gefion's association with Sjælland (cf. p. 400) is recorded by Bragi Boddason, the earliest Scandinavian poet of whom anything has been preserved. Both her name and that of Iðun can be traced in local nomenclature in the same island[1].

There remain of course a large number of less important deities who cannot be traced outside the mythology of the Edda. Many scholars hold that these were invented by Norwegian or Icelandic poets during the Viking Age ; but it is at least equally possible that our inability to trace them elsewhere is due in part to the extreme poverty of our information. One piece of evidence which tells in favour of the latter view is that the Merseburg charm preserves the name of one of the least prominent of these deities—Fulla, the handmaid of Frigg. The fact too that these poets made no attempt to incorporate Thórgerðr in the pantheon seems to show that in their time[2] the theological system of the Edda was more or less crystallised. At all events it is clear that, with the exception of Thórgerðr and Irpa, all the deities whose worship is attested were known beyond Norway, and that most of them can be traced back to the Heroic Age or still earlier times.

There is a further reason for doubting whether the theology of the Edda was a product of late Norwegian poetry. Perhaps the most striking conception in this theology is that of the 'world-tree,' Yggdrasill's Ash. I have pointed out elsewhere[3] that this conception is largely derived from a tree-sanctuary and that a fairly close parallel to it is furnished by the description

---

[1] Cf. Olrik, *Gefion* (*Danske Studier*, 1910), p. 21 ff.

[2] There is no reason for supposing that the cult of Thórgerðr was first introduced by Earl Haakon. In the Flateyiarbók, p. 408, it is stated that she had been worshipped by successive rulers of the land. Her cult too was not unknown in Iceland; according to Harðar Saga, cap. 19, Grímkell, the son of a settler from Orkadal (to the south of Trondhjem), had a temple dedicated to her.

[3] *The Cult of Othin*, p. 75 ff. Cf. R. M. Meyer, *Altgermanische Religionsgeschichte*, p. 474 ff.

of the Upsala sanctuary given in Adam of Bremen's history
(IV 26 f.) and the annexed scholia.   Similar sanctuaries may
have existed in Norway; but we have no record of one which
possessed the same characteristics, and it is extremely improbable that any of them ever attained an importance comparable with that possessed by the Swedish capital.   Again, there
are features in the picture of the 'world-tree'—I would allude
especially to the presence of snakes—for which no parallels can
be found in any Scandinavian sanctuary of which we have
record.   Yet such features do occur in the tree-sanctuaries
of more primitive peoples, especially among the Prussians and
Lithuanians.   From this it appears to me highly probable that
the conception of the world-tree dates from a comparatively
early period.   The idea of universality which it embodied cannot
be held to prove the contrary; for this idea was possessed also
by the Irminsul[1], the sacred pillar of the Old Saxons.   We have
no reason for doubting that a philosophical conception such as
this was possible before the Viking Age.

I am inclined therefore to think that the theological system
of the Edda in its main features dates from times anterior to
the Viking Age.   From earlier sources—the works of Tacitus
and various German and English authorities—we know altogether
the names of about a score of deities, half of whom belong to
either sex.   It is probable however that a much larger number
have been lost.   At all events there can be no doubt that the
religion of the Heroic Age was a highly developed polytheism.
Procopius (*Goth.* II 15), speaking of the inhabitants of 'Thule'
(Scandinavia), says that they worship many gods and demons
($\delta a i \mu o v a s$), both in the heavens and in the atmosphere, in the
earth and in the sea, besides certain other spirits ($\delta a \iota \mu \acute{o} \nu \iota a$)
which are said to be in the waters of springs and rivers.   Again,
in the preceding chapter he states that the Heruli of central
Europe worshipped a great crowd of gods ($\pi o \lambda \acute{v} \nu \ \tau \iota \nu a \ \nu o \mu \acute{\iota} \zeta o \nu \tau \epsilon \varsigma$
$\theta \epsilon \hat{\omega} \nu \ \acute{o} \mu \iota \lambda o \nu$), whom they thought it right to appease even with
human sacrifices.   Procopius' evidence is important not only
because it is almost contemporary but also because he clearly

---

[1] *Irminsul...quod Latine dicitur uniuersalis columna, quasi sustinens omnia,*
Mon. Germ., II 676.

distinguishes between the religion of the Teutonic peoples and that of the Slavs. Of the latter he says (*ib.* III 14) that "they consider one god, the creator of the lightning, to have sole control over all things, and they sacrifice to him oxen and offerings of all kinds....Yet they also reverence rivers and nymphs and some other spirits (δαιμόνια), and sacrifice to them all, using divination in these sacrifices." It will be seen that this type of religion is not very far removed from what we find among the Thor-worshippers of Iceland.

In an earlier chapter (p. 255) we quoted from the Life of St Ansgar the story of a man who claimed to have been present at an assembly of the gods. From this story it is clear that in Sweden not very long after the beginning of the Viking Age the gods were believed to form an organised community. For earlier times no such explicit information is to be found; but we can scarcely doubt that some similar belief prevailed during the Heroic Age. In the Langobardic story quoted above (p. 115) Fria (Frigg) is the wife of Wodan, as in the Edda. In the (second) Merseburg charm we find a number of deities taking part in an incantation. Of the goddesses Sunna is said to be the sister of Sinthgunt, and Volla the sister of Fria. Evidence to the same effect is furnished by a letter of Bishop Daniel of Winchester to St Boniface, in which the writer speaks of a genealogy of the gods and advises his correspondent to put awkward questions to the heathen regarding the origin, numbers and relationships of their deities[1]. It may be noted that the earlier Anglo-Saxon genealogies, which go back probably to the seventh century, trace Woden's ancestry back for five generations.

Of course it is not to be denied that some of the deities of whom we hear may have been recognised only locally or by certain nations or confederacies. Such an explanation is very likely in the case of more than one deity mentioned by Tacitus, whom we cannot identify with any probability. In later times

---

[1] Jaffé, *Bibliotheca Rerum Germanicarum*, III 71 ff.: *neque enim contraria eis de ipsorum, quamuis falsorum, deorum genealogia astruere debes...utrum autem adhuc generare deos deasque alios aliasque suspicantur? uel, si iam non generant, quando uel cur cessauerunt a concubitu et partu; si autem adhuc generant, infinitus iam deorum effectus numerus est. et quis iam inter tot tantosque potentior sit, incertum mortalibus est; et ualde cauendum, ne in potentiorem quis offendat.*

the same may be true of the god Fosite[1], to whom an island in
the North Sea—identified with Heligoland by Adam of Bremen
—was wholly dedicated.   It is quite possible too that the god
Seaxneat (*Saxnote*), who is mentioned in the Renunciation
Formula and from whom the kings of Essex claimed descent,
was worshipped only by the Saxons.

But even if such evidence was a good deal stronger than it
actually is we should not be justified in inferring from it that
the religion of the Heroic Age was of an essentially national
rather than universal character.   It is not only in Northern
records of the Viking Age or the Christian period that we hear
of families which were supposed to be descended from Othin
(Woden).   Out of the eight royal genealogies of the English
kingdoms which have come down to us seven are traced back
to the same deity; and it is highly probable that most of these
date from before the conversion[2]—i.e. from within a century of
the Heroic Age.   But Woden was not a national but a universal deity.

Moreover what little we do know of this god from English
and German sources is in full conformity with the character
which he bears in Northern records.   In the Anglo-Saxon poem
on the Nine Herbs he is skilled in magic; in the Merseburg
poem he is an expert in incantations.   In the Langobardic
story we find him represented as the giver of victory.   In
Tacitus' time he was already worshipped above the other gods;
and human victims were offered to him.   The same author
(*Ann.* XIII 57) records the custom of dedicating a hostile army
to Mars and Mercurius—a vow which entailed the total destruction of everything belonging to the enemy.   The great deposits
of antiquities which have been found at Thorsbjærg, Nydam, Vi
and elsewhere are commonly believed to be relics of such

---

[1] This explanation would not hold of course if Fosite is to be identified with Forseti
the son of Balder.   But the identification seems to me extremely problematical.

[2] Cf. Bede, *H. E.*, I 15: *Voden, de cuius stirpe multarum prouinciarum regium
genus originem duxit.*   From these genealogies and Bp Daniel's letter (quoted above)
it would seem that such compositions (including theogonies) were much in vogue
among the heathen Teutonic peoples in the period immediately following the Heroic
Age.   It is to the same period that I would ascribe the development of the theology
of the Edda, though I do not mean to suggest that the poems which have come down
to us were composed then.

dedicatory spoils. Finally, later popular belief often placed Woden at the head of the Wild Hunt or ghostly army. For the existence of a conception corresponding to Valhalla we have no explicit evidence[1]. But such a doctrine would clearly be in full accord with all that we know of the cult.

In funeral rites both inhumation and cremation were practised. The latter custom however seems to have died out almost everywhere before the introduction of Christianity—in England about the middle of the sixth century, among the Franks and Alamanni much earlier. Only among the Old Saxons it lingered apparently until towards the close of the eighth century, when it was rigorously put down after their subjugation[2]. How far the two practices were associated with different conceptions of immortality, as in the North, it is impossible to tell. In Beowulf (cf. p. 54) cremation is regarded as a pious duty owed to the dead; but all heathen references to the destiny of the soul hereafter have been removed from the poem. On the other hand there is evidence from later times for offerings at the grave, necromancy and all other practices usually associated with the cult of the dead[3].

---

[1] There is an unfortunate ambiguity about the history of the word *Áss*. In Old Norse it is applied both to Thor and Othin, as well as other gods, while *Aesir* (pl.) denotes the gods collectively and *Ásgarðr* their home (quite distinct from Valhalla). In Gothic however the same word (pl. *ansis*) seems to have meant a dead hero (cf. p. 172, note). If this was its original meaning—a view somewhat favoured by Skr. *asu*, Av. *anhu*, 'spirit,'—we must conclude that the terms *Ásgarðr* and *Aesir* (also *Áss*, as applied to Thor) have undergone a complete change of meaning in Old Norse. Such a change could be explained satisfactorily by the (poetic) inclusion of θεοὶ οὐράνιοι and θεοὶ νέρτεροι in one pantheon; but in that case the doctrine of Valhalla, or something very much like it, must be of great antiquity. This explanation is perhaps favoured by the popular use of *Aasgaardsreia* for the Wild Hunt in Norway.

[2] Cap. quae de partibus Saxoniae constituta sunt, No. VII (Mon. Germ., Leg. I 49). Whether the practice was common I do not know. References to the cult of manes occur in the same Capitula, as well as in the Indiculus Superstitionum, etc.

[3] Cremation is sometimes accompanied by a cult of the dead, e.g. among the heathen Prussians; cf. Matthias a Michov (Grynaeus, *Novus Orbis*, etc., Basel 1537, p. 520): *Habebant praeterea in syluis praefatis focos, in familias et domos distinctos, in quibus omnibus charorum et familiarium cadauera cum equis, sellis et uestimentis potioribus incendebant. Iocabant etiam ad focos huiusmodi ex subere facta sedilia, in quibus escas ex pasta in casei modum praeparatas deponebant, medonemque focis infundebant, ea credulitate illusi quod mortuorum suorum animae quorum illic*

The most important piece of evidence however on this subject
is furnished by Procopius' account of the Heruli (*Goth.* II 14).
He states that with them it was not lawful for a man to die of
old age or disease. When he felt himself to be dying he had to
request his relatives to make away with him as soon as possible.
They had then to construct a huge pyre and set the dying man
in the highest part of it. A compatriot, though not a relative
(cf. p. 346), is then sent up to stab the man, and on his return
the wood is immediately kindled. When the fire is burnt out
the remains are collected and buried forthwith, and the widow
is required to strangle herself at the tomb. Such rites as this
are commonly ascribed to the desire to set the soul free while
in possession of its faculties. But in view of the fact that in
Northern tradition cremation is bound up with the doctrine of
Valhalla[1]—a doctrine which is in no way inconsistent with this
explanation—it is certainly significant that the two rites should
be associated here, more especially since the Heruli were an
essentially military people. On the whole the evidence of this
passage is distinctly favourable to the view that a belief closely
approximating to the doctrine of Valhalla was prevalent during
the Heroic Age.

Valkyries (*walcyrgan*) are not unfrequently mentioned in

---

combusta fuerant corpora nocte uenirent escaque se exsatiarent. Inhumation however
was also practised by the same nation; cf. Erasmus Stella (Grynaeus, *op. cit.*, p. 582):
Statuit (sc. *Viduutus*) *et dies natalitios et funera pari modo celebranda, mutuis scilicet
commessationibus et compotationibus, tum lusu et cantu, absque moerore cum summa
hilaritate et gaudio, utque alterius uitae spem prae se ferrent. illo saltem ostenderunt
quod exutos spiritu armatos uestitosque ac magna supellectilis parte circumposita
humarunt. quo more usque nunc sepeliuntur,* etc. Both these notices of course refer
to a late period—the fifteenth century.

[1] Cf. p. 397 f. We may refer also to the funeral of Sigurðr Hringr, as described
in Arngrim's epitome of the lost Skiöldunga Saga, cap. 26 (Aarbøger f. nord.
Oldkynd., 1894, p. 132): *Hinc post acerrimam pugnam...Siguardus etiam male
uulneratus est. qui, Alfsola funere allato, magnam nauim mortuorum cadaueribus
oneratam solus uiuorum conscendit, seque et mortuam Alfsolam in puppi collocans
nauim pice, bitumine et sulphure incendi iubet· atque sublatis uelis in altum, ualidis
a continente impellentibus uentis, proram dirigit, simulque manus sibi uiolentas
intulit; sese tot facinorum patratorem, tantorum regnorum possessorem, more maiorum
suorum, regali pompa Odinum regem (id est inferos) inuisere malle quam inertis
senectutis infirmitatem perpeti, alacri animo ad socios in littore antea relictos praefatus,*
etc.

Anglo-Saxon literature[1], and it is clear that similar beings were
known in Germany, though this word does not occur in extant
records.   In England, as in the North, both human and supernatural beings were included under this term, though they are
not always clearly distinguished from witches.   But, more than
this, the poetic description of valkyries which we find in the
Edda[2] can likewise be traced in Anglo-Saxon poetry.   In a
charm against sudden pains we hear of mighty women who
rode over the hill, mustered their host and cast their spears.
The idea that sudden pains were due to the agency of such
beings[3] comes doubtless from popular belief; but the description
cannot be accounted for in this way.   Again, in the (first)
Merseburg charm we find supernatural women (*idisi*) taking part
in a battle; and it is to be remembered that the word *walcyrge*
can hardly mean anything else than 'chooser of the slain.'
Certainly we have no evidence to prove—or disprove—that the
valkyries were associated with Woden in early times.   But the
features noted here again point clearly to the existence of
a conception akin to Valhalla and, what is more, to the poetic
treatment of such a conception.

In the course of this discussion[4] I have endeavoured to point
out that the theological system of the Edda cannot properly be
regarded as an invention of (Norwegian-Icelandic) poets of the
Viking Age—that, on the contrary, it is derived in great measure
from much earlier times.   I do not mean to deny that the growth
of the system has been very largely influenced by poetry.   But
the evidence seems to me to show that the poetic treatment of
the subject had begun—and probably more than begun—in the

---

[1] In the glossaries the word is used to translate *Eurynis, Herinis* (i.e. Erinys),
Tisifone, Allecto, Bellona.   The first three cases occur in the Corpus glossary; hence
the suggestion that the word *walcyrge* is borrowed from Norse is inadmissible.

[2] From the inscription of Rök it appears probable that the conception of Valkyries
found in the Edda was familiar in the south-east of Sweden before the end of the
ninth century.   This is by no means the only point in which the same inscription
bears witness to a highly developed interest in antiquarian lore.

[3] An interesting analogy is furnished by the Servian belief that sunstroke is due to
arrows shot by Vile (cf. p. 317, note; and Krauss, *Slav. Volkforschungen*, p. 372 ff.).

[4] I have not attempted to give a complete list of the mythical beings mentioned in
the records.   In general we find the same classes of such beings as in the North—
elves, dwarfs, giants (Ang.-Sax. *eoten, þyrs*), etc.

Heroic Age and among many of the Teutonic peoples. It is perfectly true that the notices of Teutonic religion contained in Tacitus' works convey the impression that religion was regarded as a very serious matter and that the general attitude towards the gods was highly reverential. The same impression is conveyed by Alcuin's account of Fositesland; and probably no one will deny that the euthanasia of the Heruli was based upon a very real conception of immortality. But to compare such records with the poetry of the Edda would manifestly be absurd. For analogies to them we must turn to notices relating to actual religion, and here we shall find evidence that the people of the Viking Age were no less religious than those of earlier times. We may instance the reverence shown by Thórolfr of Mostr to his holy hill and Earl Haakon's devotion to Thórgerðr Hölgabrúðr.

On the other hand the attitude towards the gods shown in the Edda finds an exact analogy in the only record of 'theological' poetry which has survived from the Heroic Age. In the Langobardic story (cf. p. 115) the anthropomorphisation of the deities is already complete; and the chief god[1] is duped by his wife. We could scarcely wish for a better parallel to the account given in the introduction to Grímnismál. In view of this story it is scarcely possible to doubt that familiarity, not to say levity, in the treatment of the gods characterised the poetry of the Heroic Age, just as much as that of the Viking Age.

It would be well to hesitate however before assuming that the gods of Tacitus' time were treated in the same way. His account shows that Teutonic theology had then passed beyond the purely tribal stage, and that certain deities were worshipped by a number of peoples, if not universally. But it does not suggest the existence of a highly anthropomorphic conception of the gods. Further we have to bear in mind that Tacitus is separated only by a century and a half from Caesar. The account of German religion given by the latter (*B. Gall.* VI 21) is difficult to account for by any explanation. But unless we are to believe that Caesar was thoroughly imposed upon we

---

[1] It will be observed that here (as commonly in the Edda) Wodan's character as god of the dead (slain) is entirely lost sight of.

must conclude that nothing in the nature of a developed polytheism can have existed in his day. To the theology of the
Heroic Age his account of the Gaulish gods (*ib.* VI 17) would
be far more applicable than what he says regarding the worship
of the Germans.

The question we have been discussing appears to throw
some light upon the rapidity with which most of the Teutonic
peoples accepted Christianity. The facts which we know with
regard to the conversion are as follows: (1) that it almost
invariably began in the king's court; (2) that violent opposition
was offered only in kingless communities, as among the Old
Saxons, or in defiance of the king's authority, as in Norway;
(3) that after the conversion the gods (in general) disappear at
once and for good; (4) that magical practices and the belief in
spirits and even in certain female agricultural deities ('Erce,'
Holda, Berhta, etc.) lasted among the country people for many
centuries. From (4) we may probably infer that the religion
of the country people was chiefly animistic—similar no doubt
to what we find in Iceland, with the exception that we have
little evidence for the cult of the thunder-god. Again, the
explanation of (3) hangs together with (1); for the statements
of ecclesiastical writers render it clear that the religion of the
courts was essentially theistic. But it is plain from the discussion in the Northumbrian council recorded by Bede (*H. E.*
II 13)—the only discussion of this kind of which we have any
detailed account—that here at least this religion retained little
vital force[1]. This fact is fully explained if, as I have endeavoured
to point out, theology had largely passed from the realm of
dogma into that of poetry.

The conclusion then to which we are brought is that Teutonic
religion, at all events in the courts, underwent a profound change
in the course of the Heroic Age. It is to be observed that in
the earlier part of that age—as in the earlier part of the Viking
Age—we find, especially among the more northern peoples,

---

[1] We may note especially the two speeches of Coifi, the chief priest: *Nihil
omnino uirtutis habet, nihil utilitatis religio illa quam hucusque tenuimus....Iam olim
intellexeram nihil esse quod colebamus; quia uidelicet quanto studiosius in eo cultu
quaerebam, tanto minus inueniebam.*

a fanatical devotion to warfare for its own sake, accompanied by lust for destruction and apparently also by a vivid conception of a life hereafter. In the latter part of the Heroic Age these phenomena disappear, except among the Heruli who, according to Procopius, differed from all the rest of mankind. The ideal which the princes of the later period set before themselves may be gathered both from Beowulf and from Roman authorities; it was to enjoy wealth and splendour in this life and to have their fame celebrated by future generations. For their attitude towards a future life the speech of the Northumbrian councillor recorded by Bede (*l.c.*) may probably be regarded as typical[1].

In a work such as this it is scarcely necessary to give even a brief summary of the characteristics of Greek religion, since the main outlines of the subject are probably much more familiar than those of even the later religion of the North. At the same time the amount of information which has been preserved is so great and the unsolved problems presented by the subject so numerous that it is clearly better left in the hands of experts. I shall attempt no more therefore than to call attention to the salient points in which the religion of the Homeric poems differs from that of later times and to the chief characteristics in which the former resembles or differs from the religion of the Teutonic Heroic Age and the Viking Age.

The various objects of worship recognised in Greece belong in general to much the same categories as those which we have noticed above. They may be classified roughly as gods, genii locorum and manes. In the last class we may perhaps include the 'heroes,' though the position occupied by them is somewhat peculiar. They were for the most part characters of the Heroic Age, and sometimes we find the cult of the same hero recognised in a number of different states. In general the worship of the gods took a different form from that paid to the manes and heroes, though occasionally the cult of a deity seems to have been associated with, or superimposed upon, that of a hero.

---

[1] *Ita haec uita hominum ad modicum apparet; quid autem sequatur, quidue praecesserit, prorsus ignoramus.*

In the Homeric poems the gods figure much more prominently than the other classes. The most frequently mentioned of them are Zeus, Hera, Poseidon, Athene, Apollo, Artemis, Hephaistos, Aphrodite, Ares and Hermes. Zeus, as head of the divine community, corresponds to Othin (Woden); but in other respects there is little resemblance between the two. As god of the thunder his affinities are rather with Thor. Hera, as wife of the chief god, may be compared with Frigg, while Poseidon, as god of the sea, has an element in common with Niörðr; but he is also an earthquake god, which the latter is not. His characterisation also is much more clearly marked. Apollo and Artemis, as a pair of young deities, brother and sister, with certain characteristics in common, bear some resemblance to Frey and Freyia; but the sexual element, so prominent in the Northern deities, is wanting in the Homeric poems. On the whole the translator of the Icelandic New Testament seems to have been happily inspired in rendering *Diana* (Artemis) by *Gefion*[1], while Freyia's true counterpart is rather to be found in Aphrodite[2]. Hephaistos, the smith of the divine community, has no Northern god corresponding to him; as the maker of heroes' armour and other metal objects he plays the same part as Weland. Ares, as god of war, has an element in common with Týr. The Homeric Hermes bears no resemblance to Othin; his duties are to a certain extent discharged by the valkyries in Northern mythology. Athene is a character totally foreign to Northern theology.

All the above deities, together with a number of others less important, form a regularly organised community, like the Aesir. Their home is located on Mount Olympos in the north of Thessaly—a conception probably more primitive than Ásgarðr, which is never represented as a place known to the human race. But, though Olympos is the home of the gods collectively, most of them (like the Northern deities) have also one or more

---

[1] Artemis in the Homeric poems seems to be chiefly a women's deity (cf. Od. xx 59 ff.). The same may have been the case with Gefion; cf. Gylfaginning, cap. 35: "She is a maiden, and those who die in maidenhood serve her."

[2] In origin however Freyia, the daughter of Niörðr (Nerthus), corresponds probably rather to Persephone, the daughter of Demeter; cf. p. 400.

dwelling-places of their own, often in distant localities. Thus
Poseidon's home is at Aigai and Apollo's at Delphoi, though
he is also connected with several localities on the eastern side of
the Aegean—Chryse, Cille, Tenedos, etc. Athene has a home
at Athens, while Hephaistos is connected with Lemnos, Ares
with Thrace and Aphrodite with Paphos in Cyprus. Zeus
himself, apart from Olympos, has abodes at Dodona and Ida.

The belief that the gods had homes of their own in various
localities is clearly to be taken in connection with the fact that
they are said to have sanctuaries in the same places. Thus
Aigai is mentioned, together with Helice, as a place where
sacrifices were offered to Poseidon (Il. VIII 203 f.). Zeus' home
at Dodona is his sanctuary (*ib.*, XVI 233 ff.), and it is to her
sanctuary at Paphos that Aphrodite goes (Od. VIII 362 f.). We
need not doubt therefore that, as in later times, the cults of the
various deities were largely of a local character. It is a different
question of course whether the cults—or rather the deities themselves—were of local or tribal origin ; but in certain cases such
an explanation appears to be by no means improbable. Many
scholars believe that Ares was originally a Thracian deity; and
the fact that he is represented as the father of Boeotian heroes
can scarcely be regarded as conclusive evidence to the contrary.
In Il. IV 51 f. Hera states that three cities, Argos, Mycenae and
Sparta, are specially dear to her; and there is little evidence
that her cult was ever prominent in any other part of the Greek
mainland. If the same explanation is true of such deities as
Apollo and Aphrodite we must suppose either that their cults
have spread from one locality to another or that deities belonging
to different localities have been identified. The local origin of
river gods, such as Spercheios and Scamandros, is of course
clear enough ; but these are little more than genii locorum.

But the really important feature in Homeric theology is that
the various deities, whether of local origin or not, are all brought
together as members of one community, or rather family, and
that as such they are represented as meeting with universal
recognition. Indeed, they are not regarded even as peculiar
to the Greek race; the Trojans recognise the same divinities,
and Poseidon goes to receive sacrifices even from the Ethiopians.

A similar, though less important, community is that of the marine deities, one of whom, Thetis, figures prominently in the Iliad.

The spirit in which the gods are treated is in general very similar to what we find in the Edda, and in no way more reverential. Sometimes the treatment is humorous, as in Thrymskviða; sometimes again the deities are represented in a very unfavourable light. For the trick played upon Wodan by Fria in the Langobardic story (cf. p. 115) we have an interesting parallel in Il. XIV 292—353, where Hera distracts Zeus' attention from the war and coaxes him to sleep. But this is only one of a number of incidents which give a generally unpleasant picture of the domestic life of this pair, much more so than is the case with Othin and Frigg in the Edda. Again, the story of Ares and Aphrodite, which forms the subject of Demodocos' lay (Od. VIII 266—366), is very much what we should expect to find in a poem dealing at length with the scandalous charges brought against the goddesses in Lokasenna. Ares' speech in v. 292 ff.—as also Hermes' remarks in v. 339 ff.—may be compared with those of Frey in Skírnismál. In the Iliad the same two deities are more than once treated contemptuously.

The same spirit is shown in the treatment of the relations of gods with men. It is frequently recognised that deities ought to show gratitude to their worshippers for the sacrifices offered to them, as Freyia does in Hyndlulióð, though at the same time they are at liberty to refuse a petition, as in Il. VI 311—a case which may be compared with Frey's conduct in Víga-Glúms Saga (cf. p. 253). In the Iliad we find several deities taking an active interest in the fortunes of the war—Poseidon, Hera and Athene on the side of the Achaeans, and Apollo, Ares and Aphrodite on that of the Trojans. Poseidon more than once comes to rouse the Achaeans, when he thinks they are becoming slack. Apollo and Athene interfere in the struggle in a manner which strikes the reader as unfair; indeed the latter is frequently guilty of flagrantly mean and dishonourable conduct towards her opponents. The attitude of the heroes themselves to the gods is quite in keeping with the way in which the latter treat them. Achilles openly abuses Apollo for deceiving him

(Il. XXII 15 ff.); and Diomedes attacks and wounds both Ares and Aphrodite, but only after assurances or assistance from Athene. In this respect the Homeric princes are not quite so bold as the hero of Biarkamál (cf. p. 402 f.).

But it is by no means only towards communities that the deities display their favour or hatred. Indeed their attitude towards the contending forces at Troy seems to be largely determined by their relations with certain individuals, especially Helen and Paris. In the Odyssey Poseidon is represented as persecuting Odysseus, one of the Achaean leaders, for many years on account of the injury done by him to Polyphemos. On the other hand both this hero and Diomedes enjoy the special favour of Athene. It is worth noting that Diomedes appears to have inherited this favour from his father (cf. Il. V 800 ff.), and the same may be true in the case of Odysseus (cf. Od. XXIV 367 ff., 517 ff.); at all events it is continued towards his son. In neither of these cases is any hint given of conjugal relations, such as we find in the North; indeed the sexual element seems to be practically absent from Athene. Elsewhere however such relations are clearly involved, e.g. in the cases of Aineias and Achilles, who are the sons of Aphrodite and Thetis respectively. In the Odyssey (V 119 ff.) the principle is stated plainly; and the hero himself has conjugal relations with Circe and Calypso, both of whom are described as goddesses.

Of other mythical beings the genii locorum are perhaps the most prominent. The distinction between them and the class with which we have been dealing is by no means so clearly drawn as in the north of Europe (cf. p. 407 f.). Many of them are even described as gods ($\theta\epsilon o i$). River gods, such as Spercheios and Axios, are represented as the fathers or ancestors of several heroes. Among other, less important, beings of the same type we may mention the nymphs[1] to whom certain caves and springs were sacred (e.g. Od. XIII 347 ff., XVII 205 ff., 240 ff.).

References to chthonic deities are not very frequent. The Erinyes are mentioned several times, especially in curses; but

---

[1] Even beings such as these are sometimes affiliated to Zeus; cf. Il. VI 420.

they are not individualised, though the singular is occasionally used. The most important person in the under-world appears to be the queen, Persephoneia; but she is never actually brought upon the scene. Hades himself is seldom more than a name.

The sacrifices to the gods mentioned in the Homeric poems are as a rule similar to the sacrificial feasts of which we hear in the North[1]. A portion of the victims, usually bulls or rams, was offered to the deity, while the rest was consumed by the worshippers. On the other hand we hear occasionally of victims which were given wholly to the gods. Such appears to have been the case with the victims sacrificed on the occasion of a solemn oath; thus in Il. XIX 267 f. the boar is thrown into the sea[2]. It is perhaps worth noting that both here and in III 276 ff. the oath refers to chthonic deities[3], as well as to Zeus, the Sun and Earth. Victims sacrificed to the dead likewise seem to be offered entire (e.g. Od. XI 44 ff.; Il. XXIII 166 ff.). Moreover it is only in connection with funeral rites that we hear of human sacrifices, namely when Achilles puts to death twelve Trojan youths at the pyre of Patroclos (ib., 175 f.). Horses and dogs are also sacrificed on this occasion, as well as oxen and sheep, and the whole scene is in accordance with Northern custom. No mention is made in the poems of sacrifices such as that of Polyxene, which form so favourite a theme with the dramatists; but in view of the Northern evidence[4] we are entitled to doubt whether they are altogether inventions of later times.

---

[1] So also with the ceremonial drinkings, which in both sets of records form so prominent a feature in the life of human and divine communities alike. Among the Greeks the libation corresponds to the Northern 'toast' (*full*) in honour of the gods. A good example may be found in Saga Hákonar Góða, cap. 16.

[2] Reference may be made to the boar which was sacrificed to Frey (or Freyia) in Hervarar Saga, cap. 10, and on which oaths were sworn. It is not made clear however what was done with the body of the boar.

[3] With the punishment of perjurers by the Erinyes in Il. XIX 259 f. we may compare what is said regarding the fate of such persons in Völuspá, str. 39.

[4] Reference may be made to Procopius' account of the Heruli (cf. p. 411) and more especially to the stories of Ibn Dustah and Ibn Fadhlan, quoted by Thomsen, *The Relations between Ancient Russia and Scandinavia*, etc., pp. 30 f., 34. Native records preserve only somewhat vague traditions relating to such a custom; cf. *The Cult of Othin*, p. 41 f.

The theology of the Homeric poems received formal recognition in Greece down to the acceptance of Christianity; but there is no evidence that the system as a whole possessed any vital force even in the earliest times of which we have record. From the sixth century onwards poets and philosophers began to regard Zeus as much more than the chief of the gods; but even in popular religion it appears that each state honoured certain deities, while the rest were largely or altogether neglected. Thus at Athens more prominence seems to have been given to Athene, and perhaps also to Poseidon, than to Zeus, while Hera was predominant at Argos and Samos, and Apollo at Delphoi, etc. This is a feature for which the Homeric poems themselves give evidence, as we have seen, and there is no reason whatever for supposing it to be of later growth. Sometimes too we find prominence given to deities, such as Demeter and Dionysos, who seem to be of little consequence in the Homeric poems, while other cults, such as that of Serapis, were introduced from abroad in comparatively late times.

Chthonic deities are more prominent in later literature than in the Homeric poems; and many authors describe the worship paid to them down to a comparatively late period. Yet the rites seem to have been of a primitive character. But perhaps the most striking element in the religion of classical Greece was the worship of 'heroes.' Every city possessed shrines ($\dot{\eta}\rho\hat{\omega}a$), at which sacrifices were offered to heroes with rites similar in general to those used in the worship of chthonic deities. Originally these heroes seem to have been local persons and the shrines their tombs; but characters prominent in heroic poetry sometimes received worship in many different states.

In the Homeric poems there is no evidence for this hero-worship. Indeed these poems contain few traces of a cult of the manes at all, except in funeral ceremonies and in connection with the necromantic sacrifice of Odysseus. This fact has been connected with the Homeric doctrine of immortality[1], and in view of the Northern evidence (cf. p. 397 ff.) there can be little doubt that the true explanation is to be found herein. The

---

[1] Cf. especially Ridgeway, *The Early Age of Greece*, p. 512 ff.

method used in the disposal of the dead is cremation, and, as
in the North, it was believed that this sent the spirit away from
the body to a place of the dead—not a separate place for each
particular family or community but a common home for the
souls of the whole Greek race.   In Il. XXIII 65 ff. the spirit of
Patroclos comes and exhorts Achilles to pay him the last rites :
"Never again shall I return from Hades, when ye have allotted
me the due of fire" (v. 75 f.).   So also when Odysseus visits the
home of Hades the first spirit he meets is that of his follower
Elpenor, who reproaches him with not attending to his obsequies
and begs him, when he returns to Circe's island, to "burn him
up with his arms, all that he possesses."   The idea is clearly
the same as in Ynglinga Saga, cap. 8.   The honourable way
therefore to treat a fallen foe is not to strip him but to burn
him with his armour, as in Il. VI 417 ff.[1]   Even at the beginning
of the historical period this belief seems not to have entirely
died out.   According to the story told by Herodotus (V. 92),
when Periandros sent to consult the spirit of his wife Melissa,
she complained that the clothes which he had given her at her
funeral were of no use because they had not been burnt.

It has already been mentioned (p. 261) that this story seems
to show that at one time the home of the dead was located in
a definite, though probably not very well known, region ; and
the vague indications given as to the hero's wanderings in the
Odyssey can hardly be regarded as evidence to the contrary.
If this is correct the home of Hades is in one respect probably
a more primitive conception than Valhalla, just as Olympos
is more primitive than Ásgarðr.   A reasonable explanation
would be offered if we had evidence that part of the population
of Greece was believed to have come from that region[2].   An
idea of this kind was certainly in Snorri's mind when he wrote
the Ynglinga Saga; but unfortunately the account which he
has given is obviously, at least to a large extent, of scholastic
origin.

[1] Reference may be made to the story of Haraldr Hilditönn and Sigurðr Hringr ;
cf. *The Cult of Othin*, p. 22 f.

[2] The existence of a tradition to this effect is perhaps implied by Aristotle,
Meteorolog., I 14, 21 f. ; cf. p. 437, note.

In other respects however the Homeric conception of immortality appears to be less simple than the doctrine of Valhalla, as we find it in certain Northern records. The use of the verbs θάπτειν and ταρχύσουσι is probably capable of a different explanation ; but there are certain other words and expressions, e.g. κατῆλθεν, ἔνεροι, Ζεὺς καταχθόνιος (Hades; cf. also Il. XX 61 ff.), which seem to point to a belief that the world of the dead was beneath the earth. That is the conception implied in certain local beliefs which we meet with in later times, at Hermione and elsewhere, where a deep cavern or lake was supposed to lead thither. More important however is the fact that the home of Hades is totally devoid of the attractiveness of Valhalla ; the gloomy picture which is drawn of it accords rather with the Northern home of Hel. The burning of the body, together with armour and funeral sacrifices, appears to procure little real advantage to the soul ; it is regarded, as in Beowulf, rather in the nature of an honour due to the deceased. Yet in view of the parallels which we possess, both from the North and elsewhere[1], we can scarcely doubt that the custom had its origin in a much stronger motive, the force of which was scarcely appreciated in later times. For a change of feeling, if not of actual faith, positive evidence is supplied by the reprobation expressed in Il. XXIII 176—a passage as significant in its way as the homiletic verses which follow the reference to heathen sacrifices in Beow. 175 ff. (cf. p. 53).

In the course of this chapter we have noticed a considerable number of features common to Greek and Teutonic religion. Many of them are to be found in other religions also, and these we need not discuss further. Here we are concerned only to

---

[1] In addition to the examples cited by Prof. Ridgeway we may refer to the account of the Livonians given by Bartholomaeus Anglicus, *De Proprietatibus Rerum*, XV 88 : *mortuorum cadauera tumulo non tradebant, sed populus facto rogo maximo usque ad cineres comburebat. post mortem autem suos amicos nouis uestibus uestiebant et eis pro uiatico oues et boues et alia animantia exhibebant. seruos etiam et ancillas cum rebus aliis ipsis assignantes una cum mortuo et rebus aliis incendebant, credentes sic incensos ad quandam uiuorum regionem feliciter pertingere et ibidem cum pecorum et seruorum sic ob gratiam domini combustorum multitudine felicitatis et uitae temporalis patriam inuenire.* This record dates from the thirteenth century (probably about 1260) ; so that Northern influence is not impossible.

determine what may be regarded as characteristic of the Heroic
Age. In this category we may probably include the following
features.

1. The religion was predominantly a worship of gods, rather
than of spirits. Herein lies the chief contrast with the religion
of later times in both regions[1]. In Classical Greece chthonic
worship and hero worship seem on the whole to be more prominent than that of the gods. The same is true of Scandinavian
countries in the latest heathen period, though Thor is still
prominent and hero worship is scarcely distinguished from
manes worship. In Germany and England, where Christianity
was adopted during the Heroic Age or soon afterwards, the
gods disappear at once, while forms of chthonic worship survive
for centuries.

2. The same gods were, to a large extent at least, recognised
everywhere. Whether by borrowing or by identification of cults
they had ceased to be merely tribal deities. How far back this
feature goes in Greece we cannot tell. Among the Teutonic
peoples we can trace it in part back to Tacitus' time; but it
was probably intensified during the Heroic Age.

3. The conception of the gods was definitely anthropomorphic. For the Teutonic Heroic Age this is made clear
by the Langobardic story. There is no absolutely conclusive
proof that the gods in general were regarded as forming a
regularly organised community, as in the Edda and the Homeric
poems; but all the evidence which we have (cf. p. 407 f.) points
in this direction.

4. The relations between gods and human beings are of
a somewhat peculiar character both in Teutonic poetry and in
the Homeric poems; but they are almost identical in the two
cases. The gods are not treated with any very great reverence.
The conduct attributed to them is not unfrequently repre-
hensible, their purposes can often be thwarted by the help of
other gods, and the bravest warriors are sometimes even ready

---

[1] This contrast is all the more noteworthy in view of the fact that the two chief
'heroic' deities, Woden (Othin) and Zeus, are of essentially different origin. The
affinities of the former lie rather with Hades—not as a chthonic being, properly
speaking, but as lord of the spirit world.

to attack them openly. Yet the human and the divine are not confused; a man is not a god, though many heroes, both Teutonic and Greek, are sprung from gods. It should be observed that the deity from whom most English princes claimed descent is Woden, a universal and not a tribal god. This belief must be regarded as an anti-tribal force.

5. Both in Northern tradition and in the Homeric poems the practice of cremation was associated with the belief in a common home for the souls of the dead. This practice does not appear to have been common even in the earlier part of the Viking Age; and consequently the tradition probably comes down from the Heroic Age, at which time we know that cremation was widely prevalent. The cheerless home of Hades[1] differs considerably from Valhalla, though there is some ground for suspecting that the Greeks of the Heroic Age had once cherished a belief endowed with greater vitality. But both conceptions possess certain essential features in common, namely the removal of the soul to a distant place—a belief really incompatible with the local worship of heroes or manes—and the fact that this distant place of souls was a universal home and not reserved for the souls of one tribe. This belief again was doubtless an anti-tribal force of considerable importance.

Briefly then we may define as the predominant characteristic of heroic religion, both Greek and Teutonic, the subordination of chthonic and tribal cults, which as a rule go together, to the worship of a number of universally recognised and highly anthropomorphic deities—coupled with the belief in a common and distant land of souls. These characteristics, at all events

---

[1] The characterisation of the home of Hades resembles rather that of the Northern abode of Hel (cf. p. 400, note). There can be little doubt that the latter conception is founded upon a belief of considerable antiquity, though, except in the North, all our information relating to it comes from sources affected by Christian influence. From references in early poetry, as well as from popular belief in later times, it seems probable that the early Teutonic conception of Hell (Goth. *halja*, etc.) involved something more than a survival of the soul in or about the place of sepulture, though there is nothing to show that it was identical with Valhalla. For the personification of Hell definite evidence is wanting; yet note should be taken of the fact that such beings as Holda and Berhta (like Freyia and Gefion) were connected with the spirit world.

among the Teutonic peoples, seem properly to have belonged only to the religion of the royal and military classes. Hence, when the royal families are converted to a new faith, as in England, or when kingless states grow up, as in Iceland, we find in all cases more or less of a reversion to the more primitive forms of religion. It is on the same principle that I would account for the differences in religion between heroic and historical Greece.

NOTE VIII. THE SOCIAL, POLITICAL AND RELIGIOUS CHARACTERISTICS OF THE CELTIC AND SLAVONIC HEROIC AGES.

In the last three chapters we have confined our attention almost exclusively to the Teutonic and Greek Heroic Ages. It is not to be overlooked however that similar phenomena occur elsewhere. The closest and most interesting parallels, at least in Europe, are probably to be found in the history of the ancient Gauls.

It has been mentioned above that Gaulish literature has entirely perished. We are dependent therefore for our information upon a few scattered references in the works of Greek and Roman writers. These however are sufficient to show that the Gauls possessed a well-known and influential class of professional minstrels (βάρδοι), whose chief occupation seems to have been the composition of heroic poetry[1]. Like the minstrels of the Teutonic and Greek Heroic Ages these persons were attached to the courts of kings, and their poems dealt with the praises of living princes as well as with the deeds of heroes of the past[2]. With the disappearance of kingship, early in the first century (B.C.), their standing seems to have been impaired. At all events they are never mentioned by Caesar, who has so much to say about the Druids.

It is probable therefore that by this time what may be termed the Gaulish Heroic Age was already at an end. How long it had lasted we cannot tell, since all the stories have perished. We may certainly note however that the accounts of Gaulish life which have come down to us from the time before the nation became Romanised show a most striking resemblance to the conditions described in Teutonic and Greek heroic poetry. The longest of these accounts is the one given by Diodoros (v 26 ff.), where their customs are described with a considerable amount of detail. The picture which he

---

[1] Cf. Ammianus Marcellinus, XV 9. 8 (probably from Timagenes): *et Bardi quidem fortia uirorum illustrium facta heroicis composita uersibus cum dulcibus lyrae modulis cantitarunt.* Cf. also Diodoros, V 31; Strabo, IV 4. 4; Lucan, *Phars.* I 447 ff.

[2] Cf. Athenaios, VI 49 (quoting Poseidonios): Κελτοὶ περιάγονται μεθ' αὑτῶν καὶ πολεμοῦντες συμβιωτὰς οὓς καλοῦσι παρασίτους. οὗτοι δὲ ἐγκώμια αὐτῶν καὶ πρὸς ἀθρόους λέγουσιν ἀνθρώπους συνεστῶτας καὶ πρὸς ἕκαστον τῶν κατὰ μέρος ἐκείνων ἀκροωμένων. τὰ δὲ ἀκούσματα αὐτῶν εἰσιν οἱ καλούμενοι Βάρδοι· ποιηταὶ δὲ οὗτοι τυγχάνουσι μετ' ᾠδῆς ἐπαίνους λέγοντες. Reference may also be made to the story of Luernios, king of the Allobroges, and the minstrel who arrived too late (*ib.*, IV 37). Cf. also Appian, *Celtice*, § 12 (describing the arrival of an envoy sent by Bitoitos, the father of Luernios): μουσικός τε ἀνὴρ εἵπετο, βαρβάρῳ μουσικῇ τὸν βασιλέα Βιτοῖτον, εἶτ' Ἀλλόβριγας, εἶτα τὸν πρεσβευτὴν αὐτὸν ἔς τε γένος καὶ ἀνδρείαν καὶ περιουσίαν ὑμνῶν· οὗ δὴ καὶ μάλιστα ἕνεκα αὐτοὺς οἱ τῶν πρεσβευτῶν ἐπιφανεῖς ἐπάγονται.

draws of their methods of fighting, their love of boasting[1], their habits in entertaining strangers[2] and many other particulars furnishes a parallel to Homeric life closer perhaps than may be found even in Anglo-Saxon poetry.

The principle of personal allegiance seems to have been developed among the Gauls to a very high degree, although our information dates chiefly from times when kingship had almost entirely disappeared. We have scarcely sufficient evidence for determining whether the development of this principle had been accompanied by a relaxation of the bonds of kindred. But Caesar's statement (*Gall.*, VI 11) regarding the universal prevalence of party spirit points in this direction[3]; and it is perhaps worth noting that attempts were made upon the lives of more than one of the princes who had submitted to him. There is reason for suspecting that among the Celtic peoples, as among the Teutonic, the organisation of the kindred had undergone a change, probably at no very remote period. The Picts adhered to succession in the female line, at all events in the royal family, down to the eighth century; and there are said to be traces of the same type of succession in Ireland It is commonly assumed that the Pictish succession was a pre-Celtic institution; but no evidence worth consideration has been adduced in favour of this view. We need not doubt the existence of pre-Celtic inhabitants in Scotland. But the same remark applies to the rest of the British Isles and at least a considerable part of Gaul, and I see no reason why in Scotland alone (or Scotland and Ireland) so important a change should have been taken over from the aborigines. In Gaul succession certainly passed in the male line in the first century (B.C.). But in the earliest Gaulish tradition of which we have record the title to sovereignty seems to go, as among the Picts, to the sons of the king's sister[4].

The political organisation of the Gauls appears to have been similar to that of the Teutonic peoples, though kingship was dying out in the first century. We find a considerable number of comparatively small nations (*ciuitates*), each of which apparently possessed a royal family of its own. From time to time one of these acquired a position of supremacy over all or

---

[1] κατὰ δὲ τὰς παρατάξεις εἰώθασι προάγειν τῆς παρατάξεως καὶ προκαλεῖσθαι τῶν ἀντιτεταγμένων τοὺς ἀρίστους εἰς μονομαχίαν, προαναϲείοντες τὰ ὅπλα καὶ καταπληττόμενοι τοὺς ἐναντίους. ὅταν δέ τις ὑπακούσῃ πρὸς τὴν μάχην τάς τε τῶν προγόνων ἀνδραγαθίας ἐξυμνοῦσι καὶ τὰς ἑαυτῶν ἀρετὰς προφέρονται καὶ τὸν ἀντιτατγόμενον ἐξονειδίζουσι καὶ ταπεινοῦσι καὶ τὸ σύνολον τὸ θάρσος τῆς ψυχῆς τοῖς λόγοις προαφαιροῦνται (V 29).

[2] πλησίον δ᾽ αὐτῶν ἐσχάραι κεῖνται γέμουσαι πυρὸς καὶ λέβητας ἔχουσαι καὶ ὀβελοὺς πλήρεις κρεῶν ὁλομερῶν. τοὺς δ᾽ ἀγαθοὺς ἄνδρας ταῖς καλλίσταις τῶν κρεῶν μοίραις γεραίρουσι...καλοῦσι δὲ καὶ τοὺς ξένους ἐπὶ τὰς εὐωχίας καὶ μετὰ τὸ δεῖπνον ἐπερωτῶσι τίνες εἰσὶ καὶ τίνων χρείαν ἔχουσιν (*ib.* 28).

[3] We may compare also what is said (*ib.* I 20) of the relations of Diuiciacus and Dumnorix. The latter had a large comitatus of his own: *magnum numerum equitatus suo sumptu semper alere et circum se habere* (I 18).

[4] Cf. Livy, V 34.

many of the others. Sometimes too sections of the same nation appear in widely different regions. Thus we find Senones and Lingones both in Gaul and Italy, Boii in Bavaria (Bohemia) and Italy, Volcae Tectosages in Germany and the south of Gaul—Tectosages also in Galatia. There is little doubt that in such cases one of these sections is an offshoot from the other and owes its origin to some military expedition.

In regard to religion Caesar (*ib.*, VI 21) draws a striking contrast between the Gauls and the Germans, though his account of the latter in this respect will not hold good for the Heroic Age. Gaulish religion was polytheistic and highly anthropomorphic; it would seem also that the gods were regarded as forming an organised community. The method employed in the disposal of the dead was cremation; and here too this practice was associated with a vivid conception of immortality. In all these respects Gaulish religion seems to have differed little from the types which we find in the Teutonic and Greek Heroic Ages, although apparently the belief in immortality largely took the form of metempsychosis. Only in one particular can we detect a really important difference between Gaulish religion and the others, namely in the influence of the priesthood. This feature however seems to have been peculiar to Gaul itself and Britain; at all events we hear nothing of Druids elsewhere. Indeed according to Caesar (VI 13) the institution was believed to have originated in Britain; and it is by no means impossible that some of its characteristic features may have developed in this country. More than this we cannot safely say, since there is an obvious—and probably by no means superficial—resemblance between Druidism and the priesthood of the Prussians and Lithuanians.

In previous Notes (p. 101 ff.) we spoke of two other Heroic Ages—those of the Bosnian Mohammedans, in the sixteenth and seventeenth centuries, and of the Cumbrian Welsh, about a thousand years earlier. In Note VII we discussed briefly one of the leading incidents in the (Christian) Servian Heroic Age, of the fourteenth century. In all these cases the question of religion is better left out of account; for though the form taken by Christianity or Mohammedanism was doubtless influenced to some extent by national characteristics, the two religions were essentially of foreign origin.

Among the Bosnians however the influence of Mohammedanism affected also the organisation of society, while the government was in the hands of pashas sent from Constantinople. On the whole the conditions appear to have little in common with those of the Teutonic and Greek Heroic Ages. Even the principle of personal allegiance is not much in evidence.

On the other hand this principle is very prominent in the Christian Servian poems, at all events in those which deal with the battle of Kossovo. It is exemplified both in the relations of squires (such as Vaistina) with their lords and in those of the latter with the king. In the poem on the banquet (Karadžić, II 50 iii), which we have discussed above (p. 315), it is to this principle alone that Lazar appeals, when he reproaches Miloš for his suspected disloyalty; and though the latter in his reply does mention that he intends to die for the Christian faith, he too evidently regards loyalty to his king as his primary duty. My knowledge of this subject is unfortunately not sufficient to enable me to form an opinion as to whether the growth of the bond of allegiance was accompanied by a relaxation of the bonds of kinship. In the lower ranks of society however the kindred has preserved down to the present time perhaps greater vitality among the Servians than in any other European nation. The type of government which we find prevailing in the fourteenth century is far removed from that democratic system which Procopius (*Goth.*, III 14) ascribes to the Slavs some six centuries previously. The governors whom Dušan appointed in various parts of his dominions became practically independent princes after his death, although their principalities rested apparently on no national basis. Both in Servia proper and elsewhere the control of affairs seems to have been very largely in the hands of the royal family.

For the Cumbrian Heroic Age our information is sadly deficient. The evidence of the poems leaves no doubt as to the potency of the force of personal allegiance. With regard to the kindred I know of no evidence, unless we take account of the Welsh laws, which belong to a different region and to a period several centuries later. The kingdoms seem to have been fairly numerous, and there is nothing to show that their organisation differed much from that of Teutonic kingdoms of the Heroic Age. Whether they rested on any national basis we cannot tell; but it is to be noted that practically all their territories had once been included within the Roman frontiers[1].

---

[1] The rise of the Cumbrian kingdoms presents a difficulty which historians do not seem to me to have sufficiently realised. During the fourth and fifth centuries the northern parts of the province were repeatedly menaced and ravaged by Pictish invaders. Yet after the fifth century we hear practically nothing more of Picts in the south of Scotland (except in Galloway). On the other hand it was in this region that the Britons offered the most determined resistance to the English. In the latter part of the sixth century Urien is said (*Hist. Br.*, § 63) to have besieged them on one occasion in Lindisfarne (*Metcaud*); and in Strathclyde the Britons maintained their independence, except for one or two brief intervals, until long after the disappearance of the Northumbrian kingdom. It is often assumed, though on somewhat slender grounds, that the Britons held only the south-west of Scotland and that the south-east (Lothian, etc.) was Pictish before the English conquest. But this hypothesis does not get rid of the difficulties; for it is from *Manau Guotodin*, a district always regarded as Pictish, that Cunedda is said to have come (*ib.*, § 62). I suspect that the distinction between Picts and Britons was not so rigid as is commonly supposed. Unfortunately Celtic scholars have not yet been able to come to any agreement as to the character of the Pictish language. Some hold that it was British (Brythonic), others Gaelic (Goidelic), others again non-Celtic. Possibly all these views may contain a certain amount of truth. At all events it seems to me quite incredible that Gaelic was not introduced into Scotland before the sixth century. All indications appear to me to

Both these cases then appear to show a number of the features which characterise the Teutonic and Greek Heroic Ages, though scarcely to the same degree as is the case with the civilisation of the ancient Gauls. Analogies may also be found in the French and Russian Heroic Ages ; but I am not aware that either of these presents any remarkable characteristics which do not occur in one or other of those with which we have dealt. On the other hand I have no doubt that many interesting features are to be found in the Irish Heroic Age (or rather perhaps Heroic Ages[1]). This subject however is beset with such extreme difficulties of every kind that I dare not touch it.

favour the view that this language belonged to a wave of Celtic invasion earlier than the British. Yet I see no objection to supposing that in pre-Roman times the true (Gaelic) Picts—who probably included a non-Celtic substratum—may have been overlaid in part by a British element. If so, it is far from improbable that the south of Scotland in its turn received a ‘ Pictish ’ element, when that district was abandoned by the Romans. A mixed population of this kind would readily enough coalesce with the native (British) inhabitants.

[1] So also in the Heroic Ages of non-European peoples. Important parallels are certainly furnished by Sanskrit epic poetry.

CHAPTER XIX

THE CAUSES AND ANTECEDENT CONDITIONS
OF THE HEROIC AGE

In the course of the last three chapters we have observed many remarkable resemblances between the Teutonic and Greek Heroic Ages—in social organisation, in the forms of government and in religious conceptions. Further we have seen that in the former case the testimony of the poems is fully substantiated by contemporary historical authorities. In the latter case we possess no evidence which affords us ground for doubting that the poems give an equally faithful reflection of conditions and ideas which prevailed in real life. Our next and final object is to enquire into the nature of the causes to which the common characteristics of the two Heroic Ages are due.

I do not think that any one will seriously suggest the possibility of a historical connection between the two Heroic Ages, separated as they are from one another by an interval of some fourteen or fifteen centuries. It is perhaps conceivable that one or other of the common elements which we have noted may have originated in Greece and worked its way round until it appears after so long a lapse of time in the north of Europe[1]. But for the phenomena as a whole any such explanation is incredible.

---

[1] Cremation may have a common origin in the two cases ; but this practice appears to have been introduced into the North at least fifteen centuries before the Heroic Age. It has been suggested that the origin of the practice may be found in the late neolithic settlements in the district of the Dniestr and Dniepr—dating probably from the latter part of the third millennium (cf. Meyer, *Geschichte des Altertums*[2], 1 § 537). Evidence however is now accumulating to the effect that cremation was practised in Crete in Early Minoan times.

Another explanation is suggested by the fact that the Greek and Teutonic peoples are ultimately related, at least linguistically—both being members of the Indo-European family. It is only reasonable therefore to expect that they may have inherited common characteristics. But this explanation does not in itself account for the fact that the Heroic Age begins in one case some fourteen or fifteen centuries after the other. Moreover the Heroic Age of the Southern Slavs begins about a thousand years later than that of the Teutonic peoples, while we have no evidence that the Lithuanians ever had a Heroic Age. Yet both of these equally belong to the Indo-European linguistic family.

Again it may be suggested that the causes responsible for the Heroic Age are to be found not so much in ethnical affinity as in the possession of a similar stage of culture. The term 'Early Iron Age' is customarily applied to both the Teutonic and Greek Heroic Ages. But this common application of the term is misleading. In the Greek Heroic Age the use of iron, at all events for weapons, seems to have been only beginning, whereas the Teutonic peoples had been using iron weapons for at least seven or eight centuries before their Heroic Age. Moreover both the Lithuanians and the Southern Slavs have passed through similar stages of culture—in the latter case many centuries before the first Servian Heroic Age.

The suggestions put forward above may doubtless help to account for certain features in both the Teutonic and the Greek Heroic Ages ; but it cannot be contended that they are capable, whether singly or collectively, of explaining the phenomena as a whole. If we are to obtain a more satisfactory explanation we shall do well in the first place to give our attention to the outstanding characteristics of that period of history which coincides with the Teutonic Heroic Age.

This period was a momentous time in Teutonic history. In the first place it saw the conversion of most of the Continental peoples to Christianity. But probably no one will suggest that the Heroic Age was an outcome of this change. On the other hand the same period witnessed the fall of the Western Empire and the occupation of almost all its territories by Teutonic

C.

peoples. The effect of these movements must have been enormous, and in them we may reasonably expect to find at least one of the chief causes of the phenomena which we are discussing. At the same time it is to be remembered that the Vandals and Visigoths, who penetrated farthest into the empire, do not figure in stories of the Heroic Age, while even the Franks are less conspicuous than the Danes, who took no part in these movements.

In the case of the Greek Heroic Age we have unfortunately to depend upon inferences, since no historical evidence is obtainable. Not many years ago Prof. Ridgeway[1] advanced a very interesting theory, which has greatly influenced subsequent opinion, at least in this country. This theory, stated briefly, is to the effect that the Achaeans were a people from Central Europe who had made their way into Greece by way of Epeiros, not very long before the Heroic Age, and conquered the indigenous inhabitants, whom he calls Pelasgians. In support of this view he has brought forward a large number of arguments relating to physical characteristics, habits, dress, armour, social organisation, religion, funeral customs, etc., in which he shows that the affinities of the Homeric Achaeans lie with the Celtic peoples rather than with the earlier inhabitants of Greece.

It is impossible here to enter into a detailed discussion of Prof. Ridgeway's theory. The first objection which may be raised against it lies in the absence of traditional evidence for the great movement of population which it involves—evidence such as we possess for the Dorian conquest and the Ionic migration. The force of this objection depends of course a good deal upon what may be called details, e.g. the date of the invasion, the numerical strength of the invaders and the method by which the conquest was effected. A more serious objection is perhaps to be found in the conditions postulated by Prof. Ridgeway for Central Europe. Probably few who have given much attention to the subject will be inclined to dispute that the affinities of Homeric civilisation lie in many respects with that of the Celtic peoples, rather than with the earlier civilisation of the Aegean.

---

[1] *The Early Age of Greece*, Vol. I, Ch. IV and passim, together with a number of articles which have appeared in various publications.

But all the evidence at our disposal seems to indicate that among the Celtic peoples this type of civilisation belongs to a much later period. There is nothing to show that even at Hallstatt and elsewhere in the Eastern Alps the earliest use of iron[1] goes back to the beginning of the first millennium, and it is extremely doubtful whether these deposits are of Celtic origin[2]. In order to prove that Homeric civilisation came from Central Europe evidence must be adduced showing that the chronology usually accepted by archaeologists is mistaken and that a civilisation of the same type prevailed in that region far back in the second millennium. Until such evidence is forthcoming it appears more probable that both the civilisation of Central and Western Europe and the non-Mycenean elements in Homeric civilisation have radiated from a common centre, the true home of which has not yet been discovered.

These considerations however must not be allowed to obscure the fact that Prof. Ridgeway's observations have thrown light on a number of serious difficulties in early Greek history. In the first place he has rightly insisted upon a recognition of the great differences noticeable between Homeric and Mycenean civilisation—differences which can hardly be accounted for except by some such explanation as that which he has brought forward. It is now admitted by the majority of scholars that the Aegean civilisation cannot have originated with the Achaeans; but there is still great difference of opinion as to the nature of its relations with this people. Some hold that the prehistoric civilisation of Crete was non-Achaean—and indeed non-Greek— until its fall, and yet believe that Mycenae and the other cities of the mainland were always Achaean. Others again hold that the later remains both on the mainland and in Crete are Achaean, while the earlier ones, at all events in Crete, were

---

[1] I mention this point only because Prof. Ridgeway lays stress upon it. I do not myself regard the use of iron weapons as an essential characteristic of the Heroic Age. The evidence seems to me to indicate that such weapons came into use only towards the close of the period (cf. p. 199 ff.).

[2] By this term I mean 'belonging to communities which spoke Celtic languages.' It is only fair to add that Prof. Ridgeway appears to have racial (physical), rather than linguistic, characteristics in view. But I am not clear whether he means to include among his 'Celts' peoples who used other than Celtic languages.

non-Achaean. But neither of these theories accounts for the differences between Mycenean and Homeric civilisation[1]. Both alike involve the assumption that the latter is a reflection of the conditions of a later age—an assumption which, as we have seen, can scarcely be reconciled with the evidence of the poems on the use of the metals and other matters discussed above.

Secondly, Prof. Ridgeway has pointed out the groundlessness of the prevalent hypothesis that the Achaeans were the first Greek-speaking inhabitants of Greece. He has rightly insisted on the antiquity of the Arcadians and Athenians, together with certain other peoples, Ionians and Cypriotes, who had emigrated from Greece, and at the same time called attention to the fact— which is commonly overlooked—that none of these peoples claimed to be of Achaean origin[2]. The Achaean communities of historical times used dialects of the West Greek type, as distinct from Ionic or Arcadian as they are from Aeolic, and we have no evidence that they ever spoke a different type of language. On this subject however enough has been said above (p. 281 ff.). The name 'Pelasgian,' which Prof. Ridgeway applies to the earlier Greek inhabitants, seems to me to be open to objection; yet the evidence of Herodotus can be adduced in its favour.

---

[1] What I mean by the term 'Homeric civilisation' will probably be clear from Chapters X and XI. I cannot admit that a satisfactory case has been made out for believing the civilisation of the Heroic Age to have differed widely from that of the poets' own times. The excavations at Cnossos have brought to light the existence (in 'Late Minoan' times) of a highly organised bureaucratic system, for which analogies enough are to be found in Egyptian records of the same period. But the poems themselves do not give the slightest hint of acquaintance with such a system. The absence of striking inconsistencies which has been remarked above (p. 241) is unintelligible unless the civilisation with which the poets themselves were acquainted— presumably in Aeolis—was a more or less direct continuation of that of the Heroic Age. Such changes as had taken place were in general probably of a retrograde character, in spite of the growing use of iron and possibly also of riding. But there is no ground, so far as I can see, for supposing that the Homeric poems are records of the people and events of a highly civilised age preserved by the traditions of a semi-barbaric society.

[2] Both in Ionia and Cyprus there were of course cities which, according to tradition, had been founded by Achaean colonists. But the Greek population as a whole made no such claim in either case. For Cyprus cf. Herodotus VII 90.

Thirdly, when Prof. Ridgeway holds that the route by which the Achaeans made their way southwards was through Epeiros he has in his favour an argument of considerable weight in the antiquity and importance of the sanctuary at Dodona, which in historical times lay on the extreme edge of the Greek world. But, apart from this, the linguistic geography of Greece is unintelligible to me unless dialects of the Arcadian and Ionic types were once spoken over a much larger area in Greece proper than that in which we find them in historical times. All indications seem to point to the region west of Pindos as the home of that West Greek group to which the Achaean dialects belong[1].

Lastly it must be regarded as improbable that Epeiros was solely responsible for those elements in Homeric or Achaean civilisation which differentiate it from that of the Mycenean age and at the same time connect it with the civilisations of Central and Western Europe. In historical times this country had passed almost entirely into the possession of barbarian peoples owing to pressure from the north, and we have no reason for supposing that this process was new. It is commonly held that in the period preceding the Heroic Age[2] there had been great

---

[1] Aristotle (*Meteorolog.* I 14. 21 f.) applies the term Ἑλλὰs ἡ ἀρχαία to the country round Dodona and the Acheloos; but it is commonly held that in this he was following a late Molossian story relating to Dodona, rather than a genuine tradition. Yet the part played by the Acheron in Greek religion and poetry (cf. p. 422) suggests that this region was at one time traditionally regarded by a portion of the Greek race as its home-land.

[2] A different view is taken by Prof. Meyer (*Gesch. d. Alt.*[2], I § 473, note) who accepts the statement of the Lydian historian Xanthos (quoted by Strabo, XIV 5. 29 ; cf. XII 8. 3) that the Phrygian invasion took place μετὰ τὰ Τρωικά. He holds that this statement is confirmed by a passage in Proclus' epitome of the Telegony (cf. Kinkel, *Epic. Gr. Fragm.*, p. 57), where the Thesprotoi are represented as being at war with the Brygoi. But the latter are clearly the Brygoi of Albania; and there is nothing in the context to suggest that the Phrygians (of Asia) were believed to be still with their kinsfolk in the west. It seems to me that the statement of a fifth century writer, who is known only from fragments, requires stronger confirmation than this before it can be accepted as evidence for the chronological relationship of events which took place some seven centuries before his time. Especially is this the case when such a statement is directly opposed to several passages in the Iliad, which clearly recognise the presence of the Phrygians in Asia. In view of the fact that the queen (Hecabe) is said to be a Phrygian it is scarcely safe to assume that these elements are unessential or late additions to the story. But, more than this, Xanthos'

movements of population from the Balkan peninsula into the
north-west of Asia Minor—a process which likewise was repeated
in later times.   What little evidence we have for the civilisation of
these peoples does not suggest any great difference between
their civilisation and that of the Homeric Greeks.   The Homeric
poems in particular seem to draw little or no distinction in this
respect between the Achaeans on the one hand and the Trojans
and their allies on the other.   Hence, whatever may be our
attitude to the arguments based on physical characteristics, etc.,
on which Prof. Ridgeway lays so much weight, we cannot,
I think, reasonably regard it as improbable that Epeiros had long
been affected by movements from the same quarter.   Indeed the
existence of considerable ' Illyrian ' or semi-Illyrian populations

account itself does not appear to be free from Homeric influence.   The names
Βερεκύντων and 'Ασκανίας may possibly be derived from Phrygian tradition—perhaps
ultimately from the same source as Il. II 862 f.—but the leader's name (Σκαμάνδριος)
is not only Homeric but obviously a derivative of Σκάμανδρος, the name of a river in
the Troad.   It may be observed that a hero of the same name (Hector's son) figures
in a somewhat similar story recorded by Strabo elsewhere (XIII 1. 52); and for my
part I see no reason for attaching more importance to Xanthos' account than to this.
The expression ἐκ......τῶν ἀριστερῶν τοῦ Πόντου clearly suggests that he had confused
the tradition of the Phrygian invasion with certain much later movements (of the
Bithynians, Thynoi, etc.), some of which do seem to have proceeded from the quarter
indicated.   On the other hand all the evidence which we have (cf. Herodotus, VII 73
and VIII 138, and the position of the Brygoi in historical times) points to the western
part of the Balkan peninsula as the original home of the Phrygians.

As to the nationality of the Trojans themselves—the Homeric Trojans—Prof. Meyer
does not appear to have expressed an opinion.   The question will doubtless be discussed
in the next volume of his work.   His theory however would seem to involve that any
historical events which may underlie the story of the Iliad must be referred at least to
the thirteenth century ; for the date which he gives for the Phrygian invasion is about,
or shortly after, 1200.   Here again however I cannot help thinking that the evidence
is far from conclusive.   There may very well be a connection between the fall of the
Hittite kingdom, which apparently did take place about this time, and the invasion
encountered by Rameses III (cf. p. 188).   But I am by no means clear why it is
necessary to conclude that the Phrygian invasion immediately preceded these events.
If the Masa and Dardenui of the Poem of Pentaur are rightly identified with the
Mysians and Dardanoi we shall probably have to date the earliest settlements at least
a century before this time.   As for the Dardanoi—who apparently were regarded as
the parent stock of the Homeric Trojans (cf. Il. XX 215 ff.)—I see no reason for
doubting their European origin any more than that of the Phrygians (Brygoi) and the
Mysians (Moisoi), whose neighbours they were both in Asia and in the Balkans.   But
at the same time there seems to me to be equally little reason for referring the events
on which the Iliad is based to times anterior to the eleventh century.

in Italy, which certainly date from pre-historic times, shows that these movements took a south-westerly, as well as a south-easterly, course. A common centre of disturbance may be found in the highlands of Albania and Upper Macedonia, though I do not mean to deny that this area itself may have been affected by movements from more northern regions.

It may be that in the volumes of his work which have still to appear Prof. Ridgeway will be able to bring forward some stronger evidence in favour of the northern origin of the Achaeans. But even with the reservations expressed above it will be seen that this theory provides a parallel on a small scale to those historical movements which characterised the Heroic Age of the Teutonic peoples. And some such explanation is certainly required, even apart from the Homeric poems, in order to account for the archaeological phenomena and the ethnic and linguistic geography of Greece in the historical period. It is Prof. Ridgeway's great service to have pointed out that the 'Homeric question' is only a part of a much greater problem. Towards the solution of this problem little progress can be made by hypotheses like those which we have discussed in Chapters XIII and XIV—according to which one hero is derived from a god or 'tribal personification,' while another is a fictitious character which a credulous public has come to regard as historical. Even in the best of cases it is only the surface of the problem which can be touched by such investigations. Prof. Ridgeway has shown that the real problem which lies behind the Homeric poems is not, as has been said, the development of Greek heroic tradition ('die Entwickelung der griechischen Heldensage') but the character and origin of the Greek Heroic Age. This in its turn must be regarded as only one of a series of phenomena which we meet with among various peoples and at various periods of the world's history. In short the real problem presented by the Homeric poems is one not of literature but of anthropology.

We have seen that the Teutonic Heroic Age was a time of great national movements and that something of the same kind appears to have taken place in or shortly before the Greek

Heroic Age. But it is obvious enough that such movements in themselves will not account for the common characteristics of the two Heroic Ages which we have discussed in the last three chapters. In order to obtain an explanation of these phenomena we shall have to take the evidence of other Heroic Ages into consideration.

In the course of our discussion we have had occasion to refer to four other Heroic Ages, namely those of the Mohammedan and the Christian Servians, the Cumbrian Welsh and the ancient Gauls. Taking account of these and all other similar cases of which I have any knowledge I am not clear that the essential conditions requisite for a Heroic Age need involve more than may conveniently be summed up in the phrase 'Mars and the Muses.' It is to poetry that we owe the preservation of the stories—and indeed much more than this; for wherever we have any evidence as to its character heroic poetry seems to have aimed at something more than a mere record of facts. Indeed there can be little doubt that it exercised a considerable influence upon the spirit of the times.

The part played by 'Mars' is perhaps not so obvious; for it is clear from Beowulf and the Odyssey that a state of actual war is not a necessary condition either for heroic society or even for the formation of a heroic story. Yet I cannot call to mind a single story in which the hero, i.e. the leading sympathetic character, is not distinguished for personal bravery; and usually the main action of the story turns upon a situation in which opportunity is given for the display of this quality. It appears to me incredible that the types of character most prominent in all these forms of heroic poetry could have flourished in times of profound international peace and settled social conditions[1]. Indeed I cannot but think that under such conditions most of our heroes would sooner or later have found themselves in prison.

On the whole warfare is the state of affairs most commonly involved in heroic stories. It is a fact worth noting however

---

[1] Under such conditions the nearest approach to the heroic spirit is afforded by athletic contests. Such contests have at times produced what we may call 'heroic' poetry of Stage 1 (cf. p. 94). But the motive for further elaboration of the stories is wanting.

that this warfare almost invariably takes the form of hand-to-hand fighting and very frequently that of a series of single combats.   The national aspect of war is seldom brought into much prominence.   With the Teutonic and Greek evidence on this subject we have already dealt (pp. 329 f., 339 ff.); and we may perhaps remark that all the other Heroic Ages ended in periods of failure or even disaster.   In the Welsh and Servian Heroic Ages the warfare certainly has a religious side; but this aspect is not always so prominent in the poems as one might have expected.   We know too from historical sources that Welsh princes often fought in alliance with the heathen English during the first part of the seventh century.   Similar events were by no means unknown in Servian history.   The chief hero of the Southern Slavs, Kraljević Marko, was in alliance with the Turks, if he did not actually fight on their side at the battle of Kossovo.

The triumphs for which the heroes of heroic poetry hope and for which they are celebrated in the poems are primarily of a personal character and gained by personal prowess, even in times of national war; and all the stories alike are permeated by the spirit of personal adventure.   Sometimes we find this spirit indulged with a reckless disregard of consequences, as when Odysseus seeks out the Cyclops in his cave[1], or when the Beg Ljubović visits the white city of Zara.   Not unfrequently of course the object with which such adventures are undertaken is the acquisition of wealth.   But wealth itself is desired not so much in order to ensure a life of comfort or even a position of influence, but rather for the sake of display—that the hero may be able to outshine all his rivals in splendour.   Desire of personal glory—often coupled with love of adventure for its own sake— appears to be the leading motive in all the various types of heroic poetry which we have considered.

Now it has often been remarked that the savage is in many respects like a child.   We are certainly not justified in describing the people of any of the Heroic Ages treated above as savages; but it would be an equally great error to regard their civilisation, even in the best case, as mature.   And in this respect I cannot

---

[1] In the folk-tale—at least in some forms of it—the hero's arrival in the cave is involuntary.

help thinking that modern historians have tended to fall into a mistake similar to that which has sometimes been made by European governors of savage or semi-civilised communities. It is a mistake for which our historical authorities themselves are doubtless partly responsible; for we need not suppose that Greeks or Romans of the past, whether scholars or statesmen, were better able to understand the motives of heroic societies than are similar persons in our own days. The qualities exhibited by these societies, virtues and defects alike, are clearly those of adolescence. Further, we may note in this connection that the evidence of history gives us no ground for supposing that the 'heroic' spirit is an innate and permanent characteristic of certain peoples. It may be possible to point to communities in which the Heroic Age has persisted for many centuries, just as numerous peoples in different parts of the world have remained in a state of 'infancy' or savagery down to the present time. In Europe however the Heroic Age has been a transient phase. The sequel has sometimes been disastrous, sometimes comparatively prosperous; but in every case the ideas which animated the Heroic Age have ceased to retain their hold.

Thus far we have been seeking to find characteristics common to various Heroic Ages. It will be convenient here to refer briefly to the conclusions at which we arrived in the last three chapters. We saw (p. 365) that in regard to social organisation the outstanding feature both of the Teutonic and Greek Heroic Ages was the weakening of the ties of kindred and the growth of the bond of allegiance. In political organisation (p. 390 f.) the chief feature of both periods was the development of an irresponsible type of kingship resting upon military prestige, the formation of kingdoms with no national basis and the growth of relations between one kingdom and another. In religion (p. 425) the predominant characteristic in both cases was the subordination of chthonic and tribal cults to the worship of a number of universally recognised and highly anthropomorphic deities, together with the belief in a common and distant land of souls. Lastly, we observed (in Note VIII) that the Gaulish Heroic Age appears to have possessed almost all the same characteristics, while in regard to social and political organisation analogies are also to be found in the Heroic Ages of the Cumbrian Welsh and the Christian Servians, though hardly—or only to a very slight extent—in that of the Moham-médan Servians.

Now it deserves to be remarked that these characteristics are in no sense primitive. In social organisation the distin-guishing feature of the Heroic Age is in the nature of a revolt or emancipation from those tribal obligations and ideas by which the society of primitive peoples is everywhere governed. The same remark applies in principle to political organisation; the princes of the Heroic Age appear to have freed themselves to a large extent from any public control on the part of the tribe or community. The changes which we have noted in religion have a similar tendency. Tribal ideas give way to universalism both in the cult of higher powers and in the con-ception of immortality ; and in both the Teutonic and Greek Heroic Ages these changes seem to be associated with a weakening in the force of religion. Briefly expressed, the characteristic feature of both periods is emancipation, social, political and religious, from the bonds of tribal law.

It will be seen that the emancipation of which we are speak-ing is partly of an intellectual character. This applies both to religion and to those ideas which govern social relations. On the other hand it is also partly in the nature of a freedom from outside control, both in social relations and in government. The force formerly exercised by the kindred is now largely transferred to the comitatus, a body of chosen adherents pledged to personal loyalty to their chief. So also in government the council of the tribe or community has come to be nothing more than a comitatus or court. The result of the change is that the man who possesses a comitatus becomes largely free from the control of his kindred, while the chief similarly becomes free from control within his community. In both cases the only opposition that he now has to fear is from rivals who desire to take his place or from persons outside the kindred or community and in a similar position to himself. Certainly this freedom applies only to the case of kings or princes with followings of their own. But there is no reason for supposing that intellectual emancipation made much headway except among such persons and their entourages.

We have seen above that the characteristics of Heroic Ages in general are those neither of infancy nor of maturity—that the typical man of the Heroic Age is to be compared rather with a youth. The characteristics which we are now discussing are by no means inconsistent with such a view, though clearly they will not hold good for adolescence in general. For a true analogy we must turn to the case of a youth who has outgrown both the ideas and the control of his parents—such a case as may be found among the sons of unsophisticated parents, who through outside influence, at school or elsewhere, have acquired knowledge which places them in a position of superiority to their surroundings.

If we examine the history of the Teutonic Heroic Age we shall see that this analogy holds good both for individual princes and for the class as a whole. From the first century to the fifth —we may take the cases of Italicus the son of Flavus and of Theodric the Ostrogoth—it was customary for the Romans to demand the youthful sons of Teutonic kings as hostages. That the accession of such persons to power in later life would open up a channel for the introduction of foreign ideas needs probably no demonstration. But this was doubtless only one of a number of such channels. There is scarcely a single considerable deposit of antiquities dating from the first four centuries, not only in the south and west of Germany but even in Denmark and other Baltic lands, which does not contain a large proportion of Roman[1] articles. Among such articles we may mention coins, works of art (glass vases, statuettes, etc.) and, perhaps above all, armour and weapons. We may refer in particular to the Roman helmets and the large number of Roman swords and shield-bosses found in deposits on the east side of the province

---

[1] In this chapter I am using the word ‘Roman’ in a very wide sense, viz. for the civilisation of the Empire as a whole. Both the material objects and the influence of which I am speaking came doubtless rather from the provinces than from Italy itself. In many cases it would probably be more correct to use the term ‘Romanised Celtic’; cf. *The Origin of the English Nation*, p. 189 ff., though I think now that I was mistaken here in doubting the importance of (strictly) Roman influence upon the Angli— especially in military matters.

of Slesvig—a district remote from the Roman frontiers. The linguistic evidence too is in full agreement with that of the antiquities. Of the immense number of Latin loan-words which found their way into the Teutonic languages it is probable that quite a considerable proportion were borrowed in or before the Heroic Age.

Among the various channels through which Roman goods and Roman influence found entry into the Teutonic world we may mention trade, presents and subsidies, and booty gained by wars and piratical raids. But the most potent influence of all perhaps was the Roman practice of employing Teutonic mercenary soldiers—of which we hear both from inscriptions and literary works. This practice had begun as early as the first century, and it is noteworthy that those German princes who gave the Romans most trouble, such as Arminius and Civilis, were men who had previously served with their own armies. In the early part of the Heroic Age it appears that a very considerable proportion not only of the troops but also of the generals in the imperial service were of Teutonic nationality. Such forces were contributed largely by communities which had settled within the boundaries of the empire, such as the Goths and Vandals in the basin of the Danube and those smaller communities that we hear of incidentally in the east of Gaul. But it was by no means only from these dependent or semi-dependent principalities that the auxiliary troops were drawn. In the reigns of Constantius and Valentinian I the Roman army in Britain contained troops of Heruli—a nation which probably occupied the basin of the Elbe and had never been under Roman sovereignty, although a portion of it submitted to Justinian long afterwards. We have reason for believing that in the sixth century persons from the farthest parts of the Teutonic world were fighting in Italy. Otherwise it is difficult to account for the knowledge of Norway and Sweden shown by both Jordanes and Procopius.

It would be a mistake no doubt to suppose that the comitatus owes its origin to this mercenary service. The evidence for its existence goes back so far that a Gaulish derivation would be more probable, if it is not of native origin.

But there can scarcely be any question that this form of service tended to promote its development. Here too we find a satisfactory explanation of other phenomena noticeable in the Heroic Age, in particular of that military type of kingship which rests on no national basis. Further, it needs no demonstration that such service would contribute very largely to sweep away tribal prejudices and national patriotism.

On the whole then the conclusion to which we are brought is that the characteristics of the Heroic Age owe their origin not so much to the national movements which brought about the destruction of the Western Empire as to the long-standing relations between the two peoples, and perhaps more especially to the influence exercised by mercenary service. Now we obtain a more satisfactory explanation of the effects produced on the more northern peoples. It is by no means improbable that warriors even from Denmark fought in the Roman armies, while others again may have entered the service of Eormenric, Attila or Theodric. At all events we can hardly doubt that, directly or indirectly, the northern peoples were affected to no small degree by the influence of Roman civilisation and the Roman army.

I do not suppose that anyone will be inclined to question the influence of the same civilisation upon the Welsh Heroic Age. The greater part of Britain had been under the Romans for more than three centuries, though some considerable time elapsed between their retirement and the beginning of the Heroic Age. But it is to be noted that the characters who figure in heroic poetry belong partly to the west but chiefly to the north, i.e. to those parts of the country which had been less Romanised than the rest. Moreover Welsh tradition traced the ancestry of the most important western families to a certain Cunedda who, according to a statement in the Historia Brittonum which most historians seem disposed to accept, had come from a region in the north beyond the Wall about—or very shortly before—the time when the Romans evacuated Britain. The chief northern families also belonged, at least mainly, to districts which appear to have been abandoned by the Romans early in the third century, and which had probably never been effectively occupied. Dumbarton, their principal stronghold, lay far from

the frontier of the later province—indeed on the extreme edge
of the earlier frontier.   All the evidence at our disposal therefore indicates that the Heroic Age was not a product of the
Romanised part of Britain but of those communities which
remained more or less independent, more especially in the region
beyond the northern frontier.   At the same time it cannot be
denied that even these districts must have been greatly affected
by Roman influence—probably in much the same way and to
at least the same degree as the Teutonic peoples adjacent to
the Roman frontiers on the Continent.   There is little doubt
too that the inhabitants of these districts served as mercenary
soldiers[1].   The conditions then appear to have been very similar
to those of the Teutonic Heroic Age.   First we find Roman
influence, doubtless both civil and military, affecting the communities beyond the frontier.   Then, on the fall of the Roman
power, these communities, or rather their princes, step in and
take possession of part of the province.   The chief difference
between the two cases is that here the new rulers were of the
same nationality and spoke the same language as the previous
inhabitants.

The origin of the earlier Servian Heroic Age presents in
some respects rather an interesting parallel to the case we have
just been considering.   Like the northern Britons the Servians
occupied territories which had formerly been within the frontiers
of the Roman Empire.   Their possession of these territories
was recognised by the emperor Heraclius (610—640) not long
after their settlement; and from this time onwards they were
governed by a number of petty princes of their own in a state
of semi-dependence, often merely nominal, on the Greek Empire
for about six centuries.   During the whole of this period, except
perhaps for a few short intervals, when they were subject to the
Bulgarians, they were constantly exposed to the influence of

---

[1] It appears from the Notitia Dignitatum that troops of Attacotti were largely
employed by the Romans on the Continent at the beginning of the fifth century.
According to St Jerome (*Adv. Iouinianum*, II 7) the Attacotti were a British people;
and they are mentioned by Ammianus Marcellinus (XXVI 4. 5 ; XXVII 8. 5) as ravaging
the province of Britain, together with the Picts and Scots, in the reign of Valentinian I.
It is commonly held that they belonged to the south of Scotland, though opinions
differ as to whether they were Britons (properly speaking) or Picts of Galloway.

Greek civilisation. It is probable too that they were frequently employed in war by the Greek emperors, first against the Avars and later against the Magyars. On the death of Manuel I (1180), when the Empire rapidly went to ruin, Stefan Nemanja united the various principalities and formed a powerful Servian state. His work was continued and extended by several of his successors, especially by Uroš I (1242—1276) and Dušan (1331—1356), the latter of whom brought nearly the whole of the Balkan peninsula under his rule. Here again therefore, as in the Teutonic and Cumbrian Heroic Ages, we have the case of a semi-civilised and 'juvenile' nation exposed for a long period to the influence of a civilised but decaying empire. Again too, when the older power gives way, the younger nation asserts itself and takes possession of its neighbour's territories. In this respect however the affinities of the Servian state are rather with the kingdoms of the Ostrogoths in Italy or the Franks in Gaul than with the Cumbrian Welsh; for the latter apparently never succeeded in establishing a united state—at least not until their territories had been greatly diminished.

The history of the later Servian (Bosnian) Heroic Age was of a very different kind. After the Turkish conquest (1459 in Servia proper, somewhat later in the west) a large proportion of the inhabitants embraced Islam. From this time onwards their condition was somewhat comparable with that of their ancestors under the Greeks, though they were in much closer subjection to the suzerain power than the latter had ever been. Moreover, though they enjoyed a certain amount of prosperity during the sixteenth and seventeenth centuries when the Turkish empire was at the height of its power, they never again formed an independent state. There can be no question that during the whole of this period the Mohammedan Servians were exposed to foreign influence, probably to a greater extent than any of the cases with which we have dealt above. But this influence was of a very different character from the others and little calculated to produce emancipation, whether intellectual or otherwise. In estimating the value of the resemblances which their heroic poetry shows to the types discussed above account must be taken of the consideration that much has doubtless been inherited—not merely in metre and phraseology—from that of the earlier period.

In dealing with the Gauls we are placed at a disadvantage through not knowing when the Heroic Age began. But all that we do know of their early history bears a most striking resemblance to the Heroic Age of the Teutonic peoples. Our first trustworthy references to the Gauls (Κελτοί) go back to the fifth century, at which time they appear to have occupied France and some parts at least of western Germany. It is commonly held also that they had already penetrated into Spain; and there can be no doubt that by this time a considerable part of the British Isles was in the possession of Celtic peoples. By the beginning of the fourth century, if not earlier, they had effected settlements in the plain of northern Italy, from whence military expeditions frequently made their way far into the peninsula. In the latter part of the same century we hear of Gauls in the Eastern Alps, probably in the basin of the Danube. Early in the following century Gaulish armies were making expeditions throughout the greater part of the Balkan peninsula and even into Greece, while one force effected a settlement in Asia Minor.

There is no evidence that any civilised power had acquired even a nominal authority over the Gauls before their subjugation by the Romans. But it is quite clear that for many centuries they had felt the influence of the Etruscan and Greek civilisations, more especially the former. Linguistic evidence is not available here, since we know nothing of the Etruscan language and little of the Gaulish. But the fact is placed beyond doubt by the large variety of articles of Etruscan origin or Etruscan types, which have been found throughout the territories of the Gauls and even in more northern regions. The evidence seems to indicate that the influence of this civilisation was comparable with that exercised in later times by Roman civilisation on the Teutonic peoples. Unfortunately however we have no historical record of those movements which first brought the Gauls into southern Europe. All that can be said with certainty is that in the earliest times for which we have trustworthy evidence they appear usually as auxiliaries or mercenaries in the service of the Etruscans. Sometimes also they were employed by the Greeks, Carthaginians and Samnites. And it was not only the Gauls settled in Italy who were used in this way. Occasionally we hear also of Transalpine Gauls or 'Gaisatoi,' who came to their assistance. Polybius (II 22) states that the latter name means 'mercenaries' (διὰ τὸ μισθοῦ στρατεύειν); and even if his interpretation is incorrect, it is significant enough of the opinion generally entertained as to the character of these warriors. Evidence to the same effect is afforded by the consideration that in the fourth and third centuries at least half of Europe (exclusive of Russia) appears to have been under Celtic rule, while some five or six centuries later Celtic nationality had vanished almost everywhere. Such phenomena are scarcely explicable unless the Celtic conquests were largely in the nature of military occupations, like those of the Goths, Visigoths and Vandals in later times.

We have left the Greek Heroic Age until the end because in this case historical information is wanting. Here also it is clear that a high civilisation had existed in a portion of the area then occupied by the Achaeans; and there can be no doubt that the latter were deeply affected thereby. The difficulty lies in determining the relationship of the Achaeans to this civilisation. Prof. Ridgeway's theory on the question has already been discussed. At the same time however it was mentioned that there are other scholars who hold that the Achaeans themselves were partly responsible for this civilisation. Some believe that the prehistoric civilisation of Crete was non-Achaean until its fall, and yet claim an Achaean origin for the fortresses on the mainland (Mycenae, Tiryns, etc.)[1], while others attribute to the Achaeans not only the buildings

---

[1] This appears to be the view taken by Prof. Meyer (*Gesch. d. Alt.*[2], I pp. 701, 719 f.). The problem will no doubt be discussed more fully in his next volume. Here I need only mention that the recent discoveries of wall-paintings at Tiryns and elsewhere seem to me to weigh rather heavily against the view that the inhabitants of these buildings were of a totally different nationality from the 'Minoan' Cretans. It is gradually becoming clear also that—contrary to what had been supposed at first— the use of writing was not unknown on the mainland; cf. Evans, *Scripta Minoa*, I p. 56 ff.

on the mainland but also the later palaces in Crete[1]. It is recognised by the advocates of this latter view that a different type of civilisation appears in other—more western—districts which have at least as good a claim to be regarded as Achaean lands. The explanation given is that the more primitive pottery and less elaborate buildings of these districts are true products of Achaean art and handicraft, while the remains found at Mycenae and elsewhere are due to native, or rather Cretan, craftsmen and builders, who worked for Achaean lords.

Both these explanations are open, as we have seen, to the serious objection that they fail to account for the differences between Homeric and Mycenean (Late Minoan) civilisation. It has been observed that in regard to armature the affinities of the former lie apparently rather with the Warrior Vase (cf. p. 185), which belongs to a later period than the true Mycenean age. All indications favour the view that this type of armature is derived from that of the Shardina rather than from earlier Mycenean or Cretan types. Again, I do not see that the presence of vases of 'Late Minoan II' style in the tombs found at Kakovatos—which is identified with the Homeric Pylos—can fairly be held to prove that these tombs date from that period[2]; for, when the manufacture of such vases had ceased they may very well have been preserved as precious heirlooms for a considerable time. Nor can it be said with certainty that these tombs date from the Achaean period[3], or at all events from the last days of it[4]. The evidence of the pottery[5] found in the ruins of the citadel seems rather to

---

[1] Cf. especially Dörpfeld, *Ath. Mitteilungen*, XXXII 600 ff.

[2] Cf. Dörpfeld, *Ath. Mitt.*, XXXII vi ff. Dr Dörpfeld however holds (*ib.*, p. 595 ff.) that 'Late Minoan II' and 'Late Minoan III' were contemporaneous and assigns both styles to a period (B.C. 1400—1100) considerably later than English archaeologists will allow for the former.

[3] One of the chief arguments for this view is that the tombs show traces of cremation. But account must be taken of the possibility that they may have belonged to an earlier (Arcadian?) stratum of Greek population.

[4] Cf. Dawkins, *Journ. Hell. St.*, XXVII 296, where it is suggested that the tomb first explored may have belonged possibly to the ancestors of Nestor.

[5] The great majority of the sherds found in the ruins of the citadel were of that monochrome type which has been met with elsewhere on the west coast of Greece (Leucas, Olympia, etc.) and which Dr Dörpfeld regards as the native pottery of the

suggest that this site was inhabited at a later date than the tombs[1].

In the Homeric poems we certainly find the Achaeans in possession of the chief centres of the prehistoric civilisation both in Crete and on the mainland. Mycenae itself is represented as the principal seat of the most important of the Achaean dynasties. But the poems themselves do not tell us by whom these places had been founded—though the origin of Troy does seem to be known. If we are right in believing that only the stratum represented by the Warrior Vase and the Stele corresponds truly to the conditions depicted in the poems, it is a probable inference that the Achaeans came into possession of Mycenae at a very late period in its history. In that case the presence of Agamemnon in this city would be a phenomenon somewhat parallel to that of Theodric (Dietrich von Bern) in Ravenna. In later times, it is true, we meet with stories according to which Tiryns and Mycenae were founded by Proitos and Perseus, though it is not made clear whether these persons were regarded as Achaeans. But have we any reason for believing that such stories are more trustworthy than the medieval traditions which attribute the foundation of famous Roman buildings to Dietrich von Bern? In view of the parallel cases, both Teutonic and other, which we have discussed in earlier chapters, it seems to me a highly improbable hypothesis that the men of the Greek Heroic Age had long been in possession of an advanced civilisation—still more that they had themselves initiated the construction of great palace-fortresses such as those of Tiryns and Mycenae.

The problem which we are considering has been complicated by the prevalent assumption that the Achaeans were the first Greek-speaking inhabitants of the land—an assumption which seems to me to be incompatible with the evidence of linguistic geography. The objections noted above to the Achaean origin

Achaeans; cf. *Ath. Mitt.*, xxxii xv f. Some sherds of the same type were found in the tombs together with the remains of Mycenean vases. Only six fragments of Mycenean pottery were found in the citadel.

[1] This explanation is rejected by Dr Dörpfeld (*Ath. Mitt.*, xxxiii 316); but there does not appear to be any definite evidence that the citadel was destroyed soon after the construction of the tombs.

of Mycenean civilisation would not apply with the same force
to the hypothesis that this civilisation had been taken over from
an earlier branch of the Greek race, represented perhaps in later
times by the Arcadians and Ionians.   For such an explanation
a certain parallel might be found in the occupation of the
(Roman) cities in Britain by British chiefs from the north and
west (cf. p. 446 f.).   But in this case, if we wish to press the
analogy, we must bear in mind that the civilisation of the
British cities was not of native origin but superimposed on the
country by invaders from overseas.   It is by no means impossible that such may have been the case also in Greece.
Yet on the whole the complete break between the prehistoric
civilisation and that of historical times must be regarded as
an argument—not conclusive of course but weighty—against
any form of the theory that the possessors of the former were
of Greek nationality.

It may be convenient now to recapitulate briefly the various
points at issue.   In the first place account must be taken of
the undoubted existence of the prehistoric civilisation, regarding
the character of which evidence is still gradually accumulating.
Further, it is scarcely open to question that the Achaeans were
brought into contact with that civilisation in some form or
other, though almost all scholars are agreed that it did not
originate with them.   The chief questions which remain to be
settled are (i) whether the civilisation was native or introduced
from abroad (Crete or elsewhere), (ii) whether its possessors
were Greeks or non-Greeks, (iii) whether its monuments were
constructed under Achaean domination or before the centres
of civilisation fell into Achaean hands.   The first of these
questions can only be settled by a thorough examination of the
various sites, such as is now being conducted[1].   All that can

---

[1] The general effect of recent discoveries has been to bring out a closer resemblance
between the Cretan and mainland deposits than had hitherto been suspected (cf. Evans,
Scripta Minoa, I p. 55 f.).   The affinities too are by no means confined to portable
objects.   In particular note should be taken of the wall-paintings at Thebes and
elsewhere—more especially those recently discovered at Tiryns, which belong to two
distinct periods (cf. Rodenwaldt, *Ath. Mitt.*, XXXVI 198 ff.).   The resemblance of
these to similar paintings from Crete is very marked, yet perhaps scarcely sufficient as
yet to prove that the possessors of Tiryns were of Cretan origin.

be said as yet is that the buildings in several cases show work belonging to more than one period. It is now believed that the earlier parts of the fortresses at Tiryns and Mycenae go back at least to the beginning of 'Late Minoan' times, i.e. probably to the sixteenth century. On the second question something has been said above. But until further evidence is forthcoming a dogmatic expression of opinion would be out of place. With regard to the third it appears to me that such evidence as we have favours Prof. Ridgeway's view, viz. that the Achaeans came into contact with this civilisation only at its fall. In that case moreover the Greek Heroic Age will fall into line with all the other Heroic Ages which we have discussed above.

Lastly, it seems to me of essential importance that the relationship of the Achaeans to the 'sea-peoples,' more especially the Shardina, should not be overlooked. We cannot with certainty determine whether or not the Achaeans were actually descended from the Shardina. But the resemblance between the two in regard to armature scarcely leaves room for doubt that the one had at least come greatly under the influence of the other. Consequently, whatever may be thought as to the proposed identification of the Akaiuasha (cf. p. 188 f.), it is highly probable that the ancestors of the Achaeans had once been associated with the 'sea-peoples[1].'

We have seen that among the Teutonic peoples, as also among the Gauls and elsewhere, mercenary service was a factor of supreme importance in the development of those features which give to the Heroic Age its distinctive character. Now

[1] For the Aegean connections of the sea-peoples see p. 190 f. Account is also to be taken of the deposits found in the foreign settlements at Gurob and elsewhere in the Fayum, to which belonged the tomb of An-Tursha ('Pillar of the Tursha or Thuirsha'). These deposits cover a period of about two centuries, from the reign of Amenhotep III to that of Sety II or slightly later—a period corresponding practically to that in which we find historical references to the sea-peoples. They contained many stirrup-vases and other objects of Aegean origin. A peculiar custom which prevailed here was that of burning a man's personal effects—presumably at death—in a hole cut in the floor of the house. No human remains were found in these holes, the bodies being buried in cemeteries according to Egyptian fashion; but it has been suggested that the practice may have been due to a former custom of cremation (cf. Petrie, *Illahun, Kahun and Gurob*, p. 16 ff.).

it is as mercenary soldiers that the 'sea-peoples' come before
our notice from the time when they are first mentioned down
to their disappearance. We know from the Tell-el-Amarna
tablets that Shardina had entered the Egyptian service in the
reign of Amenhotep IV or his predecessor, i.e. in the first half
of the fourteenth century. Later we find them fighting under
both Rameses II and Rameses III. The references therefore
extend over a period of nearly two centuries. Nor was it only
to the Egyptians that they lent their services. The army of
the Hittites encountered by Rameses II at Kadesh is said to
have contained Shardina, and warriors of the same stock were
present in the Libyan army defeated by Merenptah.

With the Shardina we usually find a number of other
peoples associated[1]; and there is no reason for doubting that
these were employed in the same way. Reference may be made
to the description of the allies of the Hittites in the Poem of
Pentaur, where this is expressed quite clearly[2]. The Pulesatha
also represented on the monuments of Rameses III are evidently
well-disciplined professional soldiers.

There can be no question then that professional military
service, very frequently in the employment of foreign nations,
was the vocation of those bands of warriors whom we have to
regard as the predecessors of the Achaeans of the Heroic Age.
But we can scarcely suppose that this mercenary service first
began in regions so distant as Egypt. It has been mentioned
above that the earliest reference to Shardina in the Egyptian
service goes back to a time when the Cretan palaces were
probably still standing (cf. p. 184). If so and if, as is commonly
believed, the absence of fortifications in Crete was due to the
possession of a thalassocracy by its rulers, we must conclude
that these rulers permitted the early expeditions of the 'sea-
peoples.' That can scarcely mean anything else than that
the Shardina and their confederates were first employed as

---

[1] When Shardina alone are mentioned account must of course be taken of the
possibility that this name is representative of a class. The Egyptian mercenaries, ke
those of the Hittites and Libyans, may really have been drawn from a number of
similar peoples who were collectively known under the name which had first become
familiar in Egypt.

[2] Cf. the quotation given above, p. 247, note 6.

mercenaries by the Cretans themselves[1]. In that case the relations of these peoples with the civilised states of the Aegean were in all probability very similar to those of the Teutonic peoples with Rome before and after the fall of the Western Empire.

The ultimate origin of the Shardina and their confederates is a question which as yet can hardly be regarded as ripe for discussion[2]. Later discoveries may show that they were the inhabitants of the western or northern parts of Greece; or on the other hand they may confirm the view that these peoples had come in part from the western Mediterranean. All that can be said at present is that some of these peoples—the Pulesatha type—appear to have long been settled in the Aegean area[3] and that the resemblances and differences between these and the Shardina are of such a kind as to suggest that the two were peoples racially distinct[4], yet living in adjacent regions

---

[1] I am not aware that representations of Shardina have yet been found in Crete. Note must be taken however of the porcelain fragment found in the third shaft-grave at Mycenae (cf. p. 191, note 4). The date of these shaft-graves can scarcely be much later than that of the destruction of the palace at Cnossos. Indeed it appears to be the prevalent view at present that they date from 'Late Minoan I,' i.e. before the palace-period; cf. Forsdyke, *Journ. Hell. St.*, XXXI 116, Hall, *ib.*, 119. If this is correct the porcelain fragment must of course be much older than the earliest Egyptian references to the Shardina.

[2] The use of the word *ḳrn·t* in the great Karnak inscription of Merenptah has given rise to much disagreement among Egyptologists. Prof. Breasted (*Ancient Records, Egypt*, III p. 247 note) understands from it that the Shardina and their confederates were circumcised. But the allusion is clearly to something which differentiated these peoples from the Libyans. The Libyans themselves however are believed to have practised circumcision (cf. Meyer, *Gesch. d. Alt.*[2], I § 167).

[3] Cf. pp. 190 (note 2), 247. For further references see Hall, *Journ. Hell. St.*, XXXI 119 ff. In particular note should be taken of the fact that the feather head-dress is worn by Ionian or Carian mercenaries on a monument of Sennacherib (*ib.*, p. 122 f.). Sir A. J. Evans (*op. cit.*, pp. 24 ff., 285 ff.) attributes the Phaistos disk—on which this type of head-dress first occurs—to the south-west of Asia Minor. In this connection however it is perhaps worth calling to mind that according to Thucydides (I 4, 8; cf. Herodotus, I 171) the Cyclades also were originally inhabited by Carians. The reference is perhaps properly to the Leleges, a people who may have been nearly related to the Lycians.

[4] The Pulesatha are represented as beardless, whereas many of the Shardina wear beards. More important however is the difference in physiognomy between the two types. It has been observed that the Pulesatha approximate very closely to the Greek type of classical times.

and following a similar mode of life, at least so far as the military element is concerned.   On the whole the balance of probability seems at present to be in favour of the following propositions: (1) that the Shardina element was intrusive; (2) that its true home is to be looked for rather in the north than in the west[1]; (3) that its presence or influence in the Greek world is not unconnected with that series of national movements which introduced Thraco-Phrygian populations into Asia Minor[2].

[1] Attempts have been made to find traces of the Shardina in the 'nuraghi' of Sardinia and the burial-places adjacent to them; but, so far as I am aware, no definite evidence in favour of this connection has yet been obtained beyond the fact that a number of statuettes with horned helmets have been found in the island.   The chief argument against the western origin of the Shardina is the absence of evidence, either in history or tradition, for movements of population or even for cultural influence from this quarter—at least until Roman times—whereas evidence is abundant not only for cultural influence in the reverse direction but also for settlements both of ' Illyrians ' and Greeks in Italy.   On the other hand it is perhaps worth noting that a helmet somewhat similar to that of the Shardina survived in historical times among the Thracians (cf. Herodotus VII 76).   Further, from Il. XIII 576 f. we may probably infer that the Thracian peoples had early become famous for the manufacture of weapons.   Influence from this quarter may have made its way into Greece by more than one channel.   But it should be observed that Homeric poetry shows some acquaintance with the districts to the north of Epeiros and Thessaly.   In particular note should be taken of certain personal names derived from names of peoples in this region, e.g. Πελάγων, 'Ορέστης, Θυέστης.   It is perhaps not without significance that the two latter of these occur in the most important of the Achaean families, while the antiquity of the last is guaranteed by the aspirate (as against Δυέσται).

[2] The extent of these movements may be estimated by the number of names which occur both in the Balkan peninsula and on the east side of the Aegean, e.g. *Brygoi* (*Phryges*), *Dardanoi*, *Moisoi* (*Mysoi*), *Mygdones*, *Sintoi* (*Sinties*), *Pelasgoi*; and it is not to be overlooked that on the European side most of these names occur in the basins of the Axios and Strymon or the region between them.   Attention should be paid also to the common element in place-names, more especially to those (e.g. Πέργαμος) which occur in the islands (Crete, etc.) as well as in the two areas under discussion; for they seem to indicate that the movements from the Balkan peninsula were not confined to the Asiatic mainland.   Even in Asia Minor itself however the Thraco-Phrygian movements may at first have affected a much larger area than that in which languages of this type survived in historical times.   Herodotus (I 171) states that on the ground of common ancestry the Carians allowed Lydians and Mysians to use the temple at Mylasa—a privilege which they did not concede to other peoples, even to those who spoke the same language as themselves.   This passage is usually interpreted as pointing to a traditional religious federation of the indigenous peoples.   But it is a serious objection to this view that the Mysians were clearly of European origin.   If the Lydian and Carian languages were non-Indo-

It is by no means impossible that the Shardina were the direct ancestors of the Achaeans. On the other hand they may have belonged to an earlier wave of Greek invasion. Or again they may have been a non-Greek (perhaps Thraco-Phrygian) people whose relations with the Achaeans were rather in the nature of influence, however deeply this may have penetrated. That the Achaeans also were an essentially military people is shown by the tone of Homeric poetry throughout and by the story of the Iliad as a whole, as well as by many incidental passages in the Odyssey. We have good reason too for believing that their occupation was in the nature of a military rather than a tribal settlement. That is shown not only by the social and political conditions reflected in the Homeric poems[1] but also by the fact that, except in two comparatively unimportant districts, they disappeared after the Heroic Age as completely as the Ostrogoths.

The course of our investigations has led us to conclude that there is no reason for regarding the Greek Heroic Age as an exception to the general rule applying to such phenomena. Neither here nor in any other case are we justified in believing that the Heroic Age was a native outgrowth from an ancient and highly developed civilisation. It does not appear that a Heroic Age can arise from such conditions, any more than from conditions which may properly be called primitive. In four of the six cases which we have considered—and we need scarcely hesitate to reckon the Greek case as a fifth—the Heroic Age can be traced back to a similar series of causes. Firstly, we find a long period of 'education,' in which a semi-civilised people has been profoundly affected from without by the influence of a civilised people. Then a time has come in which the semi-civilised people has attained to a dominant position

European, as is commonly believed, they may have been taken over from indigenous peoples such as the Caunioi, whose language was similar to that of the Carians and who seem to have been among the peoples excluded from the temple at Mylasa. The possibility that the Carian language belonged originally to the Caunioi is suggested by Herodotus himself.

[1] In particular note may be taken of the absence of national names for the populations of several of the most important kingdoms; cf. p. 389, note.

and possessed itself, at least to some extent, of its neighbour's property. The phenomena which we have recognised as characteristic of the Heroic Age appear to be the effects produced upon the semi-civilised people by these conditions.

For the exceptional case—that of the Mohammedan Servians —a special explanation has been suggested. Whether this explanation be correct or not, I do not mean to assert that the Heroic Age is universally due to the same conditions. They can scarcely hold good for the Irish Heroic Age; and outside Europe also there are cases, e.g. among the Bantu peoples, of societies which may be called 'heroic' and yet would probably require a different explanation. All such cases doubtless postulate conditions so far advanced as to permit the existence of a class of persons who have the opportunity and the ambition to assert their individuality among and above their compatriots. To deal adequately with these cases however would require a greater amount of ethnological knowledge than I possess. I have ventured above to suggest that 'Mars and the Muses' are necessary for the formation of a Heroic Age. But beyond this I will not attempt to formulate a definition of the elements which constitute a Heroic Age in general. My object has been to call attention to certain common characteristics exhibited by a limited number of epochs in European history.

The various Heroic Ages of Europe are usually connected with considerable movements of population. There is some reason for suspecting that this may be true even of the Irish Heroic Age. But such movements do not necessarily produce a Heroic Age. We have no evidence for the existence of a Heroic Age resulting from the great movement of the Slavs into eastern Germany during the fifth and following centuries[1]. Presumably the antecedent conditions were wanting. So also with the Dorians. It was only the wreckage of the old Aegean civilisation with which they were brought into contact. The

---

[1] It may be observed also that some seven centuries elapsed between the settlement of the Servians on the lower Danube and the beginning of their (first) Heroic Age. This latter period was of course accompanied by an extension of the area occupied by the Servians, though the newly won territories were subsequently lost through the Turkish conquest.

days of mercenary service too, with all its civilising and at the same time denationalising influence, had apparently passed away long before they came to the front.

The general direction taken by these movements—though here the Irish case is an exception—was towards the culture lands of the south—i.e. the direction taken by movements of population was the opposite of that taken by movements of culture. The effect of the movements which took place in the Teutonic Heroic Age was to produce a series of inclined or tilted strata of population over a large part of Europe. Thus the Franks formed a ruling aristocracy in Gaul; but the subjects (*coloni, lati*) of the Old Saxons were in all probability largely of Frankish blood. Again, the Vandals in Africa were the wealthiest and most luxurious community known to Procopius[1]. Yet in Genseric's time (cf. p. 369) there still remained a Vandal population in the old home of the nation, of which all traces had disappeared within the next century. Presumably they had been overwhelmed by the surrounding peoples. Similar phenomena are to be found among the Goths and other Teutonic peoples, and in earlier times among the Gauls and Greeks. In the latter case we may cite as an instance the Cynurioi (on the east coast of the Peloponnesos), who were believed to be Ionians, though they had been absorbed by the Dorians of Argos. The fact therefore that we hear of no people called Achaeans in Epeiros cannot be held to prove that the Achaeans had never inhabited that region.

We hear sometimes from legends of national migrations caused by insufficiency of food. Historical records seem to show that such movements were more frequently due to pressure from neighbouring peoples. But it is greatly to be doubted whether these movements usually involved a total displacement of population. Cases like that of the Vandals indeed indicate that frequently the more enterprising part of the community were the first to move and that the chief impulse came from

---

[1] *Vand.* II 6: ἐθνῶν γὰρ ἁπάντων ὧν ἴσμεν ἡμεῖς ἁβρότατον μὲν τὸ τῶν Βανδίλων... βαλανείοις τε οἱ ξύμπαντες ἐπεχρῶντο ἐς ἡμέραν ἑκάστην καὶ τραπέζῃ ἅπασιν εὐθηνούσῃ, ὅσα δὴ γῆ τε καὶ θάλασσα ἥδιστά τε καὶ ἄριστα φέρει. ἐχρυσοφόρουν δὲ ὡς ἐπὶ πλεῖστον, καὶ Μηδικὴν ἐσθῆτα, ἣν νῦν Σηρικὴν καλοῦσιν, ἀμπεχόμενοι......καὶ ᾤκηντο μὲν αὐτῶν οἱ πολλοὶ ἐν παραδείσοις, ὑδάτων καὶ δένδρων εὖ ἔχουσι, κ.τ.λ.

the attractions offered by the chance of living upon the fruits of others' labour, whether in the form of plunder or tribute. So far as our records go back, we find among the Teutonic peoples, as among the Gauls and the early Greeks, a numerous class who prefer the military life to the labour involved in agriculture. Indeed one of the most remarkable features of the Teutonic Heroic Age—and probably of the Gaulish also[1]— is the ease with which immense hosts of warriors could be gathered for an enterprise of plunder or conquest. It is certain that these hosts were frequently drawn from far and wide. If the national kings would not embark on such enterprises their subjects were ready to embrace the service of neighbouring princes, or even that of distant or alien nations, such as the Romans. It is the existence of this military element which in various epochs of European history and under similar cultural conditions has produced the phenomena comprised under the term 'Heroic Age.' For the special characteristics however to which we have called attention above—emancipation from primitive ideas and absence of national feeling—the explanation is to be found in contact with civilised communities, especially in the form of mercenary service. The military life further had the effect of making the kings regard themselves primarily as commanders of armies. It was for their warriors that consideration was required rather than for the tillers of the soil, who were largely of alien nationality.

When this is realised it becomes easy to understand the instability of heroic society. The military followers of a peace-loving king, unless he was very wealthy and generous, were liable to drift away, while the bulk of the population counted for nothing. In the absence of any truly national organisation or national feeling all depended on the personal qualities of the leaders. Under Theodric the Ostrogoths were the chief power in Europe; but within thirty years of his death they disappear and are not heard of again. Under Dušan the Servians seemed destined to absorb all that was left of the Greek empire; after his death they failed to offer any effective resistance to the

[1] We may compare the force led by Agamemnon against Troy and the great mixed host encountered by Rameses III (cf. p. 188).

Turks. The kingdoms of the Greek Heroic Age seem to have succumbed to much less formidable antagonists. So numerous indeed are cases of this kind that one is perhaps justified in regarding national disaster as the normal ending of such epochs.

The Heroic Age, both Greek and Teutonic, presents us with the picture of a society largely free from restraint of any kind. In the higher ranks tribal law has ceased to maintain its force; and its decay leaves the individual free from obligations both to the kindred and to the community. He may disregard the bonds of kinship even to the extent of taking a kinsman's life; and he recognises no authority beyond that of the lord whose service he has entered. The same freedom is exhibited in his attitude to the deities.

It is of course in princes that we find these features most strongly developed. That which they prize above all else is the ability to indulge their desires to the full—in feasting and every form of enjoyment for themselves, in unlimited generosity to their friends, in ferocious vindictiveness towards their foes. The hero of the Odyssey, when his opportunity arrives, sets no limit to the vengeance which he exacts, from prince, goatherd and maidservant. Achilles, the chief hero of the Iliad, is transformed into a savage when he gets possession of the dead body of his enemy. His story furnishes a fitting parallel to that of Alboin, whose brutal conduct brought upon him so swift a retribution. And it is to be remembered that this Alboin's generosity was a theme of poetry from Italy to England.

The best side of heroic kingship may be seen in such a character as Hrothgar. His conception of the duties of a national ruler may have been of a somewhat elementary character. But it is rather as the head of a large household that we have to regard him; and as such he commands our esteem. Even in the Merovingian family—we may cite Gregory's description (III 25) of Theodberht—there were princes who won the respect of Roman ecclesiastics. In the courts of such princes the conditions of life were probably as good as at any time for many centuries later. We have no reason for supposing that the case was otherwise in the Heroic Age of Greece.

But above all we have to remember the heroic poems. It is not reasonable to regard the Anglo-Saxon poems, much less the Homeric poems, as products of barbarism. The courts which gave birth to such poetry must have appropriated to a considerable extent the culture, as well as the wealth and luxury, of earlier civilisations. It is to be remarked however that the hold which these poems have exercised on subsequent ages, in very different stages of culture, is due not only to their artistic qualities but also to the absorbing interest of the situations which they depict. This interest arises very largely from the extraordinary freedom from restraint enjoyed by the characters in the gratification of their feelings and desires and from the tremendous and sudden vicissitudes of fortune to which they are exposed. The pictures presented to us are those of persons by no means ignorant of the pleasures and even the refinements of civilised life, yet dominated by the pride and passions which spring from an entirely reckless individualism and untrained by experience to exercise moderation. According to the view put forward above the explanation of such features is to be found not so much in any peculiarly fertile gift of imagination by which the conventional court poetry of these periods was inspired, but rather in the circumstances of the times and in the character of the courts which produced that poetry.

ADDENDA ET CORRIGENDA.

Page 19 ff. For further information the reader may be referred to Miss Clarke's *Sidelights on Teutonic History during the Migration Period* (Cambridge, 1911), which contains a very clear and interesting account of the various characters mentioned in the heroic poems.

Page 43, ll. 5—7. This suggestion can hardly be maintained. The true name of Theodberht's son was probably Theodwald.

Page 46, l. 3 ff. The consideration of this difficult question has recently been somewhat facilitated by Richter's *Chronologische Studien zur ags. Literatur* (Halle, 1910). The general effect of Dr Richter's investigations is to confirm the view put forward by Prof. Sarazzin (*Engl. Stud.*, XVIII 170 ff.) as to the antiquity of Genesis A. Unfortunately I fear that the statistics are not complete and, further, that the evidence is not always treated with strict impartiality. Thus in Beowulf such half-verses as *to widan feore* are regarded as proofs of shortening (through loss of *h*) and reckoned in the final statistics (pp. 9, 85); but in Genesis A the metrically equivalent *on fyore lifde* is not so reckoned (pp. 24, 89). The half-verse *geseon meahton* is cited in Beowulf without qualification (p. 15), but in Exodus as doubtful (p. 18). In Beowulf *-wundor seon* is taken to be $- \times -$ (pp. 13, 15), but in Daniel A it is treated as doubtful (p. 32). Dr Richter's conclusion that Genesis A is an earlier poem than Beowulf is certainly not substantiated by the treatment of *feore* or of postconsonantal *r, l, m, n*[1], or again by that of *frea, don, gan, sie*[2]; while compounds such as *þreanyd* obviously do not stand on the same footing as case-forms like *þrea*. It is only in the treatment of intervocalic *h* that Genesis A apparently shows a more archaic character than Beowulf. In the former poem Dr Richter cites only one case of contraction (p. 28), and even this is doubtful; but the same remark applies to at least 18 of the 24 (genuine) cases which he cites for Beowulf (p. 15). Out of the five or six probable cases of contraction in this poem three occur in practically the same phrase—*in (on, to) sele þam hean*—while two of the others occur in consecutive verses (910 f.). The conclusion to which the evidence seems to me to point is that both Genesis A and Beowulf (even in its Christianised form) date from the seventh century, but that the former has been somewhat better preserved than the latter. As Genesis A is doubtless of monastic origin, we may reasonably expect that it was committed to writing at an earlier date. In the intervening period the text of Beowulf may have suffered many changes (such as the insertion of the article) at the hands of minstrels.

[1,2] As shown by Dr Richter's lists (pp. 9 ff., 24 ff. and 13 ff., 27 f.).

The further question raised by Prof. Sarazzin (*op. cit.*, p. 192 ff.) as to the relationship of Genesis A to Caedmon cannot be discussed here. But in view of the evidence brought forward I do think it would be worth while to examine and compare the characteristics of the various ' Caedmonic' poems from all points of view. Apart from the extremely improbable dating of certain sound-changes proposed by Prof. Morsbach (cf. p. 66 ff. above) and accepted both by Sarazzin and Richter, I see no reason for supposing that Caedmon's poems have entirely perished.

Page 61, l. 4 ff. Throughout this book I have followed the view generally held by scholars in the past that the expression *geongum cempan* in Beow. 2044 refers to Ingeld. In recent years several scholars have adopted a different interpretation, viz. that it means not the prince himself but a nameless member of his retinue. This interpretation is due primarily to v. 2061 f., where it has been assumed, somewhat hastily in my opinion, (1) that *se oðer* must denote the slayer and (2) that Ingeld's own country is the scene of the tragedy. On the basis of this interpretation Prof. Olrik (*Danmarks Heltedigtning*, II p. 30 ff., especially p. 37 ff.) has now put forward a theory that the episode in Beowulf has little more than the names in common with Saxo's story of Ingellus' revenge, and that the latter is in its main features the creation of a Danish poet of Harold Bluetooth's time. His explanation is certainly interesting and ingenious ; but at the same time it appears to me to be open to serious objections. Thus he has to admit (p. 39) that in the only other reference to the bridal tragedy ('bryllups-kampen') contained in the poem (v. 82 ff.) the scene is laid in the Danish king's hall. His explanation is that here we have a variant form of the story (cf. Widsith, v. 45 ff.), emanating from a different poet. But surely one cannot place much confidence in an interpretation which involves the assumption of such an inconsistency as this[1]. Still more important is the reference to Ingeld (*Hinieldus*) in Alcuin's letter to Hygebald (cf. p. 41), which Prof. Olrik seems to have entirely ignored. From this passage it would seem that Ingeld's fame was as great in England in the eighth century as it ever became in Denmark; and such fame is scarcely compatible with the passive rôle assigned to him by the theory under discussion. But, more than this, have we any ground for supposing that Alcuin did not exercise his judgment in taking Ingeld as his example of a *perditus rex*? If the story of Ingeld known to him was substantially identical with that

[1] So far as I can see the only argument for this inconsistency which Prof. Olrik brings forward is the statement (Vol. I, p. 16; cf. Vol. II, p. 38, note 1, and p. 39, note 1) that the fight at the marriage precedes Beowulf's visit to the king's hall. This however seems to mean that the present tense, which is used throughout the episode (nearly a score of examples), must be taken as a historic present—a construction which is rarely or never found elsewhere in Anglo-Saxon heroic poetry. In Beowulf only one instance (v. 1879) is cited by Nader (*Anglia*, X 547), and this is clearly erroneous. A possible case does occur in v. 1923 (*wunað*); but most recent editors either emend (to *wunade*) or regard the passage as a speech.

recorded by Saxo, as I myself believe, he could hardly have found a case in which Christian and heathen obligations presented a more glaring contrast. To the heathen this hero appealed as the pious son who exacts vengeance for his father's death; but to the Christian he was doubly abhorrent, not merely as a heathen but also as a murderer and a truce-breaker.

Like other heroic stories recorded by Saxo and Icelandic authors the story of Ingellus has without doubt a long poetic history behind it. Prof. Olrik's investigations have rendered it probable that an element in this poetry dates from the tenth century. It may be that the poem used by Saxo was actually composed—or re-cast—at that time. But I must confess to some scepticism as to the possibility of determining with certainty what proportion of the material is to be assigned to the various periods intermediate between the sixth and twelfth centuries; and I am disposed to think that in general Prof. Olrik has underrated the significance of the earlier elements.

Page 64, l. 6. It should have been mentioned that the expression "to persons born after 800" applies only to the period extending down to 975. I have not examined the evidence available for later times. About this time a new factor is introduced by the revival of interest in heroic poetry.

I would also call attention to the fact that the statistics are confined to historical documents and do not include names (of moneyers) found only on coins. My impression from a perusal of the material collected in Mr Searle's *Onomasticon Anglo-Saxonicum* is that this element will not appreciably affect the statistics.

Page 75, l. 26 ff. Reference should have been given to the Exeter Gnomic Verses, 89 ff.

Page 110. On the subject discussed at the beginning of this chapter the reader is referred to Heusler, *S.-B. d. Akad. zu Berlin*, 1909, p. 937 ff., and Van Gennep, *La Formation des Légendes*. The definitions given above may not be entirely satisfactory—mention should perhaps have been made of the 'Ortssage'—but they will probably be found sufficient for the purpose of this book.

Page 116 ff. On this subject reference should be made to Panzer, *Studien zur germ. Sagengeschichte*, I *Beowulf*, which contains a careful and detailed examination of the Märchen in question. Unfortunately I have not been able to use this work, as it did not come into my hands until the first eight chapters of my book were in print. In regard to those points on which I have chiefly laid stress, viz. that Beowulf is to be identified with Biarki and that he appears to be a historical character, Prof. Panzer's views (pp. 368 ff., 390 ff.) are practically identical with those expressed above. On the other hand he holds that the story of Biarki—the portion dealing with his origin, as well as the adventure at Leire—comes from the same folk-tale as the story of Beowulf and Grendel. His theory as a whole gives rise to important questions regarding the origin and distribution of folk-tales, which cannot be discussed here. Thus I should like to know how far the same folk-tale can arise independently in different regions. Again, the Märchen with which he deals seem to me to be highly composite structures, which I should be inclined to regard rather as aggregations of folk-tales. This is true more especially of the elements common to the stories of Beowulf, Grettir and Ormr, the close affinities of which have been brought into a much clearer light by Prof. Panzer's researches. It may be that the elaborate story which underlies all three was treated in poetry at an early date; but I see no more reason now than before for believing that the two Icelandic stories have been affected by any poem dealing with Beowulf himself.

Page 117 f. It is perhaps worth noting that Ormr Stórolfsson was related to Grettir, both being descended from Hængr, the great-grandson of that Ketill Hængr of Hrafnista whose story is largely taken up with adventures with trolls and iötnar.

Page 124. For the death of Frotho III the reader may be referred to Olrik, *Danmarks Heltedigtning*, II p. 239 ff.; and for the connection between this character and the *Beaw* of the genealogies to (*ib.*) p. 249 ff. As stated above (p. 126, note) I should prefer the form *Beowa*, for earlier *Biowi* (as *Aella* for earlier *Aelli*; cf. p. 64). The latter form may be connected with *Byggvir*.

Page 139 ff. On the Nibelungenlied reference may be made to Prof. Röthe's article *Nibelungias und Waltharius* (*S.-B. d. Akad. zu Berlin*, 1909, p. 649).

Page 161, l. 1 f. The references to Sarus (accidentally omitted here) are Olympiodoros, p. 449 (ed. Niebuhr), Jordanes, *Romana*, § 321 (*Mon. Germ., Auct. Ant.* V 41).

Page 180, l. 20 ff. It has rightly been pointed out to me by Mr C. A. Scutt that, if the statement attributed by Herodotus (VI 3) to Demaratos is to be trusted, the average length of a generation in the Spartan royal families may reasonably be expected to be somewhat longer than elsewhere. Yet in point of fact this is not borne out by the evidence available for the historical period (from the fifth to the third centuries), nor yet by that of the genealogies for the period between Theopompos and Cleomenes, if the commonly accepted date for the first Messenian war is correct.

Page 185, l. 20 ff. Recent discoveries have rendered it probable that cremation was practised in Crete in very early times. Up to now however all the evidence apparently comes from the Early Minoan period, so that the point upon which Dr Mackenzie lays stress remains practically unaffected.

Page 190, l. 2 ff. I regret that when this was written I had not observed that Prof. Meyer accepts the statement of Xanthos with regard to the Phrygian invasion. On this question see p. 437, note 2.

Page 198, l. 27 ff.   On this subject reference may be made to Shewan, *The Lay of Dolon*, which appeared too late for me to be able to make use of it.

Page 244, note 2.   A different view is taken by Allen, *Jour. Hell. St.* xxx 312 ff., where a full discussion of the Trojan Catalogue—as also of the Achaean Catalogue (*ib.*, p. 292 ff.)—will be found.   Mr Allen's conclusions differ greatly from the views expressed above.

Page 265, note 3.   In the poem Hyndlulióð (cf. p. 12) the genealogy of Óttarr the son of Innsteinn is traced back to a certain Svanr hinn rauði. The same genealogy occurs in the document *Hversu Noregr bygðist* (published in the Fornaldar Sögur Norðrlanda, II p. 6 in Dr Valdimar Ásmundarson's edition) ; and here Svanr hinn rauði is said to be the son of Finnálfr by Svanhildr the daughter of Day (*Dagr Dellingsson*) and the Sun (*Sól, dóttir Mundilfara*).   This document however belongs to a very late period—the close of the fourteenth century—and I know of no earlier authority for the first part of the genealogy.

Page 285, note 1, l. 4.   For "I p. 687" read "I ii p. 687," and similarly in all subsequent references to the second edition of Prof. Meyer's *Geschichte des Altertums*.

Page 313, note 1.   For " Pasić " read " Pavić " (and so also in the notes on the following pages).

INDEX

CAMBRIDGE: PRINTED BY W. LEWIS, M.A., AT THE UNIVERSITY PRESS